# Special Edition Using Red Hat Linux

*Alan Simpson*

*John Ray*

*Neal Jamison*

## que

A Division of Macmillan Publishing USA
201 W. 103rd Street
Indianapolis, Indiana 46290

**Associate Publishers**
Dean Miller
Tracy Dunkelberger

**Acquisitions Editor**
Gretchen Ganser

**Development Editor**
Maureen A. McDaniel

**Managing Editor**
Matt Purcell

**Project Editor**
Natalie Harris

**Copy Editor**
Suzanne Rose

**Indexer**
Chris Barrick

**Proofreaders**
Maribeth Echard
Daryl Kessler
Rebecca Salerno

**Technical Editor**
Brian Walters

**Team Coordinator**
Cindy Teeters

**Interior Designers**
Dan Armstrong
Ruth Lewis

**Cover Designer**
Maureen McCarty

**3B2 Layout Technicians**
Brandon Allen
Susan Geiselman
Brad Lenser
Cheryl Lynch

# CONTENTS

# About the Authors

**Alan Simpson** has written 72 books over the last 15 years including *Windows 95 Bible*, *The Official Netscape Composer Book*, *Mastering Microsoft Access*, *Mastering WordPerfect 8*, which was voted the best WordPerfect book of 1998 by amazon.com, and *Windows 98 Bible*, which was voted one of the top ten computer books of 1998 by amazon.com. Before becoming a full-time author, Alan was a freelance programmer and consultant, and taught introductory and advanced computer courses at San Diego State University and the University of California Extension program. Alan also runs the popular Web site coolnerds.com.

**John Ray** is an award-winning Web application and network developer for the Ohio State University. He holds a computer engineering degree from OSU and oversees network operations for one of its colleges. There, he implemented a campus-wide database for maintaining TCP/IP information for a wide range of networked computers. For the past five years, John has used Linux exclusively for his programming efforts and has championed its use for projects inside and outside the university. He provides Linux- and UNIX-based TCP/IP programming solutions to businesses nationwide. His other publications include Que's *Red Hat Installation and Configuration Handbook*, *Linux Maximum Security*, and *Special Edition Using TCP/IP*, and *Sams Teach Yourself Linux in 10 Minutes*.

**Neal Jamison** is a consultant and author specializing in Internet technologies such as Web development and administration, intranets, and Linux and UNIX system administration. As the director of the Internet Solutions Center for AnviCom, Inc., he researches and employs current and emerging Internet technologies for the benefit of his clients. Neal holds a B.S. in computer science from Virginia Tech and an M.S. in information systems from Hawaii Pacific University. He lives, works, and writes in Falls Church, Virginia with his wife and son.

# DEDICATION

To Susan, Ashley, Alec, Jeanne, Halley, and John

# ACKNOWLEDGMENTS

Every book is a team effort, and this one is certainly no exception. I'd like to thank the following individuals for their unique contributions, support, and infinite patience. At Que, many thanks to Maureen McDaniel, Development Editor; Jim Minatel and Dean Miller, Associate Publishers; and Gretchen Ganser, Acquisitions Editor. Thanks also to Jim Price.

Also many thanks to John Ray and Neal Jamison.

Thanks to the crew at Waterside Productions, my literary agency, for bringing this opportunity to me and handling all the logistics.

And of course many thanks to my family—Susan, Ashley, and Alec—and my temporary "second family"—Jeanne, Halley, and John—for their patience and support through this long and demanding project.

-Alan Simpson

# TELL US WHAT YOU THINK!

As the reader of this book, *you* are our most important critic and commentator. We value your opinion and want to know what we're doing right, what we could do better, what areas you'd like to see us publish in, and any other words of wisdom you're willing to pass our way.

As an associate publisher for Que, I welcome your comments. You can fax, email, or write to me directly to let me know what you did or didn't like about this book—as well as what we can do to make our books stronger.

*Please note that I cannot help you with technical problems related to the topic of this book, and that due to the high volume of mail I receive, I might not be able to reply to every message.*

When you write, please be sure to include this book's title and author as well as your name and phone or fax number. I will carefully review your comments and share them with the authors and editors who worked on the book.

Fax:      317-581-4666

Email:   quetechnical@macmillanusa.com

Mail:     Tracy Dunkelberger
          Que
          201 West 103rd Street
          Indianapolis, IN 46290 USA

# INTRODUCTION

## In this introduction

# WELCOME

Welcome to *Special Edition Using Red Hat Linux*, a book written to help users learn about the new, exciting, and free, UNIX-like operating system known as Linux. My goal in this book has been a simple one: to give *all* computer users—even those without UNIX system administration and network administration experience—the skills and knowledge necessary to use Linux to its fullest advantage, whether that be in the home, small office, medium-sized business, or corporation. If you've read much Linux documentation in the past, you may have felt bewildered by all the UNIX terminology that other writers assume you already know. In this book, I take a much different approach. So perhaps the first thing we should talk about here is who this book is really for.

# WHO THIS BOOK IS FOR

It seems you hear about Red Hat Linux everywhere you turn these days, not only in the computer industry press, but in the mainstream press as well. Much of the attention comes from the unique nature of how Linux was created, and how it's maintained and distributed. Unlike commercial software products with their high price tags, stiff usage requirements, and (comparatively) slow evolution, Linux is a freely distributed, full-functioning, all-in-one operating system that can play the role of a desktop OS (like the Mac OS or Windows 98), a serious Workstation (like Windows NT Workstation or Windows 2000 Professional), and a server (like Windows NT Server or Windows 2000 server).

In a sense, Linux is a clone of the old tried-and-true UNIX operating system used by the vast majority of large corporations. Because of that, much of the documentation that's written for Linux assumes that you have prior UNIX experience, and therefore already understand all the underlying concepts and jargon. This book makes no such assumptions. The reader I envisioned while writing this book has these attributes:

- Has some computer/operating system experience with Windows or a Macintosh, but is entirely new to the world of UNIX and Linux.

- Is motivated to learn what Linux is really all about, and how it can be used to create cost-effective, yet powerful, systems for general office productivity, building networks, developing application programs, and serving the Internet.

- When told what to do, would appreciate being told exactly *how* to do it, with clear step-by-step instructions, illustrations, and no jargon.

- Is specifically using Red Hat Linux Version 6.2, and wants to know how to use *that* product.

To meet those goals, you'll find that this book is organized to teach, as well as to serve as a reference.

## HOW TO USE THIS BOOK

Sometimes, it takes quite a bit of patience to learn a large complex subject. You want to take advantage of the most advanced features of a product, but are unable to because you don't understand the necessary underlying fundamentals. This book is written to explain everything you need to know, in the order you need to know it. To that end, the book is organized as follows:

- **Part I, Getting to Know Linux:** Here you'll learn the absolute basics of getting Linux up and running, and the basic skills and concepts you need to know to become productive, quickly.

- **Part II, System Administration:** This part takes you through all the aspects of managing a Linux system, including how to manage users and permissions, install packages (programs), print, and configure the various graphical desktops like GNOME and KDE.

- **Part III, Linux and the Internet:** Here you'll learn to connect your Linux computer to the Internet, and use the World Wide Web, email, FTP, the new Update Agent, and Red Hat support, which will add a lot of muscle to your ability to get the most from Red Hat Linux.

- **Part IV, Linux Network Administration:** Once you've learned the basics of system administration, you'll be able to learn how to build your own Linux local area network (LAN) or intranet. You'll learn how to share resources among Linux and Windows computers in the same network, as well as more advanced techniques for connecting your network to other networks.

- **Part V, Serving the Internet with Linux:** Whereas Part II teaches you how to use Linux as an Internet "consumer" (client), this whole part of the book focuses on the other side of the equation—using Linux to serve the Internet. Create your own Web server with Apache, and offer Usenet news, World Wide Web, Email, FTP, and other services to network consumers.

- **Part VI, Programming Linux:** For the truly motivated, this part of the book focuses on developing custom software and kernels for Linux. You'll learn about the basic scripting language such as CGI and Perl, as well as the more advanced applications-development languages like C++ and the widely popular Java programming language.

- **Part VII, Appendixes:** If you didn't buy a computer that already has Linux installed on it, the Appendixes will tell you everything you need to know about installing Linux on your computer. You'll even learn how to set up Linux so that you can keep Windows on the same computer, if you wish, so you can remain productive with Windows while learning to use Linux.

## ABOUT THE CD-ROM

Some of you may already have the Red Hat Linux 6.2 boxed set. Some of you may have bought this book instead. If you *don't* have the boxed set, you can easily install Red Hat Linux from the CD-ROM at the back of this book. See Appendix B, "Installing Red Hat Linux," for information on how to get started.

# IN CLOSING

Thank you for purchasing this book, and taking the time to read through its pages. I know your time is valuable to you, and I thank you for trusting me to teach you what you really need to know in an efficient manner. No doubt, this book will evolve through many editions, just as Red Hat Linux evolves from one version to the next. To that extent, I'm *always* open to suggestions on how to improve the book to better suit your needs. Feel free to contact me through my Web site at www.coolnerds.com, or email at alan@coolnerds.com, with any suggestions you might have.

Thanks again,

Alan Simpson

# PART I

# GETTING TO KNOW LINUX

# GETTING STARTED

**I**n this chapter

# WHAT IS LINUX?

Linux is a computer operating system (abbreviated OS). As you may know, an operating system is about the only "required" software on a computer. A computer without an operating system is like a car without a motor. Turn the key, and nothing happens. The operating system kernel is the piece of software at the center of it all; it manages the interactions between the various components that make up a computer system, including the processor, random access memory (RAM), disk drives, monitor, keyboard, and mouse.

The OS also plays a big role in determining the computer's interface. The interface is essentially the look and feel of the system from the standpoint of the user (you). For example, the look and feel of a Macintosh is not the same as the look and feel of a Windows PC because the Macintosh OS and Windows are two entirely different operating systems. The OS also determines which application programs you can and can't run, on the computer. For instance, you can't use the Windows version of Microsoft Office on a Macintosh. You can't run Macintosh programs on a PC. You can't run Windows or Macintosh programs on Linux (although there are efforts underway to make Windows programs run on Linux).

As an operating system, Linux most closely resembles UNIX, which was created in the 1969, and is still widely used in large corporations and universities. While UNIX was developed mainly to run on popular minicomputers of its day, Linux is designed to run on modern PCs. How Linux came to be is a story in itself.

## A LITTLE HISTORY

Linux got its start, indirectly, in 1984 when Richard Stallman created the GNU Project. The goal of the project was to create a UNIX-like operating system that could be distributed freely. The GNU acronym stands for "GNUs Not Unix," sort of a recursive (self-referring) acronym in that the "G" stands for GNUs. Participants in the GNU project were largely hackers (professional and skilled amateur programmers) working without pay and collaborating on the Internet. The GNU project created a ton of UNIX-based programs, commonly referred to as *GNU project utilities*, as well as a UNIX-based operating system named Minix.

Minix was difficult to install and use, and did not generate a huge following. Then, in 1991 a Finnish student named Linus Torvalds announced to a Minix newsgroup that he was working on a new UNIX-like operating system for Intel 386/486 processors—essentially the IBM PC of that time. Hundreds of programmers from around the world joined in the effort. The end result of all that was a new and improved GNU operating system now known as Linux (named after Linus, but which rhymes with Minix).

An important element of all GNU project utilities is that they are copyright-free, which means that anyone can download the operating system from the Internet and install it without charge. Even the source code is freely available. Unlike commercial software, where making copies for yourself and friends is illegal "piracy," there's no such restriction with Linux or any of the other GNU project utilities.

software product, you are really buying a license to use
lation procedure you might be forced to read the End
accept it before you can finish the installation. The
e copy of the software, and use it. But your rights stop
the software is owned solely by the holder of the
cturer. For example, Microsoft owns the rights to
he products it sells.

>uted under a different licensing scheme, known as
This is not to say that GNU software is "public
ire copyrighted. However, a secondary license,
ives everyone the rights to use, modify, and
ram derived from that code, but only if the terms
prevents a middleman from making a slight
program, slapping some new name on it, and selling it as a commercial

The copyleft license doesn't prevent a company from selling a unique version of the software.
This is why we have Red Hat Linux, as well as Debian Linux, SuSE Linux, and others. Each
version of Linux is a boxed set, with some added support, documentation, or other features,
that make it worth purchasing. However, Red Hat and the other manufacturers must
continue to make their versions freely available as well. So you could just download a copy
from the Internet and save yourself the cost of the boxed set. However, not many people do
that because the time and frustration involved in downloading far outweighs the small price
you have to pay for a boxed set.

As far as Linux and other GNU software being free is concerned—the term "free" in this
context really means "freedom" rather than "free stuff." The idea of the copyleft is that
anyone who uses the software has the freedom to make changes to the software, and the
freedom to make copies and pass it along. However, the copyleft requires that when they pass
along the software, they pass along the same copyleft distribution terms. This guarantees that
each person who uses the software has equal freedom to change and copy the software, no
matter who they got it from. If you'd like to learn more about the GNU project, the GPL, or
the history of Linux, take a look at any of the Web sites listed here:

- **GNU Project and The Free Software Foundation**: www.gnu.org
- **Open Source Software**: www.opensource.org
- **Linux International**: www.li.org
- **The Cathedral and the Bazaar**: www.tuxedo.org/~esr/writings/cathedral-bazaar
- **Red Hat's "About Us" page**: www.redhat.com/corp/about_us.html

So now you may be wondering, "If everything is 'free,' why did I have to pay for Red Hat
Linux at the store?" It's true that you cannot just walk out of your local computer superstore

with a Red Hat Linux box in your hand, unless you've paid for it. However, if you wanted to, you could download a copy of Linux from the Internet for free and install it on as many computers as you wish. You could wrap up some copies and give them away as presents, too, if you like. There's just one problem with that. Downloading an operating system from the Internet and getting it to work on your computer—without a lick of written documentation or support—is no small feat. In fact, for most people, the amount of time and frustration involved in such a feat is just downright prohibitive. It's "cheaper" (time-wise) to purchase the Red Hat Linux boxed set, which has been tweaked and refined to make installation as easy as possible. You get written documentation and 30 days free support with the Red Hat package. That's what you're really paying for when you buy a copy of Red Hat Linux from your local computer store.

## LINUX FEATURES

Though inexpensive, Linux is not a toy. It's a thoroughly modern, full-featured operating system with all the bells and whistles you'd expect to find in a modern OS. Linux is a UNIX clone, and therefore supports UNIX capabilities. For instance, Linux supports preemptive multitasking, which means it can run multiple programs at the same time. For example, as a single user you can be printing a document, formatting a disk, downloading a file, and editing some other document all at the same time. Linux is also a multiuser operating system, meaning that several people on a network can log in and use the computer resources at the same time. When you combine multiuser and multitasking capabilities, you end up with an operating system that can provide computing resources to a whole bunch of users at the same time. And ultimately, that's what networking is all about.

But there's still more to Linux that helps make it the world-class operating system it is today. Other important features include the following:

- **Portability:** Linux is portable, which means it works on a wide range of hardware platforms. Currently Linux runs Intel processors ranging from the 386 to the new Pentium III. It also runs on IBM/Motorola PowerPC, DEC Alpha, and Sun SPARC stations.

- **Security:** Linux is a secure operating system, which means you can protect sensitive data from prying eyes. You can also protect the system as a whole by denying less experienced users access to features that could lead to lost files and other mishaps.

- **Interoperability:** Interoperability (also called open systems) refers to the ability for different types of computers on a network to communicate with one another. Linux is fully compliant with the Portable Operating System Interface Specification (POSIX), which defines how systems interact.

- **SMP Support:** Some high-end workstations and servers use multiple processors to provide lightning-fast performance. Linux supports SMP (symmetric multiprocessing), which means it can take advantage of those multiple processors.

- **Open Source:** Linux source code is freely available. This is a boon to aspiring programmers who want to look inside the program to see what makes it tick. Experienced programmers can change the source code to make the program better suited to their own needs.

These features are available in all versions of Linux, whether you download a version off the Internet or purchase it at the store. The Red Hat distribution of Linux offers even more features.

## RED HAT FEATURES

Red Hat, Inc., is a software company in North Carolina that publishes the Red Hat distribution of Linux. At its core, the distribution is the same as the Linux you could download for free off the Internet. However, the Red Hat distribution comes on a CD-ROM, so there's no horrendous download to face. Also, the Red Hat Linux distribution includes much-needed (for most of us) written documentation. In addition, Red Hat has thrown in some other good, value-added stuff, including the following:

- **Simplified Installation:** Red Hat Linux 6.2 comes with its own graphical installation program, designed to make the installation as easy and painless as possible.

- **Support:** In addition to written documentation, registered Red Hat 6.2 users get 30 days of free installation support by telephone, 90 days of free installation support via the Web, and Free Priority FTP access for downloading fixes and improvements from the Internet. Register at http://www.redhat.com/apps/support.

- **Red Hat Package Manager:** Historically, installing application programs in Linux has been a complex procedure requiring substantial techno-knowledge. Red Hat Package Manager (RPM) and its graphical counterpart, GnoRPM, greatly simplify the process of installing, upgrading, and removing Linux application programs.

- **Sun Microsystems' StarOffice Deluxe:** Red Hat 6.2 comes with a copy of the popular StarOffice suite of programs that includes word processing, spreadsheet, database, presentations, and more. You'll also get all the Internet tools you need for browsing the Web, doing email, and more.

- **Modern Interfaces:** Like DOS, UNIX, and other early OS's, Linux is command-driven, which means you type in commands to get it to do things. Red Hat's distribution provides the popular GNOME, KDE, and X graphical user interfaces that bring the point-and-click convenience of the Windows and Macintosh OS to Linux.

- **Kudzu:** A feature that's specifically new to Red Hat 6.2 is a program called Kudzu, which can automatically detect and configure new hardware that you've added to your system.

In short, when you purchase Red Hat Linux, you're actually buying the convenience of having a boxed software product on CD-ROM with written documentation and added programs to simplify installation and use of Linux.

## WHERE TO USE LINUX

Part of the beauty of Linux is the fact that you can run it on a wide range of computers, from small inexpensive desktops on up to huge multi-processor servers. This wide range of applicability is especially appealing to businesses that want to build reliable, cost-effective networks. As a server, Red Hat Linux can easily be set up for use as a small intranet server or a server hosting multiple sites and hundreds of clients. All the software you need to set up an email server, Web server, DNS server, or news server is included right in the box—there's nothing extra to buy.

For more casual users and network clients, the graphical GNOME interface provides point-and-click ease of use for less experienced users. Many handy programs for email, browsing the Web, word processing, and publishing are included right in the box. In addition to the many GNU project utilities available for basic office operations, you can purchase third-party programs such as Corel WordPerfect and Applix Office. (Trial versions of both those products are included on the Red Hat Linux Applications CD.)

About the only place where Linux might not make sense is on a standalone computer that's used primarily for entertainment. For instance, I don't foresee switching my children's PCs over to Linux any time in the near future for the simple reason that the games they like to play are all Windows-based. Likewise, if you're a whiz with Windows or the Macintosh and you still need to get work done, you wouldn't want to switch to Linux all at once. Instead, you'd want to keep your existing system so that you can still get your work done and learn Linux on the side, as time permits. You can do this either by putting Linux on a separate machine or, in the case of Windows, by setting up your system to dual-boot with either Windows or Linux as the current OS.

# RED HAT LINUX SYSTEM REQUIREMENTS

Hardware requirements for Red Hat Linux 6.2 are pretty modest. So if you're at the very bottom of the learning curve, you can learn on relatively inexpensive equipment. Likewise, if you're building a business that needs networked computers, you can save quite a bit of money in both hardware and software costs. For PCs, you need at least the following hardware to run Linux:

- An Intel 386, 486, Pentium, Pentium II, Pentium III, AMD K6-2, AMD K6-3, or AMD Athlon.
- 16MB RAM (48MB recommended for graphical user interfaces).

- 500MB (1/2 a gigabyte) of free disk space.
- A CD-ROM drive and a floppy disk drive. If you can boot from your CD-ROM drive, the floppy disk drive isn't necessary.

In addition to Intel processors, Linux can be run on Dec Alpha and Sun Sparc workstations.

I don't want to imply that Linux will run in just any computer that meets the minimal requirements. There's a long list of products that are compatible with Linux and a pretty long list of products that aren't. For an up-to-the-minute list of Linux-compatible hardware products, visit the Red Hat Hardware Compatibility Lists at `http://www.redhat.com/corp/support/hardware`.

## INSTALLING RED HAT LINUX

Before you can start Linux, it needs to be installed on your computer. If you, or someone else, has already installed Linux, you're ready to roll. Just keep reading. If Linux isn't already installed on your computer, it will need to be installed first. You have a couple choices in deciding how you want Linux installed on your computer:

- If you plan to be able to use both Windows and Linux on the same computer, see Appendix A, "Dual Booting Windows and Linux," first.
- If you don't need to keep Windows on the same computer, see Appendix B, "Installing Red Hat Linux," instead.

## UNDERSTANDING USERS

As part of its built-in security scheme, Linux provides for two types of computer users. The first type is called the *superuser*, the *root* user, or the *system administrator*. Regardless of what you call the superuser, he or she is the one and only person on a Linux computer that has complete reign over the system. The superuser can do anything she wants, with no restrictions. If you're accustomed to having unlimited access to everything on your personal computer, then you're accustomed to having superuser powers. The superuser's username is always *root*, and of course the superuser can make up her own password.

The second type is a regular *user*, who has fewer privileges than the superuser. A regular user can do all the day-to-day things that most people do on a computer, such as run programs, edit, copy, and print files, and so forth. However, a regular user can't get into more sensitive areas of the operating system where a small mistake could cause large problems.

It's important to understand that, unlike standalone PCs and Macintosh computers, you cannot gain access to a Linux computer until you *log in*. And in order to log in, you need to have, at the very least, a username. If you are not the superuser of the computer you plan to run Linux on, you'll need to ask the system administrator for a username and password. If you are the superuser, then all you need to know is the superuser password. If you're also the person who installed Linux, you defined the superuser password during the installation.

# STARTING RED HAT LINUX

Starting Red Hat Linux is pretty much the same as starting any other operating system:

1. Empty all disk drives.
2. Turn on your computer.

The computer will go through its normal POST (Power On Self Test) where a bunch of technical gibberish whizzes by on the screen. Then Linux will kick in and do its own testing and configuration. At some point you'll see a LILO boot prompt. (LILO stands for Linux Loader.) That prompt will sit there for about five seconds, then still more text will whiz by on the screen.

## ENTERING YOUR USERNAME

Eventually, you may see a prompt that looks something like this on your screen:

`localhost login:`

If your computer is set up to automatically start in the GNOME user interface, within a few seconds the login prompt on the screen will be replaced with a dialog box asking you for Login and Password information. Either way you need to type your username login name, and then press the Enter key). If you are the superuser, you must enter the username root. If you are not the superuser, then you must type in the account name given to you by the computer's superuser. You can't just make up an account name on the fly. Like most things in Linux, the username you type is case-sensitive, so be sure to type in your username with the correct upper- and lowercase letters. Press Enter after typing your username.

## ENTERING YOUR PASSWORD

After typing your username and pressing Enter, you'll be prompted to enter your password. If you're at the command prompt, you'll see this prompt on the screen:

`Password:`

If you're in the GNOME user interface, the cursor will drop to the Password option in the dialog box. Either way, you need to type in your password, again being sure to use correct upper/lowercase letters. To prevent passersby from peeking over your shoulder and discovering your password, the password will not appear on the screen as you type it. After typing your password, press Enter or click the Login button, if you're in the graphical user interface.

If you installed Linux yourself, you *must* enter the superuser password you gave during the installation. If you're not the superuser, then you must type the password given to you by the superuser. If you've never been given a password, you may be able to make one up right now. If Linux came pre-installed on your system, it's hard to say exactly what the password will be. You may be able to create that password right now just by typing it in. If so, be sure to enter a password that's at least six characters in length. You'll be prompted to enter the same password a second time for verification. Go ahead and do so, pressing Enter after typing the password. If Linux came pre-installed on your computer and the login won't accept your made-up password, then you'll need to check the documentation that came with your computer to find out the correct password.

If the superuser told you to make up your password, you can do so now. Don't make the password something obvious, like your first name. Make it at least four characters long, and don't put in any spaces. Type in the password, and press Enter. You'll be asked to enter the same password again a second time, for verification. Type in the same password and press Enter.

## THE TWO FACES OF LINUX

Linux offers several *interfaces* (ways of interacting with your computer), but there are essentially two types of interfaces: a *graphical user interface* and a *character cell interface*. The differences are summarized as follows:

- **Graphical User Interface**: Abbreviated GUI and pronounced "gooey," this optional interface resembles the point-and-click interface of more modern Macintoshes and Windows computers. You have several different GUIs to choose from.

- **Character Cell Interface**: You interact with Linux by typing in commands and pressing Enter at the shell prompt (also called the *command prompt*), similar to DOS, UNIX, and other older operating systems. Rather than a lot of graphics, you see only a prompt like `[root@localhost /root]#` or `[alan@localhost alan]$`.

By default, the GUI named GNOME is the first to appear when you start Linux. GNOME stands for *GNU Network Object Model Environment*, and is yet another result of the GNU project. There are two situations, though, where GNOME might not start automatically:

- If your computer is configured to start at the command prompt, you can type `startx` and then press Enter to switch to GNOME.

- If you performed a server class installation of Linux, you'll be taken to the command prompt. If you want to use GNOME with a server installation, you'll need to install GNOME yourself, as discussed in the Case Study near the end of Chapter 9, "Configuring GNOME and Enlightenment."

**Tip**

It could take X a minute or more to start the first time, so be patient. If X gets "stuck" in an unusable state, see the Troubleshooting section at the end of this chapter for help.

If you have problems getting into the GNOME interface, please see the Troubleshooting section near the end of this chapter. The rest of this chapter will cover the most basic of "basic skills" needed to get around in the GNOME interface.

**Tip**

If GNOME doesn't look too good on your screen, try fiddling with the Brightness, Contrast, and other controls on the front of your monitor to get a better picture. If you have the ability to use multiple resolutions, you may have to tweak the monitor settings for each available resolution.

# GETTING AROUND IN GNOME

GNOME is a great graphical user interface for Linux, generally easy to learn and use. Figure 1.1 shows how GNOME looks when there are no open windows on the GNOME desktop. The names of major components that make up the GNOME interface are also pointed out there. The figure also shows GNOME with the Enlightenment *window manager* in place. The window manager is a program that gives the desktop its "look and feel," and Linux offers several to choose from. For the moment, however, it's not necessary to concern yourself with multiple window managers. We'll just refer to the screen shown in Figure 1.1 as *GNOME* throughout this chapter.

**Figure 1.1**
The GNOME graphical user interface, with the Enlightenment window manager in use.

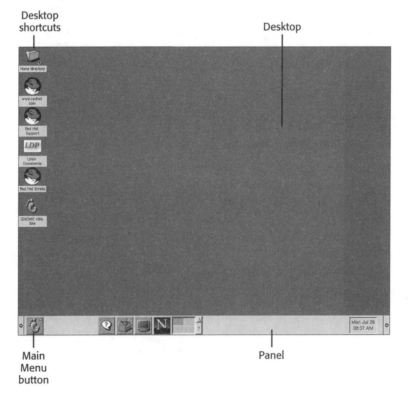

Each program that you run will appear in its own window on the Linux desktop. For example, your copy of Linux may be configured to automatically open the GNOME Help Browser and File Manager programs, as in Figure 1.2. If you logged in as the superuser, you might see a warning about opening the File Manager instead. Not to worry. If you click the OK button inside that warning dialog box, the File Manager will open.

**Figure 1.2**
GNOME with the GNOME Help Browser and File Manager windows open.

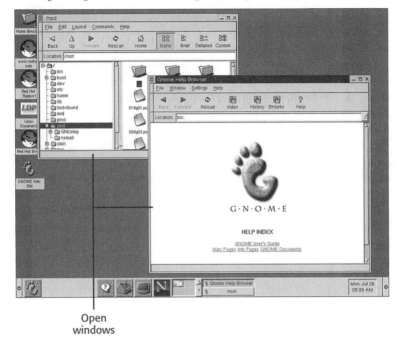

Open
windows

## POINT, CLICK, AND DRAG

Like most GUIs, GNOME provides a mouse-oriented point-and-click interface. GNOME assumes you're using a three-button mouse. But other than that, the terminology used to describe things you do with the mouse is the same as in most other GUIs:

- **Point**: To point to something, move the mouse pointer so that it's resting on the item.
- **Click**: To click (or click on) something, point to it, then press and release the left mouse button.
- **Double-click**: Point to the item, then press and release the left mouse twice in rapid succession.
- **Right-click**: To right-click something, point to it, then press and release the mouse button on the right.
- **Drag**: To drag an item, point to it, hold down the right mouse button as you move the mouse.
- **Drop**: To drop an item, drag it to some location, then release the left mouse button.
- **Mid-click**: To mid-click something, point to the item, then press and release the middle mouse button.

If your mouse doesn't have a middle button, don't worry about it. If your mouse is properly configured, you can simulate a mid-click by simultaneously clicking the left and right mouse buttons. If your mouse has a wheel, you can press and release the wheel to simulate a mid-click. If your two-button mouse or wheel won't emulate a mid-click, you probably need to reconfigure the mouse.

The mouseconfig program is an easy way to reconfigure your mouse and have it emulate three buttons. Get back to the command prompt (press Ctrl+Alt+Backspace) or open a terminal window (click the panel button that looks like a monitor) and enter the command mouseconfig. Choose your mouse from the list provided, select Emulate 3 Buttons, and then click OK.

> **Tip**
>
> You may want to reboot your computer, as discussed later in this chapter, after changing your mouse configuration. If you have any problems, see Chapter 8, "Configuring the X Window System," for more advanced configuration techniques.

## COMBO KEYSTROKES

Linux also supports the use of combination keystrokes as shortcuts to performing certain tasks. Combination keystrokes are always shown in the format *key+key*, or perhaps *key+key+key*.

Whenever you see such a combination, keep in mind that you must hold down the first key(s) while pressing the last key. Also, bear in mind that the term *press* always refers to something you do at the keyboard, not the mouse. So, for example, the instruction *press Alt+F4* means "hold down the Alt key, press and release the F4 key, then release the Alt key." An instruction like "press Ctrl+Alt+F7" means to hold down both the Ctrl and Alt keys, press and release the F7 function key, then release the Ctrl and Alt keys.

> **Tip**
>
> The Alt key is labeled Meta on some keyboards. When browsing Linux documentation, you may occasionally see *Meta*+key combinations referred to in the documentation. Just translate "Meta" to "Alt" if your keyboard has no Meta key. For example, instead of pressing Meta+PgUp, you'd actually press Alt+PgUp.

## CHANGING THE SCREEN RESOLUTION

If your screen is set up to handle multiple resolutions, such as $640 \times 480$, $800 \times 600$, and $1024 \times 768$, the first thing you'll want to do is get to the $1024 \times 768$ resolution. Smaller resolutions won't show all the components in the screen at once. You change resolutions in GNOME using the following keystrokes:

■ Press Ctrl+Alt++ (where the last + refers to the plus key on the numeric keypad) to go
to the next higher resolution.

■ Press Ctrl+Alt+- (where the - refers to the minus key on the numeric keypad) to go to
the next lower resolution.

Each time you press the three-key combination, Linux goes to the next available resolution
available on your system. In the example shown in the figure, the GNOME interface is shown
at $1024 \times 768$ resolution. If you can't get your resolution high enough to display all of the
GNOME screen, you can easily scroll any missing part into view. Just move the mouse
pointer off the edge of the screen in the direction you want to scroll. For example, moving the
mouse pointer to the bottom of the screen will scroll down. Moving the mouse pointer to the
extreme right edge of the screen will scroll to the right.

## INSTANT INFORMATION

There are a couple good tricks to know about GNOME, right off the bat. For one, if you
point to an object for a couple of seconds, you might see the name of the object or brief
instructions for using the object. For example, Figure 1.3 shows the message that appears
after resting the mouse pointer on a window's title bar.

**Figure 1.3**
Pointing to an
object in GNOME
often shows more
information about
the object.

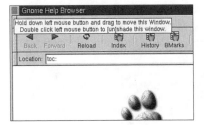

As a rule, clicking on an item opens, or activates, the item. If you're not sure what you want to
do with a particular item on the screen, try right-clicking the item. A menu of possibilities
may appear on the screen, as in the example shown in Figure 1.4. Not all items have these
right-click menus, and the options available on the menu will vary from object to object. Still,
it's worth right-clicking the item to see which options, if any, are available.

**Figure 1.4**
Right-clicking an
object on the
screen often dis-
plays a menu of
options that
pertain to that
object.

**Tip**

Often, you can change the appearance or behavior of an object on the screen simply
by right-clicking the item and choosing Properties.

## THE GNOME MAIN MENU

GNOME offers a main menu which provides easy access to some programs and features. To open that menu, click the footprint button near the lower-left corner of the screen. To view a submenu, point to any menu option that has a right-pointing triangle to the right of it, as in Figure 1.5. Getting the mouse pointer straight across to the submenu can take a little practice. Initially, you might have a tendency to move the mouse pointer up and down the Main Menu, which causes other submenus to open. If you keep the mouse pointer over to the right edge of the menu—right on the little triangles that point to the submenus—you'll find it easier.

**Figure 1.5**
The GNOME Main Menu and the Applications sub-menu.

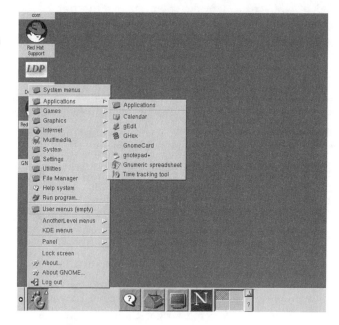

The first (topmost) option on each menu is just the menu's title. Clicking on the menu title closes the menu without making a selection. You can also close a menu, without making a selection, by using either of these techniques:

■ Click anywhere outside the menu.

■ Press the Escape key (Esc) on your keyboard.

To actually select an option from the menu, you need to click the option using the left mouse button.

As an alternative to clicking on the Main Menu button, you can get to a similar menu, shown in Figure 1.6, simply by mid-clicking the desktop. Remember, if your mouse only has two buttons, you can click the left and right mouse buttons simultaneously to simulate clicking the middle mouse button. Or, if your mouse has a wheel, you may also be able to simulate a mid-click by clicking (not turning) the wheel.

**Figure 1.6**
Click the desktop using the middle mouse button to display this menu.

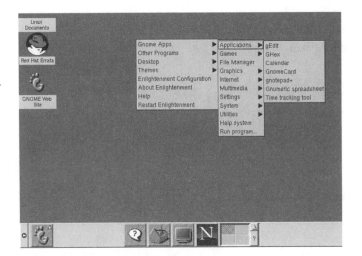

## CLOSING WINDOWS

As mentioned, when you first start GNOME on your computer, some windows may open automatically. To get to a clean desktop, you'll need to close any open windows on your desktop. To close an open window, just click the Close (X) button in the upper-right corner of the window you want to close (see Figure 1.7).

**Figure 1.7**
Click the Close (X) button in the upper-right corner of any window to close that window.

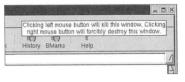

Chapter 2, "Getting Around," describes many more techniques for getting around in GNOME and managing windows on the GNOME desktop. For now, it's more important to learn that most basic of basic skills, how to log out of Linux.

## LOGGING OUT, SHUTTING DOWN

If you're going to be away from the computer for a while and you don't want anyone messing with your computer while logged in under your username and password, you need to log out. Doing so will leave the computer running, but with only a login prompt displayed on the screen. If you left any jobs running in virtual consoles, you may want to log out of those first by entering the exit command. Then, in the GNOME GUI, follow these steps:

1.  Click the Main Menu button and choose Log Out.

2.  In the dialog box that appears, choose Logout, then click the Yes button.

Within a few seconds, the Welcome To dialog box appears. To use the computer, you (or anyone else who happens to come along) needs to enter a valid username and password.

> **Caution**
>
> *Do not* just flip off the power switch when you're done using the computer, or even after logging out. You *must* shut down the computer first, as discussed under "Shutting Down Linux" later in this chapter.

# REBOOTING AND DUAL-BOOTING

In some situations you may need to reboot the computer. For example, if you set up your PC to dual-boot either Linux or Windows, you can reboot the computer to switch to Windows. In the unlikely event that your computer hangs (won't respond to the mouse or keyboard), you may need to reboot to get things going again. To do so, assuming you're in GNOME, follow these steps:

> **Caution**
>
> Rebooting is similar to shutting down, in that everything in RAM is erased. If you have any unsaved work on the screen, always save that work and close all open windows before you reboot.

1. Click the GNOME Main Menu button.
2. Choose Logout, Reboot, and then click the Yes button.

Lots of text will whiz by on the screen, the screen may go blank, and then your computer will go through its standard POST.

## REBOOTING TO WINDOWS

If you're planning to start Windows rather than Linux as the computer reboots, get your fingers on the keyboard near the letter *D* or the Tab key. Keep your eyes on the screen and watch for the following prompt:

`LILO boot:`

When that prompt appears, you have exactly five seconds to do one of the following:

- Press the Tab key to see a list of acceptable entries for this prompt.
- Type the name of the operating system you want to start.

To go straight to Windows, type dos and press Enter.

Optionally, if you want to see what boot-up options are available to you, you can press the Tab key when you see the LILO boot prompt. You'll see a list of acceptable commands followed by another boot prompt, something like this:

```
linux  dos
boot:
```

You then have another five seconds to start typing one command or the other. (By the way, dos is the correct command even if you're using Windows 95 or 98 because both of those operating system are based on the DOS kernel, which allows older 16-bit DOS and Windows 3.x programs to run on the computer.)

> **Tip**
>
> In Chapter 11, "Configuring Startup and Shutdown," you'll learn how to extend that five second LILO boot opportunity to any duration you like.

### REBOOTING TO LINUX

To get from Windows back to Linux, you need to reboot again. Remember, save and close any work in progress because rebooting wipes out everything that's not saved. Then:

1. Click the Windows Start button.
2. Choose Shut Down, Restart, and then click the OK button.

You don't need to keep a sharp eye out for the LILO boot prompt when you're booting to Linux. Even if you ignore the prompt, Linux will start automatically in five seconds.

> **Tip**
>
> To make Windows, rather than Linux, your default boot-up operating system, see Chapter 11 for details. In particular, set the default boot configuration in Figure 11.1 to dos.

## SHUTTING DOWN LINUX

It's vitally important that you always shut down Linux (or any other operating system) prior to turning off your PC because Linux uses buffers (portions of volatile RAM memory) to store information that needs to be written to the disk. It does so to decrease the number of visits to the disk and make your work flow more quickly. Shutting down Linux properly before turning off your PC ensures that all those buffers get written to disk. If you don't shut down properly, you'll not only lose any unsaved work, you may damage the filesystem so much that you can't even restart your computer. You'd need to reinstall Linux from scratch!

---

**Create a Safe Username and Password**

When you're the superuser, no restrictions are placed on what you can do with Linux. While all that power is good for the ego, there is one big downside to it. A seemingly simple typo or other mistake could have far-reaching effects on the entire system, effects so large as to wipe out the entire hard disk! (That's why you see a warning about using the File Manager as root when you first enter the GUI.)

A simple way to get some free insurance against such calamities is to create a second account for yourself that doesn't have superuser privileges. And use that account whenever you're not doing system administration. See Chapter 7, "Managing Users and Permissions," for information on creating user accounts.

---

## SHUTTING DOWN FROM THE GUI

Because of the potential for disaster, shutting down is usually a privileged command, which means only the superuser can do it. So if you're not the superuser, or the superuser hasn't granted you shutdown permission, you might not be able to shut down the PC at all. But, assuming you do have shutdown rights, here's how you do it:

1.  If you have any jobs running in virtual consoles, you'll want to finish those jobs and exit each console first.

2.  In the GUI, click the Main Menu button and choose Log Out.

3.  Choose Halt from the dialog box that appears, and then click the Yes button.

If you're not the superuser, and you really don't have the right to shut down the current computer, you may see a prompt on the screen asking for a password. You must enter the superuser password, and then click the OK button. Keep an eye on the screen as the computer shuts down. Don't turn off the computer until you see the message Power down near the bottom of the screen.

## SHUTTING DOWN FROM THE COMMAND PROMPT

If, for whatever reason, you're unable to get to the GUI and have only a command prompt to work with, you can still logout, reboot, or shut down. Chapter 2 explains all the details of using the command prompt. But for the time being, it's sufficient to know that you can use any of the following techniques at that prompt:

- To log out without rebooting or shutting down the computer, type exit and press Enter.

- To reboot the computer, press Ctrl+Alt+Del or type the command reboot and press Enter.

- To shut down the computer altogether, type halt and press Enter.

**Tip**

You can also use the conventional UNIX/Linux commands—shutdown -r now to reboot or shutdown -h now to shut down.

Remember, if you're rebooting to Windows, you need to keep an eye peeled for that LILO boot prompt as the computer is restarting. If you're shutting down the computer, don't turn anything off until you see the Power down message near the bottom of the screen.

# TROUBLESHOOTING

**When I type, nothing shows up on the screen.**

If you're trying to type your password in the Login dialog box, but your password doesn't show up as you type, make sure the cursor is in the correct field of the dialog box. Move the cursor to the field that you want to type in, and then click within that field. Then try typing again. Remember, when you type your password, nothing is supposed to appear on the screen. You just need to type your entire password without getting any real feedback from the screen, and then press Enter to complete your entry. You'll learn more about typing within dialog boxes and programs in Chapter 2.

**I get the message** Invalid username or password! after entering my username and password.

The username or password (or both) isn't a valid user account. Only the superuser can create user accounts. If you're not the superuser, you'll need to ask your system administrator to create an account for you. If you are the superuser, see Chapter 7 for information on setting up user accounts and password.

**Linux will only boot to a command prompt.**

The graphical user interfaces in Linux are optional. If, when you log into Linux, you're taken to a command prompt, type the command startx (all lowercase letters) and press Enter. If you get a message indicating that there is no such file or directory, probably no graphical user interfaces are installed on this computer. You'll need to browse through Chapter 2 to get your bearings. Then see the Case Study near the end of Chapter 9 for instructions on installing GNOME.

**Entering the command** startx **just gives me a blank (or messed-up) screen.**

If you get stuck in a mess when you try to start X, first make sure you give it a least a minute to get started the first time you use it. If nothing happens, back out of X by press Ctrl+Alt+Backspace. When you're returned to the command prompt, run the Xconfigurator program, as discussed under "Get Your GUI Working" in Appendix B.

**I get a graphical user interface when I start Linux, but it isn't GNOME.**

As discussed in Chapter 8, Linux offers several different graphical user interfaces. If you seem to be stuck in one other than GNOME, look for a window titled *xterm*. If you don't see such a menu, try clicking the desktop and choosing New Shell from the menu that appears. Click inside the xterm window, and then carefully type the following command, being sure to use all lowercase letters, forward slashes, and no blank spaces:

```
/usr/bin/switchdesk
```

Press Enter after typing the command. If all you get in response is an error message stating that there is no such file or directory, then GNOME probably isn't installed on this computer. See the Case Study at the end of Chapter 9 for information on installing GNOME.

If GNOME is installed on this computer, a dialog box titled Desktop Switcher should appear. Click the GNOME option in that dialog box, and then click the OK button. A message appears telling you that you need to restart the X Window System for the changes to take effect. Click the OK button in that dialog box to close it. To restart, click some part of the desktop to bring up a menu. Choose Exit Fvwm from that menu, then choose Yes, Really Quit from the submenu that appears. Wait for the new login dialog box to appear, and log in normally. If problems persist, see Chapter 8 for more information on the many faces of Linux.

Only a small portion of the GNOME desktop is visible on your screen, and/or things keep disappearing off the screen as you move the cursor around. These problems occur when you're using a $640 \times 480$ or $800 \times 600$ screen resolution. GNOME looks best at a $1024 \times 768$ resolution. If your computer is set up for multiple resolutions, you can hold down the Ctrl and Alt keys while pressing the + or - keys to change resolutions. If you can't get to a $1024 \times 768$ resolution, see Chapter 11 for more information on configuring your graphical user interfaces. Don't forget, too, that tweaking the controls on the front of your monitor can also help bring the overall picture into clearer focus.

**Tip**

Remember that if starting X causes a problem that makes your computer unusable, you can press Ctrl+Alt+Backspace to get back to the command prompt.

**I did a KDE Workstation installation, but always end up in GNOME.**

You've discovered a little bug in the installation program. A KDE installation installs both GNOME and KDE. While you're in GNOME, click the Terminal Emulation Program button in the panel to get to a command prompt. Then type the command `switchdesk-kde` in that window, and press Enter. Choose KDE from the Desktop Switcher window that appears, and then click its OK button.

**I can't simulate mid-click on the mouse.**

A two-button mouse needs to be configured to emulate a three-button mouse, if you want to be able to simulate a mid-click by clicking the wheel or both mouse buttons simultaneously. If your two-button mouse isn't set up for that kind of emulation, see Chapter 8 for information on reconfiguring your mouse.

# CHAPTER 2

# GETTING AROUND

## In this chapter

# MOVING AND SIZING WINDOWS

Most new programs you start will automatically appear within their own windows. As mentioned in the previous chapter, you can start most programs from the Main Menu, or the smaller menu that appears when you mid-click the desktop. For example, to run the Calendar application, you can click the Main Menu button and choose Applications, Calendar. Or, you can mid-click the desktop and choose GNOME Apps, Applications, Calendar. To open the Mahjongg game, click the Main Menu button, or mid-click the desktop and choose GNOME Apps. Then choose Games, Mahjongg. Figure 2.1 shows how the desktop might look after starting those two programs.

**Tip**

Recall from Chapter 1, "Getting Started," that if your mouse doesn't have a middle button you can simultaneously click the left and right mouse buttons, or click the mouse wheel (if there is one) to perform a mid-click.

**Figure 2.1**
The Calendar application and Mahjongg game open on the desktop. Note the location of the Tasklist.

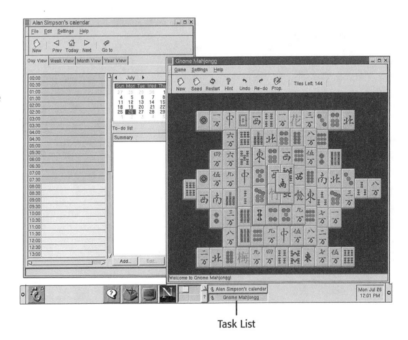

Task List

## TYPING IN WINDOWS

Whenever you have two or more open windows on the desktop, the window that's on the top of the stack is said to have the *keyboard focus* or simply *focus* for short. It's important to understand that the keyboard only works in the window that currently has the focus. There are three visual clues that you can use to tell which window currently has the focus:

- The title bar of the window that has the focus is colored differently from the title bars of windows that don't have the focus.

- As a rule, windows that don't have the focus don't overlap or secure the window that has the focus.

- The Tasklist button for the window that currently has the focus looks "pushed in."

**Tip**

In Linux, bringing a window to the top of the stack is called *raising* the window.

To give the keyboard focus to a specific window on your desktop, just click anywhere on that window. In Figure 2.1, you can see that the Mahjongg game window currently has the focus because its title bar is dark, it's not obscured by the Calendar window, and the Tasklist button has the pushed-in look.

## WINDOW WIDGETS

Each window has a similar set of *widgets*—little tools that help you manage the window. Common widgets are shown in Figure 2.2.

**Figure 2.2**
Widgets sur-
rounding a typical
window.

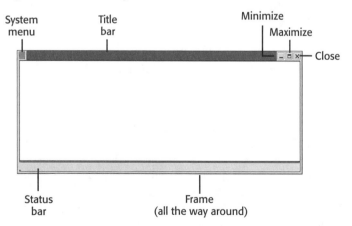

Like all GUIs, GNOME provides simple tools for managing the size and position of a window. If you point to the title bar or one of the buttons in the title bar for a couple seconds, you'll see a brief description of each button. Specific techniques for moving, sizing, and closing windows are as follows:

- To move a window, drag its title bar.
- To size a window, drag any corner or side.
- To maximize a window to full-screen, click its Maximize button.
- To restore a maximized window, click its Maximize button again.
- To minimize (or iconify) a window, click its Minimize button.
- To restore an iconified button to its previous size, click its Tasklist button (see the discussion of the Tasklist button later in this chapter if there is no such button).
- You can also minimize/restore a window by right-clicking its Tasklist button and choosing Show/Hide.
- To close a window, click the Close x button in its upper-right corner. Or, right-click its Tasklist button and choose Close.

The system menu in the upper-left corner of most windows provides an alternative technique for some of the preceding operations. To open the system menu, just click the small square near the upper-left corner of the window.

**Note** To quickly iconify all open windows on the desktop, press Alt+F4. If your Tasklist isn't set up to show minimized windows, you'll need to use the little arrow in the page to reopen the minimized windows.

You can reduce the size of a window to just its title bar as well. This might come in handy when you want to temporarily make a window as small as possible, but don't want to completely remove it from the desktop. Shrinking a window to its title bar is called *shading* because the window moves up and down like a window shade. To shade/unshade a window, do whichever of the following is most convenient at the moment:

- Double-click the window's title bar.
- Right-click the window's Tasklist button and choose Shade/Unshade.

## USING SCROLLBARS

If a window contains more information than can fit inside the boundaries of the window, one or two scrollbars will appear along the right and/or bottom borders of the window. The length (or width) of the scrollbar gives you an idea of how much information is available within the window. The raised "button" inside the scrollbar shows you how much of the overall content you're viewing at the moment. For example, the window in Figure 2.3 has a vertical scrollbar along its right border. Notice that the raised button within the scrollbar is about one-fourth the height of the window and near the top of the scrollbar. This tells you that you're viewing about the top one-fourth of the window's full contents.

**Figure 2.3**
This window has a vertical scrollbar along its right edge.

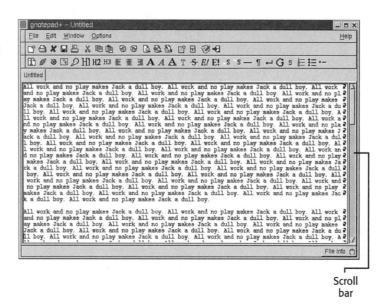

Scroll bar

You have several ways you can scroll through the contents of a window that displays scrollbars:

- Click the triangular button at the top, bottom, left edge, or right edge of the scrollbar to scroll a little bit in the direction of the arrow.

- Drag the raised button in the scrollbar to some new location along the scrollbar.

- Click on any non-raised portion of the scrollbar to jump to that section of the window.

- If your mouse has a wheel and you're using a vertical scrollbar, lay the mouse pointer on some non-raised portion of the scrollbar and turn the mouse wheel.

- If the window currently has the focus, you can use the ~UA, ~DA, ~LA, ~RA, Page Up (PgUp), and Page Down (PgDn) keys to scroll about.

**Tip**

In many windows, pressing Ctrl+Home will take you to the top of the document. Pressing Ctrl+End will take you to the bottom of the document.

# USING DIALOG BOXES

Dialog boxes provide an easy, graphical means of making selections. Many hundreds of dialog boxes are available to you, as you'll learn throughout this book. But many have certain features in common that are worth learning about now. As an example, Figure 2.4 shows the Control Center, which you can open on your own screen by clicking GNOME Configuration Tool button in the panel (it looks something like a toolbox and shows the GNOME

Configuration Tool when you point to it). Then click Background in the left column to display the Background dialog box.

The Control Center window contains two panes. The left pane contains a *menu tree*. Clicking an option in the menu tree displays a dialog box in the right pane. A plus sign (+) to the left of a menu tree option means that more options are hidden below. Clicking the + sign expands the list to show the option. A minus sign (-) indicates that all options are currently visible. Clicking that minus sign contracts the list once again.

**Figure 2.4**
The Control Center displaying the Background dialog box in the right pane.

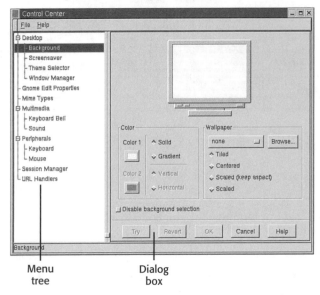

Menu
tree

Dialog
box

The dialog box itself appears to the right of the menu tree. As a rule, any option that looks "pushed in" is *selected* or *turned on*. Any option that appears "pushed out" is *notselected*, or *turned off*. To select or change an option, simply click it.

> **Tip**
>
> It's possible for a dialog box to be partially scrolled off the edge of the screen. When that happens, you can move the dialog box into a better position using the same technique you'd use to position a window: Point to the title bar of the dialog box, and drag it until the dialog box is positioned where you want it.

## DIALOG BOX BUTTONS

As a rule, selections you make from a dialog box are not applied until you click the Try, Apply, or OK button at the bottom of the dialog box. Different dialog boxes might offer different buttons. But you can generally count on a combination of the following buttons to be in just about any dialog box you come across:

- **Try**: Lets you try out a current selection without committing to it.

- **Revert:** Undoes whatever selections you activated with the Try button.

- **Apply**: Applies (permanently) any selections you made in the dialog box, and leaves the dialog box open.

- **OK**: Applies (permanently) any selections you made in the dialog box, and closes the open dialog box.

- **Cancel** the dialog box without saving any settings except those you've already activated with the Apply button.

- **Close**: Same as the Cancel button.

- **Help**: Provides help for the current dialog box. (Some will require access to the World Wide Web).

In situations where both a menu tree and dialog box appear, closing the dialog box might not close the menu tree. In that situation, you can click the Close (X) button near the upper-right corner to close the dialog box.

### DIMMED OPTIONS

Sometimes, the options in a dialog box will be dimmed, meaning they're currently unavailable. If you click such an item, nothing happens. To make the option available, you'll probably need to select some other option in the dialog box first. For example, in Figure 2.4 the Color 2, Vertical, and Horizontal options are currently dimmed and unavailable. Because it is not dimmed, you can tell the Solid option is selected within the dialog box; this tells Linux that you want to use only a single solid color as the background. Thus, the Color 2 and vertical/horizontal gradient options are irrelevant at the moment, and hence those options are dimmed.

If you were to choose Gradient in that dialog box, it would tell Linux that you want to use two colors for your background. The moment you select Gradient, the Color 2, Vertical, and Horizontal options are un-dimmed so that you can make your selections for the second color and gradient orientation. Feel free to try it yourself if you have the dialog box open. The small picture of the monitor in the dialog box gives you an idea of how your current selections will look on the actual desktop. To see your color(s) applied to the background, click the Try button. To undo the test, click the Revert button.

## USING THE PANEL

The panel along the bottom of the GNOME desktop is a very useful tool (see Figure 2.5). The Main Menu Button (footprint), as you know, opens the GNOME Main Menu. The tiny arrows at the left and right edges of the panel let you hide or display the panel. If the panel is in your way, click either button to hide the panel. Most of the panel disappears off the edge of the screen. However, an arrow remains at whichever edge you clicked. To redisplay the panel, just click the remaining arrow.

**Figure 2.5**
The GNOME panel and the names of objects on the panel.

The buttons to the right of the Main Menu button bring up specific programs. Pointing to a button for a few seconds brings up some brief text about the button. For example, if you rest the mouse pointer on the button that shows a question mark, you'll see that the button brings up integrated help. To actually select a button, just click it once. For example, if you click the button with the question mark, the GNOME Help Browser opens.

## CUSTOMIZING THE PANEL

If your panel doesn't look quite like the panels in this book, someone may have customized its appearance. You can customize its appearance as well by following these steps:

1. Right-click some neutral area of the panel or either of the small show/hide buttons at the edges of the panel.

2. Choose This Panel Properties. The Panel Properties dialog box appears with the Edge Panel tab active (see Figure 2.6).

**Figure 2.6**
The Panel Properties dialog box.

> **Tip**
>
> Keep in mind that you can change the appearance and behavior of most objects on the screen by right-clicking the object and choosing Properties from the menu that appears. If in doubt, just try it out.

Make your selections from the options that are presented and summarized here. Remember, if an option button looks pushed in, it means that the option is currently selected. To see how your selection will affect the actual screen, click the Apply button. Some dialog boxes will have a Try button. You can click that button to test your selection without actually committing to the selection. Options in the Panel Properties dialog box are summarized here:

- **Position**: Choose a position for the panel: Top, Left, Right, or Bottom.
- **Auto Hide**: If selected, the panel automatically slides off the screen when not in use. Rest the mouse pointer on the edge of the screen where the panel normally appears to bring the panel out of hiding.
- **Enable Hidebuttons**: If you de-select this option, the show/hide buttons at the left and right edge of the panel are disabled.
- **Enable Hidebutton Arrows**: If you de-select this option, the buttons at the left and right edges of the panel will be hidden.

Options on the Background tab let you customize the appearance of the panel. To switch to that other tab, just click the Background tab near the top of the dialog box (see Figure 2.7). The following are the options:

- **Standard**: Sets the panel to the default gray background color.
- **Pixmap**: Lets you choose a graphic image as a wallpaper for the panel. If you choose this option, you'll also need to specify the location and name of the graphic image.
- **Color**: Lets you choose a custom color for the panel. After selecting this option, choose a color from the Background Color button.

**Figure 2.7**
The Background tab of the Panel Properties dialog box.

After making your selections, click the OK button to save your changes and close the dialog box. To exit the dialog box without saving any changes, click the Closebutton instead. Be aware that when you click the Apply button, your changes are applied immediately and that the OK button may be dimmed. In that case, you can click the Close button to close the dialog box. The settings you have applied will remain in effect.

## CORNER PANELS

Normally, the panel extends across the width of the screen (or the height of the screen, if you move the panel to the left or right edge). You can shrink the panel down a little by changing to a corner panel. Just right-click some neutral area of the panel and choose Convert to Corner Panel. To get back to the larger view, right-click some neutral area of the panel and choose Convert to Edge Panel.

## MOVING AND DELETING PANEL APPLETS

Each tool on the panel is generally referred to as an *applet*. You can move applets around within the panel by following these steps:

1. Rest the mouse pointer on the item you want to move.
2. Hold down the middle mouse button, drag the item to the left or right, then release the mouse button. If your mouse doesn't have a middle button, drag by holding down both mouse buttons, or the mouse wheel if you have one.

> **Note**
>
> If you drag using the left mouse button, you'll end up making a copy of the applet. To get rid of either the original or copied applet, right-click it and choose Remove from Panel.

If you're not comfortable with the middle mouse button (or trying to emulate it with a two-button mouse), you can use this alternative technique instead:

1. Right-click the applet you want to move, and choose Move Applet. The mouse pointer changes to a four-headed arrow.
2. Move the mouse pointer to the left or right, depending on where you want to place the applet.
3. Click the mouse button after you've positioned the applet.

If you ever want to remove an applet from the panel, just right-click the applet and choose Remove from Panel from the menu that appears.

## CREATING QUICK PANEL SHORTCUTS

There are several more applets that you can add to the panel. To see your options, right-click anywhere on the panel and choose Add applet. From the submenu that appears, choose a category, then choose an applet. A button for starting that applet, or some other indicator, will appear on the panel. Don't worry if you don't know what an applet will do for you, there's no harm in experimenting. Have some fun. You can stick any applet that you want onto the panel. If you decide you don't like the applet, just right-click it and choose Remove from Panel.

As you gain experience using Linux, you'll probably find that you use some programs in the Main Menu more often than others. If you get sick of going through the menus to start a particular program, you can add an applet button for launching that program to the panel. To do so, click the Main Menu button, and begin making the selections you'd normally make to start the program. However, when you get to the final menu option for launching the program, don't click it. Instead, right-click the option. Then choose Add This Launcher to the Panel from the menu that appears. A new button appears in the panel. Clicking that button will now launch the appropriate program.

## CREATING MORE PANELS

If you try to add too many applets to the panel, you might soon run out of space. To get around that problem, you can create another panel, or several new panels, by following these steps:

1.  Right-click the panel that's currently visible on the screen.
2.  Choose Add New Panel from the menu that appears.
3.  To create a full-width panel, choose Edge Panel. To create a shorter panel, choose Corner Panel.

You can move or customize the new panel by right-clicking it and choosing This Panel Properties. If you want to customize two or more panels at the same time, right-click any panel and choose Global Properties instead. To delete a custom panel, right-click the panel you want to delete and choose Remove This Panel.

# USING THE PAGER

The GNOME desktop is larger than it looks. In fact, most of the time you're only seeing about one fourth of the screen. The Pager in the panel lets you move to other parts of the desktop. For example, suppose you drag an open window down toward the lower-right corner of the screen so that only the upper-left corner of the window is visible, as in Figure 2.8. If you look closely at the page, you'll see a small square straddling the lines that divide the Pager into four squares, as shown in the figure.

**Figure 2.8**
The Pager, and the upper-left corner of an open window.

The blue corner of the Pager shows you which quadrant you're in at the moment. You can click any of those small squares to visit another quadrant. When you do, you'll see whatever currently inhabits that quadrant. For example, clicking the lower-right section of the Pager takes you to the lower right quadrant, and you are then able to see the part of the window that's currently scrolled off the screen.

**Tip**

You are not limited to four virtual desktops. The section titled "Enlightenment Desktops" in Chapter 9, "Configuring GNOME and Enlightenment," explains how to add and remove virtual desktops.

When your desktop gets cluttered with open windows, you may want to consider moving some of them to other virtual desktops. You can, of course, drag the windows around, although that might be a bit tedious. Here's a cool shortcut that'll save you some time in sending any open window to any virtual desktop:

1. Right-click the title bar of window that you want to move to a virtual desktop.
2. Choose Desktop from the menu that appears.
3. Choose whichever option on the submenu best describes where you want to move the window.

For example, suppose that an open window is currently in the default upper-left virtual desktop. If you right-click the title bar in that window and choose Desktop, Move to Area Right, you'll move that open window into the virtual desktop just to the right of the current desktop. Clicking that quadrant down in the Pager will then take you to that virtual desktop, where you can see the open window.

As you change quadrants, items that are *sticky* will follow you. For example, the desktop shortcuts and the panel are both sticky, by default. So those items will be visible no matter which quadrant you're in at the moment. If you have an open window on the desktop that you'd like to make sticky (or unsticky), click that window's System Menu button. (Or right-click that window's title bar). Choose Stick/Unstick from the menu that appears. The option works as a toggle so that each time you choose Stick/Unstick, you switch from whatever the current setting is to the opposite setting.

## THE TASKLIST

The *Tasklist* in the panel shows a button for each window that's currently open. If you have a lot of windows open and they're overlapping, the Tasklist can bring any open window to the forefront (thereby giving it the keyboard focus as well). Simply click whichever button represents the window you want to give the focus to. By default, the Tasklist shows only open windows on the current desktop (quadrant) and only windows that aren't minimized at the moment. (However, you can change that default, as you'll learn in a moment.) To see a more thorough list of open windows, click the small up-pointing arrow just to the right of the Pager.

## CUSTOMIZING THE PAGER AND TASKLIST

To change the appearance or behavior of the Pager, click the Question Mark (?) button next to the Pager. The GNOME Pager Settings dialog box shown in Figure 2.9 appears with the Pager tab active. Options in that dialog box are as follows:

**Figure 2.9**
The GNOME Pager Settings dialog box.

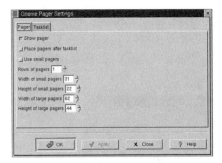

- **Show Pager**: If selected, the Pager is visible in the panel. If de-selected, the Pager is not shown.

- **Place Pagers After Tasklist**: If selected, this option moves the pagers to the right of the Tasklist, rather than the left.

- **Use Small Pagers**: If selected, this option shrinks the size of the Pager. De-select to return to the Pager to its previous size.

- **Rows of Pagers**: This option determines how many rows of pagers appear in the panel. Changing this option has no effect unless you set up change the number of separate desktops available to you (see Chapter 9).

The items beneath the Rows of Pagers option let you set the exact pixel size of small and large pagers—in case you happen to be *really* fussy about these things.

The following are the options on the Tasklist tab of the GNOME Pager Settings dialog box (see Figure 2.10):

- **Show Tasklist Button**: Shows or hides the buttons to the right of the Pager desktops.

- **Show Tasklist**: Shows or hides the list of open windows. If you clear this option, you should enable the Show Tasklist button option, so that you have some means of displaying buttons for all open windows.

- **Show Button Icons**: Determines whether or not the little icon at the left of each open window's button is visible.

- **Show All Tasks**: If selected, the Tasklist shows tasks that are currently in normal (open) windows, as well as tasks that are in minimized windows.

- **Show Normal Tasks Only**: If selected, the Tasklist shows only tasks that are currently in normal (open) windows. Tasks in minimized windows are not listed.

- **Show Minimized Tasks Only**: Opposite of Show Normal Tasks Only. If selected, the Tasklist shows only tasks that are currently in minimized windows. Tasks in normal open windows are not listed.

- **Show All Tasks on All Desktops**: Extends the Tasklist to include windows on all virtual desktops, not just the desktop you're in at the moment.

- **Show Minimized Tasks on All Desktops**: As preceeding, but shows minimized tasks on all the virtual desktops.

- **Geometry**: The various options under Geometry let you define exact size and appearance of the Tasklist.

**Figure 2.10**
The Tasklist tab of the GNOME Pager Settings dialog box lets you customize the Tasklist.

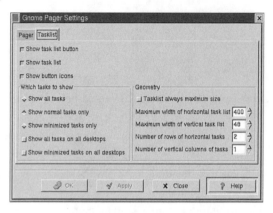

As always, you can click the Apply button to activate any settings that you've changed in the dialog box. When you're done, click the OK button to close and save (or click the Close button if you've already applied all your settings).

**Tip**

If you don't enable the Show All Tasks on All Desktops and Show Minimized Tasks on All desktops options, you'll need to click the triangle button to the left of the Tasklist whenever you want to see a complete list of open windows.

# USING DESKTOP SHORTCUTS

To move a desktop shortcut, just drag it to some new location on the screen. If you move desktop icons around and things get messy, you can easily tidy up. Right-click any area of the desktop and choose Arrange Icons from the menu that appears.

You can move or copy panel buttons to desktop shortcuts. Just drag (using the left mouse button) the applet you want to copy from the panel onto the desktop, then release the mouse button. If you don't want to keep a copy of the shortcut in the panel, just right-click the original panel applet and choose Remove from Panel.

# USING SCREENSAVERS

Any time you leave your computer unattended for 20 minutes or more, a screensaver will kick in. The screensaver keeps motion on the screen and is so named because if you leave an unchanging image on the screen for too long, burn-in can occur on some monitors (mostly older monitors). That burn-in causes the monitor to get blurry. Once the screensaver kicks in, moving the mouse or tapping any key on the keyboard should stop the screensaver activity.

If your screensaver is set up to keep unauthorized people from using your computer, you'll be greeted with a skull-and-crossbones dialog box that requests your password. To get out of the screensaver and back to work, you need to type in your password and press Enter.

If you want to change the screensaver, the time it takes for the screensaver to kick in, or the need to re-enter your password when stopping the screensaver, you can change your screensaver properties. Here's how:

1. Click The GNOME configuration tool button in the panel (the one that shows a toolbox).

2. In the Control Center that appears, click Screensaver in the left column. The options shown in Figure 2.11 appear.

**Figure 2.11**
You can customize your screensaver using the Screensaver dialog box in the GNOME configuration tool.

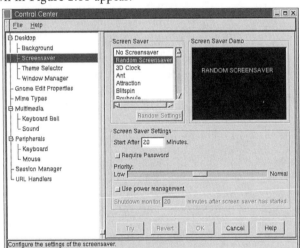

By default, the Random Screensaver option is selected in the list of screensaver names. That option tells Linux to pick a screensaver at random. To see what some of the other screensavers look like, just click any screensaver name in the list. The Screen Saver Demo to the right of the list shows you what that screensaver will look like.

> **Note**
>
> Some screensavers require a high color depth setting on your monitor. If a particular screensaver won't appear in the demo, it may be that your color depth setting is too low for that one. Try a different screensaver. Or, if you want to change the color depth setting of your GNOME display, see Chapter 9.

You can fine-tune the appearance and behavior of some screensavers. When you select a screensaver that has adjustable options, the Settings button directly under the list of screensaver names will be made available. You can click that button to see what additional options are available.

If your computer is new enough to have built-in energy-saving features, you can select the Use Power Management option to take advantage of your monitor's capability to shut itself down when not in use. After you select the Use Power Management option, you can then set the number of minutes to wait, after your screensaver kicks in, before the monitor shuts down. If you just want to use power management, and no screensaver, set that delay to 0 (zero) minutes.

As always, you can save your new settings and exit the dialog box by clicking the OK button. Then close the Control Center by clicking its Close (X) button. Remember, the screensaver or power management won't kick in until neither the mouse nor keyboard has been used for the amount of time specified in the Screensaver dialog box.

There's a lot more you can do with the GNOME interface, as you'll learn in upcoming chapters. And, you'll find many alternative GUIs that you can use in Linux. For now, though, you've learned enough to get around GNOME. Basically, it all boils down to pointing at some item, then clicking on it. Or, if you're not sure what you want to do with a specific item, you can right-click it to see which options, if any, appear. If you want to change the appearance or behavior of an item, try right-clicking it and choosing Properties. Next, we'll look at the other main interface offered by Linux, the character cell interface.

# THE CHARACTER CELL INTERFACE

If your computer experience goes back to the early days of UNIX or DOS, you're probably familiar with the "command prompt" mode of doing things. The screen shows a prompt, and you simply type in a command and press Enter. As soon as you press Enter, the command you typed is sent to the computer, which carries out the command.

Just as Linux has multiple GUIs to offer, it also offers multiple command prompt shells. (They're called "shells" because they sort of protect the underlying operating system.) The default shell, and the one you're most likely to encounter, is named *bash* for *Bourne Again Shell*. In GNOME, you can call up a *terminal window* that provides a command prompt. To open a terminal window, do whichever of the following seems most convenient at the moment:

- Click the Terminal emulation program button in the panel (it shows a picture of a computer monitor).
- Click the Main Menu button and choose Utilities, GNOME Terminal.
- Mid-click the desktop and choose GNOME Apps, Utilities, GNOME Terminal.
- For a more colorful display, click the Main Menu button and choose Utilities, Color XTerm.

The terminal window will open, looking similar to the example shown in Figure 2.12. Before you start typing commands, make sure the terminal window has the keyboard focus. Just click anywhere within the window to give it the focus.

**Figure 2.12**
A GNOME terminal window open on the desktop.

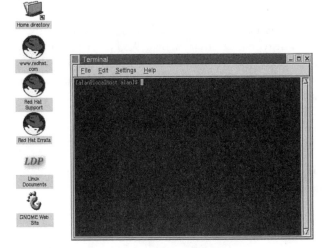

## THE SHELL PROMPT

How your particular shell prompt will look on the screen depends on your user name and your computer's name. However, the prompt will probably look something like this:

```
[root@localhost /root]#
```

The first part will be your user name. If you're logged in as the superuser, then your username is root and that's what appears in the prompt. If you're logged in as a regular user, your prompt may look more like the following one, with your name in place of alan in the example.

```
[alan@localhost alan]$
```

Where the example shows localhost, the name of your computer will appear. Your computer may also be named localhost, if nobody has ever given it a different name. The text after the space generally shows the name of the directory you're in at the moment. Chapter 3, "Understanding the Linux Filesystem," discusses directories in detail. The pound sign (#) character at the end of the prompt appears only if you're the superuser. If you're logged in as a regular user, a dollar sign appears instead of the pound sign.

The command prompt appears in the character cell interface whenever Linux is ready to accept a new command. Before you enter a command, you need to understand these three important rules:

■ **Everything in Linux is case-sensitive**. When typing commands, you must use the correct upper- and lowercase letters. As a rule, most commands are lowercase.

- **Spaces count**. When you see a command like ls -a ¦ lpr and you want to try that command, be sure to include all the blank spaces. Typing ls-a¦lpr won't work.
- **You must press Enter after typing the command**. The command isn't actually sent to the computer until you press the Enter key.

So, whenever you see an example of a command in this book (or on the Web or wherever), remember that you must type it exactly as shown. And don't forget that you have to press Enter afterward. For example, consider the bash command, which will start the bash shell (or do nothing, if you're already in the bash shell). First, to make sure you're in the bash shell right now, type the following:

```
bash
```

Then press the Enter key. If you're already in the bash shell, no harm done. A new, fresh command prompt will appear on the screen. Another example of a simple command is clear, which clears all clutter from the terminal window or screen, and displays a new command prompt. To try the command, type the following:

```
clear
```

Then press Enter.

## ERROR MESSAGES

If you type a command incorrectly and press Enter, you'll see an error message that follows this general pattern:

```
bash: problem: errormessage
```

bash is the name of the shell you're in, problem points out the part of the command that caused the problem, and errormessage is a brief description of the problem. For example, if you enter the command CLEAR (uppercase letters), the following message would appear, followed by a new command prompt:

```
bash: CLEAR: command not found
```

The problem is that Linux cannot find a command named CLEAR to execute. Linux can't find the command because Linux is case-sensitive, and the correct syntax for the command is the word *clear* in lowercase letters. (See, I'm not kidding about case-sensitivity!)

As another example, suppose you're logged in as a regular user. You try to access a directory that only the superuser can access, such as /root. The error message you get might look something like this:

```
bash: /root: Permission denied
```

The Permission denied message indicates that you do not have permission to do whatever the command requested. You can't get around an error like that. You either need to be the superuser to gain permission or you must get the superuser to grant you permission to whatever the command might be.

The shell prompt always reappears just under the error message, so you can try entering some other command. Rather than typing a new command from scratch, you can access and modify any previously entered commands to make corrections, thanks to the command history.

## COMMAND HISTORY

Bash keeps track of every command you enter in its command history. You can use the command history to bring back commands you entered previously. This saves typing when you want to enter a new command that's similar to one you just entered. You can also use it to make corrections to a command. For example, if you enter a command, press Enter, and don't get the results you want, you may have typed the command incorrectly. To view, and possibly repair that command, press ~UA to bring the command back to the prompt.

PART

I

CH

2

**TABLE 2.1    KEYS USED TO MOVE THROUGH THE COMMAND HISTORY**

| Key | Purpose |
| --- | --- |
| ~UA or Ctrl+P | Move back through command history |
| ~DA or Ctrl+N | Move forward through command history |
| Alt+Shift+< | Move to first command in history |
| Alt+Shift+> | Move to last command in history |

When you have a command back at the prompt, you can use the editing keys described next to make additions or corrections. Then press Enter to enter the new version of the command.

## MAKING CORRECTIONS AT THE SHELL PROMPT

We all make typing errors. When typing a command at the command prompt, there are a few keys you can use to make changes and corrections prior to pressing Enter to enter the command. These keys are listed in Table 2.2.

**TABLE 2.2    KEYS FOR MAKING CHANGES AND CORRECTIONS AT THE SHELL PROMPT**

| Key | Purpose |
| --- | --- |
| Backspace | Erase character to left of the cursor |
| ~LA or Ctrl+B (Back) | Move cursor left one character |
| ~RA or Ctrl+F (Forward) | Move cursor right one character |
| Alt+B (Back word) | Move to start of previous word |
| Alt+F (Forward word) | Move to end of next word |
| Ctrl+A | Jump to start of line |
| Ctrl+E | Jump to end of line |
| Ctrl+L | Clear screen except this command |
| Ctrl+D (Delete) | Delete character at cursor |

**TABLE 2.2  CONTINUED**

| Key | Purpose |
|---|---|
| Ctrl+U (Undo) | Erase all text at the prompt |
| Ctrl+W (Delete word) | Delete from cursor to start of word |
| Ctrl+T (Transpose letters) | Transpose this character with character at left |
| Ctrl+C (Cancel) | Cancel command |
| Other key | Inserts text at cursor |

You'll learn a lot more about its capabilities as we progress through the chapters. For now, it's sufficient to know that when typing commands, you need to type them correctly (usually in all lowercase). Once the command is typed, you need to press Enter to send the command to Linux.

The terminal window, in which you type commands, can be closed like any other window. Just click the Close x button near its upper-right corner.

# UNDERSTANDING VIRTUAL CONSOLES

As a multiuser operating system, Linux supports the concept of virtual consoles or virtual terminals. This allows you to operate up to seven different "monitors" from a single mouse and keyboard. These aren't actual physical monitors that take up space on your desktop. Rather, they're virtual monitors that use your single physical monitor. The monitors are numbered 1 through 7. To switch from one monitor to another, hold down the Alt and Ctrl keys, then press the function key that represents the monitor you want to switch to. For example, pressing Alt+Ctrl+F2 takes you to console number 2. Pressing Alt+Ctrl+F5 takes you to console number 5.

**Note**

Virtual consoles are not the same as GNOME virtual desktops described earlier in this chapter. Virtual consoles exist "outside" the GUI, each with its own shell command prompt. Virtual desktops, on the other hand, are portions of the screen that exist only within the GUI.

Each virtual console is like a full-screen terminal window, in that you can work only at the command prompt. When you first log into a new virtual console, you're taken to the login prompt. You can log in using the same username that you originally logged in with or a different username. Once you've logged in, you have all the capabilities you had on your original login. You can start another lengthy job and switch to yet another console, or just stay in the console for more routine work.

Virtual consoles are handy for running jobs that take a long time to complete. You can start a job in one virtual console and let it get going. Rather than waiting around for that job to finish, you can switch to another virtual console and perform some other work, just by holding down the Ctrl+Alt keys while pressing one of the function keys F1 through F7. You'll learn many Linux commands as you progress through this book. For the time being, though, it's sufficient to know that as an alternative to using a terminal window to enter commands, you can use a virtual console.

---

**Virtual Consoles 1 and 7**
Virtual consoles are used both for X, the program that allows you to work with GNOME, and other GUIs. Console 7 actually shows the GUI; Console 1 just shows some messages that occur as the GUI is running. Normally, you'd never really use Console 1. But, if something weird happens in the GUI, you can often find out what happened by taking a peek at Console 1.

For example, suppose you try to run some program in GNOME, you briefly see the mouse pointer turn to the "wait" (watch) symbol, and then nothing happens. If you press Ctrl+Alt+F1 to switch to Console 1, there's a good chance you'll see some kind of message describing why the program wouldn't start.

---

## EXITING A VIRTUAL CONSOLE

When you've finished working in a virtual console, you should close it, just to make sure you don't leave any unfinished work hanging around. To exit the console you're in at the moment, type exit and then press Enter. You'll be prompted to log in again. Assuming you're done with this virtual console, you would then hold down the Ctrl+Alt keys and press one of the function keys F1 through F7 to go to another virtual console.

## RETURNING TO THE GUI

Virtual consoles 1-6 are always command prompt consoles. Console 7 is always the GUI interface. Any time you want to get back to the GUI, simply press Ctrl+Alt+F7.

# PROJECT PAGE

Now that you've learned some basic "getting around" skills in Linux, why not challenge yourself a little and see if you can complete some of the following small projects on your own:

■ **Run the System Info program to see a brief description of the hardware in your PC.** You haven't seen this program yet, but here's a hint. It's under Utilities on the GNOME Main Menu. See if you can find it, run it, take a look, and then close it on your own.

- **Try to set up a theme on your PC.** Even though I didn't discuss themes in this chapter, you can probably figure out what they are and try some out, on your own. I'll tell you how to get started, though. Open the GNOME Configuration Tool, and click Theme Selector in the menu tree. Use the Preview and Try buttons in the dialog box to check out some of the available themes. To get back to the original theme, choose Default from the list of themes.

- **Move some windows around the virtual desktops.** Open any four programs that you can think of, then move three of them to other virtual desktops. Remember, an easy way to move a window to a different virtual desktop is to right-click its title bar, then choose an option from the Desktop menu. After you've put each of the four windows into a separate virtual desktop, go to each of those desktops and close its open window.

# CHAPTER 3

# UNDERSTANDING THE LINUX FILESYSTEM

**I**n this chapter

# UNDERSTANDING LINUX FILES

In a computer, virtually all information that's stored on a disk is stored within a *file*. Programs, documents you create, settings you've made, Linux itself—all these things are stored in files. And therefore, your hard disk may well contain hundreds, or even thousands, of files. The way in which these files are named and organized is called the *filesystem*. The Linux filesystem follows rules and conventions that are different from other operating systems, like the Macintosh OS or Windows.

You probably know that every file in a filesystem has a *filename* that (hopefully) gives some clue as to the contents of the file.

If you are using special (non-alphanumeric) characters in a filename, you must place the filename in quotes when you refer to it.

To pay special attention to the filename, many people use periods, hyphens, and underscore characters in place of blank spaces. For example, all the filenames shown here are perfectly valid in Linux because they contain letters, numbers, and the dot, hyphen, or underscore:

- `fd`
- `e-conf`
- `bash_history`
- `.gimp`
- `xmorph-1996.07.12`
- `panel.dl`
- `wanda.bea.starr`
- `Snaffle Waffle (tooth).txt`

If you're accustomed to DOS or Windows, the multiple dots in the filename might seem strange. But the characters following the last dot represent the filename extension and can be used to associate document files with programs. (More on this topic in Chapter 4.)

> **Tip**
>
> If you plan on copying files from Linux to Windows, you can give your filenames Windows-like extensions. When copied or transferred, those extensions will play their normal roles in Windows.

## CASE SENSITIVITY

Everything in Linux is case-sensitive, even filenames. Hence, files named *myfile*, *myFile*, *MyFile*, and *MYFILE* are four completely separate and independent files, just as four files named *apples*, *bananas*, *cherries*, and *dingleFritz* are four separate, independent files. Linux and UNIX users tend to stick with lowercase letters in filenames so that upper- and lowercase letters in filenames don't become a confusing issue, although, there are exceptions to the rule. Some people prefer to capitalize each "word" within the filename, as in *AnotherLevel* or *libNoVersion*. So you can't rely on all filenames to contain lowercase letters only.

## HIDDEN FILES

Files can be hidden from view. For example, many files that contain system settings, which only the superuser should mess with, might be hidden from regular users. And individuals might want to hide a file from other users. To create a hidden file, one just needs to make the first character of the file a dot. For example, the following are all examples of valid, hidden filenames:

- `.bash_history`
- `.Xclients`
- `.wm_style`
- `.gnome-help-browser`

PART

**I**

CH

**3**

Hidden files aren't really too terribly hidden. In fact, it's pretty easy to view hidden files. People tend to use hidden files as a means of keeping certain filenames out of the way while casually browsing around a disk. Hiding a file doesn't necessarily protect that file from unauthorized access. As you'll learn later in this chapter, though, there are other ways to set *permissions* on files which prevent unauthorized access to those files.

> **Tip**
> Chapter 7 will discuss the "how-tos" of granting permissions to access files in depth.

## FILE TYPES

Linux views each file on the system as being an *executable file*, a *system file*, or a *user data file*. The difference between the three types is summarized here:

- **Executable files**: These files contain instructions that tell the computer to do something. Programs and scripts that the computer "runs" are always executable files.
- **System data files**: These files contain information that is used by executable programs. System administrators and programmers can often tweak the contents of a system data file to make a program run differently.
- **User data files**: These files contain the text and data that we humans create and use.

Linux usually assigns file types automatically, so you needn't concern yourself too much with types. Although, if you're coming from a DOS or Windows environment, it's helpful to know that Linux doesn't make any assumptions about the type of file based on filename extensions.

For example, while an .exe file in Windows is always assumed to be an executable program file, the .exe extension in Linux doesn't presume anything about the file type.

**Tip**

As in Windows, you can associate filename extensions with programs to make it easy to open documents in the most appropriate program. Use the Mime Type Capplet discussed in Chapter 9 to create such associations.

## OWNERS, PERMISSIONS, AND GROUPS

Linux is very much a secure operating system. An individual user can protect his or her files by deciding which users can, and cannot, view or change that file. The buzzwords that go along with security at the file level are *owner*, *group*, and *permission*. Linux assigns an owner to every file in the filesystem. For example, when a user creates and saves a file, that user automatically becomes the owner of that file. The owner of the file has the right to determine who can, and cannot, access the file by granting permissions to other users.

The owner can grant or deny himself and other users three kinds of permissions:

- **Read**: Making a file readable allows other users to view the contents of the file. But they cannot change the contents of the file. If the owner makes the file "not-readable," then other users cannot even see the contents of the file.

- **Write**: If the owner of a file makes the file "writeable," then other users can view and change the contents of the file, even delete the file. If the owner declares the file "not-writeable," other users cannot change or delete the file.

- **Execute**: If the file that the owner created is an executable file (that is, a script or program), the owner of that file can grant execute permissions to allow others to run the file or deny that permission to prevent others from running the file.

The owner of a file need not grant these permissions on a user-by-user basis. To do so, in fact, would be tedious. For example, what if the owner wanted to grant "read" permissions to everyone in a company, or everyone on the Internet? It would be difficult, if not outright impossible, to grant permission to everyone who might want to take a look at the file. So rather than granting permissions to individuals, the owner of a file grants permissions to groups of individuals.

A group is a set of people to whom the owner of a file can grant permission. Each owner can assign permissions to three groups named Owner, Group, and World:

- **Owner**: The owner of the file (typically one person).

- **Group**: The group that the owner belongs to. This might be the owner's co-workers in a company department.

- **World**: Everyone else in the world.

Let's take a look at an example. Suppose the superuser at Company X creates groups of users named *acct* and assigns every user in the accounting department to that group. Furthermore, let's say a user named Lana belongs to that group.

**Note** The superuser can create groups as well as individual user accounts. Chapter 7 will explain how.

One day, Lana uses WordPerfect (or a similar program) to create and save a file that contains some payroll information. By virtue of the fact that Lana created the file, she automatically becomes the owner of that file. Lana doesn't want anyone but herself tinkering with the payroll file she created. But she needs to allow other members of the accounting department to see the contents of the file. People outside the accounting department shouldn't be able to see the contents of the file at all. So how does Lana set up the file permissions to make this all happen?

Easy. Lana grants herself (Owner) Read and Write permission to the file. That way, she can view and change the file any time she wants. She then grants Read permission to Group-(other people in the Accounting department)so they can view the file's contents, but not change the file. And lastly, Lana grants no permissions to the rest of the World, thereby denying everyone else any access to the file's contents.

What about Execute permissions? In this example, Lana created the file using WordPerfect, which implies that the file is a document (user file), as opposed to a program. So the Execute permission doesn't really apply. Therefore, no one can be granted Execute permission in this example. However, let's say Lana also creates a program or script that can be run on the computer to perform some task. Lana can easily determine who can and can't run the program or script by granting Execute permissions to only those people or groups that she wants to be able to execute the program, and denying Execute permission to people who shouldn't be running that program.

**Tip** You can also assign permissions to a directory as a whole. For example, Lana could create an entire directory of files that only she can change and only the accounting department can view. More on directories a little later in this chapter.

For the moment, it's not necessary to know how to grant permissions and such. Chapter 7 will cover all of that. For now it's sufficient to know that unlike a standalone desktop operating system, which has little or no file security, Linux is a complete network operating system with extensive security. As a user, you have the ability to protect files from other users. And other users have the ability to protect their files from you as well. (Unless you're the superuser, in which case you can do pretty much anything you want!)

# UNDERSTANDING DIRECTORIES

If you were to place all the files on your hard disk in one place, you'd end up with a really lengthy list of filenames to contend with. Doing so would be similar to taking everything out of a file cabinet and dumping it all into one big box. You'd have to dig through the entire box every time you went looking for a particular file. Fortunately, your file cabinet lets you organize your files into folders, which makes it a lot easier to find things. Linux allows you to organize your files into *directories*, which are also called *folders* in some operating systems.

A directory, then, is just some part of the hard disk that contains its own files. In fact, in Linux, a directory is really just a file that contains still other files. The rules that apply to filenames—and all the business with ownerships and permissions—apply equally to directory and filenames. For example, our pal Lana from the previous example could create a directory named Lanas-Secret-Stuff. By granting herself full permissions to the contents of that directory and granting no permissions to anyone else, she automatically protects every file in that directory from unauthorized access.

## THE INVERTED TREE

The directories in the Linux filesystem are arranged in a hierarchy, also called an *inverted tree*. At the top of the hierarchy (or upside-down tree) is the *system root* a directory that's always named simply / (a forward slash). Just beneath the system root are the first-level directories. Any directory can contain still more directories (sometimes called *subdirectories*). Figure 3.1 shows an example, using an abridged version of the actual Linux filesystem. You can see that the system root (/) is at the top of the hierarchy. That system root contains still more directories named bin, dev, mnt, and home. The home directory contains still more directories, named alan, alec, and lana.

**Figure 3.1**
A sample directory hierarchy. The system root (/) is always at the top.

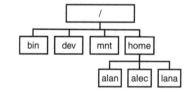

## PARENTS AND CHILDREN

It's common practice to define the relationships among directories using the same language one might use when describing a family tree. A *parent directory* is a directory that contains still more directories. For example, in Figure 3.1, the system root (/) is the parent to the bin, dev, mnt, and home directories. Likewise, bin, dev, mnt, and home directories are all children of the system root, /.

The home directory is the parent to the alan, alec, and lana directories. And alan, alec, and lana are all children of the home directory. I suppose we could say that alan, alec, and lana are all "grandchildren" of the system root (/), although you never hear the term "grandchildren" used in the computer world. Similarly, we could say that alan, alec, and lana are all siblings to one another because they share the same parent, although you don't hear the term "sibling" used too often either.

## PATHS

A *path* is the complete list of directories one needs to follow to get to a specific file or directory in the filesystem. The path always starts with a slash, to indicate the system root at the top of the directory tree. Then, each directory name in the path is followed by a forward slash to separate its name from the parent directory name. For example, the following path

/home/alec/myresume.txt

specifically refers to a file named myresume.txt that's in the directory named /alec. The /alec directory, in turn, lives inside the /home directory. And the home directory is directly under the system root. The path leaves no ambiguity as to the exact location of the file named myresume.txt.

**Caution**

Windows users beware. Linux uses forward slashes (/), whereas Windows uses backslashes (\) in path names. You'll need to break the habit of using backslashes because they don't work in Linux!

## STANDARD DIRECTORIES

The inverted tree example shown previously in Figure 3.1 represents only a small portion of the actual Linux filesystem. When Linux is first installed, it automatically creates many directories. The directory names are by no means arbitrary. Rather, they follow the Linux Filesystem Standard (FSSTND). The standard is a great thing because it provides some predictability as you go from one Linux (or UNIX) machine to another. It also makes it easier for authors like me to describe where a file can be found. For example, rather than referring to a file just by its name like "the fstab file (somewhere on your hard disk)," I can pinpoint the file for you, as in "the /etc/fstab file."

**Note**

If you want to learn more about the Linux Filesystem Standard, visit http://www.pathname.com/fhs on the Web.

Although it's not necessary to know exactly what's in each directory, it's good to have a sense of which kinds of files are stored in the different directories. The contents of the system root, and the immediate children of the root directory, are summarized here:

- **/**: The root of the entire filesystem, it contains all the following directories, plus any other directories you create at that level.
- **/bin**: Contains binary files (programs) that are part of the Linux operating system.

- **/boot**: Contains the Linux kernel and files needed by LILO to boot the computer.
- **/dev**: Contains device drivers for connected hardware devices. Linux treats all connected devices as files within this directory.
- **/etc**: Contains most system configuration files for the computer.
- **/home**: Each regular user on a Linux system has his or her own home directory. All those home directories are contained within this /home directory. (They should have named this one /homes, since it contains a home directory for each user!)
- **/lib**: Contains library files that are required to start the computer and run some programs and commands.
- **/lost+found**: Files that, for whatever reason, get lost in the filesystem end up in this directory when the fsck (FileSystem ChecK) program is run.
- **/mnt**: Contains mount points for removable media such as floppy disks and CD-ROMs. Red Hat Linux automatically creates one subdirectory named floppy and another named cdrom within this directory, and makes the files from mounted floppies and CD-ROMs available within those subdirectories.
- **/proc**: Used by Linux for handling processes (running programs) and for managing system information.
- **/root**: This is the home directory for the root user (superuser). Regular users can't get to this directory. Don't confuse the /root directory with the system root named /. (Maybe they should have named this directory /super or /sysadmin or something.)
- **/sbin**: Contains the superuser's binary files (programs). Only the superuser can run the programs that are stored in this directory.
- **/tmp**: Stores temporary files. Any user can place temporary files here. Files in this directory are erased each time you start or reboot the computer. So don't use it for storing anything that you want to keep!
- **/usr**: Contains files that are accessible to all users, not just the superuser.
- **/var**: Contains files whose contents vary (change) frequently, such as log files that are created and maintained automatically by Linux, and files that are waiting to be printed.

Linux also creates many subdirectories beneath the first-level directories. Some of those subdirectories have names that are similar to parent directories, which could potentially be confusing. However, if you always use the complete path to refer to a directory, there can be no doubt which directory you're referring to. For example, the /usr directory of the filesystem contains subdirectories named /bin and /etc. When referring to a directory, you always need to include the parent directory name. So the /bin directory always refers to the directory named bin that's just beneath the system root, whereas /usr/bin always refers to the directory named bin that's a child to the /usr directory.

If you were to explore your filesystem and check out the contents of the /usr directory, you'd see that it contains quite a few subdirectories, not just /bin and /etc. Again, it's not necessary to memorize the contents of every single directory and subdirectory. But to give you a sense of what the /usr directory contains, the following is a summary of the contents of those subdirectories:

- **/usr/X11R6**: Contains files required by the X Window graphical user interface, Version 11, Release 6.
- **/usr/bin**: Contains binary files (programs) that are available to all users.
- **/usr/doc**: Contains documentation available to all users.
- **/usr/games**: Contains games that are available to all users.
- **/usr/include**: Contains header files that can be included with custom C and C++ programs, and also parts of the X Window system.
- **/usr/lib**: Contains library files for programming languages that are accessible to all users.
- **/usr/local**: Contains programs written by users on the local computer.
- **/usr/man** Contains user manuals that are accessible to all users.
- **/usr/sbin**: Contains superuser binary files (programs) and files that the superuser can tweak to refine the behavior of some programs.
- **/usr/src**: Contains the source code for the Linux operating system, which users can modify.

**PART**

**I**

**CH**

**3**

> **Tip**
>
> When you're looking around for some written documentation on a particular program, the /usr/doc directory is a good place to start your exploration.

## THE HOME AND WORKING DIRECTORIES

While you're learning Linux, you'll often come across the terms *home directory* and *working directory*. The definitions of those terms are as follows:

- **Home directory:** The directory that a user is taken to automatically just after logging in.
- **Working directory:** The directory that the user is "in" at the moment. (Sometimes referred to as the current directory as well.)

Every user has a home directory, which is sort of the default place for putting that user's files. The user's home directory name generally contains the user's username. For everyone except the superuser, home directories are actually subdirectories of the /home directory. For example, the home directory for a user named alan will be /home/alan. The home directory for a user named Lana will be /home/lana.

The superuser, as you know, always logs in with the username root. The superuser's home directory is not a subdirectory of /home. Instead, it's a child of the parent directory and is named /root. This is potentially confusing because you'll often hear the system root—the one named just / at the top of the directory tree—referred to as the *root directory*. Rest assured, though, that throughout this book, whenever I refer to the directory named /root, I'll always use the complete path, which is /root, so as not to confuse it with the system root.

---

**The / and /root Directories**

It's unfortunate that someone decided to make up the rule that the superuser is named *root*, as there's the potential for confusion. Since the name of a user's home directory generally contains the user's name, the home directory for the superuser is /root. But that directory is entirely separate from the system root named / at the top of the directory tree. The fact that, verbally, the system root is sometimes called the "root directory" only compounds the confusion.

Had someone decided to assign a different username to superusers, something like superuser or sysadmin or honcho, the home directory for the superuser could have then been named accordingly. For example, the home directory for the superuser could have been /superuser or /sysadmin or /honcho, which isn't easily confused with the synonym "root directory" sometimes used to refer to the system root. But, for reasons unbeknownst to me, they had to complicate things by naming the superuser "root." Go figure.

---

Whenever a user first logs into Linux, she's automatically taken to her home directory. At that moment, the home directory is also the working directory, the one that the user is in right at the moment. If the user switches to another directory, say the one named /usr/doc, then at that moment the /usr/doc directory is that user's working directory. But her home directory remains the /home/*username*directory at all times.

# USING FLOPPIES AND CD-ROMS

If you grew up on Windows or the Macintosh, you're probably familiar with the concept of "disk drives," also called "drives" for short. For example, the non-removable hard disk (which is always in the computer) is usually called drive C:. You may also have some removable drives—disk drives that allow you to easily pull out a disk and replace it with another disk. Floppy, CD-ROM, Zip, and JAZ drives are all examples of removable drives. In a Windows system, each removable drive also has its own drive letter. For example, your floppy disk might be drive A:, and your CD-ROM drive might be drive D:. Each disk that you place in a removable drive has its own filesystem, which means each floppy disk and each CD-ROM is likely to have its own unique set of directories and files. In Linux, there's no such thing as drive letters, like A:, C:, and D:. Instead, each drive is referenced by the location of its device driver within the filesystem.

## DEVICE NAMES

Every piece of hardware that's connected to your computer, including floppy disk and CD-ROM drives, is a *device*. The program that allows your computer to interact with that device is called a *device driver* because the program drives the device to work correctly. Linux has a unique way of identifying devices attached to your system. Rather than using drive letters like A: and C:, each device is identified by the location of its driver in the filesystem. All the device drivers are stored in the directory named /dev. So you know that whenever you see a path like /dev/*whatever*, you're probably looking at a reference to a specific hardware device.

Each device is given an abbreviated name and a number. For example, floppy disks are named *fd*. The first floppy disk is fd0, the second floppy disk (if any) is fd1, and so forth. The path /dev/fd0 refers to the first floppy disk in the system—the one you'd call drive A: in DOS and Windows. A CD-ROM drive is generally just referred to as /dev/cdrom.

Hard disk drives that use IDE (Integrated Device Electronics) connections are named *hd* followed by a letter and a number. If a computer has only one IDE hard drive, it's named *hda*. If a given computer has two IDE hard drives, they'll be named *hda* and *hdb*. Any drive can be divided into *partitions*. A partition is just a section of the drive that's used for some specific purpose. The first partition on the first IDE hard drive would be referred to as hda1. The second partition on that drive would be called hda2, and so forth. If there were a second IDE drive in that same computer, and it too was divided into partitions, those would be named hdb1, hdb2, and so forth.

Disk drives that are connected to the computer using the SCSI (Small Computer System Interface, pronounced *scuzzy*) interface are named sd followed by a letter and a number. The first SCSI drive on the system, which would typically be a SCSI hard disk is named sda. A second SCSI drive would be named sdb, and so forth. SCSI disks can also be segmented into partitions. And Linux uses numbers here as well to identify each partition. For example, the first partition on the SCSI device would be sda1, the second partition would be sda2, and so forth. If there were a second SCSI drive with multiple partitions attached to that same computer, they'd be named sdb1, sdb2, and so forth.

Remember that these device names actually refer to the device driver file for the device, and that the device drivers are all stored in the /dev directory. For this reason, a given device name will usually be something like /dev/hda1 for the first partition on the first IDE hard drive. Table 3.1 shows some examples of device names which may, or may not, be available on your computer.

PART

I

CH

3

**TABLE 3.1  EXAMPLES OF LINUX DEVICE NAMES**

| Device Name | What It Refers To |
| --- | --- |
| /dev/fd0 | First floppy disk (drive A: in DOS/Windows) |
| /dev/cdrom | CD-ROM drive |
| /dev/hda1 | First partition on IDE hard drive |
| /dev/hda7 | Seventh partition on IDE hard drive |
| /dev/sda1 | First partition on SCSI hard disk |
| /dev/sda6 | Sixth partition on SCSI hard disk |

Confused yet? I hope not. Because it gets a little more complicated.

## MOUNT POINTS

In addition to having a device name, each removable drive also has a *mount point*. The mount point is just another directory in the filesystem, usually a subdirectory of the /mnt directory. Whereas the /dev/*devicename* name refers to a device driver, the mount point refers to the place in the filesystem where the *contents* of a disk in that drive are made available. In most cases—and this is what you're interested in—the directories and files on a particular disk happen to be its drive at the moment. When installed, Linux sets up a couple of mount points automatically and gives them names that are pretty easy to grasp:

- **/mnt/floppy:** The contents of the current floppy disk are visible in this mount point.
- **/mnt/cdrom:** The contents of the CD currently in the CD-ROM drive are visible in this mount point.

In short, when you want to see the contents of, say, a floppy disk, you don't go looking for drive A:, or even /dev/fd0. Instead, you look into /mnt/floppy to see what's on the disk. Unfortunately, it's not sufficient to simply stick a disk into a removable drive, then peek at its contents because the Linux filesystem won't "see" the contents of a floppy disk or CD-ROM until that disk has been *mounted*, as discussed next.

## MOUNTING REMOVABLE DISKS

GNOME comes with a program called the User Mount Tool that makes its easy to mount and unmount disks. To start that program, follow these steps:

1. Click the GNOME Main Menu button.
2. Choose System, Disk Management.

If you see a message stating that there are no user mountable filesystems, that probably means you don't have permission to mount disks. By default, only the superuser can mount disks. However, the superuser can grant permission to other users to mount disks as well. (If you are the superuser, see the Case Study at the end of Chapter 6 for instructions on granting disk-mounting permissions to users.) If you do have permission to mount disks, you'll see the User Mount Tool on the screen, as in Figure 3.2.

**Figure 3.2**
The GNOME User Mount Tool lets you mount and unmount floppy disks and CD-ROMs.

PART

I

CH

3

**Tip**

Don't forget that you can easily create a panel button for any program you need to start often. If you'd like to create a panel button for opening the User Mount Tool, click the Main Menu button, choose System, then right-click (don't click) the Disk Management option. Choose Add This Launcher to Panel.

Notice how the User Mount Tool displays information in columns titled Directory, Device, and Type, and a couple of columns of buttons. Here's what each column offers:

- **Directory:** The mount point for the drive; that is, where the contents of the drive will be available in the filesystem.

- **Device:** The name of the device that's available at the mount point (after the disk in the device is mounted).

- **Type**: The format of the disk in the device. In Linux, hard and floppy disks are generally formatted according to the ext2 specification, and CD-ROM discs follow the ISO 9660 specifications.

- **Mount/Unmount button**: The button in the fourth column lets you mount or unmount the disk. If the disk is already mounted, the button is labeled Unmount. If the disk is *not* mounted, then the button is labeled Mount.

- **Format button**: Allows you to format the disk in the drive. Generally only available for floppy disks and other formattable disks.

**Caution**

Never unmount the /dev/pts, /proc, /boot/, or / directories because these are needed by Linux. Only an advanced system administrator who has good reason to unmount those items should do so.

Many of the directories in the example shown in Figure 3.2 are already mounted. The first two, /dev/pts and /proc, are special mount points used by Linux, and for the time being you can ignore those. The last two, /boot and /, relate to partitions on the hard disk. As a rule, you don't want to mess with any of those four items in the list. The two items in the middle, /mnt/cdrom and /mnt/floppy, are the mount points for the CD-ROM and floppy disk drives. The names of those devices are /dev/fd0 and /dev/cdrom, as discussed earlier in this chapter. In Figure 3.2, neither of those devices currently contains a mounted disk, and hence their buttons are presenting the opportunity to mount a disk in the drive.

**Note**

Ext2 is the format on Linux disks. ISO 9660 is the format used on all CD-ROMs for the PC class of computers.

**Auto-Mounting CD-ROMs**

The Gnome and KDE desktops in Version 6.2 of Red Hat Linux are both capable of *auto-mounting* CD-ROMs. With auto-mounting, there's no need to take an extra step to mount the CD-ROM drive. Rather, just put the CD into its drive and wait about 15 seconds or so. If a file manager window opens on the screen displaying the contents of the CD, you'll know that the CD has indeed been mounted automatically already. In fact, if you open the User Mount Tool (described next) after the file manager window appears, you'll see that the CD has, indeed, already been mounted, because its Mount button will be labeled Unmount. So before you make an effort to mount a CD-ROM manually, just take a quick peek at the screen to see if it has already been mounted automatically for you.

## MOUNTING A FLOPPY OR CD-ROM

Once you're in the User Mount Tool, mounting a CD-ROM or floppy disk is easy. Follow these steps:

**Note**
The User Mount Tool will only mount floppy disks that are formatted for Linux. If you need to mount a floppy disk formatted for DOS, Windows, or some other operating system, see Chapter 12.

1. If there is already a mounted disk in the drive, click that drive's Unmount button. Then remove that disk from the drive.
2. Put the Linux-formatted floppy disk, or a CD-ROM, into its drive.
3. Click the Mount button for that device in the User Mount Tool program.

Nothing too exciting happens. In fact, the only change you might notice is that the button for the mounted drive is now labeled Unmount rather than Mount because the disk in the drive is already mounted. Once the disk is mounted, you can close the User Mount Tool if you wish, or just leave it open. Either way, the disk in the drive will stay mounted until you specifically unmount it.

**Tip**
The section titled "Creating Shortcuts from File Manager" later in this chapter shows how to create quick desktop shortcuts for mounting and viewing the contents of floppy disks and CD-ROMs.

## UNMOUNTING A FLOPPY OR CD-ROM

It's important to remember that you should always unmount a floppy disk or CD-ROM before you remove the disk from its drive. In fact, with a CD-ROM drive, the eject button on the front of the drive might not work until you've unmounted the CD in that drive! So you really need to try to get into the habit of unmounting disks before removing them from their drives. With the User Mount Tool, unmounting is just as easy as mounting:

1. If the User Mount Tool isn't already open, go ahead and open it (click the Main Menu button and choose System, Disk Management).

2. Click the Unmountbutton for the device you want to unmount.

3. Remove the disk from its drive.

The button is relabeled Mount, so that you can mount a different disk in the drive when you want to.

> **Tip**
>
> You can also mount and unmount disks from the Bash shell command prompt, using the mount and umount commands. More on this topic later in this chapter.

PART

**I**

CH

**3**

## FORMATTING A FLOPPY DISK

A brand new, unformatted floppy disk needs to be formatted before Linux can use it. It's important to understand, however, that whenever you format a disk, you *permanently delete all files on the disk*! So you never want to format a floppy disk that already contains files. Some people assume that if they take a floppy disk that contains DOS or Windows files, then format that floppy disk into the Linux ext2 format, they'll be able to access the files on the disk. No, it doesn't work that way. I'd hate to have you lose any important files on a floppy disk, so let me restate the warning here.

> **Caution**
>
> Never format any disk unless you're absolutely sure you can live without the files on that disk for all time. Formatting a disk permanently deletes all files on the disk. There is no way to "unformat" the disk to get its original contents back.

If you're sure you want to format a floppy disk as a Linux floppy, you can follow these steps to do so:

1. If the User Mount Tool isn't already open, click the Main Menu button, and choose System, Disk Management.

2. If another floppy disk is already mounted in the floppy drive, click the drive's Unmount button, then remove the floppy from the drive.

3. Insert the disk to be formatted into the floppy drive, then click the Format button for that drive in the User Mount Tool.

4. You'll see a Confirm dialog box. Make sure the Do Low-Level Format option is selected (pushed in) as in Figure 3.3.

5. To start the formatting, click the Yes button. Be careful; this is your last chance to change your mind. If you change your mind, click the No button and the floppy disk will retain its current format and contents.

**Figure 3.3**
When formatting
floppy disks,
choose the Do
Low-Level Format
option.

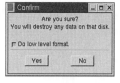

 **Tip**

You can access files and format DOS/Windows floppies in Linux. You just can't do so with the User Mount Tool. See Chapter 12 for more information.

The format process should begin right away. It could take two minutes or more, and you won't see any progress indicator on the screen. If the computer is nearby, however, you'll probably be able to hear the floppy drive running.

If you see any kind of error message, click OK to clear the message. It may be that the disk is already low-level formatted for Linux, and therefore only needs high-level formatting. Click the Format button again, this time de-select the Do Low-Level Format option, and then click the Yes button. If problems persist, try using a different floppy disk.

When the disk has been successfully formatted, the Confirm dialog box closes, and you're returned to the User Mount Tool. If you plan to use the disk right away, click its Mount button first to mount it. But you can move and copy files to the disk using the GNOME File Manager.

# EXPLORING WITH THE GNOME FILE MANAGER

Linux comes with a program called the GNOME File Manager that makes it easy to explore your filesystem. Not to confuse things, but I should point out that the File Manager goes by several different names. The program is actually a specialized version of the Midnight Commander file manager. So the File Manager is sometimes referred to as GNOME Midnight Commander, or GMC for short. But menu commands for launching the program just refer to it as File Manager, so I'll stick with that simple name in this book.

**Tip**

If you have Internet access, you can see more examples of using the GNOME File Manager at www.gnome.org/users-guide/gmc.html.

Depending on how your computer is configured, the File Manager might open each time GNOME starts. But, you can open the File Manager at any time using any one of these simple methods:

■ Double-click the Home Directory desktop icon.

■  Click the GNOME Menu button and choose FileManager.

■  Mid-click the desktop and choose GNOME Apps, File Manager.

If you're logged in as root, you may see the warning message shown in Figure 3.4. It's there to remind you that as superuser, you have unrestricted access to the entire filesystem. This means you also have the power to make a mistake that could mess up the whole system. You can click the OK button to clear the message and open the File Manager.

**Figure 3.4**
Warning that appears when a superuser opens the File Manager.

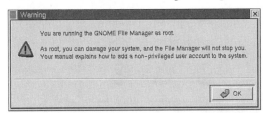

> **Tip**
>
> If it were up to me, I'd reword the vague and intimidating warning that appears to something like "Remember that you're logged in as superuser, and can do whatever you want in File Manager. Don't go around deleting, moving, or renaming files at random, or you might make a big mess of things."

When the File Manager opens, it initially displays the contents of your home directory. The home directory, in turn, is simply the name of the directory you're automatically taken to when you first start Linux. When you log in as superuser, your home directory is /root. When you log in as a regular user, your home directory is likely to be /home/*username*, where *username* is the username you logged in with.

The left column of the File Manager lists all the directories that are currently available in the filesystem, in a vertical *directory tree* format. A plus sign (+) next to a directory name tells you that there are subdirectories contained within the current directories, but that they're hidden. Clicking the + sign expands the line so that you can see the list of subdirectories within the directory. The plus sign also changes to a minus sign. Clicking the minus sign collapses the tree, thereby hiding the names of subdirectories. Figure 3.5 shows the File Manager with just the system root (/) open. You can see the first level of subdirectories—bin, boot, dev, and so on, listed beneath the system root. These are the default directories discussed earlier in this chapter that Linux creates automatically during installation.

> **Tip**
>
> If there's no plus or minus sign next to a directory's icon, and you think there should be, click the directory's icon. If the directory has children, the + sign should appear.

**Figure 3.5**
The left column of the GNOME File Manager showing the root and first-level directories.

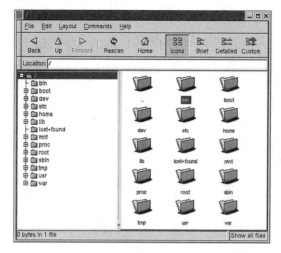

The right pane in File Manager shows the contents of whatever directory is currently highlighted in the left column. For example, in Figure 3.5 the right pane is currently showing the contents of the system root (/) because that's the name highlighted in the left column. In that figure, File Manager is also set up to display information in the right column using the Icons view, which you can get to simply by clicking the Icons button in the toolbar. In Icons view, different icons are used to display different kinds of files. The three most common icons are the file folder, which represents a directory. The "sheet of paper" icon represents a *document*, such as a file you create on your own using a word processing program or spreadsheet. The piston icon represents an executable file—a program or script that you can run.

> **Tip**
>
> The File Manager's title bar and Location box always display the name of the directory whose contents are currently being displayed in the right pane.

An international "No" symbol in an icon means that you don't have permission to access the directory or file. A small bent arrow indicates that the file isn't really a file, but just a shortcut (a.k.a. *symbolic link*) to some other file.

In the Brief, Detailed, and Custom views, files are color-coded by type. Directories are listed in blue text, files in black text, and symbolic links in green text.

## THE .. DIRECTORY

Most directories will display a folder icon with a pair of periods (..) beneath it. The .. symbol is used throughout Linux (and other operating systems) to stand for "parent directory." Double-clicking the .. folder in the right pane of File Manager always takes you to the parent directory of the current directory. You can also get to the parent of the current directory by clicking the Up button in the toolbar, or by simply clicking the name of that directory in the left column.

| Tip | Think of a single dot (.) as standing for "this" (directory), and two dots (..) as standing for "up one" directory. |
| --- | --- |

## VIEWING FLOPPY DISK AND CD-ROM CONTENTS

Recall that when you mount a floppy disk, its contents become available in the /mnt/floppy directory. The contents of a mounted CD-ROM become available in the /mnt/cdrom directory. To view the contents of a mounted floppy or CD-ROM, simply open the appropriate directory. For example, in Figure 3.6, I've opened the /mnt/cdrom directory. You can see the highlighter on that directory in the left column of the display. The right pane in the figure is showing the contents of the CD, which is mainly a bunch of directories.

| Tip | If GNOME or KDE can auto-mount the CD you put into a CD-ROM drive, the file manager will open automatically, with the left column highlighter already on the /mnt/cdrom mount point. |
| --- | --- |

**Figure 3.6**
Opening the /mnt/cdrom directory displays the contents of the CD currently mounted in the CD-ROM drive.

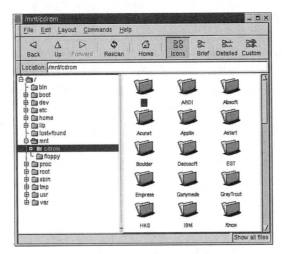

If you want to view the contents of a mounted floppy disk, simply open the /mnt/floppy directory.

## FILE MANAGER TOOLBAR BUTTONS

Toolbar buttons just beneath the File Manager menu bar provide quick access to common activities. The role of each button is described here:

PART

I

CH

3

■ **Back:** Takes you back to the directory you were visiting prior to the directory you're visiting now.

■ **Up:** Takes you to the parent directory of the current directory.

■ **Forward:** Available only after you've clicked the Back button, this button takes you to wherever you were before you clicked on the Back button.

■ **Rescan:** Rereads filenames off the directory to make sure the display is up-to-date.

■ **Home:** Takes you to your home directory.

■ **Icons:** Displays files in the right pane as large icons.

■ **Brief:** Lists filenames with only small icons.

■ **Detailed:** Lists filenames, their size, and the date that the file was last modified (MTime).

■ **Custom:** Lets you set up the right pane to your own liking.

The Custom view provides the greatest flexibility in determining exactly what information appears in the right pane of File Manager.

## CUSTOMIZING THE FILENAME DISPLAY

You have several options for deciding how you want the File Manager to organize filenames in the right panel. For starters, you can choose the Icons, Brief, Detailed, or Custom view simply by clicking the appropriate button in the toolbar. All but the Icons view display file information in a list. For example, Figure 3.7 shows File Manager displaying filenames in a Custom view. In that view, directories are listed first in alphabetical order. Only directory names have the file folder icon to the left. The display there shows the Name, Size, Permission, Owner, and Mtime (date and time that the file was last modified) of each file.

**Figure 3.7**
The Custom View in File Manager can provide detailed information about each file in a directory.

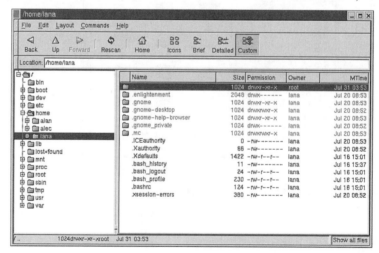

In the Custom view, you can choose how much information about each file the right pane of File Manager displays. To change the Custom view, choose Edit, Preferences from File

Manager's menu bar. You'll be taken to the Preferences dialog box. Click the Custom View tab to get to the options shown in Figure 3.8. To add a column to the display, click its name in the left column, then click the Add button. To remove a column from the display, click its name in the right column and then click the Remove button.

**Figure 3.8**
The Custom View tab of the File Manager Preferences dialog box lets you choose how much information you want the right pane to display.

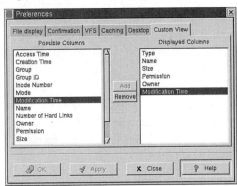

PART
I
CH
3

### SHOWING HIDDEN FILES

As mentioned earlier in this chapter, Linux usually hides files whose names begin with a period, such as .gimp, .gnome. Those files generally won't appear in the right pane of the File Manager. But if you need to see them, it's easy to take them out of hiding. Follow these steps:

1. From File Manager menu bar choose Edit, Preferences.
2. Select the Show Hidden Files option so that its button looks pushed in.
3. Click the OK button.

When viewing a directory that contains hidden files, the hidden files will typically be listed in alphabetical order after any directories in the display and before any files whose names don't start with a period.

### SIZING COLUMNS

In the Custom view, you have some flexibility in setting the width of each column you display. To change a column width, move the mouse pointer to the dark line separating any two column headings. Then drag that line to the right or left. If the column springs back to its previous size, you've tried to make the column too narrow to fill the pane. Try resizing the neighboring column instead.

### SORTING (ALPHABETIZING) THE DISPLAY

You can instantly sort by any column simply by clicking the column heading. For example, to sort files by size (smallest to largest), click the Size column heading. To reverse the sort order so that it goes from largest, click the column heading a second time. You can also choose a sort order (even in the Icons view), by choosing Layout, Sort By from the File Manager's menu bar. A dialog box titled Sort By appears.

To choose which column is used to sort the filenames in the display, click the Sort files by button and choose an option. If you want filenames to be alphabetized without regard to upper/lowercase differences, choose the Ignore Case Sensitivity option. If you want to reverse the sort order, like from Z to A or from largest to smallest, choose the Reverse the Order option. Click OK after making your selections.

### SHOWING DIRECTORY SIZES

File Manager doesn't bother to calculate the sizes of directories when you first open it because it takes a few seconds to calculate that information. If you want to see the true sizes of directories listed in the File Manager's right pane, choose File from the File Manager's menu bar, then select the Show directory sizes option.

**Note**
The . . directory, which is really just a quick link to the parent of the current directory, is always shown as being 1024 bytes in size. You can't change that.

You can even choose to mix directory and filenames together and then have them display in alphabetical order in one long list. To mix directory and filenames in the right pane of File Manager, follow these steps:

1. Choose Edit, Preferences from the File Manager menu bar.

2. Choose the Mix Files and Directories option.

3. Click the OK button to close the dialog box.

### HOW FILE PERMISSIONS ARE DISPLAYED

When defining a Custom view, you can choose to display Permissions in the right pane of File Manager, as in the example shown in Figure 3.7. The permissions are displayed in a very succinct format that looks something like this:

drwxr-xr-x

This strange-looking string of letters composes four groups of information about permissions (see Figure 3.9).

**Figure 3.9**
How file permissions are displayed in Linux.

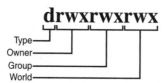

The first character indicates what type of item the line represents, as summarized here:

- **d**—Indicates that the item is a directory.
- **l**—Indicates that the item is a symbolic link (shortcut) to another file.
- **- (hyphen)**—Indicates that the item is a file, as opposed to a directory or a link.

The rest of the letters in the first column are divided into three groups, each consisting of three letters. The first three letters indicate permissions granted to the owner of the file. The next three letters indicate permissions granted to the group that owns the file. And the last three letters show permissions for everyone else in the world. The letters within each three-letter section are organized as the following:

- read permission
- write permission
- execute permission

A hyphen indicates "permission not granted." So, let's say a line starts with these characters:

`-rwxr-x---`

The first character, the hyphen, indicates that this item is a regular file. The first three letters after that, rwx, indicate that the owner of the file has permission to read, write, and execute the file. The following set of letters, r-x, tells us that the file's owning group has permission to read and execute the file, but they are not allowed to write to the file. The last three characters, ---, tell us that the rest of the world has no permissions at all with regard to this file.

Said another way, only the owner of the file can do anything she wants with it. Other members of the owner's group can view and execute the file, but they're not allowed to make any changes. The rest of the world is outta luck. They can't view, change, or run the file. You'll learn how to change file permissions in Chapter 7.

## SEARCHING FOR A FILE WITH FILE MANAGER

If ever you're in a situation where you know the name of the file you're looking for, but not its location in the filesystem, you can use the File Manager to search the entire filesystem for that file. If you don't know the exact name of the file you're looking for, you can use *wildcard characters* to stand for individual characters or groups of characters. Exactly which characters you use depends on whether File Manager is set up to use *shell patterns*, or *regular expressions*. Shell filter wildcard characters resemble those of DOS and Windows, like the following:

- **?**—Stands for any single character.
- **\***—Stands for any groups of characters.

Regular expressions follow Linux rules for specifying wildcard characters, and follow UNIX standards. The difference is that you use a period (.) rather than a question mark to stand for a single character, as follows:

- ■  .—Stands for any single character.
- ■  *—Stands for any groups of characters.

The only advantage to using regular expressions is that they are the same as those used at the Linux command prompt. So deciding between one style or the other is simply a matter of personal taste. To choose one format or the other, follow these steps:

1. Choose Edit, Preferences from the File Manager's menu bar.

2. If you want to use shell patterns, where the question mark stands for a single character, select the Use Shell Patterns Instead of Regular Expressions option. If you prefer to use the period as the single-character wildcard, de-select that option.

3. Click the OK button.

Now, let's assume you're looking for files that have something to do with a program from Applix, and you know that the company name appears somewhere in the filename. A search for `applix*` would show the names of all files that begin with the letters *applix*. A search for `*applix*` would search for all files that have the word applix anywhere in the filename. A search for `applix?`(using shell patterns) or `applix.` (using regular expressions) would search for a filename that starts with *applix* followed by any single character. To perform a search, follow these steps:

1. Choose Commands, Find Files from the File Manager's menu bar. The Find File dialog box appears, shown in Figure 3.10.

**Figure 3.10**
The first Find File dialog box to appear lets you specify a starting directory for the search, and a filename or text within a file to search for.

2. Next to Start At, type the name of the directory where you want to start the search. The directory you specify, and all subdirectories beneath it, will be searched. So, for example, to search the entire filesystem (including any mounted floppies or CDs), simply type /. Or, to search just a CD-ROM drive, you'd type /mnt/cdrom.

3. In the Filename textbox, type the name of the file you're looking for or just type part of the name using wildcard characters to stand for unknowns. For example, a search for `*howto*` would find all files that have the letters *howto* in them.

**Caution**

Searches are case-sensitive, so watch those upper/lowercase letters. If in doubt, use all lowercase letters because that's the most common method of naming files in Linux.

4. Optionally, if you don't know the name of the file you're looking for, but know something about the file's contents (that it starts with the salutation *Dear Dr. Groff*, for example), you can type that chunk of text in the Containing textbox.

---

**Caution**    Searching for a file based on its contents can take a *really* long time because Linux needs to read the contents of every file! Try to avoid that kind of search if possible.

---

5. Click the OK button to start the search.

The File Manager will start scouring the filesystem or whatever portion of the filesystem you specified in step 2 of the search. As it encounters files that match the name you specified, it will list those files preceded by the name of the directory that the file was found in. Remember that directory names always start with a forward slash (/). Filenames within a directory are indented and don't have a leading slash. For example, Figure 3.11 shows the results of a search for *howto*. One file, named howto.txt, was found in the directory named /usr/share/im/doc. Another file named ppp.howto.html was found in the directory named /usr/lib/exmh-2.0.2/html, and so on. To open any listed directory, click its name in the Find File list. Then click the Change to This Directory button. File Manager will instantly display the directory contents.

**Figure 3.11**
The results of searching for a file named *howto*.

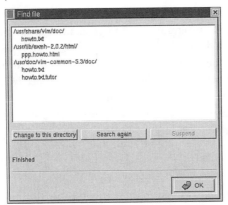

If the file you specified isn't found, you might try searching for a different name or a different pattern. To do that, just click the Search Again button and change the Filename entry in the small Find File dialog box.

## CREATING DIRECTORIES IN FILE MANAGER

Directories, as you know, are a way of organizing files into groups. For example, you might want to keep all the documents in your own home directory so that it's easy to find them later. If you have, or plan to have, a lot of files, you might want to categorized those files by type, such as "photos" and "text." To do so, you could simply create subdirectories within your home directory. When you're in the File Manager, you can quickly jump to your own home directory by clicking the Home button in the File Manager's toolbar. To create a directory in File Manager, follow these steps:

1. First, make sure you go to the parent of the directory you want to create. For example, to create a subdirectory within your own home directory, first go to your home directory.

2. Next, use either of the following techniques to create your directory:
    - Right-click any white space in the right pane of File Manager, and choose New Directory from the menu that appears.
    - Choose File, New Directory from the File Manager menu bar.

3. In the dialog box that appears, type the name of the new directory and then click the OK button.

Linux will allow you to include blank spaces in the directory name. However, it's not a good idea to use blank spaces in directory and filenames because not all programs will support such names. You're better off using an underscore, hyphen, or period in the name. After you click the OK button, an icon for the directory will appear in the pane, most likely already alphabetized within existing directory names.

## OPENING FILES IN FILE MANAGER

To "open" a file means different things with different types of files. For example, when you open an executable program file, the program runs and generally appears in its own window on the desktop. When you open a document file, such as a letter you typed or a photo you took, Linux will try to open the document in the program that you used to create that document. If it cannot, it will display a dialog box where you can specify the program you want to use to view or edit the file. If the file you open is actually a directory, then the File Manager will only show the contents of that directory. There are lots of ways to open a file in the right pane of the File Manager:

- Double-click the file's icon.
- Right-click the file's icon and choose Open.
- If you want to be able to specify the program that will be used to open the file, right-click the icon and choose Open With.
- After clicking the file's icon, press the F3 key or choose File, Open from the menu bar.

**Tip**

> You can right-click a file and choose View to see its contents without opening a specific program. However, many programs store their documents in a binary format that's incomprehensible to humans. So that view might not do you any good.

If you're trying to open a document and Linux can't decide which program to use to open that document, you'll see the dialog box shown in Figure 3.12. You can expand any category by clicking the + sign to the left of the category. To select the program to use to open a document, click the program name, and then click the OK button at the bottom of the dialog box. For example, in Figure 3.12, I'm about to use the GIMP, a Linux graphics program, to open a document file I double-clicked in the File Manager.

**Figure 3.12**
This dialog box appears when you choose Open With, or when Linux doesn't know which program would be best suited for opening a document file.

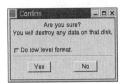

PART

I

CH

3

**Note**    You'll learn more about using programs to create and edit documents in Chapter 4.

If you're fairly certain that the file you're opening contains only text, you can use the Text File Viewer to view the file's contents. You can find the Text File Viewer under the Utilities category. To view and edit the file, you can use any of the many Linux text-editing programs, including gEdit available in the Applications category.

**Tip**    To simplify editing text files, click the GNOME Main Menu button, choose Settings, GNOME Edit Properties, and then choose gEdit from the drop-down list that appears. From that point on, you'll be able to right-click any text file's icon in the File Manager and choose Edit to open it in gEdit.

## RENAMING FILES IN FILE MANAGER

You can easily change the name of any file (or directory) in the filesystem. However, you never want to do so without good reason because Linux and other programs often depend on certain files in the filesystem. And if you rename one of the dependent files, you might have problems. As a rule, it's best to rename only files you create yourself. If you're sure you want to change the name of a file, follow these simple steps:

1. Right-click the file's icon in File Manager.

2. Choose Properties from the menu that appears.

3. On the Statistics tab of the dialog box that appears, type the new name in the File Name text box.

4. Click the OK button.

You can also rename a file by double-clicking its filename (not the icon!). The filename becomes selected (has a blue background). You can click a third time to position the cursor within the existing name. When the cursor appears in the filename, you can type new characters, and delete existing characters using the Delete and Backspace keys. After changing the filename, pressing Enter or clicking anywhere outside the file's icon will save the change.

## SELECTING FILES IN FILE MANAGER

You can move, copy, or delete a whole bunch of files at a time by first *selecting* the files you wish to operate on. When you select a file, its name is highlighted in some manner (usually with a blue background) to let you know the file has been selected. There are lots a ways to select files:

- If you want to select just one file, click that file's icon.
- To add more files to the selection, hold down the Ctrl key while clicking the icon of the file you want to add to the selection.
- To extend the selection from the currently selected file to some other file in the display, hold down the Shift key and click the icon of the file you want to extend the selection to.
- To select all the files in the right pane of the File Manager, choose Edit, Select All from the File Manager's menu bar, or just press Ctrl+A.
- To de-select a single selected file, Ctrl+click it (hold down the Ctrl key as you click the icon).
- To de-select all selected files, click the white space behind the icons.

You can also select multiple files by "lassoing" them. Click just outside the icon of the first file you want to include in the selection. Then hold down the left mouse button and drag the mouse pointer to the icon of the last file you want to include in the selection. Then release the mouse button. If you get too many or too few files in the selection, you can Ctrl+click individual files to add them to, or remove them from, the current selection.

You can invert a selection so that the files that are currently selected are no longer selected, and all files that aren't selected become selected. Just choose Edit, Invert Selection from the menu bar. You can also select a bunch of files using a shell pattern or a regular expression (depending on how you've set up the File Manager preferences).

To get started, choose Edit, Select Files from the menu bar. In the dialog box appears, enter the Shell pattern (called a filter in the dialog box), or a regular expression that defines the pattern of the files to be selected. For example, to select all files that contain the letters *fig* you'd enter *fig*. (Shell patterns and regular expressions both use an asterisk as the wildcard to match combination of characters, so in this case you don't need to worry about the difference between shell filters and regular expressions.) After you've typed the pattern, click the OK button. You can then scroll up and down through the right pane of the File Manager window to verify that you've selected all the appropriate files for the job. You can Ctrl+click icons to add files to the selection, or remove files from the selection.

## DELETING FILES IN FILE MANAGER

Deleting a file is always serious business. You never, ever want to delete a file unless you know what it contains, and are certain you (and Linux) can live without it. There is no way to "undelete" a file via File Manager, so please use caution! To delete a file or file(s), follow these steps:

1. If you want to delete two or more files, select those files first.

2. Choose File, Delete from the File Manager menu bar. Or right-click the file's icon, or any of the selected icons, and choose Delete.

In most cases, you'll be given a chance to change your mind, thanks to a dialog box that appears. If you're sure you want to delete the file, choose Yes. If you change your mind, choose No.

> **Note**
>
> The confirmation dialog box won't appear unless the Confirm When Deleting File option is selected in the File Manager's Preferences dialog box. To get to that dialog box, choose Edit, Preferences, and then click the Confirmation tab.

PART

I

CH

3

If you're deleting an entire directory and that directory contains files (or subdirectories), you'll be given a warning that the directory is not empty, and asked if you want to delete it recursively. If you're sure you want to delete the directory and all its contents, choose Yes. Otherwise, choose No to leave the directory intact.

## OPENING A SECOND FILE MANAGER WINDOW

When it comes time to move or copy a file to a directory or disk, your best bet is to open a second File Manager window. This is simple to do. Just choose File, Create New Window from File Manager's menu bar. You can then use the two windows independently. For example, when you're moving or copying files, you always have a source and a destination. The source is where the files are right now; the destination is the directory that you're planning on moving or copying the files to.

For example, suppose you plan to copy some files from your home directory on the hard disk to a floppy disk you've mounted in the floppy disk drive. First, you could choose the source directory in the File Manager that's already on your screen, just by clicking the appropriate directory in the left column. Then, to open a second window, choose File, New Window from the File Manager menu bar. In the new window, open the destination directory, again by simply clicking its name in the left column. (Remember that in Linux, a mounted floppy disk is actually accessible as the directory named /mnt/floppy.) Figure 3.13 shows just such an arrangement where the top-left window is showing the contents of /home/alan, and the lower-right window is showing the contents of a floppy disk.

After you've opened a second window, you can use the simple drag-and-drop technique to move or copy files, as discussed in the next two sections.

**Figure 3.13**
The contents of the /home/alan and /mnt/floppy directories in two separate file manager windows.

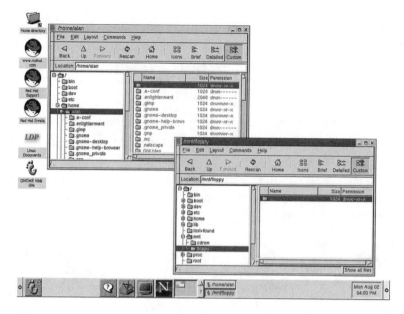

## MOVING AND COPYING FILES IN FILE MANAGER

With the ability to open two or more File Manager windows comes the ability to move and copy files using simple drag-and-drop techniques. Remember that there are always two directories involved when moving or copying files: the *source directory*, which contains the files you want to move or copy, and the *destination directory*, where you want to place the moved or copied files. Either directory can be a mount point that represents a mounted disk in a removable drive. You can't, however, copy files to a CD-ROM disc, so using /mnt/cdrom as a destination directory wouldn't make any sense. However, the following are the steps for moving or copying one or more files, using the drag-and-drop method:

1. Open the File Manager, if you haven't already done so, and open the source directory in the left pane.

2. Choose File, Create New Window to open a second File Manager window. Within that second window, open the destination directory.

3. If you want to move or copy two or more files, select those files in the right pane of the File Manager window that's displaying the source directory.

4. Point to the file you want to move or copy, or to any one of the selected files that you want to move or copy, then hold down the middle mouse button.

5. Hold down the middle mouse button, and drag the file or selection to the right pane of the File Manager window that's displaying the destination directory.

6. Release the middle mouse button.

7. From the menu that appears, choose Move Here if you want to move the files to the destination directory, or choose Copy Here if you want to copy the files to the destination directory.

| Caution | When copying files to a floppy disk, don't remove the disk until the copy is complete and the light on the floppy disk drive goes off. |
|---|---|

You can also move or copy files using a single File Manager window, if you're so inclined. Open the source directory in File Manager. If you want to move or copy multiple files, select them first. Then right-click the file, or any selected file, and choose Move if you want to move the files, or Copy if you want to copy the files. Or, if you prefer, you can choose File, Copy or File, Move from File Manager's menu bar. Either way, a dialog box titled Move or Copy will appear asking for the destination directory. There you can type the path to the destination directory (such as /home/alec). Or, you can choose the destination directory (if available) from the drop-down list (click the down-pointing arrow to the right of the textbox). Or, you can click the Browse button and navigate to the destination directory in the directory tree that appears on the screen.

## FINE-TUNING THE FILE MANAGER

You can change several settings to fine-tune the behavior and performance of the File Manager. First, there's the option to turn confirmation dialog boxes on or off. Choose Edit, Preferences from File Manager's menu bar, then click the Confirmation tab in the Preferences dialog box that appears. The options there are as follows:

- **Confirm When Deleting Files:** Selecting this option ensures that you're prompted for confirmation whenever you're about to delete a file via the File Manager.

- **Confirm When Overwriting Files:** Select this option if you want to protect yourself from overwriting a new file with an old file by the same name when moving or copying files. The confirmation box will alert you when you're about to overwrite an existing file, giving you a chance to change your mind.

- **Confirm When Executing Files:** Ensures that a confirmation dialog box appears whenever you try to run a program from within the File Manager.

- **Show Progress While Options Are Being Performed:** When selected, this option ensures that a progress odometer appears whenever you're using the File Manager to perform some task that takes a long time.

The VFS tab in the Preferences dialog box allows you to adjust settings for the Virtual File System (VFS). The Virtual File System, in turn, gives you File Manager access to files that aren't on your own PC, but rather located on some other computer connected via a network. There are two different versions of VHS: ftpfs, which allows you to manage files via the Internet's FTP (File Transfer Protocol). The other is tarfs, which allows the File Manager to manipulate files that are compressed inside tar files. You'll learn more about these topics in Chapter 16. But if you're already familiar with VFS, FTP, proxy servers, and the like, the following are your options:

PART

I

CH

3

- **VFS Timeout:** Determines how long you can stay connected to a Virtual File System without using it before being disconnected. The default setting is 60 seconds.

- **Anonymous FTP Password:** Lets you set your password for logging into anonymous FTP sites. Typically, you'll want this to be the same as your email address.

- **Always Use FTP Proxy:** If your network connection goes through a proxy server, select this option to allow FTP to work through that proxy server.

Options on the Caching tab let you control the overall speed of the File Manager by tweaking cache settings. A cache (pronounced *cash*) is a place in fast random access memory (RAM) that stores information from a disk for quick access. Your options are as follows:

- **Fast Directory Reload:** When selected, tells File Manager to update directory listings from a cache rather than directly from the disk. If File Manager seems slow, selecting this option can speed things up. However, you'll need to rescan the directory from time to time, using the Rescan button in the toolbar, to keep the cache in sync with the disk.

- **Compute Totals Before Copying Files:** When selected, makes File Manager calculate information about files that you're about to copy so it can present that information during the copy procedure.

- **FTP Directory Cache Timeout:** Determines how long to keep directories that you're connected to via FTP in the cache. The default is 1800 seconds.

- **Allow Customizations of Icons in Icon View:** If selected, lets you customize icons in the File Manager's Icons view.

The last option pertains only to the Icons view in File Manager. As you'll learn in a moment, you can always customize icons that appear on the desktop. But you can only customize icons in File Manager when you're using its Icons view, and only if you've selected this option. The disadvantage to selecting this feature is that allowing customization of icons in File Manager can slow down your system.

On the Desktop tab, you'll find options that pertain to the desktop as a whole:

- **Use Shaped Icons:** When selected, displays shaped icons on the desktop. If icons don't look right, you can de-select this option to see if the situation improves. The default setting is "on" (selected).

- **Auto Place Icons:** When selected, forces icons on the desktop to be placed into position automatically so they can't get scattered around the screen as you move them.

- **Snap Icons to Grid:** When the above feature is disabled and this feature is enabled, any icons you move on the desktop will automatically snap into place on an invisible grid. This makes it easier to line the icons up neatly when moving them about the desktop.

## CREATING SHORTCUTS FROM FILE MANAGER

While the File Manager is open, you can create a quick shortcut to any directory or file in the filesystem and place that shortcut on the desktop, in the panel, or both. Shortcuts in Linux may be called links, symbolic links, or aliases. But regardless of what you call them, each is just an icon that provides instant access to the file or directory, without actually moving or copying the directory.

Probably the most common use of shortcuts is to create desktop or panel shortcuts to favorite directories. For example, you might want to put a single icon on your desktop or panel that displays the contents of the currently mounted floppy disk or CD-ROM. To create a desktop shortcut from File Manager, follow these steps:

1. Click on the directory to which you want to create a shortcut. Or, click on the name of the file you want to create a shortcut to in the right pane of File Manager.

2. Hold down the middle mouse button, and drag the file or directory name to the GNOME desktop, or to the panel.

3. Release the mouse button. If you dragged to the panel, a button will appear automatically. If you dragged to the desktop, you'll need to choose Link Here to create a shortcut.

If you dragged to the desktop, the new icon will display a shortcut arrow, indicating a link. For example, in Figure 3.14 I created shortcut icons to the /mnt/floppy and /mnt/cdrom directories, which will allow me to view the contents of any disk currently mounted in those drives. Double-clicking the shortcut icon on the desktop or clicking its button in the panel opens the File Manager, already navigated to the floppy disk or CD-ROM drive. In fact, you can mount a floppy disk or CD-ROM by right-clicking that icon and choosing Mount device. You can unmount a disk by right-clicking its shortcut icon and choosing Unmount device. Pretty handy, as it allows you to mount and unmount without opening the User Mount Tool.

PART

I

CH

3

**Figure 3.14**
Shortcuts for viewing the contents of a mounted CD-ROM and floppy disk on the desktop.

If you create a shortcut to a program or document file, rather than to a directory, then double-clicking that icon on the desktop (or clicking the panel button) will open the document or program. However, a document file will open in the correct program only if the file's filename extension is defined as a MIME type, as discussed in Chapter 4.

## CUSTOMIZING ICONS

You can customize icons on your desktop at any time. You can also customize icons that appear in File Manager while you're using its Icons view. However, you can only do so if you've activated the Allow Customization of Icons option in the Icon View feature in

Preferences, as described in the previous section. Since customizing icons in File Manager can slow its performance, you might want to limit yourself to customizing icons on the desktop. To customize an icon, follow these steps:

1. Right-click the icon you want to customize.

2. Choose Properties from the menu that appears.

A dialog box appears with three tabs: Statistics, Options, and Permissions. On the Statistics tab, you can change the label that appears beneath the icon by changing the File Name option. On the Options tab, you can click the button that shows the current icon to view a list of other icons that are available. To choose a different icon, just click on it and then click the OK button. For example, in Figure 3.15, the labels and icons for the shortcut icons to the CD-ROM and floppy disk drives have been changed.

**Figure 3.15**
The CD-ROM and floppy disk short-cut icons with new labels and pictures.

CD-ROM Drive

Floppy Drive

> **Tip**
>
> To view more icons to choose from, use the Browse button in the Select an Icon dialog box to select the `/usr/share/pixmaps`, `/usr/share/icons`, and `/usr/share/pixmaps/mc` directories.

Shortcut icons that lead to removable disk drives automatically get a right-click menu that includes the option to mount or unmount the disk that's currently in the drive. So if you create shortcut icons to your floppy and CD-ROM drive, and you have permission to mount and unmount those types of disks, you won't have to go through the User Mount Tool to mount and unmount disks anymore. Instead, simply right-click the drive's shortcut icon and choose Mount device or Unmount device. You can also choose Eject device from that same menu to eject the disk currently in that drive, provided the drive supports that capability.

## MANAGING FILES FROM THE SHELL PROMPT

Anything you can do in GNOME, you can also do at the shell prompt. It may see odd to care. After all, if you can get a task done just by clicking a few icons or buttons, why type some esoteric command to perform the same task? It's true that, in the vast majority of situations, the GUI will get the job done faster and easier than the command prompt. However, there are some good reasons to at least familiarize yourself with the command-prompt alternatives to doing things:

■ You can print the output of commands. For example, you can create a printed list of your directories, or all the files in a directory.

**Tip**

> If your printer isn't working in Linux, it probably needs to be installed. Chapter 14 explains how to do that.

- You can build scripts (called *batch files* in DOS) that contains several commands. You can then perform all those commands just by running the script.

- Some written documentation in Linux will contain instructions that require you to enter commands at the shell prompt. An awareness of what the commands do will make those instructions seem less arcane.

- It's possible you'll someday get into a situation where the GUIs break or won't work on a particular computer. Being able to fall back on the command prompt can get you out of such jams like a pro.

Recall that you can enter commands in a GNOME terminal window, or a virtual console. To get to a terminal window, click the Terminal Emulation Program button in the panel. To get to a virtual console, press Ctrl+Alt, then one of the function keys F1 through F6. Remember that if you use a virtual console, you can get back to GNOME by pressing Ctrl+Alt+F7.

For the rest of this chapter, we'll look at the commands you can use to perform most of the tasks you already learned to perform via the GNOME File Manager. But in the interest of brevity, I won't go into extensive detail on each and every command. There's really no need for me to do that because you can get plenty of additional information right on your screen. One way to do so is to type the command followed by a space, two hyphens, and the word *help*. For example, to get help with the ls (list) command, you enter the following command:

```
ls --help
```

If the help information whizzes by too quickly, you can pipe it into the less program, discussed in more detail later in this chapter, by following the entire command with a pipe character (|) and the word *less*. For instance, entering this command would display help for the ls command:

```
ls --help ¦ less
```

Once the documentation appears on the screen, you can scroll up and down using the ~UA, ~DA, Page Up (PgUp), and Page Down (PgDn) keys. At the bottom of the display you'll see a colon (:) as in the example shown in Figure 3.16. Typing the letter **q** at the prompt quits the less program and returns you to the command prompt. When you're at the end of a page, the colon will be replaced by the highlighted word (END) which indicates that you cannot scroll down any farther. Typing a **q** at the (END) prompt will also bring you back to the command prompt.

**Figure 3.16**
When viewing help or man pages with `less`, entering q at the colon (:) prompt near the bottom of the window will exit back to the shell command prompt.

Not all commands support the `-help` option. But you can always find detailed information about a command in the *man pages* (manual pages). If you can't get the information you need using `--help`, try entering man followed by a space and the name of the command you wish to look up. For example, the following command would show the man page for the `ls` (list) command:

```
man ls
```

The man pages are also displayed by the `less`program, so you can scroll up and down using the ~DA, ~UA, Page Down (PgDn), and Page Up (PgUp) keys. Type **q** to quit and return to the command prompt. Chapter 5 will explain the man pages and other sources of information in greater detail. For now, it's sufficient to know that more information about each of the following commands is available, right at your fingertips.

## THE "WHERE AM I NOW?" COMMAND

The `pwd` command shows you the complete path to your current working directory, giving you a better idea of where you really are in the overall filesystem at the moment. You enter this command as you would any other. Just type the following and press Enter:

```
pwd
```

The path to your current directory appears on the screen, just below the command you typed. So, if you're logged in as the superuser and haven't left your home directory, you'll see the following:

```
/root
```

If you're logged in as a regular user, such as `alan`, you'll see the complete path to your current working directory as shown here:

```
/home/alan
```

**Note**

In case you're wondering, *pwd* stands for *print working directory*. The word *print* in Linux doesn't necessarily refer to the printer. Feedback from commands is generally "printed" on the screen.

## MOUNTING DISKS WITH mount AND umount

You can mount removable disks from the shell prompt using the mount command with the following basic syntax:

```
mount devicemount-point
```

device is the name of the device (that is, /dev/fd0 for the floppy disk, or /dev/cdrom for the CD-ROM drive). The mount-point is the name of an existing directory that will display the contents of the disk. Recall that Red Hat Linux has already created the /mnt/floppy and /mnt/cdrom mount points for these devices, so you can just use those mount point names. So, to mount a CD-ROM from the command prompt, enter the following command:

```
mount /dev/cdrom /mnt/cdrom
```

To mount a Linux-formatted (or ext2) floppy disk, you need to enter this command:

```
mount /dev/fd0 /mnt/floppy
```

> **Tip**
>
> The syntax shown for the mount command is "proper" Linux. But your Red Hat installation will probably let you omit the device name. For example, try entering mount /mnt/floppy to mount a floppy disk, and mount /mnt/cdrom to mount a CD-ROM.

To unmount a disk from the shell prompt, use the following syntax:

```
umount mount-point
```

mount-point is the current mount point of the drive that you want to unmount. (Notice that the command is umount, not *unmount!*) For example, to unmount the currently mounted floppy disk, you'd enter the command:

```
umount /mnt/floppy
```

To unmount a CD-ROM from the shell prompt, you'd enter the following command:

```
umount /mnt/cdrom
```

The effect is exactly the same as clicking the Unmount button in the User Manager Tool. The contents of the disk are no longer accessible to the Linux filesystem. The disk can be safely removed from its drive.

> **Tip**
>
> If you want to access a DOS/Windows floppy disk, you must enter the command mount -t msdos /dev/fd0 /mnt/floppy. Chapter 12 discusses this and other techniques for accessing Windows resources in depth.

## FORMATTING FLOPPIES WITH fdformat

The fdformat (floppy disk format) command lets you format a floppy disk to Linux's ext2 filesystem format. The basic syntax is as follows:

```
fdformat /dev/fdndsize
```

*n*is the device number (for example, 0 for the first floppy disk), and d represents the size and density of the floppy disk as summarized here:

- **d:** Low-density 5.25 inch
- **D:** Low-density 3.5 inch
- **h:** High-density 5.25 inch
- **H:** High-density 3.5 inch

The size parameter represents the disk capacity in kilobytes. Possible values are 360, 720, 1200, and 1440. Most modern floppy disk drives support high-density 3.5 inch disks with a capacity of 1440KB. To format such a disk, you'd enter the following command:

```
fdformat /dev/fd0H1440
```

## CHANGING DIRECTORIES WITH cd

To switch to another directory, use the cd (change directory) command. The following is the syntax for this command:

```
cd path
```

path is the complete path to the directory you want to switch to. For example, to go to the topmost system root, /, enter this command:

**cd /**

> **Caution**
>
> DOS users need to be aware the Linux uses forward slashes (/) where DOS and Windows use backslashes (\). Backslashes don't work in Linux! Also, the blank space after the cd command is required. You cannot omit it as you can in DOS.

If you mount a CD in your CD-ROM drive and you want to make that CD your current working directory, enter the following command:

```
cd /mnt/cdrom
```

If you want to go to the directory named /usr/doc, enter this command:

```
cd /usr/doc
```

### RELATIVE REFERENCING

The path name, /usr/doc in the sample cd /usr/doc, is an *absolute reference* to that directory. The path starts at the system root, /, then points to the user directory, and finally the doc directory. In some cases, you can save some typing by using a *relative reference* to a directory. A relative reference refers to some directory in relation to the current directory rather than the system root. For example, if you want to go to a directory that's directly below the current directory, you don't have to type the absolute path to that directory. Instead, you can just enter the directory name.

For example, if you're currently in the /usr/doc directory and you want to drop down to a directory named /usr/doc/bash-1.14.7, you could enter this command:

```
cd bash-1.14.7
```

Notice that the path name in the above example does not start with a slash. Omitting the slash tells Linux to "start from here" as opposed to "start from the system root."

In Linux, a single dot (.) always represents the current directory, and two dots (..) represent the parent of the current directory. The parent symbol, .., is a handy shortcut when used with the cd command. To go to the parent of the current directory, you can simply enter this command:

```
cd ..
```

To move to the current directory's "grandparent" (up two levels from the current directory), you could enter this command:

```
cd ../..
```

PART

I

CH

3

**Tip**

Absolute references always start with a / character. Relative references never start with a slash character.

## Going Home

Linux also provides a quick and easy way to return to your home directory from anywhere in the directory tree. Just enter the cd command with no pathname, as follows:

```
cd
```

You can also use the tilde character (~) to refer to your home directory. So, let's say you have a subdirectory named spreadsheets in your home directory. No matter where you are in the directory tree at the moment, you could enter this command to get to that subdirectory:

```
cd ~/spreadsheets
```

If you wanted to get to your home directory's parent directory quickly from any place in the directory tree, you could enter this command:

```
cd ~/..
```

The tilde takes you straight to your home directory, the .. then moves you up to the parent of that directory. The slash is needed to separate the tilde from the dot pair.

**Note**
If you try to go to a directory that you don't have permission to access, the cd command will display Permission Denied, and leave you in the current directory.

## CREATING DIRECTORIES WITH mkdir

To create a directory via the shell prompt, use the mkdir (make directory) command. If you just follow the command with the name of a directory, then the directory you create becomes a subdirectory of the directory you're in at the moment. For example, suppose you're in your home directory, and that directory is named /home/alan and you enter the following command:

```
mkdir spreadsheets
```

You'd end up with a new directory named spreadsheets within your home directory. So the full path to that new directory would actually be /home/alan/spreadsheets.

## VIEWING DIRECTORY CONTENTS WITH ls

To see what's available in a directory, use the ls (list) command. Entering the ls command with no path name lists the contents of the current directory. For example, if you enter the following command

```
ls
```

you see the contents of whatever directory you're in at the moment. To see the contents of a specific directory, follow the ls command with an absolute or relative reference to the directory whose contents you wish to view. For example, to view the contents of the system root (/), you'd enter the following command

```
ls/
```

The resulting list of names would look something like Figure 3.17. Notice that the names are displayed in five columns, and alphabetized vertically. Since the cd / command shows the contents of the system root, the directory names that appear on the screen should be similar to the directory names in Figure 3.1, shown near the beginning of this chapter.

**Figure 3.17**
Contents of the root (/) directory as displayed by an ls command.

To see the contents of the /usr/doc directory, you could enter this command:

```
ls /usr/doc
```

To see the contents of your home directory, you could enter this command:

ls ~

To see the contents of a CD-ROM that's currently mounted in the CD-ROM drive, you'd enter this command:

ls /mnt/cdrom

### ls COMMAND OPTIONS

Like many commands in Linux, the ls command offers some options that you can use to customize the behavior, or results, of the command. Some of the more commonly used options are shown in Table 3.2. When using options in a command, don't forget to put in a blank space before the hyphen(s). If you'll be typing more text after the option, another blank space is needed.

**TABLE 3.2:    COMMONLY USED OPTIONS FOR THE ls COMMAND**

| Option | Meaning |
| --- | --- |
| -a | Lists all files and directories, including those that start with a dot (.) |
| -l | Lists in long (verbose) format including each file's type, permissions, owner name, group name, size, and timestamp |
| -p | Adds a one-letter abbreviation for file type to each listed filename |
| -r | Reverses sort order of display |
| -s | Shows the size of each file, in kilobytes, to the left of each filename |
| -t | Sorts files by date (timestamp) rather than alphabetically |
| -u | Sorts files by date of last access rather than timestamp |
| -x | Sorts horizontally rather than down columns |
| --color | Shows directory names in dark blue, symbolic links in light blue |

Linux filenames that begin with a dot are normally hidden from the ls command's display. Linux uses these dotted filenames for files that your average user doesn't need access to, such as files that it creates and maintains on its own. The -a option tells the ls command to go ahead and show them. So, for example, you could use the -a option to see all the filenames in your home directory, including files that are normally hidden from ls, by entering this command:

ls -a ~

The resulting display might look something like this:

```
.          .Xdefaults         .bash_logout    .bash_rc      .tshrc
..         .bash_history      .bash_profile  .cshrc
```

The normally hidden dotted filenames (which you really don't ever need to mess with) are visible in the display now.

PART

**1**

CH

**3**

If you have a color monitor, the `--color` (note the two hyphens) colorizes your display a little. Directory names are shown in navy blue, symbolic links (shortcuts) are shown in green. The names of regular files are displayed in the normal white color. So entering the following command would list all files and directories within the current directory. The directory names would be dark blue:

```
ls -a --color
```

The `-l` option (that's a lowercase letter *l*) displays a long list (also called a verbose list) of file and directory names, as well as extended information about each item in the list. For example, to view the contents of the /usr/doc directory in long format, you'd enter the following command:

```
ls -l /usr/doc
```

You can combine multiple hyphenated options after a single hyphen. For example, if you want to view the contents of the current directory in long format, and you also want to see hidden files, you can use both the `-a` and `-l` options with a single hyphen, as follows:

```
ls -al
```

Options that start with two hyphens need to be listed separately. For example, the following command adds color to the previous command:

```
ls -al -color
```

**Tip**

Red Hat Linux offers two alternatives to the `ls` command not found in most versions of Linux. You can use the DOS `dir` command to display file names, similar to using the `ls` command. You can use the `vdir` command to display the verbose list.

### REDIRECTING ls

Normally, any command that you enter is going to display its output on the screen. But you can use the *pipe* character (¦) to redirect that output to some program, a file, or the printer. For example, the `less` program takes whatever information is piped into it, and displays it one "page" at a time on the screen. Thus, to see the verbose contents of the /usr/doc directory, one page at a time, you'd enter the command:

```
ls -al /usr/doc ¦ less
```

Use `lpr` as the device name for the printer when you want to pipe output to the printer. For example, to print the verbose list of files on the /usr/doc directory, enter the following command:

```
ls -al /usr/doc ¦ lpr
```

### `ls` Wildcards

If you're only interested in viewing the names of files that match some pattern in a directory, you can use the ? and * characters as wildcards. The ? matches any single character, and the * matches any group of characters. If you want to look into some directory other than the current working directory, use the wildcard characters in the filename portion of the path. For example, to see the names of files that begin with the letters *READ* on the currently mounted CD, enter the command:

```
ls /mnt/cdrom/READ*
```

For a verbose listing of those files, add the `-l` option to the command, as follows:

```
ls -l /mnt/cdrom/READ*
```

### `ls` Subdirectories

The `ls` command's `-R` option (uppercase) recursively displays the contents of subdirectories within directories. The term "recursive" means to "call one's self." In the `ls` command, recursion happens as follows. If `ls` encounters a subdirectory within the directory it's currently examining, it calls upon itself to display the contents of that subdirectory, and then goes back to displaying the contents of the current directory. If you want to see a list of every directory and file on your hard drive, you need to view the contents of the system root with recursion turned on. If you want to display that information in the long format and be able to scroll through the information using the `less` program, enter this command:

```
ls -Rl / ¦ less
```

You can quit the `less` program at any time by typing the letter q and pressing Enter. You'll be returned to the shell command prompt.

## Finding Files at the Shell Prompt

We all have occasion to know or remember a filename without knowing exactly where it's located in the filesystem. Fortunately, Linux offers a `find` command that can scour the entire filesystem—or any directory on the filesystem—for files that match some name or pattern. The syntax for the command is as follows:

```
find startingPoint -name regularExpression
```

`startingPoint` is the directory where the search should begin. That directory and all subdirectories within it will be searched.

`regularExpression` specifies the name of the file to look for, or an expression that provides a skeletal structure of the name you're looking for.

As an example, suppose you've been using Linux for a long time, and you want to find a document named `wilbur-letter` that you created a long time ago. The only problem is, you've forgotten where you put it. If you want to search the entire filesystem for `wilbur-letter`, you'd enter this command:

```
find / -name wilbur-letter
```

The / in the sample command tells the `find` command to start searching from the system root. The `-name` option is required when you're searching for a filename. And `wilbur-letter` is the name of the file you're looking for.

You can use wildcard characters in the `find` command as well to locate files that match some pattern. As an example, let's say you want to search the entire filesystem for all files that contain the characters *howto* in lowercase letters only. The command to enter at the command prompt would be the following:

```
find / -name *howto*
```

The `-name` option in the command specifies a case-sensitive search. If you want to perform the search without regard to upper/lowercase letters, use `-iname` (*ignore casename*) instead of `-name`. So, for example, to locate all files in the filesystem that contain the letters *howto* without regard to upper/lowercase letters, you'd use `-iname` rather than `-name` as in the following example:

```
find / -iname *howto*
```

If the results of the search whiz by too quickly on the screen, you can pipe the output of the `find` command to the `less` program or printer, using the standard pipe character (¦). For example, to search the entire filesystem for files that contain the letters *readme*, without regard to case, and send that output to the `less` program, you'd enter the command:

```
find / -iname *readme* ¦ less
```

## Viewing a File's Contents from the Shell

You can use the `less` program to view the contents of any text file. Just type the command `less` followed by the path to the file you want to view. If the file is in the current working directory, you can use just the filename. For example, suppose you want to view the contents of a file named README in the `/usr/man/man1` directory. Entering this command would do the trick:

```
less /usr/man/man1/README
```

Or, if you switched to that directory first using the `cd` command, the following would also work:

```
cd /usr/man/man1
```

Then you could view the contents of the README file in that directory using just the filename:

```
less README
```

Once the `less` program displays the contents of the file, you can browse through the file using the various navigation keys provided by `less`. You can type a q to quit `less` and return to the shell prompt at any time.

Don't forget that case-sensitivity counts in the `less` command. For example, let's suppose you enter a `find` command to locate all files that contain the phrase *howto* regardless of case, as in the following:

```
find / -iname *howto*
```

The command lists a bunch of filenames that contain the letters *howto*. Now, suppose one of those files is `/usr/doc/dosemu-0.99.10/dosemu-HOWTO.txt`. When you want to view the contents of that file, don't forget that you have to use the same upper- and lowercase letters when entering the `less` command, as in the following:

```
less /usr/doc/dosemu-0.99.10/dosemu-HOWTO.txt
```

**Tip**

The `head` and `tail` commands let you peek at the first few lines or last few lines of a file, but they don't allow you to scroll through the file. Nonetheless, they can be handy for taking a quick peek into log files, as you'll learn in Chapter 17.

## DELETING FILES WITH `rm`

Deleting files is always risky business, so you want to proceed with caution here. It's probably safest to use the GNOME File Manager to delete files. But if you must use the shell prompt, the command you'll need is `rm` (short for remove). If the file you want to delete is in the current working directory, then you only need to follow the `rm` command with the name of the file you want to delete. For example, the following command deletes the file named `mystuff.txt` from the current working directory:

```
rm mystuff.txt
```

The `rm` command asks for permission before deleting a file:

```
rm: remove 'mystuff.txt'?
```

To delete the file, you must type the letter **y** and press Enter. Any other entry (including just pressing Enter) will cancel the deletion and keep the file intact.

If you want to delete a file that's not in the current directory, simply specify the path to the file you want to delete. For example, if you want to delete `/home/alec/mystuff.txt`, but you're not in that directory at the moment, just enter the following command:

```
rm /home/alec/mystuff.txt
```

You can use wildcard characters in the `rm` command as well. But be careful! You might end up deleting more than you bargained for. For safety, you should always test the wildcard first using the `ls` command. For example, let's say you were pretty sure you wanted to delete all files in the working directory that start with the letters *01fig* (that is, all files that match the pattern *01fig\**). Before you commit to this decision, you could enter the following command to see exactly what you'll be deleting:

```
ls 01fig*
```

Review the list of filenames that appears on the screen, and make sure you really want to delete all those listed files. If you are sure, use that same skeleton in the rm command to remove the files:

```
rm 01fig*
```

You'll be prompted for confirmation before each file is deleted. So you can still decide to delete, or keep, each file that matches the wildcard pattern.

### DELETING DIRECTORIES WITH rmdir

If you try to delete a directory using the rm command, Linux will (thankfully) ignore your request. After all, deleting a directory deletes *everything* in that directory and its subdirectories. And you never want to delete an important directory by accident. To delete a directory, use the rmdir command with the following syntax:

```
rmdir directoryname
```

where directoryname is the complete path, or a relative reference to a directory. For example, suppose you want to delete a subdirectory named spreadsheets from your home directory. The following command would do the trick:

```
rmdir ~/spreadsheets
```

If the directory you're trying to delete isn't empty, you'll see a Directory not empty message. Linux will keep the directory as well. Before deleting the directory, you should open it and use the ls command to make sure you really want to delete every file in that directory. Then use the rm and rmdir commands within that directory to delete files and subdirectories individually, or by using wildcard characters.

## COPYING FILES WITH cp

The shell command for copying files is cp with basic syntax:

```
cp sourcedestination
```

source is the directory and file you're copying from, and destination is the directory you're copying to. You can use wildcard characters in the source to specify filenames that match some pattern. For example, suppose you have files named 01fig01.pcx, 01fig02.pcx, 01fig03.pcx, and so forth in your home directory. You want to copy all those files to a floppy disk that's currently mounted as /mnt/floppy. The following command would do the trick:

```
cp ~/01fig* /mnt/floppy
```

(~ is the shortcut name for your home directory.) If you were already in your home directory, then you could omit the ~/ and enter the command, as in the following:

```
cp fig* /mnt/floppy
```

Copying files can be riskier than you might think because Linux will overwrite a newer file with an older file by the same name, without warning. For example, suppose your home directory on the hard disk contains a file named myLetter that you last modified a week ago.

The floppy disk in your drive also contains a file named myLetter that you last modified several months ago. If you copy myLetter from the floppy disk to the hard disk, you'll replace the newer myLetter with the older one. And there's nothing you can do to bring back the newer version of the file.

You can avoid these kinds of problems by using the -i (interactive) switch in the cp command, which gives you a chance to change your mind before copying a file. For example, the following command tries to copy all files from the floppy disk to your home directory:

```
cp -i /mnt/floppy/* /~
```

However, the -i switch prompts before overwriting any files on the home directory. So if something looks fishy, you can cancel the copy until you have a chance to compare the contents of the two files to see which one you really want to keep on your hard disk.

The cpcommand also accepts multiple filenames to copy. Just separate each filename with a blank space. For example, if you specifically wanted to copy files named 01fig01.pcx and myChapter.txt from the current directory to a floppy disk, you could enter this command:

```
cp 01fig01.pcx myChapter.txt /mnt/floppy
```

PART

I

CH

3

**Note**    You can copy files from a CD-ROM. But you cannot copy files to a CD-ROM because CDs are a Read-Only medium. Nor can you delete, rename, or move a file from a CD-ROM because doing so would require the ability to change the CD's contents.

## MOVING AND RENAMING FILES WITH mv

To move or copy a file from the shell prompt, use the mv command with the following syntax:

```
mv sourcedestination
```

source is the file to be moved or renamed, and destination is the new name, or the name of the new directory for the file. For example, let's say you just want to rename the file myStuff.txt in the current directory to giddyup.txt. The command to enter would be as follows:

```
mvmyStuff.txt giddyup.txt
```

If, on the other hand, you want to keep the name myStuff.txt, but just move that file to some other directory (such as .mnt/floppy), you'd enter this command:

```
mv myStuff.txt /mnt/floppy
```

You can use wildcard characters in the mv command. For example, suppose you have a subdirectory named myBackups in your home directory. Currently you have files named 01fig01, 01fig02, 01chap, and so forth in your working directory that you'd like to move to the myBackups directory. Given that you can always use a tilde (~) to represent the current working directory, the following command would copy all files that start with *01* from your home directory to the ~/myBackups directory:

```
mv ~/01* ~/myBackups
```

Remember, you can get more detailed information on any of the file management commands described in this chapter by simply entering the man (manual) command followed by a blank space and the command you want help with. For example, to get help with the mv command, you'd enter the following at the shell prompt:

```
man mv
```

Also, don't forget that just about anything you can do at the shell prompt, you can probably do in the GNOME File Manager more intuitively. So don't wear yourself out studying and memorizing commands.

# CASE STUDY: CREATING SCREEN SHOTS

Lana Leulu needs to make some screen shots of Linux to be used in a presentation she plans to give at work. Using her Linux PC at home, she figures out how to use the Screen Shot extension of the GIMP (a graphics program that comes with Linux) to create the screen shots. She takes several shots and saves them as files in her home directory with names like figure1.gif, figure2.gif, and so forth. Now she needs to copy those screen shots to a floppy disk to take to work. Lana has permissions to mount floppy disks on her current PC, so how does she copy the files from her home directory to the floppy drive?

First, Lana needs to put a floppy disk into the floppy drive. Then she opens the User Mount Tool (Main Menu, System, Disk Management). If a floppy disk is currently in the floppy drive, she unmounts it using the Unmount button in the User Mount Tool. Then she puts her empty floppy disk into the floppy drive. If that disk has never been formatted for use in Linux, she can use the Format button in the User Mount Tool to format the disk. Finally, she mounts the floppy disk using the Mount button in the User Mount Tool. So now the floppy disk is mounted and ready to accept files.

Next, Lana needs to get a couple of File Manager windows open so that she can copy files using drag-and-drop. Clicking the Home Directory icon on her desktop opens up the GNOME File Manager, already pointing to her home directory. Then she chooses File, Create New Window from the File Manager's menu bar. When the second File Manager window opens, she moves it down and to the right so that it's not covering the original File Manager too much. Then she points that File Manager window to her floppy disk by opening the /mnt/floppy folder in that second window.

To copy files, Lana needs to go back to the first File Manager window and select the files she wants to copy. She can do this by "lassoing" them, or by Ctrl+clicking each file she wants to copy. Then she drags—using the middle mouse button—any selected file into the right pane of the File Manager window that's displaying the contents of the floppy disk. After she releases the middle mouse button, she chooses Copy Here from the menu that appears. When the copy is complete, she unmounts the floppy disk from the drive, again using the User Mount Tool. Then she removes the floppy disk from the floppy drive and is ready to roll.

# CHAPTER 4

# RUNNING AND MANAGING PROGRAMS

**In this chapter**

# RUNNING PROGRAMS

As you probably know, the terms *program*, *application*, and *app* all refer to the same thing—a piece of software that you can run on your computer to do some work. Your Red Hat Linux package comes with many free applications. Some are installed automatically during the installation. Others can be installed separately using the Red Hat Package Manager (RPM). Linux apps come in three main "flavors," which describe a little about the interface the program uses—GNOME apps, X apps, and command-prompt apps.

## GNOME APPS

GNOME apps are all graphical in nature and share a common look and feel. An easy way to open and explore some of the GNOME applications installed on your system is to follow these steps:

1. Mid-click the desktop.
2. Point to GNOME Apps.
3. Choose a program from the menu or any submenu that appears.

Most GNOME apps have all the graphical elements you'd expect to find in a graphical application, including a menu bar, toolbar, tools around the window border for moving and sizing the app's window, and so forth. Most GNOME apps also offer *tear-away menus*. When you click an item in the menu bar, you see a little dashed line across the top of the menu. Clicking that dashed line puts a copy of that menu, in the "open" position, on your desktop. You can drag that open menu anywhere onto the screen so that it stays open, but out of your way. For example, in Figure 4.1 I tore away a few menus from the GNOME Gnumeric spreadsheet application and placed them around the desktop. To close the torn-away copy of the menu, just click the dashed line again, or click the menu's Close (X) button.

The menu bar and toolbar, as well as any other bars that appear beneath the title bar are also movable. You can drag the little pad at the left edge of the bar to move the bar to anywhere on the desktop. You can also "anchor" the bar to any edge of its program by dragging the pad right to the border that you want to anchor it to and dropping it there. For example, Figure 4.1 shows the Gnumeric window with the toolbar anchored to the left edge of the window border. A toolbar can also float freely, like a tear-away menu. To return a bar to its original position, just drag its little pad back to that original position, and drop it there.

GNOME apps can also span multiple virtual desktops, which means your work area can be as much as four times the size of the screen (even larger if you allow more virtual desktops). Just drag the program's window so that it spans two or more virtual desktops, then use the Pager to visit various corners of the program's window. Enlarge the window by dragging any edge or border within that virtual desktop. Figure 4.2 shows an example where the Gnumeric spreadsheet is sized to take up almost four virtual desktops. If you look at the Pager in the panel of that figure, you'll see a large square covering the four panes of the pager. That huge square represents the Gnumeric window. You can easily jump to any corner of the application by clicking on that corner in the page.

**Figure 4.1**
Gnumeric spread-sheet with its toolbar moved to its left edge, and some torn-away menus off to the right.

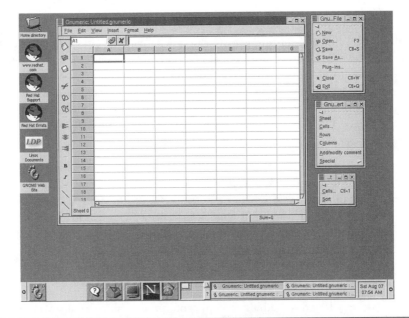

**Tip**

If your hands happen to be on the keyboard, you can jump to any virtual desktop by holding down the Alt+Shift keys, then pressing the ~RA, ~DA, ~LA, or ~UA to indicate which direction you want to jump.

**Figure 4.2**
The Gnumeric spreadsheet sized to fill almost all four virtual desktops. Notice its size in the pager.

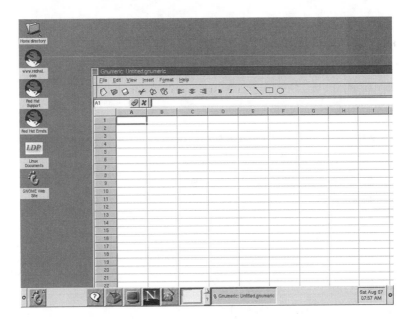

Right-clicking is widely supported in GNOME apps. For example, you can right-click any cell in the Gnumeric spreadsheet to get a quick menu of options that are relevant to spreadsheet cells. Many (though not all) GNOME apps include a Preferences dialog box that you can use to tweak the program to your own tastes. You may have to look around for the Preferences option by checking each pull-down menu in the program. But once you find it, you can generally figure out what to do just by experimenting with settings that the dialog box presents. The status bar along the bottom of most GNOME apps can often be turned on and off using an option in the Preferences dialog box.

Cut and paste is also widely supported across GNOME apps. The techniques are virtually identical to those used in Windows. First you need to select the thing you want to move or copy. You can usually select text or a portion of a graphic image just by dragging the mouse pointer through or around it. Or, to select an entire picture, as in a graphics program, click it once. Many programs that let you type text allow you to select a single word by double-clicking it or select an entire paragraph by triple-clicking it. If appropriate to the program you're using at the moment, the ability to select the entire current document may be available by choosing Edit, Select All from the menu bar.

After you've selected something to copy, you can probably use at least one of the following techniques summarized to copy it to the clipboard:

**Tip**
If you happen to be familiar with Windows, you'll probably notice that GNOME's Cut and paste methods are virtually identical to those used in most versions of Windows.

- Click the Copy button in the toolbar.
- Right-click the selection and choose Edit, Copy.
- Choose Edit, Copy from the program's menu bar.
- Press Ctrl+C.

If you want to move the selection to the clipboard (so the original no longer exists), use one of these techniques instead:

- Click the Cut button in the toolbar.
- Right-click the selection and choose Edit, Cut.
- Choose Edit, Cut from the program's menu bar.
- Press Ctrl+X.

To paste the selected item elsewhere, first click the spot where you want to paste the item. Then do any of the following:

- Click the Paste button in the toolbar.
- Right-click where you want to paste the selected item and choose Paste (or Edit, Paste).

- Choose Edit, Paste from the menu bar of the program you're pasting into.
- Press Ctrl+V.

A shortcut for copy and paste supported in many GNOME apps is to simply select the item you want to copy. Then, mid-click the spot where you want to paste a copy of that selection. *Very* quick and easy! Many GNOME apps also support undo, which you can access by right-clicking the spot where you made a change, and choosing Undo or Edit, Undo from the menu that appears. Pressing Ctrl+Z often works as well.

> **Tip**
>
> After you click the Main Menu button and open a submenu, you can drag that submenu by its title to the panel for one-click access to the menu in the future. Dragging a document file from File Manager onto a specific application's icon will open that document in that program, if at all possible.

Most GNOME applications have Help options on their menu bars. So, to learn more about the abilities and techniques of a specific GNOME app, check its Help menu. For general help with GNOME, click the Integrated Help System button (the one with a question mark) in the panel. Chapter 5, "Getting Help," discusses still other sources of documentation for GNOME, GNOME apps, and Linux in general.

PART

I

CH

4

## X Apps

X, also called *X11*, the *X Window System*, and even *X Windows* (though the latter is often frowned upon), is another graphical interface that Linux supports. X apps are very similar to GNOME apps in look and feel, but may not offer all the conveniences of GNOME apps. For example, not all X apps have tear-away menus. But you can run X applications from GNOME. In fact, many of the programs that are available from the GNOME menus are actually X apps.

> **Tip**
>
> The specific version of X that ships with Red Hat Linux 6 is Version 11, Release 6. The short notation for expressing that is X11R6. You'll learn more about X in Chapter 8, "Configuring the X Window System."

The GIMP (GNU Image Manipulation Program) is an example of an X application. You can start the GIMP by clicking the Main Menu button and choosing Graphics, the GIMP. The first time you start the GIMP, you may have to go through a brief installation procedure. But that's just a matter of clicking the Install and Continue buttons that appear on the screen. When the GIMP first opens, all you'll see is a "Tip of the Day" and a set of tools in a small window. But you can open a blank document to work on in the GIMP by choosing File, New, OK from the menu bar near the top of the window that shows all the tools. The new blank document floats in its own separate window. In Figure 4.3, I used the Text tool to add the words Hello and World to the empty document. (That tool displays the hint "Add text to the image" when you rest the mouse pointer on it.)

**Figure 4.3**
The GIMP is an X app, and a little unusual in that virtually all of its tools are free-floating.

You can open additional tools by choosing File, Dialogs, and then an option that appears on the submenu. Each dialog appears in its own little window, which is different from what you might expect with a GNOME app (or Windows app, for that matter). For example, in Figure 4.3 I've opened several dialogs, and each appears in its own window. But all the same basic rules apply. Clicking the X in the upper-right corner of the window closes the window. Right-clicking the document or anything you've placed in the document provides quick access to options that are relevant to the item you right-clicked. Again, you can learn more about an individual application from its Help menu or other documentation. But it's safe to click around and experiment, just using basic point-and-click (and right-click) techniques.

## COMMAND-PROMPT APPS

Command-prompt apps are few and far between in the modern era of graphical computing, but you can still find some hanging around in Linux. Command-prompt apps simply take over the command prompt, and it's up to you to know what to type at that point. The bc calculator is an example of such a program. To start it, you need to get to a command prompt. The easiest way to do that is to click the Terminal Emulation Program, which will open a window that displays the Linux command prompt.

---

**Giving New Windows the Keyboard Focus**
In Windows, any newly opened window immediately gets the keyboard focus so that anything you type goes right into that window. It doesn't work that way in Linux. Often, you'll be typing along, assuming that whatever you're typing is going into a recently opened window or dialog box. But when you look at the screen, there's no text! You need to click exactly where you want to type, then start typing all over again.

If that drives you crazy, here's a quick cure. Click the GNOME Configuration Tool button in the panel. In the Control Center that appears, click on Window Manager (under the Desktop category), then click the Run Configuration Tool or Enlightenment button. Click on Behavior in the left column. Then choose the first two options on the Advanced Focus tab so that both are selected (their buttons looked pushed in). Click the OK button. Then click the Close (X) button in the upper-right corner of the Control Center window. From now on, when you open a new window (including a terminal window), whatever you type should appear in the new window. You'll learn more about customizing Enlightenment (the default window manager for GNOME) in Chapter 9, "Configuring GNOME and Enlightenment."

To run bc, the command-prompt calculator, follow these steps:

1.  Click anywhere inside the Terminal window.
2.  Type **bc** and press Enter.

A copyright notice appears, followed by some (non-) warranty information, and not much else seems to have happened. But if you look closely, you'll realize that the Linux command prompt is gone. And, if you enter a common Linux command like **ls** to list the contents of the current directory, you don't get such a list. Instead, you get the number zero! That's because bc has "taken over" the command prompt, and the commands you enter are executed by bc rather than Linux.

The bc calculator lets you do math, not enter Linux commands. So, for instance, if you were to type

`10+10`

and press Enter, the screen would display 20, the sum of 10 plus 10. If you type

`sqrt(81)`

and press Enter, the screen displays 9, the square root of 81.

That's all well and good. Eventually, though, you're going to ask, "How do I get out of here?" Well, it depends which command-prompt app you happen to be using at the moment. Usually, though, typing the command **quit** and pressing Enter, as in Figure 4.4, will do the trick. (If quit doesn't work, try **help** or **exit**). When the Linux command prompt reappears, you know you can start entering normal Linux commands again.

PART
I

CH
4

**Figure 4.4**
A little session with bc, terminated by a quit command.

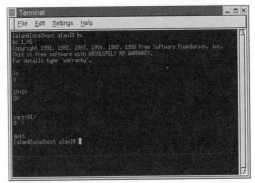

Fortunately, the vast majority of Linux applications are graphical, so you won't have to spend too much type typing commands at the command prompt. Unfortunately, there are so many apps to choose from, there's not really space in this book to discuss them all in any depth. Linux, proper, is bound to consume all the pages we can squeeze into this book. But where there's an app, there's usually documentation. Typically, just selecting Help from a graphical program's menu bar will get you pointed in the right direction. In Chapter 5, you'll learn about the many sources of documentation available on your local PC, as well as on the Web.

# OPENING FILES

The Main Menu doesn't necessarily give you access to all the programs that are installed on your hard disk. For example, newly installed programs may not be accessible from the menu. Some of the more advanced programs for programmers and such are also inaccessible from the menus. Likewise, there may be many *documents*, files that contain text or data used by some program, that aren't accessible from the menus. For example, Linux comes with many README and HOWTO files that contain just simple text, which you can open with virtually any text viewer or editing program. But, you can't get at those documents straight from the menus. There are three techniques that you can use to open *any* file, be it a program or a document:

- From the GNOME File Manager
- From the Run Program dialog box
- From the Linux command prompt

## OPENING FROM THE FILE MANAGER

Double-clicking the icon of just about any file in File Manager will open that file. As a rule, it's not a good idea to just double-click icons at random. Typically, you'll do this only when trying to follow someone's directions that tell you to open some file. What happens when you double-click a filename depends on the characteristics of the file that you double-clicked. Basically, here's how it works:

- If you double-click the icon for a document file that's associated with some program, the document opens within that associated program.
- If you double-click the icon for a document that's not associated with a program, a dialog box appears asking which program you want to use to open the document.
- If you double-click the icon for a graphical program, the program opens in a window, just like programs you start from the Main Menu.
- If you double-click the icon for a program that runs from the command prompt, often nothing happens on your screen. The program, instead, runs in virtual console 1 (Ctrl+Alt+F1).

Let's take a look at some examples. As an example of opening the first type of file—a document that's associated with some program—let's suppose you've read an instruction that tells you to see the /usr/doc/HTML/index.html file. How do you go about opening that file? From File Manager, you simply have to work your way to the /usr/doc/HTML directory. Let's assume that the file is truly where it's supposed to be and the icon that got that file appears in the right pane of the File Manager, as in Figure 4.5.

**Figure 4.5**
After opening the /usr/doc/HTML directory, an icon for the in-dex.html ap-pears in the right pane.

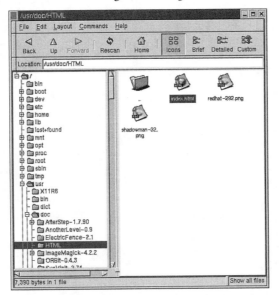

It just so happens that document files with the .html extension are associated with the Netscape Navigator Web browser. So when you double-click the index.html filename, its contents will appear within that browser. (The first time you run Navigator, you may get some extra dialog boxes of information. You can close those by clicking the Accept or OK button within each open dialog box.) Figure 4.6 shows how index.html looks when opened in Navigator. Notice, too, that the Location bar near the top of Navigator's window verifies that you are indeed viewing the file /usr/doc/HTML/index.html. When you've finished viewing the file, you can just click the Close (X) button in the upper-right corner of Navigator's window to close it.

**Tip**

You can create and change associations between document filename extensions and the applications that open them using the MIME Types section of the GNOME Control Panel, as discussed in Chapter 9.

If a document file is not associated with a particular program, you'll be asked which application you want to use. For example, let's say that, for whatever reason, you want to view the /usr/doc/enlightenment-0.15.5/README file. The procedure would be the same as with any other file; work your way to the /usr/doc/enlightenment-0.15.5 directory, and you should see an icon named README in the right pane. When you double-click that icon, a dialog box titled gmc (for GNOME Midnight Command) appears.

**Figure 4.6**
Viewing the contents of `/usr/doc/HTML/index.html` with Netscape Navigator.

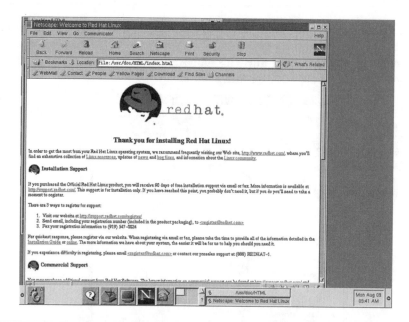

**Tip**

The easiest way to view a text file's contents is to right-click its icon and choose View from the menu that appears. If you'd like to use the simple gEdit program to edit text files, click the Main Menu and choose Settings, GNOME Edit Properties, and the gEdit from the drop-down list. Choose OK to save the change. After that, you can right-click any text file's icon and choose Edit to open that file in gEdit.

Because README files are generally all plain text files, a simple text file viewer will do the trick. To get to the Text File Viewer, you first need to scroll down to and expand the Utilities category; then scroll down to and click Text File Viewer. If you look at the Program to run section of the dialog box, you'll notice that this option actually runs a program named `gless` (see Figure 4.7). That little tidbit of information may come in handy later. But for now, you just need to click the OK button to open the README file in `gless`. Sure enough, the README file opens and appears within the `gless` program window. You can, of course, close `gless` and the README file at any time by clicking the Close (X) button at the upper-right corner of the `gless` window.

You can also start a program from the File Manager. For example, let's say that you want to open the gless program. You cleverly use the Commands, Find File option in File Manager to search the entire filesystem (starting at /) for a file named `gless`. And you discover that `gless` is stored in the `/usr/bin` directory. Within File Manager, you then work your way to the `/usr/bin` directory, scroll down a bit in the right pane and find that there is, indeed, an icon for `gless` in that directory. It has a piston icon, as shown in Figure 4.8, which indicates that `gless` is an executable program file. Double-clicking that icon opens the Text File Viewer program. The program's document window is empty because you just opened the program, not a specific document.

**Figure 4.7**
The gmc dialog box appears when GNOME doesn't know which program to use to open a document. The Utilities, Text File Viewer option is good for opening plain text documents like README files.

**Figure 4.8**
Opening the /usr/bin directory in File Manager shows that there is an icon for gless in that directory.

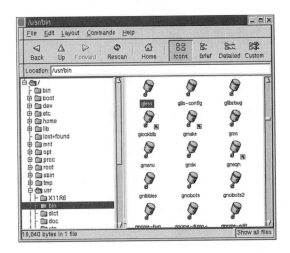

> **Tip**
>
> The /usr/doc directory is home to much of Linux's user documentation. The /usr/bin directory is home to many of Linux's *user* programs (also called binary files).

## OPENING DOCUMENTS FROM WITHIN PROGRAMS

Most graphical applications that you open with have a File menu that contains an Open option. When you choose File, Open, you'll be taken to a dialog box that's like a mini File Manager. You can browse through directories in the left column or jump to any parent of the current directory by clicking on the button centered near the top of the dialog box. That button always shows the name of the directory whose contents are currently visible in the right pane. For example, in Figure 4.9 I'm currently viewing the contents of the /usr/doc/dosemu-0.99.10 (DOS Emulator) directory. To open the README.txt file in that directory using gless, just click its icon and then click OK. Or, if you prefer, you can just double-click the icon. Assuming the file is indeed a text file that `gless` can read, it opens inside the `gless` document area.

**Figure 4.9**
Many graphical programs offer a File, Open command, which leads to a dialog box similar to the Open Text File dialog box shown here. You can browse around the filesystem and select a file to open.

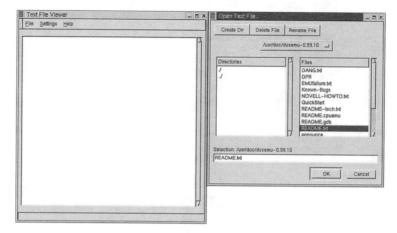

## OPENING FROM THE RUN PROGRAM DIALOG BOX

Using the File Manager is a nice, graphical way to locate a file to open, but it's not the only choice available to you. If you know the path to the file you want to open, you can also use the Run Program dialog box. To get there, follow these simple steps:

1. Click the GNOME Main Menu button.
2. Choose Run Program.

A tiny dialog box titled Run Program appears. Simply type the complete path to the program you want to run, then click the OK button. For example, let's suppose you want to run the / usr/bin/gless program. Type that path into the text box (being careful about case-sensitivity as in Figure 4.10) and then click the Run button. Optionally, you can use the Browse button in the Run Program dialog box to browse your way to the program's directory and icon.

**Figure 4.10**
About to start the `gless` program from the Run Program dialog box.

The Run Program dialog box only works with programs. If you try to open a document file from Run Program, the result will likely be nothing—the Run Program dialog box closes without showing the contents of the document file. When that occurs, you're better off using the File Manager to open the document file.

An error message describing what happened before the Run Program dialog box disappeared may appear in Virtual Console 1, although the message might not do you any good. It's better to just use File Manager to open the document file, or the `gless` program, as discussed next.

> **Tip**
>
> Actually, if the program is in the /usr/bin directory, you don't need to type the directory name. For example, just entering the command gless in the Run Program dialog box will start that program. That's because /usr/bin is one of the directories in the Linux default Path environmental variable, which you'll learn more about in Chapter 11, "Configuring Startup and Shutdown."

## OPENING FROM THE COMMAND PROMPT

Keep in mind that there are two major types of command prompts. There's the command prompt that you can access in the terminal window from GNOME (or whatever GUI you're using at the moment). And then there's the more "pure" command prompt that you get when you have no GUI installed, or when you go to one of the virtual terminals 1 through 6.

You can run any application from the terminal window by entering its path and filename. For example, if you open the Terminal Emulation Program from GNOME's panel, and enter the path **/usr/bin/gless** the Text File Viewer will pop up in its own window. However, this isn't a great way to run the program because when you close the Terminal window, the gless program will close as well. Typing a path to a non-graphical application generally runs that program inside the terminal window, as the previous example demonstrated with the bc program.

From a virtual console outside the GUI (Ctrl+F2 through Ctrl+F6), you can run only nongraphical applications. For example, attempting to run /usr/bin/gless from a virtual console only displays the following error message:

```
Gtk-warning **: cannot open display
```

What the message is really saying is that no GUI is in this console to run gless. You have to run gless from inside the GUI (the Ctrl+Alt+F7 console).

However, you can certainly run a non-graphical application from any terminal. For example, entering the command **bc** at any virtual console starts bc right up and lets it take over the command prompt. Entering the **quit** command exits bc and returns you to the command prompt.

Associations between document files and programs don't really exist at the command prompt either. For example, if you try to open a README file from a command prompt (either in terminal emulation or a virtual console) by entering the following command, you'll likely get a Permission Denied error message:

```
/usr/doc/enlightenment-0.15.5/README
```

You're much better off trying to open document files from within the GNOME file manager.

If you can't get into the GNOME File Manager and really need to see the contents of a text file, you can pipe those contents into the `less` program, which is a non-graphical version of the `gless` program. The syntax is as follows:

```
less path
```

`path` is the path to the name of the file you want to view. For example, entering the following command will indeed show the contents at the command prompt, inside the `less` program:

```
less /usr/doc/enlightenment-0.15.5/README
```

The `less` program will "take over" the command prompt until you type the letter **q** to quit. Needless to say, going through the GNOME File Manager is a lot easier because there's a lot less typing to do. But in a pinch, you can use the `less` program at the command prompt to view a document file's contents.

> **Tip**
>
> For help with the `less` program, you can enter the command **less - ?** at any command prompt.

# SAVING DOCUMENTS

Most application programs will let you create and edit as many documents as you wish. As with any operating system, if you create a document in some program and want to have access to it again in the future, you need to save that document. The standard procedure is to choose File, Save from the application menu bar. Typically, this will open a dialog box that's already pointed to your home directory (for instance, /home/*username*). Your home directory is a good place to save documents because it makes them easy to find in the future. In fact, whenever you choose File, Open in order to reopen a document from this same application, it will take you to your home directory. If you have lots of documents to keep track of, you can create subdirectories within your home directory and organize your files into the subdirectories.

---

**Creating Subdirectories in Your Home Directory**

Chapter 3, "Understanding the Linux Filesystem," discussed general techniques for creating directories. To specifically add subdirectories to your own home directory, double-click the Home Directory icon on the desktop. This will open File Manager with your home directory (such as /home/*username*) already selected in the left column. To create a subdirectory there, right-click any empty area (not on an icon) in the right pane and choose New Directory. Type a name for the directory, and then click the OK button. The new directory appears in your home directory instantly with the standard "folder" icon.

---

To name your file, type in a valid filename where prompted. For example, in Figure 4.11, I created a simple workbook using Gnumeric. (To start that program, click the Main Menu button and choose Applications, Gnumeric Spreadsheet). To save the workbook I created, I chose File, Save from the Gnumeric menu bar. It just so happens that I have a subdirectory named workbooks within my home directory, and so I opened that directory before typing a filename. The button centered near the top of the dialog box shows that the file I'm about to save will go into /home/alan/workbooks. Down at the bottom of the dialog box I've typed NerdToysQuarterlySales as the filename. Gnumeric will automatically add the filename extension .gnumeric to whatever filename I provide so clicking the OK button now saves the workbook to /home/alan/workbooks/NerdToysQuarterlySales.gnumeric.

**Figure 4.11**
About to save a Gnumeric workbook with the filename NerdToysQuar-terlySales in the workbooks subdirectory of my home directory.

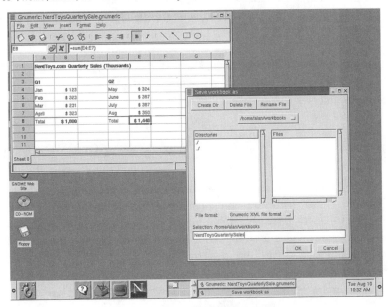

To reopen that document in the future, I could start up Gnumeric, and choose File, Open from its menu bar. The Load File dialog box that appears would initially point me to my home directory. In this case, I'd need to move down to the workbooks directory first and then choose NerdToysQuarterlySales.gnumeric from the list of filenames that appears.

> **Tip**    The user's manuals for Gnumeric are accessible from Gnumeric's Help menu.

It just so happens the .gnumeric filename extension is a registered MIME type. This means if I double-click a file with that extension in File Manager, the document automatically opens in Gnumeric. So I really don't have to open Gnumeric first; instead, I can just use File Manager to browse to my /home/alan/workbooks directory. Double-clicking on the icon for NerdToysQuarterlySales.gnumeric in the right pane of File Manager opens the Gnumeric spreadsheet automatically, and loads the NerdToysQuarterlySales.gnumeric document into that program.

> **Tip**    You'll learn how to create and edit MIME types of your own in Chapter 9.

# CUSTOMIZING THE MAIN MENU

If your Main Menu offers programs you really don't need access to, and/or doesn't provide easy access to programs that you need to run often, you can change the menu. First, you need to be aware that there are actually two separate menus that can be modified:

- **System menu**: Available to all users. Only the superuser can change the System menu.
- **User menu**: Available only to the user who is currently logged in. Any user can change his/her own User menu without superuser privileges.

The program used to edit the Main Menu is named, aptly, Menu Editor. And any user can start that program by following these simple steps:

1. Click the Main Menu button.
2. Choose Settings, Menu Editor.

If you prefer, you can mid-click the desktop and choose GNOME Apps, Settings, Menu Editor.

When the Menu Editor opens, its left pane shows an entry for each submenu that branches off from the Main Menu. Expanding a menu name, by clicking its + sign, allows you to see all the options that are currently on that menu. For example, Figure 4.12 shows the contents of the Applications submenu on the Main Menu. As you can see, the options listed beneath Applications in the Menu Editor exactly match the options available under Applications on the Main Menu.

**Figure 4.12**
Options under Applications in the Menu Editor reflect the options that are visible under Applications on the Main Menu.

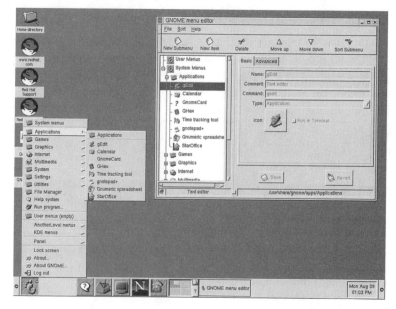

When you click a menu option in the left pane, the right pane displays the information that's associated with that menu option. This same information is also used for any other launchers, such as a panel button or desktop shortcut, that you might create to gain access to the program. For example, in Figure 4.12 the highlighter is currently on the gEdit entry in the left pane. The right pane shows the following information about that menu entry:

- **Name**: The text of the menu item.
- **Comment**: The Tooltip that appears when a user points to the launcher's icon.
- **Command**: The command that's executed when someone clicks on the menu option.
- **Type**: The type of file that the menu item is attached to, either Application for a program, or Directory for a submenu.
- **Icon**: The icon displayed by the launcher.
- **Run in Terminal**: De-selected if the program runs in a GUI; selected if the program must be run in a terminal window. For example, if the bc program were accessible from the menus, its entry would show Run in Terminal as being selected, since bc runs only at the command prompt.

If you're logged in as root, all the options are available for change because the superuser has the right to change the System menu. If you're logged in as a regular user, the options will be dimmed, indicating that you cannot change them.

## CREATING YOUR OWN USER MENUS

Every user can create his or her own custom menu, called a *user menu*, which is accessible from the Main Menu. The option groups for that user menu appear under the User Menus heading on the Main Menu. For example, in Figure 4.13 I created a user menu that has two categories beneath it, one named My Games and the other named My Apps. Currently in the figure, the mouse pointer is resting on the My Apps menu group. As you can see, I've added menu options titled My Calendar, Color Terminal Window, gEdit, Spreadsheet, and Text File Viewer to that menu submenu.

To create or customize the user menu, click User Menu at the top of the left column in the GNOME Menu Editor. Then, if you want to create a new submenu, like the My Games or My Apps example from Figure 4.13, click the New Submenu button in the toolbar. In the dialog box that appears, type the option name as you want it to appear in the user menu (for example, My Games or My Apps). You can leave the Comment option blank. There's no need to change the icon either because the suggested "folder" icon is a good choice for a submenu.

PART
I

CH
4

**Tip**

If you want to create a menu option that duplicates an option on the System menu, but you don't know the command you need, there's an easy way to find out. Open the appropriate category under System Menus, and click the option you want to duplicate. The Command entry in the right pane tells you exactly what you need to type into the Command text box when creating your own custom user menu option.

**Figure 4.13**
The Main Menu has two new categories under User Menus, one named My Games, the other named My Apps. The My Apps submenu is currently open.

To create a menu option that opens a program, follow these steps:

1. If you want to put the option in a submenu, first click the name of that subfolder in the left pane so that it's highlighted.

2. Click the New Item option in the Toolbar. Or choose File, New Item from the menu bar. The right pane displays *untitled*.

3. Fill in the Name, Comment, and Command options. Make sure you type the command exactly, as these are case sensitive!

4. The Type option will automatically be set to Application; you needn't change that.

5. If you want to select an icon for your menu option, click the Icon button. In the Choose an Icon dialog box that appears, click whichever icon tickles your fancy, then click the OK button.

6. If the program that the menu option opens is not graphical, select the Run in Terminal option.

7. Click the Save button.

You can repeat the preceding steps to add as many menu items as you wish to the submenu.

You can also control the order in which the items in the menu or submenu appear. To alphabetize the items on the menu or submenu, first click on the parent (that is, click My Apps, if you want to sort the items in a submenu named My Apps). Then do one of the following:

■ Click the Sort Submenu item in the toolbar.

■ Right-click the highlighted submenu name and choose Sort. Or just press Ctrl+S.

■ To sort the current menu and the contents of all submenus beneath it, right-click and choose Sort Recursive or press Ctrl+R.

Linux always alphabetizes things so that uppercase letters are listed before lowercase letters. So, the items might not look alphabetized in the normal sense of the term. You can easily move items around within the submenu by clicking the option you want to move. Then click the Move Up or Move Down button in the toolbar to move the item. Optionally, you can right-click the highlighted item and choose Move Up or Move Down.

To test your new menu at any time, close the GNOME Menu Editor by clicking its Close (X) button. Then click the Main Menu button to see your new user menu(s). Click any option to test it out.

**Tip**

Your user menus are also accessible from the menu that appears when you mid-click the GNOME desktop.

If you discover any mistakes while testing your user menu, you can go back into the Menu Editor and make changes. But an even simpler method is to right-click the item you want to change, then choose Properties. The Desktop Entry Properties dialog box that appears gives you immediate access to the Name, Comment, Command, Type, Icon, and Run in Terminal options for that menu option. Just make your changes, and then click the OK button.

If you want to re-order menu items, move things around, or delete items, you'll need to reopen the Menu Editor and make your changes there. If you want to delete a menu option or submenu while in the Menu editor, click the item you want to delete. Then click the Delete button in the toolbar, or right-click the item you want to delete and choose Delete. Or, if your hands happen to be on the keyboard, you can delete the currently highlighted item by pressing Ctrl+D.

**Note**

According to the official GNOME documentation at http://www.gnome.org, you should be able to move items within the Menu Edit by dragging them around. But that feature doesn't work on any of my computers.

All of these techniques also work with the System menu, provided you're logged in as root. Just make sure you click System Menus, or any option under System Menus, in the Menu Editor before making your changes.

## UNCLUTTERING THE MAIN MENU

You can alter the overall availability of options on the Main Menu, making it either more or less extensive. For example, if you'd like a smaller, tighter main menu, you can move some items into submenus, or even hide them completely. To do so, follow these steps:

1. Right-click the Main Menu button.
2. Choose Properties. The Menu Properties dialog box appears (see Figure 4.14).

PART

I

CH

4

**Figure 4.14**
The Menu Properties dialog box lets you control the overall appearance of the Main Menu.

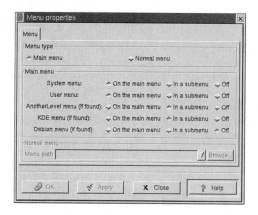

Under Menu Type, choose Main Menu to give yourself the most flexibility. If you choose Normal Menu, you'll only have a tiny menu to work with, so you probably won't want to choose that option. The various options in the center of the dialog box let you place submenu options on the main menu, in a submenu, or not at all (Off). For example, you can have all the options on the System menu be readily visible on the main menu by choosing On the Main Menu next to System Menu. Or, if you'd like to unclutter your main menu, choose In a Submenu instead. System Menu will then become a single option on the Main Menu, which you can point to in order to view its submenus. If you want to remove the System Menu from the main menu altogether, choose Off instead.

The AnotherLevel menu, KDE menu, and Debian menu all refer to menus that are generally available in desktop environments other than GNOME. You'll learn about those other desktop environments in Chapter 8. By default, the AnotherLevel and KDE menus are available via a submenu, mainly so that people who are already familiar with those desktops will have access to menus they're confortable using. If you're not familiar with AnotherLevel or KDE, and you find those options on the main menu to be distracting, you can hide the menus by choosing Off.

Figure 4.15 shows a modified version of the Main Menu where only user menus are displayed on the Main Menu. In that example, I moved the System menu to a submenu and turned off the AnotherLevel, KDE, and Debian menus. So my user menus are now available at the top of the menu, and the System Menus are visible only when that option is highlighted. The AnotherLevel, KDE, and Debian menus are not on the Main Menu at all. Options beneath System Menus, Panel, Lock Screen, About, and so forth, are permanent and can't be removed via the Menu Editor.

Don't be afraid to experiment with the Menu Properties dialog box a bit. Taking a menu "off" the Main Menu doesn't delete it from existence. If you turn a menu off and then later change your mind, simply reopen the Menu Properties dialog box and move the menu back to a submenu or the Main Menu.

**Figure 4.15**
A customized main menu with System Menu options moved to a submenu, and the AnotherLevel and KDE menus removed altogether.

# LAUNCHING APPS FROM THE PANEL

You can create a panel button for any item that's available in your main menu, even options that you've added to your user menu. Just click the Main Menu button, point to the menu option you'd like to copy to the panel, right-click that option, and choose Add This Launcher to Panel. A button for that menu appears on the panel instantly. If you change your mind later, you can remove the panel button by right-clicking it and choosing Remove from Panel.

## PANEL DRAWERS

If your panel starts getting a bit crowded with buttons, you can create a *drawer* (see Figure 4.16). As you can see in the figure, a drawer is just a panel button that, when clicked, stretches upward to display more buttons. Each button appears as a Tooltip (comment) when you point to the button. To close an open drawer, click the Hide button at the top of the drawer. Or just click the drawer's panel button again.

**Figure 4.16**
A drawer added to the panel.

It's easy to add a drawer to the panel. You can right-click the panel and choose Add Drawer. Or you can click the Main Menu button and choose Panel, Add Drawer. To move a button off the panel and into a drawer, open the drawer. Then use the middle mouse button to drag any button from the panel into the open drawer. The following are some other handy techniques for working with drawers:

■ To change a drawer's Tooltip, right-click the drawer, choose Properties, and change the Tooltip/Name option. You can control the appearance of the little Hide button that appears at the top of the open drawer from this same dialog box.

■   To move a drawer, just drag it, using the middle mouse button, to anyplace on the panel.

■   To move a button out of the drawer and back onto the panel, drag it—again using the middle mouse button—from the drawer onto the panel.

■   To delete a drawer, right-click its button and choose Remove from Panel.

You can even create a drawer that duplicates the System Menu, your user menu, or any other menu that's visible on your main menu. Just click the Main Menu button, then point to the title of the menu at the top of the menu you want to make into a drawer. For example, you could right-click User Menus if you wanted to make a drawer of your own user menu. Choose Add This as Drawer to Panel from the menu that appears, and your drawer appears in the panel. When you point to the drawer, its Tooltip will be the same as the name of the menu it represents.

## DESKTOP LAUNCHERS FOR APPS

Any item from the main menu, as well as any button on the panel, can easily be copied to the desktop as well. Just point to the item to which you want to create a desktop shortcut. Then hold down (but don't click) the left mouse button. Drag the item to the desktop and release the mouse button. If you want to get your desktop icons aligned, right-click the desktop and choose Arrange Icons. If you change your mind and want to delete the desktop shortcut, use the standard technique—right-click the item and choose Delete.

## USING GNOME SESSION MANAGEMENT

GNOME offers a feature called Session Management that any user can use to save the current appearance of his desktop when logging out. This feature will even "remember" which programs were open when the user logged out and re-open those programs when the user logs back in. In fact, GNOME even has the ability to remember which document was open in each program and can re-open those documents when the user logs in as well. Unfortunately, this last feature isn't widely supported in the current generation of GNOME apps. So it's still important to *always* save your documents before logging out.

Using Session Management is easy. Simply log out as you normally would; that is, click the Main Menu button and choose Logout. You'll notice the Save Current Setup option near the top of the dialog box (see Figure 4.17). Clicking that button, so it looks pushed in, will save your current desktop settings. Next, choose Logout (or Halt or Reboot) and then click the Yes button. If you're taken to the Linux command prompt, don't forget to enter the `logout` command to complete your logout. The next time you log in under your current username, the application programs you left on the desktop should appear on the screen as soon as you get into the GNOME desktop.

**Figure 4.17**
Use the Save Current Setup button to make GNOME remember which programs you had open next time you log in.

**Tip**

To add a Logout button to your panel, right-click the panel and choose Add Log Out Button.

# CASE STUDY: ADDING STAROFFICE TO YOUR DESKTOP

The StarOffice 5.1 CD that comes with your Red Hat package includes StarOffice, a suite of programs designed to aid in general office productivity. Like other office suites, StarOffice offers word processing, a spreadsheet, a database, a program for preparing presentations, and more. In this case study, you'll go through the steps required to install StarOffice and set up some icons to make it easy to access.

PART

I

CH

4

**Caution**

Package installation is privileged, meaning only the superuser can do it. You must be logged in as root to perform the installation discussed in this Case Study.

## MOUNTING THE STAROFFICE CD

The first step to installing StarOffice is to mount the Red Hat Linux StarOffice CD-ROM. If you set up a desktop shortcut to your CD-ROM drive as suggested in Chapter 3, you can follow these steps:

1. If there's already a CD in your CD-ROM drive, right-click the CD-ROM's icon and choose Unmount Device.

2. Remove any CD from your CD-ROM drive and put in the Red Hat Linux StarOffice CD.

3. Wait a few seconds and if the File Manager opens showing the contents of /mnt/cdrom, then the CD-ROM is already mounted and you can skip to step 6. Otherwise, continue on.

4. Right-click your CD-ROM shortcut icon and choose Mount Device.

---

**Note**

If you didn't set up that desktop shortcut to your CD-ROM drive, you'll need to use the User Mount Tool discussed in Chapter 3 to unmount the existing CD, if any. Then mount the StarOffice CD.

5. Open the GNOME file manager (double-click the Home Directory icon on the GNOME desktop).

6. Work your way to the /mnt/cdrom/linux/office51 directory in the left column of the file manager, as in Figure 4.18.

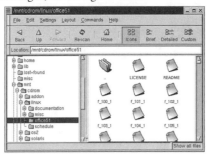

**Figure 4.18**
The GNOME file manager showing the contents of the /mnt/cdrom/ linux/office51 directory of the StarOffice 5.1 CD.

## INSTALLING STAROFFICE

The /mnt/cdrom/linux/office51 directory contains a file named setup that you can run to launch the installation. Perhaps I should point out that this is somewhat unusual in the Linux world. As you'll learn in Chapter 13, "Managing Packages with RPM," you're more likely to use RPM or GnoRPM to install most programs. On the other hand, if you're accustomed to installing Windows programs, the approach used by StarOffice will probably seem pretty familiar. Anyway, to start the installation, follow these steps:

1. With file manager displaying the contents of the /mnt/cdrom/linux/office51 directory, scroll down to the bottom of the right pane where you'll see a "piston" icon titled *setup*. Double-click that icon.

2. Within a minute or so, the StarOffice 5.1 installation program will begin. Just read the instructions on each screen, then press the Next button. (You'll see some tips for installing StarOffice and licensing information. You can just keep clicking the Next button until you get to the Enter User Data box.

3. Fill in the Enter User Data box, and click Next.

4. When you get to the Select Installation Type screen, choose Standard Installation unless you already have StarOffice experience and know exactly which components you do/don't want to install. Click Next.

5. When you get to the Select Installation Directory screen, it will probably suggest installing StarOffice in your home directory (root/Office51). I suggest you change that to a more widely accessible directory, such as /usr/office51, and then click Next.

6. If told that /usr/Office51 doesn't exist, just click Yes to create the directory now.

7. Click the Complete button to start the actual installation.

8. If you see a dialog box indicating that no Java Runtime Environment was found, just click OK to move ahead with the installation.

The installation process begins, and a progress meter will keep you informed of how the various steps are going. You may see a couple of messages along the way. Just click each message's OK button to clear the message and move along. When the installation is completed, you'll see a message telling you so. Click its Complete button, and you'll be returned to the GNOME desktop.

## ADDING StarOffice TO THE SYSTEM MENU

With StarOffice successfully installed, you can create some menu items and icons to make it easy to start the program. The startup program is in `wherever_you_put_it/bin/soffice` where `wherever_you_put_it` refers to the directory you specified while installing StarOffice. In my example, where I installed StarOffice in `/usr/Office51`, the complete startup command would be `/usr/Office51/bin/soffice`. In fact, entering that as a command in a GNOME terminal window would launch the StarOffice program.

If you want the option to start StarOffice from the GNOME System menu, follow these steps:

1. Click the Main Menu button and choose Settings, Menu Editor.

2. To put StarOffice under Applications, click Applications in the left column of the GNOME Menu Editor that appears.

3. Click New Item in the toolbar.

4. Fill in the blanks as follows (make sure you get the upper/lowercase letters right when typing the Command entry):

   Name: `StarOffice`

   Comment: `StarOffice 5.1 Suite`

   Command: `/usr/Office51/bin/soffice`

> **Caution**
>
> If you didn't install StarOffice in the `/usr/Office51` directory on your computer, be sure to make the appropriate change when typing the path in the Command box.

   Type: `Application`

5. To choose a different icon, click the Icon button. A new dialog box titled Choose an Icon appears. There's a custom icon in the directory to which you installed StarOffice (`/usr/Office51` in my example). To get to it, work your way to that directory. Then scroll down to, and click on the file named `1_soffice.xpm`. Click the OK button.

6. Click the Save button. Your Menu Editor dialog box should look something like Figure 4.19.

**PART**

**I**

**CH**

**4**

**Figure 4.19**
An option for
starting StarOffice
added to the Sys-
tem menu, via the
GNOME Menu
Editor.

7.   Close the GNOME Menu Editor by clicking its Close button.

When you click the Main Menu button and point to Applications, you should see StarOffice
listed along with other programs in that category (see Figure 4.20). As always, you can right-
click that menu option and choose Add This Launcher To Panel if you want to create a panel
button for launching StarOffice. You could then drag that button off the panel, and drop it
into the desktop, to create a desktop shortcut icon to the same program.

**Figure 4.20**
A menu option for
launching StarOf-
fice has been
added to the Ap-
plication menu.

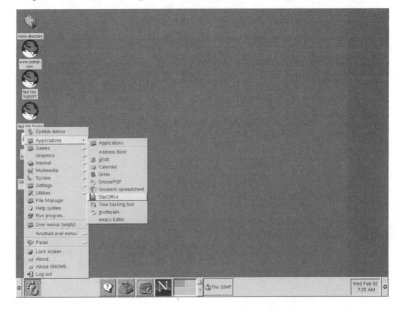

Other users who log into this same computer will be able to start StarOffice by clicking the GNOME Main Menu button and choosing Applications, StarOffice. If those users want to add buttons to their panel, or desktop shortcuts, they can use the standard techniques to do so.

To get help in learning how to use StarOffice, your best bet is to start with the most basic help. That is, after you start StarOffice, choose Help, Contents, and you'll be taken to the introductory-level help screens. To learn more about StarOffice online, visit Sun's Web site at www.sun.com/staroffice.

PART

I

CH

4

# CHAPTER 5

# GETTING HELP

In this chapter

# EXPANDING YOUR RESOURCES

A big part of learning to use Linux is knowing where to look to get information. Obviously, this book is one resource. But there are mountains of documentation available right from your hard disk, as well as from the Internet, in the form of Guides, man pages, HOWTOs, FAQs (Frequently Asked Questions), magazines, journals, and more. There's also support in the form of newsgroups, which are probably the best places to post questions as they arise.

Be forewarned, though: Much of the documentation is written for Linux system administrators, network administrators, and other more experienced users. What you've learned in the first four chapters of this book won't be sufficient to grasp all the technical information available to you. This book makes no attempt to repeat all the information available from those resources. Rather, the primary goal of this book is to provide the basic knowledge that the more advanced documentation presumes you already have. A semi-famous quote sums it up perfectly: "There are two kinds of knowledge: Either we know a subject ourselves, or we know where we can find information about it." In the ever-evolving world of Linux and the ever-changing world of high-tech in general, knowing where to find information is often the most useful knowledge of all.

# USING THE MAN PAGES

Man (manual) pages in Linux provide detailed (though terse) information for virtually every command in Linux. The GNOME Help Index provides quick access to a Table of Contents for all the man pages. To get to the Table of Contents, assuming you're working in GNOME at the moment, follow these steps:

1. Click the Integrated Help System (question mark) button in the GNOME panel, or click the Main Menu button and choose Help System from the System menu.

2. Click Man Pages near the bottom of the window that opens.

The Table of Contents categorizes man pages as User Commands, System Calls, and so forth, as shown in Figure 5.1. At this juncture, you'd probably be the most interested in User Commands, which includes all commands to which users have access, such as ls, cp (copy), and others described in earlier chapters. Also, under Admin Commands you'll find commands that are typically for the superuser only, such as mount and umount. Within each category, commands are listed in the semi-alphabetical order that Linux imposes, where uppercase letters precede lowercase letters. To view the man page for any command, just click the command.

**Note**   If the man pages aren't installed on your hard disk, you can use GnoRPM (see Chapter 13, "Managing Packages with RPM") to install them. Install the files named man-*version* and man-pages-*version* on your Red Hat Linux CD #1.

**Figure 5.1**

The GNOME Help Browser's Table of Contents for man pages.

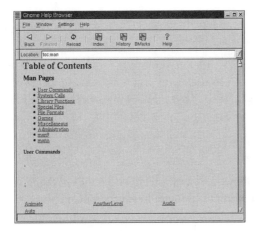

For example, clicking User Commands takes you to that section of the Table of Contents. You'll see lots of commands that you're not familiar with yet, if you're new to Linux. But don't let that intimidate you. All you need right now is to know that the man pages exist and how to get to them. You can find man pages for commands that have already been covered in this book. For example, scrolling all the way down to the commands that start with a lowercase *l* takes you to the section that includes the man page for the ls (list directory contents) command. Clicking ls there displays the man page for ls, as shown in Figure 5.2.

**Figure 5.2**

The man page for the ls command, as viewed through the GNOME Help Browser.

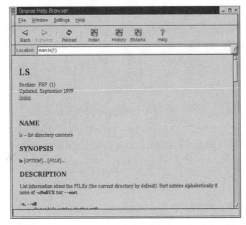

PART

I

CH

5

As you can see in the figure, the man page starts out with the name of the command followed by a brief description. The synopsis shows the general syntax of the command. For ls the synopsis shows the following:

```
ls [OPTION]... [FILE]...
```

The square brackets indicate parts of the command that can be omitted. For example, just entering the command ls by itself is okay because the other parts of the command are optional. If you do use one of the optional components of the command, don't type the square brackets. Those brackets are included in the syntax merely to show that the component is optional—you never actually type the brackets. The ellipses (...) show that multiple components of the type are allowed.

Under DESCRIPTION, you see all the different options that can be used in the [OPTION] part of the command. For example, you can use -a or -all (either one) to show filenames that start with a dot, which are normally hidden. That means you can use either of these commands to view all files, including hidden files:

ls -a

ls -all

Since multiple [OPTION]s are allowed, you can string on a bunch of them. It's not necessary to type all the hyphens though. For example, the following command uses the -a and -s options:

ls -a -s

But this command accomplishes exactly the same thing:

ls -as

Double-hyphenated options should be used independently. For example, the --help option displays help for the ls command. So, to get help with that command, you could enter the command:

ls --help

**Tip**

Many commands support the –help switch, so it never hurts to try it. Simply enter the command you need help with, followed by --help to see if it works. If it doesn't work, no biggie. Just view the man page instead.

The [FILE] option indicates that you can type a filename, or a *regular expression* (such as a filename skeleton that uses * to represent any group of characters) that limits the description of the filenames to view those that follow some pattern or contains certain characters. For example, the following command lists all files that start with the characters *fig*:

ls fig*

If you want to use options and a filename in a command, place the options first, as indicated by the synopsis section of the man page. For example, the following command lists all files, including hidden files, that begin with the letters *.bash* in the current directory:

ls -a .bash*

The [FILE] option can include a path, as well as the ~ shortcut, which always represents your home directory. For instance, this command shows all files that start with *.bash* in the directory named /etc/skel:

ls -a /etc/skel/.bash*

The following command shows all files that start with *.bash* in your home directory. The tilde (~) is always an acceptable abbreviation for "my home directory":

```
ls -a ~/.bash*
```

All these commands work because they follow the syntax that the SYNOPSIS section of the man page requires.

**Tip**

To view the man page for the man command, enter `man man`.

The NAME, SYNOPSIS, and DESCRIPTION sections are pretty standard in man pages. Some man pages will also contain some combination of the sections summarized here:

- **ACCESS CONTROL**: Describes who can use the command, and when.
- **FILES**: Lists files used by, or related to, the command.
- **BUGS**: Lists any known bugs (problems) or deficiencies with the command.
- **AUTHOR**: Name of the person who wrote the man page.
- **SEE ALSO:** Lists related commands and the section of the manual that contains that command.

## XMAN

xman is an alternative to the GNOME Help Browser for getting information from the man pages. You might want to give it a try; some people like it better. Also, xman runs in any of the graphical user interfaces (discussed in Chapter 8, "Configuring the X Window System"), not just GNOME. To open xman from GNOME, click the Main Menu button, choose Run Program, type xman into the Run Program dialog box that appears, and click the Run button. Or open a terminal window, type **xman**, and press Enter. At first, only a tiny window titled *xman* appears containing three buttons:

- **Help:** Shows instructions for using xman.
- **Quit:** Quits xman and closes all open xman windows.
- **Manual Page:** Initially shows the same page as the Help button, but with two active buttons at the top of the window titled Options and Sections.

Clicking the Manual Page button opens a larger window titled Manual Page. Near the upper-left corner of that window are two buttons titled Options and Sections. Clicking either button displays a menu. You can use the Sections button to choose a section of the manual to focus on, such as Section 1, User Commands or Section 8, System Administration Commands.

The Options menu provides some basic options you may want to experiment with. The Show Both Screens option lets you divide the xman window into two panes. The top pane lists commands in the section of the manual that you're currently viewing. The lower pane displays the man page for whatever command you click in the upper pane. You can adjust the relative heights of the panes by dragging the little black square on the separator line up or down. I should point out that the scrollbars in these panes work a little differently than most. They're on the left side of the window rather than the right, which is a little unusual. Also, to scroll up, you right-click anywhere on the scrollbar. To scroll down, you left-click anywhere on the scrollbar. Mid-clicking a point in the scrollbar jumps the gray scrollbar to that section of the bar.

Other than that, things are pretty self-explanatory. For example, if you choose (1) User Commands from the Sections menu, the top pane lists all user commands in that weird uppercase-letters-first alphabetical order. Clicking any command in the top pane shows the man page for that command. For example, in Figure 5.3 I've clicked the ls command, and the lower pane now shows that man page.

**Figure 5.3**

The xman manual browser, with the larger window split to show the Table of Contents in the top pane.

You can also search man pages with xman. Choose Search from the Options menu in the Manual Page window. The tiny Search dialog box shown in Figure 5.4 appears. To search for a specific command, type that command beneath the Type String to Search For prompt, and click the Manual Page button. xman also supports the *apropos* facility of man pages, which allows you to enter any word, then find appropriate commands that relate to that word. For example, you could type copy as the string to search for, and then click the Apropos button to find commands that have the word *copy* in them.

> **Tip**
>
> The word *string* in computer science refers to any string of characters, be it a word like *howdy* or a phrase with multiple words, like *hello there*.

**Figure 5.4**
The Search dialog box for xman lets you search for specific commands or commands that are appropriate to some action you want to perform.

If you do a Manual Page search, rather than an apropos search, for the word *copy*, you'll get nothing because there is no copycommand. The command for copying files is cp.

xman will display a list of commands that have your keyword somewhere in the program's description (see Figure 5.5). You can use the scrollbars to scroll up and down the list. The number next to each command tells you which section of the Table of Contents contains that command. For example, the following line tells you that the cp command can be used to copy files and directories:

```
cp (1)    -copy files and directories
```

The (1) tells you that the command is referenced in section 1. So to find the command, you first need to click the Sections button near the top of the Manual Page window, and choose (1) User Commands. You'll then find cp in the alphabetized list of commands in the upper pane of the xman window.

**Figure 5.5**
Results of doing an apropos search for the word *copy* in xman.

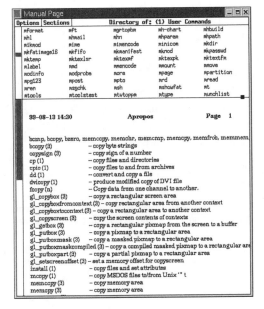

PART

I

CH

5

If your apropos search returns nothing, look to the right of the Sections button for a description of what may have gone wrong. If apropos never seems to find anything, see the sidebar titled "Apropos Never Finds Anything" in this chapter for an easy fix.

## COMMAND PROMPT MAN PAGES

At the command prompt, you can view the man page for any command by entering the following:

```
man command
```

command is the command you want to look up. For example, to get information on the ls command, you'd simply type the following and press Enter:

```
man ls
```

For example, Figure 5.6 shows the results of entering the man ls command in a color terminal window (though, I guess you can't see the colors here.) Under the NAME heading, you see the name of the command and a brief description.

**Figure 5.6**

The man page for the ls command, viewed in a color terminal window.

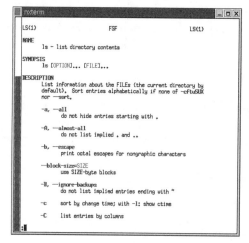

The colon (:) at the bottom of the page is a prompt indicating that more pages follow. You can press Enter to scroll down a line. You can also scroll using the ~UA, ~DA, Page Up, and Page Down keys. When you're ready to leave the man page and return to the command prompt, type the letter q (for quit) at the colon prompt.

---

**Apropos Never Finds Anything**

The apropos feature of the man pages searches a database of commands and keywords. That database isn't installed automatically with Red Hat Linux; instead it is created by a *cron job* (a task scheduled to take place at a certain time) somewhere between 4:00 and 7:00 a.m. If you always shut your computer off at night, the database will never be created. Thus, apropos will never find anything.

Fortunately, it's easy to create that database, although you do need superuser status to create the database. If you're currently logged in as root, just enter the following command at the command prompt:

**/usr/sbin/makewhatis**

If you're not logged in as root, but know the root password, you can enter this command instead:

**su -c /usr/sbin/makewhatis**

The latter command will prompt you for the root password before executing the command.

You may see a Read File error appear on the screen. Ignore that, and wait for the program to finish. You'll know the program is finished when the shell command prompt reappears. Although there's no feedback on the screen, the makewhatis program has created a file named /usr/man/whatis. And it's *that* file that the apropos program needs to do its job.

You can also search for commands that are appropriate to a certain keyword from the command prompt, using either of the following two syntaxes:

```
apropos keyword
man -k keyword
```

keyword is the word that you're looking for. For example, the following command lists commands that contain the word *print*:

```
apropos print
```

The following command does exactly the same thing:

```
man -k print
```

Either way, the results look something like Figure 5.7. Note that the list is formatted exactly like the list that appears when you do an apropos search in xman. The number next to each command tells you which section to look in for the command. However, since using the man command at the command prompt always searches all the man page sections, you really don't need to worry about the section number. For example, banner(6) lets you print a large banner on a printer. To learn more about the banner command, simply enter the following command at the command prompt:

```
man banner
```

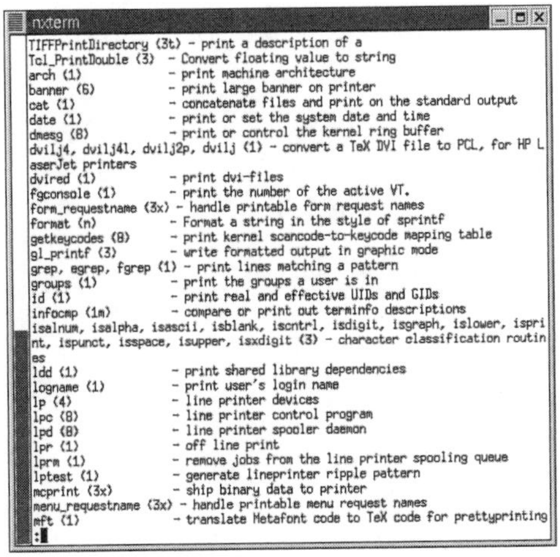

**Figure 5.7**
Results of entering the command
apropos print
in a color terminal window.

PART

I

CH

5

You need not bother with the section number. But, in the unlikely event that your computer takes a long time to locate man pages, you can speed things up by including the section number, preceded by a -S, at the end of the command. Doing so limits the search to that particular section of the manual. For example, the following command searches only section 6 (Games) of the man pages for the command banner:

```
man -S6 banner
```

### whatis SEARCHES

The command prompt also supports a whatis, which simply returns the brief description of the command. The syntax is as follows:

```
whatis command
```

command is the command you're wondering about. For example, entering the following tells you a bit about the su (substitute user) command:

```
whatis su
```

For more information about that command you could, of course, enter **man su**. If whatis always returns "nothing appropriate," you'll need to take a moment to create the whatis database as discussed in the previous sidebar.

## INFO PAGES

Info pages are similar to man pages, but tend be more descriptive and less terse than the man pages. There don't seem to be quite as many info pages as man pages either. But if you're looking for more information on a command, it never hurts to give the info pages a shot. The syntax at any command prompt is as follows:

```
info command
```

command is the command you're interested in learning more about. For example, entering the command

```
info ls
```

displays an info page about the ls command, as shown in Figure 5.8. Within the info page, you can scroll up and down using the ~UA, ~DA, PgUp, and PgDn keys. To quit the info page and return to the command prompt, just type the letter **q**.

**Figure 5.8**
The results of entering the command `info ls` in a color terminal window.

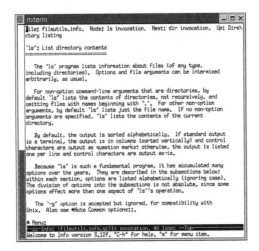

# HOWTOS AND FAQS

HOWTO documents are a great resource for finding our how to accomplish a given task or how to configure and use a specific type of hardware. When you find yourself wondering "How do I do *such-and-such*?," you'd do well to browse through the HOWTO filenames and see if you can find one that might answer your question. The HOWTO documents aren't stored on your hard disk. In the interest of saving space, they're kept on your Red Hat Linux 6.2 CD #1. To get to them, mount that CD and, using the GNOME File Manager, browse to the `/mnt/cdrom/doc/HOWTO` directory. Some HOWTOs are stored in that directory, others are categorized under the `/mini`, `/unmaintained`, and `/unmaintained/mini` directories, as you can see in Figure 5.9.

> **Tip**
>
> If you want to copy the HOWTO pages to your hard disk, use GnoRPM to install the "how-to..." file from the Red Hat Linux CD #1 (see Chapter 13). Once installed, you'll find them in `/usr/doc/HOWTO`.

For your convenience, Table 5.1 lists all the HOWTOs, in alphabetical order, and pinpoints where each is located on the CD.

> **Tip**
>
> Since both Linux and Windows use the ISO 9660 format for CD-ROMs, you can browse the HOWTO and FAQ directories using Windows My Computer or Windows Explorer. To open any text file on the CD, just double-click its icon (or single-click if you're using Web View). Then choose a text editor such as NotePad or Wordpad from the Open With dialog box that Windows presents.

PART

**I**

CH

**5**

**Figure 5.9**
Results of mounting the Red Hat Linux 6.2 CD and browsing to the /mnt/cdrom/doc/HOWTO directory.

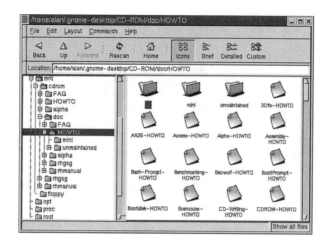

## TABLE 5.1   HOWTOs Located on the Red Hat Linux CD

| Topic | Where Located |
|---|---|
| 3-Button-Mouse | /doc/HOWTO/mini |
| 3Dfx-HOWTO | /doc/HOWTO |
| Access-HOWTO | /doc/HOWTO |
| ADSL | /doc/HOWTO/mini |
| ADSM-Backup | /doc/HOWTO/mini |
| Advocacy | /doc/HOWTO/mini |
| AI-Alife | /doc/HOWTO/mini |
| Alpha-HOWTO | /doc/HOWTO |
| Alsa-sound | /doc/HOWTO/mini |
| Apache+SSL+PHP+fp | /doc/HOWTO/mini |
| Assembly-HOWTO | /doc/HOWTO |
| Automount | /doc/HOWTO/mini |
| AX25-HOWTO | /doc/HOWTO |
| Backup-With-MSDOS | /doc/HOWTO/mini |
| Bash-Prompt-HOWTO | /doc/HOWTO |
| Battery-Powered | /doc/HOWTO/mini |
| Benchmarking-HOWTO | /doc/HOWTO |
| Beowulf-HOWTO | /doc/HOWTO |
| Boca | /doc/HOWTO/mini |
| BogoMips | /doc/HOWTO/mini |
| Bootdisk-HOWTO | /doc/HOWTO |
| BootPrompt-HOWTO | /doc/HOWTO |

**TABLE 5.1    CONTINUED**

| Topic | Where Located |
| --- | --- |
| Bridge | /doc/HOWTO/mini |
| Bridge+Firewall | /doc/HOWTO/mini |
| Busmouse-HOWTO | /doc/HOWTO |
| Bzip2 | /doc/HOWTO/mini |
| Cable-Modem | /doc/HOWTO/mini |
| CDROM-HOWTO | /doc/HOWTO |
| CD-Writing-HOWTO | /doc/HOWTO |
| Chinese-HOWTO | /doc/HOWTO |
| Cipe+Masq | /doc/HOWTO/mini |
| Clock | /doc/HOWTO/mini |
| Coffee | /doc/HOWTO/mini |
| Colour-ls | /doc/HOWTO/mini |
| Comeau-C++ | /doc/HOWTO/unmaintained/ mini |
| Commercial-HOWTO | /doc/HOWTO |
| Config-HOWTO | /doc/HOWTO |
| Consultants-HOWTO | /doc/HOWTO |
| COPYRIGHT | /doc/HOWTO |
| Cyrillic-HOWTO | /doc/HOWTO |
| Cyrus-IMAP | /doc/HOWTO/mini |
| Danish-HOWTO | /doc/HOWTO |
| DHCP | /doc/HOWTO/mini |
| DHCPcd | /doc/HOWTO/mini |
| DHCPcd | /doc/HOWTO/unmaintained/ mini |
| DHCPd | /doc/HOWTO/unmaintained/ mini |
| Diald | /doc/HOWTO/mini |
| Dial-On-Demand | /doc/HOWTO/unmaintained/mini |
| Dip+SLiRP+CSLIP | /doc/HOWTO/unmaintained/mini |
| Diskless | /doc/HOWTO/mini |
| Distribution-HOWTO | /doc/HOWTO |
| DNS-HOWTO | /doc/HOWTO |
| DOSEMU-HOWTO | /doc/HOWTO |
| DOS-to-Linux-HOWTO | /doc/HOWTO |
| DOS-Win-to-Linux-HOWTO | /doc/HOWTO |
| DPT-Hardware-RAID | /doc/HOWTO/mini |

PART

I

CH

5

**TABLE 5.1 CONTINUED**

| Topic | Where Located |
| --- | --- |
| Dynamic-IP-Hacks | /doc/HOWTO/unmaintained/mini |
| ELF-HOWTO | /doc/HOWTO |
| Emacspeak-HOWTO | /doc/HOWTO |
| Esperanto-HOWTO | /doc/HOWTO |
| Ethernet-HOWTO | /doc/HOWTO |
| Ext2fs-Undeletion | /doc/HOWTO/mini |
| Fax-Server | /doc/HOWTO/mini |
| Finnish-HOWTO | /doc/HOWTO |
| Firewall-HOWTO | /doc/HOWTO |
| Firewall-Piercing | /doc/HOWTO/mini |
| French-HOWTO | /doc/HOWTO |
| Ftape-HOWTO | /doc/HOWTO |
| GCC-HOWTO | /doc/HOWTO |
| German-HOWTO | /doc/HOWTO |
| GIS-GRASS | /doc/HOWTO/mini |
| Glibc2-HOWTO | /doc/HOWTO |
| Gravis-Ultra-Sound | /doc/HOWTO/unmaintained/mini |
| GTEK-BBS-550 | /doc/HOWTO/mini |
| GUI-Development | /doc/HOWTO/unmaintained/mini |
| HAM-HOWTO | /doc/HOWTO |
| Hard-Disk-Upgrade | /doc/HOWTO/mini |
| Hardware-HOWTO | /doc/HOWTO |
| Hebrew-HOWTO | /doc/HOWTO |
| HTML-Validation | /doc/HOWTO/unmaintained/mini |
| INDEX | /doc/HOWTO/mini |
| INDEX.html | /doc/HOWTO |
| INDEX.html | /doc/HOWTO/mini |
| INFO-SHEET | /doc/HOWTO |
| Installation-HOWTO | /doc/HOWTO |
| Install-From-ZIP | /doc/HOWTO/mini |
| Intranet-Server-HOWTO | /doc/HOWTO |
| IO-Port-Programming | /doc/HOWTO/mini |
| IP-Alias | /doc/HOWTO/mini |
| IPCHAINS-HOWTO | /doc/HOWTO |

**TABLE 5.1   CONTINUED**

| Topic | Where Located |
|---|---|
| IP-Masquerade | /doc/HOWTO/mini |
| IP-Subnetworking | /doc/HOWTO/mini |
| IPX-HOWTO | /doc/HOWTO |
| IR-HOWTO | /doc/HOWTO |
| ISP-Connectivity | /doc/HOWTO/mini |
| ISP-Hookup-HOWTO | /doc/HOWTO |
| Italian-HOWTO | /doc/HOWTO |
| Java-CGI-HOWTO | /doc/HOWTO |
| JAZ-Drive | /doc/HOWTO/unmaintained/mini |
| JE | /doc/HOWTO/unmaintained/mini |
| Kerneld | /doc/HOWTO/mini |
| Kernel-HOWTO | /doc/HOWTO |
| Keyboard-and-Console-HOWTO | /doc/HOWTO |
| KickStart-HOWTO | /doc/HOWTO |
| Large-Disk | /doc/HOWTO/mini |
| LBX | /doc/HOWTO/mini |
| Leased-Line | /doc/HOWTO/mini |
| LILO | /doc/HOWTO/mini |
| Linux+DOS+Win95 | /doc/HOWTO/unmaintained/mini |
| Linux+DOS+Win95+OS2 | /doc/HOWTO/mini |
| Linux+FreeBSD | /doc/HOWTO/mini |
| Linux+FreeBSD-mini-HOWTO | /doc/HOWTO/mini |
| Linux+NT-Loader | /doc/HOWTO/mini |
| Linux+OS2+DOS | /doc/HOWTO/unmaintained/mini |
| Linux+Win95 | /doc/HOWTO/mini |
| Linux+WinNT | /doc/HOWTO/unmaintained/mini |
| LinuxDoc+Emacs+Ispell-HOWTO | /doc/HOWTO |
| Loadlin+Win95 | /doc/HOWTO/mini |
| Loopback-Root-FS | /doc/HOWTO/mini |
| Mac-Terminal | /doc/HOWTO/mini |
| Mail2News | /doc/HOWTO/mini |
| Mail-HOWTO | /doc/HOWTO |
| Mail-Queue | /doc/HOWTO/mini |
| Man-Page | /doc/HOWTO/mini |

PART

I

CH

5

**TABLE 5.1 CONTINUED**

| Topic | Where Located |
| --- | --- |
| META-FAQ | /doc/HOWTO |
| MGR-HOWTO | /doc/HOWTO |
| MIDI+SB | /doc/HOWTO/unmaintained/mini |
| MILO-HOWTO | /doc/HOWTO |
| MIPS-HOWTO | /doc/HOWTO |
| Modem-HOWTO | /doc/HOWTO |
| Module-HOWTO | /doc/HOWTO/unmaintained |
| Modules | /doc/HOWTO/mini |
| Multiboot-with-LILO | /doc/HOWTO/mini |
| Multicast-HOWTO | /doc/HOWTO |
| Multi-Disk-HOWTO | /doc/HOWTO |
| NCD-X-Terminal | /doc/HOWTO/mini |
| NET-3-HOWTO | /doc/HOWTO |
| Netrom-Node | /doc/HOWTO/mini |
| Netscape+Proxy | /doc/HOWTO/mini |
| Netstation | /doc/HOWTO/mini |
| Networking-Overview-HOWTO | /doc/HOWTO |
| News-HOWTO | /doc/HOWTO/unmaintained |
| News-Leafsite | /doc/HOWTO/mini |
| NFS-HOWTO | /doc/HOWTO |
| NFS-Root | /doc/HOWTO/mini |
| NFS-Root-Client | /doc/HOWTO/mini |
| NIS-HOWTO | /doc/HOWTO |
| Offline-Mailing | /doc/HOWTO/mini |
| Online-Support | /doc/HOWTO/unmaintained/mini |
| Optical-Disk-HOWTO | /doc/HOWTO |
| Oracle-HOWTO | /doc/HOWTO |
| Pager | /doc/HOWTO/unmaintained/mini |
| PalmOS-HOWTO | /doc/HOWTO |
| Parallel-Processing-HOWTO | /doc/HOWTO |
| Partition | /doc/HOWTO/mini |
| Partition-Rescue | /doc/HOWTO/mini |
| Path | /doc/HOWTO/mini |
| PCI-HOWTO | /doc/HOWTO |

**TABLE 5.1   CONTINUED**

| Topic | Where Located |
| --- | --- |
| PCMCIA-HOWTO | /doc/HOWTO |
| Pilot-HOWTO | /doc/HOWTO |
| PLIP | /doc/HOWTO/mini |
| Plug-and-Play-HOWTO | /doc/HOWTO |
| Polish-HOWTO | /doc/HOWTO |
| Portuguese-HOWTO | /doc/HOWTO |
| PostgreSQL-HOWTO | /doc/HOWTO |
| PPP-HOWTO | /doc/HOWTO |
| PPP-over-ISDN | /doc/HOWTO/unmaintained/mini |
| PPP-over-minicom | /doc/HOWTO/unmaintained/mini |
| Pre-Installation-Checklist | /doc/HOWTO/mini |
| Print2Win | /doc/HOWTO/unmaintained/mini |
| Printing-HOWTO | /doc/HOWTO |
| Printing-Usage-HOWTO | /doc/HOWTO |
| Process-Accounting | /doc/HOWTO/mini |
| Proxy-ARP | /doc/HOWTO/unmaintained/mini |
| Proxy-ARP-Subnet | /doc/HOWTO/mini |
| Public-Web-Browser | /doc/HOWTO/mini |
| Qmail+MH | /doc/HOWTO/mini |
| Quake-HOWTO | /doc/HOWTO |
| Quota | /doc/HOWTO/mini |
| RCS | /doc/HOWTO/mini |
| Reading-List-HOWTO | /doc/HOWTO |
| README | /doc/HOWTO |
| README | /doc/HOWTO/mini |
| README | /doc/HOWTO/unmaintained |
| RedHat-CD | /doc/HOWTO/mini |
| Remote-Boot | /doc/HOWTO/mini |
| Remote-X-Apps | /doc/HOWTO/mini |
| Root-RAID-HOWTO | /doc/HOWTO |
| RPM+Slackware | /doc/HOWTO/mini |
| RPM-HOWTO | /doc/HOWTO |
| SCSI-HOWTO | /doc/HOWTO/unmaintained |
| SCSI-Programming-HOWTO | /doc/HOWTO |

PART

I

CH

5

**TABLE 5.1 CONTINUED**

| Topic | Where Located |
|---|---|
| Secure-POP+SSH | /doc/HOWTO/mini |
| Security-HOWTO | /doc/HOWTO |
| Sendmail+UUCP | /doc/HOWTO/mini |
| Sendmail-Address-Rewrite | /doc/HOWTO/mini |
| Serial-HOWTO | /doc/HOWTO |
| Serial-Programming-HOWTO | /doc/HOWTO |
| Shadow-Password-HOWTO | /doc/HOWTO |
| SLIP+proxyARP | /doc/HOWTO/unmaintained/mini |
| SLIP-PPP-Emulator | /doc/HOWTO/mini |
| Slovenian-HOWTO | /doc/HOWTO |
| Small-Memory | /doc/HOWTO/mini |
| SMB-HOWTO | /doc/HOWTO |
| Software-Building | /doc/HOWTO/mini |
| Software-RAID | /doc/HOWTO/mini |
| Software-Release-Practice-HOWTO | /doc/HOWTO |
| Soundblaster-16 | /doc/HOWTO/unmaintained/mini |
| Soundblaster-AWE | /doc/HOWTO/mini |
| Sound-HOWTO | /doc/HOWTO |
| Sound-Playing-HOWTO | /doc/HOWTO |
| Spanish-HOWTO | /doc/HOWTO |
| SRM-HOWTO | /doc/HOWTO |
| StarOffice | /doc/HOWTO/mini |
| Swap-Space | /doc/HOWTO/unmaintained/mini |
| Term-Firewall | /doc/HOWTO/mini |
| Term-HOWTO | /doc/HOWTO/unmaintained |
| TeTeX-HOWTO | /doc/HOWTO |
| Text-Terminal-HOWTO | /doc/HOWTO |
| Thai-HOWTO | /doc/HOWTO |
| Tiny-News | /doc/HOWTO/unmaintained/mini |
| Tips-HOWTO | /doc/HOWTO |
| TkRat | /doc/HOWTO/mini |
| Token-Ring | /doc/HOWTO/mini |
| Ultra-DMA | /doc/HOWTO/mini |
| UMSDOS-HOWTO | /doc/HOWTO |

**TABLE 5.1    CONTINUED**

| Topic | Where Located |
|-------|---------------|
| UNIX-Internet-Fundamentals-HOWTO | /doc/HOWTO |
| Update | /doc/HOWTO/mini |
| Upgrade | /doc/HOWTO/mini |
| UPS-HOWTO | /doc/HOWTO |
| User-Group-HOWTO | /doc/HOWTO |
| UUCP-HOWTO | /doc/HOWTO |
| VAIO+Linux | /doc/HOWTO/mini |
| VAR-HOWTO | /doc/HOWTO |
| Vesafb | /doc/HOWTO/mini |
| Virtual-Services-HOWTO | /doc/HOWTO |
| Virtual-Web | /doc/HOWTO/unmaintained/mini |
| Visual-Bell | /doc/HOWTO/mini |
| VME-HOWTO | /doc/HOWTO |
| VMS-to-Linux-HOWTO | /doc/HOWTO |
| VPN | /doc/HOWTO/mini |
| Win95+Win+Linux | /doc/HOWTO/unmaintained/mini |
| Windows-Modem-Sharing | /doc/HOWTO/mini |
| WordPerfect | /doc/HOWTO/mini |
| WWW-HOWTO | /doc/HOWTO |
| WWW-mSQL-HOWTO | /doc/HOWTO |
| X-Big-Cursor | /doc/HOWTO/mini |
| Xfree86-HOWTO | /doc/HOWTO |
| Xfree86-Video-Timings-HOWTO | /doc/HOWTO |
| Xfree86-Xinside | /doc/HOWTO/mini |
| X-Notebook | /doc/HOWTO/unmaintained/mini |
| Xterminal | /doc/HOWTO/unmaintained/mini |
| Xterm-Title | /doc/HOWTO/mini |
| Xwindow-User-HOWTO | /doc/HOWTO |
| ZIP-Drive | /doc/HOWTO/mini |
| ZIP-Install | /doc/HOWTO/mini |

PART

**I**

CH

**5**

When you double-click a HOWTO file's icon, you'll get the usual gmc dialog box listing programs that you can use to open the file. Or, you can right-click the page's icon and choose View.

Tip

You can also find HOWTOs on the Internet at `http://metalab.unc.edu/LDP/HOWTO` and at `www.redhat.com/mirrors/LDP/HOWTO/HOWTO-INDEX-3.html#ss3.1`.

The Red Hat Linux CD-ROM also contains lists of FAQs (Frequently Asked Questions). To get to those files, mount the CD and browse to the directory `/doc/FAQ`. The FAQs are available in three different formats, as indicated by the subdirectories that appear within that directory: HTML (can be viewed with any Web browser), ps (PostScript for printing on PostScript printers), and txt (text files you can view with any text editor or the Text File Viewer). You may find it easiest to use the HTML directory since your Linux installation probably already installed Netscape's Web browser. Just double-clicking any filename with the `.html` extension should open that file in Netscape's browser without your having to go through the middle step of choosing a program.

The files titled `Linux-FAQ-1.html` through `Linux-FAQ-13.html` contain the most general FAQs about using Linux. The PPP FAQs all have to do with access the Internet via a modem and PPP (Point-to-Point Protocol). You can also find a list of current Linux FAQs on the Internet at `http://metalab.unc.edu/LDP/FAQ`.

Tip

You can find a whole lot of documentation on many topics by browsing around the `/usr/doc` (that is, user documentation) directory with GNOME's File Manager.

# THE locate COMMAND

Although the `locate` command doesn't display any documentation, per se, it is an easy tool for finding out if a particular file is installed on your computer, and where the file is installed. For example, suppose you come across a piece of documentation that tells you that you need to have a program named `slang` on your computer in order to compile some other program. A quick way to find out if there's anything named *slang* installed on your hard disk is to enter the `locate` command followed by a blank space and the name you're looking for. So, to see if there is anything named *slang*, simply enter the following command at the Linux command prompt:

```
locate slang
```

Filenames and directory names that contain that word will be listed on the screen. If the list is lengthy and whizzes by too quickly on the screen, pipe the output into the `less` program, as in the following example:

```
locate slang ¦ less
```

The `locate` command searches a database for its information. Normally that database is created by a cron job (scheduled job) that runs in the early morning hours. If you don't leave the computer running 24 hours a day, seven days a week, the database might not yet exist on your computer. If that's the case, any attempt to use the locate command will likely return an error message that looks something like this:

```
locate:decode_db():open:(2) No such file or directory
```

Fortunately, this problem is easily solved. Simply log in as root and enter the following command at the Linux command prompt:

```
/usr/bin/updatedb
```

Or, if you're not logged in as root but know the root password, you can enter this command instead:

```
su -c /usr/bin/updatedb
```

## PACKAGE DOCUMENTATION

Red Hat Linux comes with many *packages*, which are programs that you can use with Linux. The documentation for most packages is available in the User Documentation directory, /usr/doc, on your hard disk. If you simply browse to the folder in the GNOME File Manager, you'll see that the right pane contains a bunch of subdirectories (see Figure 5.10). Each of those icons actually leads to a subdirectory of documentation for the package. The name of the package and its version number make up the name of the directory. For example, the Xconfigurator-4.2.3 directory contains information on the Xconfigurator program version 4.2.3. (You'll learn what Xconfigurator is about in Chapter 8.)

**Figure 5.10**
The /usr/doc directory contains subdirectories of information on a variety of Red Hat Packages.

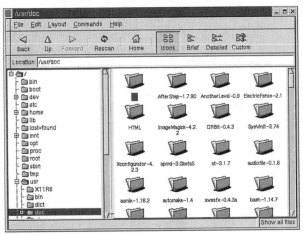

PART

I

CH

5

The package documentation can be very technical. You probably don't want to just browse around and read these at random. Rather, when you're interested in installing or using a specific package or program, you'd look to the /usr/doc directory for any information about that particular program or package. You'll learn about installing and using packages in Chapter 13.

# SUPPORT ON THE WEB

As one might expect, the World Wide Web is a great resource of Linux knowledge. You can, of course, use any computer and any Web browser to access those resources. The general search engines such as www.altavista.com, www.aol.com/netfind, www.excite.com, www.goto.com, www.hotbot.com, www.infoseek.com, www.looksmart.com, www.lycos.com, www.snap.com, www.webcrawler.com, and www.yahoo.com are all good resources. But for Linux-specific information, you'll want to take a look at the Web sites listed in the sections that follow.

> **Tip**
>
> Tip: At my own Web site at http://www.coolnerds.com, you'll find a Search box that lets you type a search word or phrase once, then search any of the engines just mentioned using a simple drop-down list.

## RED HAT

Red Hat maintains its own Web site, which is, of course, an ideal resource for Red Hat Linux. Red Hat's home page is http://www.redhat.com. There you'll find news, links to user groups, a Knowledge Base, Red Hat White Papers, and more. Red Hat's support site at http://www.redhat.com/support provides installation support, hardware compatibility lists, product updates, fixes, errata, downloads, tips and tricks, HOWTOs, and online versions of the printed documentation that comes with the Red Hat Linux boxed set. If you bought the Red Hat Linux boxed set, you're entitled to 30 days of free installation support via telephone, 90 days via the Web, if you register your product. You can find links for registering on that support page. For a list of Frequently Asked Questions at Linux Support, see http://www.redhat.com/cgi-bin/support?faq.

> **Tip**
>
> If you're thinking about installing Linux on a portable computer, you'll be interested in their laptop page at http://www.redhat.com/mirrors/laptop/welcome.html.

## LINUXCARE

At about the same time I started writing this book, linuxcare.com began a project to beef up their documentation for Linux newbies. By the time this book gets into your hands, they may actually be posting those pages. Linuxcare.com also offers training, support, and newsgroup-style question and answer forums. You can find Linuxcare at http://www.linuxcare.com.

### THE LINUX DOCUMENTATION PROJECT

Probably the best resource for discovering all the sources of information available to you online would be the Linux Documentation Project Web site at http://metalab.unc.edu. Red Hat maintains a *mirror* (exact duplicate) of that site at http://www.redhat/com/mirrors/ LDP. Going to either site will take you to a list of still more mirrors. You may want to find the site nearest you, and add it to your list of bookmarks or favorites. The site also has an LDP Search page where you can hunt for any word or phrase within all the LDP Web pages. This is a great place to get started in expanding your informational horizons.

The Excite Search engine, which is accessible from the Linux Documentation Project Search page, is a great place to look for project guides and HOWTOs dealing with any subject. You can jump straight to that page via the URL http://amelia.db.erau.edu/Excite/AT-LDPquery.html.

### GNOME DOCUMENTATION

Documentation on the GNOME desktop environment is available at http://www.gnome.org. The site includes a User's Guide, a collection of GNOME-related mailing lists, and a GNOME FAQ. Some information on specific GNOME applications, such as Gnumeric, is available from the GNOME Office Suite link on that first page (or just browse straight to http://www.gnome.org/gw.html). The Hosted Web Sites page at http://www.gnome.org/ hostedsites.shtml also provides links to pages dealing with GNOME applications, including GMC (GNOME Midnight Command), also known as the GNOME File Manager.

> **Tip**
>
> The GNOME Help browser that's on your Linux computer is also a good resource for GNOME. Just click the Integrated Help (question mark) button on the Linux panel to open the help browser.

PART

**I**

CH

**5**

### THE GNU PROJECT

The GNU project home page is a great resource for learning not just about Linux, but the entire GNU project from which Linux was formed. The home page for the GNU project is http://www.gnu.org. The Manuals Online page there (http://www.gnu.org/manual/ manual.html) provides manuals for specific GNU project programs, such as the bash shell, bc, Emacs (a text editor), and more.

## NEWSGROUPS AND MAILING LISTS

Newsgroups are always a great resource for information. I've posted my share of questions to newsgroups, and have *always* gotten an answer! While visiting a newsgroup, I also try to answer whatever questions I can—to give back to the community, so to speak. Many other newsgroup users do the same. So it seems that no matter what question you pose, you'll find someone who knows the answer at a newsgroup.

Before you post a question to a newsgroup, you might want to check to see if it's already been answered. Deja News on the Web provides a great service that will scan multiple newsgroups for any word or phrase you give it. You can access Deja News through any Web browser at the URL http://www.deja.com. The following is a list of Linux-related newsgroups that you can access individually using any Internet newsreader:

- alt.fido.linux
- alt.hacking
- alt.linux
- alt.os.linux
- alt.os.linux.caldera
- alt.os.linux.mandrake
- alt.os.linux.slackware
- alt.uu.comp.os.linux.questions
- at.linux
- aus.computers.linux
- comp.os.linux.advocacy
- comp.os.linux.answers
- comp.os.linux.development.apps
- comp.os.linux.development.system
- comp.os.linux.hardware
- comp.os.linux.m68k
- comp.os.linux.misc
- comp.os.linux.networking
- comp.os.linux.setup
- comp.sys.amiga.misc
- de.comp.os.unix.linux.misc
- de.comp.os.unix.linux.newusers
- deja.public.review.test
- es.comp.os.linux
- fa.linux.kernel
- fido7.linux
- fido7.ru.linux
- hun.lists.mlf.linux
- hun.lists.mlf.linux-kezdo
- it.comp.linux
- it.comp.linux.setup

- linux.act.admin
- linux.act.apps
- linux.act.bbsdev
- linux.act.chaos_digest
- linux.act.configs'linux.act.compression
- linux.act.c-programming
- linux.act.debian
- linux.act.dec_alpha
- linux.act.doc
- linux.act.ftp
- linux.act.hams
- linux.act.kernel
- linux.act.linuxnews
- linux.act.lugnuts
- linux.act.msdos
- linux.act.newbie
- linux.act.normal
- linux.redhat
- linux.redhat.announce
- linux.redhat.applixware
- linux.redhat.axp
- linux.redhat.devel
- linux.redhat/development
- linux.redhat.digest
- linux.redhat.install
- linux.redhat.list
- linux.redhat.misc
- linux.redhat.pam
- linux.redhat.ppp
- linux.redhat.rpm
- linux.redhat.sparc
- nl.comp.os.linux
- nl.comp.os.linux.discussie
- nl.comp.os.linux.installatie
- pl.comp.os.linux

- `redhat.config`
- `redhat.general`
- `tw.bbs.comp.linux`
- `uk.comp.os.linux`

Mailing lists are similar to newsgroups, but require only basic email services. For a current list of Red Hat Mailing Lists, visit their page at `http://www.redhat.com/community/list_subscribe.html`.

# PROJECT PAGE

1. In several places this chapter briefly mentions the `su` command, which allows you to run a privileged command without actually being logged in as the superuser. See if you can locate the man page for the `su` command and determine what the `-c` switch does.

2. On your Red Hat Linux CD-ROM, locate and browse through the FAQ titled `Linux-FAQ-1.html`.

3. Suppose you have a SoundBlaster AWE 32 sound card, and need some help in getting it to work in Linux. Using Table 5.1 in this chapter and your Red Hat Linux CD-ROM, see if you can locate and open the appropriate HOWTO page for using that card in Linux.

# PART II

# SYSTEM ADMINISTRATION

# CHAPTER 6

# SYSTEM ADMINISTRATION BASICS

In this chapter

# WHAT IS SYSTEM ADMINISTRATION?

System administration is all about having complete control over Linux and the computer. In large corporate environments where everyone has a specific job title, computer *users* are assumed to have just enough knowledge to run whatever programs their jobs require, manage files, and perhaps tailor their own desktops. Users should also have some ability to find information from time to time, so they're not entirely dependent on the system administrators. In short, a user would be able to do most or all the things discussed in Chapters 1-5 of this book.

The system administrator (a.k.a. *sysadmin*) has a lot more responsibility and is assumed to be something of the company or department computer guru. The responsibilities of the system administrator include the following:

- Create and manage user accounts
- Install and configure hardware and software
- Make and maintain backups
- Mount devices
- Shut down the system (if those privileges have not been granted to other users)
- Log and keep track of system changes
- Make sure the system is secure
- Train and advise users

---

**Need to Get Online?**

If you're anxious to get access to the Internet from your Linux computer, and you're planning to connect through a modem, you can skip ahead to Part III (Chapter 18, "Connecting to the Internet") to get connected now. It's not necessary to know everything here in Part II to connect your computer to the Internet. However, after you get through Part III and all connected to the Internet, you'll want to come back here before moving on to Part IV.

---

Smaller businesses usually don't have an "official" system administrator. They just tend to wing it with their computers and get by the best they can. When things get too out of control, they may call in a consultant. That consultant will—hopefully—have about the same level of knowledge as a system administrator in a large corporation. So whether your goal is to get a full-time job as a system administrator or act as a freelance Linux consultant, you'll need to be able to perform system administrator duties.

If your goal is to set up a Web server, conduct e-commerce using a Linux computer, or create an ISP (Internet Service Provider) business, you'll need to know a lot of system administration. On top of that, you'll need to learn the job of network administrator as well. But to make it as a network administrator, you'll need to understand system administration first. The goal of this chapter is to teach you the basic skills that you need to get started in making the transition from casual user to system administration.

# LINUX CONFIGURATION BASICS

The first step to learning system administration is to understand that Linux is a *very* configurable operating system. Just about every feature of Linux can be changed and configured to better suit any given situation. The configuration information that Linux uses to make decisions is stored in a variety of *configuration files* through the filesystem. The system administrator needs to learn where all these configuration files are stored and how to change them when needed. All configuration files are plain text files that can be edited using any simple text editor. So part of the job is to learn to use at least one text editor. Red Hat Linux also comes with a program named *linuxconf* (for Linux Configuration), which provides a fairly easy-to-use point-and-click interface for changing many configuration options.

> **Tip**
>
> The letters *conf* in a program or filename imply that the program is used to configure Linux or the file stores configuration information. However, not all configuration programs and files have the letters *conf* in their filenames.

> **Caution**
>
> Never change the contents of a conf file just to "see what happens." Doing so can make a real mess of things. If you open or edit a conf file by accident, try closing it without saving it.

For future reference, keep in mind that Linux configuration is usually a privileged activity. You must be logged in as root to do anything other than some basic desktop customization. Also, many configuration files and directories that contain configuration files have names that begin with a dot (.), so they're hidden from view. If you can't find a configuration file, but know you're looking in the correct directory, chances are the file is just hidden. To bring those files out of hiding in the GNOME File Manager, you need to choose Edit, Preferences from the File Manager menu bar. Then select the Show Hidden Files option on the File Display tab. If you're working from a command prompt, remember that you have to include the -a switch in the ls command to show all files, including hidden files.

## USING LINUXCONF

LinuxConf offersthe easiest and safest way to configure Linux. As with any graphical program, you simply make your selections from the controls presented. Or in some cases, you might type small chunks of text into textboxes. The likelihood of making errors, using this approach, is less than the likelihood of making errors when opening and editing configuration files manually. The configuration options that Linuxconf presents are presented in a cascading menu, like the left pane of File Manager, which makes it easy to find the options you want to configure. There are three ways to start LinuxConf, and you can use whichever is most convenient at the moment:

- From GNOME, click the Main Menu button and choose System, LinuxConf.

- Click the GNOME Main Menu button, choose Run Program, type `linuxconf`, and then click the Run button.

- At any command prompt, type `linuxconf` and press Enter.

LinuxConf will open on your screen. Down the left pane you see categories that can be expanded and collapsed by clicking the + and - symbols to the left of any category, just like in the GNOME File Manager. When you click on an option within a category, the dialog box options for that category appear in the right pane. For example, Figure 6.1 shows LinuxConf after clicking on the User Accounts category under Config, User Accounts, Normal.

**Figure 6.1**
LinuxConf open on the desktop, showing user accounts.

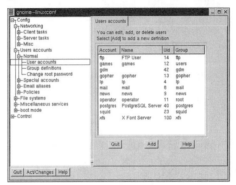

As would be expected, you can scroll through options in the left pane using the scrollbars. You can also widen or narrow the left column by dragging, to the left or right, the tiny raised square near the bottom of the vertical scrollbar. Each time you select an option from the left pane, its dialog box is added to the right pane. If you have more than one dialog box open at any time, you can switch between them by clicking the tabs near the top of the right pane.

---

### Character Cell and Web-based LinuxConf

LinuxConf is one of the few graphical programs that has a non-graphical counterpart. If you enter the `linuxconf` command at a command prompt outside the GUI, such as in a virtual console or on a computer that doesn't have the X Window program installed, a character cell, or "text-mode" version of Linuxconf will open. Initially, it looks like the left pane of the graphical LinuxConf, but you can't use your mouse in the text-mode version. You need to move around from item to item using the arrow keys. To expand or contract a category, move the highlighter to a + or - sign and press Enter. To select an option inside a category, highlight it and press Enter.

After you've selected an option, the dialog box for that option appears on the screen. Once again, you use the arrow keys to move from option to option, press Enter to select the Currently Highlighted option. To select a button at the bottom of a dialog box, press Tab or Shift+Tab until the button you want is highlighted, then press Enter.

If you're out on the road and need to perform some administrative tasks on your Linux computer, you can also access LinuxConf from any Web browser-equipped computer. Just make sure that "linuxconf" is enabled in your /etc/inetd.conf file and then connect to port 98 of your computer using a browser:
`http://yourlinuxmachine.com:98/`.

---

Buttons at the bottom of the dialog box in the right pane pertain to the current dialog box only. To close a dialog box, click its Quit or Accept button. Many dialog boxes will include a Cancel button, which allows you to close the dialog box without saving any changes. To ensure that any changes you make to settings while in LinuxConf are activated, click the Quior Act/Changes at the bottom of the left pane. If you've indeed made any changes that haven't been activated yet, a dialog box titled Status of the System appears in the right pane (see Figure 6.2).

**Figure 6.2**
The Status of the System dialog box in LinuxConf appears whenever you try to exit without activating your changes.

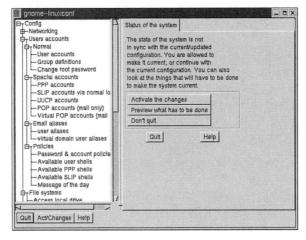

Your options there are as follows:

- **Activate the Changes:** Clicking this button activates all settings made while in LinuxConf, and then closes LinuxConf.

- **Preview What Has to Be Done:** Displays a list of tasks that need to be performed to activate your changes. If you still want to activate your changes after viewing the list, click the Activate the Changes button. Otherwise, just click the Quit button to close without saving your changes.

- **Don't Quit:** Lets you stay in the LinuxConf program.

If you simply want to leave LinuxConf without saving any of your recent changes, click on the Quit button at the bottom of the Status of the System dialog box without first clicking the Activate the Changes button.

LinuxConf is distributed under the GNU General Public License, and has its own Web site and mailing lists. To visit the Web site and learn more about the mailing lists, point your Web browser to http://www.solucorp.qc.ca/linuxconf. The page provides links to easy forms for subscribing to the LinuxConf mailing list.

While LinuxConf provides easy access to many of Linux's configurable options, it can't cover them all. Linux is just too configurable for a single program to cover all the bases. So there may be times when you need to edit a configuration file directly. The remainder of this section discusses the many different ways that you can manually edit configuration files.

PART

**II**

CH

**6**

## EDITING CONFIGURATION FILES MANUALLY

Editing configuration files isn't terribly difficult. However, you must keep in mind two rules: First, there's no real margin for error. Like the commands you enter at the command promptthe lines you add to a configuration file must follow exact rules of syntax. Assume that everything is case-sensitive, and that blank spaces are important. Typing a line that's "sort of" correct just won't cut it. You need to be a perfectionist.

Secondly, configuration files must be saved as plain ASCII text. Never use a word processing program—or any other program that allows advanced formatting—to change a configuration file. Doing so could add hidden formatting characters to the file, which will cause problems later when Linux tries to interpret the file. You can use any of the text editors discussed in the sections that follow to edit configuration files—there's no "right" or "wrong" editor. Choosing one editor over the other is simply a matter of personal taste, perhaps tempered by what's available on the machine you're configuring at the moment.

## CONFIGURATION FILE COMMENTS

When you open a configuration file, you may see one or more lines that start with a pound symbol (#), as in the example shown in Figure 6.3. Any line that begins with that # sign is a *comment*, which means "For human consumption only." Linux ignores those lines altogether, so changing a comment line will have no effect on the behavior of your system. You can add your own comments, if you like, by typing them with the # symbol as the first character in the line. For example, when you change a configuration file, you might want to put in some comments summarizing the date, time, and purpose of your change. That way, you can keep a record of changes you've made to the configuration files as you go along.

**Figure 6.3**
Any line that starts with a # character is a comment that's ignored by Linux. You can use comments to write notes to yourself or other system administrators.

## BACKING UP CONFIGURATION FILES

When you're working with configuration files, it's always a good idea to make a backup of the file you're about to edit. That way, if you somehow make a mess of things, you can replace the messed-up copy with the original copy. In the GNOME File Manager, you can easily make a quick backup by following these simple steps:

1. Right-click the configuration file you're about to edit.

2. Choose Copy from the menu that pops up.

3. Click anywhere within the existing path to get the cursor in there, then press the End key to move to the end of the path.

4. Type some word that will make it easy to see the file later. For example, I often add *Orig* or *Original* to the end of the existing filename to make it easy to spot the original.

5. Click the OK button.

If you're working at the command prompt rather than in the File Manager, you'll need to enter a `cp` command to make the copy. For example, suppose you want to make a backup of the `/etc/fstab` file before editing it. Entering this command gets you to the correct directory:

```
cd /etc
```

Then enter this command to create a duplicate of the fstab file, named fstabOrig:

```
cp fstab fstabOrig
```

## EDITING WITH GNOME GEDIT

The GNOME gEdit text editor is a small, lightweight text editor that's ideal for editing configuration files and other small ASCII text files. To start gEdit from within GNOME, do one of the following:

- Click the GNOME Main Menu button and choose Applications, gEdit.

- To open a file for editing from within the File Manager, right-click the file you want to edit, choose Open With, and then select Applications, gEdit from the menu that appears.

- If you make gEdit your default GNOME menu, you can right-click any file's icon and choose Edit to edit the file with gEdit.

PART
**II**

CH
**6**

**Tip**

To make gEdit your default GNOME editor, click the GNOME Main Menu button and choose Settings, Default Editor. Choose gEdit from the drop-down list. Make sure the Run In Terminal button is *not* selected (pushed in). Then click the OK button and close the Control Center window.

- Click the GNOME Main Menu button, choose Run Program, type gedit, and then click the Run button.

- In any terminal window, enter the command gedit &.

When you're using either of the last two methods, you can follow the gedit command with a space and the path to the file you want to edit. For example, entering the following command

```
gedit /etc/fstab &
```

opens gEdit and the fstab configuration file in the /etc directory, ready for editing.

> **Tip**
>
> The & at the end of the sample commands makes gEdit run as a separate process, rather than as a child process to the terminal window. Thus, you can close the terminal window without having gEdit shut down with it.

If you don't open a file to edit while starting gEdit, you can always open the file right from the gEdit menu bar or toolbar. Choose File, Open from the gEdit menu bar or click the Open button in the toolbar. The standard Open File dialog box appears. You can use the button at the top of the dialog box and the list of directory names at the left side of the dialog box to work your way to a specific directory. Then, click on the name of any file in the right column and click the OK button to open that file.

You can open and edit multiple files in a single gEdit session. Each open document's filename will appear as a tab, usually in the left column. To switch from one document to another, just click its filename tab:

### gEdit Preferences

When editing configuration files—where line breaks are important—you might want to turn off the Autoindent, Wordwrap, and Linewrap Settings in gEdit. Also, make sure the Readonly setting is turned off. To do so, click on Settings in the menu bar and make your choices from the menu that appears. To make your new settings the default for future sessions, choose Settings, Save Settings from the gEdit menu bar (see Figure 6.4).

**Figure 6.4**
These gEdit settings are a good choice for editing configuration files.

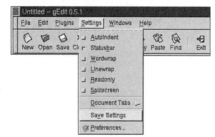

### POSITIONING THE CURSOR IN GEDIT

gEdit follows the standard cursor-positioning scheme used by most modern text editors. You can move the cursor to any character in the document simply by clicking the spot that you want to move the cursor to. You can also use the cursor-positioning keys available on most modern keyboards, as summarized in Table 6.1.

**TABLE 6.1  CURSOR-POSITIONING KEYS IN GEDIT**

| Key | Effect |
| --- | --- |
| ~UA or Ctrl+P | Up one line |
| ~DA or Ctrl+N | Down one line |
| ~RA or Ctrl+F | Right one character |
| ~LA or Ctrl+B | Left one character |
| Home | Start of line |
| End | End of line |
| Page Up (PgUp) | Up a screen |
| Page Down (PgDn) | Down a screen |
| Ctrl+Home | To top of document |
| Ctrl+End | To end of document |
| Shift+*key* | Select text |
| Backspace | Delete character to left |
| Delete (Del) or Ctrl+D | Delete character to right |
| Ctrl+U | Delete entire line |

### CUT AND PASTE IN GEDIT

You can select, copy, cut, and paste text in gEdit using the same techniques that most modern text editors and word processing programs support. For example, you can select text by dragging the mouse pointer through it or by holding down the Shift key as you press the arrow or other cursor-positioning keys. Double-clicking a word selects that word. Triple-clicking a line (or paragraph) selects that paragraph. To select all the text in a document, choose Edit, Select All from the gEdit menu bar. Then, to work with the selected text, choose one of the following:

- To copy the selected text, choose Edit, Copy or press Ctrl+C.
- To cut the selected text, choose Edit, Cut or press Ctrl+X.
- To delete the selected text, press the Delete (Del) key.

If you cut or copied the selected text, you can paste it anywhere in any open document. Just move the cursor where you want to place the text and choose Edit, Paste or press Ctrl+V.

Tip

gEdit has its own Web site at http://gedit.pn.org. You can subscribe to gEdit mailing lists from the Web page too.

## FIND AND REPLACE IN GEDIT

To quickly locate a specific chunk of text or a specific line in gEdit, click the Find button in the toolbar, or choose Edit, Find from its menu bar, or press the F6 key. The dialog box shown in Figure 6.5 appears. In the Search text box, type the word or phrase you want to search for. Then you can choose where to begin the search, either from the current cursor position or from the top of the document. If you like, you can turn on case-sensitivity so that only words that have the same uppercase/lowercase letters as your search string will be found. Click the OK button to perform the search. The cursor will jump to the first occurrence of the string you specified.

**Figure 6.5**

The Search dialog box in gEdit helps you locate a specific line of text in an open document.

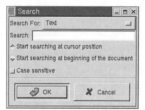

If the text that gEdit finds isn't the text you were looking for, you can easily search for the next occurrence of that same string. Press the ~RA key to move the cursor off the current character, then press Shift+F6 to locate the next occurrence of the text.

To locate a specific line rather than a chunk of text, choose Line Number from the Search For button. Then type in the number of the line you want to jump to, and click the OK button.

You can globally replace text throughout a document using the gEdit Replace option. Choose Edit, Replace from the menu bar, or press the F7 key. The Search and Replace dialog box appears (see Figure 6.6).

Note

Globally searching and replacing text is not the kind of thing you'll do often when editing configuration files. You usually need to make very small, specific changes in configuration files. Use Replace only when you're sure that you must change all occurrences of a word or phrase within the configuration file.

In the Search textbox, type the text that needs to be replaced. Decide whether you want to start the replacement from the current cursor position or from the top of the document. If you want to replace words that match the upper/lowercase letters of your search string, choose the Case Sensitive option. Then, type the new text that will replace the old text. If you

**Figure 6.6**
Use the gEdit Search and Replace dialog box to globally change text throughout a document.

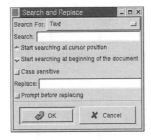

want to be prompted for permission before each change is made, choose the Prompt before replacing option. Then click the OK button to perform the Replace operation.

### SAVING YOUR CHANGES IN GEDIT

When you've finished making your changes to a configuration file in gEdit, you can save your work and close gEdit by clicking the Exit button in the toolbar, by pressing Ctrl+Q, or by choosing File, Exit from the gEdit menu bar. If you've made any changes to the document that haven't been saved, you'll see the message *"filename" has been modified. Do you wish to save it?*

Choose Yes to save your changes and exit gEdit. If you're concerned that you might have made a mistake while editing the configuration file, choose No to close gEdit without saving your changes. To stay in gEdit you can click the Cancel button.

## EDITING WITH XEDIT

Another graphical text editor you can use in Linux is named xedit. This one is not quite as user friendly or intuitive to use. It has no menus, and no form of help. However, it works in virtually any of Linux's GUIs. So if you happen to be working on a computer that has X installed, but not GNOME, you can use xedit to edit configuration files.

| Tip | Other X GUIs are discussed in Chapter 8. If you performed a server-class installation of Linux, your system has no GUI capabilities at all. So you can only run text-mode editors like vi and emacs, which are discussed later in this chapter. |

As with most programs, you can use several different methods to start xedit. In GNOME, you can click the Main Menu button, choose Run Program. Or, in any GUI you can open a terminal window. Either way, you can then type the following command:

```
xedit path
```

*path* is the location and name of the file you want to edit. For example, entering the command

```
xedit /etc/fstab
```

opens the file named `fstab` from the `/etc` directory, ready for editing in xedit, as in the example shown in Figure 6.7.

**Figure 6.7**

The `/etc/fstab` configuration file open for editing in xedit.

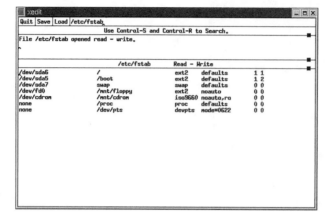

If you omit the path in the command, then xedit opens with no document. To open a document in xedit, click just to the right of the Load button near the top of its window. Type in the complete path to the file you want to edit (`/etc/fstab`, for example), then click the Load button.

As you perform actions in xedit, feedback messages appear in the narrow pane below the "Use Ctrl-S and Ctrl-R to Search" message. The document you're editing appears in the bottom pane. You can adjust the relative size of the panes by dragging the sizing handle (the little black square) at the top of each pane up or down.

### CURSOR-POSITIONING IN XEDIT

You can position the cursor to any place in your text simply by clicking the spot that you want to move to. A caret (^) points to where the next text you type will appear. When you've clicked somewhere within the document to get the cursor there, you can also use the keys listed in Table 6.2 to position the cursor and delete text.

**TABLE 6.2   CURSOR-POSITIONING KEYS IN XEDIT**

| Key | Effect |
| --- | --- |
| ~UA or Ctrl+P | Up one line |
| ~DA or Ctrl+N | Down one line |
| ~RA or Ctrl+F | Right one character |
| ~LA or Ctrl+B | Left one character |
| Ctrl+A | Beginning of line |
| Ctrl+E | End of line |
| Home | Top of document |
| End | Bottom of document |

**TABLE 6.2    CONTINUED**

| Key | Effect |
| --- | --- |
| Page Up (PgUp) | Up a screen |
| Page Down (PgDn) | Down a screen |
| Backspace, Ctrl+D, or Delete (Del) | Delete character to left |

> **Caution**
>
> If you're accustomed to a modern text editor like gEdit, using xedit can be dangerous. Many of the commands you're accustomed to in other editors will have no effect, or strange effects, in xedit. If you make a mess of things, click the Quit button near the upper-left corner twice to close xedit without saving your changes.

xedit really offers nothing beyond the most rudimentary editing capabilities of positioning the cursor and adding or deleting text. But in a pinch, where no other text editor is available, it'll do. Typically, changes you make to a configuration file will be small and simple anyway, so you normally won't need a powerful editor anyway.

> **Note**
>
> Theoretically, you're supposed to be able to search and replace text in xedit by pressing Ctrl+S or Ctrl+R. But that feature doesn't work on any of my computers!

### SAVING, CLOSING, AND BAILING IN XEDIT

If you're happy with the changes you've made to a document in xedit, and want to save the modified file, click the Save button near the upper-left corner of the xedit window. You'll see a small Saved file message, which is your only indication that the file has been saved.

To close xedit, click the Quit button. If you haven't saved recent changes to the document you're working on, you'll see the message Unsaved changes. Save them, or Quit again.

If you want to bail out and not save your current changes, click the Quit button a second time. Otherwise, if you forget to save your changes, click the Save button, then click the Quit button again.

## EDITING WITH VI

Should you ever find yourself working on a Linux computer that has no GUI installed (or, at least none that's working properly), you can always edit configuration files using the character cell editor named vi. A throwback to the early '70s when computer monitors could display text but not graphics, vi offers nothing in the user-friendliness department. But in a pinch—when you need to change a configuration file without the benefit of gEdit or xedit—it will do. To start vi, without any particular document, just enter vi at the command prompt.

PART

**II**

CH

**6**

However, most of the time you'll probably want to use the following syntax to open a specific configuration file with vi to edit it:

```
vi path
```

path is the location and filename of the configuration file that you want to edit. For example, if you want to open a configuration file named fstab in the /etc directory, enter the following command:

```
vi /etc/fstab
```

> **Note**
>
> Even though you use the command vi to start the program, Red Hat Linux actually ships with vim (*vi improved*), which is a newer version of vi.

The file opens at the top of the screen. Any blank lines at the bottom of the file are indicated by a tilde (~) character, as in the following example (see Figure 6.8).

**Vi modes**

**Figure 6.8**
About to edit the contents of the /etc/fstab file using vi.

vi works in two modes: the *command mode* and the *insert mode* (or *append mode*). In command mode, every character you type is assumed to be part of a command that you're about to send to vi. Those characters don't appear within your document. If you want to insert text into your document, you must do the following:

1. Move the cursor, using keys summarized in Table 6.3, to wherever you want to insert text.

2. Type a lowercase a to append text at the cursor position. The word INSERT appears at the bottom of the screen to let you know you're in insert mode.

3. Type the text you want to insert.

4. To return to command mode, press the Esc key. The INSERT indicator at the bottom of the screen disappears.

**TABLE 6.3   KEYS USED TO POSITION THE CURSOR IN THE VI COMMAND MODE (WHEN INSERT ISN'T VISIBLE AT THE BOTTOM OF THE SCREEN)**

| Key | Effect |
| --- | --- |
| ~UA or k | Up one line |
| ~DA or j | Down one line |
| ~RA or l | Right one character |
| ~LA or h | Left one character |
| Home | Start of line |
| End or $ | End of line |
| Page Up (PgUp) or Ctrl+U | Up a screen |
| Page Down (PgDn) or Ctrl+F | Down a screen |
| 1G | Go to top of document (line 1) |
| Delete (Del) or x | Delete character at cursor |
| dw | Delete from cursor to end of word |
| d$ | Delete from cursor to end of line |
| dd | Delete entire line |
| o | Open new line below cursor and enter Insert mode |
| O | Open new line above cursor and enter Insert mode |
| Esc U | Undoes previous command |

**Tip**

If you press Esc to go to command mode and you're already in command mode, you'll hear a beep. That's not a problem—just vi's way of telling you, "You're already in command mode, so go ahead and enter commands."

More powerful commands for opening files to edit, saving your changes, abandoning your changes, and quitting vi are summarized in Table 6.4. Note that after you type a command that starts with a colon (:), you need to press Enter to actually send the entire command to vi. So to enter :q! type those exact three characters (lowercase "q"), then press Enter.

**TABLE 6.4   COMMANDS FOR OPENING, SAVING, ABANDONING FILES AND CLOSING VI**

| Command | What It Does |
| --- | --- |
| :help (or press F1) | Get onscreen help |
| :x | Exit help and return to document |
| :r *filename* | Read (open) filename |
| :q! | Exit vi without saving changes to document |

PART

**II**

CH

**6**

**TABLE 6.4 CONTINUED**

| Command | What It Does |
|---------|-------------|
| :wq | Save changes and exit vi |

After exiting vi, you'll still see your document and perhaps some tildes on the screen, followed by a new Linux command prompt. To clean up the screen, enter the usual `clear` command.

The basics covered here should be sufficient for editing configuration files when you have no GUI to work from. For more information, you can view the vi man page (man vi). There's also a vi Web site at `www.vim.org`.

If you're accustomed to a graphical computing environment, hopefully you won't have to do too much editing with vi. In the unlikely event that vi isn't available on the Linux computer you're sitting at, or if you find vi just too weird to work with, there's yet another text editor you can use to edit configuration files without the benefit of a graphical user interface. It's called Emacs.

## EDITING WITH EMACS

An alternative to vi for editing in character cell mode is the Emacs editor. Emacs, which stands for *Editor Macros*, is a favorite text editor among UNIX programmers and has a lot of features that you really don't need to do simple editing of configuration files. If you're accustomed to working with a mouse, Emacs will almost surely drive you crazy because it offers no mouse support whatsoever, unless you run it from a terminal window in a GUI. But if you're already in a GUI, it will almost surely be easier to use gEdit or xedit to edit a configuration file, unless you happen to be intimately familiar with Emacs already.

To start Emacs, type `emacs` at the command prompt and press Enter. If you want to start Emacs and open a file at the same time, just follow the `emacs` command with a blank space and the path and filename of the file you want to open. For example, entering `emacs /etc/fstab` opens the file named `fstab` in the `/etc` directory in Emacs, ready for editing.

### WHAT'S ON THE EMACS SCREEN?

The Emacs screen is divided into several components. Along the top of the Emacs window is the menu bar. In a GUI, you can access the menu with the mouse. In character-cell mode, you have to press the F10 key. When you do, the screen divides into three *buffers* (areas where information is stored and displayed), as shown in Figure 6.9. In the top buffer, named Fundamental, you'll usually see the document you're editing. The middle buffer, named Completion List, will display some help text telling you how to complete the task you just started. In this example, you just pressed F10, which brings up the Menu bar line in the small bottom buffer, which is called the *minibuffer*. In the minibuffer you can press the ~UA and ~DA keys to scroll through menu options. They'll appear in the minibuffer as h==>help, b==>Buffers, s==>Search, and so forth. Each option that appears represents a command from the menus that you can select.

**Figure 6.9**
The three buffers sometimes visible in Emacs.

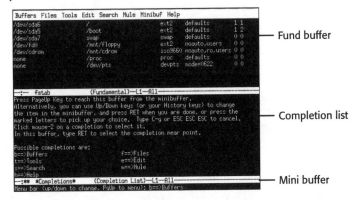

— Fund buffer

— Completion list

— Mini buffer

Within the middle pane you'll often see combination keystrokes referred to using the syntax C-key, M-key, and ESC. The C- refers to the control (Ctrl) key, the M- refers to the Meta key (labeled Alt on PC keyboards). ESC refers to the Escape key. Table 6.5 shows examples of how you can translate those combination keystrokes to the format used in this book, and it explains exactly what each example means.

**TABLE 6.5  EMACS COMBINATION KEYSTROKES TRANSLATED TO THE FORMAT USED IN THIS BOOK**

| Emacs Example | Equivalent | Means |
| --- | --- | --- |
| C-g | Ctrl+G | Hold down Ctrl, press G |
| M-f | Alt+F | Hold down Alt, press F |
| ESC ESC ESC | Esc Esc Esc | Press the Esc key three times |

Emacs comes with a brief tutorial that can help you learn the basics. To start the tutorial, assuming you're in Emacs at the moment, follow these steps:

1. Press F10 to display menu options in the minibuffer.

2. Type b to select the Buffers menu option.

3. Type t to select Tutorial.

Because you're working in a character cell mode, the tutorial text looks exactly like text in a document. In fact, all text looks exactly alike because there's only one way to display text in character cell mode. (Emacs was invented back in the early days of simple terminals that had no graphics capability at all.) You can scroll through the tutorial using the ~UA and ~DA keys. The tutorial will teach you about basic navigation keys and more.

To get out of the tutorial, press F10 again to bring up the menu in the minibuffer. Next press b to select Buffers, then f to select the Fundamental buffer, where the document you're editing resides. If you get stuck in the minibuffer, press Ctrl+G or tap the Esc key three times to get out. To get back into the minibuffer at any time, press the F10 function key. If you feel like a complete klutz for a while, don't feel bad. I'm sure everyone who has ever ventured into Emacs has felt exactly the same way.

### POSITIONING AND DELETING IN EMACS

Moving the cursor around and deleting text in your document really isn't too terribly challenging. First, remember that to get rid of all the extra buffers and view only the document you're working on, you need to press F10 and then type the letters bf to get to the Fundamental buffer. If it doesn't work, you are probably in the minibuffer already, in which case you can press ESC ESC ESC to get out of that buffer. Press Ctrl+X1 to reduce the display to a single buffer. Next, try the F10, b,f business again. Then you can use the keys listed in Table 6.6 to do all your basic cursor navigation and text deleting.

### TABLE 6.6   CURSOR-POSITIONING KEYS IN EMACS

| Key | Effect |
| --- | --- |
| ~UA or Ctrl+P | Up one line |
| ~DA or Ctrl+N | Down one line |
| ~RA or Ctrl+F | Right one character |
| ~LA or Ctrl+B | Left one character |
| Alt+F | Forward one word |
| Alt+B | Backward one word |
| Ctrl+A | Beginning of line |
| Ctrl+E | End of line |
| Alt+A | Beginning of sentence |
| Alt+E | End of sentence |
| Home or Alt+Shift+< | Top of document |
| End or Alt+Shift+> | Bottom of document |
| Page Up (PgUp) or Alt+V | Up a screen |
| Page Down (PgDn) or Ctrl+V | Down a screen |
| Backspace or Delete (Del) | Delete character to left |
| Ctrl+D | Delete character to right |

### OTHER COMMON EMACS COMMANDS

As with any text editor, you can open files to edit, save your work, and exit Emacs at any time. Table 6.7 lists the combination keys you can use while working in a document to perform those tasks. Note that you can hold down the Ctrl key, tap the first key, then tap the second key before you release the Ctrl key. For example, to type Ctrl+xf, hold down the Ctrl key, tap the x key, tap the f key, then release the Ctrl key.

**TABLE 6.7  COMMANDS FOR OPENING AND SAVING DOCUMENTS, HIDING BUFFERS, AND EXITING EMACS**

| Key | Effect |
| --- | --- |
| Ctrl+xf | Open a file to edit |
| Ctrl+xs | Save changes without closing |
| Ctrl+x1 | Hide all but one buffer |
| Ctrl+xc | Exit Emacs |

When you exit Emacs, the command prompt will appear at the bottom of the screen. But you'll still see the remnants of Emacs above the command prompt. To clear that stuff off, simply enter the clear command to clear the screen.

What you've learned about Emacs here should be sufficient to help you edit configuration files, should a GUI and vi not be available. If you'd like to learn more about Emacs, you can visit their Web page at http://www.emacs.org, as well as the man page (man emacs).

# CASE STUDY: LETTING USERS MOUNT DISKS

Samantha Sysadmin is tired of having users bug her to mount and unmount CD-ROMs and floppy disks. She learns from the man pages for the mount command and fstab (*filesystem table*) file that by adding the users option to the drive's entry in the /etc/fstab file, she can grant mounting capabilities to users. The users option needs to be in the last section of the drive options. The example given in the man page for the mount command shows an example using the user option as with the following:

```
/dev/cdrom /cd iso9660 ro,user,noauto,unhide
```

Samantha has learned that if she makes the option singular (user), then only the user who mounted a disk can unmount it. If she makes it plural (users), then any user can unmount a disk. So she decides to go with the plural users option.

## EDITING fstab WITH GEDIT

The user that needs mounting capability has a machine that runs GNOME, so Samantha knows she can edit fstab with gEdit. She needs superuser power to make this change, so she logs into that machine as root. She wants to play it safe, so first she gets to the /etc directory via the File Manager and makes a copy of the fstab file, naming the copy fstabOrig. Then she right-clicks the original fstab file icon and chooses Open With, Applications, gEdit. When the file first opens, it looks like Figure 6.10.

She adds a comma and the users keyword (no blank spaces) to options for the floppy disk drive (/dev/fd0) and the CD-ROM drive (/dev/cdrom) (see Figure 6.11).

To finish up, she closes gEdit and chooses Yes when asked if she wants to save the changes to the file.

**Figure 6.10**
The fstab file as it first looks when opened in gEdit.

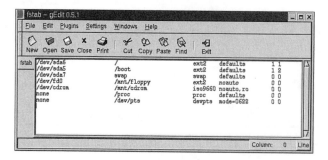

**Figure 6.11**
The users option added to the /dev/fd0 and /dev/cdrom drive entries in fstab.

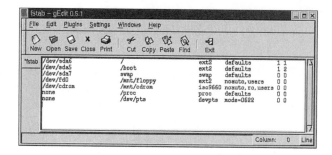

To test, Samantha will need to log in as a regular user. She can reboot to ensure that she's starting fresh (Main Menu, Log Out, Reboot, Yes). When asked to log in, she logs in under a regular user's name and password. If all went well, she should be able to mount and unmount a floppy disk or CD-ROM without her superuser powers.

It just so happens that this user has desktop shortcuts to the CD-ROM drive and floppy disk drive on his desktop. So Samantha right-clicks those icons and, sure enough, just like the superuser, this user now has a Mount Device option on the icon's right-click menu. To test, she puts a disk in each drive, mounts each drive, then views its contents by double-clicking the shortcut icon. The contents of each disk appear in the File Manager, so she knows she was successful. She can now unmount each disk by right-clicking the drive's shortcut icon and choosing Unmount Device. To eject the unmounted CD-ROM, she right-clicks the CD-ROM drive's icon and chooses Eject Disk.

If you have no interest seeing how this change could be done in vi, you can skip the next section. But don't miss the section titled "More on fstab" at the end of this chapter.

## EDITING fstab WITH VI

Let's say that Samantha also has another user, named Harry Humble, who also wants to be able to mount disks. Harry's computer doesn't have the hardware horsepower to use any GUI, so Harry works at the command prompt exclusively. (He doesn't mind because he's been a programmer since 1975 and can type 6,000 words per minute.) To grant mounting privileges to Harry, Samantha will need to log in as root on Harry's system and edit his fstab file using vi.

Samantha goes to Harry's computer and enters the su (substitute user) command to give herself superuser power. She then makes a backup copy of his fstab file, just to play it safe, by entering the following command:

```
cp /etc/fstab /etc/fstabOrig
```

To edit Harry's fstab file, she then enters the command vi/etc/fstab. His fstab file opens, and she gingerly moves the cursor to the options for the /dev/fd0 device. She then types a to enter insert mode and types in the comma and user's keyword. Then, she presses Esc to return to command mode and carefully deletes any blank spaces she added by positioning the cursor and pressing the Delete key. She does the same for the /dev/cdrom device. The completed file is shown in Figure 6.12.

**Caution**

No spaces are allowed within the options. Each option must be separated by a single comma only. There must be at least one blank space between the full set of options and the 0 that follows the options, as shown in Figure 6.12.

**Figure 6.12**
The users option added to the /dev/fd0 and /dev/cdrom devices in vi.

To save the modified fstab file, Samantha presses Esc to make sure she's in command mode. Then she types :wq and presses Enter to save her changes and exit vi. To clear the screen, she enters a clear command. To give up her superuser powers, she enters an exit command. The command prompt shows a $ sign rather than # sign, indicating that her superuser powers are indeed gone.

**Caution**

When mounting disks from the command prompt, users must use a syntax that's a little different from the superuser's syntax. To mount a CD-ROM from the command prompt, the user must enter the command mount /dev/cdrom. To mount a floppy from the command prompt, the user must enter the command mount /dev/fd0.

To test her changes to the fstab file, Samantha places a Linux-formatted (ext2) floppy disk in the floppy drive and a CD in the CD-ROM drive. Since she's now logged in as a regular user, she enters a mount /dev/fd0 command to mount the floppy. To verify that she can view the contents of the floppy disk, she then enters the command ls /mnt/floppy. To mount the CD,

PART

**II**

CH

**6**

she enters the command mount /dev/cdrom. To view the contents of the CD, she then enters the command ls /mnt/cdrom. It all works, so she knows that Harry can mount his own disks. She just has to tell him how to do it now.

## MORE ON fstab

The user's option in the fstab file doesn't give the average user quite as much mounting power as the superuser has. For example, the user can mount only CDs and Linux-formatted floppy disks, no DOS/Windows formatted disks. The user cannot run programs from the mounted drives (unless you add an exec option to their fstab file). Nor can they view hidden files on the mounted disks (unless you add a nohide option to their fstab file.) For more information about fstab and powers you can grant to regular users, see the man page for the fstab file (man fstab) and mount command (man mount). The CD-ROM HOWTO also contains useful information. That HOWTO is available on your Red Hat Linux CD as well as on the Web at http://www.redhat.com/mirrors/LDP/HOWTO/CDROM-HOWTO.html. There's also a helpful FAQ at http://www.redhat.com/mirrors/LDP/HOWTO/CDROM-HOWTO-6.html#ss6.1 on the Web.

For information on creating desktop shortcuts to the floppy and CD-ROM drives, see the section titled "Creating Shortcuts from File Manager" in Chapter 3.

CHAPTER **7**

# MANAGING USERS AND PERMISSIONS

## In this chapter

# WHY CREATE GROUPS AND USER ACCOUNTS?

As you may recall from Chapter 3, "Understanding the Linux Filesystem," users on a Linux system can control access to their files by assigning permissions to themselves, their group, and everyone else in the world. In the example there, the user Lana from the accounting department created a document and saved it in a file. She granted herself permission to read (view) and write (change) the file. She wanted other people in her department to be able to view (read) the file, but not change it. People outside her department, she decided, should have no access to the file whatsoever. That is, they had neither read nor write permission.

> **Tip**
>
> The user/group structure of Linux will be familiar to those with Windows NT experience.

To make all that happen, Lana needs to put the document (or a copy of the document) in a directory that other people on the system have access to. This could be a directory that's accessible only to people in the accounting department. Optionally, she can put the document in a directory that's accessible to everyone. However, she first needs to set up the properties of the file so that she (the owner) has read/write permission, everyone else in the accounting department has read permission, and the rest of the world has no permission. Figure 7.1 shows how she would set up the properties for such a file after right-clicking the file and choosing Properties. Notice that Lana (User) has Read/Write permission, her Group has Read permission, and everyone else (Other) has no permission. At the bottom of the dialog box you can see that the Owner of the file is Lana. By default, the person who creates a file is the owner. The Group option beneath the owner is acct (short for accounting).

**Figure 7.1**
The owner of this file has granted herself permission to read and write the file, the group permission to read the file, and everyone else no permission.

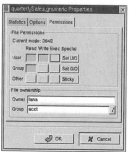

> **Tip**
>
> For reasons that defy any sort of logic, the three buttons that define the owner's permissions are labeled User, rather than Owner, on the Permissions tab. But those top three buttons really do represent the owner's permissions.

Now, before Lana can do *any* of this, there needs to be a group named acct on the computer (or somewhere in the network). And of course, Lana needs to have a user account so she can get on the computer in the first place. Which brings up the question, "Who creates these group and user accounts?" The answer, as you may suspect, is the superuser. Only the superuser (or users with equivalent power) can create groups and users, which is what allows security to be built in to the system in the first place. Just as the root of a plant "grows" the branches and leaves of the rest of the plant, the superuser (also called the *root* user) "grows" the users and groups that make up the user base of the system. Exactly *how* the root creates users and groups is the main subject of this chapter.

# CREATING AND MANAGING GROUPS

The first step to creating groups is to do a little planning. Certainly different types of businesses will require different kinds of groups. And it's not always easy to foresee exactly how all the users in a system might be best grouped. Fortunately, you don't need a crystal ball. You can create a group and add users to it any time. And, a user can belong to any number of different groups, so there's tremendous flexibility there. But still, it makes sense to think about what kinds of groups might be useful before you actually sit down and create them.

Sticking with our accounting department example, it probably makes sense to create an Accounting group. After all, members of that accounting department will probably want to share some files among themselves, but not share those files with people outside the accounting department. The same could be said of the marketing, sales, and IT (information technology) departments, or any other departments within the organization. Creating groups for individual departments is a pretty common way to get started.

The easiest way to create groups is probably via the LinuxConf program. As you may recall from Chapter 6, "System Administration Basics," when logged in as root, you can start LinuxConf using either of the following methods:

- Click the GNOME Main Menu button and choose System, LinuxConf.

- Or, enter the command linuxconf in the GNOME Run Program dialog box or in any terminal window.

---

**Character Cell LinuxConf**
Throughout this chapter I'll show the graphical X Window version of LinuxConf, under the assumption that the superuser has GNOME or some other GUI on the computer. However, there is a character cell version of LinuxConf that runs from the command prompt without a GUI. That character cell version of LinuxConf provides the same capabilities that the graphical version does except that it doesn't support a mouse. To get around in character cell LinuxConf, you need to move the highlighter around using the arrow keys, Tab, and Shift+Tab keys. To select the currently highlighted option or expand the currently highlighted category, press Enter.

---

When LinuxConf starts, a "tree menu" appears in the left column. As in all tree menus, you can click any + sign to expand a category, click the - sign to collapse the category. To get to the options for managing users and groups, you need to open the Config, Users Accounts, and Normal categories. Clicking on Group definitions within the Normal category displays a list of all existing groups in the right pane of the window, as shown in Figure 7.2.

**Figure 7.2**
The default list of user groups that the Red Hat Linux installation creates appears in the right panel of LinuxConf when Group definitions is selected.

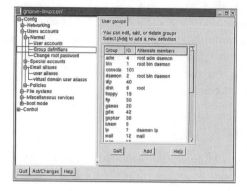

Right off the bat, you'll see that a lot of groups already exist. When you installed Red Hat Linux, it automatically created those groups, and each group serves a purpose. Each group has a group ID (GID). Some groups have alternate members; for example, the root, bin, and daemon groups are alternate members to the bin group. As you learn more about configuring services and granting permissions in upcoming chapters, you'll see when these predefined groups can come in handy. For now, your best bet is to leave them alone. Stick with creating your own groups and modifying only the groups you've created, until you learn more about the predefined groups.

To create a new group, click the Add button. You must type in a group name. I suggest you keep it brief, use only lowercase letters, and don't use spaces or any other punctuation marks. Each time you create a group, LinuxConf will automatically assign it a unique number, starting at 500. There's really no need to change that value; it's best to leave it as is. If you know ahead of time that you'd like to add some alternate member groups, you can list those in the last field. You *must* enter only valid group names and separate the group names with a single space. You can also leave this option blank if you don't want alternate members (or don't want to think about what those alternate member might be at the moment!). Figure 7.3 shows an example of a new group named acct (for accounting) that has been created.

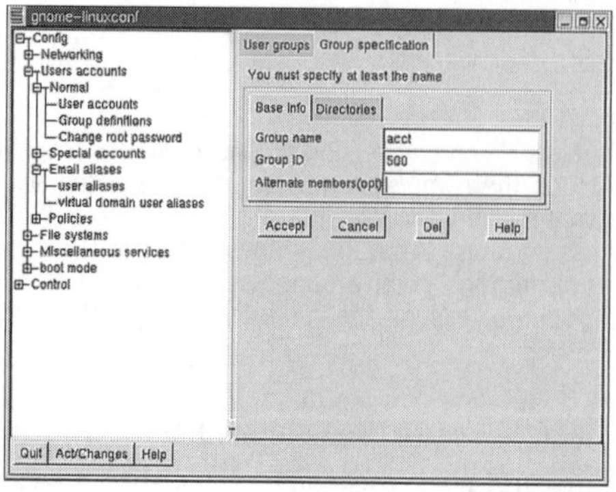

**Figure 7.3**
A new group named acct created within Linux-Conf.

You can give a group its own directory, where members of that group can place files that they want to share with one another. To do so, click the Directories tab. In most cases, you'll want users to have their own private home directories, so leave the Different Directory for Eeach Members option selected. To give the group a directory for shared files as well, type the complete path to that directory in the Home Base directory field. Making the shared directory a subdirectory of /home puts it near the home directories of all users, which makes for easy access. The Creation Permissions setting of 700 is a setting that affects only spool files used for printing, and can be left at that value. Figure 7.4 shows an example where the superuser has specified a directory named /home/accounting for the members of the accounting department to store their shared files.

**Figure 7.4**
Members of the accounting department will be able to use the /home/account-ing directory to store their shared files.

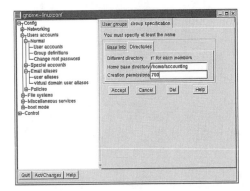

Click the Accept button to complete your entries. If you specified a nonexistent directory as the home for the group, you'll see a message asking you for permission to create that directory. Click the Yes button. LinuxConf closes, and the group now exists. To verify, you can reopen LinuxConf and take a look at the Group definitions again. You should see your new group within the list of existing groups. (The groups are alphabetized by name). When you quit LinuxConf, be sure to select the Activate the Changes button if presented. To verify that the directory was created, open File Manager and go the parent directory of the directory you specified. You should see the new directory listed in the right pane of the File Manager.

You can create as many or as few groups as you wish using the same techniques just described. If at any time you need to change or delete a group in the future, you can use LinuxConf to do that too. Simply go back to the Group Definitions category and click the name of the group you want to modify or delete. Make your changes in the Base Info and Directories tabs that appear. Or, click the Del button if you want to delete the group entirely. Don't forget to click the Accept button when you're done, and choose Act/Changes when you quit LinuxConf, if that option is presented to you.

PART
**II**

CH
**7**

# ADDING AND MANAGING USERS

As you know, only a user with a valid user account can log on to a Linux computer. You must be logged in as root to create user accounts. Of course, it's a good thing that only the superuser can create accounts; otherwise, anyone could just walk up to the machine and create an account for himself! A user account consists of a username, password, and some privileges that define what that user can and cannot do.

You can use LinuxConf to create and manage user accounts. Just fire up LinuxConf and open the Config, Users Accounts, and Normal categories. Click Users Accounts to view a list of all existing user accounts, as in Figure 7.5.

**Figure 7.5**
LinuxConf showing current users on the Users Accounts tab.

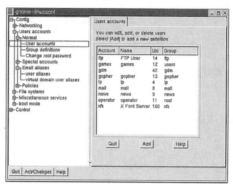

> **Note**
>
> The root user's account is never listed in the Users Accounts dialog box. But just as an FYI, the root's user ID is 0.

Once again you'll find that your Red Hat Linux installation has already created several user accounts. However, those accounts don't really apply to human beings. Rather, they are used internally within Linux to grant permissions to specific services and programs. You'll learn more about those predefined user accounts as you learn to set up and configure services in future chapters. For now, your best bet is to leave those accounts alone—don't change them and don't delete any of them.

To create a new user account, click the Add button. The User Account Creation tab appears. Select options and fill in the blanks for one new user based on the following:

- **The Account Is Enabled:** If you want this user to have immediate access to his account, select the The account is enabled option so that it looks pushed in. If you don't want the user to have immediate access to the system, de-select this option. You can enable the account at any time by returning to this dialog box and selecting the option.

- **Login Name:** Every user must have a unique username. The standard practice is to use all lowercase letters with the user's first initial, followed by their last name, as in gjones for George Jones. However, you can use any scheme you like provided you don't put any blank spaces into the user name.

- **Full Name:** Although optional, you should type the user's complete name here. For example, George Jones for the gjones account.

- **Group:** Fill in the group to which this user will belong to or leave this option empty. Ideally, you're better off leaving it empty because in doing so you give the user his own private group, which will be the same as the user's username. Even if this user will be the member of some group, like acct, it's best to leave this option blank and use the next option, Supplementary Groups, to define other groups this user belongs to.

- **Supplementary Groups:** If you leave this option blank, the user will be assigned to no supplementary groups. If you've already created one or more groups, and know you want this user to be a member of the group, type the group name(s) here. Be careful: You must use exact upper/lowercase letters. If this user will be a member of two or more groups, make sure you separate each group name with a single blank space.

- **Home Directory:** If you leave this option blank, the user's home directory will be /home/*username* (that is, /home/gjones). This is the recommended default, even if you've set up a shared directory for the user's groups. Every user likes having a private home directory for "personal" stuff. Leaving this option blank will ensure that the user gets such a directory.

- **Command Interpreter:** Specifies which command shell will be loaded for this user when he logs in. If you leave this blank, the bash shell will be loaded, which is a perfectly fine choice.

- **User ID:** By default, each user is also granted a numeric user ID (UID) that Linux uses internally. Leave this option blank to let Linux determine a user ID automatically. Regular users all have numeric UIDs equal to 500 or greater.

Figure 7.6 shows a completed form for creating a new user account for Louise Ana with the username lana. The account is enabled, and this user will have access to the acct group files, but only as a supplemental group. Leaving all option fields blank ensures that LinuxConf will automatically create a personal home directory and User ID for this new user.

The Mail Aliases tab lets you define multiple email names for this user. If you've already set up email services on this computer, you can direct email messages with certain addresses to this user. If you haven't set up email services yet, you can leave those options blank. If need be, you can always come back and set up email aliases after you've configured mail for this computer.

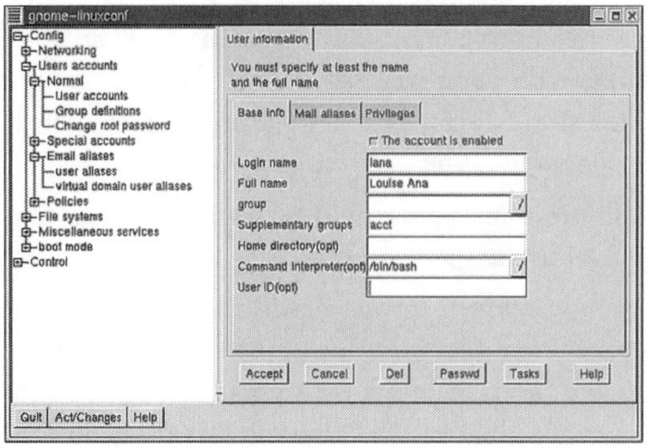

**Figure 7.6**

A new user account created for Louise Ana with the username lana.

Clicking the Privileges tab brings up a set of options broken into four tabs titled General System Control, Services, Miscellaneous, and User Accounts (see Figure 7.7). These options grant the user permissions that apply only to LinuxConf. The most basic—May Use LinuxConf—really needs to be granted before the others really make much sense. The remaining permissions define what that user can do within LinuxConf.

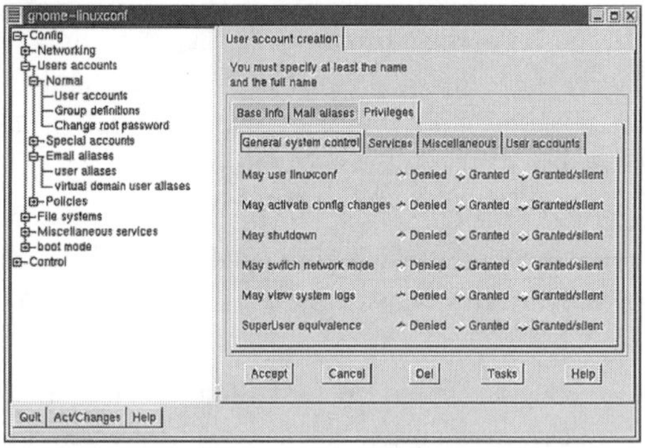

**Figure 7.7**

The special privileges in this dialog box grant the user permissions that apply only to using the LinuxConf program.

For each privilege, you can select from the following options:

- **Denied:** The user is denied this privilege.
- **Granted:** The user is granted the privilege, but will have to re-enter his password before performing the privileged task. This option adds a little extra security to the system by ensuring that if someone finds the computer unattended but still logged in under this username, he won't be able to do anything too drastic.
- **Granted/Silent:** Grants the privilege to the user. The user won't have to re-enter his password to exercise this privilege. This is more convenient for this user, but not quite as secure as the Granted option.

Most of the privileges are pretty self-explanatory, but the following is a quick summary of all the options presented on all four tabs. If you're not exactly sure at this juncture what a specific privilege does, you can leave it in the default setting of Denied. You can always change your mind later and grant the privilege after you have a better understanding of what the privilege is really about.

- **May Use linuxconf:** If granted, the user can start and use LinuxConf to explore the system, although not necessarily to change the system.

- **May Activate config Changes:** If granted, the user is allowed to make changes to configuration files via linuxconf, and activate them immediately upon saving them.

- **May Shutdown:** When granted, allows the user to shut down his own computer by entering the command `linuxconf -shutdown` at a command prompt or by opening the Control, Control Panel, Shutdown/Reboot categories of the left pane of LinuxConf.

- **May Switch Network Mode:** When granted, gives the user the ability to use LinuxConf's Switch Network Mode capability.

- **May View System Logs:** When granted, lets the user view system logs via LinuxConf, which normally only the superuser can view.

- **SuperUser Equivalence:** When granted, gives this user the same power and flexibility that the superuser has while working in LinuxConf. Be very careful with this one. Omnipotence without omniscience can be a dangerous thing!

- **Apache Administration:** If granted, this user can configure the Apache Web server from within LinuxConf.

- **Mail to Fax Manager:** If granted, this user can send mail to the LinuxConf fax manager.

- **Message of the Day:** If granted, the user sees the "message of the day" when first logging in.

- **POP Accounts Manager:** If granted, this user can manage POP (Post Office Protocol) accounts (which are involved in email) from within LinuxConf.

- **PPP Accounts Manager:** If granted, this user can manage PPP (Point-to-Point) accounts from within LinuxConf. PPP accounts are involved in dial-up network connections with modems.

- **UUCP Accounts Manager:** If granted, this user can manage UUCP (UNIX to UNIX Copy) accounts from within LinuxConf.

When you've finished setting up the new user account, click the Accept button. You'll come to the Changing Password tab shown in Figure 7.8. You need to enter a valid password for this user. Users can always change their own passwords in the future, but to test the account you should enter a password now and jot it down on a piece of scratch paper so that you don't forget. Or, you can simply make up an easily remembered generic password for all new users, like *newuser*, so you don't forget. Just make sure that users come up with their own unique passwords sometime in the near future. Otherwise, you may be presenting yourself with a bit of a security risk if users realize that all new accounts have the same password.

PART

II

CH

7

**Figure 7.8**
After clicking the
Accept button to
define a new user,
you're prompted
to enter a pass-
word for that
user.

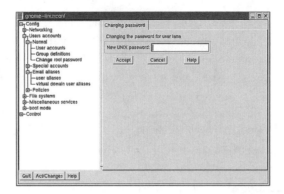

I should point out that Linux prefers passwords that don't contain just dictionary words, that don't resemble the user's username, and that contain a wide variety of characters, such as *snork928blar*. However, it doesn't insist on these passwords. You can type in any password that's at least six characters in length, then click the Accept button. If it's not a great password, you'll see a BAD PASSWORD message. Click the OK button to get past the error message. You'll be prompted to re-enter the password. Should you decide to ignore the BAD PASSWORD advice, simply retype the same password for verification, then click the Accept button. You'll be returned to the list of existing users, and you should be able to see the new account you created listed, in alphabetical order, along with other existing user accounts.

To complete the account, click the Quit button down near the lower-left corner of the LinuxConf window. You'll see the Status of the System tab with its options. Click the Act/Changes button. LinuxConf will set up the account and create a home directory for the user. When convenient, you can test the account by logging out, then trying to log back in under the new user's username and password.

You can, of course, create as many user accounts as you wish. Just remember that when defining a new user, if you already have a group in mind for that user, you'll want to add the group name to the user's Supplemental Groups option.

**Tip**

> If you grant a user special permissions to use LinuxConf, but they don't seem to get those permissions, you'll need to change the permissions of the LinuxConf file itself. Get to a command prompt and enter the command `chown root.root /bin/linuxconf` and then enter the command `chmod 4t55 /bin/linuxconf`.

## MORE ON PERMISSIONS

As superuser, you'll want to make sure that the shared directory for a group is accessible to everyone in that group. And you may also want to make sure the directory is inaccessible to people outside the group. You do this by setting permissions on the directory. In the preceding example, the superuser made `/home/accounting` the shared directory for the group. To put some controls on that directory, the superuser needs to get into the GNOME File

Manager (or a similar tool), get to the /home directory, right-click the accounting directory icon, and choose Properties. Then, on the Permissions tab, she wants to make sure that the owning group of that directory is indeed the accounting group (acct) and that members of that group have permission to read, write, and execute files in the directory. To keep other people out, she can remove all permissions for Other users (regular users outside the group), as in Figure 7.9.

**Figure 7.9**
Superuser has granted full access to the /home /accounting directory members of the acct group, and no access at all to "Other" users.

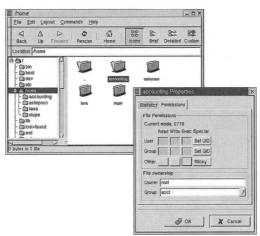

Users will also need to keep in mind that only the files that they move or copy to that shared directory will be visible to other people in the group. So, when Lana creates a document that she wants to share with other members in the accounting department, she needs to move or copy that file to /home/accounting. To allow them to view, but not change that file, she needs to set the Group permissions to Read Only (see Figure 7.10).

**Figure 7.10**
The owner of this file has granted herself Read/ Write permissions, other members of the acct (accounting) group Read permissions, and no permissions to the rest of the world.

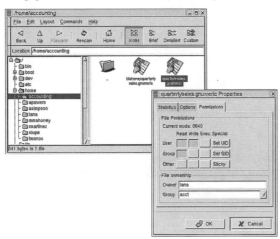

PART

II

CH

7

In these last two examples, the superuser set permissions for the /home/accounting directory, and the user Lana has set permissions for a specific file she owns. Permissions placed on directories have a slightly different meaning than permissions placed on files, as summarized in Table 7.1.

**TABLE 7.1   THE MEANING OF READ, WRITE, AND EXECUTE PERMISSIONS ON FILES AND DIRECTORIES**

| Permission | Effect on File | Effect on Directory |
|---|---|---|
| Read | Can view file's contents | Can view directory contents but not change those contents |
| Write | Can change file's contents | Can create and delete files in the directory |
| Execute | Can run file if it's a script or program | Can change to the directory, making it the working directory |

As you may recall from Chapter 3, this information is displayed in the highly compact format shown in Figure 7.11. A leading *d* indicates that the file is actually a directory; a leading hyphen indicates that the file is a regular file. An *r* stands for read, *w* for write, and *x* for executable. If the file doesn't have a certain permission assigned to it, a hyphen replaces the r, w, or x.

**Figure 7.11**
How permissions (mode) are displayed in an ls -l command and in the Permission column of a Custom File Manager view.

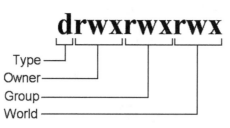

So, if a user were to view the contents of the /home/accounting directory using an ls command with the -l (long) option or File Manager view in a custom view that includes permissions, the permissions for the file shown in Figure 7.10 would look like this:

-rw-r-----

The leading hyphen indicates that it's a file rather than a directory, the owner has *read* and *write* permissions, the group has *read* permissions, and nobody has execute permissions (because the file is a document, not an executable script or program).

Note the line that reads Current mode: 0640 on the Permissions tab in Figure 7.10. Internally, Linux keeps track of a file permission using a single number that's called the *mode*. It just so happens that the number that defines the -rw-r----- permission is 0640. Exactly how Linux converts the permissions into a numeric mode is covered under the discussion of the chmod (change mode) command later in this chapter. For now, though, it's important only that you see how all the pieces of the puzzle—users, groups, and permissions—all fit together. As superuser in charge of overall system security, all this business of users, groups, and permissions will eventually have to become second nature to you. And it will, as you gain experience. The Set UID (Set User ID), Set GID (Set Group ID), and Sticky buttons in the Permissions tab are only relevant to executable files, and should generally be left in the "Off" position. There are some tricky things you can do with those settings. However, a discussion of those settings makes more sense within the context of securing executable program files in Chapter 17, "Advanced System Administration." For now, you're better off staying focused on managing users and groups.

### ENABLING AND DISABLING USERS ACCOUNTS

A user account can be disabled—without wiping it out completely—should you need to suspend the user's access to the computer. One example might be where an Internet service provider needs to suspend access to a user account when that user has gotten woefully behind in his monthly payments. To disable a user account, start LinuxConf and go to the Users Accounts list, just like when you first created the account. Then click the user's entry in the list and de-select The account is enabled option. Click the Accept button. The next time that user tries to log in, he won't be allowed to.

To re-enable the user's account in the future, simply go back to the Users Accounts tab in LinuxConf and select The Account Is Enabled Option again. Then click the Accept button. The user will be back in good standing, and able to log on to the system.

## CHANGING A USER'S ACCOUNT OR PASSWORD

The same techniques that you use to create a user account can be used to modify it. Go back to the Users Accounts list in LinuxConf, and click the account that you want to modify. Make any changes in the fields that you need to. If you specifically need to change the user's password, click the Passwd button, type in the new password, and click the Accept button. You'll be prompted to enter the same password again for verification.

## CHANGING THE SUPERUSER'S PASSWORD

For security reasons, changing the superuser's password is a little trickier than changing regular passwords. Of course, you first need to be logged in as the superuser if you want to change the superuser password. Then, in LinuxConf, you need to open the Config, Users Accounts, and Normal categories. Then click Changing the Password for User Root. The dialog box shown in Figure 7.12 appears.

**Figure 7.12**
Although it looks as if it's asking for a new root password, this dialog box is actually asking for the current root password.

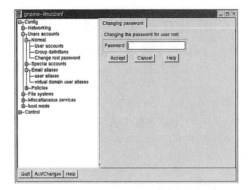

You need to type in the existing root password first, to verify that you know it! (There is no prompt on the screen informing you of this fact, though). Click the Accept button after entering the existing root password. Then, enter the new password and click the Accept button. Type in that same password a second time, for verification, click the Accept button, and the superuser's password is now changed. (Don't forget to enter the new password next time you log on!)

## DELETING A USER ACCOUNT

When a user leaves the system permanently and there's no chance of them ever needing an account again, you can delete the user's account in its entirety. You need to get back into LinuxConf and get to the list of current users. Click the account that you want to delete to bring up its details in the right pane. Then click the Del button. You'll be presented with three options for handling the user's account information, home directory, and any remaining mail in his inbox (see Figure 7.13).

**Figure 7.13**
Three options are presented whenever you delete a user account.

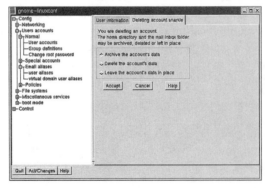

These options are as follows:

- **Archive the Account's Data:** The user's home directory, its contents, and email are compressed into a single file, then placed in the /home/oldaccounts directory. The name of the file consists of the user's login name, date the account was archived, and a job number followed by .tag.gz (for example, asimpson-1999-09-15-4243.tar.gz). The superuser can decompress the file (see Chapter 16, "Archiving, Backing Up, and Restoring") and recover its contents if need be.

- **Delete the Account's Data:** The user's home directory, its contents, and messages are permanently deleted from the system. There's no way to recover the deleted directory or messages.

- **Leave the Account's Data in Place:** The user's home directory, files, and messages are left as is, but the account is disabled so the user cannot log in.

Of the three options, deleting the user's data is the most severe because it doesn't leave the superuser any chance of reinstating the account in the future or recovering files or messages that the user left behind. The archive approach is safer because there is some hope of recovering messages or lost files. The last option is the same as temporarily suspending the user's account.

# COMMANDS FOR MANAGING USERS, GROUPS, AND PERMISSIONS

LinuxConf isn't the only way to manage user accounts. In fact, LinuxConf is just an alternative to using Linux commands to manage users. The sections that follow will discuss the many commands and behind-the-scenes files involved in managing user accounts.

## THE adduser AND passwd COMMANDS

The adduser command lets the superuser create a new user account right from the command prompt. The syntax for the command is either of the following:

```
adduser username
useradd username
```

username is the unique username that you want to apply to this new user. After creating the user account, the system administrator then needs to use the passwd command to define the password for that user. The syntax for assigning a password to a specific user is as follows:

```
passwd username
```

username is, of course, the username of the account to which you want to assign a password. So, as an example, let's say the superuser wants to create an account for Roberto Martinez with the username rmartinez. First she enters the following:

```
adduser rmartinez
```

Assuming there isn't already a user with that username, Linux accepts the command and displays another command prompt. To set up a password, the superuser then needs to enter this command:

```
passwd rmartinez
```

The prompt New UNIX password: appears on the screen. Type in a valid password (at least six characters in length, no blank spaces), and press Enter. The prompt Retype new UNIX password: appears on the screen. Type the same password a second time, and press Enter. After successfully entering both commands, the message passwd: all authentication tokens updated successfully appears on the screen. A home directory, named /home/rmartinez in this example, will be created automatically for the new user.

### USERS CAN CHANGE THEIR OWN PASSWORDS

A regular user can change his own password at any time. Click the GNOME Main Menu button and choose System, Change Password. As prompted on the screen, the user must first enter his current password, then click the OK button. Then, the user needs to enter his new password, following the instructions on the screen. Users will need to understand the "rules" of UNIX passwords for this to work (that is, at least six characters in length, no spaces).

A regular user can also change his password at the command prompt. Entering the command passwd at the command prompt will display the prompt (current) UNIX password:. The user needs to type in his current password and press Enter. The prompt New UNIX password: appears. The user needs to type in a new password, press Enter, retype the same password, and press Enter again. If the user really makes a mess of things, the superuser can always create a new password for the user via LinuxConf or the passwd username command syntax.

The adduser (or useradd) command automatically creates a home directory for the new user, following the standard /home/username practice. It does so by copying a directory named /etc/skel (for skeleton) into the /home directory. I mention this last tidbit of information so that if you ever wonder why there's a directory named /etc/skel on your system, you'll know that the adduser command (and LinuxConf as well) use that as the "skeleton" to create home directories for new users.

## THE who AND finger COMMANDS

The who command lists all users that are currently logged in to the system. On a single system, this will include any logins made in virtual consoles. Just enter the command who at any command prompt, and you'll receive some feedback like this:

```
root        tty1    Aug 30    14:30
asimpson        tty2    Aug 30    14:35
```

The first column tells you the username of the person logged in (that is, root and asimpson are logged in). The tty1 and tty2 tell you that root is logged into virtual console 1 and asimpson is logged onto virtual console 2. (The tty stands for "teletype," a throwback to the days when people actually logged into mainframe computers on teletype machines. Some people say tty stands for "terminal," though even that term is pretty dated!) The remaining two columns are the login date and time.

**Tip**    In GNOME, you can click the Main Menu button and choose Utilities, User Listing to view a list of all logged in users.

Adding a -u option, as shown here, adds another column that displays how long it has been since that user was active (actually did anything):

```
who -u
```

For example, suppose the command returned the following:

```
root       tty1    Aug 30    14:30       .
asimpson          tty2    Aug 30    14:35    00:45
```

You'd know that the root user (probably yourself) hasn't been inactive, whereas the user asimpson has been inactive for the last 45 minutes. The -count option displays the number of users that are currently logged in. For more options, see the man page for who.

> **Tip**
>
> Remember, *all* Linux commands have man pages. So to learn more about any command discussed in this book, just enter the command man *command*, where command is the command you want to learn more about.

The information displayed by who comes from a file named /var/run/utmp, which keeps track of all users currently logged in.

The finger command returns information about any user who has an account on the system. You must provide the username, though. For example, entering the following command

```
finger lana
```

might return something like the information shown here (assuming someone on the machine has the username lana):

```
Login: lana          Name: Louise Ana
Directory: /home/lana      Shell: /bin/bash
Last Login: Thu Aug 19 12:02 (PDT) on tt1
No mail
No plan
```

Most of this information reflects what the superuser enters when creating a user account. The username lana is for Louise Ana, her home directory is /home/lana, and she logs into the bash shell. The date and time of her last login is noted, and she has no outstanding mail messages, nor a plan. A *plan* is a file in the user's directory that contains information that the user wants displayed when someone fingers them. That file must be named .plan, and can be created with any text editor by any user. Most of the information that finger displays actually comes from a file named /etc/passwd, which you'll learn about a little later in this chapter.

> **Tip**
>
> Any user can add an office number, work phone, and/or a home phone number to their finger information. In GNOME, click the Main Menu button and choose System, About Myself. At the command prompt, enter the command chfn. The superuser can change any user's finger information using the syntax chfn *username*. Commas are *not* allowed in any of the fields.

## THE su, whoami, AND exit COMMANDS

The su (substitute user) command allows one user to temporarily become another user. Typically, it's used to allow the superuser to temporarily become a regular user, or to allow the superuser, when logged in as a regular user, to temporarily regain superuser powers. When you're logged in as a regular user and need to turn on your superuser powers, you can enter the following command all by itself:

```
su
```

A prompt appears asking for the password. You must type the superuser password and press Enter. The command prompt will change from the $ for regular users to the # sign for the superuser. You won't, however, be switched the /root home directory for the superuser. The su command never changes the current working directory.

When you've finished doing whatever you need to do as superuser and want to go back to your regular "safe" account, enter this command:

```
exit
```

The command prompt regains the # character that's used to indicate superuser powers.

If you're logged in as superuser and want to switch to another user's account, the command to enter is the following:

```
su username
```

username is the name of the user you want to log in as. For example, to log in as asimpson temporarily while in superuser mode, enter this:

```
su asimpson
```

The username asimpson appears in the prompt, and the prompt ends with the $ shown to all regular users. After doing whatever needed to be done while logged in as asimpson, enter the following command to go back to your original login account, root, in this example:

```
exit
```

If you try to log out by entering a logout command and see an error message that looks like this

```
logout: Not login shell: use 'exit'
```

that means you're currently operating under a substitute user name, and you're no longer logged in under the username you entered to log in to the computer (that is, you're no longer in your "login shell"). You'll have to enter an exit command to return to your original login shell. If you've entered several su commands, switching from one username to another, you'll have to keep entering exit commands until Linux finally accepts your logout command.

If you ever lose track of who you're logged in as, you can enter the command whoami. The screen will show the username you're currently logged in under then display a fresh command prompt. If you're trying to remember the name you initially logged in to the system with, enter the command logname instead.

If you're logged in as superuser, and simply want to execute one command that requires superuser status, you can use the following syntax:

```
su -c command
```

command is the command you want to execute. For example, if you're not logged in as root and you enter the command linuxconf, you'll get a Permission Denied error message. But if you enter this command, you'll be prompted for the superuser password:

**su - c linuxconf**

If you enter the correct password, you'll be taken into the character cell version of LinuxConf. When you quit LinuxConf and return to the command prompt, you'll still be logged in under the original "safe" username, rather than as root.

## chown: CHANGING OWNERS

Every file (including directories) is owned by someone. In a sense, the root (superuser) owns everything because the superuser can change file ownerships and bypass any permissions that the true owner has set on a file. The superuser is, after all, omnipotent. Either the owner of the file, or the superuser, can change a file's ownership using the chown (*change own*er) command. The following is the basic syntax for entering a chown command:

```
chown [options] [newUserID][[:newGroupID]] file
```

options are letter and/or word options associated with the command, newUserID is the name or number of the new owner to assign to the file, newGroupID is the name or number of new group that owns the file, and file is the name of the file, a list of filenames delimited by blank spaces, or an expression representing multiple files on which to perform the command. Valid usernames and the number associated with each are listed in the /etc/psswd file, valid group names and the number associated with each are listed in the /etc/group files. Both files are described in detail near the end of this chapter.

You can use a period (.) rather than a colon (:) to separate the newUserID and newGroupID values. You can omit the :newGroupID argument if you want to change only the owner. If you want to change only the group, you can omit the newUserID option, but you must precede the new group name with either a colon or a period. For example, either of the following commands changes the owner of the file named whatever.gnumeric in the current directory to lana, and the group to acct:

```
chown lana:acct whatever.gnumeric
chown lana.acct whatever.gnumeric
```

This command changes the owner of whatever.gnumeric to root, without changing its group ID:

```
chown root whatever.gnumeric
```

The following command changes the group ownership of all files in the /home/accounting directory to the group named acct:

```
chown :acct /home/accounting/*
```

PART

**II**

CH

**7**

The next command uses the period rather than the colon, but has exactly the same effect:

```
chown .acct /home/accounting/*
```

Assuming that the acct group has the group ID of 500, the following commands will have exactly the same effect as the preceding commands:

```
chown :500 /home/accounting/*
chown .500 /home/accounting/*
```

The -R (recursive) option extends the effect of the chown command to all files in all subdirectories beneath the current subdirectory. For example, the following command changes the ownership of all files and directories beneath the /whatever directory to root:

```
chown -R root /whatever/*
```

Like most Linux commands, the syntax for chown is terse. And as superuser, you can make a large, sweeping change by entering a brief command. So it's vitally important that you use commands cautiously with an understanding of what you're doing.

I suppose I should mention that there is also a chgrp (change group) command that you can use in place of chown when you're interested in changing only the group ID of a file or files. The basic syntax for chgrp is as follows:

```
chgrp [options] [newgroupID] [files]
```

Basically, it's the same as chown, but you don't need to precede the groupID with a colon or period. For example, the next command changes the groupID of a file named whatever.txt to the group named acct:

```
chgrp acct whatever.txt
```

If the group ID number associated with the acct group happens to be 500, the following command will have exactly the same effect:

```
chgrp 500 whatever.txt
```

## chmod: CHANGING PERMISSIONS

The chmod (change mode) command gives the superuser, and the owner of a file, a means of changing the permissions assigned to a file or group of files. The (rather hairy) syntax for chmod is as follows:

```
chmod [options]  [[u][g][o][a]] [=/+/-] [[r][w][x]]  [files]
```

options are any options supported by the command, and files is the name of the file to change, a set of filenames delimited by blank spaces, or an expression that defines a group of files. The u, g, o, and a parameters define which set of permissions are to be changed, as follows:

- **u**   user (owner)
- **g**   group

- ■  **o**  other (rest of the world)
- ■  **a**  all

The =, +, and - symbols represent how the change is to be made:

- ■  =  The file's permissions are set to exactly the specified permissions.
- ■  +  The permissions specified in the command are added to existing permissions.
- ■  -  The specified permissions are removed from the file.

The r, w, and x represent the read, write, and execute permissions. Thus, the following command sets the group permissions for the file named whatever.txt to read, write, and execute:

```
chmod g=rwx whatever.txt
```

The following command removes execute permissions for *o*ther users (the rest of the world) from all files in the current directory:

```
chmod o-x *
```

This command grants read permissions to everyone (*a*ll users) for files that end in *.txt within the current directory:

```
chmod a+r *.txt
```

You can set multiple permissions by adding multiple definitions separated by commas to the command. For example, the next command adds Read and Write permissions (rw) to whatever the *u*ser (owner) and *g*roup permissions are currently set to. It also adds Read (r) permissions to whatever the other (rest of the world) permissions are currently set to. It does so that every file in the directory named /home/accounting can be read and written to by its owner and group members, but can be only read by the rest of the world:

```
chmod ug+rw, o+w /home/accounting/*
```

As mentioned earlier in this chapter, Linux actually stores the mode (full set of permissions) for every file as a single brief number. It does this mainly because computers "like" numbers, in the sense that they process data more efficiently when information is expressed as a number rather than a string of characters. As you choose permissions from the Permissions tab of a File Properties dialog box, the number next to Current Mode changes to reflect the current set of permissions. At first glance, there may seem to be no rhyme or reason as to how the number correlates to the selected permissions. But, in fact, a fairly simple scheme is going on behind the scenes that makes it all happen. First, each possible permission—r, w, and x—has a numeric value associated with it, as summarized in Table 7.2.

TABLE 7.2 NUMERIC VALUES ASSOCIATED WITH READ, WRITE, AND EXECUTE PERMISSIONS

| Permission | Numeric Value |
| --- | --- |
| Read (r) | 4 |
| Write (w) | 2 |
| Execute (x) | 1 |

If permission is turned off, its value is zero. The sum of the numbers defines the full set of permissions. Thus, if a file read, write, and execute permissions (for example, rwx), the resulting sum is 7, or 4+2+1. If a file has read and execute permissions, but no write permissions (for example, r-x), then the sum is 4+0+1, or 5. If a file has only execute permissions (-x), the value is 0+0+1, or 1. No permissions (for example, ---) produces 0+0+0, which equals 0.

There are three types of users to whom permissions can be assigned: *owner* (also called *user*), *group*, and *other*. A simple three-digit number, then, is all it takes to express the permissions for all three groups. For instance, if a file's owner, group, and other permissions are all "turned on," as in rwxrwxrwx, each three-digit set has a sum of 7, so the number 777 is all it takes to express that. If a file has read/write permissions only (rw-) or Owner, the numeric value for the owner permission is 6. If that file has only read permissions for the group, then the group permission is 4+0+0, or 4. If everyone else (Other) has no permission, the number is 0+0+0, or 0. Thus, that full set of permissions can be expressed either as rw-r----- or 640.

**Tip**

The permission mode 0755 is fairly common because it grants everyone Read and Execute permissions, and it grants Write permissions to the Owner only.

When working in the Permissions tab of a File Properties dialog box, the current mode is generally expressed as a four digit number, such as 0640. For the time being, you can ignore the first digit. However, I will mention that the first digit does get a value if you choose the Set UID, Set GID, or Sticky button. But a detailed discussion of those permissions is best reserved for Chapter 17, where it will be easier to understand its relevance and context.

The chmodcommand will accept a number when setting permissions. For example, the command shown here sets the permissions of the file named annualSales.gnumeric in the current directory to 640, or rw-r-----:

```
chmod 640 annualSales.gnumeric
```

## MORE COMMANDS FOR MANAGING USERS AND GROUPS

LinuxConf is probably the easiest and safest way to manage users and groups. However, there are still more commands that you can use at the command prompt to perform those tasks. Rather than discuss each at length, however, it would probably be more efficient to just tell you what they are. Should you ever need to change or delete a user or group from the command prompt, you can always just open the man page for any of the following commands to get the syntax and full set of options that the command supports:

- **chfn:** Changes finger information for a user and allows them to add a work room number, work phone number, and home phone number in their finger information.

- **chsh:** Changes the user's default login shell (usually set to bash).

- **groupadd:** Creates a new group, and adds it to the /etc/group file.

- **groupdel:** Deletes a group from the /etc/group file.

- **groupmod:** Changes an existing group name or Group ID.

- **groups:** Lists all groups that a specific user belongs to.

- **id:** Displays a user's numeric UID (user ID) and group ID (GID), and supplemental groups.

- **newgrp:** Allows a user to log in to a different group.

- **userdel:** Deletes a user account and all related information about that user.

- **usermod:** Can be used to change any information about a user's account including full name, home directory, expiration date, group, supplementary groups, and more.

## WHERE USER AND GROUP INFORMATION IS STORED

All the information about users and groups exists in two simple files on your Linux system. User information is stored in /etc/passwd and group information is stored in /etc/group. Both are plain text files, so you can view their contents with the less program, or any text file viewer. For example, at the command prompt, you could enter either of these commands to view the contents of either file:

```
less /etc/passwd
less /etc/group
```

In the GNOME File Manager, you could open the /etc directory, right-click either the group or passwd filename's icon, and choose View to view the contents of either file.

You can edit either file directly using any text editor. However, doing so could be *very* dangerous because if you make even a tiny mistake, you could gum up the works so bad as to make the system unbootable. It's no exaggeration to say that the very reason for the existence of LinuxConf and all the commands discussed in this chapter is to discourage you from making changes to /etc/passwd and /etc/group files manually through a text editor. LinuxConf and the commands all verify what you're trying to do and make sure that the file is changed correctly, so it becomes impossible to make a small error with devastating consequences.

PART

II

CH

7

**Caution**

If you must edit /etc/passwd or /etc/group manually, make sure you make a backup copy of the file first. And make sure you have a Rescue disk available should you make a mistake that prevents the machine from booting correctly.

## THE etc/passwd FILE

While it's not my intent to encourage you to mess with these files directly, as superuser it's probably good to know how the information is arranged within each file. In /etc/passwd, each record (row) represents one user. Fields within each record are delimited with colons as shown in Figure 7.14.

**Figure 7.14**
The contents of a sample /etc/passwd file, which stores user account information on a Linux system.

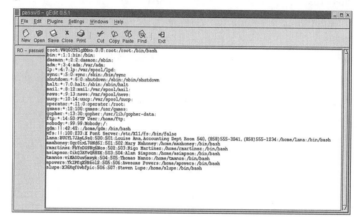

The order of fields in each record is as follows:

userName : encryptedPassword : UID : GID : comment : homeDir : loginShell

Each field is described in more detail here:

- **userName:** The user's username, or simply the name of the account for special (nonhuman) accounts like "bin" and "daemon."

- **encryptedPassword:** The user's password, encrypted to be unreadable. An asterisks (*) indicates no password and is common in nonhuman accounts. An *x* indicates a shadow password is in use (see Chapter 17).

**Note**

Actually, you can't change a user's password by editing /etc/passwd directly because the password is encrypted. You need to use LinuxConf or the passwd command to change a user's password.

- **UID:** The user's numeric ID, typically greater than or equal to 500 for human user accounts.

- **GID:** The user's numeric group ID, typically 500 or greater for human user accounts.

- **comment:** Information that appears when the user is fingered. Typically, this includes the user's full name for human accounts as well as office, work phone, and home phone delimited by commas if the user entered that information.

- **homeDir:** The user's home directory, typically /home/*username* for humans.

- **loginShell:** The command shell given to the user at login time, typically /bin/bash for humans.

## THE etc/group FILE

The /etc/group file contains information about groups and supplemental groups that various users belong to. The contents of a sample /etc/group file are shown in Figure 7.15.

**Figure 7.15**

The contents of a sample /etc/group file.

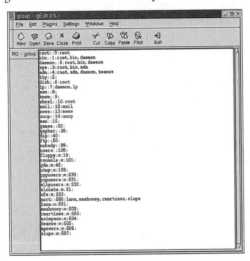

Each record in the file represents a group. The information for each group is divided into four fields separated by colons as follows:

*groupname : password : GID : usernames*

Each field contains the following information:

- **groupname:** The name of the group.

- **password:** Usually left blank or entered as a * because groups rarely have passwords. If a group does have a password, it will be encrypted.

- **GID:** The numeric group ID, usually 500 or greater for groups of human users.

- **usernames:** List of all users who belong to the group delimited with commas.

Both files are surprisingly simple in their formats, especially when you consider how confusing it can be—for a human—to keep track of all these users, groups, and permissions. The beauty of it all is that it really is, beneath the surface, quite simple. Every file has an owner, a group that it's associated with, and a set of permissions that decide how much access the owner, group, and everyone else has in accessing that file. All the users, and information

PART

**II**

CH

**7**

about each user, are listed in /etc/passwd. And all the group information, including who belongs to each group, is listed in the /etc/group file. And that, in a nutshell, is how it all works.

# CASE STUDY: RECOVERING FROM FORGOTTEN PASSWORDS

Forgotten passwords and usernames are a common problem. If a user forgets their username and/or password, they can't log in. As superuser, you can easily look up the user's username and assign them a new password if need be. First, you'll need to log in to the system as root. If you need to check the user's username, you can enter the following command to browse through the /etc/passwd file to discover the username:

```
less /etc/passwd
```

The password will be encrypted, so you can't read that. But you can certainly assign a new password to the user. Just enter this command:

```
passwd username
```

username is the username of the person whose password you're creating. Enter the new password and press Enter. You'll be prompted to type it again for verification. Go ahead and do so, and press Enter. The user should be able to log in with their username and password immediately.

## DEALING WITH A FORGOTTEN ROOT PASSWORD

Now, maybe that first troubleshooting problem wasn't so challenging. But suppose you forget the root password? Without the root password, you can only log in as a regular user, which wouldn't give you the power you need to create a new root password. Hmmmmm. What to do? There is a little trick you can perform to create a new password for the superuser, without even knowing the current superuser password. Here's how it works:

1. Power up the computer normally, and watch for the LILO boot prompt.
2. Within five seconds, type in the name of your Linux boot partition, followed by a blank space and the word single. Unless you specifically renamed the boot partition, it will be named linux (all lowercase), so you want to type in linux single and press Enter. (The *single* keyword tells Linux to boot up in a special single-user mode.)
3. The machine will go through a normal boot up, then stop at a prompt that looks like this:
   bash#
4. Type the command passwd and press Enter.
5. When the New UNIX password: prompt appears, type in a new root password and press Enter. Make sure the password is at least six characters long and contains no blank spaces.

6. If you see a BAD PASSWORD message, but the `Retype new UNIX password:` prompt appears anyway, don't worry about it. Just go on to the next step.

7. Retype the same password that you typed in step 5 and press Enter.

You should see a message that says `passwd: All authentication tokens updated successfully` followed by another `bash#` prompt. Now, reboot the machine by entering this command:

```
shutdown -r now
```

The machine will go through its usual shutdown procedure, then start booting up again. This time, when you see the LILO boot prompt, do nothing. Eventually you'll get to the login prompt, which will look something like this (although localhost will be replaced by the actual hostname of the machine):

```
localhost login:
```

Type `root` as usual and press Enter. At the Password prompt, type the new password you entered back in step 5 and press Enter. You should now be logged in as the superuser. From now on, log in with your new password. The password you forgot is now ancient history.

This time, don't forget the root password. And by the way, don't be telling a whole lot of people about this little trick. It'll be our little secret.

# CHAPTER 8

# CONFIGURING THE X WINDOW SYSTEM

## In this chapter

# UNDERSTANDING X

As you now know, you have two very different modes of interacting with Linux: The command-driven approach—where you're pretty much limited to typing one command at a time and pressing Enter—dates back to the earliest days of computing. (The first Apple computers and PCs with DOS were all command-driven, as were the earliest versions of UNIX.) As computer hardware became more powerful, though, the possibility of having the second approach of point-and-click graphical user interface (GUI) became a reality. By the late 1980s and early 1990s, the Apple Lisa, the Macintosh, and Microsoft's Windows had brought the GUI to personal computers. In the mainframe and UNIX world, it was a product known as the X Window System, or just X for short, that brought the GUI to mainframes.

Creating a GUI for UNIX posed some special problems because the UNIX platform has always been a multiuser network operating system, and different parts of the overall system could reside on different computers. So X was never really designed as a GUI, per se. Rather, it was designed as a program that would allow GUIs to function in a networked environment. There are really two components to X. The X *server* controls the keyboard, monitor, and mouse, but does not provide any specific look. The menus, borders that surround windows, and all the other "decorations" that give the GUI its look and feel come from the X *clients*. Hence, with X, you have a choice of exactly how you want your desktop to look and behave. Unlike the Macintosh and Windows environments—where what you see on the screen is what you get—X truly gives you the ability to choose a GUI that best suits your own tastes. You're not locked in to a particular GUI at all.

When you purchased Red Hat Linux, you also got a specific version of X known as XFree86. The "free" part stems from its origins in the GNU project and Free Software Foundation. The 86 part refers to its being built for the Intel 80x86 family of microprocessors which includes the 386, 486, Pentium, Pentium II, Pentium III, and "clone" chips like those from AMD and Cyrix. More specifically, you got Version 11, Release 6 of Xfree86. Hence, you'll sometimes see the version of X that came with your Red Hat package referred to as X11 or X11R6. But don't let that confuse you. Pretty much any name that starts with an uppercase X (including file and directory names) has something to do with X.

> **Tip**
>
> Like most GNU project programs, XFree86 has its own Web site. To visit, point your Web browser to www.xfree86.org.

# STARTING X

While installing Red Hat Linux, you were probably asked if you want to start X automatically when Linux first starts. If you selected Yes in response to that question, then you shouldn't have to do anything to start X—you'll automatically be taken into X when Linux starts. If you didn't opt to start X automatically, then when you first start Linux, you'll be taken to a command prompt. After entering your username and password, you need to enter the `startx` command to start X:

```
startx
```

If you've set up X so that it can handle multiple color depths, you can specify a color depth by following the `startx` command with a space, two hyphens and another space, -bpp (for bits per pixel), another space, and the color depth. For example, to start X with a color depth of 16, enter the following command:

```
startx -- -bpp 16
```

To start X at a color depth of 24, enter the following command:

```
startx -- -bpp 24
```

You should see GNOME (or perhaps another window manager) start up soon. Some good keystrokes to know about when X first starts are listed here:

- **Ctrl+Alt++on numeric keypad:** Switches to next highest resolution.
- **Ctrl+Alt+-on numeric keypad:** Switches to next lowest resolution.
- **Ctrl+Alt+Backspace:** Stops the X session and takes you back to the command prompt or to a graphical login prompt.
- **Ctrl+Alt+F1:** Takes you to the virtual console where some X error messages may be displayed.
- **Ctrl+Alt+F7:** Takes you from any virtual console back into the X GUI.

---

**Tip**

If the `startx` command produces only a gray screen with an *x* in the middle, give it a few minutes. The very first time X is started on a computer, it can take quite a while for it to pull all the necessary pieces together to get the proper display on the screen.

---

Entering the `startx` command may display an error message like this one:

```
bash: startx: command not found
```

If so, make sure that you typed the command correctly using all lowercase letters. If the error persists, then X isn't installed. The Red Hat documentation recommends that, if you encounter this problem, you should reinstall Red Hat Linux using Appendix B as your guide. Your best bet, at this time, would be to perform a GNOME Workstation class install, especially if you're new to Linux. The Server class install doesn't install X or any of the GUIs, which will make learning Linux more difficult. Should you opt for a Custom class install or upgrade, you'll eventually come to a screen that asks which components to install. At that screen you should choose at least the following options:

- The X Window System
- GNOME

- Mail/WWW/News Tools
- File Managers
- Console multimedia
- X multimedia support
- Emacs
- Emacs with X Window

If, after reinstalling Linux, you still can't get X to start, look through the Troubleshooting section at the end of this chapter. If you cannot get X to start under any circumstances, the most likely problem is that your video card isn't compatible with X. The only solution might be to replace your existing card with a new one. If you have a spare PCI slot inside your computer, a PCI card will be your best bet since XConfigurator (described in the next section) is capable of detecting certain PCI cards, which makes installation easier. Appendix C lists video cards for the Intel (PC) platform that X supports and the X Server that each card requires. For an up-to-the-minute list of video cards supported by X, and DEC Alpha and SPARC hardware, visit Red Hat's Hardware Compatibility Lists at `http://www.redhat.com/corp/support/hardware/index.html`.

## STARTING X MANUALLY OR AUTOMATICALLY

You're free to choose whether you want to start X manually or automatically at any time. In the real world, I suppose most system administrators and other more advanced users will want to start X manually because this gives you easy access to the command prompt without having to go through a terminal window. Your more casual users may prefer to have X started automatically, so they never have to encounter that "scary command prompt thing."

If you want to switch from a manual start to an automatic start on a computer, you must make absolutely sure that X is working properly on that computer first. Your best bet is to run a quick test using the telinit program. You should be logged in as root and at a command prompt, with no GUI running. Then, at the command prompt, enter the following command:

```
/sbin/telinit 5
```

After a short delay, you should see the Login screen for X. Go ahead and log in to make sure that GNOME (or any other GUI) appears on the screen. If you can't get a GUI to appear, you'll need to solve whatever problems are preventing X from starting before you try to make X start automatically on the computer. But, assuming that X did start up fine, you can use any of the following techniques to configure Linux to have X start automatically, or manually. Using LinuxConf, you can do the following:

1. In GNOME, click the Main Menu button and choose System, LinuxConf. Or enter the command `linuxconf` at a command prompt.

2. Open the Config, Boot Mode, and Mode categories, and then click Default Boot Mode (see Figure 8.1).

**Figure 8.1**
The Default Operation Mode option lets you choose between booting into a GUI (Graphic & Network), or to the command prompt (Text Mode & Network).

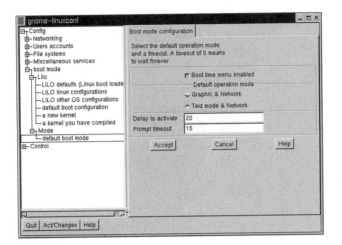

3. Under Default Operation Mode, choose Graphic & Network if you want X to start automatically, or choose Text Mode & Network if you want to boot into the command prompt.

4. Click the Accept button.

5. Click the Quit button in the lower-left corner of the LinuxConf window.

6. Click the Activate the Changes button.

The configuration file that LinuxConf modifies to store your preference is /etc/inittab. If LinuxConf isn't handy on a particular machine, or you have some other reason to edit that file manually, you can use any text editor to make the change. Follow these steps:

> **Caution**
>
> Use extreme caution when manually editing /etc/inittab. Specifically, make sure you enter the id:3:initdefault: or id:5:initdefault: command *exactly* as shown (with colons, no blank spaces). A faulty line in /etc/inittab can really mess up your Linux boot-up procedure!

1. Open /etc/inittab using any text editor.

2. Look for the line that reads id:3:initdefault: or id:5:initdefault:.

3. To start X manually, change the 5 to a 3. To start X automatically, change the 3 to a 5. *Do not make any other changes!*

4. Save and close the inittab file.

> **Tip**
>
> In case you're wondering what's with the 3 and the 5, it all has to do with Linux *runlevels*, which you'll learn about in Chapter 11. By default, the character cell login prompts appear in runlevel 3 at bootup. X starts in runlevel 5.

## OVERRIDING THE DEFAULT SETUP

Whether you choose to start X manually or automatically, you can always override that decision for a single session, without changing the inittab file. This is an especially good thing to know for a system administrator because if you set up all your users' machines to start X automatically, you can boot yourself to a command prompt whenever it becomes necessary to do so. If the machine is already running, you'll want to reboot it using the shutdown -r now or the Reboot option in GNOME's Logout dialog box. As the computer is booting up, keep an eye on the screen and watch for the LILO boot prompt (remember, it stays on the screen for only five seconds, so you have a narrow window of opportunity there). When the LILO boot prompt appears, enter the following command:

linux 3

If, for whatever reason, you actually do want to go straight into the GUI, you could enter this command instead:

linux 5

> **Tip**
>
> You can change how long the LILO Boot prompt stays visible on the screen by modifying the Prompt Timeout in Seconds option in LinuxConf, available under the Config, Boot Mode, LILO, Mode, Default Boot Mode Categories. Chapter 11 discusses this topic in more depth.

You can then log in as root and do whatever configuration is needed on that machine.

# CONFIGURING X FOR YOUR HARDWARE

To get X working correctly on your computer, you need to tell it about your video hardware and mouse. The easiest way to do so is through a program called Xconfigurator. That program is automatically run during installation of Red Hat Linux so you shouldn't need to run it again after a successful installation. However, if you change your video card—or just can't seem to get X to run correctly—making another pass through Xconfigurator might help.

Xconfigurator will ask you some detailed questions about your video hardware, and you'll need to answer those questions *accurately* to get a good result. So before you run Xconfigurator, try to gather as much of the information below as possible. (You might not need it all. But if you do, it will be handy to have it ready when asked for it.)

- The make and model of your mouse (usually printed on the bottom of the mouse), and whether it plugs into a serial port (rectangular) or PS/2 port (round) on the back of the computer.
- The type of keyboard you have. The brand name is usually sufficient.

- The make and model of your monitor, usually printed on the front or back of the monitor.

- If you have an unsupported monitor, you'll need to know your monitor's vertical and horizontal refresh rates.

- The make and model of your video card. If the video card isn't a PCI card that Linux Setup can probe, you'll need to know how much video memory the card has and which clockchip (if any) it uses.

You should also grab your original Red Hat Linux 6.2 CD-ROM #1 (for Intel) that came with your Red Hat boxed set because you may need it during the X installation.

**Tip**

Technical information about your monitor and video card is usually available in the manual that came with those components or with your computer. If you can't find those, consider contacting your computer manufacturer, monitor manufacturer, and/or video card manufacturer (if known). Most companies have Web sites that provide this technical information or a Customer Support line you can call.

When you've gathered as much information as you can, you can start Xconfigurator by entering the following command:

```
Xconfigurator
```

(Note that only the X is uppercase in the command.) At the Welcome screen that appears, press Enter to choose OK. What happens next all depends on the hardware installed in your system, as discussed under the heading "Get Your GUI Working" in Appendix B. Turn there now to continue with the Xconfigurator program. Should you encounter a problem accompanied by the error message `Server doesn't exist, can't continue`, you'll need to come back to the Troubleshooting section at the end of this chapter and follow the instructions under the heading that matches that error message.

## CONFIGURING X HARDWARE MANUALLY IN XF86CONFIG

The information that X needs to communicate with your hardware is stored in the configuration file `/etc/X11/XF86Config`. Normally, Xconfigurator creates and maintains that file. But, as with any configuration file, you have the option of opening and editing it yourself using any text editor, such as gEdit. (Start gEdit from the GNOME Main Menu button and Applications menu. Then choose Open from gEdit's toolbar and open `/etc/X11/ XF86Config`.) Figure 8.2 shows how the top part of XF86Config looks when open in gEdit.

**Note**

It's important to make a backup copy of *any* configuration file before you edit it, just in case you make some drastic mistake. If you need a reminder on how to do that, see "Backing Up Configuration Files" in Chapter 6.

**Figure 8.2**

The /etc/X11/ XF86Config file, open for editing in gEdit.

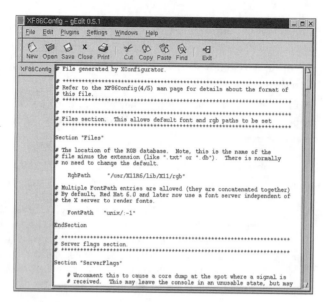

The XF86Config file is broken into several major sections titled Files, ServerFlags, Keyboard, Pointer, Monitor, GraphicsDevice, and Screen.

As you may recall from Chapter 6, any line that starts with a hash mark (#) in a configuration file is a comment, which means the Linux completely ignores that line. Many of the comments explain what the various lines do, and why you might want to uncomment a particular command. So in some ways, the best source of documentation for XF86Config is the file itself.

As you look through the XF86Config file, you'll notice that most of the lines in it are commented out. The vast majority of those lines are plain-English descriptions of the various commands within XF86Config. And those should always remain commented. Occasionally, you'll come across an actual command that's been commented out, such as the following:

#NoTrapSignals

The command is there just as an option. To activate the command, you'd need to remove the # character in front of it. Of course, you don't want to uncomment commands at random. You should know why you want to uncomment a command before you do so. The plain-English comment above a commented-out command usually describes why the command is currently commented out. This chapter will also explain which commands you might want to uncomment, and why.

**Tip**

The XF86Config file has its own man page, which also describes the commands in the file. Enter the command man xf86config at any command prompt to view the man page.

In the sections that follow, we'll look at the options in XF86Config most likely to be used by Red Hat Linux 6.2 users on an Intel platform (PC). For more detailed technical information and additional options, see the man page for XF86Config. You'll also find many documents dealing with specific hardware devices in the /usr/X11R6/lib/X11/doc folder. From File Manager, you can simply right-click any document icon and choose View to read the file. From the command prompt you can use the *less* program. For example, entering the command cd /usr/X11R6/lib/X11/doc will take you to the appropriate directory. Entering the ls command will list filenames in that directory. To view a document, type the less command followed by a blank space and the name of the document to view, such as less VideoModes.doc.

## THE Files SECTION

The Files section of XF86Config defines the locations of the X RGB (Red, Green, Blue) database, which in turn contains information about colors used in X. Normally, this is set to /usr/X11R6/lib/X11/rgb and shouldn't be changed, unless you specifically want to use some other color database. To view the contents of the default RGB database and the color name associated with each color, view the contents of the file /usr/X11R6/lib/X11/rgb.txt using any text file viewer or editor.

Likewise, the FontPath setting is set to unix/:-1 and should not be changed. Earlier versions of Red Hat Linux listed paths to specific fonts here. The version of X that comes with Red Hat 6.2 uses the xfs font server to manage fonts. xfs gets paths to installed fonts from its configuration file /etc/X11/fs/config file. The fonts themselves are available in /usr/X11R6/lib/X11/fonts.

## THE ServerFlags SECTION

The ServerFlagssection provides options that determine how X behaves. The three options in this section are initially commented out, but you can activate any option by removing the # sign at the start of the line. The three settings are summarized here:

- **#NoTrapSignals**—If activated, causes a core dump at the point where a signal is received. Activating this option can cause problems. The option should be activated only by X programmers who need to do some debugging.

- **#DontZap**—If activated, disables the Ctrl+Alt+Backspace key, which provides a quick exit out of X. This should not be enabled unless there's some really compelling reason to disallow the Ctrl+Alt+Backspace keys.

- **#DontZoom**—When activated, disables the Ctrl+Alt++ and Ctrl+Alt+- keystrokes used to change resolutions on-the-fly. The only reason to use this option is to lock the user into the default screen resolution.

## THE Keyboard SECTION

The Keyboard section defines how your keyboard operates in X. The default protocol is Standard, and should only be changed on systems that use the Xqueue event driver. With

Xqueue, the Protocol Standard should be commented out, and Protocol Xqueue should be activated. If you don't know what Xqueue is, then you probably don't have it.

The AutoRepeat setting determines how the typematic feature of the keyboard acts under X, using the parameters *delay* and *rate*. The delay is the length of time that the key must be held down before it starts repeating itself. The default is 500 milliseconds (about half a second). The rate is how quickly it repeats itself when the delay period is up. The default is 5 times per second.

The ServerNumLock option, when activated, forces the server to handle the Num Lock key internally. With most keyboards you'll get the best use of the Num Lock key and numeric keyboard by leaving this option commented out. The Xleds section determines how keyboard LEDs (lights) for the Scroll Lock, Num Lock, and Caps Lock keys on the keyboard function. Leaving this option disabled allows the LEDs on most keyboards to function normally. Setting any value to a negative number disables the key's LED.

The LeftAlt, RightAlt, ScrollLock, and RightCtrl options define the roles played by the Alt keys, the Scroll Lock key, and the Control key on the right side of the keyboard. The default settings make the Alt key behave like the UNIX Meta key, the Scroll Lock key as the UNIX Compose key, and the right Control key behave as a Control (Ctrl) key. This is the best setting for most modern keyboards.

The XkbDisable option determines whether or not XKB keyboard extensions are processed or executed. Typically, you'll want to leave this option commented out so that XKB extensions are enabled. The lines that follow this section provide some examples of XKB extensions, and explanations of why you might want to change some of them.

### THE Pointer (MOUSE) SECTION

The Pointer section defines the mouse, and how it behaves in X. The protocol setting should be PS/2 for a PS/2 mouse, Auto for a serial mouse, or BusMouse for a bus mouse. Most of the non mouse pointing devices will also work. For example, the trackballs on most laptops can be configured as PS/2 mice, by setting the protocol setting to PS/2. If you have an ALPS GlidePoint, you can set the protocol to serial.

The Device setting should point to the device driver for the mouse, typically /dev/mouse. The BaudRate and SampleRate options should be left commented out, except for LogiTech mice that require those settings. The Emulate3Buttons option is a must for two-button mouse users. It allows simultaneous clicking of the left and right mouse buttons to simulate a click on the middle button of the three-button mouse.

The Emulate3TimeOut option determines how closely together, timewise, the two mouse buttons have to be pressed in order to count as a middle mouse click rather than a separate left click and right click. The default setting of 50 milliseconds should be adequate for most mouse devices. The ChordMiddle option handles three-button mouse devices that don't treat the middle mouse button as a separate button. The LogiTech Mouseman is such a mouse; pressing the middle button sends a simultaneous left and right click to the computer. If your middle mouse button doesn't do what it's supposed to do, try activating the ChordMiddle option in your XF86Config file.

### THE Monitor SECTION

The Monitor section defines the characteristics of your monitor. Most of the information in this section comes straight from the Xconfigurator program, and you shouldn't make any changes unless you're sure there's a good reason. In particular, you don't want to change the HorizSync or VertRefresh options because if you set them too high, you could damage your monitor.

The long list of standard mode timings at the end of the section contains mostly commented-out lines. The only active, uncommented lines are the ones that Xconfigurator determined will work with your monitor. If you really want to tweak those settings, make sure you understand your monitor's capabilities. You might also want to read the Video Timing HOWTO at /etc//usr/X11R6/lib/X11/doc/VideoModes.doc.

### THE Graphics Device SECTION

The Graphics Devicesection defines your video card. Again, most of this information comes from the Xconfigurator program and should be changed only when you're sure a change needs to be made. Strangely, though, the VideoRam setting is commented out in most XF86Config files, despite the fact that you may have had to go to great lengths to find that information to enter it into the Xconfigurator program. You can uncomment that if it appears to be set to the correct value for your video card.

> **Tip**
>
> See the README files in /usr/X11R6/lib/X11/doc for details on specific video cards.

### THE Screen SECTION

The Screen Section tells X which X Server to use, what color depth to use, and which screen resolutions are available on the machine. If you selected multiple color depths and resolutions in XConfigurator, as in Figure 8.3, you'll see a subsection for each color depth listed under the Accelerated Servers option.

There's a subsection for each color depth, 8, 16, and 24. The resolutions available at each color depth are listed next to the Modes heading. The first-listed resolution is the default resolution that's used when X first starts. To choose a default resolution for when X first starts, you can reorder the resolutions so that your favorite is first. Just make sure each resolution is enclosed in a pair of quotation marks and separated by a blank space:

```
# The accelerated servers (S3, Mach32, Mach8,
# 8514, P9000, AGX, W32, Mach64 I128, and S3V)
Section "Screen"
  Driver   "accel"
```

```
Device    "ViRGE/VX"
Monitor   "Nokia 447X"
Subsection "Display"
  Depth    8
  Modes    "640x480" "800x600" "1024x768"
  ViewPort  0 0
EndSubsection
Subsection "Display"
  Depth    16
  Modes    "640x480" "800x600" "1024x768"
  ViewPort  0 0
EndSubsection
Subsection "Display"
  Depth    24
  Modes    "640x480" "800x600" "1024x768"
  ViewPort  0 0
EndSubsection
EndSection
```

**Figure 8.3**
This S3 video card is capable of handling lots of resolutions and color depths. I've selected nine in the sample XConfigurator screen.

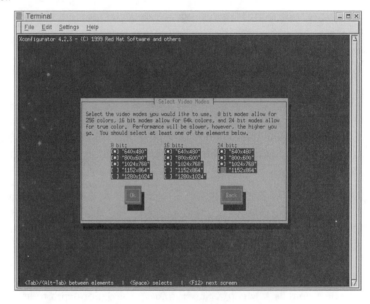

For example, if you want $1024 \times 768$ to be your default resolution, change the Modes entry as shown here:

```
Modes    "1024x768" "800x600" "640x480"
```

Remember that, if you want to choose one of the color depths listed in this section of XF86Config, you need to use the following syntax when entering the startx command:

```
startx -- -bpp xx
```

xx matches one of the Depth numbers (8, 16, or 24 in the example shown). Entering the startx command without the -bpp option defaults to a color depth of 8bpp (also known as *256 colors*).

**Getting X to Fit the Screen**
If you get X running, but it occupies only a part of the screen or seems to be off to one side, you can do a couple of things to rectify the situation. First, start with your highest resolution (the one that shows the most stuff on the screen) by pressing Ctrl+Alt++ (using the + key on the numeric keypad) until you reach the highest resolution. Then, use the controls on the front of your monitor to adjust the display width, height, vertical, and horizontal centering, and pincushion (roundness) until you get a perfect fit, or the best possible fit.

If you can't get a perfect fit, you can use the xvidtune program to try for a better fit. In a terminal window, enter the command xvidtune. Read the warning, and then click its OK button. Then, experiment with the Left, Right, Wider, Narrower, Up, Down, Shorter, and Taller buttons. Each time you click one of those buttons, click the Test button to see its effect so that you can monitor your progress. Click the Apply button to save the change if you like it. When everything looks pretty good, click the Quit button. More information on using xvidtune is available in the file /usr/X11R6/lib/X11/doc/VideoModes.doc. If you're using multiple resolutions, you'll probably have to repeat the process for each resolution.

# UNDERSTANDING DISPLAY MANAGERS

Display managers are programs that provide a graphical login screen, as opposed to the command prompt login. Red Hat Linux ships with three display managers, each with its own unique graphical login box.

The three display managers are as follows:

- **xdm (X Display Manager):** The most basic display manager, this one provides a simple graphical login screen with no options.

- **gdm (GNOME Display Manager):** The login screen you use when logging into GNOME. Its Options button provides some added flexibility for making decisions about how you want to log in. It also provides options for choosing a language, rebooting the computers, and shutting down.

- **kdm (KDE Display Manager):** Like GNOME, KDE is a complete desktop environment with its own unique X login window. You'll learn about KDE in Chapter 10.

With so many display managers available to you, things can become confusing at times. The startx script that starts X from a command prompt is designed to "remember" which display manager the user last logged out from, and then use that same display manager to log them back in the next time. This is fine for users who work only within one display manager (provided they don't do too much exploring!). But as system administrator, you need to be aware that you can also start X with the display manager of your choice, entering the command xdm, gdm, or kdm where you would otherwise enter the startx command. The graphical login dialog box for that display manager will appear on the screen.

**Note**
The kdm display manager will be available only if you install the KDE desktop environment, as discussed in Chapter 10.

If you get lost in other display managers or window managers, you can always use switchdesk to get back. Open a terminal window in your current GUI and enter the command `switchdesk`. Choose GNOME from the Desktop Switcher, then click the OK button. Click the OK button, and then log out of your current GUI using the Exit or Logout command on its main menu. When you get to the gdm, choose Sessions, GNOME from the Options button, then log in normally.

**Tip**
To pick a single default display manager, you can create or modify the `/etc/sysconfig/desktop` file, as discussed later in this chapter.

## EXPLORING THE WINDOW MANAGERS

A window manager is the highest-level component of the X Window system, and ultimately defines the specific look and feel of the GUI. The borders that surround windows on the screen, the little buttons inside the window border, the various *widgets* (controls) that appear within dialog boxes, and other details belong to the window manager. In fact, if you were to run X without a window manager, you'd still see open windows on the desktop. But you wouldn't see any window borders, buttons, desktop shortcuts, or any other "decorations" that the window managers provide. You could make this happen by choosing Options, Sessions, FailSafe from the gdm login window. Without any decorations, however, you'll only be able to type commands in the terminal window, and bail out by pressing Ctrl+Alt+Backspace.

The sections that follow will briefly discuss the window managers that come with Red Hat Linux 6, and some that don't. I suspect that in most modern work environments, users will prefer to work in the more integrated desktop environments like GNOME or KDE. But as system administrator, you should at least be aware that there are many window managers to choose from, and have a sense of what each looks like on the screen. In the interest of brevity, I'll show what each window manager looks like, point out some of the more interesting features, and point you to sources of additional information.

**Tip**
The Web site at `http://www.plig.org/~xwinman` offers a guide to window managers for the X Window system, with sample screen shots of each. In color, of course!

## THE ANOTHERLEVEL WINDOW MANAGER

The AnotherLevel window manager that comes with Red Hat 6 is actually a version of the fvwm window manager, configured to work well with the Red Hat Linux distribution. The *vwm* part of the name stands for Virtual Window Manager. Nobody is quite sure what the *f* stands for anymore. At one time, "Feeble" seemed to be favored; you can find a list of words that the *f* might stand for, posted in the FAQs at the fvwm Web site (`www.fvwm.org`). AnotherLevel is also called fvwm2 and fvwm95 in some circles (which really helps to confuse things!).

Figure 8.4 shows how AnotherLevel looks when it first appears on the screen. AnotherLevel's greatest strengths are its flexibility and small memory footprint, which allows it to run on computers with limited RAM. AnotherLevel is popular among experienced UNIX users who often have to work with Windows machines because the look and feel of AnotherLevel is similar to that of the newer versions of Windows, including Windows 95, 98, and 2000. For example, you can see a taskbar and Start button along the bottom of the screen. Mouse buttons and shortcut keys are also similar to those in Windows. Its File Manager, named xfm, is reminiscent of the My Computer file manager in many version of windows.

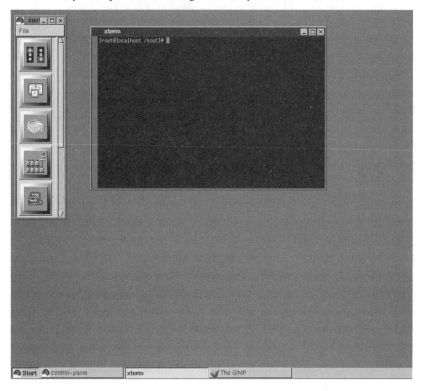

**Figure 8.4**
The AnotherLevel window manager, also known as fvwm2 or fvwm95.

If you're in GNOME or at the command prompt and want to see the AnotherLevel, AfterStep, or LessTiff window managers, you should first load the xdm display manager. From the command prompt, just enter the command xdm. If you're in GNOME, you can use the Desktop Switching Tool to switch to AnotherLevel first. Use either of the following techniques:

- Click the GNOME Main Menu button and select KDE Menus, System, Desktop Switching Tool.

- In a terminal window in any GUI, enter the command switchdesk.

Either way, you'll come to the Desktop Switcher dialog box. Choose Another Level, then click the OK button. You'll see a message about restarting X. Click its OK button and close any other open windows on your desktop. Then click the GNOME Main Menu button and choose Logout, Logout, Yes. You should come to the login dialog box for xdm. (If you end up at the command prompt, enter the command xdm). Log in normally.

The list of buttons near the upper-left corner of the desktop is the Control Panel. The buttons provide quick access to some of the configuration tools that system administrators need to set up printers, modems, a network and other Linux features. You can point to any button to see its tooltip; click any button to select it. The large dark window titled nxterm is a terminal window where you can enter Linux commands. To view the AnotherLevel Start menu, click the Start button or click any part of the desktop. You can also right-click the desktop to get the more familiar System menu onto the screen. The menus all work as you would probably expect. Point to any item that has a triangle at its right edge to view a submenu. Click any item to select it. Applications and utilities on the Programs menu are categorized in much the same way they are in GNOME.

Switching to another window manager from within fvwm95 is easy. Open the Start menu and choose Exit Fvwm, Switch To. A list of other installed window managers that are immediately accessible appear on a submenu (see Figure 8.5).

**Figure 8.5**
Use the Switch To option on AnotherLevel's Exit menu to switch to another window manager.

To learn more about AnotherLevel, you can visit the AnotherLevel and fvwm man pages. You'll also find some README files and other documentation in the /usr/doc/fvwm2-2.2 and /usr/doc/fvwm2-2.2/docs directories. The official home page for fvwm is at http://www/fvwm.org. There are also two mailing lists, which you can join from the fvwm Web site.

## THE AFTERSTEP WINDOW MANAGER

The AfterStep window manager was originally based on the look and feel of the NeXTSTEP interface used on the NeXT computers. Over the years, however, it has evolved into a very configurable animal, and you can change its look and feel to resemble many different operating systems. Still, it's probably most widely used by UNIX users who also work on NeXT machines.

If you're in the fvwm window manager, you can switch to AfterStep by choosing that name from the Switch To menu. When AfterStep first appears on the screen, it will look something like Figure 8.6. The Control Panel appears in the upper-left corner of the desktop. An nxterm terminal window is also open on the desktop. The thin bar across the top is actually a set of buttons, each representing an open window on the desktop. You can quickly raise an open window to the forefront by clicking its button. The column of buttons along the lower-right edge of the screen, called Wharf, provide quick access to commonly used features. The topmost button opens up some documentation for AfterStep. You reduce and expand the size of Wharf by right-clicking it.

**Figure 8.6**
The AfterStep window manager borrows its look and feel from the NeXT family of computers.

To open the main menu in AfterStep, just click anywhere on the desktop. Options with submenus are indicated with a couple of dots to the right of the option label. By default, the current menu disappears as soon as you make a selection from it. But you can make a menu sticky by clicking its title bar before you make a selection. When you do, a Close (X) button appears at the top of the menu. And the menu remains open until you click that Close button.

AfterStep offers many different looks and feels. If you open the main menu and then the Desktop menu, you'll see many options for controlling the desktop. For example, in Figure

8.7 I've opened the Desktop menu and, from there, the Look, Feel, and Update menus. To try a different look and feel, simply choose an option from the Feel, Look (or both menus). Then click the Update Look and Feel option in the Update menu. Couldn't be any easier! To switch to another window manager from within AfterStep, choose Quit, Switch To from the AfterStep main menu, then choose a window manager from the submenu that appears.

**Figure 8.7**
The Look, Feel, and Update menus under the Desktop main menu option provide options for changing the look and feel of the AfterStep window manager.

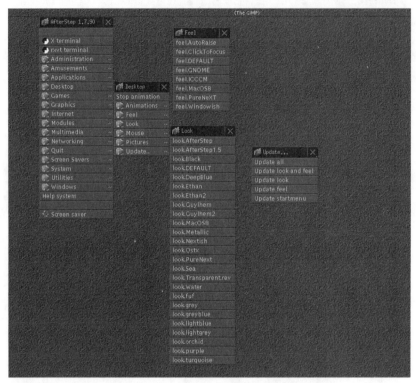

Documentation for AfterStep is available by simply clicking the AfterStep button at the top of the Wharf button bar. The official Web site for AfterStep is at www.afterstep.org. You can view FAQs and documentation at that site, as well as subscribe to mailing lists. Closer to home, there's a man page for Afterstep (man afterstep).

## THE LESSTIF WINDOW MANAGER (MWM)

The LessTif window manager is based on the commercial OSF/Motif window managers popular in the UNIX sector. It's actually a modified version of the fvwm2 window maker with a Motif look and feel, and it sometimes goes by the acronym mwm (for *Motif window manager*). Motif is a commercial product, whereas LessTif is distributed freely under the terms of the GNU GPL. Hence, LessTif is sometimes called "the poor man's Motif." Its main strength is its ability to run programs that were designed for the Motif window manager. The programmers maintain a list of Motif apps that currently do, and don't, work with LessTif at http://www.lesstif.org/apps.html.

As you can see in Figure 8.8, LessTif is fairly spartan in its appearance. Windows don't have a Close button, and the Maximize button is where you'd normally expect to find the Close button. To close a window, you need to double-click the button at the upper left corner of the window, or click that same button and choose Close from the menu that appears. The LessTif Start menu is accessed by clicking any part of the desktop. You can add a taskbar and the Wharf button bar to the desktop by choosing the appropriate options from the System Utilities option on the Start menu. You can switch to another window manager by opening the Start menu and choosing Exit, Switch To.

**Figure 8.8**
The LessTif window manager is based on the Motif window manager that's widely used in the UNIX community.

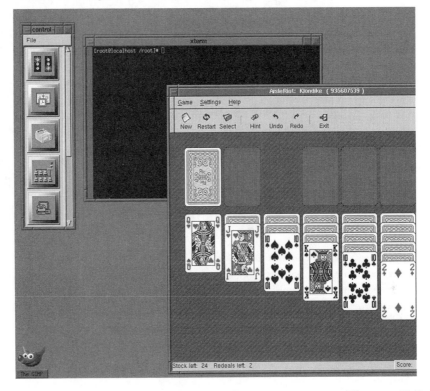

As one might expect, there is a Web page for LessTif at www.lesstif.org. There you'll find FAQs, documentation, access to mailing lists, and more.

## THE WINDOW MAKER WINDOW MANAGER

Window Maker is designed to provide the look and feel of the NeXTSTEP operating system, with support for GNUstep applications (see Figure 8.9). GNUstep (www.gnustep.org) is an attempt to provide applications that follow the framework specified by the OpenStep (www.openstep.org) specification, developed by NeXT, which is now part of Apple computer. The GNUStep group plans to track the development of the MacOS X system and remain compatible with its offerings. In short, Window Maker is the window manager for people who like the look and feel of OpenStep/Apple application programs.

**Figure 8.9**
The Window Maker window manager.

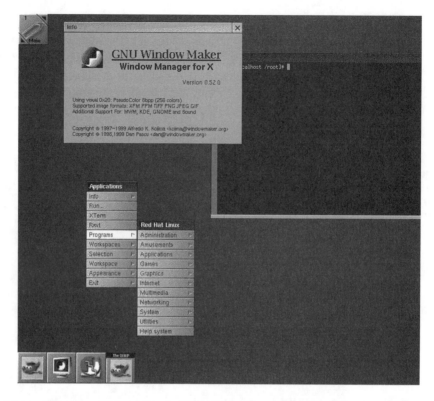

Window Maker includes a clipboard and a Wharf-like button bar. Minimized application icons appear as buttons near the bottom of the desktop. To open the main menu, right-click anywhere on the desktop. To get a menu to stay open, click its title bar. To close an open menu, click its X button.

Window Maker is included with Red Hat Linux 6.1, but isn't installed by default. To use it you have to install two packages from the Red Hat CD-ROM—libPropList*.rpm and WindowMaker*.rpm. You can use either GnoRPM or the rpm command at the command prompt to do so. After you install both packages, you need to run the script /usr/X11R6/bin/wmaker.inst from the command prompt or a terminal window. After you've done so, you should find that Window Maker has been added to the list of xdm window managers (that is, AfterStep, fvwm95, and LessTif), as shown in Figure 8.10.

**Note**

Chapter 13 will discuss the ins and outs of RPM in detail.

**Figure 8.10**
Once Window
Maker has been
installed, you
should find it in
your list of win-
dow managers
that you can
choose from.

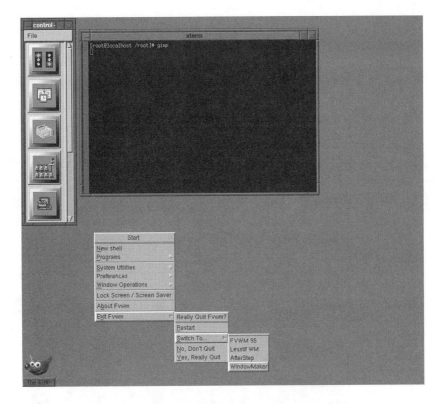

You can find more information about Window Maker at (you guessed it) www.
windowmaker.org. You'll find access to mailing lists there as well. If you install Window
Maker from your Red Hat CD-ROM, you'll also find a lot of documentation in the /usr/
doc/WindowMaker-0.52.0. The README file implies that there's an INSTALL document
that you can read for installation help.

## THE ICE WINDOW MANAGER

The ICE window manager (Ice WM) is designed to provide the look and feel of Motif, OS/2
Warp 4, OS/2 Warp 3, and Windows such as 95. It's highly compatible with GNOME and
can be configured via the GNOME control center (Chapter 9). It offers a wide variety of
"focus models," which gives you lots of leeway in deciding how and when windows on the
desktop get the keyboard focus. When installed and running in GNOME, it gives a slightly
different look to window borders and the panel (see Figure 8.11).

Ice WM doesn't come with your Red Hat package, but you can download a copy from
http://www.kiss.uni-lj.si/~k4fr0235/icewm. You'll find several different files to download
from that site. You only need to download the .rpm file for Red Hat Linux. (The version I
downloaded was icewm-0.948-1.i386.rpm, but there may be a newer version by the time you
get there.) Once downloaded, you can install Ice WM using GnoRPM or the rpm -i
command at the command prompt. When the installation is finished, you'll find that Ice WM

has been automatically added to your list of window managers in GNOME (open the GNOME Configuration Tool from the panel and choose Window Manager under the Desktop category). You'll also find several documentation files in your /usr/doc/ icewm-0.9.48. (The numbers at the end of that directory name will match whichever version of Ice WM you downloaded.)

The official Web site and access to mailing lists for Ice WM are at www.kiss.uni-lj.si/ ~k4fr0235/icewm.

**Figure 8.11**
The ICE window manager, running in GNOME.

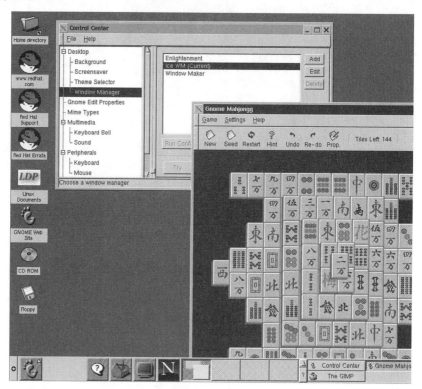

## WHAT ABOUT GNOME AND KDE?

You may wonder why I haven't mentioned GNOME, which you've seen in earlier chapters, and KDE, which you may have heard about elsewhere. Although those two products certainly do provide a look-and-feel, both are actually better described as *desktop environments* because they offer much more than your basic window decorations. GNOME, as you saw in Part I of this book, offers extensive drag-and-drop, desktop shortcuts, the panel, special applications, and other goodies. KDE offers a similar range of capabilities. Each is unique enough to warrant its own chapter, coming right up.

# Choosing a Default Display Manager

As you may recall, the display manager appears on the screen as a graphical login box, and there are three to choose from: gdm (GNOME), kdm (the KDE display manager), and xdm. If you hop around from one display manager to the next, you can easily lose track of which one will be used to log in a user. There are a couple of ways you can get a grip on which display manager becomes the default. If you've set up Linux so that X starts automatically, you can create or edit the `/etc/sysconfig/desktop` file to choose a default display manager. That file must contain one of the following three words to define which display manager is the default, and hence which login box will appear on the screen:

- **GNOME**: Makes gdm the default display manager
- **KDE**: Makes kdm the default display manager
- **AnotherLevel**: Makes xdm the default display manager

**Caution**

> Don't use the KDE magic word unless you've already installed KDE, as discussed in Chapter 10.

You can create or edit `/etc/sysconfig/desktop` using any text editor. For example, if you're working in GNOME and want to use gEdit to create or edit that file, follow these steps:

1. Click the GNOME Main Menu button and choose Run Program.
2. Type `gedit /etc/sysconfig/desktop` and press Enter.
3. If there's already a "magic word" in that file, delete it using the Delete key.
4. Type your new magic word (such as GNOME) using the exact upper- and lowercase letters shown in the list.
5. Click the Exit button in the toolbar or choose File, Exit from the menu bar, and choose Yes when asked about saving the file.

If you're working at the command prompt, you can use vi to create or edit the `/etc/sysconfig/desktop` file by following these steps:

1. Enter the command `vi /etc/sysconfig/desktop`.
2. If there is already some magic word there that you want to replace, type the letters `dd` to delete that line.
3. Type the letter a to go into insert mode.
4. Type your new magic word, (GNOME) and make sure you use the correct upper- and lowercase letters.
5. Press Escape to return to command mode.
6. Type `:wq` to write (save) the file and exit vi.

## SETTING THE DEFAULT SESSION TYPE

If Linux isn't configured to start X automatically, you can still control the type of session that appears after entering the `startx` command. To do so, you need to create or edit the `.xinitrc` file in your home directory. That file can contain any one of the following three magic words to choose the default session type:

- **exec gnome-session**: Starts a GNOME session.
- **exec startkde**: Starts a KDE session (don't use this unless you've already installed kde).
- exec /usr/share/apps/switchdesk/XClients.anotherlevel: Starts an xdm session.

As usual, you can create or edit the `.xinitrc` file using any text editor. Each user can have their own `.xinitrc` file in their home directory. So if you want to pass this default onto another user, copy your modified `.xinitrc` file to that user's home directory.

For more information on startup defaults, see Chapter 11, and also the man pages for X, `xinit`, `startx`, and `wmconfig`.

## CHOOSING THE DEFAULT XDM WINDOW MANAGER

Each user's home directory will contain a file named `.wm_style`. This file stores the name of the window manager to use if the user logs in via xdm. Normally, it gets its value from the current window manager. For example, if the user is using AfterStep, then `.wm_style` contains AfterStep. If the user switches to LessTif, then the `.wm_style` file instantly changes to MWM. The `startx` command always looks in `.wm_style` to determine which xdm window manager the user was last in to determine which window manager to start in the current session.

Normally, every time a user switches to another window manager, the contents of the `.wm_style` file are automatically changed to reflect the current window manager. For example, the `.wm_style` file might contain any one of the magic words in the left column of Table 8.1, depending on which window manager is in use at the moment.

**TABLE 8.1   MAGIC WORDS FOR XDM WINDOW MANAGERS IN EACH USER'S `.wm_style` FILE**

| Magic Word | xdm Window Manager |
|---|---|
| AfterStep | AfterStep |
| Fvwm95 | AnotherLevel |
| MWM | LessTif |
| WindowMaker | Window Maker |

You could force the user to always start in a specific window manager by using any text editor to type the appropriate magic word in the `.wm_style` file. If you also remove all the Write permissions to that file, its contents can't change. So no matter which window manager is in use when the user logs out of X, the window manager name you put into the .wm_style file will always be used when she first logs in via xdm.

# GETTING BACK TO GNOME

If you get lost in all of the window managers and desktops, and want to get back to GNOME and Enlightenment, there are a couple of things you can do. First, press Ctrl+Alt+Backspace to exit your current window manager. If you end up at the command prompt, enter the command gdm to start the GNOME display manager. When the login dialog box for GNOME appears, click the Options button and choose Sessions, GNOME, then log in normally.

If you can't get back to the GNOME login box at all, you'll have to reboot and make sure that X doesn't start up automatically. In any terminal window, you can enter the command **reboot** to reboot. If your computer is set up to start X automatically, keep your eye on the screen and watch for the LILO Boot prompt. When you see it, enter linux 3 to make sure you go straight to the command prompt. There, enter the command gdm to start the GNOME display manager. Click its Options button, choose Sessions, GNOME, then log in normally.

To get Enlightenment, the default Window Manager for GNOME, to "stick" better, run switchdesk by entering the command switchdesk in the GNOME terminal window, or by choosing KDE menus, System, Desktop Switching Tool from the main menu. Choose GNOME and Change Only Applies to Current Display, then click the OK button. Click the OK button to close the message that appears about restarting X. Click the Main Menu button, choose Logout, Logout, Yes. Then log back into GNOME.

> **Tip**    You'll learn more about the Enlightenment window manager in Chapter 9.

# TROUBLESHOOTING X STARTUP PROBLEMS

The following sections describe some common error messages that may appear when trying to run an X session. If you see any of those error messages, try the recommended technique to get things working. If problems continue, try the sources listed under "More X Support."

## CANNOT OPEN MOUSE (NO SUCH DEVICE)

This error message could mean that your mouse is not connected at all. Make sure your mouse is plugged in to the PC. If it is, you may have selected the wrong mouse during setup, or perhaps you've changed to a different mouse. To fix the problem, you can either re-install Linux or you can edit the Pointer section of XF86Config file manually, as discussed under "Configuring X Hardware Manually in XF86Config" in this chapter, and specify the correct mouse.

## DEVICE BUSY

If you get an error message saying that a device is busy after you enter a `startx` command, the most likely culprit is a program named gpm, which allows some character cell programs to use the mouse. To end the gpm session, try entering the following command:

```
gpm -k
```

Then enter the `startx` command again. The following error message occurs when you try to start X despite the fact that it's already running:

```
Server is already active for display 0
```

To get to X, you should switch to its virtual console instead by pressing Ctrl+Alt+F7.

## SERVER DOESN'T EXIST, CAN'T CONTINUE

If you run into an error message similar to this section's title, you'll need to install the correct X server for your video card. If you run XConfigurator and it detects your video card correctly, it will tell you the name of the X server you need. If XConfigurator can't detect your card, you can try looking up that card in Appendix C to see if you can determine which server you'll need. If all else fails, you can try the SVGA server, which is sort of a plain-vanilla server that works with most modern video cards and monitors. After you've determined the X server you need, you can follow these steps to install it:

1. Insert the Red Hat Linux CD-ROM that came with your boxed set into your CD-ROM drive.

2. If the CD doesn't mount automatically, mount it by entering the command mount / dev/cdrom/mnt/cdrom at the command prompt. You'll probably see a message about mounting the disk read-only, followed by a fresh command prompt.

3. Locate your required X server in the left column of Table 8.2. Use the text in the right column, including the ending asterisk, to complete your rpm command.

### TABLE 8.2 SELECT YOUR NEEDED X SERVER FROM THE LEFT COLUMN

| X Server | Replace yourservername with... | Replace Yourlinkname with... |
| --- | --- | --- |
| 8514 | 8514* | XF86_8514 |
| ACX | AGX* | XF86_AGX |
| I 128 | I128* | XF86_I128 |
| Mach 32 | Mach32* | XF86_Mach32 |
| Mach 64 | Mach64* | XF86_Mach64 |
| Mach 8 | Mach8* | XF86_Mach8 |
| Mono | Mono* | XF86_Mono |
| P 9000 | P9000* | XF86_P9000 |
| S3 | S3* | XF86_S3 |
| S3 Virge | S3V* | XF86_S3V |

| TABLE 8.2 CONTINUED | | |
|---|---|---|
| **X Server** | **Replace** yourservername **with...** | **Replace** Yourlinkname **with...** |
| SVGA | SVGA* | XF86_SVGA |
| VGA 16 | VGA16* | XF86_VGA16 |
| W 32 | W32* | XF86_W32 |

4. Type the following command, but replace yourservername with the appropriate text from the center column of Table 8.2. For example, if you need a Mach 64 server, replace yourservername with Mach64* so that your command reads rpm -i /mnt/ cdrom/RedHat/RPMS/XFree86-Mach64*:

   ```
   rpm -i /mnt/cdrom/RedHat/RPMS/XFree86-yourservername
   ```

5. Press Enter. If you typed the command correctly, you should return to a fresh command prompt. If you get an error message instead, try retyping the command correctly, and pressing Enter.

> **Caution**
>
> Don't forget that Linux is case-sensitive. If you get one upper- or lowercase letter wrong, the command won't work!

6. Enter the following commands at the command prompt to set up required symbolic links:

   ```
   cd /usr/X11R6/bin
   ln -sf xserver-wrapper ./X
   ```

7. Create a symbolic link to your X server by entering the following command, but replace yourlink namewith the name from the third column of Table 8.2:

   ```
   ln -sf /usr/R11X6/bin/yourlinknamehere /etc/X11/X
   ```

The problem should be resolved. Try starting X again.

## No Server Was Installed

This error can happen if either the appropriate X server isn't installed, or the appropriate links haven't been set up. See the section titled "Server Doesn't Exist, Can't Continue" in this section for instructions on installing an X server and creating the necessary links.

## More X Support

Probably the best resource for fixing common problems with X is the FAQ at the XFree86 Web site (http://www.xfree86.org/FAQ). The FAQ contains a list of dozens of problems and provides solutions for each. It's a "must know about" page for superusers.

When you purchased your Red Hat Linux boxed set, you were also granted 90 days of free Installation Technical Support. And getting X to work seems as though it should come under the heading of "Installation." Before you contact anyone though, gather as much information as you can. Your best bet is to create a log of error messages that occur when X fails to start. You can do so by entering this command at the command prompt:

```
startx &> startx.out
```

When X fails, you'll be returned to the command prompt. (If X hangs, rather than fails, press Ctrl+Alt+Backspace to get back to the command prompt. To view the contents of the startx.out command, enter the following:

```
less startx.out
```

The information available in that file should help Red Hat support pinpoint the problem. On the Web you can get to Red Hat's support via http://support.redhat.com. If you haven't already done so, you'll need to register your product using the code on the back of the jewel case that your Red Hat CD-ROM came in. Telephone installation support is available at the following numbers:

- **1-800-348-2451** (Monday - Friday 9 a.m. - 9 p.m. EST, US and Canada Only)
- **+1-716-784-2082** (Monday - Friday 9 a.m. - 9 p.m. EST, International Calls, English Only)

# CHAPTER 9

# CONFIGURING GNOME AND ENLIGHTENMENT

In this chapter

# USING THE GNOME CONTROL CENTER

If you read Part I of this book, you already know quite a bit about GNOME and how to use it. Chapters 1 and 2 covered basic skills for getting around the GNOME desktop. Chapter 3 covered basic skills for using gmc, the GNOME Midnight Commander file manager, and GNOME's many drag-and-drop features. Chapter 4 covered techniques for running GNOME clients (that is, applications and programs), as well as some cool techniques for personalizing your GNOME desktop. There you also learned about GNOME's unique ability to perform *session management*, where you can save your entire desktop before logging out and return to that exact desktop when you log back in. The GNOME Help Browser, which you can open at any time by clicking the ? button in the panel, was discussed in Chapter 5.

> **Tip**
>
> If you performed a server-class installation and want to add the GNOME interface, see the Case Study at the end of this chapter.

In this chapter we'll go beyond the basics of using GNOME, pop open the hood, and take a look at tools for configuring GNOME. Like most modern graphical desktop environments, GNOME provides an easy-to-use graphical tool, called the Control Center, that gives you access to all the configuration options you could want. You have a couple of ways to open the Control Center:

- Click the button labeled The GNOME Configuration Tool in the panel.
- Click the Main Menu button and choose Settings, GNOME Control Center.

When the Control Center opens up it will look something like Figure 9.1. The categories in the left panel that are marked with + and - signs can be clicked to show or hide specific *capplets*. The term capplet is short for *configuration applet*, or a small configuration program. Clicking on the name of a capplet opens its window in the right column of the window.

**Figure 9.1**
The GNOME Control Center provides easy access to GNOME configuration tools.

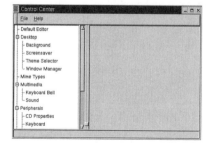

> **Tip**
>
> GNOME's Control Center also has its own help system, which you can open by choosing Help, Help from its menu bar.

## THE BACKGROUND CAPPLET

The Background capplet shown lets you choose a background color for the desktop. If you choose the Gradient option, you can select two colors for the background and a vertical or horizontal aspect. (That background, by the way, is also called the *desktop* and even the *root window* by hardcore techies.) For example, in Figure 9.2 I've created a horizontal gradient using dark and light shades of blue (although they no doubt look gray in this book!).

**Figure 9.2**
A color gradient used for GNOME's background.

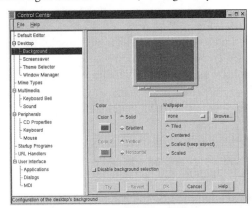

You can also use a graphic image as wallpaper, rather than a color, for your background. Click the Browse button under Wallpaper, and you'll be taken to a dialog box titled Wallpaper Selection. Initially you'll be viewing the contents of the /usr/share/pixmaps/ backgrounds directory, where many sample backgrounds are stored. You can then double-click a subdirectory name in the left column to view background images in that directory. (The Propaganda category is further subdivided into volumes, but you can double-click on volume name to see its files.) When you see a list of filenames in the right column, simply click any filename to see a thumbnail-sized preview of the picture off to the right. When you find an image you like, just click the OK button.

You have four options in choosing how you want the image displayed on your screen:

- **Tiled:** The image is repeated like tiles to fill the screen.
- **Centered:** The image is displayed alone in the center of the screen.
- **Scaled (Keep Aspect):** The image is enlarged to fill the screen, but not stretched or distorted.
- **Scaled:** The image is enlarged to fill the screen and may be distorted.

To try out different renditions of your selected background color or image, click the Try button. If you don't like what you see, click the Revert button. Should you decide to dispense with a wallpaper altogether, choose the None button within the Wallpaper pane. When you're happy with your selection, you can click the OK button. You can then stay in Control Center to make more selections, or you can close it by clicking its Close (X) button or by choosing File, Exit from its menu bar.

**Tip**

You can also get to the Background capplet by right-clicking the desktop and choosing Configure Background Image. Various options in the Settings submenu of the GNOME Main Menu also act as shortcuts to specific capplets.

## THE SCREENSAVER CAPPLET

The Screensaver capplet, shown in Figure 9.3, gives you precise control of the xscreensaver that's used to protect your screen when the computer is sitting idle. You can choose from a wide variety of options in the Screen Saver list. Clicking an option presents a preview of it in the Screen Saver Demo box. Some screensavers have additional settings you can adjust. If the screensaver you're previewing at the moment has such settings, the button beneath the list will be enabled, and you can click that button to access those additional settings. The two options at the top of the list, No Screensaver and Random Screensaver, let you disable the screensaver or let GNOME pick a screensaver at random.

**Figure 9.3**
The Screenaver capplet of the GNOME Control Center.

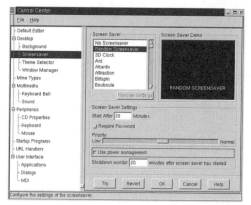

To choose how long the computer needs to sit idle before the screensaver kicks in, set the Start After *xx* Minutes option to however many minutes you want. To protect your screen while you're away, you can choose the Require Password option, so that only people who know your account login password can get out of the screensaver and back to the desktop.

If your monitor supports power management, you can activate that feature by choosing the Use Power Management option. When you select that option, you can set the number of minutes that the computer must remain idle before the monitor is shut off.

## THE THEME SELECTOR CAPPLET

A theme (or *GTX theme* as it's officially called) is a collection of *GTK widgets*—the individual controls such as text boxes, drop-down lists, buttons, and so forth that appear in dialog boxes. The Theme Selector capplet, shown in Figure 9.4, offers quite a few themes for you to choose from. Just click a theme name in the Available Themes list. If the Auto Preview option is selected, a preview of that theme appears in the Preview pane of the dialog box. If Auto Preview isn't selected, click the Preview button to preview the currently highlighted theme.

**Figure 9.4**
The Theme Selector capplet lets you choose a GTK widget set, which defines the appearance of buttons, check boxes, and other controls that appear in dialog boxes.

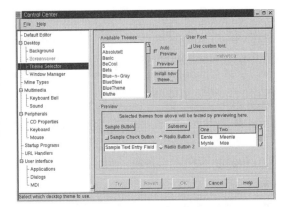

**Tip**

Microsoft Corporation is in Redmond, Washington. If you've ever used Windows, the Redmond95 theme will look pretty familiar to you.

You can also choose a custom font for the text labels that accompany widgets. Choose the Use Custom Font option and click the large button beneath that option. In the Pick a Font dialog box that appears, choose your font, style, and size, then click the OK button in that dialog box.

You can find additional themes online at the Web site http://www.themes.org. There you'll find themes for many different programs and window managers, including GNOME (listed under GTX+), Enlightenment, and IceWM. If you find a theme you like, download it by clicking the download link for that theme. The downloaded file will be a compressed *tarball*, as indicated by the .tar.gz at the end of the filename. To install the downloaded theme, click the Install New Theme button. Use the Select a Theme to Install dialog box that appears to navigate to whichever directory you download the tarball to. Click the name of the tarball file in the right column, then choose OK. The new theme will appear in the list of available themes. Click its name to take a look.

**Tip**

The Enlightenment window manager has a few themes of its own. To try them out, mid-click the desktop and choose Themes from the menu that appears.

## THE WINDOW MANAGER CAPPLET

The Window Manager capplet, shown in Figure 9.5, shows you which window manager you're currently using in GNOME, as indicated by the word Current next to the window manager's name. You can also use this capplet to choose any other installed window managers. Simply click the window manager you want to try, then click the Try button to test it out, or the OK button to switch to that window manager.

Initially, only Enlightenment is presented in the list, because that window manager is currently the only one available that's 100% GNOME-compliant (although, that may change by the time you read this). If you use a window manager that's only partially GNOME-compliant, you may very well lose some of the unique capabilities of GNOME, such as the ability to create a desktop link by mid-dragging any file or directory icon out of the File Manager and dropping it onto the desktop. But if you're willing to settle for less than perfect compliance, you can take a look at some of the partially compliant window managers listed here:

**Icewm:** `http://www.kiss.uni-lj.si/~k4fr0235/icewm`

**FVWM:** `http://www.fvwm.org`

**Window Maker:** `http://www.windowmaker.org`

**Figure 9.5**
The Window Manager capplet lets you choose a window manager for use in GNOME, add new window managers, and configure window managers that have configuration tools.

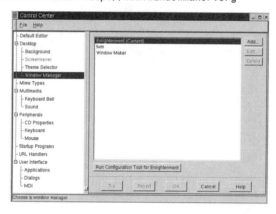

You can add new window managers to your list of available window managers in several ways. Some window managers will add themselves to the list automatically when you install them. For example, when I installed ICE and Window Maker, as discussed in Chapter 8, both of those programs added themselves to the list of available window managers without any intervention on my part.

You can also add a window manager manually by clicking the Add button. You'll be presented with a dialog box asking for information about the Window Manager. There, you must fill in the blanks using information you've garnered from the documentation that came with the window manager you downloaded. Fill in the blanks as follows:

- **Name:** This is the name as it will appear in the list (you can make up any name you like).

- **Command:** The command required to open the window manager.

- **Configuration Command:** The command required to open the window manager's configuration tool, if it has one.

- **Window Manager Is Session Managed:** Choose this option only if you're absolutely certain the window manager you're adding is session managed.

If the currently selected window manager has a configuration tool, the Run Configuration Tool For button will be made available. You can click that button to configure the window manager. The section "Configuring Enlightenment" later in this chapter will show you how to configure that window manager.

## CHOOSING A DEFAULT EDITOR

Whenever you right-click an icon in File Manager and choose Edit, that file (if it's editable) opens up in some text editor. By default, that editor will be Emacs. The GNOME Edit Properties dialog box lets you choose some other editor as the default. For example, if you're coming from a Windows or Macintosh background, you'll probably find gEdit much easier to use than Emacs. Just click the drop-down list button and choose gEdit, or any other editor you like, from the list that appears, as in Figure 9.6. You need only choose the Run in Terminal option if the editor you selected isn't capable of running in X. It's definitely *not* needed for gEdit, which is very much an X text editor, particularly well-suited for use in GNOME.

**Figure 9.6**
You can choose which editor appears when you right-click a file's icon and choose Edit.

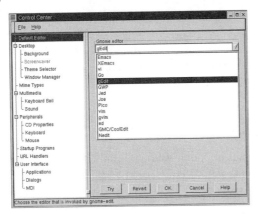

## THE MIME TYPES CAPPLET

Mime is an acronym for *Multipurpose Internet Mail Extensions*, and was originally developed to allow email messages to carry different types of files as attachments. However, the concept has grown to allow different types of document files, such as graphics, spreadsheets, and word processing documents to be associated with specific applications via a filename extension. For example, if you often work with JPEG graphic images and use the GIMP as your graphics editing tool, you can associate the filename extensions .jpg and .jpeg with the GIMP application program. That way, whenever you double-click the icon of a file that has either of those extensions, the file will automatically be opened in the GIMP. You won't have to go through the Select an Application dialog box every time you open the file from File Manager or the desktop. You can also choose which application you want to view or edit the file after you right-click the file's icon and choose View or Edit. You can even choose which icon you want those files to display.

The Mime Types capplet in the GNOME Control Center lets you create and edit mime types. When you choose that option, a long list of known mime types appears in the left column, as in Figure 9.7. The column to the right lists filename extensions used to identify that mime type. For example, any file with the extension .JPG, .jpg, .jpeg, or .jpe is assumed to be of the mime type image/jpeg.

**Figure 9.7**
The Mime Types capplet lets you change or create associations between filename extensions and applications.

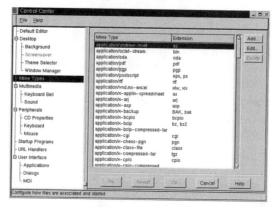

An easy way to discover if a particular filename extension is already listed as a mime type is to open the file manager and locate any filename that has that filename extension. If you double-click that file's icon and it opens, then you know there's an Open application for that mime type. If you right-click the icon and choose View, you know there's already a View application associated with that filename extension. Likewise, if you right-click and choose Edit, you know there's an Edit application for that extension as well.

If a filename extension is already associated with any application (be it Open, View, or Edit), it means that the filename extension is already listed in the mime types. If you want to change the application used to open, view, or edit that type of file, locate the filename extension in the right column of the list of mime types. Click that line and then click the Edit button to the right. You'll see a dialog box like the one in Figure 9.8. You can see the icon used to display files that contain a jpeg image, as well as the programs used to open and view that file type, ee (Electric Eyes) in the example shown.

**Figure 9.8**
The Set Actions for Image/jpeg dialog box lets you define the icon used to display jpeg images, as well as the applications used to open, view, and edit those files.

Suppose you decide that you'd rather use the GIMP, the GNU Image Manipulation program, to open and edit JPEG images. The first thing you need to know is which command is used to start the GIMP. If you don't know offhand, you can easily find out:

1. Click the GNOME Main Menu button and work your way to the option that starts the program that you want to use. However, don't select that option, just point to it.

2. Right-click the menu option and choose Properties. In the dialog box that appears, the startup command appears next to Command. For the GIMP, the startup command is `gimp`.

3. Click Close to close the dialog box.

Next, if you want to choose a different icon for this type of file, click the icon button, then choose an icon from the Select an Icon dialog box that appears. Click OK to close that dialog box. Then, you need to specify which applications you want to use for opening the file. In my example, if you want to use the GIMP to open and edit JPEG images, you need to set up the dialog box as in Figure 9.9. Be sure to follow the command with a blank space and %f. That %f is a placeholder that passes the name of the file to be edited to the `gimp` command.

**Figure 9.9**
The Open and Edit actions for JPEG images changed to the GIMP.

Click the OK button when you're done. To test the new association, close the Control Center by clicking its OK button to save your changes, then clicking its Close (X) button. Use the File Manager to locate any file that has the extension you just modified. If you set up an Open action, double-click the file to make sure it opens in the appropriate program. Likewise, if you set up View or Edit actions, you should right-click the file's icon and choose View or Edit to test those options.

Chances are there's already a mime type for any type of file that you'd like to associate with a specific application. The primary authorities for issuing Internet standards are the Internet Assigned Numbers Authority (IANA) at http://www.iana.org and the Internet Architecture Board (IAB) at www.iab.org. In a nutshell, there are already seven main mime types defined, as summarized here. Every mime type is followed by a slash and a *subtype* that further defines the type of data stored in the file:

■ **text:** Textual information that contains no hidden formatting codes and can be displayed without any special programs. For example, text/html is the mime type for Web pages.

- **image:** Image data that requires some type of special program or device to be viewed, such as a graphics program or fax machine. For example, image/tiff is the mime type for *Tagged Image File Format* images.

- **audio:** Audio data that requires some type of special program and/or device to be heard. For example, audio/x-wav is the mime type for wav files.

- **video:** Video data that contains moving images and needs specialized hardware and/or software to be viewed. For example, video/mpeg is the mime type for mpeg videos.

- **application:** Some other kind of data, typically binary data, that can be interpreted only with a particular type of program such as a spreadsheet or word processing application. For example, application/ms-excel is the mime type for Microsoft Excel spreadsheets.

- **multipart:** Data consisting of multiple data types. For example, multipart/alternative describes a file that contains the same data in two or more alternative formats.

- **message:** An encapsulated message that may or may not contain other data types. For example, message/partial refers to a file that contains a partial RFC 822 message.

Detailed information on each mime type is available in RFC 2046, which you can view online at http://www.oac.uci.edu/indiv/ehood/MIME/2046/rfc2046.html.

> **Tip**
>
> RFC stands for "Request for Comments," and is used to describe any document that defines Internet standards. You can usually find a specific RFC by going to any search engine and searching for the document name.

There is no rule that states you must use the conventional MIME types. You can, in fact, make up your own MIME type names. However, before you do so, you'd be wise to check whether the standards committee has already suggested a type/subtype pair that describes the type of document you're defining. You can see the current list of existing types and subtypes at ftp://ftp.isi.edu/in-notes/iana/assignments/media-types/media-types. Most Web browsers will let you view the document.

To add a new mime type to the list, click the Add button and type in Mime Type name and filename extensions for that mime type. For example, in Figure 9.10 I've created a new mime type named image/pcx for graphic files that I create and save in the pcx format. I've opted to associate the .pcx and .PCX filename extensions with that mime type. Click OK after defining the mime type.

To choose applications to associate with that mime type, click on the new mime type name in the list of available mime types. Then click the Edit button. Choose an icon and specify an application for opening, editing, and/or viewing files of that type.

**Figure 9.10**
A new mime type, image/pcx, added to GNOME's list of known mime types.

## THE KEYBOARD BELL CAPPLET

The Keyboard Bell capplet, as you might guess, lets you control the little beep you hear when some event triggers the bell. You can click the Test button to hear the current bell. Then experiment with the Volume, Pitch, and Duration options until you find one you like. Simply click the Test button to try out your new settings.

## THE SOUND CAPPLET

The Sound capplet lets you associate sounds with events that occur on your computer. For these to work you must have a sound card installed and working speakers. You must also make sure the sound card is properly configured, as covered in Chapter 15. On the General tab of the capplet, you need to activate the GNOME Sound Support option to ensure that the GNOME sound engine kicks in each time you start GNOME. To hear sounds that are triggered by GNOME events, you'll also need to click the Sounds Events option.

To associate a sound with a particular event, click the Sound Events tab. You'll see a list of GNOME clients (mostly programs) that can generate sounds, as shown in Figure 9.11. Events that have sounds associated with them are listed under each program name. To hear the sound currently associated with the event, click the Play button. To change the sound associated with the currently selected event, use the Browse button to find a different sound on your hard disk. After you've selected a sound, you can click the Play button to test it.

**Figure 9.11**
The Sound Events tab in the Sound capplet lets you assign sound effects to events that occur in various GNOME clients.

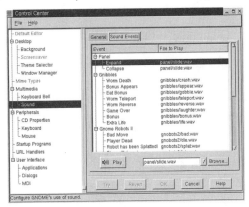

## THE CD PROPERTIES CAPPLET

The CD Properties capplet lets you control how GNOME responds to a newly inserted CD in your CD-ROM drive (see Figure 9.12). The first set of options apply only to data CDs. They're pretty self-explanatory, but just to clarify, they are as follows:

- **Automatically Mount CD When Inserted:** If selected, a newly inserted CD is mounted automatically to the mount point /mnt/cdrom, so you don't have to mount the CD manually using the mount command or User Mount Tool.

- **Automatically Start Auto-Run Programs on Newly Mounted CD:** If selected, GNOME will search a newly mounted CD-ROM for a script or program named autorun, and then will run that script or program.

- **Open File Manager Window for Newly Mounted CD:** If selected, the GNOME file manager will open, displaying the contents of the /mnt/cdrom mount point (and hence, the contents of the CD-ROM) as soon as the CD is mounted.

**Figure 9.12**

The CD Properties capplet lets you decide what happens when you put a data or audio CD into your CD-ROM drive.

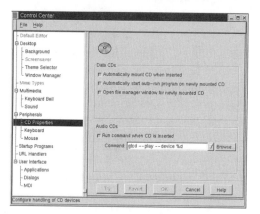

The lower pane in the CD Properties capplet lets you decide how a newly mounted audio CD is treated. The default setting is to use the GNOME CD Player, gtcd, to start playing the audio CD automatically.

## THE KEYBOARD CAPPLET

The Keyboard capplet lets you fine-tune the performance of your keyboard. However, it doesn't work with all keyboards, so don't get your hopes up too high. The Auto-Repeat option sets the "typematic" features of your keyboard, which is the way that holding down a key causes that key to be repeated as although you were rapidly tapping the key. The Enable Auto-Repeat option must be selected for auto-repeat to work. The Repeat Rate defines how quickly the key repeats, the default being 5 times per second. The Repeat Delay option defines how long the key must be held down, in milliseconds, before auto-repeat kicks in. The default is 500 milliseconds (one half of a second).

The Keyboard Click option, when selected, provides some auditory feedback each time you press a key. If you select this option, you can then adjust the volume of the clicks. To test your settings, click anywhere in the Test Settings textbox to get the cursor there. Then type or hold down a key to see the results of your current selections.

## THE MOUSE CAPPLET

The Mouse capplet lets you fine-tune your mouse, providing your mouse has the ability to be configured in this manner. The Mouse Buttons options let you choose between a left-handed or right-handed mouse. If you select Left-Handed, the left and right mouse buttons change roles. For example, to view a file's options or an item's properties, you click that option using the left mouse button. To open an item, you'd click or double-click it using the mouse button on the right.

The Acceleration option determines how fast the mouse pointer moves in relation to how fast you move the mouse. The higher the setting, the faster the pointer moves. The Threshold setting defines how quickly the mouse must actually be moving before the accelerated speed kicks in. Be aware that if you make the acceleration fast and the threshold small, the mouse will always move very quickly across the screen. That can make it difficult to zero in on small objects, like the Close button at the upper-right corner of a window.

## THE STARTUP PROGRAMS CAPPLET

The Startup Programs capplet configures features of GNOME's session management capability, originally discussed back in Chapter 4. Session management is GNOME's ability to remember certain settings and which application programs were on the desktop when you logged out, making it so they pop up on the desktop automatically the next time you log in. To activate session management, simply choose the Save Current Setup option that appears in the Really Log Out? dialog box (it opens when you log out using the Log Out option in GNOME's main menu). You can also click the Main Menu button and choose Settings, Save Current Session to save your current session at any time.

To fine-tune session management via the Startup Programs capplet, choose from the options described here (and shown in Figure 9.13):

- **Prompt on Logout:** This option must be selected if you want the Save current setup option to appear in the Really log out? dialog box.
- **Automatically Save Changes to Session:** When selected, this option makes GNOME save your current session automatically whenever you log out.

---

**Caution**

Currently, no *data-aware* applications are available that can take full advantage of GNOME's session management. This means that GNOME won't save the document you're currently working on in a program and won't bring the document back up when you log in. Therefore, you should *always* remember to save your work before you log out of GNOME.

PART

**II**

CH

**9**

**Figure 9.13**
The Startup Programs capplet lets you fine-tune session management and automatically start GNOME-compliant programs that don't support session management.

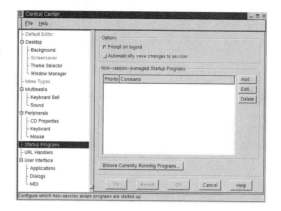

The Non-Session-Managed Startup Programs list lets you automatically start GNOME-compliant programs that don't have session management capabilities each time you log in to GNOME. To add such a program to the list, click the Add button, then type in the startup command for the program or browse to the file used to start the program. You can give each program a priority to determine when it loads. By default, each program is given a priority of 50, so that no program has any priority. The lower the priority you assign to a program, the sooner it starts. However, until you learn about program priorities in Chapter 17, you should leave each program's priority setting at 50. The Edit and Delete buttons to the right of the list let you change or delete programs currently in the list.

It's important to remember that only GNOME-compliant programs that don't support session management should be added to the list. Programs that are not GNOME-compliant or GNOME programs that do support session management shouldn't be included in that list.

> **Tip**
>
> You can save non-GNOME-compliant programs by simply choosing the Save Current Setup option from the Logout dialog box when logging out. You can't add those programs to the list of GNOME-compliant programs that don't support session management.

The Browse Currently Running Programs button lets you see which programs are currently running. You can use that option to shut down any open programs that you don't want to be started the next time you log in. However, when you click that button you'll see a long list of programs, most of which are running behind the scenes. Some of those programs are *required* for GNOME to run. So it's vitally important that you do not shut down any programs that you don't recognize. You should only shut down programs that you're familiar with and are certain you don't want appearing in your next GNOME session.

## RESETTING YOUR GNOME DESKTOP

If your desktop gets too cluttered with windows or something goes awry and GNOME won't start correctly, you can get back to a clean GNOME desktop. Log in to GNOME or start X as you usually do, and hold down the Ctrl + Shift keys. You'll see a dialog box with the two options described here:

- **Start with Default Programs:** Choosing this option starts GNOME with default programs listed in the Session Manager capplet, but makes no attempt to open programs that were saved at the end of the previous session.

- **Reset All User Settings:** Starts with a clean slate, resetting all options to their original defaults. Erases custom settings you've made to the Session Manager capplet, the GNOME File Manager, the Panel, and GNOME-compliant applications. Don't use this option unless you're certain you want to lose all your custom GNOME settings.

## THE URL HANDLERS CAPPLET

The URL Handlers capplet decides how various GNOME help files are displayed. If you open the help browser and click on GNOME User's Guide, you'll notice that the URL in the Location box reads `ghelp:users-guide`. The URL handlers capplet is currently set up to send any URL that starts with `ghelp:`, `info:`, or `man:` to the GNOME help browser. The default URL handler for other types of URLs is the current Mozilla browser, as detected by the gnome-moz-remote program in `/usr/bin`. There's probably no reason to ever change any of these settings.

## THE USER INTERFACE CAPPLETS

The URL handlers capplet determines the general appearance and behavior of 100% GNOME-compliant application programs, dialog boxes, and Multiple Document Interface (MDI) mode. The specific options within each capplet are pretty self-explanatory:

- **Applications:** Determines behavior, appearance, and features available from all 100% GNOME-compliant application programs, such as whether or not tear-away menus are supported.

- **Dialogs:** Determines the general appearance and behavior of dialog boxes presented by GNOME and GNOME application programs.

- **MDI:** Determines how applications that allow you to work on more than one document at a time treat the multiple documents. Really for advanced users only.

If you open one of the preceding capplets and want more information about the options it presents, click the Help button near the lower-right corner of the GNOME Control Center window.

# CONFIGURING ENLIGHTENMENT

Some window managers have their own configuration tools that you can access from within the GNOME Control Center. Enlightenment, being 100% GNOME-compliant, definitely has such a tool. Its name is e-conf, and you can get to it by opening the Window Manager capplet in the Control Center, then clicking the Run Configuration Tool for Enlightenment button. If the Control Center isn't open at the moment, there are a couple of shortcuts you can take. One is to mid-click the desktop and choose Enlightenment Configuration from the menu that pops up. Or enter the command e-conf & in a terminal window. No matter which method you use, you'll come to the Enlightenment Configuration Editor shown in Figure 9.14.

**Figure 9.14**
The Enlightenment Configuration tool lets you tweak your Enlightenment window manager.

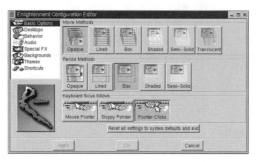

The list in the upper-left corner of the Enlightenment Configuration Editor lists categories of options that are available to you. Clicking any item in that list displays those options in the panes to the right of the list. To activate any options you select and try them out, click the Apply button that appears in the right pane.

## ENLIGHTENMENT BASIC OPTIONS

The Basic Options category lets you choose the animation style that's used when you move and size windows on the desktop. Each button illustrates how the animation will look. The Keyboard Focus Follows option lets you decide how windows get the keyboard focus. As you may recall, anything you type at the keyboard goes into only one open window on the screen, which is the window that's currently highlighted. You have three ways to pass the keyboard focus to a window in Enlightenment:

- **Mouse Pointer:** The window that the mouse pointer is over at the moment is highlighted and has the keyboard focus.

- **Sloppy Pointer:** Same as above, but the window retains the focus if you move the mouse pointer to the desktop or some other area of the desktop that isn't a window.

- **Pointer Clicks:** To pass the focus to a window, you need to actually click on the window.

To try out any of the keyboard methods, open a few windows including a terminal window. Choose an option, then click the Apply button. Then move the mouse pointer around on the screen and watch how windows get highlighted. If you type characters when the terminal window is highlighted, you'll see that the characters show up just fine. If you type when that window isn't highlighted, the characters don't show up in that window.

## ENLIGHTENMENT DESKTOPS

The Desktops category, shown in Figure 9.15, lets you choose how many virtual desktops you want to be available on your screen. As you may recall from Chapter 2, your screen is initially divided into four virtual desktops. The pager in the panel shows all those desktops, with the one you're in at the moment highlighted. If you want more or fewer desktops, just adjust the sliders along the top and left edge of the virtual screen to however many desktops you want. You can also adjust the edge resistance, which defines how long you must hold the mouse pointer at the edge of the screen to move to the next desktop. The default setting of 1.0 offers very little resistance. So the moment the mouse pointer touches a screen edge, you're moved to the next virtual desktop and all your non-sticky open windows seem to disappear. That can drive you crazy if you're not accustomed to it.

**Figure 9.15**
The Desktops options let you decide how many virtual desktops you want and how long you have to point to the edge of the screen to flip from one desktop to the next.

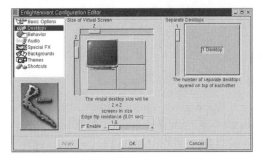

If you want to slow down how quickly the mouse pointer takes you to another desktop, make sure the Enable option under Edge resistance is selected. Then drag the slider to the right. To test your current setting, click the Apply button, then move the mouse pointer to the right or left edge of the screen to jump to another desktop. The higher the setting on the slider, the longer you have to hold the mouse pointer at a screen edge before you flip to the next desktop.

> **Tip**
> Turning on the "Desktops slide in when changed" special effect can also make desktop switching a lot less sudden. See "Enlightenment Special FX" later in this chapter for more information.

You can even layer desktops one atop the other. Move the Separate Desktops slider to however many desktops you want, then click the Apply button to try it out. The panel will display a pager for each virtual desktop. To switch from one layer to the next, just click the appropriate pager in the panel.

You can also stack pagers vertically in the panel so they don't take up so much width. Right-click any pager in the panel and choose Properties. Use the Rows of Pagers option to define how many rows of pagers you want stacked up in the panel. (Click the Apply button to test your current selection). To keep the panel from becoming exceptionally tall, you can choose the Use Small Pagers option in that same dialog box.

## ENLIGHTENMENT BEHAVIOR OPTIONS

The Behavior options let you customize how Enlightenment reacts to various events. The Advanced Focus tab, shown in Figure 9.16, let you precisely control how and when windows get the keyboard focus. Your options are as follows:

**Figure 9.16**
The Advanced Focus tab of Enlightenment's Behavior options give you tight control over when windows receive the keyboard focus.

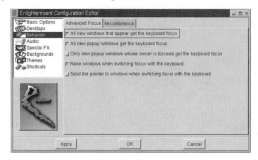

- **All New Windows That Appear Get the Keyboard Focus:** Ensures that any new window that opens automatically gets the focus. (Windows works like this.)

- **All New Popup Windows Get the Keyboard Focus:** Ensures that any small pop-up windows, such as error messages, get the keyboard focus as soon as they pop up.

- **Only New Popup Windows Whose Owner is Focused Get the Keyboard Focus:** Small pop-up windows get the focus only if the window that generated the pop-up window currently has the focus.

- **Raise Windows When Switching Focus With the Keyboard:** Ensures that when you use the keyboard to switch from one open window to the next, the current window is raised and not overlapped by any other open windows.

- **Send the Pointer to Windows When Switching Focus With the Keyboard:** When selected, makes the mouse pointer follow the focus when switching among open windows with the keyboard.

> **Tip**
> To shift the focus among open windows using the keyboard, press Alt+Tab to shift to the next window or Alt+Shift+Tab keys to shift to the previous open window.

The Miscellaneous tab of the Behavior options, shown in Figure 9.17, provides still more flexibility in controlling the behavior of Enlightenment:

- **Tooltips ON/OFF & Timeout:** Tooltips are tiny hints that appear when you rest the mouse pointer on certain objects. To allow tooltips to appear, you must select the Enable option. The slider lets you determine how long the mouse pointer must rest on an object (in seconds) before the tooltip appears.

- **Automatic Raising of Windows:** If enabled, ensures that any window you point to is raised and gets the focus. The slider determines how long the mouse pointer must rest on the window (in seconds) before the window is raised.

- **Transient Popup Windows Appear Together with Leader:** Select this option to make error messages or other pop-up windows appear on or near the window that created the pop-up window. If you don't select this option, a pop-up window might appear anywhere on the screen.

- **Switch to Where Popup Window Appears:** If selected, the mouse pointer and keyboard focus automatically jump to any pop-up window that appears on the screen.

- **Display Icons When Windows Are Iconified:** When selected, displays an icon for each minimized window.

> **Tip**
>
> Minimized windows are always accessible from the Tasklist. You can also make them visible in the pager by modifying the pager properties. See "Using the Pager" in Chapter 2 if you need some reminders.

- **Place Windows Manually:** If you select this option, you can position any window using the mouse immediately after the window opens, without even holding down a mouse button.

**Figure 9.17**
The Miscellaneous tab of the Behavior options controls tooltips, icons, and more.

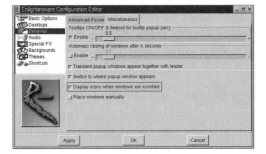

## ENLIGHTENMENT AUDIO

If selected, this option activates Enlightenment's own unique sound events. Your sound card must be configured correctly before this option will work (see Chapter 15). If not selected, you'll still get GNOME sound effects, provided your sound card is configured correctly and you've enabled audio through the Sound capplet.

## ENLIGHTENMENT SPECIAL FX

The Special FX options let you activate or deactivate various special effects that Enlightenment offers. Most special effects are disabled by default because they consume considerable system resources. This makes them dreadfully slow on any computer that doesn't have the hardware horsepower to spare. The following list shows your options. (Note that for those options that allow you to adjust timing, the lower end of the slider represents slower speeds.)

- **Window Sliding Methods:** Defines how new windows are opened when the "Windows slide in then they appear" option is selected.

- **Windows Slide in When They Appear:** When selected, this option causes new windows to "slide" onto the screen rather than appear suddenly. You can set how long it takes for windows to slide in using the slider bar.

- **Windows Slide About When Cleanup in Progress:** Makes windows move about the screen when you select the Cleanup Windows option from the Enlightenment menu (the menu that appears when you mid-click the desktop), or when you press Ctrl+Alt+Home.

- **Desktops Slide in When Changed:** When selected, prevents that sudden screen change that occurs when switching from one virtual desktop to the next. Adjust the slider to adjust the speed of the change.

- **Window Shading Speed:** If this option is selected, you can shade or unshade any open window by double-clicking its title bar. The slider adjusts the speed at which the window appears and disappears.

- **Drag Bar:** Some Enlightenment themes offer a *drag bar* that lets you peek in on other desktops. If your current theme offers this feature, the drag bar will be visible only if you select this option. When selected, you can use the Location option to choose where you want the drag bar to be positioned.

- **Animate Menus:** Some Enlightenment themes offer animated menus. This option allows you to turn that feature on and off.

- **Reduce Refresh (Use SaveUnders):** Speeds up access to menus by placing them in system memory (RAM). Use only if your system has lots of RAM, and if selecting this option doesn't cause problems with other applications running out of memory.

Another special effect that Enlightenment offers is called FX Ripples. This effect works only if you have some kind of image or pattern on your background—a solid color won't show the effect. Also, the effect appears at the bottom of the screen, so to see it, you'll need to hide the panel (right-click the panel, choose This Panel Properties, and select the Auto Hide option.) To turn on the ripple effect, mid-click the desktop to bring up the Enlightenment menu, then choose Desktop, FX Ripples. If you look to the bottom of the screen, you'll see an effect that looks like rippling water. If you open a window and drag it down toward the bottom of the screen, you'll see that window's reflection in the ripples. If you get tired of the effect, repeat the same procedure you used to start the effect.

## ENLIGHTENMENT BACKGROUNDS

Enlightenment has its own set of backgrounds. Any background you select from e-conf will automatically override the background you specified in the Background capplet. When you choose the Background category, you'll see a collection of background images as in

Figure 9.18. If you have multiple layers of virtual desktops, you first need to choose which desktop you want to apply the background to, using the desktop button. The first desktop is always number 0. If you only have one virtual desktop, that's number 0 as well. To choose any of the existing background images, click the image you want, and then click the Apply button.

**Figure 9.18**
The Background option in the Enlightenment Configuration Editor let you choose a Background image or color.

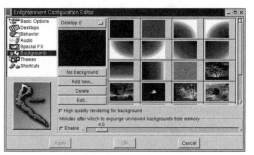

You can also change any existing background, or create your own. To change an existing image, click on it, then click on the Edit button. To create a new background from scratch, click the Add New button. The Enlightenment Edit Background dialog box shown in Figure 9.19 appears. Use the three tabs to define three characteristics of your background:

**Figure 9.19**
The Enlightenment Edit Background dialog box lets you change or create Enlightenment backgrounds.

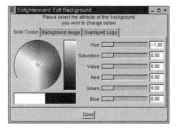

- **Solid Colour:** Defines the solid color of the background. This will show through only if you don't also add a full-sized background image.
- **Background Image:** Use the Browse button to open any image file on your hard disk. Use the Image Display options to define how you want the image displayed.
- **Overlayed Logo:** Use the Browse button to locate a graphic image that will be overlayed on top of the selected color or background image. Use the Image Display buttons to choose how you want the overlayed logo to appear.

After making your selections, click the Done button. The background image will be added to the collection of existing backgrounds. To activate the background, click its thumbnail button, then click the Apply button. To delete a background image from the collection, just click its thumbnail button and then click the Delete button.

The High Quality Rendering for Background option provides the best quality for displaying background images, at the cost of using a little more memory. If memory is tight in your system, you can de-select this option to regain some of that memory. The next option, if enabled, allows you to remove unused backgrounds from memory after $x$ number of minutes, again to conserve system memory.

To turn off the background you chose in Enlightenment, choose No Background from the button just above the Add New button. Next, click the OK button to save the change and return to the desktop. Any background image you previously set with the Background capplet will be lost as well. However, you can always re-open the GNOME control panel and choose a background from the Background capplet.

## ENLIGHTENMENT THEMES

Enlightenment themes set the look and feel of your window manager. When you click the Themes option in the Enlightenment Configuration Editor, you'll be taken to a list of possible themes. To try a theme, click its name, then click the Apply button. The theme mainly affects window decorations like the title bar and the buttons in that bar. So you might want to open some windows to get the full effect, and point to some buttons to see how tooltips are displayed in the theme. To get back to the original theme, choose CleanBig from the list of available themes.

> **Tip**
>
> If selecting a theme wipes out our selected background, you can just click the Backgrounds option and apply any background you like.

There's a collection of themes for Enlightenment at www.e.themes.org. You can choose Theme Gallery from the left frame to browse through the collection. To download a theme, click the Download link that appears with that theme. If the theme is delivered as a tarball (.tar.gz file), you must decompress it to get to the .etheme file inside. Copy the .etheme file to the .enlightenment/themes subdirectory of your home directory (that is, ~/.enlightenment/themes) to add it to the list of available themes in Enlightenment.

## ENLIGHTENMENT SHORTCUTS

The Shortcuts category, shown in Figure 9.20, lets you define keyboard shortcuts that work whenever you're using the Enlightenment window manager. The list at the top half of the dialog box shows the default shortcut keys that Enlightenment comes with. You may just want to review the keys, without changing them, to see that those defaults are there. Keep in mind that much of the documentation for Enlightenment refers to these default shortcuts when telling you how to do things. If you change them, you'll be out of sync with that documentation. If you're not worried about that, although, you can use the bottom half of the dialog box to change existing shortcut keys or create new ones.

To edit an existing shortcut key, click on the shortcut in the top half of the dialog box. Then choose options from the bottom half of the dialog box. To create a new shortcut key, click the New button in the top half of the dialog box instead. Either way, your next task will be to define the shortcut key in the bottom half of the dialog box.

**Figure 9.20**
You can change and create Enlightenment keyboard shortcuts in this dialog box.

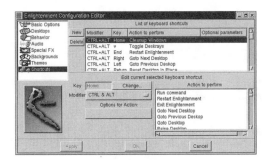

Step 1 is to decide which key you want to use for the shortcut and the modifier key(s), such as Ctrl, Shift, or Alt, that will precede that key. Click the Change button, then press the key that will be the main key (a letter, number, function, or navigation key). Then click the Modifier button and choose a modifier from the list shown. Next, choose the action to perform from the list of possible actions. If you choose an action that allows options, the Options for Action prompt will allow you to enter options. For example, if you choose Run command, you can then type in the command you want to run such as gimp, if you want the shortcut key to start the GIMP program. Click the Apply button when you're done. To test the shortcut key, press the keys you defined. For example, if you defined Alt+Shift+g as a shortcut key that does the Run Command action and the GIMP as the option for the action, then pressing Alt+Shift+g now should start up the GIMP. A handy way to create quick keyboard shortcuts to your favorite programs!

## ENLIGHTENMENT MENUS AND THEMES

One thing you do need to be aware of is that the Enlightenment menus are tied to the theme you're using at the moment. So every time you try to switch to another Enlightenment theme, you might wind up with a slightly different set of menus. In general, however, you can bring up the main Enlightenment menu by mid-clicking any part of the desktop. Once open, the menu will probably provide some or all of the options shown in Figure 9.21.

- **GNOME Apps:** Essentially identical to the System portion of the GNOME main menu.

- **Other Programs:** The same as the User menu that's accessible from the main menu.

- **Desktop:** Includes options to clean up your desktop (rearrange its windows), or go to another desktop.

- **Themes:** A quick way to switch to a different Enlightenment theme.

- **Enlightenment Configuration:** Takes you straight to the Enlightenment Configuration Editor, e-conf.

- **About Enlightenment:** Presents general information about the version of Enlightenment you're using.

- **Restart Enlightenment:** Restarts just the Enlightenment window manager. If you're looking to restart your whole X session, use the Logout option on the GNOME Main Menu instead.

**Figure 9.21**
Mid-clicking the desktop will bring up the Enlightenment Main Menu, which may vary slightly from one theme to the next.

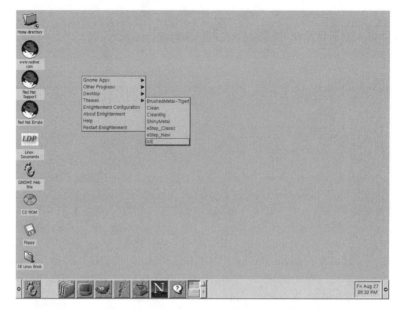

Each Enlightenment theme also has its own set of menus for managing individual windows. One way to bring up this menu is to hold down the Alt key and right-click the window you want to work with. In most themes, you can also just click the box in the upper-left corner of the window. The menu that appears will look like Figure 9.22.

**Figure 9.22**
Enlightenment's window menu might vary from one theme to the next, but will generally contain the options shown here.

The options on the menu are summarized here:

- **Close:** Closes the window normally.
- **Annihilate:** If a window is hung and will not close normally, this option will force it to close.
- **Iconify:** Minimizes the window to an item in the Tasklist. Or, in configurations that don't use a tasklist, will minimize the window to an icon on the desktop.
- **Raise:** Brings the window to the top of the stack so no other windows obscure it.
- **Lower:** Moves the window down to the bottom of the stack.
- **Shade/Unshade:** Shades or unshades the window. When a window is shaded, only its title bar is visible.

- **Stick/Unstick:** Sticks or unsticks the window. A sticky window is one that remains visible even when you switch to another virtual desktop.
- **Desktop:** Provides options for moving to other virtual desktops.
- **Window Size:** Provides options for sizing the current window.
- **Remember State:** Lets you save or cancel attributes defined using the options on this menu.
- **Set Stacking:** Lets you move the stacking position of the window.
- **Set Border Style:** Lets you change the border style of the window.

# UPGRADING GNOME

Red Hat keeps GNOME and Enlightenment bug fixes and changes at its Errata site at `www.redhat.com/errata`.

Table 9.1 lists the base set of packages that make up GNOME and Enlightenment in your Red Hat Package. So as soon as you get your Linux computer connected to the Internet, you may want to use the Update Agent (Chapter 21) to get the most recent versions. Optionally, you can download the most recent files using your Web browser (Chapter 19) by visiting `www.redhat.com/support/errata`.

> **Tip**
>
> Any time you have problems with any Linux feature or program, you should check out the Red Hat Errata page to see if it's something that's already been fixed.

**TABLE 9.1** THE BASE SET OF PACKAGES THAT MAKE UP RED HAT'S DISTRIBUTION OF GNOME AND ENLIGHTENMENT

| RPM Package File | What It Contains |
| --- | --- |
| ORBit-0.5.0-3.i386.rpm | CORBA object requestor |
| audiofile-0.1.9-3.i386.rpm | Library used by esound |
| control-center-1.0.51-3.i386.rpm | GNOME Control Center |
| desktop-backgrounds-1.1-1.noarch.rpm | GNOME backgrounds |
| ee-0.3.11-1.i386.rpm | Electric Eyes |
| enlightenment-0.15.5-48.i386.rpm | Enlightenment window manager |
| enlightenment-conf-0.15-9.i386.rpm | E configuration tool |
| esound-0.2.17-2.1386.rpm | Enlightened sound |

**TABLE 9.1 CONTINUED**

| RPM Package File | What It Contains |
| --- | --- |
| freetype-1.3.1-5.i386.rpm | TrueType font rendering |
| gdm-2.0beta2-23.i386.rpm | GNOME display manager |
| gedit-0.6.1-3.i386.rpm | GNOME text editor |
| gftp-2.0.6a-3.i386.rpm | GNOME FTP client |
| glib-1.2.6-3.i386.rpm | C library |
| glib10-1.0.6-6.i386.rpm | Another C library |
| gmc-4.5.42-10.i386.rpm | GNOME file manager |
| gnome-audio-1.0.0-8.noarch.rpm | Sound for gnome |
| gnome-audio-extra-1.0.0-8.noarch.rpm | Extra gnome sounds |
| gnome-core-1.0.55-12.i386.rpm | Main GNOME files |
| gnome-games-1.0.51-4.i386.rpm | GNOME games |
| gnome-libs-1.0.55-12.i386.rpm | Required GNOME libraries |
| gnome-linuxconf-0.25-2.i386.rpm | Graphical LinuxConf |
| gnome-media-1.0.51-2.i386.rpm | GNOME CD player and other multimedia |
| gnome-objc-1.0.2-6.i386.rpm | Objective C libraries |
| gnome-pim-1.0.55-1.i386.rpm | GNOME personal information manager |
| gnome-users-guide-1.0.72-1.i386.rpm | GNOME documentation |
| gnome-utils-1.0.50-4.i386.rpm* | GNOME calendar, calculator, other utilities |
| gnorpm-0.9-15.i386.rpm | Graphical RPM |
| gnotepad+-1.1.4-3.i386.rpm | A GNOME text editor with HTML |
| gnumeric-0.48-3.i386.rpm | GNOME spreadsheet |
| gqview-0.7.0-4.i386.rpm | GNOME image viewer |
| gtk+-1.2.6-7.i386.rpm | GIMP toolkit |
| gtk+10-1.0.6-6.i386.rpm | Another GIMP toolkit |
| gtk-engines-0.10-3.i386.rpm | Graphical engines |
| gtop-1.0.5-1.i386.rpm | System monitor |
| guile-1.3-10.i386.rpm | Library for Scheme language |
| imlib-1.9.7-3.i386.rpm | Image handler |
| imlib-cfgeditor-1.9.7-3.i386.rpm | Imlib configuration app |
| libghttp-1.0.4-1.i386.rpm | HTTP request library |
| libgtop-1.0.6-1.i386.rpm | System monitor |
| libxml-1.8.6-2.i386.rpm | XML file manipulator |
| mc-4.5.42-10.i386.rpm | Midnight Commander |

TABLE 9.1    CONTINUED

| RPM Package File | What It Contains |
| --- | --- |
| umb-scheme-3.2-11.i386.rpm | Scheme language |
| xchat-1.4.0-1.i386.rpm | A GNOME IRC client |
| xscreensaver-3.23-2.i386.rpm | Cool screensavers for GNOME |

PART

II

CH

9

**Tip**    To see what version of a package is currently installed on your computer, enter the command rpm -q *name* where name is the name of the package you're curious about. For example, to see what version of Enlightenment is currently installed, you'd enter the command rpm -q enlightenment.

If you're a programmer and interested in developing or modifying GNOME software, you will also want to install the packages listed in Table 9.2.

TABLE 9.2    PACKAGES ALLOWING PROFESSIONAL PROGRAMMERS TO MAKE CONTRIBUTIONS TO GNOME AND RELATED PRODUCTS

| Optional GNOME Developer's Package | What It Contains |
| --- | --- |
| ORBit-devel-0.5.0-3.i386.rpm | CORBA for programmers |
| audiofile-devel-0.1.9-3.i386.rpm | Libraries to write audio |
| control-center-devel-1.0.51-3.i386.rpm | Capplet developer tools |
| esound-devel-0.2.17-2.1386.rpm | esound developer tools |
| fnlib-devel-0.4-10.i386.rpm | 24-bit color development tools |
| glib-devel-1.2.6-3.i386.rpm | GIMP libraries |
| gnome-core-devel-1.0.55-12.i386.rpm | GNOME panel developer tools |
| gnome-games-devel-1.0.51-4.i386.rpm | Game developer tools |
| gnome-libs-devel-1.0.55-12.i386.rpm | GNOME app developer tools |
| gnome-objc-devel-1.0.2-6.i386.rpm | Objective C developer tools |
| gnome-pim-devel-1.0.55-1.i386.rpm | GNOME PIM developer tools |
| gtk+-devel-1.2.6-7.i386.rpm | GIMP toolkit |
| imlib-devel-1.9.7-3.i386.rpm | Image rendering tools |
| libghttp-devel-1.0.4-1.i386.rpm | HTTP developer tools |
| libgtop-devel-1.0.6-1.i386.rpm | GNOME app developer tools |
| libxml-devel-1.8.6-2.i386.rpm | XML developer tools |

The developers of GNOME and Enlightenment often release updates of packages to add functionality or to fix bugs. The update packages are available from their Web sites at www.gnome.org and www.enlightenment.org. If you're the type of person who must always have the latest or greatest, or you encounter some bug that you hope an update will fix, you may want to go to these sites to see what the latest release is. However, if you're new to Linux you're probably better off limiting your updates to those from the Red Hat server. Because you know the updates from Red Hat are sure to work with your distribution of Linux, whereas a generic update might not work as well.

# CASE STUDY: ADDING GNOME TO A SERVER CLASS INSTALLATION

In the real world, there's usually no reason to put a fancy interface on a server since nobody actually sits at the server to do work. Fancy interfaces are best reserved for workstations rather than servers. But if you're just learning and want to work with a server installation through the relatively easy GNOME interface, there's no harm in adding it to your existing installation. When you're done learning all the ins and outs of Linux, you can always reinstall or remove packages that you don't need.

While this case study uses adding X and GNOME to a server class installation of Red Hat Linux 6.2, the general technique will probably work with any installation of Linux that currently has no GUI.

## GETTING STARTED

Every GUI requires the X be installed first. To determine whether X is already installed, enter the following command at any command prompt:

```
rpm -q Xfree86
```

If X is installed, you'll see its name followed by the version number that's installed, so there is no need to reinstall X. You can go straight to the "Installing GNOME" section later in this chapter.

> **Caution**
>
> Be sure you're logged in as root before you try to install X and/or GNOME.

If, on the other hand, the rpm command tells you that the XFree86 package is not installed, you'll need to keep reading and install X first.

## INSTALLING X

If X isn't installed on your Linux computer already, you'll need to log in as root, put the Red Hat Linux CD-ROM #1 into your CD-ROM drive, and then enter this command to mount the CD:

```
mount /dev/cdrom /mnt/cdrom
```

You'll see a message indicating that the CD was mounted Read-Only, which is fine. Next, enter the following command to switch to the /RedHat/RPMS directory on the CD-ROM, which is where all the installable Red Hat packages are kept:

```
cd /mnt/cdrom/RedHat/RPMS
```

Finally, to install all the appropriate X files in one fell swoop, enter this command (type it as one big long line, even although it will wrap to two lines on the screen):

```
rpm -Uvh X11R6-contrib* XFree86-3.3* Xconfigurator* gtk+-1* xinitrc*
```

You'll see a little progress meter on the screen as each package is installed. When you're returned to the command prompt, the installation is complete. Your best bet now would be to run the Xconfigurator program to get X in sync with your video hardware. See the section "Get Your GUI Working" in Appendix B for instructions. After you've run Xconfigurator, be sure to return to this section of the book. You'll then be ready to install GNOME, as discussed next.

## INSTALLING GNOME

To install GNOME, you'll need to insert and mount the Red Hat Linux 6.2 CD-ROM #1. If you *didn't* already do that to install X, right now you'll want to insert the CD into its drive, then enter the following commands to mount the CD and switch to the directory that contains the Red Hat packages:

```
mount /dev/cdrom /mnt/cdrom
```

```
cd /mnt/cdrom/RedHat/RPMS
```

Next, you'll need to enter a whole bunch of rpm commands to install the many files that make up GNOME. As always, be careful with upper/lowercase letters and blank spaces as you enter each command. Allow one command to complete before entering the next one. Of course, you can use the ~UA key to re-type the rpm -Uvh part of the command each time, and just Backspace over the package name from the previous command.

**Tip**

The rpm command is described in detail in Chapter 13, "Managing Packages with RPM." Once you've installed GNOME, you'll be able to use the Gnorpm program described in that chapter to install future packages.

Enter the following rpm commands:

```
rpm -Uvh ORBit-0*
rpm -Uvh audiofile-0*
rpm -Uvh esound-0*
rpm -Uvh gnome-audio*
rpm -Uvh gnome-users*
rpm -Uvh gtk+-1*
rpm -Uvh libghttp-1*
rpm -Uvh libxml-1*
rpm -Uvh libxml10*
rpm -Uvh mc*
rpm -Uvh libgr-progs*
rpm -Uvh libungif-4*
rpm -Uvh imlib-1*
rpm -Uvh xpm*
rpm -Uvh gnome-libs-1*
rpm -Uvh xload*
rpm -Uvh xscreensaver*
rpm -Uvh control-center-1*
rpm -Uvh ee*
rpm -Uvh esound-0*
rpm -Uvh extace*
rpm -Uvh gdm*
rpm -Uvh gmc*
rpm -Uvh gnome-media*
rpm -Uvh gnome-pim-1*
rpm -Uvh gtk-engines*
rpm -Uvh imlib-cfg*
rpm -Uvh libglade-0*
rpm -Uvh libgtop-1*
rpm -Uvh pygtk*
rpm -Uvh magicdev*
rpm -Uvh fnlib-0*
rpm -Uvh enlight*
rpm -Uvh gnome-core-1*
```

```
rpm -Uvh umb-scheme*

rpm -Uvh guile*

rpm -Uvh gnome-games-1*

rpm -Uvh gnome-utils-1*

rpm -Uvh pygnome-1*

rpm -Uvh gnumeric-0*

rpm -Uvh xchat*

rpm -Uvh usermode*

rpm -Uvh gnorpm-0*

rpm -Uvh gedit-0*

rpm -Uvh gnome-linuxconf*
```

When you've finished, switch back to your home directory and unmount the CD-ROM by entering the following commands:

```
cd ~
umount /mnt/cdrom
```

Then remove the CD using the button on the drive or the `eject` command. Log out of the system to end your current session:

Log in again normally when given the login prompt. Then enter this command to start X and GNOME:

```
startx
```

You should find yourself in a working GNOME environment. If you haven't used GNOME before, see "Getting Around in GNOME" in Chapter 1 for the basics.

# CHAPTER 10

# INSTALLING AND USING KDE

## In this chapter

# WHAT IS KDE?

KDE is a complete desktop environment for Linux, in much the same way that GNOME is a desktop environment. If you're looking to build a cost-effective network for a small- to medium-sized business and you want users to have a simple, intuitive interface to work with, KDE may be just the ticket. It includes all the best ease-of-use features of GNOME and popular desktop operating systems like Windows and the Macintosh OS. But unlike a commercial OS, KDE is freely distributed under the GNU General Public License.

In the ease-of-use department, KDE is tough to beat. There's extensive use of drag and drop, a trashcan for recovering deleted files, a graphical file manager and graphical configuration tools. There are currently well over 100 clients (programs) that run under the KDE framework, all sharing a common look and feel for easy transfer of skills from one product to the next. KOffice (http://koffice.kde.org) is an ambitious project to create a free "office suite" of applications for KDE including KWord (word processing), KSpread (spreadsheet), KPresenter (presentations), KIllustrator (drawing), KDiagramm (charting), and Katabase (database management). As I write this chapter, the KOffice apps are still in the alpha stage of development and not quite ready for prime time. But perhaps by the time you read this, they'll have packages that you can easily download and install.

By the way, in case you're wondering, KDE stands for K Desktop Environment. The K doesn't really stand for anything, though some people maintain that it really stands for "Kool."

# INSTALLING KDE

Your Red Hat boxed set comes with the complete desktop environment right on the Red Hat Linux CD. If you didn't perform a KDE Workstation, or didn't choose KDE during a custom installation, you can install everything you need right from the Red Hat Linux CD-ROM. Here are the exact steps, assuming you'll be starting from the GNOME interface:

1. Insert the Red Hat Linux CD-ROM into your CD-ROM drive. If the CD doesn't mount automatically, go ahead and mount it using the User Mount Tool or the `mount /dev/cdrom /mnt/cdrom` command in a terminal window.

**Tip**

> You can skip steps 2-9 by entering four commands in a terminal window. First enter the command `rpm -i /mnt/cdrom/RedHat/RPMS/qt1x-1*` and when the command prompt returns, enter the command `rpm -i /mnt/cdrom/RedHat/RPMS/qt-1*`. Then enter the commands `rpm -i /mnt/cdrom/RedHat/RPMS/kde*` and `rpm -i /mnt/cdrom/RedHat/RPMS/switchdesk-kde*`.

2. If GnoRPM doesn't open automatically after you've inserted the Red Hat Linux CD, click the Main Menu button and choose System, GnoRPM to start GnoRPM yourself.

3. Click the Install button in the GnoRPM toolbar. The Install dialog box opens.

4. Click the Add button in the Install dialog box to open the Add Packages dialog box.

5. If the button at the top of the Add Packages dialog box isn't pointing to /mnt/cdrom/ RedHat/RPMS, click that button and navigate to that directory now.

6. Click each of the files listed in Table 10.1, then click the Add button to copy the file to the Install dialog box.

**TABLE 10.1    PACKAGES THAT MAKE UP THE KDE DESKTOP ENVIRONMENT AVAILABLE ON YOUR RED HAT CD-ROM**

| Package Name | What It Contains |
| --- | --- |
| kdeadmin-1.1.2-6.i386.rpm | KDE system administration tools |
| kdebase-1.1.2-33.i386.rpm | Core applications for KDE |
| kdebase-lowcolor-icons-1.1.2-33.i386.rpm | Custom icons for KDE |
| kdegames-1.1.2-3.i386.rpm | KDE games |
| kdegraphics-1.1.2-3.i386.rpm | Graphic viewers and editors |
| kdelibs-1.1.2-15.i386.rpm | Core libraries required by KDE |
| kdemultimedia-1.1.2-7.i386.rpm | Multimedia apps for KDE |
| kdenetwork-1.1.2-13.i386.rpm | Internet and network applications |
| kdesupport-1.1.2-12.i386.rpm | KDE support libraries |
| kdetoys-1.1.2-3.i386.rpm | Fun KDE toys (optional) |
| kdeutils-1.1.2-4.i386.rpm | Text editors, calculator, and more |
| qt-2.1.0-4.beta1.rpm | Toolkit used to develop KDE |
| qt1x-1.45-3.i386.rpm | Shared library for the QT GUI toolkit |
| switchdesk-kde-2.1-1.i386.rpm | KDE desktop switching tool |

7. Close the Add Packages dialog box by clicking its Close button. The Install dialog box will show names of packages to be installed with checkmarks to the right, as in Figure 10.1.

**Figure 10.1**
GnoRPM showing packages to be installed (those with check marks).

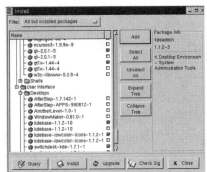

8. Click the Install button at the bottom of the Install dialog box.

9. Wait until all the files have been installed, and then you can close the Install dialog box and GNOME RPM window.

# RUNNING KDE

Once KDE is installed, you can enter the following command at the command prompt or in a terminal window, to bring up the desktop switching tool and switch to the KDE desktop:

```
switchdesk-kde
```

The desktop switching tool opens up looking something like Figure 10.2. Choose the KDE option, choose Change Only Applies to Current Display, then click the OK button. You'll see a message indicating that the desktop configuration has been updated. Click its OK button. Then, click the Main Menu button and choose Logout, Logout, Yes. If your computer isn't set up to start X automatically, you can simply enter the `startx` command to start X. Otherwise, you'll be taken to the kdm login menu, where you can log in with your usual username and password.

> **Tip**
>
> Any time you want to get back to GNOME, just follow the instructions under "Getting Back to GNOME" near the end of this chapter.

**Figure 10.2**
The Desktop Switcher gains KDE as an option after you've installed KDE.

The first time you start KDE, it will create a subdirectory named desktop in your home directory, and you'll see a little message telling you so. Click the OK button, and you'll be taken into KDE, which will look something like Figure 10.3. If you've set up X to use multiple resolutions, you may need to use the Ctlr+Alt++ or Ctlr+Alt+- keys (using the + and - keys on the numeric keypad) to get to the $1024 \times 768$ resolution shown in the figure.

## KDE DESKTOP COMPONENTS

The tools on the KDE desktop will probably seem pretty familiar to you now. Here's a quick rundown:

- **Taskbar:** Each open window on the desktop has a button on the taskbar. Clicking that button raises the window to the forefront. If the window is minimized, clicking its button restores the window to its previous size.

**Figure 10.3**
The KDE desktop environment at 1024 × 768 resolution.

- **Desktop (a.k.a. root display or root window)**: Your basic work area. Mid-clicking brings up a menu of virtual desktops and open windows. Click any option to jump to that desktop or window. Right-click the desktop for help, arranging icons, logging out, and other options.

- **Desktop icons:** Shortcuts to favorite programs. The Trash icon is permanent and can be used to hold files that you've "semi-deleted," but haven't fully committed to deleting yet (more in this subject later in the chapter). To create a link to a favorite directory, document, or program, drag its icon out of the File Manager (discussed in a moment), drop it onto the desktop, and choose Link. Right-click any desktop icon to delete it or change its properties.

- **K button (a.k.a. the pplication Starter or the Main Menu button)**: Offers access to programs and utilities through a standard menu structure. You can customize the menu using the Menu Editor. To get to the Menu Editor, click the K button and choose Utilities, Menu Editor.

- **Panel:** Offers quick-access buttons to commonly used applications. Pointing to most buttons will display a tooltip. Buttons with an up arrow are like GNOME drawers, and clicking one presents a menu of more options. Right-click the panel and choose Configure to see options for customizing the panel. To add a button to the panel, click the K button and choose Panel, Add Application.

■ **Pager:** The One, Two, Three, and Four buttons represent the four virtual desktops, and you can click any button to get to that desktop. X and lock buttons provide quick access to logging out and locking the screen. To increase or decrease the number of virtual desktops available to you, right-click the panel, choose Configure, and make your selections from the Desktops tab in the K Panel Configuration dialog box that appears.

## KDE HELP

The Help system in KDE is easy to get to, easy to use, and contains lots of handy hyperlinks for cross-referencing within the help system. You can get to the opening Help page using any of the following methods (see Figure 10.4):

■ Click the KDE Help button in the panel.

■ Right-click the desktop and choose Help on the Desktop.

■ Click the K button and choose KDE Help.

**Figure 10.4**
Opening page of the KDE Help system.

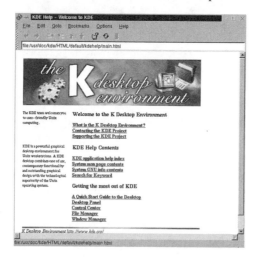

The following are some particularly useful links on the opening Help page:

■ **A Quick Start Guide to the Desktop:** An absolute must-read for any KDE newbies, it explains how to do all the basic tasks.

■ **Search for Keyword:** Search the KDE documentation and/or online manuals (man pages) for a specific word or phrase.

■ **KDE Application Help Index:** Offers a list of programs available for KDE.

Most applications also have their own context-sensitive help, which you can access by opening the Help option in that application's menu bar. Or in many cases, pressing the Help (F1) key will open up the appropriate help for that program.

The KDE Web site at www.kde.org adds a lot more documentation to the built-in help. There you'll find the Quick Start Guide, a more extensive User's Manual, and the ever-important FAQs. The KOffice Web site (http://koffice.kde.org) is the place to check on that project's progress. There were no RPM packages available when I wrote this chapter because the product hadn't been officially released yet. But by the time you read this—who knows?

## KDE KEYBOARD SHORTCUTS

KDE has some keyboard shortcuts that are handy when your hands happen to be on the keyboard rather than the mouse. Keys that work at the desktop and when you're working with open windows are summarized in Table 10.2.

**TABLE 10.2    SHORTCUT KEYS FOR THE KDE DESKTOP**

| Key | Purpose |
| --- | --- |
| F1 | Context-sensitive Help |
| Alt+F1 | Opens the Main Menu |
| Alt+F2 | Opens a box for entering a single Linux command |
| Alt+Tab | Switches to next open window |
| Ctrl+Tab | Switches to next virtual desktop |
| Ctrl+Esc | Switches to another virtual desktop or log out |
| Alt+F3 | Shows options menu for the currently window |
| Alt+F4 | Closes the current window |
| Alt+mid-click | Raises the current window to the top of the stack |
| Ctrl+F$n$ | Takes you to virtual desktop $n$ |
| Ctrl+Alt+Backspace | Closes KDE without saving |
| Ctrl+Alt++ (numeric keypad) | Cycles to next screen resolution |
| Ctrl+Alt+- (numeric keypad) | Cycles to previous screen resolution |

## ENTERING COMMANDS IN KDE

KDE doesn't prevent you from using the command prompt. You can pop open a terminal window at any time using whichever technique is most convenient:

- Click the Terminal Emulation (kvt) button in the panel.
- Click the K button and choose Utilities, Konsole.
- Click the toolbox button in the panel (the one showing a box, wrench, and hammer) and choose Konsole from the button bar that pops up.

If you want to enter a single command and then have the command window disappear automatically, you can do either of the following:

- Right-click the desktop and choose Execute Command.
- Press Alt+F2.

# MANAGING FILES IN KDE

The KDE graphical file manager, named kfm, aims to be as user-friendly as a file manager can be. It also doubles as a Web browser, FTP client, and tar archive utility. To open, click the panel button showing a folder with a little house in front (its tooltip reads This folder contains all your personal files). Optionally, you can click the K button and choose Home Directory. Initially, the file manager will point you to your home directory. If you'd like to see the directory tree in the left pane as in Figure 10.5, choose View, Show Tree from kfm's menu bar.

**Figure 10.5**
The KDE File Manager, kfm, with the directory tree displayed in the left column.

Superusers can open up a copy of file manager that provides much greater privileges by clicking the K button and choosing System, File Manager (Super User Mode). If you're not logged in as root, you'll be prompted for the root password before the file manager will open.

**Caution**

Files whose names begin with a dot are hidden by default in kfm. To bring the dot out of hiding, choose View, Show Hidden Files from the kfm menu bar.

To move and copy files, you can open a second file manager window by choosing File, New Window (or simply press Ctrl+N). Use the standard tools to navigate through directories. To select multiple files to move or copy, drag a frame around them using the mouse, or hold down the Ctrl key while clicking file icons. Then drag the selected file(s) to any directory or directory icon. When you release the mouse button, you'll be given the options to Copy, Move, or Link (create a symbolic link or "shortcut icon" to the original file). In this manner you can quickly create desktop shortcuts to favorite directories, programs, and other files.

As in the GNOME file manager, if you want to rename a file, you need to right-click it and choose Properties. Then use the File Name textbox to change the name of the file. You can also use the Properties dialog box to change the file permissions, ownership, and icon.

You have a couple of ways to delete files in KDE. When you right-click a file's icon (or any selected icon), you'll be given two deletion options on the context menu that appears: Move to Trash and Delete. The Delete option is permanent. Once you delete a file, there's no way to undelete it. You'll see a warning to that effect. If you choose Move to Trash, the file is simply moved into the Trashcan directory.

> **Tip**
>
> You can also search the filesystem for a file based on its name, date modified, type, content, or size. Click the Find Utility button in the panel, or click the K button and choose Find Files.

## USING THE TRASHCAN

The Trashcan is simply a directory for storing files that have been deleted from their original location, but not yet permanently deleted from the disk. You can use a couple of quick shortcuts to get to the Trashcan directory:

- Click the Trash button on the desktop.
- Click the K button and choose Trashcan.

To rescue files from the Trashcan, you need to open that directory, then move the files to some other directory. To remove the files from the disk permanently and therefore recover the disk space they're using, choose File, Empty Trash Bin from the Trashcan menu bar. Be careful, though—the files are permanently deleted right away, and there's no way to get them back.

# MOUNTING DISKS IN KDE

Mounting and unmounting removable disks in KDE is easy, because its desktop provides two simple icons—CD-ROM and floppy. To mount a disk, put it into the appropriate drive. Then right-click the drive's desktop icon and choose Mount (see Figure 10.6).

**PART**

**II**

**CH**

**10**

**Figure 10.6**
Floppy and CD-ROM icons to the KDE desktop make it easy to mount disks and access those drives.

> **Tip**
>
> Remember, if you want regular users to be able to mount removable disks, you need to add the users option to /etc/fstab, as discussed at the Case Study near the end of Chapter 6, "System Administration Basics."

Once the disk is mounted, double-clicking the icon will open the K file manager and display the contents of the disk that's currently in the drive. When you want to unmount a mounted disk, right-click its icon and choose Unmount from the menu.

---

**Bug or Feature?**

In the version of KDE I used to write this passage, I discovered that a user can't unmount a CD-ROM using her desktop icon. Trying to do this displays a message like /dev/hdd (or /dev/scd0) doesn't exist, and you are not root. My workaround was to open /etc/fstab and copy the line that defines /dev/cdrom to a new line. In that new line, change /dev/cdrom to either /dev/hdd or /dev/scd0, depending on what your error message shows. Of course, if this is a little bug, it may be fixed by the time you read this.

---

> **Tip**
>
> To format floppy disks, use the KDE Kfloppy tool. Click the K button and choose Utilities, Kfloppy.

## AUTOSTARTING PROGRAMS IN KDE

KDE is session-managed, so that when you log out, it can remember which programs were open and redisplay them the next time you log in. But, it only works with programs that *can* be session-managed. If you want a particular program, say Konsole, to start automatically at log in, you need to drag that program's startup icon into the folder named Autostart on the KDE desktop. The startup icons for most programs on the system can be found in the /usr/bin (user binaries) directory. You can test the icon before you drag it into the Autostart program by clicking it to make sure that it opens the program you want.

For most programs, the name of the file that starts the program is the same as the program name, although, it may be longer and will probably be in lowercase. You can use the KDE Find Utility to search for the appropriate file. Click the Find Utility button in the panel, or click the K button and choose Find Files. Type the name of the program you want to search for, in lowercase, followed by an asterisk (as in konsole*). To search the entire filesystem, set the Look In option to / and check the Include Subfolders option. Then click the Start Search button in the toolbar to start the search.

If you end up with a whole lot of files, the one whose name exactly matches the program's name or the one that's in the /usr/bin directory will probably be the one you want. When the Find Utility has finished its search, you can double-click whichever icon seems to be the most likely for starting the program to see if it actually *does* start the program. If the program you want opens up on the screen, you've found the correct icon for starting that program.

## DEFINING DEFAULT KDE DESKTOPS

When KDE is first installed, it sets up a default skeleton desktop in the /etc/skel/Desktop directory. Any time you add a new user, that user's desktop will receive whatever icons and settings are defined within that directory. As root, you can open /etc/skel/Desktop and put whatever desktop icons you wish into it. Also, if users enter the startx command to get to their GUIs, you can create or edit the .xinitrc file in each user's home directory. If there is no .xinitrc file in the user's home directory, you can create one and put it in the command startkde. If the user does have a .xinitrc file, you'll first want to check to see if it already contains a line that calls a window manager, such as exec gnome-session; if there is, replace that line with startkde.

> **Tip**
>
> To get out of KDE altogether and return to GNOME or another desktop environment, open the Desktop Switching Tool by clicking the K button and choosing System, Desktop Switching Tool. Or enter the command switchdesk-kde in a terminal window or the Command dialog box that appears after you press Alt+F2.

# CONFIGURING WITH THE KDE CONTROL CENTER

Configuring KDE is pretty easy, thanks to its extensive Control Center. To open the Control Center, do one of the following:

- Click the KDE Control Center button on the panel.
- Click the K button and choose KDE Control Center.
- Enter the command kcontrol in a terminal window.

Whichever method you use, the KDE Control Center will open up, initially looking something like Figure 10.7. As you may have guessed, options down the left panel represent categories of options. Clicking the + sign next to a category expands it. Clicking an option within a category displays the dialog box for configuring that component of KDE.

**Figure 10.7**
The KDE Control Center provides easy configuration of virtually the entire K Desktop Environment.

When you click an option to display its dialog box, most options you see should be pretty self-explanatory. If not, you can click the Help button down near the bottom of the Control Center. You'll get a Help screen that describes, specifically, the controls in the dialog box you're working with at the moment. The Help screens are free of the heavily technical jargon used in other forms of Linux documentation, so you shouldn't have any problems configuring KDE to your needs.

Customizing the Main Menu is handled as a separate Menu Editor app. You can start that app by clicking the K button and choosing Utilities, Menu Editor. When the Menu Editor window opens, you can press F1 or choose Help, Contents from the Menu Editor's menu bar to get all the information you need to edit KDE's menus. KDE also has its own tool for adding and managing users. To get to it, click the K button and choose System, User Manager.

## GETTING BACK TO GNOME

Any time you feel like returning to GNOME, just re-run the desktop switching tool and choose GNOME. Here are the exact steps to follow from the KDE desktop:

1. Click the K button.
2. Choose Red Hat, System, Desktop Switching Tool.
3. Choose GNOME in the window that appears, and then click its OK button.
4. Click OK when told about restarting X.
5. To restart X, click the K button and choose Logout, Logout.
6. If you're returned to the command prompt, enter the command startx once again to restart X. The GNOME desktop should appear.

Remember that you can use the Desktop Switching Tool at any time to switch desktops. If you're in GNOME, and want to switch to KDE, follow these steps:

1. Click the GNOME Main Menu button and choose System, Desktop Switching Tool.
2. Choose KDE and click the OK button.
3. Click the OK button in response to the message about restarting X.
4. Then click the GNOME Main Menu button and choose Logout, Logout, Yes.
5. If you're returned to the command prompt, enter the command startx to restart x.

## PROJECT: BECOMING A KDE GURU

I realize that this chapter has been something of a whirlwind tour of KDE. I'm sure one could write a pretty good-sized book just about KDE, and certainly about KDE with KOffice combined. But given the fact that this is a book about Linux, I need to keep this chapter brief so I can have room for all the Linux-specific topics to come.

Fortunately, you can find lots of documentation and other support for KDE both on your computer and online. The help system described earlier in this chapter is a great resource. If you can get into the habit of pressing the F1 key or choosing an option from the Help option on the menu bar when problems arise, you'll probably find the answers to most of your questions in a jiffy.

There's a more detailed and extensive User's Guide at the KDE Web site that is very informative. The last time I checked, the address was `http://www.kde.org/documentation/userguide/index.html`. But if they move it, you should be able to get to it from the KDE home page at `www.kde.org`. Click the Documentation link, then click User's Guide. You'll also find the Quick Start Guide and FAQs under the Documentation link.

The Mailing List archive is another great resource of information. That too is accessible from the KDE home page, and also at `http://lists.kde.org`. As a newbie, you'll probably find the kde-user list to be your best starting point. To subscribe to that list, address an email message to `kde-user-request@kde.org`. In the Subject line, type the word `subscribe` followed by a blank space and your email address. You can leave the body of the message blank, and send it off normally.

PART

**II**

CH

**10**

# CHAPTER 11

# CONFIGURING STARTUP AND SHUTDOWN

## In this chapter

# HOW THE BOOT PROCESS WORKS

Before a computer can do anything, it needs to "pick itself up by the bootstraps" by loading an operating system. The operating system, in turn, defines the whole user interface and manages all the various devices attached to the computer, such as disk drives, printers, and so forth. Every program you use is actually an *application* of the operating system it runs on. Hence, you can run Macintosh applications on the Mac OS, but you can't run those applications on a Windows or Linux PC. Anyway, the act of loading an operating system at startup is called *booting up*(due to the bootstrap analogy). And as you've no doubt seen when watching your computer screen while Linux is booting up, a whole lot of stuff happens. But all that activity can be broken down into smaller stages. Starting at the moment you start your machine, the following sections describe what happens.

## THE POWER ON SELF TEST (POST)

First the computer performs a Power On Self Test (POST) where you see that certain components get checked. There's really no software involved at this point. After the test the computer loads information from the BIOS (Basic Input Output System), which is actually a chip on the motherboard inside the computer. On most machines you have a brief moment to change the information stored in the BIOS by pressing some key. For example, you might see the message `Press Del to Enter Setup` or `Press F1 to Enter Setup`. Typically, the only time you'd need to go into the BIOS setup would be if you changed or added a disk drive, processor, memory, or mouse. The instructions that came with that new device would describe what needs to be done within BIOS setup. The documentation that came with the computer (or the motherboard, if you built the computer yourself) would also provide more information about the BIOS setup.

> **Tip**
>
> The BIOS information is actually stored in a chip on the computer's motherboard. It retains any information you place in it, even when the power is off, thanks to a small battery or capacitor on the motherboard.

The normal procedure, of course, is to simply ignore the prompt that allows you to enter BIOS Setup and let the boot process continue.

## SCSI DEVICES

If your computer has SCSI devices attached, those are tested and initialized during the POST as well. Most SCSI devices have their own BIOS setup that's separate from the regular BIOS setup on the motherboard. If your computer contains a SCSI *host adapter* (typically a card on the motherboard that SCSI devices plug into), you may see a message likes `Press <CTRL><A> to Enter SCSISelect Utility`. Again, the only reason to go into the SCSI Setup program is if you add or remove a SCSI device and need to make some changes to your SCSI settings.

Specific instructions on what to do would be provided with the SCSI device itself or with the documentation that came with the SCSI host adapter.

> **Tip**
>
> New SCSI hard drives often need to be "low-level formatted" before they can be formatted for a particular filesystem. Low-level formatting is usually done through the SCSI Setup program.

Assuming you don't enter the SCSI Setup program, the boot process continues. After all the SCSI devices are taken care of, the POST is done and the computer goes looking for a *Master Boot Record* (MBR), a *boot loader*, or a *boot manager* that will load an operating system into memory.

So far, everything that's happened is independent of the particular operating system you're using. This "wake up" procedure is built into the PC hardware. At this point, the computer can load any operating system that's available on the computer. In Red Hat Linux, a program named LILO takes over, and lets you choose your operating system.

## LILO THE BOOT LOADER

PART
**II**

CH
**11**

When hunting for a Master Boot Record, most computers will first check the floppy and CD-ROM drives. If those drives contain disks, it looks to the first sector of those disks. If one of those disks does not contain a boot loader or MBR, the machine might just hang and do nothing. However, if the floppy and CD-ROM drives are empty, which is usually what you want when starting a computer, the computer looks to the first sector of the hard drive. On your typical Linux PC with only Linux installed, or Linux plus DOS, Windows 3/95/98 installed, the computer should find LILO, the Linux Loader, on that first sector. Unlike an MBR, which loads a specific operating system, LILO pauses for a moment to allow the user sitting at the machine to choose an operating system to run or to pass options to the operating system that will be run.

If you've never messed with the LILO default settings, LILO will present a LILO boot prompt on the screen for about five seconds shortly after the POST is finished. During those five seconds you can press the Tab key to see a list of installed operating systems that you can boot from. For example, if you have both Linux and Windows 95/98 installed, you'd see something like this:

```
linux    dos
```

If you type dos and press Enter, you're taken to Windows (or DOS, if that's your other OS).

If you type linux or do nothing within those five seconds, LILO begins to load the Linux kernel.

> **Note**
>
> Dec Alpha machines use MILO, rather than LILO, to load the kernel. Sparc workstations use SILO. Third-party loaders like System Commander use their own programs, which are described in the documentation that comes with those programs.

---

**DOS, Windows, NT, 2000, and OS/2**

In case you're wondering, Windows 3, 95, and 98 are all built around the DOS kernel and are collectively referred to as DOS in Linux literature. Those "consumer" operating systems keep the DOS kernel for compatibility reasons—popular DOS/Windows games still require a DOS kernel. Windows NT and 2000 are built around the NT kernel, which is an altogether different animal. Dual-booting with NT or 2000 is not the same as dual-booting with DOS. The mini-HOWTO *Linux+NT-Loader* explains how to do it.

---

To dual-boot with OS/2, you need to install the OS/2 Boot Manager in the MBR, and LILO on your Linux /root partition. The mini-HOWTO *Linux+DOS+Win95+OS2* and the unmaintained mini-HOWTO *Linux+OS2+DOS* discuss strategies for dual-booting with OS/2. For a reminder on accessing HOWTOs, see "HOWTOs and FAQs" in Chapter 5.

As I write this chapter, there are no HOWTOs for dual-booting with Windows 2000 because that product is still in the beta test phase. But you can check the latest HOWTOs online at `http://metalab.unc.edu/LDP/HOWTO` to see if anyone has written one.

## LOADING THE LINUX KERNEL

Once you've made your selection from LILO, or the LILO boot prompt has timed out, the last phase of the startup procedure begins. This last phase is where the operating system kernel (core) is actually loaded into RAM. Assuming you chose Linux as your OS, the kernel goes through an initialization process, often referred to as *init*. In a nutshell, the initialization process loads some vital processes (programs), presents the Login prompt, and stores some information about the current session in environment variables. As you'll learn later in this chapter, there are lots of ways to configure the init process. Before we get into the details of all that, though, some words of advice.

# PREPARING FOR THE NEW CONFIGURATION

Much of the information that follows in this chapter is about customizing, configuring, or repairing your boot process. However, there's an inherent risk in doing these things because you could make a mistake that prevents the computer from booting up at all! You want to be prepared for the worst-case scenario before you get started, just in case....

## KNOW YOUR BOOT PARTITION(S)

You never know when you'll need to know your Linux boot partition, and perhaps the boot partitions of other operating systems on the same computer. So it's good to get this information while things are working correctly, and jot it down for future reference. LinuxConf will gladly display the information you need. Recall that, to run LinuxConf, you can click the Gnome Main Menu button and choose System, LinuxConf from the menu. Or just enter the command `linuxconf` at any command prompt or terminal window.

From the tree menu in LinuxConf, open the Config, boot mode, and LILO categories, then click default boot configuration, as in Figure 11.1. In the example shown, /dev/sda6 is the boot partition for Linux. The /boot/vmlinuz-2.2.12-20 is the actual kernel that's loaded at bootup time. The boot partition for DOS/Windows, in that example, is /dev/sda1.

**Figure 11.1**
LinuxConf can display your current boot partitions, information you should jot down and keep safe for future reference!

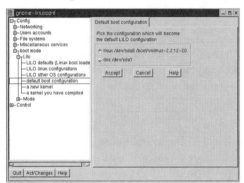

PART

**II**

CH

**11**

After jotting down the information, quit LinuxConf without saving any changes. Just keep clicking Cancel and Quit buttons until LinuxConf closes.

## ALWAYS COPY YOUR ORIGINAL CONFIGURATION FILES

Don't forget that whenever you change a configuration file, you run the risk of making an error that makes the file unusable. Always make a copy of any configuration file you're about to change, using the `cp` command or any file manager, before you make your changes. In particular, you want to make copies of the following configuration files any time you'll be editing them directly, and even before using LinuxConf to tweak your startup configuration (because LinuxConf stores your selections in those files):

- **/etc/liloconf**: LILO's configuration file
- **/etc/inittab**: Initialization Table, controls the behavior of the `init` process

## CREATE AN EMERGENCY BOOT DISK

An emergency boot disk can come in very handy when a problem occurs that prevents LILO or Linux from starting from your hard disk. This disk works when your hard disk and Linux are basically intact, but you just can't get to a LILO boot prompt. While "Emergency Boot Disk" is not the official name of this disk you're about to create, I'll refer to it as that throughout this book to differentiate it from the Red Hat boot disk you use to install Linux on your computer. Grab a blank floppy disk (or one with stuff that you don't care about anymore), and label it *Red Hat Linux 6.2 Emergency Boot Disk*. If there's already a mounted floppy disk in your floppy drive, dismount it by entering the command:

```
umount /mnt/floppy
```

Next, put the disk you labeled "Emergency Boot Disk" into the floppy drive. At the command prompt or in a terminal window, enter the following command to determine the current release version number of your Linux kernel:

```
uname -r
```

You should see something like 2.2.14-5.0. Next, enter the command:

```
mkbootdisk --device /dev/fd0 2.2.14-5.0
```

but replace 2.2.14-5.0 with whatever release number the uname -r command returned. Follow the instructions on the screen. When you're returned to the command prompt, store that new boot disk in a safe place where you'll be able to find it when you need it.

## CREATE A RESCUE DISK

A rescue disk will come in handy should your boot disk find it impossible to gain access to your hard drive. Chances are you created a rescue disk when you first installed Linux. If you happened to read Chapter 2 of the *Reference Guide* that came with your Red Hat package, you might have noticed the instructions for creating the rescue disk. If you tried following those instructions, you will have probably discovered that they don't work. That's because the rescue.img file needed to create the rescue disk isn't on the Red Hat CD-ROM. In fact, as I write this chapter, a rescue.img file specifically for Red Hat 6.2 doesn't exist anywhere.

Perhaps by the time you read this, Red Hat will have made a rescue.img file available from its Errata page (www.redhat.com/errata), and/or from ftp.priority.redhat.com. If so, you'll want to use that image file to create your rescue disk. Otherwise, it seems safe to use the rescue.img filefrom Red Hat 6.0, which is available on that CD as well as online at ftp://ftp.redhat.com/redhat/old-releases/redhat-6.0/i386/images.

Once you get a hold of the rescue.img file, you can easily create a rescue disk. You'll need a blank floppy disk (or one with stuff you don't care about anymore). Label it *Red Hat Linux 6.1 Rescue Disk* or some such thing, perhaps jotting down the date you created the disk as well. Put that disk into the floppy drive and enter the following:

```
dd if=path/rescue.img of=/dev/fd0 bs=1440k
```

path is the path to wherever you put the rescue.img file. For example, if you put the rescue.img file in the /root directory, the command would be as follows:

```
dd if=/root/rescue.img of=/dev/fd0 bs=1440k
```

After you've entered the command, you'll get a little feedback on the screen, perhaps hear some disk activity, and then be returned to the command prompt. When the command prompt is back on the screen and the light on the floppy drive goes out, you're done.

Store the rescue disk in a safe place, where you'll be able to find it if needed, along with your emergency boot disk.

## Using the Boot and Rescue Disks

If you ever have trouble getting to the LILO boot prompt, or for some reason can't get Linux to boot from the hard disk, you can follow these steps to boot from your emergency boot disk:

1. Put your emergency boot disk into the floppy drive.

2. Make sure the CD-ROM and any other disk drives are empty.

3. Turn on the computer.

4. You'll see a LILO message followed by brief instructions. Press Enter or wait 10 seconds to try to boot from the hard disk.

> **Tip**
>
> If you have a recent computer, chances are you have a bootable CD-ROM drive and can simply boot from the Red Hat Linux 6.2 CD-ROM! Doing this eliminates the need to keep a separate disk around to access your system. Simply pop in the CD and choose the option you need from the main menu.

**PART**

**II**

**Ch**

**11**

If you can make it to the command prompt or GUI, then Linux is still intact. You'll have access to your entire Linux filesystem, and hopefully, you'll be able to fix whatever was causing your problem. Unfortunately, I can't help you much in this case because I have no idea of what the problem might be. However, if you recently changed some configuration file, a good starting point would be to delete the customized version of that file, and replace it with the backup copy you (hopefully) made beforehand. If the problem is that LILO has been overwritten or deleted—as may very well be the case if you installed another operating system after installing Linux—you can reinstall LILO as discussed in the section "Installing or Reinstalling LILO" later this chapter.

If the emergency boot disk cannot gain sufficient access to the hard disk in order to boot correctly, you'll need to fall back on the rescue disk. This, unfortunately, won't give you access to your entire Linux filesystem. However, it will give you access to some commands that might help you solve the problem. To use the rescue disk, you need to first boot from the emergency boot disk by following the steps 1-3 just discussed. Optionally, you can boot from the Red Hat Boot Disk that you used to install Linux. But this time, when you get to the boot prompt, type rescue and press Enter. Follow the instructions that appear on the screen to boot from the rescue disk.

Eventually you'll get to a message telling you that you're using the rescue disk, followed by the # character, which is the rescue disk version of the superuser command prompt. If you enter the command ls -a, you'll see a list of all the directories on the disk, which are similar to the directories that are available on your hard disk. Most of the commands you're likely to need will be found in the /bin directory, which you can get to by entering the command cd/bin.

Unfortunately, I have no way of telling you what to do from this point forward. That all depends on the problem you're trying to solve, and obviously, I have no way of guessing what that might be. However, I can tell you that the rescue disk contains the programs listed in Table 11.1, which should help you fix any problems. For more information on any program, check the index at the back of this book, the command's man page on the Red Hat CD-ROM, the Linux Documentation Project Mirror at http://www.redhat.com/mirrors/LDP, or any other resource discussed previously in Chapter 5, "Getting Help."

**TABLE 11.1 COMMANDS AVAILABLE FROM A BOOTED RESCUE DISK**

| Command | Purpose |
|---------|---------|
| badblocks | Searches a device for bad blocks |
| bash | Run the Bourne Again Shell |
| bzip2 | Compress files |
| cat | Concatenate (join) files |
| chmod | Change file permissions |
| chroot | Change root directory |
| cp | Copy file or directory |
| cpio | Copy files to and from archives |
| dd | Convert and copy a file |
| e2fsck | Create Linux second extended filesystem |
| fdisk | Manage disk partitions |
| grep | Locate lines that match a pattern |
| gunzip | Decompress .gz files |
| gzip | Compress a file |
| head | Display first 10 lines of a file |
| ifconfig | Configure network interface |
| init | Initialize process control |
| ln | Create a symbolic link |
| ls | List directory contents |
| lsmod | List loaded modules |
| mkdir | Create a directory |
| mke2fs | Make a Linux filesystem |
| mknod | Create special file type |
| mount | Mount a filesystem |
| mt | Control a tape drive |

**TABLE 11.1    CONTINUED**

| Command | Purpose |
| --- | --- |
| mv | Move or rename files |
| open | Open a file and return a file descriptor |
| pico | A simple text editor |
| ping | Send echo request to network host |
| ps | Display process status |
| restore | Restore backup |
| rm | Remove (delete) file |
| route | Show/change IP routing table |
| rpm | Install/remove/query Red Hat packages |
| sed | Perform text transformations on input stream |
| sh | Run shell command |
| swapoff | Stop swapping to device |
| swapon | Start swapping to device |
| sync | Flush filesystem buffers |
| tac | Concatenate  (join) files in reverse |
| tail | Display last 10 lines of file |
| tar | Manage .tar (Tape archive) files |
| traceroute | Track route a network packet follows |
| umount | Unmount a file system |
| vi | Simple text editor |
| vim | Improved vi text editor |

PART

**II**

CH

**11**

When you use the rescue disk to boot your computer, you should enter the command exit at the # prompt before shutting down the computer or rebooting. Remove the rescue disk from its drive (because you can't boot directly from that disk!).

# CONFIGURING LILO

LILO, as you now know, is your boot loader. Its job is to locate the operating system kernel and get it loaded into memory. If your computer has two or more operating systems on it, LILO can pause to give you time to choose an operating system to load. You can also pass *parameters* (options) to LILO to configure your Linux bootup process on-the-fly.

## PASSING PARAMETERS TO LILO

If you have problems booting up from your hard disk, you can pass parameters to LILO to boot into special modes that may help you fix the problem. When the LILO boot prompt appears on the screen, you can type any of the following parameters to change the normal startup procedure. With dual-boot configurations, you should first type the word `linux` followed by a space, then the parameter (as in, `linux single`):

- `single` (or 1): Loads Linux in a simplified single-user mode that prevents other users from logging on and can be used to fix problems that prevent normal bootup.

- `rescue`: Allows you to boot from a floppy rescue disk, and enters the single-user mode.

- `root=device`: Allows you to specify the *device* that should be mounted as the root filesystem. For example, `root=/dev/fd0` mounts the floppy disk's filesystem as the root.

- `vga=mode`: Allows you to choose a VGA monitor mode, where *mode* can be normal, extended (or ext), ask, or a number, usually between 0 and 6, representing a mode for your monitor. Enter `linux vga=ask` for a list available VGA modes.

- *x*: Where *x* is a number 0-6, starts at that runlevel. For example, `linux 3` boots up at runlevel 3 (command prompt).

Many of the parameters previously listed are settings that can be placed in the LILO configuration file, `lilo.conf`. But any time you use one of the those parameters, your entry will override the settings that are currently in that `lilo.conf` file.

## CONFIGURING LILO WITH LINUXCONF

You can use LinuxConf to configure LILO. Remember, to start LinuxConf, you can enter the command `linuxconf` (all lowercase letters) in a terminal window or at the command prompt. In Gnome, you can click the Main Menu button and choose System, LinuxConf. When LinuxConf opens, you want to open the Config, Boot Mode, and LILO categories. You'll see several categories listed under there. Each is described in the sections that follow. Note that changes you make to LILO via LinuxConf will automatically be placed in the LILO configuration file, typically `/etc/lilo.conf`.

**Note** It would be a good idea to make a backup copy of your `/etc/lilo.conf` file before you start LinuxConf. Options you select in LinuxConf will be saved in your `lilo.conf` file.

## LINUXCONF LILO DEFAULTS

The LILO Defaults dialog box lets you reconfigure your default Linux bootup procedure—the bootup procedure that occurs when you let the LILO boot prompt time out or when you choose Linux as your OS (see Figure 11.2). A word of advice—if your Linux bootup procedure is working, don't fix it! If you're going to change some settings, you'd be better off to first create a new Linux configuration with those settings in it so that you can test the new configuration. When you're sure it's working, *then* you can make those new settings part of your new bootup configuration.

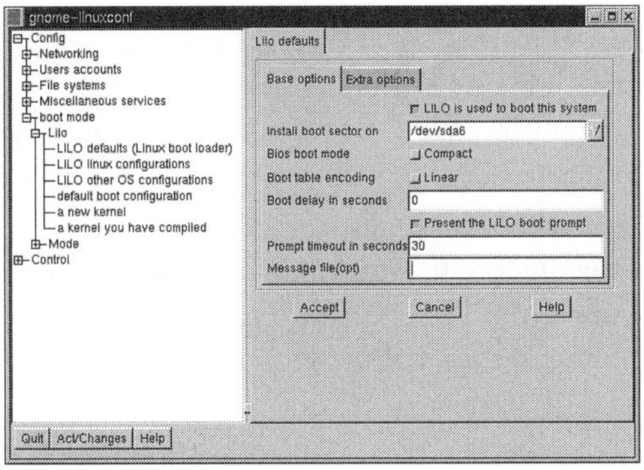

**Figure 11.2**
The base options for configuring LILO defaults in LinuxConf.

If you're just learning, and all you know is what you've learned so far in this book, some of these options will be a bit over your head. Even so, I think it's best to describe them all together. I'll refer back to this section of the chapter, where appropriate, as you gain knowledge in future chapters. Also, I'll point out other sources of information near the end of this section. For now, notice that the LILO defaults are spread across two tabs titled Base Options and Extra Options. The following are descriptions of what each option offers:

- **LILO Is Used to Boot This System:** This option must be selected if, and only if, LILO is indeed used to boot this computer. De-selecting that option will not remove LILO or prevent the computer from booting via LILO. It will simply tell LinuxConf not to go looking for LILO on the hard disk.

- **Install Boot Sector On:** You can install the boot sector on any partition you like, or even on a floppy disk. In general, though, you want the boot sector to be installed at your Linux root partition—the one named /. You can look up the device name of that partition in the /etc/fstab file if need be. If you have another boot manager installed, such as the OS/2 Boot Manager, then the safest choice is to put LILO on the Linux root partition.

- **Bios Boot Mode:** The Compact option, if selected, supposedly allows a system to boot more quickly. However, the folks at LinuxConf don't recommend using this option. So your best bet is to leave the button turned off.

- **Boot Table Encoding:** LILO creates and uses a table to locate kernel files to load. The encoding in these files in a track/head/sector format, or in a linear block number. The most common setting is to leave the Linear button turned off. But if you have a large drive or boot partition that requires a linear block number address, you can select this option.

- **Boot Delay in Seconds:** If LILO is not configured to display the LILO boot prompt, this option determines how long, in seconds, LILO will wait before loading the Linux kernel. Without the prompt visible on the screen, you can press Shift+Tab during that delay to bring up a boot prompt.

- **Present the LILO Boot Prompt:** Select this option if you want LILO to display its LILO boot prompt before it loads the Linux kernel. If, for whatever reason, you don't want the LILO boot prompt to appear on the screen, de-select this option (so the button no longer looks pushed in).

- **Prompt Timeout in Seconds:** Determines how long, in seconds, the LILO boot prompt stays on the screen before it automatically starts loading the Linux kernel. If you leave this option empty, the LILO boot prompt will stay on the screen until the user responds. This option requires that the Present the LILO boot prompt option is also selected.

- **Message File (Opt):** You can have LILO display a custom message before it displays the LILO boot prompt. The message must be stored in a text file. This option should specify the path and filename of that text file (as in, /root/lilomessage.txt).

The Extra Options tab allows you to further refine boot options:

- **Root Partition:** The partition that will be mounted as the root filesystem.

- **Ramdisk Size (Opt):** If selected, puts a limit on the size of the boot ramdisk. If omitted, the ramdisk is sized automatically.

- **Boot Mode:** Selects the Read Only option to have the boot process initially load the filesystem in Read Only mode, to protect file timestamps from being altered during bootup.

- **VGA Mode:** The VGA mode used for startup. The default setting is Normal, which uses standard VGA settings.

- **Boot Options:** If booting from a non-standard device, such as a CD-ROM drive, you may need to enter text here to identify the device (such as hdb=cdrom) to treat the CD-ROM drive as a second IDE hard disk.

- **Initial Ramdisk (Opt):** Specifies the initial ramdisk used for booting.

- **Password (Opt):** If this bootup is to be password-protected, enter the password here.

- **Restricted Access:** Choose this option to password-protect this startup configuration, and make sure you define the password in the textbox above this one.

If you make any changes and want to save them, don't forget to click the Accept button.

## LINUXCONF LILO LINUX CONFIGURATIONS

The LILO Linux Configurations tab in LinuxConf lets you define additional "optional" LILO configurations and give each one a label (name) (see Figure 11.3). This is a safe way to create and test a new configuration before making it your default. For example, after you learn about creating custom kernels (see Chapter 37, "Configuring the Kernel"), you can create an optional configuration too. Also, you can create different bootup configurations for different scenarios, and choose the configuration you want to use for the current session when you're at the LILO boot prompt. For example, you might have one configuration for booting up the machine as a standalone desktop computer and another for booting up as a network workstation.

**Figure 11.3**
The LILO Linux Configurations tab lets you create additional configurations for booting Linux.

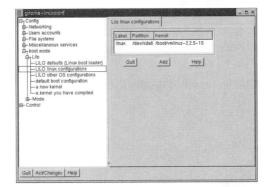

The options that appear when you click the Add button are basically the same as the options used to alter the default configuration:

- **Label:** The name of this configuration, as it will appear when a user presses Tab at the LILO boot prompt. Use one brief word, no spaces.

- **Partition:** The partition that will be mounted as /, the filesystem root.

- **Kernel:** The location and name of the kernel image file to use. Can be a custom kernel you compiled yourself.

## LinuxConf LILO Other OS Configurations

The LILO Other OS Configurations tab, shown in Figure 11.4, lets you define other, non-Linux operating systems to boot on your system. To add access to another installed operating system, click the Add button. Enter a label, a short descriptive name for the other operating system, and the boot partition for that OS. In the future, when you get to the LILO boot prompt, you'll be able to start that operating system by typing whatever label you gave the OS. If you press Tab at the LILO boot prompt, you'll also see this new operating system listed as one of your available options.

**Figure 11.4**
The LILO Other OS Configurations options in Linux-Conf.

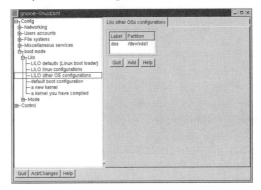

## CHOOSING YOUR DEFAULT OPERATING SYSTEM

If your computer is configured to dual-boot, the LinuxConf Default Boot Configuration option will let you decide which operating system is started when you press Enter at the LILO boot prompt or when you let the LILO boot prompt time out. Figure 11.5 shows how those options appear on a computer that has both Linux and either DOS, Windows 3, Windows 95, or 98 installed on the computer.

**Figure 11.5**

The Boot Mode Configuration dialog box lets you choose between a graphic X (GUI) and text (command prompt) boot, and a delay and prompt timeout.

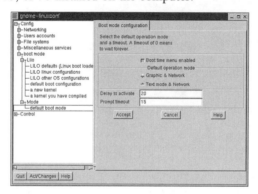

## MANUALLY EDITING lilo.conf

Options for controlling LILO's behavior are in its configuration file `lilo.conf`. The full path to that file is typically `/etc/lilo.conf`, and of course you can change it using any text editor you like. Don't forget to make a backup copy of `lilo.conf` before making any changes. Remember, too, that `LinuxConf` is a safer alternative to making changes to `lilo.conf` because you're less likely to make typographical errors that way. When you open the `lilo.conf` file, it will contain settings as in the following example:

```
boot=/dev/sda
map=/boot/map
install=/boot/boot.b
prompt
timeout=50
image=/boot/vmlinuz-2.2.14-5.0
    label=linux
    root=/dev/sda6
    initrd=/boot/initrd-2.2.14-5.0.img
    read-only
other=/dev/sda1
    label=dos
    table=/dev/sda
```

The options correspond to similar items presented in LinuxConf, though the wording isn't always the same. I'll briefly describe the purpose of each option, as well as a few common ones that don't appear in the previous example. For a more thorough and detailed description of the options, see the man pages for LILO and `lilo.conf` (enter the commands `man lilo` and `man lilo.conf`):

- **boot=**: Sets the name of the device that contains the boot sector, typically a hard drive.
- **compact:** If included, forces LILO to read requests for adjacent sectors into a single request. Can speed up booting from floppy disks, but it's risky.
- **default=**: Specifies which operating system is run when the user presses Enter at the LILO boot prompt, or when that prompt times out.
- **image=**: Specifies the location and filename of the Linux kernel boot image file, typically the `vmlinux` file in the `/boot` directory.
- **initrd=**: Specifies the initial RAM disk used at startup, usually `/dev/initrd` device. See `man initrd` for technical information.
- **install=**: Defines the file to be used as the new boot sector, typically the LILO `boot.b` file in the `/boot` directory.
- **label=**: Label that appears for this type of boot when user presses the Tab key at the LILO boot prompt.
- **map=**: Specifies the location and filename of the boot map, `/boot/map` by default.
- **message=**: Specifies the location and name of a text file that contains text to be displayed on the screen before the LILO boot prompt appears.
- **other=**: Specifies the boot partition for an optional operating system that can be loaded. Options that follow `other=` refer to that specific operating system.
- **prompt:** If included, shows the LILO boot prompt on the screen at startup.
- **read-only:** If included, mounts the root filesystem read-only, which provides safety. The system startup procedure then remounts the filesystem as read/write before the user has access.
- **root=**: Specifies the device that should be mounted as the filesystem root (`/`). Typically the device defined as the `/` partition in `/etc/fstab/`.
- **table=**: Specifies the device that contains the partition table, used primarily with non-Linux operating systems.
- **timeout=**: If prompt is included, specifies how long the LILO boot prompt stays on the screen, in tenths of a second, before LILO loads Linux. Setting this value to `-1` makes the LILO boot prompt stay on the screen until the user responds.

## TESTING LILO RECONFIGURATIONS

LILO configuration is unique in one important way. Any time you manually edit `lilo.conf`, you need to rerun LILO from the `/sbin` directory before you test your changes. Simply enter the command `/sbin/lilo` at the command prompt, and then you can reboot to see how well your configuration is working.

If a custom configuration hangs and the computer won't start, press Ctrl+Alt+Delete to reboot. When the LILO boot prompt appears, enter `linux` at the LILO boot prompt to get

PART

II

CH

11

back to your original Linux configuration, assuming that one is still working. If you altered that configuration and have problems, you can boot from the emergency boot disk previously described in this chapter.

## INSTALLING OR REINSTALLING LILO

Though LILO was probably installed when you first installed Linux, it certainly is possible to install LILO on a machine that has never had LILO installed. In fact, LILO comes with a program named QuickInst that's designed expressly for that purpose. You can learn more about QuickInst by opening the file /usr/doc/lilo-0.21.

If you install another operating system *after* you've installed Linux, chances are you'll overwrite LILO and lose it. You could also lose LILO if you inadvertently replace it with another file, erase it, uninstall it—whatever. If you're not installing LILO for the first time, you'd be better off reinstalling from the emergency boot disk already discussed in this chapter, rather than through the QuickInst program. To do so, follow these steps:

1. Shut down your computer.
2. Put the emergency boot disk in your floppy drive.
3. Turn the computer back on.
4. Press Enter at the boot prompt or just wait for it to time out.
5. Log in as root.
6. Type the command /sbin/lilo -v and press Enter.
7. Remove the emergency boot disk from its drive.
8. Enter the command shutdown -r now to reboot the computer from your hard disk.

You should get the LILO boot prompt from now on whenever you boot up. If you somehow also lost your /etc/lilo.conf file, you'll need to re-create that. If you had a backup, you can copy that backup to /etc/lilo.conf. If you need to create one from scratch, you can do so using any text editor. Assuming DOS or Windows is installed on the same computer, the lilo.conf should contain at least the following lines. However, the three items in italics will need to be customized for your system as summarized here:

- ▪ */sda:* Needs to be the name of the disk you boot from. If you have an IDE rather than SCSI drive, this is likely to be /hda.

- ▪ */sda6:* Needs to refer to the root directory of your filesystem (the partition named / in your /etc/fstab file).

- ▪ *2.2.12-20:* Should refer to the version number of your Linux kernel. This would be different only if you've upgraded your kernel since initially installing Red Hat Linux 6.2.

```
boot=/dev/sda
map=/boot/map
install=/boot/boot.b
prompt
timeout=50
```

```
image=/boot/vmlinuz-2.2.14-5.0
    label=linux
    root=/dev/sda6
    initrd=/boot/initrd-2.2.14-5.0.img
    read-only
other=/dev/sda1
    label=dos
    table=/dev/sda
```

> **Note**    If DOS/Windows isn't installed on the same computer, leave out the last three lines of the sample `linux.conf` file shown.

## UNINSTALLING LILO

If, for whatever reason, you want to uninstall LILO, simply enter the command `/sbin/lilo -u` in any terminal window or at the command prompt. If you want to overwrite LILO with a DOS/Windows Master Boot Record so that the computer boots to DOS or Windows only, you need to boot to a DOS command prompt. At the DOS command prompt, enter the command `fdisk /mbr`.

## MORE ON LILO

The full range of LILO's capabilities go beyond the scope of this chapter. If you need to configure Linux to boot on diskless workstations, to co-exist with operating systems other than DOS/Windows, or have gotten to a point where you can create your own kernels and such, there is plenty of documentation available to help you along. Complete documentation for LILO can be found on your hard disk in the directory `/usr/doc/lilo-0.21`. See the README file in that directory for starters.

The following HOWTOs contains LILO examples and related topics. Remember that HOWTOs can be found in the `/doc/HOWTO` directory of the Red Hat Linux CD-ROM 1, as discussed in Chapter 5. They're also available at the Red Hat Index of HOWTOs at `http://www.redhat.com/mirrors/LDP/HOWTO/HOWTO-INDEX-3.html#ss3.1`:

- **Bootdisk HOWTO:** Creating boot and maintenance floppy disks.
- **BootPrompt HOWTO:** Boot-time parameters and overview of booting software.
- **Diskless HOWTO:** How to set up a diskless Linux workstation.
- **LILO mini-HOWTO:** Examples of LILO installations.
- **Linux+DOS+Win95+OS2 mini-HOWTO:** How to use Linux, OS/2, DOS, and Windows on a single computer.
- **Linux+NT-Loader mini-HOWTO:** How to use Linux and the Windows NT on the same computer.
- **Linux+Win95 mini-HOWTO:** How to use Linux and Windows 95 together.
- **MILO HOWTO:** How to use the Dec Alpha Miniloader.

PART

II

CH

11

You can also enter any of these commands to view LILO-related man pages:

- `man lilo`
- `man lilo.conf`
- `man initrd`

On the Web, as we go to press, a LILO site was under construction, which may be open for business by the time you're reading this.

So much for LILO. Once LILO has finished its job and the user has opted to start Linux, then the kernel kicks in, and the entire Linux startup process kicks in as well, as described next.

# UNDERSTANDING LINUX INITIALIZATION

The bulk of the startup procedure starts after LILO has finished its small job and loaded the Linux kernel into memory. When that happens, you see the `Loading Linux...` message on the screen followed by still more messages and lots of descriptions of various *processes* (programs) being started. That whole process is sometimes referred to as init, for initialization. Behind the scenes, the kernel is actually running some programs, which in turn are gathering data from several configuration files. Here, in a nutshell, is what the kernel does:

- The kernel runs the `/sbin/init` program (a.k.a. `init`).
- `init` gets some information about how to proceed from the configuration `/etc/inittab`.
- The `init` program then runs a shell script at `/etc/rc.d/rc.sysinit` (*resource control system init*ialization).
- The `rc.sysinit` file does some startup initialization and sets some system *environment variables*.
- The `init` program then runs the `/etc/rc.d/rc.local` script.
- If all goes well, a login prompt appears on the screen.
- The user logs in, some information about that user is stored in environment variables, and the command prompt (or GUI) appears.

Exactly what happens during those steps depends on the *runlevel* that the procedure is trying to achieve. So let's discuss that first.

## CHOOSING THE RUNLEVEL

Linux offers several *runlevels*. Each runlevel is essentially the end goal of the initialization procedure. There are seven different runlevels, numbered 0 through 6. Each is designed to achieve a particular state by the end of the initialization process, as summarized in Table 11.2.

**TABLE 11.2   DIFFERENT METHODS OF BOOTING LINUX ARE CALLED RUNLEVELS AND ARE IDENTIFIED BY NUMBERS 0 THROUGH 6**

| Runlevel | Goal |
|---|---|
| 0 | Halts the machine. For shutdown only; never use this setting in your /etc/inittab file. |
| 1 | Single-user mode. No other users can log in; can be used when a network or other problem prevents normal bootup. |
| 2 | Multiuser mode without NFS; that is, multiuser mode when not attached to a network. |
| 3 | Full multiuser mode with networking; starts at command prompt. |
| 4 | Unused; you can create your own runlevel here. |
| 5 | Like 3, but takes the user straight to a GUI rather than to the command prompt. |
| 6 | Reboots the machine. For rebooting only; *never* use this setting in your /etc/inittab file. |

The information about which runlevel to use comes from two sources. If, at the LILO boot prompt, you enter a runlevel parameter number, such as `linux 3` for command prompt startup, or `linux 5` for a GUI startup, then that's the runlevel to use. If you do not specify a runlevel at the LILO boot prompt, then the selected runlevel comes from the /etc/inittab file. Specifically, this line in /etc/inittab is similar to one of the following:

```
id:3:initdefault:
id:5:initdefault:
```

The number is what defines the runlevel. You can see from Table 11.2 why only a 3 or a 5 would likely be used in the /etc/inittab file. Under normal circumstances you want to boot to the command prompt (3) or the GUI (5). You can change your default runlevel using LinuxConf, as discussed later in this chapter. However, you could also just use any text editor to change the 3 to a 5, or vice versa, in the /etc/inittab file.

Back to the startup procedure. When the desired runlevel is ascertained, init runs all the *processes* (programs) needed to achieve that runlevel. init accomplishes this task by running numerous other scripts on the computer including /etc/rc.d/rc.sysinit, /sbin/update, /sbin/mingetty, and /etc/X11/prefdm. You can view, and optionally change, the contents of those scripts using any text editor. However, now is not a good time to do so, unless you're already fluent in shell scripting (a topic this book will cover in Chapter 34, "Shell Programming and Scripting").

## PROCESSES

As you may recall, Linux is a multitasking operating system, which means that many separate programs can all be running at the same time. Processes that aren't "in your face" at the moment (that is, doing something on the screen) are said to be running in the background.

PART

**II**

CH

**11**

Some processes are *daemons*, which are really just programs that keep an eye out for certain events to occur. For example, a mail daemon might do nothing most the time. But as soon as an email message arrives, the daemon goes into action, accepts the messages, and stores them in the user's mailbox. When it has finished that job, it goes back into the mode of just "keeping an eye out" for new incoming messages. The filenames of most daemons end in the letter *d*, such as inetd, lockd, and nfsd. Some processes are called *services* because they provide a particular service. But all in all, they're basically software programs.

We tend to think of processes by names that describe what they do. But Linux keeps track of them by number. Each running process is assigned a unique Process ID (PID). Before any process can be run, a process needs to be installed that's capable of spawning other processes. That mother of all processes is the init process that's launched right at the beginning of the boot process. That process is always given a PID of 1. The processes that init starts are then numbered as they're started.

Future chapters will discuss the many processes that Linux offers. For now, it's sufficient to know that whenever you're using Linux, processes are going on in the background, and each of those processes has a unique ID number. You can also start or stop (kill) a process at any time, as you'll learn in future chapters.

For now, if you'd just like to take a peek at the processes currently running on your Linux machine, you can use the ps (Process Status) command with the -agux arguments. That is, in any terminal window or command prompt, enter the following command:

```
ps -augx
```

The list will probably whiz by pretty quickly. If you really need to take a close look, you can pipe the output to the less program by entering this command instead:

```
ps -augx | less
```

Then use the ~DA and ~UA keys to scroll through the output at your leisure. Remember that to quit less and get back to a command prompt, you need to type the letter q for quit.

The pstree command also displays running processes and lists them in the order in which they were started. At the top of the list you'll find init, which is always the first process started.

**Tip**

The ps and pstree commands have their own man page (man ps). If you find them unintelligible at your current skill level, don't worry about it. You'll learn more about managing processes in Chapter 17, "Advanced System Administration." For now, it's sufficient to know that they exist.

There's no need to get into too much detail about individual processes right here and now. But for your general edification, Table 11.3 lists some of the more common processes you may find running in the background at any given time, depending on how your machine is configured. Don't worry if your process list has fewer items, or items not listed. You'll learn how to configure services, start processes, kill processes, and more in upcoming chapters.

> **Tip**
>
> Many processes have their own man pages. So if you're really curious, simply enter the man command followed by a space and the process name.

**TABLE 11.3  SOME COMMON LINUX PROCESSES AND WHAT THEY DO**

| Process | Purpose |
| --- | --- |
| amd | Automounts services daemon |
| apmd | Advanced power management daemon |
| atd | Daemon that manages jobs scheduled for later execution |
| bash | The Bourne Again shell |
| crond | Daemon that runs jobs schedules for regular intervals |
| dhcpd | Dynamic Host Configuration Protocol daemon |
| gpm | Mouse server used for cut-and-paste |
| httpd | Runs the Apache Web server |
| inetd | Internet super-server daemon; listens for Internet requests |
| inmd | Usenet news server daemon |
| login | Allows user login |
| lpd | Controls print spooling services |
| named | Provides DNS name services |
| network | Controls all network services |
| nfs | Network File Systems services |
| nfsfs | Mounts/unmounts Network File System services |
| pcmcia | Provides PCMCIA card services |
| portmap | Controls Remote Procedure Call services |
| postgresql | Runs postgres database and SQL services |
| rpc.mountd | NFS disk-mounting daemon |
| rpc.nfsd | Network File System daemon |
| sendmail | Controls sending of email |
| syslogd | System logging daemon |
| xfs | The X Window system font server |

PART

**II**

CH

**11**

## THE SYSTEM LOG FILE

As processes are started to achieve the goals of the desired runlevel, arcane messages whiz by on the screen, followed by an OK if the process started correctly or a FAILED if the process wasn't started correctly. Similar information is also stored in the /var/log/messages file, which you can view with any text file viewer or editor, should you ever want to study what happened during bootup more closely. Entries are listed in chronological order, so you'll need to scroll to the bottom of the list to study the messages that occurred during the most recent bootup.

## ENVIRONMENT VARIABLES

Eventually the bootup procedure displays the login prompt. The user logs in, and the system is up. While everything else was going on, Linux created some *environment variables*. These are little chunks of information stored in memory for the duration of the session that can be used by many different scripts and programs on the system. Some examples include the USERNAME environment variable, which holds the name of the user that's currently logged in. The HOME environment variable holds the path name of the current user's home directory. The PATH environment variable tells Linux which directories to search when a user enters a command, and so forth. Although it's not critical at this point to understand all the environment variables, you may just want to take a peek at them. Should you get into shell scripting (see Chapter 34), you may need to get at the data stored in some of these variables. You can view the environment variables that are currently defined by entering the command env at the command prompt or in a terminal window.

> **Tip**
>
> Entering man env at a command prompt displays the man page for the env command. However, you needn't get too deep into environment variables until you learn shell scripting in Chapter 34.

## HOW init WORKS

The program that controls the whole initialization procedure is /sbin/init. The main configuration file for that program is /etc/inittab (for *ini*tialization *tab*le). If you were to open the /etc/inittab file in gEdit, or any other text editor, and scroll down past the comments (lines that start with #), you'd see something like Figure 11.6.

The first uncommented line, shown here, tells init what the desired runlevel is:

```
id:3:initdefault:
```

You've seen this line discussed earlier. Basically, your only options here are to change the number within the line. Only runlevel 3 (for the command prompt) or 5 (for the GUI) make any sense in this configuration file. However, if you were to design your own runlevel for unused number 4, you could change the number to a 4 instead.

**Figure 11.6**
A sample /etc/ inittab file open in gEdit. Lines that start with # are comments; some are scrolled out of view.

**Tip**

Remember, entering a value at the LILO boot prompt, as in linux 5, will override the setting in inittab.

The next lines in /etc/inittab look something like this:

```
# System initialization.
si::sysinit:/etc/rc.d/rc.sysinit
```

These tell the init script to run the /etc/rc.d/rc.sysint script. That script, in turn, does several jobs, including setting the initial PATH environment variable, configuring networking, mounting filesystems, and in general does most of whatever is needed to get the system going. It does so by running all the programs in the directory /etc/rc.d/init.d directory, shown in Figure 11.7.

**Figure 11.7**
The /etc/rc.d/ init.d directory contains links to services that are launched at startup.

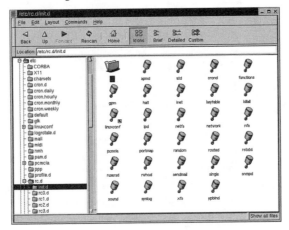

PART
**II**

CH
**11**

Next, `inittab` runs one of the following lines, depending on the desired runlevel. All the runlevels are listed in `/etc/inittab`, but the `init` script knows to execute only one of those lines—the line whose number matches the desired runlevel. For example, if the desired runlevel is 3, `init` runs the line `13:3:wait:/etc/rc/d/rc 3`. That line, in turn, runs the `/etc/rc.d` script, passing to it the number 3. The `wait` tells the rest of this script to wait for that task to finish its work before moving on:

```
l0:0:wait:/etc/rc.d/rc 0
l1:1:wait:/etc/rc.d/rc 1
l2:2:wait:/etc/rc.d/rc 2
l3:3:wait:/etc/rc.d/rc 3
l4:4:wait:/etc/rc.d/rc 4
l5:5:wait:/etc/rc.d/rc 5
l6:6:wait:/etc/rc.d/rc 6
```

The `rc.d` script starts or stops all the processes needed to achieve the desired runlevel. It does so in an interesting way. Each runlevel has its own directory of files associated with it, named `/etc/rc.d/rc0.d` for runlevel 0, `/etc/rc/d/rc1.d` for runlevel 1, and so forth, up to `/etc/rc.d/rc6.d` for runlevel 6. If you were to peek inside the `/rc0.d` (halt) or `/rc6.d` (reboot) directories, all of the icons that launch processes have filenames that begin with the letter K. The K indicates that the process is going to be killed (stopped), which of course is necessary when shutting down or rebooting. The `rc3.d` (start at command prompt) and `rc5.d` (start at GUI, shown in Figure 11.8) directories contain a lot of icons whose names begin with the letter S because those icons start the necessary process. The `/etc/rc.d` script simply runs all the scripts within the appropriate directory to achieve the desired runlevel.

**Figure 11.8**

The `/etc/rc/d/rc5.d` directory contains scripts that are necessary to achieve runlevel 5 at startup.

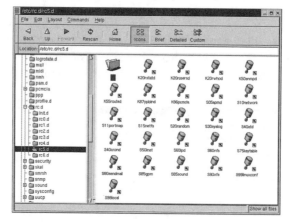

Although it seems pretty complicated, in the long run this approach actually simplifies things for the system administrator. Because rather than writing a bunch of complex code to define processes to start and stop for a given runlevel, the administrator only needs to create links to the desired processes within the appropriate directory. Better yet, LinuxConf can handle the job quite eloquently. You'll learn how it's all done in Chapter 17. For now, it's sufficient to understand the basic concept of runlevels and that the processes used to define a runlevel are actually just links to the appropriate programs within a directory.

**Tip**

If you happen to be coming from a UNIX background, you might be interested to know that the Linux `init` command is compatible with the System V `init` command.

You probably won't need to change any of the remaining settings in /etc/inittab. But just to give you a sense of what else is defined in there, the following line tells init to run the program /sbin/update one time. As the comment above the line indicates, that script performs tasks that apply to every runlevel:

```
# Things to run in every runlevel.
ud::once:/sbin/update
```

The following lines define the function of the Ctrl+Alt+Del keypress. By default, that keypress gives the system three seconds (-t3) to kill all the running processes before rebooting (-r) the system:

```
# Trap CTRL-ALT-DELETE
ca::ctrlaltdel:/sbin/shutdown -t3 -r now
```

**Note**

Shutdown command options are described in the section "Shutting Down" a little later in this chapter.

The following line in inittab defines what happens if an Uninterruptible Power Supply (UPS) sends a "power failure" signal to the computer. By default, init will execute a shutdown -f -h +2 "Power Failure; System Shutting Down" shutdown command, giving all terminals a two-minute warning before halting the system:

```
pf::powerfail:/sbin/shutdown -f -h +2 "Power Failure; System Shutting Down"
```

The line shown here defines what happens if the UPS sends a "Power Restored" signal during the two-minute delay between execution of the shutdown command and actual shutdown. In this case, init will cancel the shutdown using the -c switch and broadcast a "Power Restored; Shutdown Cancelled" command. Of course, the power failure commands will work only if your computer is connected to a UPS, and the UPS is configured to send the appropriate signals in the event of a power failure:

```
pr:12345:powerokwait:/sbin/shutdown -c "Power Restored; Shutdown Cancelled"
```

The following settings use the mingetty program to set up virtual consoles 1 through 6 (the ones you get to by pressing Ctrl+Alt and a function key) for runlevels 2, 3, 4, and 5. mingetty is a compact version of the getty program, which uses set up terminals, presents the login prompt, and processes a login for the user. Essentially, it's this series of settings that displays the Login prompt on each of the virtual consoles 1 through 6:

```
# Run gettys in standard runlevels
1:2345:respawn:/sbin/mingetty tty1
2:2345:respawn:/sbin/mingetty tty2
3:2345:respawn:/sbin/mingetty tty3
```

```
4:2345:respawn:/sbin/mingetty tty4
5:2345:respawn:/sbin/mingetty tty5
6:2345:respawn:/sbin/mingetty tty6
```

Lastly, if the default runlevel is set to 5 for GUI startup, the following line executes the /etc/X11prefdm script which, in turn, displays the xdm, gdm, or kdm graphical login dialog box. That will also replace the textual Login prompt on virtual console 1, which you may have noticed appears briefly on the screen if you boot up in a GUI:

```
x:5:respawn:/etc/X11/prefdm -nodaemon
```

Although there's no setting in inittab to indicate it, the init script runs another script named /etc/rc.d/rc.local before it's done. The rc.local script sets up a small file named /etc/issue that contains specific information about the operating system and machine architecture of the local computer. For example, /etc/issue would contain the following lines if installed on a Pentium (i686, in Linux-speak). Information from /etc/issue is used elsewhere throughout the system:

```
Red Hat Linux release 6.2 (Zoot)
Kernel 2.2.14-5.0 on an i686
```

# CONFIGURING STARTUP AND SHUTDOWN WITH LINUXCONF

LinuxConf is filled with options for configuring your system, and many of those options directly affect how your system starts. You'll learn about the many ways that you can use LinuxConf to configure services that start automatically when booting as you learn about those services in future chapters. For starters, there's a simple way to adjust the runlevel defined in inittab, via LinuxConf, without editing the inittab file directly. Just start LinuxConf and open the Config, Boot Mode, Mode, Default Boot Mode categories. You'll come to the options shown in Figure 11.9. Choose the Graphic & Network option to start in the GUI (runlevel 5) or Text Mode & Network to start at the command prompt (runlevel 3). If you change and accept the current setting, LinuxConf will update the line that defines the default runlevel in /etc/inittab (for example, id:3:initdefault:).

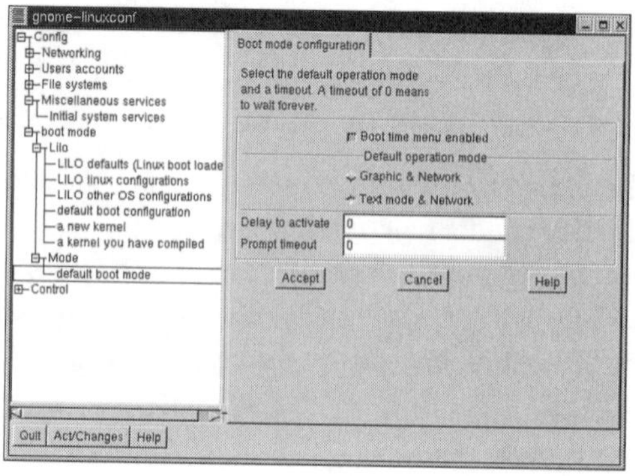

**Figure 11.9**
LinuxConf Boot Mode Configuration options let you choose a default runlevel.

PART

II

CH

11

**Note**

> Other options in that dialog box are stored in `conf.linuxconf`, which is a configuration that's relevant only to LinuxConf. Red Hat doesn't show `conf.linuxconf` in its initialization. So those other options won't have any effect on your startup procedure.

You can also set a default runlevel for initialization using the Initial System Services dialog box under Config, Miscellaneous in LinuxConf.

# CHOOSING STARTUP SERVICES

As you know, many programs (services) are launched automatically at startup. Ultimately, all those services become processes that are running in the background, and they're all child processes of the init process. Red Hat Linux provides several tools that greatly simplify the task of choosing what services you want to start automatically at startup, and which services you want to terminate gracefully at shutdown:

- At the command prompt, enter the command `ntsysv` to get to the options shown in Figure 11.10. To change a runlevel other than the current runlevel, you need to enter the command `ntsysv --level` *n* where *n* is the number of the runlevel you want to modify.

**Figure 11.10**
The ntsysv program is a character cell interface for selecting which services to run at startup.

- In GNOME, click the Start button and choose System, Control Panel. Then click the Runlevel Editor button at the top of the Control Panel that appears. You'll be taken to the SYSV Runlevel Manager (see Figure 11.11).
- In KDE, click the K button and choose System, SysV Init Editor to get to the window shown in Figure 11.12.

**Note**

> System V (SysV) is originally from Unix, and is the init process that Red Hat Linux uses at startup to launch services. For more information on System V Init, see `http://www.redhat.com/corp/support/docs/Boot-Process-Tips/Boot-Process-Tips-3.html`.

**Figure 11.11**
GNOME's Runlevel Editor also lets you choose which services you want to run at startup.

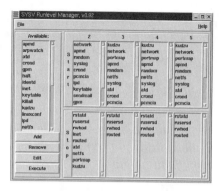

At this stage of the game, it's not terribly important to know what each an every service provides. But you do want to be aware that there are tools available to you that let you pick and choose services as you learn more about what those services are. The services summarized in Table 11.3 describe the more commonly used services available to you.

**Figure 11.12**
KDE's SysV Init Editor is yet a third tool for choosing which services to run at startup.

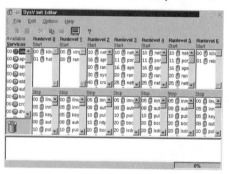

> **Tip**
>
> To view which services are currently started and stopped at various runlevels, enter the command `chkconfig --list`.

# SHUTTING DOWN

As you know, the `shutdown` command lets you shut down your computer. You can enter the command `shutdown -h now` to shut down the system or `shutdown -r now` to reboot the system. Both shutting down and rebooting are actually runlevels of `init`, numbered 0 and 6, respectively. Both options ensure that all processes are killed (stopped) before the computer is powered down. The reboot runlevel is also able to bring everything back up from scratch. The complete syntax for the shutdown command is as follows:

```
shutdown [-t seconds] -cfFhknr  time [warning message]
```

The following are your options:

- seconds is the number of seconds to wait before shutting down.
- time the number of minutes to wait preceded by a + sign, or the time of day in 24-hour (military) format, or the word *now*.
- warning message is the message to display prior to shutting down.
- -rkhncfF is any of the following listed options:
    - **-c:** Cancel an already-running shutdown
    - **-F:** Force fsck (filesystem check and repair) on reboot
    - **-f:** Do a fast reboot by skipping fsck
    - **-h:** Halt after shutdown
    - **-k:** Don't shut down, just send warning message
    - **-n:** Don't use init to shutdown (not recommended)
    - **-r:** Reboot after shutdown

If you're working on a standalone computer, it may seem odd to have so many options for shutting down. But in a distributed system, where any number of people might be in the middle of some work, a warning message is a must. If you omit the optional warning message, a default message will still be displayed on everyone's monitor. Make sure you give them some time to save their files. For example, if you enter the following command, the computer will shut down in five minutes:

```
shutdown -h +5 WARNING
```

The following message displays:

```
WARNING
The system is going down
System halt for in 5 minutes will be broadcast to all computers in the network.
```

> **Tip**
>
> Entering the command date at the command prompt will show you the current system date and time.

If you want to cancel a timed shutdown, enter the command shutdown -c. If you can't get to a command prompt, press Ctrl+C instead.

## SHUTTING DOWN WITH LINUXCONF

The superuser (any user who has been granted Shutdown permission in LinuxConf) can shut down the system using this command:

```
linuxconf --shutdown
```

If you enter the command from a terminal window or Run Command dialog box, LinuxConf displays the Shutdown Control Panel dialog box (see Figure 11.13). You can choose to shut down or reboot. Optionally, you can enter a delay time in minutes and a message to broadcast to other terminals.

**Tip**

If you enter the `linuxconf --shutdown` command from a character cell command prompt, you'll see a similar dialog box. But your mouse won't work in that one. You need to use the Tab and Shift+Tab keys to move from option to option, and the spacebar to select an option button.

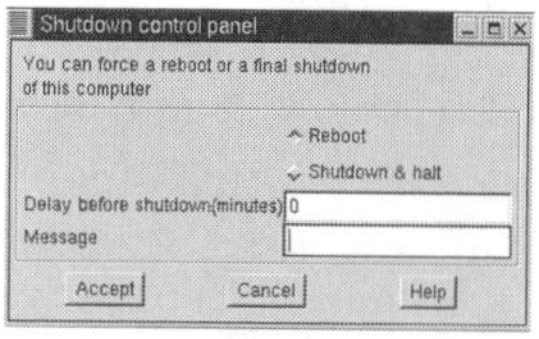

**Figure 11.13**
The LinuxConf Shutdown Control Panel dialog box lets you choose a shutdown type, delay, and warning message.

To grant, or deny, a user permission to shut down using the `linuxconf --shutdown` command, you need to get to the user's privileges. Run LinuxConf and open the Config, User Accounts, Normal, User Accounts categories. Then click the name of a user in the right column. Click the Privileges tab to get to the options shown in Figure 11.14. Then choose one of the following summarized options from the May Shutdown options:

- **Denied:** The user cannot shut down.
- **Granted:** The user can shut down with the `linuxconf --shutdown` command, but must enter his password.
- **Granted/silent:** Same as Granted, but no password required.

**Figure 11.14**
This user has been granted permission to shut down, without entering his password, using the `linuxconf --shutdown` command.

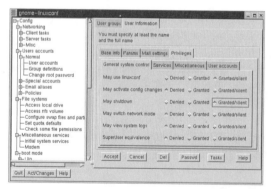

**Tip**

In Gnome and KDE, logging out of the system will take you to another graphical login box if the system is set up to start in a GUI automatically. But you can choose Shutdown from either the gdm or kdm dialog box options to shut down from there.

### HALT, REBOOT, AND CTRL+ALT+DEL

In addition to the `shutdown` command and LinuxConf, you can shut down or reboot the computer by entering these commands:

- **halt:** Shuts down the computer; requires superuser privileges.
- **reboot:** Reboots the computer; requires superuser privileges.
- **Ctrl+Alt+Del:** In the absence of any command prompt, pressing Ctrl+Alt+Del will reboot the computer. As you saw in `.etc/inittab`, pressing these three keys is the same as entering `ashutdown -t3 -r now` command.

# PROJECT: MAKE THOSE BOOT DISKS!

Your project for this page is pretty simple, although it will take a few minutes of your time. If you didn't already, go ahead and create the boot disk described earlier in this chapter now. If you wait until you really need it, it will be too late!

PART

**II**

CH

**11**

CHAPTER **12**

# USING DOS AND WINDOWS

**I**n this chapter

# ACCESSING DOS/WINDOWS DISKS

Linux has the unique ability to read disks in a variety of formats, including the DOS format used by DOS, Windows 3, Windows 95, and Windows 98. So if you have your computer set up to dual-boot with Linux and DOS, Windows 3, Windows 95, or Windows 98, you can mount your DOS/Windows disks to Linux mount points (directories). Then you can move and copy files between your Linux and DOS/Windows disks using the GNOME File Manager or the KDE File Manager, or Linux commands at the command prompt.

## MOUNTING DOS/WINDOWS FLOPPIES

To mount a DOS floppy disk, use the mount command with the `-t vfat` option. Here are the exact steps, working from a terminal window or the command prompt:

1. If a mounted floppy disk is in the floppy drive, unmount it using the command `umount_/mnt/floppy`.

2. Place the DOS-formatted disk in the floppy drive.

3. Enter the following command to mount the disk:

   `mount -t vfat /dev/fd0 /mnt/floppy`

To verify that you can view the contents of the drive, enter the command `ls /mnt/floppy`. After the disk is mounted, you can access it as you would any other disk. For example, you can get to its contents by going to the `/mnt/floppy` directory in any graphical file manager. You can copy files to and from the floppy using the standard drag-and-drop techniques for your file manager or you can use the Linux `cp` command. As an example of the latter, the following command copies all the file from the DOS-mounted floppy into the current user's home directory (abbreviated as ~ in the command):

`copy /mnt/floppy/* ~`

---

**Tip**

The `vfat` format is similar to the MS-DOS format for floppies, but supports the long filenames that were added in Windows 95.

---

If you have a heterogeneous environment of both Windows and Linux machines, you can greatly simplify things by standardizing on just one floppy disk format. To do so—and also ensure that regular users can mount and dismount DOS floppy disks—you'll need to edit your `/etc/fstab` file, as discussed in the case study at the end of Chapter 6, "System Administration Basics." Make sure that the line that defines the floppy drive, `/dev/fd0`, uses vfat as the disk format, and also includes the users option (see Figure 12.1).

When you've done this, any user should be able to mount a DOS/Windows floppy disk by entering the following command

`mount /mnt/floppy`

or by right-clicking the Floppy icon on his desktop and choosing Mount Device.

**Figure 12.1**
This /etc/fstab file has been edited to allow any user to mount and unmount DOS-formatted floppy disks.

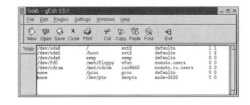

The superuser can still mount Linux `ext2` formatted floppy disks in that drive by entering the following command:

```
mount -t ext2 /dev/fd0 /mnt/floppy
```

## MOUNTING WINDOWS/DOS PARTITIONS

If you dual-boot with Windows, you have at least one partition for Windows, which is acting as drive C: in Windows. You can mount any Windows (or DOS) partition and treat it like a directory within your Linux filesystem. Since partitions on hard disks don't change often like disks in removable drives, the smart thing to do here is to simply have the Windows partition mounted automatically at bootup. To see which device your Windows partition is, you can enter the following command at the command prompt or any terminal window to display the current partition table:

```
fdisk -l /dev/drive
```

`drive` is the name of the drive on which you want to check partitions. If you're using an IDE hard drive, that's most likely to be had. If you're using a SCSI hard drive, then replace `drive` with `sda`. Mountable DOS/Window partitions will be listed as FAT 16. For example, if you have a Windows drive C: you might see an entry like this one:

```
Device   Boot   Start    End      Id   System
/dev/sda1  *     1   255  2048256   6   FAT16
```

In this example, bootable partition `/sda1` is the Windows C: drive. Let's say you want that drive to be mounted automatically at startup when you're using Linux. Furthermore, you want the Windows C drive to be available in the Linux filesystem as `/mnt/winc`.

First, you need to create the mount point for the partition. As you may recall, a mount point is usually just an empty directory—a "placeholder" of sorts—that's used to mount disks. Because mount points are just empty directories, you can use the `mkdir` command to create a mount point. For example, to create a directory named `/mnt/winc`, which will act as the mount point for your Windows C: drive under Linux, enter the following command in any terminal window or at the command prompt:

```
mkdir /mnt/winc
```

PART
II

CH
12

Next, you need to tell the /etc/fstab file that you want to mount the Windows partition at the mount point. Using any text editor, add the following line to your /etc/fstab files, as in Figure 12.2:

```
/dev/sda1     /mnt/winc  vfat     defaults    0 0
```

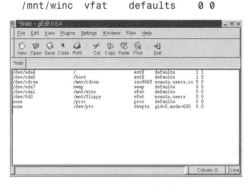

**Figure 12.2**
Entry for /dev/ sda1 will auto-mount Windows drive C: at startup, as /mnt/winc in the Linux filesystem.

---

**Tip**

You can also manipulate the contents of the /etc/fstab file through LinuxConf, under the Config, File Systems, Access Local Drive category.

---

The fstab file is executed at startup. So, after you save and close that file, you'll need to reboot using shutdown -r now or the reboot option when you log out of your GUI. When you're back in Linux and logged in as root, you can view the contents of the Windows partitions using the ls command, followed by the mount point, as in ls /mnt/winc. In KDE or GNOME, you can open the File Manager as you normally would. Then just open the /mnt/winc directory to access files on the DOS/Windows partition. In essence, your DOS/ Windows partition is now like any other directory in your filesystem.

# USING DOS COMMANDS IN LINUX

If your experience with PC computers goes back to the 1980s or earlier, you probably had some experience with DOS. MTools is a program that comes with your Linux package that allows you to manage files on DOS/Windows disks using commands that resemble DOS commands. Essentially you use the normal DOS syntax, but add a lowercase *m* to the start of the command. For example, rather than DIR, it's mdir. Rather than COPY, it's mcopy.

For the most part, mtools is designed to work with floppy disks as well as other removable media such as JAZ and Zip drives. When mtools is active, you can refer to the floppy drive as A:, just as you do in DOS. JAZ and Zip drives are generally referred to as J: and Z:, respectively. Also, as in DOS, there's no need to mount or unmount removable disks. You can just change disks on the fly as you would in DOS.

## CONFIGURING mtools

To use mtools effectively, you first need to tell it a bit about your hardware. You do so by editing the /etc/mtools.conf configuration file using any text editor of your choosing. When you first open that file, it will already contain many lines that define common hardware storage devices (see Figure 12.3). The vast majority of those lines are commented out (preceded with a # character) to be ignored because, obviously, nobody has all those devices attached to their computer! Your job is to uncomment the lines that are relevant to your hardware, and comment out any lines that aren't relevant.

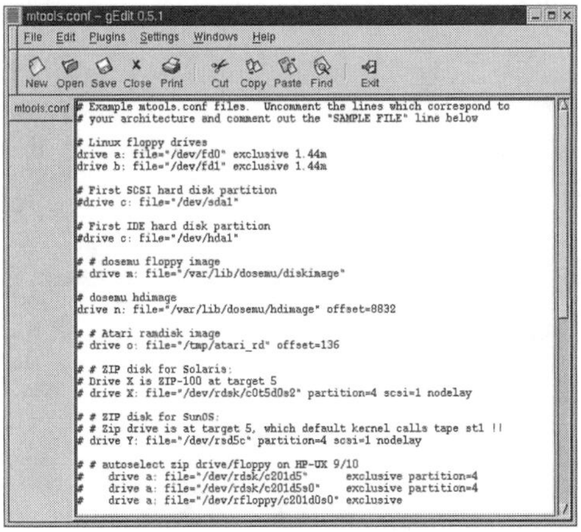

**Figure 12.3**

The /etc/ mtools.conf file, here open in gEdit, lists common DOS hardware devices.

---

**Note**

If mtools isn't already installed on your hard disk, you can install it from your Red Hat Linux CD-ROM #1 using GnoRPM or the command rpm -i /mnt/cdrom/ RedHat/RPMS/mtools* at the command prompt. If you need more information on RPM, see Chapter 13, "Managing Packages with RPM."

PART

**II**

CH

**12**

---

For example, on my computer I have only one floppy drive—the typical 3.5-inch variety that reads 1.44Mb floppy disks. I also have a SCSI hard disk, which Linux defines as /dev/sda. And Windows is installed on the first partition of that drive. In other words, my Windows drive C: is defined as /dev/sda1 in Linux. I know this because entering the command fdisk -l /dev/sda at the Linux command prompt lists all my partitions. And I know that the any listed as FAT16 or VFAT are DOS/Windows partitions. Thus, I would want to uncomment the line that defines that device, and comment out the rest of the lines. So I'd remove the # symbol in from the the lines that define drives A: and C: in /etc/mtools.conf as follows:

```
#Linux floppy drives
drive a: file="/dev/fd0" exclusive 1.44m
#drive b: file="/dev/fd1" exclusive 1.44m

#First SCSI hard disk partition
drive c: file="/dev/sda1"
```

```
#First IDE hard disk partition
#drive c: file="/dev/hda1"
```

Make sure you scroll through the entire /etc/mtools.conf file and comment out any uncommented lines that aren't relevant to your computer. Close and save the file when you're done.

## USING MTOOLS

To start mtools, you'll need to get to a terminal window or virtual console command prompt and enter the following command:

mtools

You'll see a list of supported commands, followed by the normal Linux command prompt. You still have the full range of Linux Bash commands at your disposal. But you also have the mtools commands, listed in Table 12.1, at your disposal.

TABLE 12.1   NEW COMMANDS THAT THE mtools BRINGS TO YOUR LINUX COMMAND PROMPT

| mtools Command | Purpose |
| --- | --- |
| mattrib | Changes DOS file attributes |
| mbadblocks | Scans a DOS floppy for bad blocks |
| mcd | Changes DOS current directory |
| mcopy | Copies DOS file(s) |
| mdel | Deletes DOS file(s) |
| mdeltree | Deletes a DOS folder (directory) |
| mdir | Shows DOS folder (directory) contents |
| mdu | Shows the space occupied by a directory |
| mformat | Formats a DOS floppy disk (after Linux low-level format) |
| minfo | Displays information about a DOS filesystem |
| mlabel | Labels a DOS disk |
| mmd | Creates a DOS folder (directory) |
| mmount | Used to mount DOS disks with unusual geometries |
| mpartition | Creates DOS filesystems as partitions (dangerous!) |
| mrd | Removes a DOS directory |
| mmove | Moves DOS file(s) |
| mren | Renames a DOS file or directory |
| mshowfat | Shows FAT entries for a file |
| mtoolstest | Tests mtools configuration |
| mtype | Displays the contents of a DOS file |
| mzip | Issues zip disk-specific command in Solaris or HPUX |

The syntax of each command is identical to its counterpart in DOS. For example, the syntax of the `mdir` command is identical to the syntax of the DOS `DIR` command. So to view the contents of a the DOS floppy disk currently in drive A:, you'd enter the command `mdir a:`. When specifying directories, you can use either a forward slash or a backslash as the delimiter. So, assuming that the floppy disk in drive A: contained a directory named `mystuff`, you could view the contents of that directory using either of the following commands:

```
mdir a:/mystuff
mdir a:\mystuff
```

```
If the directory name contains spaces, you need to enclose the expression in
quotation marks. For example, if the floppy disk contains a folder named More of my
stuff, you'd use one of these commands to view the contents of that directory:mdir
"a:/More of my stuff"
```

```
mdir "a:\More of my stuff"
```

Like DOS, `mtools` converts filenames that don't comply with the original 8.3 naming convention of DOS in both an abbreviated format using the first six characters of the filename followed by a tilde (~) and a number. That abbreviated format removes blank spaces and any DOS-illegal characters, and is always shown in all uppercase letters. The last column of the `mdir` display shows the true name of the file or directory. For example, assuming the floppy disk currently in drive A: did indeed contain the two directories just mentioned entering the `mdir a:` command would list something like this:

```
MYSTUFF     <DIR>    09/08/2000    10:09    MyStuff
MOREOF~1    <DIR>    09/08/2000    10:09    More of my stuff
```

You can use the abbreviated name in your `mtools` commands, without quotation marks and without regard to case. Thus, a third alternative to viewing the contents of the folder named `More of my stuff` on the floppy in drive A: would be the following:

```
mdir a:\moreof~1
```

> **Tip**
>
> As in DOS with the DOSKEY option enabled, you can scroll through your command history using the ~UA and ~DA keys. This is actually a standard feature of the Bash shell, but works very much like DOSKEY.

Undoubtedly, the most common use of `mtools` will be to copy files to and from the floppy or other removable disk. The `mcopy` command provides that service, and follows the standard DOS syntax of `mcopy source destination`. If you omit the drive letter in either the source or destination and use forward slashes, then `mcopy` assumes you're referring to a Linux directory or file. Thus, to copy the file `a:\MyStuff\01selinux.doc` to your home directory (always abbreviated ~ in Linux), you could enter this command:

```
mcopy a:/mystuff/01selinux.doc ~
```

Or, using the abbreviated filename, you could enter this command:

```
mcopy a:/mystuff/01seli~1.doc ~
```

When copied, the file on your hard drive will have whatever name you used in the mcopy command. Don't forget that if your DOS directory contains blank spaces, you need to enclose the entire reference in quotation marks. For example, suppose you want to copy all the HOWTOs that start with the characters DOS- from the Linux /usr/doc/HOWTO directory to the directory named More of my stuff on the floppy disk in drive A:. Simply enter the following command:

```
mcopy /usr/doc/HOWTO/DOS-* "a:/More of my stuff"
```

---

**Tip**

As in DOS, you can use the * character to stand for any number of characters, and the ? to stand for any single character in a filename.

---

Linux text files use a different end-of-line character than DOS text files. So if you view a Linux text file using Notepad or some other simple text editor in Windows, you'll get a strange-looking result with little squares representing linebreaks. You'll get much better results if you use WordPad to view the Linux text file. Optionally, you can use the -t option in mcopy to convert the copied files to DOS text format. Place the -t just after the mcopy command as in the following:

```
mcopy -t /usr/doc/HOWTO/DOS-* "a:/More of my stuff"
```

You can open files copied using the -t switch using either Notepad or WordPad in Windows.

## FORMATTING FLOPPIES FROM MTOOLS

To format DOS/Windows floppy disks using mtools, you first have to low-level format the disk using the Linux fdformat command. The following is the syntax for 3.5-inch 1.44Mb floppies:

```
fdformat /dev/fd0H1440
```

---

**Caution**

Don't forget that formatting a disk wipes out its existing content. Typically, you only need to format brand-new, unformatted floppy disks.

---

When fdformat has finished its job and you're returned to the command prompt, you can enter the following command to format the floppy disk (assuming it's in drive A:):

```
mformat a:
```

That command only takes a few seconds to place a DOS filesystem structure on the low-level formatted floppy.

## More on mtools

Though copying files to and from DOS floppies is likely to be the most common use of mtools, it does have a wide range of other capabilities. To learn more about mtools, consult the following resources:

- mtools man page (man mtools at the command prompt)
- mtools Web site and mailing list at http://www.tux.org/pub/knaff/mtools
- DOS-to-Linux-HOWTO
- DOS-Win-to-Linux-HOWTO
- man fdformat for low-level formatting help.

# Using the DOS Emulator (DOSEMU)

DOSEMU, as the name implies, emulates DOS on a Linux computer. In essence, this allows you to run some DOS programs (but no Windows programs) in Linux without rebooting to DOS or Windows. So if you happen to have one of the supported DOS programs listed here and don't have a means to boot to DOS/Windows, you can run those programs under Linux:

- 4DOS 4.0
- a86 and d86 (assembler and debugger)
- Alpha-4 2.1
- Big Mouth Voicemail card
- Borland TASM/TLINK
- Checkit
- ColorView/386
- dBASE III+
- Doskey
- DR-DOS 6.0
- Elvis 1.5
- FoxPro 2.0
- HelpPC 2.1
- Lotus 1-2-3 v2.2
- Managing Your Money
- Microsoft Multiplan 4.2
- Microsoft Word 5.0
- Microsoft Word 5.5
- Minitab
- MKS utilities

- MouseSystems mouse and MicroSoft mouse driver (`mscmouse.com`)
- Norton Utilities v6.0
- PC Tools PCShell
- pkzip 2.04e
- QEdit
- Quicken 4.0
- SimEarth
- Stacker
- SuperStor
- Telix & Kermit (at low baud rates)
- Turbo C++ 1.0
- Turbo Debugger 3.0
- Turbo Pascal 5.5
- uEmacs
- WordPerfect 5.0

DOSEMU can be tricky to install. Because there is a risk of messing things up in such a way as to make your machine unbootable, I recommend backing up any important files before you proceed. Of course, if you don't really need this capability, it might be best to ignore it altogether. For example, if you have Windows 95/98 installed on the same machine, it might be easier just to boot to Windows to run your DOS apps.

If I may be so bold as to assume that few, or none, of you has a burning need to run any of those supported programs in Linux, I'll leave it at that and just refer the rest of you to places where you can find more information. DOSEMU is already installed if you performed a GNOME Workstation-class installation, or if you selected DOS/Windows Connectivity during a custom installation. If you need to install DOSEMU, you can use RPM or GnoRPM (see Chapter 13) to install the packages `dosemu-0.99.13-1.i386.rpm` and `xdosemu 0.99.13-1.i386.rpm`. If mtools hasn't been installed already, you'll also need to install the package `mtools-3.9.1-5.i386.rpm`.

> **Tip**
>
> To find out if dosemu is installed, enter the command `rpm -q dosemu`. To find out is mtools is already installed, enter the command `rpm -q mtools`. If you get any message other than `...not installed`, then the package is already installed and you don't have to do anything else.

When the installation is complete, you can view all the documentation files by using your favorite File Manager to get to the directory `/usr/doc/dosemu-0.99.13`. Or, you can enter the following commands to view the names of the DOSEMU documentation files:

```
cd /usr/doc/dosemu*
ls
```

The QuickStart, README.txt, and dosemu-HOWTO.txt provide all the information you need to configure and use DOSEMU after it's installed. Optionally, you can preview those documents, without installing, by visiting the DOSEMU home page at http://www.dosemu.org. The HOWTO is also available from Red Hat's HOWTO index at http://www.redhat.com/mirrors/LDP/HOWTO.

# Running Windows Programs in Linux

Before you get too excited here, let me tell you that Wine's ability to run Windows programs in Linux is currently a *goal*, not a reality. It's not likely that you'll be able to run *all* your favorite Windows applications while booted into Linux. More likely than not, you'll still need to boot to Windows to run your favorite Windows apps. But, there is a project known as Wine (short for *Win*dows *E*mulator) that's well underway, and doing a pretty good job of running quite a few Windows programs under Linux. You'll probably still need to have a Windows partition installed in the same computer. But Wine will allow you to run some Windows apps right on your Linux X desktop without rebooting to Windows. If you are interested in a solution that will let you actually run the entire Windows operating system, including Windows 2000 under Linux, take a look at the product "Vinware" at http://www.vmware.com/.

Wine doesn't come with your Red Hat Linux CD-ROM. So if you want to take it for a spin, you'll need to download its RPM file from http://www.winehq.org. You'll find many different formats for downloading there. Make sure you choose the .rpm package for Red Hat Linux 6.2.

After the .rpm file is downloaded, you can install Wine using GnoRPM or the rpm command, both of which are discussed in Chapter 13. When the installation procedure is complete, you'll have two new files on your hard drive: /usr/bin/wine, which is the actual Wine program, and /etc/wine/wine.conf, which is Wine's configuration file. Before you can use Wine, however, you need to edit one line in Wine's configuration file. You can use any text editor to do so. Figure 12.4 shows the /etc/wine/wine.conf file opened in the GNOME gEdit editor.

Within that file you need to locate the [Drive C] and Path lines, which will look like these:

```
[Drive C]
Path=/c
```

Your job is to replace the c with the mount point for your Windows C: drive. For example, if you mount your C: drive automatically in fstab to the mount point /mnt/winc, then you need to change the Path line to read:

```
Path=/mnt/winc
```

**Figure 12.4**

The `/etc/wine/ wine.conf` configuration file for Wine.

In Figure 12.4 I've already made that change to `wine.conf`. If you mount the Windows C: drive manually using a command like `mount -t vfat /dev/sda1 /mnt/winc`, then the `Path` line needs to be changed to the following:

`Path=/mnt/winc`

Close and save that file, and you're ready to try your luck. I've had the best luck launching Windows apps using the Open With option on the right-click menu. To do that, open your File Manager, then open the directory (mount point) that represents your Window C drive (as in `/mnt/winc`). From there, work your way to the icon that represents the program you want to start. Then, right-click that icon and choose Open With. In the GMC dialog box that appears, type `wine` under Program to run, then click the OK button. It might take a few seconds, so be patient. If Wine is able to run the app, it'll open on your Desktop eventually. Figure 12.5 shows Windows WordPad running on the GNOME desktop.

**Figure 12.5**

Running Windows WordPad on the GNOME desktop, thanks to Wine.

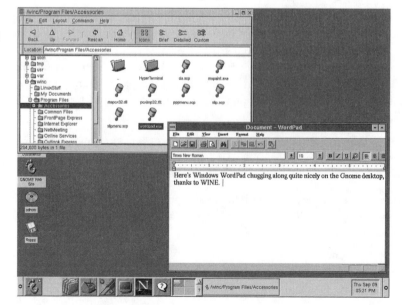

You can also launch Windows apps from a terminal window by entering the command wine followed by the full path to the Windows program you want to run. For example, I could have also run WordPad by entering this command in a terminal window:

```
wine "/mnt/winc/Program Files/Accessories/wordpad.exe"
```

You can learn more about Wine from the following sources, though the two man pages won't be available until after you've installed Wine:

- Wine Headquarters at www.winehq.com
- man wine
- man wine.conf
- The Wine FAQ at www.winehq.com/faq.html
- The Wine Newsgroup at comp.emulators.ms-windows.wine

Also, unless you're a programmer, you can probably ignore all the information on compiling Wine on your computer. The Red Hat RPM file that you download contains the compiled file and additional files needed to run Wine.

# LAUNCHING LINUX FROM DOS (LOADLIN)

You can start your computer in DOS or Windows, then load the Linux kernel into memory and start using it. This technique is especially handy if you have trouble using a DOS/Windows modem, sound card, or other device in Linux. The program you use to load Linux from DOS is named LOADLIN.EXE, and is included on your Red Hat Linux CD-ROM #1. To use it, you'll first need to make sure you know the Linux device name of your Linux root (/) partition. To get that info, start LinuxConf, then open the Config, File Systems, Access Local drive, and look for the device name to the left of the Mount Point named /. Mine happens to be /dev/sda6 but yours could be anything. Jot it down on a piece of scratch paper. Then click Quit buttons until LinuxConf closes.

Next, you'll need to boot up in DOS/Windows. If you're in GNOME, click the Main Menu button and choose Log out, Reboot, Yes. If you're at a command prompt, you can use the reboot or shutdown -r now command. Watch for the LILO boot prompt. When it appears, type dos and press Enter to start up in DOS or Windows.

When you get to the Windows desktop, put your Red Hat Linux CD-ROM #1 in your CD-ROM drive. Open your My Computer icon, and double-click the icon for your CD-ROM drive. You should see a folder named dosutils. Double-click that folder to open it up. You'll need to copy a couple of files from that folder to your DOS C: drive.

PART
II

CH
12

**Tip**

If My Computer is set up to display only one window at a time on your system, you can get to a C icon for your hard drive by opening a second copy of My Computer.

Next, you need to copy `loadlin.exe` (it may appear as simply loadlin in My Computer) from that `dosutils` folder to your C: drive. To do so, you can just drag, using the right mouse button, the `loadlin` or `loadlin.exe` file from `d:\dosutils` to the icon for your C: drive. Choose Copy Here after dropping the icon onto your C: drive's icon. Then, back on your D: drive, open the `\dosutils\autoboot` folder. Copy the `vmlinuz` file's icon from there to your C: drive. If you look at the contents of your C: drive, you should see icons for `loadlin` (or `loadlin.exe`) and `vmlinuz`. And that's it for copying. You can close your My Computer windows, and remove the CD from your CD-ROM drive. You can't load Linux directly from Windows—you need to do that from a DOS command prompt. So if you're at the Windows desktop, you need to click the Start button and choose Shut Down, Restart in MS-DOS Mode, OK. Enter this command to get to the topmost folder of your C: drive:

```
cd \
```

To use `loadlin`, you need to enter the command `loadlin vmlinuz root=xxx ro` but replace *xxx* with your own computer's device name. In my case, where the Linux root directory is `/dev/sda6`, I would enter the following command:

```
loadlin vmlinuz root=/dev/sda6 ro
```

If all goes well, Linux will go through its normal startup routine, and you'll be able to log in normally. For more information on loadlin, and help getting around any problems it presents, see author Chris Fischer's `Linux+Windows 95 Reference Page` at `http://www.eskimo.com/~praxis`. The site includes custom scripts and tips on using `loadlin` specifically with Windows 98.

# CASE STUDY: SAVING LINUX FILES TO WINDOWS

One of the tricks of writing this book was to capture screens that are used in the figures and zip them up in Windows, with the rest of the chapter material to be sent to the publisher. Fortunately, once I had added a line to my `/etc/fstab` file, this was pretty easy to do. As in the example presented earlier in this chapter, I added a line to `/etc/fstab` file to treat my Windows C: drive as a directory named `/mnt/winc` in Linux. Once in Linux, I could get to that drive at any time by simply opening `/mnt/winc` on the GNOME File Manager.

I decided to put all this book's chapters in a subfolder named SELinux under the My Documents folder of Windows. So I just had to open My Documents in GNOME's File Manager, right-click the pane on the right, choose New Directory, type in the folder name (`SELinux`), and then click the OK button. Then I switched to that new directory just by double-clicking its icon in the right pane, and used the same right-click technique to create a separate folder for each chapter. Thus, whenever I browsed to `/mnt/winc/My Documents/SELinux`, I had access to all my Windows files for this book, as shown in Figure 12.6.

Unlike Windows, pressing the Print Screen key in Linux doesn't take a snapshot of the screen, but several screen capture programs are available. I used the GIMP for most of my screen shots. Assuming it's installed, you can start the GIMP by clicking the GNOME Main

Menu button and choosing Graphics, The GIMP. In the small window that appears, choosing Xtns, Screen Shot presents a dialog box for capturing the screen.

**Figure 12.6**
Once drive C: is mounted via /etc/fstab, you can get to it by opening its mount point (/mnt/winc in my example) in any file manager.

When the screen was captured, the computer would beep a couple times and the screen shot would appear on the screen. To save the screen shot, I just had to right-click any part of it and choose File, Save As. In the Save Image dialog box, all I needed to do was browse to the appropriate directory (such as /mnt/winc/My Documents/SELinux/12Chap), type in the filename and extension (as in 12fig06.pcx to save in PCX format), and click the OK button. After the file was saved, I could just right-click the graphic image on the screen, choose File, Close, and I was back to my real desktop.

Putting the graphic images directly onto the Windows C: drive saved me the added step of moving or copying them later. Most graphic image file formats are device-independent, so it really doesn't matter which operating system or program you use to create the image. I used the .pcx format because that was the publisher's preference. But I could just as easily saved the files as .gif, .jpeg, or any other format the GIMP supports.

PART
**II**

CH
**12**

CHAPTER 13

# MANAGING PACKAGES WITH RPM

**In this chapter**

# UNDERSTANDING PACKAGES

If you cruise around the Internet looking for free programs to download, you'll find that the programs come in many different formats. There's *source code*, which is the actual programming code that the programmers have created. They share this with other programmers who might be interested in contributing to the product. If you download the source code yourself, you'll typically need to *compile* it before it will run on your computer. Compiling is a step that takes the programmer's source code and translates it to executable code, instructions that Linux can "follow" whatever it is that the program makes the computer do. To compile a program, you often need to have numerous other files, in the form of programmer's toolkits, on your computer as well. If you're not a programmer, the whole business can be pretty confusing, and you may not be up to the many challenges that compiling source code presents.

Sometimes, you can download *tarballs* of programs. A tarball is a single file that can contain several files. A tarball filename will typically end with the extension .tar or .tar.gz if it is compressed. You'll learn how to create and decompress tarballs in Chapter 16, "Archiving, Backing Up, and Restoring." But if you're just looking to download a program, there's no guarantee that the tarball is going to make life any easier. The tarball may contain a bunch of separate source code files that still need to be compressed.

> **Tip**
>
> The tarball is roughly equivalent to a .sit file on the Macintosh, or a .zip file on Windows. The tar format, however, is not compressed, while .sit and .zip are.

The third way that Linux programs are transported from one computer to another is through Red Hat packages, often called *packages* for short. Unlike source code and tarballs, packages are created for everyday computer users, as opposed to programmers. A package contains all (or most) of the files needed to run the program, already compiled and ready to go. The filename extension for such packages is always .rpm, which makes it a little easier to identify a package when faced with a lot of different possible file formats to download. After you download a package, you need to *install* the package on your computer before you can use whatever program is inside the package. You can use either GnoRPM or the rpm command at the command prompt to install any package. Most of the time, it's pretty easy and most definitely does not require that you be a professional programmer. Many packages even add themselves to your GNOME or KDE menus automatically. So once the package is installed, starting the program is a simple matter of finding its entry in your Main Menu.

# USING GNORPM

GnoRPM is the graphical version of the Red Hat Package Manager. In GNOME, you can start GnoRPM using either of the following methods:

- Click the Main Menu button and choose System, GnoRPM.
- Mid-click the desktop and choose GNOME Apps, System, GnoRPM.

In any other GUI, you can enter the command gnorpm in a terminal window to fire up GnoRPM. The left column of GnoRPM is called the *package panel*. It consists of several groups of packages categorized as Amusements, Applications, Development, and so forth. Groups that contains subgroups can be expanded or collapsed by clicking the + or - sign to the left of the group name. The pane on the right is called the *display panel*. When you open a category in the package panel, the display panel shows an icon for each installed package within that category. Each icon is labeled with the name and version number of the installed package, as in the example shown in Figure 13.1. There, you can see that several packages from the Amusements/Graphics groups are installed on that computer.

**Figure 13.1**
The GnoRPM window initially displays a categorized list of packages that are already installed on your computer.

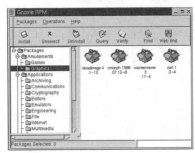

> **Note**
>
> Keep in mind that all the packages that are visible through the initial GnoRPM window are already installed. They don't need to be installed again!

## QUERYING PACKAGES IN GNORPM

To find out what the heck a given package is for, you *query* the package. Simply click the icon for the package you're curious about, and then click the Query button in the toolbar. The package name and version number appear centered at the top of the Package Info dialog box that appears (see Figure 13.2):

- **Size:** How much disk space (in bytes) the package occupies.
- **Build Host:** Where the package can be found on the Internet.
- **Distribution:** Who is responsible for creating and distributing the package.
- **Group:** How this package is categorized within GnoRPM, usually as *Category/ Subcategory*.
- **Install Date:** When the package was installed on this computer.
- **Build Date:** When this build (version) of the program was released to the public.

- **Vendor:** Who sells or provides the package.

- **Packager:** Who created the package; often doubles as a clickable URL for visiting the Packager's Web site.

- **URL:** If there's a Web site dedicated to the current package, its URL will be displayed. If that URL is blue and underlined, a click will take you to the appropriate page.

**Figure 13.2**
Results of querying the xscreensaver package in GnoRPM.

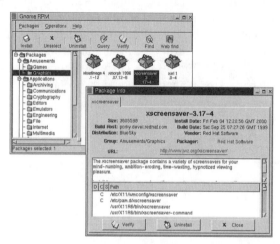

---

**Tip**

If you select multiple icons before clicking the Query button, the Package Info dialog box will display information about all the selected packages, each on its own tab within the Package Info dialog box.

---

The files that make up the package are listed beneath the package description. There's no need for you to read through the entire list or memorize all the files that make up a package. But, if you're wondering where a particular package is installed on your hard disk, the directory name that each file is stored in is included in the filename. Furthermore, the columns titled D, C, and S provide some useful information:

- **D:** Indicates a documentation file, which contains information about using the program.

- **C:** Indicates a configuration file, which can be used to tweak the installed program.

- **S:** Indicates the status of the file. Typically left blank unless there's a problem, such as the file is missing.

Unfortunately, there's no quick and easy way to open a documentation file directly from the Package Info dialog box. So if you want to check out the documentation right away, you'll need to open your File Manager, get to the directory that houses the documentation file, then double-click the documentation filename within that directory. If you can't find a given package in your Main Menu and are trying to figure out how to start the darn thing, the documentation file is definitely a good place to look for that information.

If you need to make sure that a package is fully and correctly installed, click its icon, then click the Verify button in the toolbar. GnoRPM will quickly check to ensure that all the necessary files are where they're supposed to be. Any problem files will be listed in the Verifying Packages dialog box that appears. If that dialog box is empty, that's good. It means all the files are indeed in place. If you do find a problem, the simplest way to fix it will be to reinstall or upgrade the package from its original source, as discussed later in this chapter.

## INSTALLING PACKAGES WITH GNORPM

To install a new package, you first need to know where the package (the .rpm file) is located. Many optional packages are available on your Red Hat Linux CD-ROM #1, in the directory named /RedHat/RPMS. The World Wide Web is home to many more packages, most of which you can download and install for free.

Before you go exploring on the Web, however, take a moment to create a directory on your hard disk for storing downloaded packages. You can put that directory in your home directory, or anywhere else for that matter. Give the new directory any descriptive name, such as DownloadedRPMs. Whenever you come across an .rpm file that you think you'd be interested in exploring, go ahead and download it, putting into your DownloadedRPMs directory. Putting all your downloaded RPMs into a single directory will make it easier to install, review, and manage the packages later via GnoRPM.

> **Note**
>
> You must be logged in as *root* (the superuser) if you want to install, upgrade, or remove a package.

Red Hat also maintains a Web site of packages. To get to it, just click the Web Find button in the GnoRPM toolbar. In the Rpmfind window that appears, you'll see a long list of packages that are available for downloading from the Web site. The vast majority of those packages are also readily available on your Red Hat CD-ROM so you really don't need to spend a whole lot of time downloading files from the Web. However, if you must have the latest and greatest version of a program, you can always check the Red Hat Web site to see if the version that's currently posted there is newer than the version that's already installed on your computer. To install or upgrade a package, just click the package name, then click the Install or Upgrade button at the bottom of the RPMfind dialog box.

To install packages from your Red Hat CD-ROM, you need to first put that CD into your CD-ROM drive. If your system is set up to automount and autostart CDs, you'll be taken into GnoRPM automatically, in which case you can go straight to step 1. If the CD doesn't auto mount, you'll need to mount the CD first. If you're using GNOME or KDE and have already created a desktop shortcut to your CD-ROM drive, you can just right-click that icon and choose Mount device. Optionally, you can use the User Mount Tool to mount the disk or enter the command mount /mnt/cdrom in a terminal window. Then, in GnoRPM, follow these steps:

1. Click the Install button in the GnoRPM toolbar. A dialog box titled Install appears (later, it will list packages you've opted to install).

2. Click the Add button in the Install dialog box to choose packages to install.

3. In the Add Packages dialog box that appears, navigate to the directory that contains the package(s) you want to install.

When you're looking to install from the Red Hat Linux CD-ROM #1, the directory to navigate to will be /mnt/cdrom/RedHat/RPMS. If you're not taken there automatically when the Add Packages dialog box first opens, you'll need to use the Directories list in the left column to navigate to that directory. When the Add Packages dialog box is pointed to a directory that contains one or more .rpm files that you can install, the name of those files will be listed in the right column. For example, Figure 13.3 shows the packages available for installation from the /mnt/cdrom/RedHat/RPMS directory.

**Figure 13.3**

Packages available for installation from the /mnt/cdrom/ RedHat/RPMS directory when the Red Hat Linux CD-ROM is mounted in your CD-ROM drive.

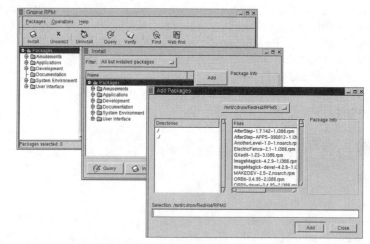

If you want to install packages from some other location, you need to navigate to the appropriate directory for those packages. For example, if you have an .rpm file on a floppy disk and you've already mounted that disk, you'll want to navigate to /mnt/floppy in the Add Packages dialog box. If you download .rpm files from the Internet, you need to navigate to whatever directory you saved those downloaded files into.

You can scroll through the Files list to view all the packages that are available for installation from the current directory. To choose a file to install, simply click its name, then click the Add button at the bottom of the Add Packages dialog box. That package will be added to the list of packages to be installed in the Install dialog box. For example, in Figure 13.4 I've selected the package xfishtank-2.0-14 for installation.

**Figure 13.4**

In this example, I've selected for installation the package xfish-tank-2.0-14 from the Red Hat Linux CD-ROM.

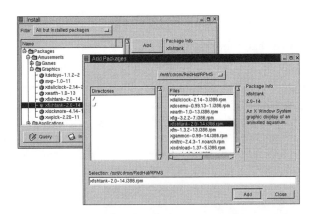

Packages that have -devel- in their filenames are for programmers who want source code to contribute to the package. If you're just looking to use a program, you can ignore the -devel- package.

When you've finished selecting packages for installation, click the Close button at the bottom of the Add Packages dialog box. The Install dialog box will contain a list of packages you've chosen to install. In the Install dialog box, only packages that are selected will actually be installed. (By "selected" in this context, I mean that the package's check box contains a check mark.) You can select and de-select individual packages by clicking their check boxes.

The filename for a package consists of the package name, version number, and architecture that the package was compiled for, followed by .rpm. Packages for the PC class of computers will be identified as .i386. Packages that contain programs that aren't, or don't need to be, compiled for a specific architecture will be identified as *noarch*. It's always safe to install noarch packages from your Red Hat CD-ROM.

Before you actually install a package, do yourself a favor and Query the package, using the Query button at the bottom of the Install dialog box. The Package Info dialog box will tell you some important information about where the installed package will end up. For example in Figure 13.5, I can see that once installed, the xfishtank package file will be in the path /usr/X11R6/bin, under the filename xfishtank. Nearer the top of the Package Info dialog box, the Group entry tells me that after the package is installed, I can find it under the Amusements/Graphics group in the left column of the main GnoRPM window.

Larger packages may contain many files. You'll want to scroll through the list and pay particular attention to the names and locations of any documentation files (marked D in the left column), in case you need additional information to get the program going after it has been installed. Note, too, the paths of files to be installed, so you won't be completely clueless

PART
**II**

CH
**13**

about where to go hunting for the package startup file. You can close the Package Info dialog box after you've reviewed that information.

Finally, to actually install the selected packages listed in the Install dialog box, click the Install button near the bottom of that dialog box. GnoRPM will first go through a series of steps to verify that the program will work correctly when installed on your hard disk. If no problems arise during that phase of the installation, you'll see a progress indicator that keeps you posted as to how things are progressing. If problems do arise, you'll see an Installation Problems dialog box on the screen, briefly describing the problem. If that occurs, see the later section, "Installation Problems."

**Figure 13.5**
Querying a package before actually installing it tells you useful information about where the installed package will end up on your hard disk.

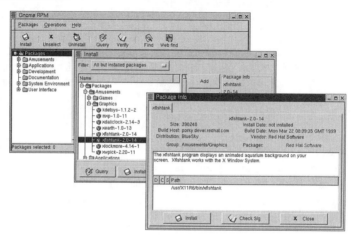

## RUNNING THE INSTALLED PACKAGE

Assuming that no problems arise, the package will install, and you'll be returned to the Install dialog box. You can close that dialog box if you're finished installing packages for now. Most likely, you'll want to start the installed package and take it for a spin. Many packages automatically add startup icons to your main menu. So starting an installed package might be as easy as finding, and clicking on, its menu icon.

Unfortunately, starting an installed application is not always quite that easy. Sometimes, you'll need to go digging around to find out exactly where the package was installed and which command you need to enter in order to start the program. If you queried the package before you installed it and noted which group the package was installed under, you can now find that package icon in the main GnoRPM window simply by opening the appropriate groups. For example, to query the xfishtank package after it has been installed, first open GnoRPM and then open the Amusements, Graphics groups in the left column. An icon for the installed package should appear in the display pane. To query the installed package, click its icon, then click the Query button in the toolbar. Remember, if a package contains many files, documentation files are marked with a D in the left column.

You can also search for an installed package based on its name. In GnoRPM click the Find button, then choose Match Label from the button that appears near the top of the dialog box. Type in the first few letters of the package name, then click the Find button. The Find Packages dialog box will list all installed packages that contain whatever name you typed in. When you find the installed package you were looking for, select it by clicking on it. Then click the Query button at the bottom of the Find Packages dialog box to query that installed package.

When you've determined how to start the program, you can enter the appropriate path and filename at a command prompt or in a terminal window. (Definitely in a terminal window if the package contains an X graphical application program!) For example, to start xfishtank, I'd open up a terminal window in GNOME and enter the following command:

```
xfishtank &
```

Note that the ampersand (&) at the end of the command makes xfishtank its own process, so that xfishtank will run and let you continue to interact with your terminal window.

**Tip**

In lieu of extensive documentation, xfishtank does offer a small list of optional parameters. Enter the command xfishtank --help to see them.

**Command Not Found Errors**

In the xfishtank example, it wasn't necessary to enter the complete path name, /usr/X11R6/bin/ xfishtank because I happen to know that the /usr/X11R6/bin directory is already included in the PATH environment variable. I know this because entering the command env displays all such variables, and I could see next to PATH= that /usr/X11R6/bin is one of the directories that will be searched whenever I enter a command. As discussed in Chapter 11, "Configuring Startup and Shutdown," the PATH environment variable is defined during the Linux initialization (startup).

The PATH environment variable tells Linux which directories to search when a user enters a command that is not a built-in command or when the name of a file is not in the current working directory.

By default, Linux usually sets up the PATH environment variable to search the /usr/bin, /sbin, /bin, /usr/sbin, /usr/X11R6/bin, and /root/bin directories before returning a "command not found" error message. Many packages are installed in those directories to make startup easier.

Then again, there's always the exception. For example, as discussed in the Case Study at the end of Chapter 6, the StarOffice suite of applications startup file is stored in /opt/Office50/bin, which obviously is not in the PATH. But, it's fairly easy to create icons for launching that application, as was also demonstrated in that case study.

## INSTALLATION PROBLEMS

The two most common installation problems that arise are "already installed" and "dependency problem." The first problem is simply GnoRPM telling you that you're about to reinstall a package that's already installed. The only downside to doing so is that, if you've made any custom configurations to that installed program, you'll lose those if you reinstall the package. In other words, the newly installed program will have all the original default options selected for that particular program. If that doesn't worry you, click the Yes button to replace your existing installed package.

If you are installing a new version of a package and want GnoRPM to try to keep your existing configuration options within that program, click the No button to leave the Installation Problems dialog box. You'll see a message indicating that the installation failed, and you'll be returned to the Install dialog box. To upgrade, rather than reinstall, that package, click the Query button at the bottom of the Install dialog box. Then, in the Package Info dialog box that appears, click the Upgrade button rather than the Install button. You may still see a message telling you that the package is already installed. But, since you're upgrading rather than installing, you can choose Yes to proceed.

## FAILED DEPENDENCY PROBLEMS

The dependency problem is a little trickier. Most programs consist of several files. In fact, many programs depend on other files being on your hard disk already, even before you install the package. At first glance, they may seem odd. After all, what good is a package if it doesn't already contain all the files needed to run the program? The answer to that has to do with certain common *library files* that many different programs share and depend on. Those library files are created and distributed independently of the programs that rely on them. So rather than forcing you to use "version x" of some library file, RPM uses whatever version of that file is already on your hard disk. Hence, you can always have the latest and greatest library files installed without worrying about a particular package overwriting your library file with an older version of the same file.

Dependency problems occur when the required library file doesn't exist at all on your hard disk. In this case, a dialog box titled Dependency Problems appears before the package is installed. That dialog box will tell you which files are missing from your hard disk. For example, Figure 13.6 shows what happens if you try to install only the gnuchess package from the Red Hat CD-ROM.

**Figure 13.6**
If a package needs another file in order to run correctly, the Dependency Problems dialog box will list the required file(s).

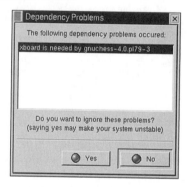

There, the dialog box tells you that in order for gnuchess to run correctly on your system, you'll also need to install package named xboard. The smart thing to do here is to choose No so that you don't proceed with the installation. Then click the Add button in the Install dialog box again, and look around for the other package that needs to be installed. Add that package to the list of packages to be installed. Then try again by clicking the Install button at the bottom of the Install dialog box. Although the circumstance is rare, you may have to make more than one visit to the Add Packages dialog box to choose all the packages needed for a successful installation.

### FINDING OBSCURE FILES

Sometimes a dependency check will fail because of a single missing file, rather than a missing package. A lot of library files (which tend to have filenames containing the letters *lib*) fall into this category. For example, a dependency might fail because the package being installed needs a file named `libgtk.so.1` or some such thing. If the missing `libgtk.so.1` isn't a package, then it must be a file that's inside some uninstalled package. The question is, *which* uninstalled package contains the needed file, `libgtk.so.1` in this example?

Fortunately, there's an easy way to find out. You need to use the `rpm` command with the `-q` (query) and `--redhatprovides` options. Get to a terminal window or command prompt (if you're not already at one) and enter a command that looks like this:

```
rpm -q --redhatprovides mysteryfilename
```

Replace *mysteryfilename* with the name of the file you're looking for. So for example, to discover where `libgtk.so.1` is hiding I would enter this command:

```
rpm -q --redhatprovides libgtk.so.1
```

It would return the following:

```
gtk+10-1.0.6-6
```

That means that I have to install `gtk+10-1.0.6-6` from the Red Hat CD-ROM #1 before I install the program that failed to install. Thus, I would enter the following command to do that installation:

```
rpm -ivh /mnt/cdrom/RedHat/RPMS/gtk+10-1.0.6-6*
```

After that package has installed, I must go back and try to install the package that originally caused the failed dependency. The previously missing `libgtk.so.1` file is now installed on my hard disk as a result of installing the `gtk+10-1.0.6-6*` file.

PART

II

CH

13

> **Tip**
>
> The name of the actual package file is likely to be longer than the name shown on the screen. The actual filename for the package might be something like gtk+10-1.0.6-6.i386.rpm. Using the * in the `rpm -I` command covers whatever those additional filename letters might be.

It's possible that you might have to install two or more packages before you can get a specific package installed. Often, it's a matter of using the `--redhatprovides` option to work your way to a file that can be installed without failing the dependency check.

### UNINSTALLING PACKAGES WITH GNORPM

Uninstalling a package removes all the files that make up the package from your hard disk. However, if GnoRPM detects that other installed packages are dependent on some part of the package you're about to uninstall, it will pop up a dialog box and ask for confirmation before deleting the file. In general, you *don't* want to delete those files, as doing so might cripple other packages that are dependent on that file. To uninstall a package, follow these steps:

1. Open GnoRPM (Main Menu, System, GnoRPM).

2. In the left pane of GnoRPM, open the category that contains the package you want to remove.

3. In the right pane, select the package you want to remove by clicking its icon.

4. Click the Uninstall button in the toolbar.

> **Note**
>
> If you try to uninstall a package without being logged in as root, you get the rather unhelpful error message `Failed to open /var/lib/rpm/packages/rpm` when you click the Uninstall button. You must be logged in as root to uninstall packages.

A dialog box titled Continue Removal appears and asks for confirmation. If you're sure you want to remove the package, click the Yes button.

## USING THE RPM COMMAND

As with most of Linux, GnoRPM is a graphical interface to the RPM program, which can also be used at the command prompt without a GUI. Should you ever need or want to manage packages without GnoRPM, you can enter RPM commands directly at the command prompt. The following is the general syntax for using RPM at the command prompt:

```
rpm -switches [--options] [packagename]
```

*switches* is any combination of switches summarized here:

- **-e**—Erase (uninstall) package.
- **-F**—Freshen outdated files only.
- **-h**—Show hash marks (#) as progress meter, fifty hash marks indicate 100% completion.
- **-i**—Install package.
- **-q**—Query package.
- **-U**—Upgrade package.
- **-v**—Verify, and show what's happening.

The *--options* component, as the name implies, are optional settings that you can add to refine the command. Commonly used options include the following:

- **--excludedocs:** Prevents the installation of documentation files
- **--force:** Forces the package to be installed despite any problems that may arise
- **--hash:** Same as using -h; shows progress as a series of hash marks
- **--help:** Shows help (use rpm --help ¦ less to scroll through help)
- **--includedocs:** Ensures that documentation files are installed (the default, even if you don't use this switch)
- **--nodeps:** Eliminates dependency checking prior to installation
- **--oldpackage:** Allows "downgrading" of a newer installation to an older version
- **--percent:** Displays percentage progress as files are installed
- **--replacefiles:** Allows files in an existing installation to be replaced by newer files
- **--replacepkgs:** Allows installed package to be replaced by new package
- **--test:** Goes through a package installation without actually installing, so you can test for potential problems that might arise during the installation

The *packagename* is the name of the package you wish to install. All RPM package names follow this standard format:

```
name-version-release.architecture.rpm
```

So you can tell a lot about a package just from its name. For example, the following package name tells you that the package contains version 2.0, release 4, of the package named xsomething, and that this is the package to use on i386 architectures:

```
xsomething-2.0-4.i386.rpm
```

The i386 architecture covers essentially all the PC class computers, including those based on Intel 386, 486, and various versions of the Pentium CPU, as well as the AMD and Cyrix chips.

## INSTALLING WITH RPM

As with GnoRPM, you'll need to know the location and name of the package (.rpm) file that you want to install before you enter the RPM command. If you'll be installing from a CD-ROM or floppy disk, you'll also want to mount that disk before you enter the RPM command. Recall that, at the command prompt, you can enter the command mount /mnt/floppy to mount a floppy disk, or the command mount /mnt/cdrom to mount a CD.

To install a package, use the -i switch. If you'd also like to verify the installation and show a progress bar of hash marks on the screen as the package is being installed, use a combination of the i, v, and h switches. For example, to install and verify a package named xsomething-2.0-4.i386.rpm from the mounted Red Hat Linux CD-ROM number 1, you'd enter the following command:

```
rpm -ivh /mnt/cdrom/RedHat/RPMS/xsomething-2.0-4.i386.rpm
```

PART

II

CH

13

As the installation progresses, you'll see a progress bar composed of hash (#) characters on the screen. If a problem arises during the installation, you'll see an error message instead. You can use the various options to override these error messages if the current situation warrants that. For example, the error message `package is already installed` means that you're trying to reinstall a package that has already been installed. If your intent is to upgrade the existing package, you can use the -U switch, as here:

```
rpm -U /mnt/cdrom/RedHat/RPMD/xsomething-2.0-4.i386.rpm
```

If you want to replace the installed package with the one you're about to install, as when you're trying to repair a faulty installation, use -i with the --replacepkgs option as in the following:

```
rpm -ivh --replacepkgs /mnt/cdrom/RedHat/RPMD/xsomething-2.0-4.i386.rpm
```

If the package you are attempting to install contains a file that has already been installed as part of some other package, you'll see an error message like *filename* `conflicts with file from` *package*. To override the problem and install the package anyway, use the -i and --replacefiles options as in the following example:

```
rpm -ivh --replacefiles xsomething-2.0-4.i386.rpm
```

If you try to install a package that depends on some file that isn't on your system and isn't included in the package, you end up with an unresolved dependency. The error message for this sort of problem reads something like `failed dependencies,` *file* `is needed by` *package*. Ideally, you'll want to install the missing package first. However, if (for whatever reason) you want to go ahead and install the current package first, you can use --nodeps to get past this error message. However, you'll eventually need to locate and install the file on which the package depends.

## FRESHENING PACKAGES WITH RPM

The rpm command offers one switch that has no equivalent in GnoRPM. The -F switch allows you to freshen an installed package by installing only files that are newer than existing files from a package. Freshening is different from upgrading in that the freshen option will not install a package if a version of that package is not already on the hard disk. The Upgrade option, on the other hand, will install the package even if the package has never been installed.

As an example of freshening a package, suppose you download a package named *xsomething*-2.04-19.rpm from the Web. You save it in the DownloadedRPMs subdirectory of your home directory. Furthermore, you already have an earlier version of xsomething installed on your hard disk. Now you want to bring any older files up to date with any newer files that are in the package. The command to enter in this case is as follows:

```
rpm -Fvh /~/DownloadedRPMs/xsomething-2.04-19.rpm
```

## QUERYING WITH RPM

You can query any installed package using the -q option in the rpm command. You need only specify the name of the package after the -q switch. For example, to see which version of xfishtank (if any) is currently installed on your hard disk, enter the following command:

```
rpm -q xfishtank
```

You'll see the name of the package file that the program was installed from. In the xfishtank example, you might see xfishtank2.1tp-1, which lets you know that you currently have version 2.1tp-1 installed on your system.

You can also use the -q switch to query multiple packages. Rather than providing a specific package name after the -q switch in the command, you can use one of the Package Specification options summarized as follows:

- **-a**—Queries all currently installed packages
- **-f** *file*—Queries the package that owns the specified *file*
- **-p** *packagefile*—Queries the .rpm file specified by *packagefile*, rather than the installed package

Let's say you want to see a list of all the packages that are currently installed on your system. Entering the following command would do the trick:

```
rpm -qa
```

If the information whizzes by too quickly on the screen, you can pipe its output to the *less* program, as in the following:

```
rpm -qa | less
```

You're not limited to querying for the package name and version number. From the command prompt, you can gather the same information that the Package Info dialog box in GnoRPM provides. Use any combination of the switches below to specify the type of information you're looking for in your query. Just follow the -q with any of the following combination of letters (no blank spaces):

- **i:** Displays extensive information including name, description, release, size, install date, and so forth
- **f** *file*: Queries the package that owns the *file* (that is, the package that the named *file* came from)
- **l:** List of files that make up the entire package (also referred to as the files that the package owns)
- **c:** Lists the files that act as configuration files for the installed package
- **d:** Lists the files within the package that contain documentation
- **s:** Checks the status of each file in the package
- **v:** Used in conjunction with c, d, l, and s options to include permission and ownership information in a format similar to the way the ls -l command lists files

PART

**II**

CH

**13**

> **Tip**
>
> The options listed in the preceding list are officially named Information Selection Options, just in case you come across that term in your Linux documentation meanderings.

Let's say you want to find out which documentation files exist for the package named AnotherLevel. Entering this command would fill you in:

```
rpm -gd AnotherLevel
```

To see a list of all the files that make up the AnotherLevel package, including ownership and permission information, enter this command:

```
rpm -qlv
```

As always, if the information whizzes by on the screen too quickly, you can tack on ¦ less to pipe the output into the *less* program ( rpm -qlv ¦ less). To reduce the amount of detail that the command presents, eliminate the v option (as in, rpm -ql).

> **Tip**
>
> Don't forget that you can also use the -whatprovides switch with -q to find out what package provides a specific file, as discussed in the section "Finding Obscure Files" earlier in this chapter.

## VERIFYING PACKAGES WITH RPM

Verifying a package involves comparing the installed files from a package with the set of files that the package originally contained. Thus, if any problems arise using a particular program, you can check to see whether one of its files has been lost or corrupted by comparing the installed files to the original, intended files. Use the -V switch to verify a package. You can follow -V with any of the Package Specification options -a, -f file, or -p package described in the earlier section, Querying with RPM," to specify the file or package you're interested in. If you follow the -V option with just the name of a package, then the command compares the installed files on the hard disk to the files in the original package and points out any discrepancies between the two. For example, this command verifies the installed AnotherLevel package against the original owning package.

```
rpm -V AnotherLevel
```

If the command returns nothing, that's good because it means there are no discrepancies.

If you want to verify that all the installed packages on your hard disk match their original owning package files, you'd enter this command:

```
rpm -Va
```

If a discrepancy does arise, you'll see an eight-character string consisting of some combination of the characters 5SLTDUGM. Each letter indicates the results of a test comparing the installed file to the file in the owning package. A period in place of one of those characters means the file passed that test, and hence, there is no problem. If the file is a configuration file, the letter *c* will follow the eight-character string. That's for information only, not an indication of a problem. The letters and numbers in the eight-character string represent the following tests and potential problems:

- **5:** File failed MD5 checksum test (installed file is not identical to package file)
- **S:** Installed file is not the same size as package file
- **L:** Symbolic link status of installed file doesn't match the status of the original package file link
- **T:** Modification time of installed file does not match modification time of original file
- **D:** Owning device of installed file doesn't match owning device of the original file
- **U:** Owner of installed file doesn't match owner of original package file
- **G:** Group that owns installed file isn't the same as group that owns the original file
- **M:** Mode (permissions and file type) of installed package doesn't match the original file

If you've intentionally changed a file's ownership or permissions, then the resulting text might not be an indication of an actual problem. For example, if the program is working fine with the new permissions you've assigned to a file, there's no need to "correct" the problem. However, if the installed program isn't working correctly, the results of the verification could be telling you why. If there is no other way to fix the problem, your best bet would probably be to uninstall the package. Then reinstall it from scratch.

### UNINSTALLING WITH RPM

To uninstall packages using the RPM command, use the -e switch followed by the name of the package to uninstall. In this command, the name of the package is sufficient, and you don't have to include a pathname or filename. For example, if you installed the gnuchess and xboard packages and now want to remove them using the rpm command, you'd enter these commands:

```
rpm -e gnuchess
rpm -e xboard
```

# GNORPM AND RPM RESOURCES

The information presented in this chapter will probably cover just about everything you'd ever want to do with RPM and GnoRPM. However, both packages do contain more (and often obscure) options. Plus, GnoRPM has its own configuration file that you can tweak to alter the default behavior of GnoRPM. You can get to GnoRPM's configuration options by choosing Operations, Preferences from its menu bar. Additional sources of information are listed below. Note that some of the more technical information is intended only for programmers who wish to create .rpm files to simplify installation of their programs for users:

PART

II

CH

**13**

- RPM Man page (man rpm).

- RPM Web site at http://www.rpm.org.

- RPM HOWTO at http://www.rpm.org/support/RPM-HOWTO.html.

- Using GNOME RPM and RPM at http://www.redhat.com/support/manuals/ RHL-6.1-Manual/getting-started-guide/ch-rpmlite.html.

- *Maximum RPM* by Ed Bailey, available as a 442-page book, and online in PostScript and LaTeX formats from www.rpm.org.

- RPM Mailing List at rpm-list@redhat.com, archived at http://www.redhat.com/ support/mailing-lists. To subscribe to the mailing list, send an email with the word *subscribe* in the subject line to rpm-list-request@redhat.com.

- RPM Newsgroup at linux.redhat.rpm and through DejaNews at http://www.deja.com/topics_if.xp?search=topic&group=linux.redhat.rpm.

- Terse help can be brought onto the screen by entering the command gnorpm –help or rpm –help.

### PROJECT: QUERYING AND INSTALLING A PACKAGE

In this project you'll use GnoRPM to install the xboing package (if it isn't already installed). And also, you'll query that package to learn more about its files. To get started, make sure you log in as root, and get into your favorite GUI. Either GNOME or KDE will work best here. Then follow these steps:

1. Put your Red Hat Linux CD-ROM #1 into your CD-ROM drive. If GnoRPM starts automatically, skip to step 4.

2. Mount the CD by right-clicking its desktop icon and choosing Mount Device or by opening a terminal window and entering the command mount /mnt/cdrom.

3. Start GnoRPM by clicking the GNOME Main Menu button and choosing System, GnoRPM. In KDE, press Alt+F2 and enter the command gnorpm.

4. Click the Install button in the GnoRPM toolbar.

5. Click the Add button in the Install dialog box that opens.

6. If you're not taken to the CD-ROM automatically, work your way to the /mnt/cdrom/ RedHat/RPMS directory in the Add Packages dialog box.

7. Scroll down to and click the xboing RPM, and then click the Add button at the bottom of the Add Packages dialog box.

8. Click the Close button at the bottom of the Add Packages dialog box to close it. The xboing package should now be listed and checked in the Install dialog box (see Figure 13.7).

9. Click the Query button. As Figure 13.8 shows, once installed, this package will appear under the group Amusements/Games. The startup command will be xboing. Documentation will be stored as /usr/X11R6/man/man1/xboing.1x (which, due to the /man in the path, would indicate a man page).

**Figure 13.7**
The xboing package added to the Install dialog box and selected for installation.

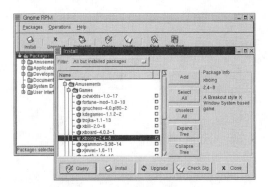

**Figure 13.8**
Results of querying the xboing package prior to installing it.

10. Click the Close button at the bottom of the Package Info dialog box.

11. Click the Install button at the bottom of the Install dialog box.

If xboing hasn't been installed yet, it will install now. If xboing has already been installed, you'll see the Installation Problems dialog box. There's really no need to reinstall it, so simply click the No button and "pretend" you've just now installed xboing. The remainder of this project will work the same way regardless. (Linux doesn't care *when* xboing was installed, just whether or not it is installed.) You can then close all remaining open windows.

From what we saw while querying the package, there appears to be a man page for xboing. To find out, enter the following command in a terminal window or at the command prompt:

man xboing

Sure enough, the man page shows up. The command for starting the game is simply xboing. Just entering that command at a command prompt should start up the game—although, I can't guarantee that it will start on every computer, because X programs can be tricky, even simple games. But the goal of this project wasn't really to teach you how to play xboing, per se; but rather, just to provide you with a little hands-on experience with installing a Red Hat package file.

# CHAPTER 14

# PRINTING FROM LINUX

**In this chapter**

# IDENTIFYING LINUX-COMPATIBLE PRINTERS

Every printer that is connected to a computer is driven by a file called a *driver*. The driver is essentially a program that allows the operating system and printer to communicate with one another. In the Linux world, modern printers are driven by *Ghostscript drivers*, so named because they emulate Adobe's PostScript printing language. Ghostscript also supports Adobe's Portable Document Format (PDF), which is commonly used on the Internet to format pages so that they can be viewed in multiple operating systems. More information about Adobe's products is available at their Web site at www.adobe.com.

Trying to determine whether a particular printer is compatible with Linux is a matter of understanding which Ghostscript drivers are available and which printers are supported by those drivers. Table 14.1 lists printers that are fully compatible and the GhostScript driver that each type of file will use. However, as discussed in a moment, a printer that *isn't* listed in Table 14.1 could very well be fully compatible with Linux.

## TABLE 14.1  SUPPORTED PRINTERS

| Printer Models | Ghostscript Driver |
| --- | --- |
| Apple ImageWriter LQ | iwlq |
| Apple ImageWriter, hi-res | iwhi |
| Apple ImageWriter, low-res | iwlo |
| C. Itoh M8510 | m8510 |
| Canon BJ103 | bj10e |
| Canon BJC-210, 240, 250, 70, 200 | bj200 |
| Canon BJC-610 | uniprint |
| Canon BJC-70, 210, 600, 610, 4000, 4100, 4200, 4300, 4550, C2500240 | bjc600 |
| Canon BJC-800, 7000 | bjc800 |
| Canon LBP-8II | lbp8 |
| Canon LIPS III | lips3 |
| DEC LA50 | la50 |
| DEC LA70 | la70 |
| DEC LA75 | la75 |
| DEC LA75 Plus | la75plus |
| DEC LJ250 | lj250 |
| DEC LN03 | ln03 |
| Epson AP3250 | ap3250 |
| Epson dot-matrix printers | epson |
| Epson LQ-2550 | epsonc |

**TABLE 14.1** CONTINUED

| Printer Models | Ghostscript Driver |
| --- | --- |
| Epson Stylus 800 | st800 |
| Epson Stylus Color, Color II, 500, 600, 800 | stcolor |
| Epson Stylus Color, II, 500, 600, 800, 1520 | uniprint |
| Epson-compatible 9-pin printers | eps9mid (lo res), eps9high (hi res) |
| Fujitsu 1200, 2400 | epsonc |
| HP 2563B | lp2563 |
| HP 500C, 510, 520, 540C, 693C | cdjmono (no color) |
| HP DesignJet 650C | dnj650c |
| HP DeskJet 400, 500C, 540C, 690C, 693C | cdj500, cdjcolor (24-bit color) |
| HP DeskJet 500 Portable | djet500 |
| HP DeskJet 500C | cdeskjet, djet500c |
| HP DeskJet 550C | uniprint |
| HP DeskJet 550C, 560C, 600, 660C, 682C, 683C, 693C, 694C, 850, 870C | cdj550 |
| HP DeskJet 600, 870Cse | ljet4 |
| HP DeskJet 600, LaserJet 4 | lj4dith |
| HP DeskJet 600m 1200C, 1600C | pjx1300 |
| HP DeskJet, DeskJet Plus | deskjet |
| HP LaserJet 4, 5, 5L, 6L | ljet4 |
| HP LaserJet IId, IIp, III | ljet2p |
| HP LaserJet III | ljet3 |
| HP LaserJet IIId | ljet3d |
| HP LaserJet Plus | ljetplus |
| HP PaintJet | paintjet |
| HP PaintJet XL | pj, pjxl |
| HP PaintJet XL300 | pjxl300 |
| IBM Jetprinter | jetp3852 |
| IBM Proprinter | ibmpro |
| Imagen Impress | imagen |
| Mitsubishi CP50 printer | cp50 |
| NEC P2X | uniprint |
| NEC P6, P6+, P60 | necp6 |
| NEC SuperScript 860 | ljetplus |

PART

**II**

CH

**14**

**TABLE 14.1  CONTINUED**

| Printer Models | Ghostscript Driver |
| --- | --- |
| OCE 9050 | oce9050 |
| Oki OL410ex | ljet4 |
| Ricoh 4081, 6000 laser | r4081 |
| Sony NWP533 | newp533 |
| StarJet 48 | sj48 |
| Tektronix 4693d | t4693d2, t4693d4, t4693d8 |
| Tektronix 4695, 4696 | t4696 |
| Xerox XES 2700, 3700, 4045 | xes |

> **Tip**
>
> The latest list of supported printers and other hardware is is available online at www.redhat.com/support/hardware.

If you don't see your specific printer in the table, don't panic. Many printers are compatible with multiple drivers. So often you can get everything you need from your printer by choosing a device driver that's similar to, if not exactly like, the driver your printer really needs. Check the manual that came with your printer to see which other printers it can emulate. For example, while perusing the manual for my Hewlett-Packard OfficeJet printer, I found the information shown in Table 14.2, which tells me there are quite a few drivers I can use to get that printer going.

**TABLE 14.2  HP OFFICEJET PRINTER DRIVERS AND PRINTER SUPPORT**

| Printer Driver Selection | Printer Support |
| --- | --- |
| HP DeskJet 520 printer | All printer features |
| HP DeskJet 510 printer | All printer features |
| HP DeskJet 550C printer | All printer features |
| HP DeskJet Portable printer | All printer features except envelope printing |
| HP DesktJet 500 printer | All printer features except fonts and envelopes |

So according to Table 14.2, I can use any GhostScript driver that supports the HP DeskJet 510, 520, or 550C printer to drive my HP OfficeJet. In a pinch, I could use the DeskJet Portable or DeskJet 500 drivers, with some limitations. If you don't have your printer manual handy, just guessing and experimenting will often do the trick. You'll want to try to match the printer manufacturer and model number as closely as possible.

---

**More Supported/Unsupported Printers**

Red Hat's Hardware Compatibility List at www.redhat.com/support/hardware/ also lists compatible printers. Grant Taylor maintains a current list of compatible and incompatible printers at http://www.picante.com/~gtaylor/pht. Of particular interest is the Printer Compatibility Database, which rates how various printers work under Linux. The ratings range from "Perfectly" to "Paperweight." If you discover that your existing printer gets the Paperweight rating, don't get your hopes up. If you're considering buying a printer, anything rated "Perfectly" will be the way to go.

Currently, the most problematic printers under Linux are the "Windows Only" printers from Hewlett-Packard, which are based on the their new PPA (Printing Performance Architecture) architecture. Fortunately, there is hope even for those printers. Tim Norman's PPA drivers for Linux will allow you to use the HP 710C, 712C, 720C, 722C, 820Cse, 820Cxi, 1000Cse, and 1000Cxi under Linux. See his site at http://www.httptech.com/ppa for details and instructions.

---

In some cases, you'll find that several different drivers will work with your printer. As a rule, you can simply pick any compatible driver. If you discover any limitations with the driver you selected, you can always go back and try a different compatible driver. You'll learn how to install a printer and select a driver a little later in this chapter.

# LINUX PRINTING CONCEPTS

As a system administrator, it's good to know what's going on "behind the scenes" when a file is being printed. It's usually not a simple matter of sending the document straight to the printer and waiting for the job to be finished. Thank goodness—or you wouldn't be able to use your computer while the printer was running! Instead, when you print a file, a copy of the file gets sent to a *print spooler*. The print spooler is basically a directory that contains one or more files waiting to be printed.

A program named lpd, and called the *printer daemon*, automatically looks at the print spooler directory from time to time to see if anything is waiting to be printed. If the daemon finds a file there, it ships it off to the printer. All of this happens as a separate process behind the scenes, so you never have to wait for a print job to finish in order to continue using your printer. Of course, you can also "pile up" documents to be printed without waiting for the current print job to complete first.

**Note**

A *print job*, as you may have guessed, is a single request to print one file or document. Thus, if you print three separate documents or files, each of those is one print job.

The printer daemon gets information about available printers from a configuration file named /etc/printcap (*printer cap*abilities). Like any configuration file, you can edit etc/printcap manually to define or change printers. But Red Hat Linux comes with a program named PrintTool that simplifies the task of managing the printcap file. You'll learn how to use PrintTool later in this chapter when you install a local printer.

## PRINTER DEVICES

In Linux, printers are treated as files, in much the same way that removable drives and other devices are treated as files. Like removable drives, printers have mount points in the filesystem that provide access to the printer. Printer mount points are all in the /dev (device) directory. By far and away, the vast majority of modern printers are *parallel printers* that attach to the parallel port(s) on the back of the computer. Table 14.3 lists the names of the parallel printer ports, from Linux's perspective. The table also includes the equivalent DOS name, I/O address, major device number, and minor device number, although things are not quite as complicated as the table makes them seem. Typically, you just plug one printer into the parallel port at the back of your computer and refer to it as /dev/lp0 from within Linux.

### TABLE 14.3 DEVICE NAMES FOR PARALLEL PRINTERS

| Linux Name | Represents | DOS name | I/O Address | Major # | Minor # |
|------------|-----------|----------|-------------|---------|---------|
| /dev/lp0 | First parallel printer | LPT1 | 0x3bc | 6 | 0 |
| /dev/lp1 | Second parallel printer | LPT2 | 0x378 | 6 | 1 |
| /dev/lp2 | Third parallel printer | LPT3 | 0x278 | 6 | 2 |

**Tip**

The abbreviation *lp* stands for *line printer*, and is a vestige from the early days of computers and printers that printed one line of text at a time (no graphics). Nowadays, we just call them *printers*, and they do much more than print lines of text. But the lp abbreviation lives on.

Linux also supports serial printers, which connect through the smaller COM ports on the back of the PC. But serial printers are rare these days—I can't even remember the last time I saw one—so I won't confuse things by getting into serial printers. If you have a serial printer that you need to connect to your Linux computer, you can get all the necessary instructions from the Printing HOWTO and other resources listed near the end of this chapter.

## FORMATS AND FILTERS

Printable documents come in a wide variety of formats, ranging from simple text to more complex formats that support graphics and fonts. The most common print formats in the Linux (and UNIX) world are as follows:

- **Text:** Files contain only text, no graphics or fonts.
- **PS (PostScript):** Can contain fonts, graphics, special formatting options.
- **DVI (TeX files):** Contains page layout instructions.
- **TR (troff files):** Contains special formatting tags. (Man pages are troff files.)

Red Hat Linux uses a relatively new feature called *magic filters* that automatically detects the file's print format and prints it accordingly. This means that when you're working in GNOME or KDE, printing a file is simply a matter of dragging its icon to a Print icon or button, and dropping it there. Details are presented a little later in this chapter.

# INSTALLING A LOCAL PRINTER

A local printer is any printer that's physically connected to the current computer via a cable. There are several ways to get a printer hooked up and working.

## CHECK YOUR /etc/conf.modules FILE FIRST

The first thing you want to do is check to see if Linux is currently set up to detect and install a parallel printer (assuming you're installing a parallel printer). To do that, you need to open the /etc/conf.modules file using gEdit or any other text editor of your choosing. Then look for the following line within that file:

```
alias parport_lowlevel parport_pc
```

If you don't see that line, type it in exactly as shown (all lowercase with underscore characters as shown). Doing so allows low-level parallel ports for printers to be detected at startup, which in turn simplifies the whole printer installation procedure. If, indeed, you did need to add that line to /etc/conf.modules, be sure to save and close the file. You might as well shut down the computer after making that change, so you can connect your printer, as discussed next.

## CONNECTING THE PRINTER

If the printer isn't already connected to the computer, you'd do well to shut down Linux. Then plug the printer into the parallel 1 port (or LPT1 port) of your computer. Turn on the printer, get some paper in, and so forth, so that it's ready to print. Then turn your computer back on and log in as root. You need to be logged in as root to add a new printer to the system. Once installed, however, any user can have access to the printer. Once you're booted up, start your favorite GUI, be it GNOME or KDE.

## STARTING PrintTool

The easiest way to install and configure a new printer is through the PrintTool utility, which is automatically installed when you install Red Hat Linux. To start the utility in GNOME, open up a terminal window and enter the command printtool &. In KDE, you can press Alt+F2 and enter the command printool &. You may see a couple of error messages telling you that Samba isn't installed and that you won't be able to print to NetWare printers. But these messages are irrelevant to the task at hand (installing a local printer), so you can just click the Ignore buttons to close them. The Red Hat Linux Print System Manager dialog box opens up (see Figure 14.1).

PART

**II**

CH

**14**

**Figure 14.1**
The PrintTool utility is titled Red Hat Linux Print System Manager when it opens on your screen.

To install a local printer, follow these steps:

1. Click the Add button. A dialog box titled Add a Printer Entry appears.

2. Choose Local Printer from the options presented, and then click the OK button.

3. A new dialog box appears telling you which parallel ports (if any) were detected. Typically, at least /dev/lp0 will be detected, and hopefully that's the port you've plugged your printer into. Click the OK button.

4. A new dialog box titled Edit Local Printer Entry appears. As the title implies, you can use this dialog box to define or change a printer. Fill in the blanks as summarized here:

   - **Names:** A printer can have multiple names (but no spaces or punctuation). One printer, which will act as the default printer for the current computer, should be named lp. To give the current printer both a descriptive name and the lp name, type the descriptive name first, followed by a pipe character (¦) and then the lp name. In my HP OfficeJet example, I named the printer officejet¦lp.

   - **Spool Directory:** The default entry of /var/spool/lpd/lp is perfect for installing a local printer. No need to change this.

   - **File Limit in KB (0=no limit):** Some older printers on large networks get hung up if sent files that are extremely large. In this situation that's a very unlikely problem, so you can leave this setting at 0 to specify "no limit."

   - **Printer Device:** This is where the printer device appears in the filesystem. For a printer connected to the first parallel printer port (for example, LPT1), this should be set to /dev/lp0.

   - **Input Filter:** Click the Select button next to this option to see the list of supported printers, as in Figure 14.2. In the left column, choose the Printer Type that best matches your printer, or a printer that yours can emulate. For example, I could choose HP DeskJet 550C/560C/6xx Series for my HP OfficeJet based on the information presented in Table 14.2. You may want to test the printer before selecting other options.

   - **Suppress Headers:** Headers are pages that are printed before the actual print job to indicate the source of the print job. These are generally used in large network environments to help people sort out different print jobs. You can keep this option in its "selected" state to suppress headers for local printing.

Figure 14.3 shows how my Edit Local Printer Entry dialog box looks after making selections that are appropriate for that printer. You can click the OK button in the Edit Local Printer Entry dialog box to close it. You should now see your printer listed in the Print System Manager dialog box.

**Figure 14.2**

The Configure Filter dialog box lets you choose a Printer Type (driver) to control your printer.

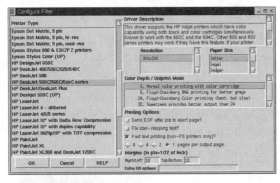

**Figure 14.3**

The Edit Local Printer Entry dialog box after defining the HP OfficeJet printer that's connected to Parallel Port 1 (LPT1) of the current computer.

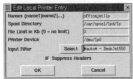

**Tip**

You can also launch PrintTool from the Control Panel. In GNOME, click the Main Menu button and choose System, Control Panel. In the panel that appears, click the Printer Configuration button.

## TESTING THE LOCAL PRINTER

Now comes the acid test. Make sure your printer is turned on, online, has paper, and is ready to accept output from the computer. Then, in the Print System Manager dialog box, click the name of the printer you want to test (there will probably be only one printer in the list) so that its line is selected (appears to be slightly raised). To test the printer, follow these steps:

1. Choose Tests, Print ASCII Test Page from the Print System Manager menu bar.

2. Click the OK button to close the Info dialog box. Don't worry if the page is not ejected from the printer.

3. Choose Tests, Print Postscript Test Page from the Print System Manager menu bar.

4. Click the OK button to close the Info dialog box.

PART

**II**

CH

**14**

5. Choose Tests, Print ASCII Directly to Port from the Print System Manager menu bar.

6. Click the OK button to close the Info dialog box.

If the first page you printed didn't eject automatically when printing was finished, and/or that page showed only one short line of text, see the section "Poor ASCII Test Page Results" later in this chapter.

If the PostScript test produced bad results, see the section "Poor PostScript Page Results" later in this chapter.

If the last test failed, then chances are that all three tests failed. This is indicative of a hardware problem rather than a software problem. See the "Printer Hardware Problems" section later in this chapter. On the other hand, if the first two tests failed and the third test passed, that's indicative of a software problem having to do with the spooling system. Your best bet is to read through the rest of this chapter to try some other things, and see what kinds of error messages you get. Then look through the "Troubleshooting Printer Problems" section near the end of this chapter for help with specific problems.

# HOW TO PRINT

Just about any program that you use to create documents will have a menu option for printing those documents. Many programs have a Print option right on the toolbar and on the File pull-down menu. For specific information, however, you may have to dig through the program's help. Once you've opted to print, you may be faced with a dialog box before printing. For example, Figure 14.4 shows the dialog box that appears when you print a gEdit document. Figure 14.5 shows the Print dialog box for printing Web pages from Netscape Navigator.

**Figure 14.4**
The Print dialog box for gEdit asks for a print command. Just click OK to print to the default printer.

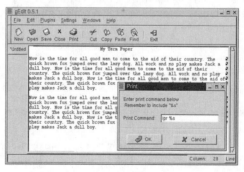

If you set up gEdit as your default GNOME editor, printing a file is as easy as opening it:

1. In the File Manager, right-click the icon for any file you want to view or print.

2. Choose Edit.

3. When the file appears in gEdit, click the Print button in the toolbar.

4. Click OK to accept the default command: lpr %s.

**Figure 14.5**
Netscape Navigator offers many options for printing. If you simply click the Print button, the page will be printed to the default printer.

**Tip**

If you need help setting up gEdit as your default editor in GNOME, see "Choosing a Default Editor" in Chapter 9.

The same basic principal applies to text files you view from the KDE File Manager:

1. Right-click the icon for the file you want to view or print and choose Text Editor to open the file in kedit.

2. Click the Print button the kedit toolbar.

3. Click the OK button in the dialog box that appears.

## ADDING A PRINTER APPLET TO GNOME

You can add a Printer applet to your GNOME panel to make printing files as easy as dragging and dropping. To add the applet, click the GNOME Main Menu button and choose Panel, Add Applet, Utility, Printer Applet. A new icon titled Print appears in the panel (see Figure 14.6). You can drag any printable file from the File Manager to that applet to print it. For example, in that same figure, the File Manager is currently showing files in /usr/man/man1, home of the man pages for user commands. To print one of those man pages, simply drag an icon onto the Print applet, and drop it there.

**Tip**

When you enter a command such as man lpr to view a man page, you'll see a number such as LPR(1) in parentheses at the top of the page. That number tells you which subdirectory the page resides in. Thus, the man page for the lpr command can be found in the /usr/man/man1 directory.

PART

**II**

CH

**14**

**Figure 14.6**
The Printer applet added to the GNOME panel, next to the Main Menu button.

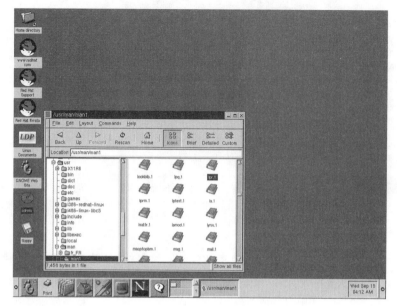

## KDE PRINTING

If you use the KDE desktop manager, you'll see an icon titled Printer on your desktop. You can drag any file icon from the KDE File Manager onto the icon to print it. For example, to print a man page, navigate to /usr/man/man1 in the KDE file manager, drag any icon from the right column onto the Printer icon on the desktop, and drop it there.

> **Tip**
>
> Double-clicking the Printer icon on the KDE desktop displays the print queue. If KDE is installed, but GNOME is your current interface, you can click the GNOME Main Menu button and choose KDE Menus, Utilities, Printer Queue to get to the same display.

## PRINTING FROM THE COMMAND PROMPT

At the command prompt, you can use the lpr command followed by the name of any text file to print to the default printer. LPR is sometimes called the *user spooling command* because it allows any user (not just root) to send a file to the print spooler for printing. The following is the syntax for the lpr command:

```
lpr [options] [filename...]
```

filename is one or more files to be printed, including the path if not in the current working directory. When printing a plain text file, you can omit the options, although the printed output is very plain. For example, the following command prints the file named README in the directory /usr/doc./printtool-3.40 (assuming such a file exists):

```
lpr /usr/doc/printtool-3.40/README
```

The following are major options for the `lpr` command:

■ **`-Pprintername`:** To print to a specific printer rather than the default print, specify the printer name after the `-P` as in `lpr -Pepsoncolor somefile.txt`. The epsoncolor printer must be accessible somewhere in the network from the current computer (see Chapter 24, "Sharing Linux/Windows Resources with Samba").

> **Tip**
>
> Entering the command `lpc status` lists names of printers that are available from the current computer. The information comes from the `/etc/printcap` configuration file.

■ **`-#numberofcopies`:** Determines the number of copies to print. For example, `lpr -#2 somefile.txt` prints two copies of the specified file.

■ **`-d`:** Print using DVI (TeX) instructions embedded in the file.

■ **`-t`:** Print using troff formatting instructions. (Use `-t` when printing man pages.)

■ **`-p`:** Break long lines of text to fit onto the page.

Using the `lpr`command can be awkward, especially if you're not sure of the format of the file you're trying to print. Dragging files to Print/Printer icons in GNOME/KDE is far simpler because each file type is detected automatically, and print content is translated (that is, "filtered") so that it comes out looking right on the printed page.

## PRINTING COMMAND OUTPUT

You can also send the output from most commands to the printer by using the redirection character (>) followed by a space and the `lpr` abbreviation for the default printer. For example, let's say you've mounted Red Hat Linux CD-ROM #1 and want to print out the filenames of all the HOWTOs in its `/doc/HOWTO` directory. Just tacking `> lpr` onto the end of the `ls` command would do the trick, as in the following:

```
ls /mnt/cdrom/doc/HOWTO > lpr
```

# MANAGING PRINTERS AND PRINT JOBS

Linux offers several programs for managing printers, print jobs, queues, and the like. All users can manage the print jobs they own using these programs. By default, the person who started a print job owns that print job. The superuser can control all print jobs. Furthermore, the superuser can control all printers, spoolers, and printing daemons.

## VIEWING THE PRINT QUEUE WITH `lpq`

The `lpq` command lets any user view the print queue of any printer. Each print job is automatically assigned a job number and is ranked according to when it will be printed in

PART

**II**

CH

**14**

relation to other documents in the queue. For example, entering the command `lpq` might return something like this:

```
lp is ready and printing
Rank      Owner    Job    Files           Total Size
active    lana     12     whatever.txt    10034 bytes
1st       root     13     something       32343 bytes
2nd       lana     11     BashPrompt-HOWTO  61127 bytes
```

The job ranked `active` is the one currently being printed. Remaining jobs will be printed in the order shown in the left column. The job number is arbitrary and not indicative of when the job will be printed.

> **Tip**
>
> Double-clicking the Printer icon on the KDE desktop offers a nice graphical interface to the print queue.

To query a print queue other than the default printer for the current computer, use the `-P` switch followed by the name of the printer. For example, the following command displays the print queue for the printer named epsoncolor:

```
lpq -Pepsoncolor
```

## CANCELING A PRINT JOB WITH `lprm`

To cancel a print job, the owner of the job (or superuser) can enter an `lprm` (lp remove) command followed by a blank space and the job number. For example, either the superuser or the user named Lana can cancel the print job ranked second in the previous example by entering the following command:

```
lprm 11
```

To cancel all print jobs that you own, use a hyphen rather than a specific job number in the `lprm` command. If the job is being handled by a printer other than the default printer for the current computer, use the `-P` option to specify the printer name, as in the example below:

```
lprm -Pepsoncolor 11
```

## MANAGING PRINTERS WITH `lpc`

The `lpc` (printer control) command lets the superuser manage printers and print queues. The simplest form of the command is as follows:

```
lpc status
```

This displays the names and status of all printers that are accessible from the current computer. For example, the command might return the following:

```
officejet:
    queuing is enabled
    printing is enabled
no entries
no daemon present
```

This indicates that a printer named officejet is accessible from this computer. Queuing and printing are enabled, though at the moment there are no entries in the queue and nothing is being printed (no daemon present). The latter is not an indication of a problem, since the daemon is only present when the printer is actually printing.

The superuser can use the lpc command to control printers and queues. Entering the command lpc alone enters the lpc program and replaces the bash command prompt with an lpc> prompt. At that prompt you can enter the follow commands and arguments to control printers. Note that the word *printername* must be the name of a printer that's accessible from the current machine:

- **abort [all¦*printername*]:** Terminate the active spooling daemon and disable printing.
- **clean [all¦*printername*]:** Remove *cruft files* (temporary, control, and data files that cannot be printed) from the queue.
- **disable [all¦*printername*]:** Turn off the printer queue to disallow any new print jobs.
- **down [all¦*printername*] *message*:** Turn off the specified printer's queue, disable printing, and broadcast *message* to users.
- **enable [all¦*printername*]:** Enable print spooling (opposite of disable).
- **exit:** Leave lpc and return to the bash command prompt.
- **help [*command*] or ? [*command*]:** Show help for specified command (for example, help clean).
- **quit:** Same as exit; leave lpc and return to the bash command prompt.
- **restart [all¦*printername*]:** Re-enable the printer daemon.
- **start [all¦*printername*]:** Enable printing and start a spooling daemon.
- **stop [all¦*printername*]:** Stop spooling after current job completes, then disable printing.
- **up [all¦*printername*]:** Reinstate queuing and printing, the opposite of down.

# More Printing Documentation

The topics here should get you going on printing. Once you've installed a printer, printing documents is as easy as choosing File, Print from a program's menu bar or dragging a document file onto a Print or Printer icon. Should you need to get into greater technical detail on any of the subjects discussed in this chapter, you have a wide selection of man pages, HOWTOs, and FAQs to choose from:

- **man gs:** Previewing and printing with Ghostscript.
- **man lpc:** Using the lpc program to control print jobs.
- **man lpd:** How to manage the lpd printer daemon.
- **man lpq:** How to examine print spools.
- **man lpr:** How to use the lpr command for printing.
- **man lprm:** Removing jobs from the print queue.
- **man printcap:** How to manually configure a printer in /etc/printcap.
- **Printing HOWTO:** How to set up printers in Linux.
- **Printing Usage HOWTO:** How to print and manage print jobs.

# TROUBLESHOOTING PRINTER PROBLEMS

This chapter has focused on installing and using a local printer (one that's attached directly to your computer). Network printing will be discussed in Chapter 24. Before you can print through the network, the printer will have to be working on its local computer, for sure! The sections that follow describe the solutions to common (and some not so common) problems in using a local printer.

## POOR ASCII TEST PAGE RESULTS

If you're reading this, I suppose your Print ASCII Test Page didn't turn out too well. Try the following:

1. Make sure the printer that caused the problem is still selected in the list of available printers in the Print System Manager dialog box.
2. Click the Edit button at the bottom of that dialog box.
3. Click the Select button next to Input Filters:
    - If the page did not eject from the printer after printing was completed, select the Send EOF After Job to Eject Page option.
    - If you only got one short line of text on your printed page, choose Fix Stair-Stepping Text.
4. Click the OK button at the bottom of the Configure Filter dialog box to close it, then click OK to close the Edit Printer Entry dialog box.
5. Choose Test, Print ASCII test page from the Print System Manager window's menu bar to retest the page.

## POOR POSTSCRIPT TEST RESULTS

Linux works on a concept of *magic filters*, where any specially formatted text is automatically sent through a Ghostscript driver that converts the file's contents to a format that's appropriate for your printer. If the PrintTool PostScript Test Results gives you poor results, your best bet will be to try a different filter (that is, Printer Type). As mentioned earlier, if your exact computer is not included in the list of Printer Types, try checking its manual for other supported printer drivers or printers that yours can emulate. If you can't find the manual, perhaps you can get the information from the printer manufacturer's Web site or (heaven forbid) technical support.

In PrintTool, click the name of the printer that needs to be fixed, then click the Edit button to get back to the Edit Local Printer Entry dialog box. Click the Select button next to Input Filter, and try a different printer from the list of available Printer Types. Click OK to save your changes and close both open dialog boxes. Then choose Tests, Print PostScript Page again.

## PRINTER HARDWARE PROBLEMS

If you can't get the printer to work at all, the problem is most likely something to do with the hardware. The problem is almost certainly hardware if your printer failed the Print ASCII Directly to Port test in PrintTool, as that test bypasses all the spooling software. The best thing to do would be to follow these steps:

1.  Shut down the computer.
2.  Turn off the printer.
3.  Carefully check both ends of the cable to ensure they're both fully plugged in.
4.  If you have multiple parallel ports on the back of your computer, make sure the printer is plugged into the correct port. Remember that /dev/lp0 usually corresponds to printer port 1 (or LPT1).
5.  Make sure the paper and ink cartridge (if any) are properly installed.
6.  Turn the printer back on. If the printer has a Test button, try it.
7.  If there is on Online/Offline button on the printer, make sure the printer is online.
8.  Restart the computer and log in as root.
9.  Try running the PrintTool Print ASCII Directly to Port test again.

## ONLY PART OF JOB IS PRINTED

If large jobs are partially printed, then poop out, the mx# (maximum file size) setting in the /etc/printcap file is too small. You can edit that file using any text editor. If you set its value to zero, as in the following example, you remove the maximum size altogether, which should definitely solve the problem:

```
mx#0
```

As an alternative to editing /etc/printcap directly, you can edit the printer's entry in PrintTool, and set the File Limit in KB option to zero (0).

## PRINT JOB IS ACCEPTED, BUT NOTHING PRINTS

Few things are as irritating as successfully submitting a job to be printed, without anything coming out of the printer. In some cases, this could be a hardware problem. You need to make sure the printer is turned on, online (if it has an Online/Offline switch), and so forth, as discussed previously under Printer Hardware Problems.

Check the printer queue by running the lpq program. If the job is in the queue but won't print, it's possible that the printer is disabled. Use the lpc program discussed earlier in this chapter to make sure the printer is enabled and ready to accept jobs. Enter the command lpc up or lpc restart to get the printer and queue running again.

The problem could also be that the print daemon isn't running. Go into PrintTool and choose lpd, Restart lpd to make sure the daemon is running.

> **Tip**
>
> The print daemon normally starts automatically at bootup due to the line daemon.lpd in the /etc/rc.d/init.d/lpd file.

Finally, if the printer still refuses to print, go back to the section titled "Check Your /etc/conf.modules File First" earlier in this chapter, and make sure the /etc/conf.modules file contains the alias parport_lowlevel parport_pc line. If it doesn't, be sure to add that line, save and close the file, then reboot the computer. Run PrintTool again to make sure the /dev/lp0 port (or whatever port your printer is connected to) is detected by PrintTool. Then install the printer and try again.

## JOB QUEUED BUT CANNOT START DAEMON

This error message means that the print job is in the queue, but the daemon isn't there to respond. Choose lpd, Restart lpd from the PrintTool menu bar to restart the daemon.

## PRINTER QUEUE IS DISABLED

As the message states, the print queue is disabled. As the superuser, enter the command lpc enable to enable the printer queue.

CHAPTER **15**

# USING YOUR SOUND CARD

## In this chapter

# GETTING INFORMATION ABOUT YOUR SOUND CARD

If your PC contains a sound card and has speakers attached, you can configure Linux to play sound. This includes special sound effects, as well as the ability to play audio CDs in your CD-ROM drive. Linux has the ability to detect and automatically configure many different types of sound cards. However, there's always the outside chance that you'll need to configure the card manually. In case you need to do the latter, you'll need to know your sound card's make and model, I/O Port, IRQ, and DMA addresses.

If you printed out a System Summary Report before you repartitioned your hard drive or before you replaced Windows with Linux, you can look under IRQ Summary to find the IRQ that your sound card uses. Typically you'll find your sound card make and model number next to IRQ 10 (or perhaps IRQ 5—it can be any IRQ). Under IO Port Summary, you'll find your sound card listed next to one of the I/O Port Ranges. 0220h is a common starting range, but again it can be any range. DMA channels are listed under DMA Usage Summary in that report. You should find two numbers, such as 03 and 06, pointing to your sound card.

If you don't have the printout, but Windows is still installed on your computer, you can boot to Windows and follow these steps to get information about your sound card:

1. Click the Start button and choose Settings, Control Panel.
2. Double-click the System icon.
3. Click the Device Manager tab.
4. Expand the Sound, video, and game controllers category.
5. Click the make and model of your sound card, and then click the Properties button.
6. Click the Resources tab to get to the settings shown in Figure 15.1. Get ready to jot down some info on a piece of scratch paper.

**Figure 15.1**
If Windows is still installed on your system, you can use its Device Manager to check your sound card's current properties.

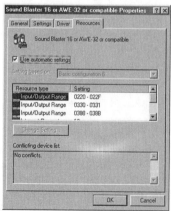

7. The make and model of your sound card are centered near the top of the dialog box, "Sound Blaster 16 or AWE-32 or Compatible" in the example. Jot that down as your Card Type.

8. The starting address of your sound card will be the first number listed as Input/Output Range (0220 in the example). Jot that down as your I/O Port.

9. If you scroll down a little in the Resource Type listing, you'll find the sound card's IRQ listed next to Interrupt Request (10 is a typical, though by no means mandatory, setting). Jot that number down as your IRQ.

10. Scroll down a little more and jot down the numbers next to Direct Memory Access as DMA 1 (for the first one) and DMA 2 (for the second one).

11. Click the Cancel button.

12. You might as well print out a System Resource Summary now; it may come in handy later in this chapter. Click the Print Button, choose System Summary, then click OK.

13. Click Cancel to close the System Properties dialog box.

As an example for future reference, here's what I was able to determine about my own sound card while going through the preceding steps. Remember, your settings will likely be completely different, so don't try to copy mine when configuring your own sound card (tempting as it may be):

```
Card Type: Sound Blaster 16 or AWE-32 or Compatible
Input/Output Range: 0220
IRQ: 10
DMA1: 03
DMA2: 06
```

When you're ready to get back to Linux, click the Windows Start button and choose Shut Down, Restart, OK to reboot. Boot into Linux as root because you'll need superuser status to configure the sound card.

It would also help to have a copy of the manual that came with your sound card. Among other things, the manual will be able to tell you what drivers are compatible with your card. It may describe them as sound cards that your card can emulate, rather than as drivers per se. Knowing that will make it easier to pick a driver in Linux, in case you can't find your sound card's exact make and model while making selections within Linux.

Finally, you should be aware of the sound cards that Linux supports. I've provided a quick list here. If you ever want to look at a more recent list, check out Red Hat's Hardware Compatibility List at www.redhat.com/support/hardware:

- Acer Notebook Sound
- AdLib
- Advance Logic ALS-007
- Compaq Deskpro XL sound
- Crystal CS423x sound chip
- Ensoniq Audio PCI 1370 (SoundBlaster 64/128 PCI)
- Creative/Ensoniq Audio PCI 1371
- Ensoniq SoundScape

- ESS688 AudioDrive
- ESS1688 AudioDrive
- ESS1868 AudioDrive
- Gravis UltraSound
- Gravis UltraSound MAX
- Gravis UltraSound PnP
- Logitech SoundMan Games (not SM16 or SM Wave)
- MediaTrix AudioTrix Pro (MT-0002-PC Control Chip)
- MediaVision Jazz16 (ProSonic, SoundMan Wave)
- Mozart/MAD16 (OPTi 82C928)
- MAD16 Pro (OPTi 82C929/82C930)
- miroSOUND PCM12
- OPL3-SA1 sound chip
- OPL3-SA2/3/x sound chip
- Pro Audio Spectrum/Studio 16, Logitech SoundMan 16
- PSS (Orchid SW32, Cardinal DSP16)
- S3 SonicVibes
- Sound Blaster
- Sound Blaster DS
- Sound Blaster Pro
- Sound Blaster 16/PNP
- Sound Blaster 32/64 AWE
- The Sound Blaster Wave FX PNP card*
- Turtle Beach MultiSound Classic/Monterey/Tahiti
- Turtle Beach MultiSound Pinnacle/Fiji
- Windows Sound System (AD1848/CS4248/CS4231)

*The Sound Blaster Wave FX PNP card works only in 8-bit mode, not in 16-bit mode.

# CONFIGURING YOUR SOUND CARD

Before you get started here, make sure your speakers are ready. They need to be plugged into the sound card. And, if they have their own power, they should be plugged in or have batteries inserted. If the speakers have their own on/off switch, make sure they're turned on. If they have their own volume switch, make sure the volume is turned up a little, but not so high as to startle the daylights out of you when you get them working! The sound configuration program has a character cell interface, so it will be easiest to read if you work from the command prompt rather than a GUI. If you're in an X GUI, you can press Ctrl+Alt+F2 to get to a new terminal window. Be sure to log in as root. Then, follow these steps:

1. Enter the command sndconfig at the Linux command prompt.

2. Press Enter to choose OK when presented with the opening screen.

3. If you get a message saying that no PnP or PCI cards were found, press Enter to choose OK. Otherwise skip to step 8 now.

4. In the Card Type list that appears, use the ~UA and ~DA keys to move the highlighter to whichever name best matches your sound card (I chose Sound Blaster AWE-32/64 for mine). Then press Tab and Enter to choose OK.

5. Specify your sound cards I/O Port, IRQ, DMA 1, and DMA 2 by pressing Tab to move from one column to the next, and using the ~UA and ~DA keys to highlight a selection within each row. Figure 15.2 shows the settings I chose to configure my own sound card.

**Figure 15.2**
Choosing sound card settings in sndconfig, using my own sound card as an example.

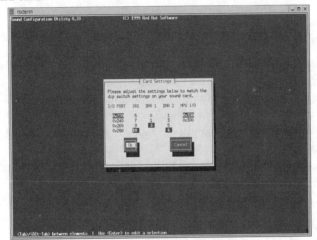

6. The MPU I/O setting has to do with MIDI music. In your printed Resource Summary under IO PORT SUMMARY, look up the addresses starting with either 0330h or 0300h. Whichever one points to your sound card, choose that as your MPU I/O.

7. Press Tab and then press Enter to choose OK.

8. You'll see a message telling you that sndconfig is going to make a backup copy of your existing configuration file as /etc/conf.modules.bak. Press Enter to choose OK.

9. Now you can just follow the instructions on the screen.

You'll be given two test sounds. The first is Linus Torvalds saying, "Hello, this is Linus Torvalds and I pronounce Linux, as Linux." If you hear the sound, choose Yes. Otherwise, choose No, and you'll be taken back to step 3 to choose different settings. Make sure your speakers are turned up loud enough to hear the sound (if they have their own volume control) before you actually change any of the settings you made on the first pass through.

If your sound card has MIDI capabilities, you'll be given an opportunity to test a MIDI sound. When it plays, you should hear a piano riff. If you hear the sound, choose Yes, and you're done. If you don't hear the sound, you'll be taken back to step 3 shown earlier. This time, when going through the settings screens, try using the other MPU I/O setting.

**Note**

If you cannot get MIDI to play, your card may not have MIDI capabilities. Or, you may need to adjust the dip switches on the card to use 0x300 or 0x330 as your MPU I/O Port. Only your sound card manual can help you accomplish that goal!

When you've finished configuring your sound card, you'll be taken back to the bash command prompt. Before you go any further, I suggest you reboot your system to get a fresh reading of all your configuration files. Enter the command reboot or shutdown -r now to reboot your computer.

# USING YOUR MIXER

Your sound card can play many different types of sounds, from a variety of sources. Initially, each different type of sound, except the microphone, is given roughly equal volume by the sound card. The microphone is intentionally turned down low so that random sounds that the microphone picks up are not amplified through your speakers. Should you ever want to adjust the relative volume of one type of sound over another, you can use the GMX audio mixer to do the job. In GNOME, just click the Main Menu button and choose Multimedia, Audio Mixer. You'll come to the window shown in Figure 15.3.

**Figure 15.3**
The GMX Audio Mixer allows you to adjust the relative volume of different sound sources.

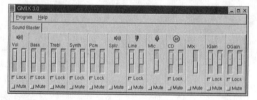

You can adjust the relative volume of any sound source by dragging its sliders up and down. The Lock button, when pressed in, keeps the left and right speakers at equal levels. If you turn off the lock, you can adjust the volume of the left and right speakers independently. The Mute button, if selected, keeps all sound from that source from reaching the speakers. You can leave the mixer open while playing a variety of sounds so that you can hear the effects of your changes. When you've finished with the mixer, choose Program, Exit from its menu bar.

**Tip**

Remember, if your speakers have their own volume control button, they can limit how loud the sound can go if turned down low.

# PLAYING AUDIO CDs

You can play audio CDs (the kind you usually play in a stereo) in your CD-ROM drive. First, follow these steps to start up the CD Player:

1. If there's currently a mounted CD in your CD-ROM drive, unmount it, then remove it from the drive. Close the CD-ROM drive tray.

> **Tip**
>
> If you're using GNOME, and it's set up to auto-play audio CDs, the CD should just start playing in a minute or so. See the section titled "CD Properties Capplet" in Chapter 9 for more information.

2. In GNOME, click the Main Menu button.
3. Choose Multimedia, CD Player. The CD Player opens (see Figure 15.4).

> **Tip**
>
> In KDE click the K button and choose Multimedia, CD Player. That player looks a little different than GNOME's but offers many of the same features.

**Figure 15.4**
The GNOME CD Player can play audio CDs that you normally listen to on a stereo.

4. Click the Eject button in the CD Player that appears. The CD-ROM drive should open.
5. Insert an audio CD and close the CD-ROM drive.
6. Give the CD Player a few seconds to scan the disk, and then click the Play button.

You should be able to hear the music coming through the speakers. You can adjust the volume by dragging the slider along the bottom of the player. The rest of the buttons work the way they do on a real CD player. Point to each button to see its tooltip. The down-pointing button lets you skip to a specific track (song) on the CD.

You can keep track of CD titles, artists, and songs using the Track Editor (see Figure 15.5). To open that editor, just click the Open Track Editor button in the CD Player. When you open the Track Editor, you're given a dialog box where you can fill in information about the CD. If you have Internet access, you may be able to download all the information without typing it in by visiting the CDDB database. That database is an enormous collection of information about countless music CDs. And if the CD you're playing at the moment is in that database, CDDB will fill in the blanks for you. To try it, click the CDDB Status button at the bottom of the Track Editor dialog box.

**Figure 15.5**
The Track Editor lets you build a library of audio CDs, including artist, title, and tracks (songs) on each CD.

The Preferences button lets you change the appearance and behavior of the CD Player. You can choose a default behavior that occurs when CD Player opens and when it closes. You can also change the font and color of text in the window. The Show Handles option adds a dragging handle to the left of the player window that you can use to drag the window out of the player. If you select this option, you'll need to close, then reopen the CD Player to see the handle.

## PLAYING WITH SOUND EFFECTS

Both GNOME and KDE let you assign sound effects to various events. To get to GNOME's sound effects, open the GNOME Control Center using the "toolbox" button in the panel, or Main Menu, Settings, GNOME Control Center. Under the Multimedia category, click Sound. On the General tab (shown in Figure 15.6), make sure that the GNOME Sound Support and Sounds for Events options are both selected. If they weren't selected originally, you'll need to close the dialog box, log out of GNOME, and then restart GNOME to activate the option.

**Figure 15.6**
The Multimedia, Sound category in GNOME Control Center lets you enable sounds and sound events in GNOME.

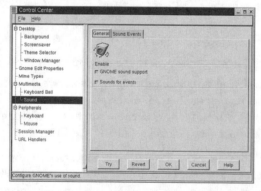

The Sound Events (shown in Figure 15.7) tab lets you assign sounds to various events that happen while you're using GNOME. The first pair of options lets you assign a sound effect to the opening and closing of the panel. The next two are specifically for the Gnibbles and GnobotsII games available under Games on the GNOME main menu. Down near the bottom of the list you'll find more general events to which you can assign sounds.

**Figure 15.7**
Use the Sound Events tab to assign sounds to events that occur while you're using GNOME.

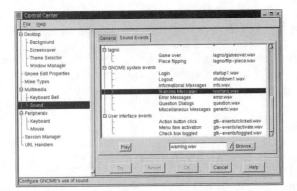

To hear or change the sound assigned to an event, click the event to highlight the entire line. Click the Play button to hear the sound that's currently assigned to the event. Use the Browse button to choose a different sound for the event. To remove a sound from an event, select the event, then delete the sound filename from the box next to the Browse button. When you're finished, click the OK button to save your changes. Then you can close the Control Center by clicking its Close (X) button.

## KDE SOUND EFFECTS

The K Desktop Environment also allows you to assign sound effects to events. Click the KDE Control Center button in KDE's panel, or click the K button and choose Settings, Sound, System Sounds. Select the Enable System Sounds option, as shown in Figure 15.8. Then select an event from the left column and a sound to associate with that event from the right column. To hear the currently selected sound, click the Test button. To associate the event and sound, click the Apply button.

**Figure 15.8**
KDE's System Sounds dialog box lets you assign sound effects to KDE events.

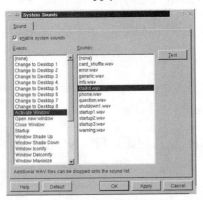

You can add new sounds (.wav files) to the list of sounds by dragging them from the K File Manager into the right pane of the System Sounds dialog box. By default, that pane lists sounds that are in the /usr/share/sounds directory. So any sounds you copy or download to that directory will also be listed in that right column.

**Tip**

KDE looks for a file named /etc/sysconfig/sound for sound card information. But the sndconfig file stores its information in /etc/sysconfig/soundcard. If you have trouble getting sound to work in KDE, create a symbolic link from the sound file to the soundcard file by entering the command

ln -s /etc/sysconfig/soundcard /etc/sysconfig.sound.

## CONFIGURATION FILES AND MORE INFO

You shouldn't ever have to manually edit configuration files to get your sound card working: the sndconfig program takes care of that for you. But just so you know, if your sound card is Plug and Play, information about the card is stored in the /etc/isapnp.conf configuration file. Information about modules that need to be loaded in order for your sound card to work is stored in the /etc/conf.modules configuration file. You can also find out more information from the following sources:

- Sound HOWTO
- Sound Playing HOWTO
- Soundblaster AWE mini-HOWTO
- Sound & MIDI Software for Linux at http://sound.condorow.net
- Jeff Tranter's *Linux Multimedia Guide*, published by O'Reilly and Associates (ISBN 1-56592-219-0)
- SoX Sound eXchange at http://www.spies.com/Sox
- Open Sound System's Web site at http://www.opensound.com

For some interesting tidbits on adding audio to email messages, see the following man pages:

- man audiocompose
- man audiosend
- man showaudio

## PROJECT: BUILDING YOUR COLLECTION OF WAVE FILES

You can add your own sound events by adding .wav files to your /usr/share/sounds directory. The World Wide Web is home to thousands of wave files that you can download for free. If your Internet connection is working, use Netscape Navigator to go to any search engine (for example, www.altavista.com). Search for "free wave files" or "free .wav files." You'll no doubt find lots of links to sites offering such files. Most sites will let you test the sound. When you click the sound file link, Navigator will display the Save As dialog box. (If not, you can right-click the link and choose Save Link As). When the Save As dialog box appears, be sure to specify /usr/share/sounds as the directory for storing your downloaded .wav file before clicking the OK button.

Next time you assign sound events in GNOME or KDE, you should see those new sound files available for selection. For example, in Figure 15.9, you can see some new "boing," "bonk," and other sound files that I downloaded from various Web sites on the Internet and saved in my /usr/share/sounds directory.

**Figure 15.9**
New "boing,"
"bonk," and other
sound files I
downloaded from
the Web and
saved in my
/usr/share/
sounds directory.

# CHAPTER 16

# ARCHIVING, BACKING UP, AND RESTORING

## In this chapter

# UNDERSTANDING ARCHIVES

An *archive* is a file that contains one or more files. Archives are generally created to simplify backing up a large number of files onto some external medium such as floppy disks, Iomega or JAZ disks, tape backups, and so forth. Closely related to the concept of an archive is *compression*, where the file is put through an algorithm that reduces excess space and makes a smaller copy of the file. The advantages of compression are that the compressed file takes up less disk space (such as on a backup medium), and the compressed file can be transferred more quickly over network lines.

A *compressed archive*, as the name implies, is an archive of files that has been compressed or a collection of compressed files all stuffed into a single file. The four most common archive and compression formats in the Linux/UNIX world are .tar, .gx, .tar.gz, and .zip. Table 16.1 summarizes what each type of file contains and the programs used to create and unpack the files. To simplify matters, though, I'll use the term "archive" throughout this chapter as the general term for compressed files, archives, and compressed archives.

**TABLE 16.1  COMMON TYPES OF ARCHIVES**

| Extension | Type | Create | Open |
|-----------|------|--------|------|
| .gz | compressed file | gzip | gunzip |
| .tar | archive | tar -c | tar -x |
| .tar.gz | compressed archive | gzip & tar | gunzip and tar |
| .zip | compressed archive | zip | unzip |

> **Tip**
>
> Compressed archives that have the extension .tar.gz are often referred to as *tarballs*.

For starters, we'll look at dealing with archives under the assumption that you've downloaded an archive from the Internet or elsewhere, and are wondering what to do with it now. We'll look at how you can open those files using both GNOME's file manager, gmc, and KDE's file manager, kfm. If you haven't already done so, you may want to create a directory specifically for storing downloaded files. It can be a subdirectory of your home directory, perhaps named Downloads.

# USING ARCHIVES IN FILE MANAGERS

Graphical file managers, like GNOME's gmc and KDE's kfm, are  the easiest tools for managing directories and files on disks. Both file managers offer some tools for viewing and unpacking tarballs and zip files. We'll take a look at techniques for viewing and unpacking archives in GNOME's file manager first.

## WORKING WITH ARCHIVES IN GNOME'S FILE MANAGER (gmc)

Tarballs (compressed archives with the filename extension .tar.gz) are very common in the Linux/UNIX world. Essentially, the tarball is a directory whose contents have been archived into a single file (.tar). That archive is then compressed using GZip to make the file smaller (.gz). When you unpack a tarball in GNOME's file manager, the directory and all its contents suddenly appear within whatever directory you're currently working in. To avoid overwriting existing directories and files on your hard disk, you might want to unpack a new tarball in a new, temporary directory. If you're not 100% sure of the source of the tarball, you may want to run the new directory through your virus scanner, just to be on the safe side.

PART
II

CH
16

> **Tip**
>
> Packages, with the extension .rpm, are the preferred format for downloading application programs. See Chapter 13, "Managing Packages with RPM," for more information on using packages.

To create a new directory in gmc, navigate to what you want the parent directory to be, right-click anywhere in the right pane, choose New Directory, and type in the directory name. Next, open the new directory and move the tarball into that new directory. (You can use the basic drag-and-drop technique discussed in Chapter 3, "Understanding the Linux Filesystem," to move the file.) Figure 16.1 shows an example in which I've created a directory named /root/eetarball, and have already moved a downloaded tarball named ee-0.3.9.tar.gz into that directory.

**Figure 16.1**
A downloaded tarball in a directory named /root/ eetarball.

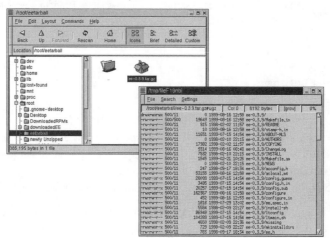

To take a peek inside the tarball before you unpack it, right-click its icon and choose View. You'll see a list similar to the one shown in Figure 16.1 that displays the permissions, sizes, dates, and names of files within the tarball. Note that the permissions of the first file start with drwx. The "d" indicates a directory. Thus, all the files beneath that first listed row were originally in a directory named ee-0.3.9. After viewing the contents of the tarball, you can close the viewing window by clicking its Close (X) button.

To unpack a tarball, double-click its icon. Almost instantly, gmc creates a new subdirectory beneath the current directory. That directory has the same name as the tarball file, followed by the phrase #utar (which, I imagine, stands for *untarred*). Contained within that new subdirectory are the complete contents of the .tar.gz file, now decompressed. For example, in Figure 16.2 unpacking the ee-0.3.9.tar.gz file created a subdirectory named ee-0.3.9.tar.gz#utar. The subdirectory named ee-0.3.9 within that directory contains all the uncompressed files and subdirectories from the tarball.

**Figure 16.2**
Decompressing the ee-0.3.9.tar.gz file in GNOME's File Manager yields a subdirectory named ee-0.3.9 that contains all the uncompressed files and subdirectories.

> **Tip**
>
> You can move the entire directory, if you want, just by dragging it to a new parent directory, and dropping it there.

## MANAGING ZIP FILES IN gmc

The same basic techniques used to view and unzip a .tar.gz file will also work for .zip files. For example, to view the contents of a zip file in GNOME's file manager, right-click the zip file's icon and choose View. A window will open listing the contents of the .zip file. To unzip the .zip file, double-click its icon. A new subdirectory, with the same name as the zip file but with #zip tacked onto the end, appears beneath the current directory. Opening that new directory reveals the contents of the zip file, all unpacked and ready for action.

For example, in Figure 16.3 I unzipped a file named 09chap.zip that was originally in the /root/zipfiles directory. Doing so created the 09chap.zip#zip directory. The contents of that directory are the decompressed files from the zip file.

**Figure 16.3**
Double-clicking a zip file's icon in GNOME's file manager creates a subdirectory containing all its decompressed files.

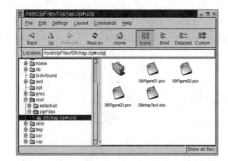

## MANAGING ARCHIVES IN KDE

KDE comes with a program called Ark (sort of an abbreviation for "Archiver"), that can handle archives quite nicely. You'll use it in conjunction with kfm, KDE's file manager. If you're in the KDE desktop, you can click the Home Directory button in the panel or click the K button and choose System, File Manager. If KDE is installed, but you're in GNOME at the moment, it's not necessary to switch desktops. Instead, you can click the GNOME Main Menu button and choose KDE Menus, Home Directory. Navigate to the directory that contains the tarball or zip file that you want to inspect and/or unpack.

To open Ark, right-click the archive's icon and choose Ark. Ark opens up and displays a list of all the files in the archive (see Figure 16.4). You can view the contents of any text file in the archive simply by clicking its name within Ark's window. This is handy if you want to take a peek at the README file or other document files before you actually unpack the archive.

**Figure 16.4**
Opening a .zip or .tar.gz file in kfm automatically opens Ark, which lists the names of files in the archive.

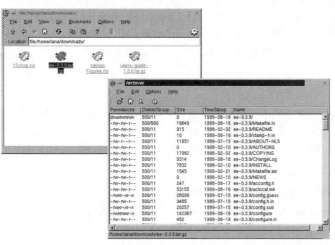

When you're ready to unpack the archive, choose File, Extract To from Ark's menu bar. You'll come to a dialog box titled Extract. Next, you need to decide where you want to put the extracted files. If you don't already have a directory in mind, you can create a new directory for the extracted files on-the-fly. Just type the complete path (for example, /root/ downloadedEE) into the Destination text field of the Extract dialog box. Click the OK button. When the extraction is complete, you can close Ark. Then go back to kfm and navigate to the directory that you extracted the files to. You'll find the extracted files (or, in the case of a tar file, the topmost directory of the archive) in that directory. With a tar file, you'll need to open that parent directory to get to the actual files that were in the archive.

# COMMANDS FOR MANAGING ARCHIVES

The command prompt offers the widest range of options for working with archives, including commands for creating them. We'll start with tar, the command for creating tar files, then look at gzip, the program that's often used to compress a tar file into a tarball (such as a .tar.gz file). Last, we'll look at the zip and unzip programs, which let you create and manipulate zip files.

## COMMANDS FOR .tar FILES

Tar, an abbreviation for *Tape Archive* utility, is one of the most widely used archiving formats in the UNIX/Linux world. It doesn't compress files, but rather archives a group of files into a single file for easy transfer over network lines or for backup onto tape or another medium. Despite the name Tape Archive, tar files are very often used for archiving files on a hard disk into a single *tar file*. The archived file always has the filename extension .tar.

Perhaps the most important point to remember about archiving with tar is that you don't actually compress files. Instead, you combine files into a single directory. So, all the files that will go together within a tar file should be placed in a single directory first, before being "tarred." That directory can contain subdirectories, and those subdirectories can contain files. When you tar the parent directory, the resulting tar file will contain all the files in the parent directory, all the subdirectories, and all the files in the subdirectories. In other words, the tar file will contains the entire *directory structure* with all its files. The basic syntax for the tar command is as follows:

```
tar options tarfilename directory
```

tarfilename is the name of the archive you'll be creating (add a .tar extension to the name, so people will know it's a tar file.) The directory portion is the name of the directory that contains the files you want to archive. Main options are summarized here:

- **-c:** Create tar file.
- **-f name:** Use archive file or device *name*.
- **-r, -append:** Append files to end of existing archive file.
- **-t, -list:** List contents of archive.
- **-u, -update:** Append only files that are newer than ones in the archive.
- **-v:** Verbose (display progress).
- **-x, -extract, -get:** Extract files from an archive.

### CREATING A TAR FILE

The -c option lets you create a tar file. You can add the -v option to get feedback on the screen as the tar file is created. And you can use the -f option to give the tar file a specific filename. As an example, let's say I need to gather all the files I created when writing Chapter 9 of this book and put them into a tar file for backing up to some other disk, or for attaching to an email and sending to the publisher. Furthermore, let's say that all the files are stored in the directory /home/SELinux/09chap. I want to name the tar file 09chap.tar and put it in the same directory as the other files in that chapter. First, to save myself some typing, I could make /home/SELinux/09chap my working directory by entering the following command:

```
cd /home/SELinux/09chap
```

To create a tar file, I'd use the -cvf options with the filename of the resulting tar file following the -f option. To specify that I want all the files from the current working directory to be placed in the tar file, I could use the shortcut symbol for the current directory, which is a single period. Hence, this command would do the trick:

```
tar -cvf 09chap.tar .
```

To verify that the tar file exists in the working directory now, I could just enter the ls command to list the names of all files in the current directory. The 09chap.tar file should be included with the rest of the filenames in that directory. For future comparison, I note that the tar file is 5,529,600 bytes in size.

### VIEWING THE CONTENTS OF A TAR FILE

When you receive a tar file, you might want to take a look at its contents before you commit to pulling out its contents and placing them on your hard disk. You can use the -t (tell) or –list option for that. For example, suppose I sent my chap08.tar file to the publisher, and he wants to take a look inside the file before unpacking it. He would simply enter the command shown here:

```
tar -tf 09chap.tar
```

If only one tar file is in the directory, you can use an asterisk instead of the filename. For example, as an alternative to the preceding command, they could have entered tar-tf *.tar. If an archive contains a great many files and the file list whizzes by so quickly you can't see it, pipe the output to the less program. Then scroll up and down through the output using the arrow or Page Up and Page Down keys. Just tack ¦ less onto the end of the tar command, as in the following:

```
tar -tf *.tar ¦ less
```

### UNPACKING A TAR FILE

You use the tar command with the -x switch to unpack a tar file. The files will be unpacked into a subdirectory of the current working directory. To avoid overwriting any files or subdirectories that have the same name, you might want to create a temporary directory, move the tar file into it, and unpack it there. That way, you can look through the unpacked files and subdirectories first, then decide where you might want to move them or how you might want to rename them.

As an example, let's say that the superuser at the publishing company who got my `09chap.tar` file wants to create a subdirectory named `tempch09` within the root directory, then move the `.tar` file into that directory. The following command would do the trick, assuming that the working directory is the same directory that the tar file is in at the moment:

```
mkdir /root/tempch09
```

These next commands would then move (`mv`) the tar file into the `/root/temp` directory, make `/root/tempch09` the current working directory, and list that directory's contents just to make sure the `09chap.tar` file is indeed in that directory:

```
mv *.tar /root/tempch09
cd /root/tempch09
ls
```

To unpack the tar file in the `/root/tempch09` directory, enter the command:

```
tar -xvf *.tar
```

When unpacking is finished, entering an `ls` command will show that the current directory now contains a new subdirectory. In this example, that new directory will be named `09chap` because I created the original tar file from a subdirectory named `09chap` on my computer. The publisher can then enter the following commands to get to his new `09chap` subdirectory and view its contents:

```
cd 09chap
ls
```

The three uses of tar files covered here will probably be sufficient for all your tarring needs. But, as you might expect, there are many more options you can use to tweak your tar files. For the full suite of options you can use with the `tar` command, see `man tar`.

## COMMANDS FOR .gz FILES

UNIX uses three programs—compress, uncompress, and zcat—to manage and create archive files that have a `.z` filename extension. The GNU project folks realized that using those specific programs and archiving formats could eventually involve getting licensing fees to distribute such files, and they came up with a "free software" alternative known as GZip (for GNU Zip). GZip archives normally have the filename extension `.gz`. But you can also decompress `.z` files using GZip.

Unlike tar and zip files, a `.gz` file is not an archive containing multiple files. Instead, when you GZip a file, you end up with a slightly smaller version of that one file and the letters `.gz` added to the filename. People sometimes GZip tar files to make them smaller before transferring them over the Internet. Therefore, you often find tarballs—files with the extension `.tar.gz`—on the Internet when visiting pages that offer downloads.

### COMPRESSING WITH GZIP

To compress a file using `gzip`, use the following syntax:

```
gzip filename
```

`filename` is the name of the file you want to compress. For example, to compress my `09chap.tar` file (assuming its directory is my current working directory), I would enter this command:

```
gzip 09chap.tar
```

Using `ls` to view the contents of the current directory, I see that my `09chap.tar` file has been renamed to `09chap.tar.gz`. The size of that file is now 939,254 bytes, considerably smaller than the original `.tar` file which was 5,529,600 bytes.

### DECOMPRESSING WITH GZIP

Suppose that rather than sending my publisher the `.tar` file, I sent this `.tar.gz` file instead. The transfer would go more quickly because the file is smaller. But to get the original tar file out of its compressed format, it needs to be decompressed first. You can use the `gzip -d` command or `gunzip` command (it doesn't matter which) to decompress a `.gz` file. Thus, if the publisher went to the directory that contains the `.tar.gz` file and entered the following command

```
gunzip 09chap.tar.gz
```

He'd end up with the larger `09chap.tar` file, and the `09chap.tar.gz` file would no longer exist. That `09chap.tar` file is now just a regular archive (no compression). And the publisher can view its contents or unpack it using the `tar` command, as described earlier in the sections "Viewing the Contents of a Tar File" and "Unpacking a Tar File."

That covers the most common uses of the `gzip` and `gunzip` commands. As is so often the case, there are many other options you can use with these commands to further tweak your compression and decompression activities. See `man gzip` and `man gunzip` for all the gory details. For summary help, enter the command `gzip -h` or `gunzip -h`.

## COMMANDS FOR `.zip` FILES

Zip files are popular in the DOS/Windows arena, largely due to the success of programs like PKZip (www.pkware.com) and WinZip (www.winzip.com). A zip file is an archive, like a tar file. But every file in the archive is compressed before it gets placed in the archive. Hence, you get archiving and compression in one fell swoop. Compressed archives created with zip always have the filename extension `.zip`. In Linux, you use the `zip` and `unzip` commands.

### CREATING A ZIP FILE

To create a zip file, use the following general syntax:

```
zip zipfilename filestozip
```

*zipfilename* is the name of the zip file you're creating, and *filestozip* is the name of the file, or a regular expression that specifies several files, that will go into the compressed archive. If you want to put all the files from the current working directory into the zip file, you can use the * symbol to represent "all files."

As an example, suppose I want to compress all the files from my /home/SELinux/10chap directory into a single archive file named 10chap.zip. First I'd go to the appropriate directory by entering this command:

```
cd /home/SELinux/10chap
```

Next I'd enter the following command to create the zip file (where * stands for "all the files in this working directory"):

```
zip 10chap.zip *
```

Entering a ls command shows me that—in addition to the files that were originally in that directory—I now have a file named 10chap.zip. I know that the 10chap.zip contains a compressed copy of every other file in that same directory.

> **Tip**
>
> Unlike Tar, which generally assumes you're placing all the contents of a directory into a single tar archive, Zip lets you zip specific files, regardless of what directory they're in.

### UNZIPPING ZIP FILES

So now, let's say I ship 10chap.zip off to the publisher. How might he'd go about peeking into its contents and unzipping its contents into normal files? To avoid getting its files mixed in with his existing files, let's say the superuser decides to create a subdirectory in his /root directory, named tempch10. The following is the command to do this:

```
mkdir /root/tempch10
```

Next, he decides to move the 10chap.zip file into that new directory. Assuming the directory that contains the 10chap.zip file is his working directory, he would enter this command to move the file into his temporary directory:

```
mv 10chap.zip /root/tempch10
```

To get to this new directory and verify that the 10chap.zip file is indeed in that directory, he should enter the following commands:

```
cd /root/tempch10
ls
```

To see a list of files within the archive before you unzip, use the -l option in the unzip command. So if the publisher wants to take a peek at the contents of 10chap.zip before unpacking it, he'd enter this command:

```
unzip -l 10chap.zip
```

To unzip the files into the current directory, use no option and specify only the name of the zip file. Thus to unpack 10chap.zip into the current /root/tempch10 directory, the publisher would enter the following command:

```
unzip 10chap.zip
```

That covers the most common uses of the zip and unzip commands. If you want to get fancier than that, see the /usr/doc/zip-2.1/zip.doc file or enter the command man zip for additional options and details. You can also get brief "reminder" help by entering the command zip or unzip without any parameters.

PART

II

CH

16

**The New BZip2**

BZip2 is a newcomer to the world of zipping and archiving. Compressed files and archives in this format have the extension .bz2. There's an rpm package containing bzip2 on your Red Hat Linux CD-ROM #1 that you can install using GnoRPM or RPM (Chapter 13). Once installed, you can find documentation in /usr/doc/bzip2. In particular, you'll want to right-click the manual_toc.html file in that directory and then view it with Netscape Navigator. After it's installed, you can enter man bzip2 to see its man page.

# BACKING UP YOUR HARD DISK

Backups are an important part of the system administrator's job. You just never know when someone is going to accidentally delete or overwrite an important file or directory. You can prevent accidental deletions and overwrites simply by copying a file to another file with the same name. The easiest way to protect against these hazards is to simply make backups of files and directories either on an as-needed basis or on a schedule. You can use the cp (copy) command with the -a (archive) option to make a quick backup of a user's home directory, or the entire /home directory, to protect user files. For example, the command

```
cp -a /home /root/homebackup
```

copies the current contents of the /home directory to a directory named /root/homebackup. If anything in the /home directory gets lost, you can simply copy the original from the /root/homebackup directory to the /home directory.

**Tip**

As mentioned, whenever you plan to manually edit a configuration file, you should first make a quick backup copy of that file in case your edits render the original configuration useless.

The small backups don't protect against bigger disasters, though. For example, a hard drive crash could take all the data on the hard disk (including your backups) with it. Beyond that, there may be a risk of fire, flood, theft, or some other natural disaster that could render the entire system unusable. For these situations, you need off-site backups—tapes, disks, or whatever—to be kept at a separate location so they don't get stolen or destroyed along with the main system.

You have many different media to choose from for storing backups off-site. Choosing one over the other is largely a matter of cost and convenience. The cheapest, of course, is the floppy disk, which just about any PC has from the moment of purchase. But floppies can also be the least convenient, especially when you consider that it could take several hundred, or even several thousand floppies, to back up an entire hard disk! The alternatives to floppies include the following:

- **CD-R, CD-RW:** Drive that can "burn" 680MB of data to a CD. Linux has limited support for this medium so unless you're a Linux guru, you might want to consider one of the following alternatives.

- **Magnetic Tape:** Magnetic tape can hold a lot of data, but backing up can be slow. On the other hand, if you use KDE, you might find its tape backup utility, KDat, to be the easiest tool around for managing your backups.

- **Removable Disks:** Zip drives and JAZ drives (www.iomega.com) provide quick and efficient backups. JAZ cartridges can handle up to 2GB of data, or up to 4GB of compressed data from your hard disk. External drives tend to be easier to install and manage in Linux.

Beforeyou purchase a specific device, you'll want to check the latest Hardware Compatibility List at Red Hat's site, to ensure that you're getting something that's gonna work! The list is available online at www.support.redhat.com.

> **Tip**
>
> The CD Writing HOWTO explains how to write to CDs under Linux. The Ftape-HOWTO covers techniques for QIC, Iomega, and Ditto tape drives. The Zip Drive mini-HOWTO offers instructions on setting up and using the Iomega zip drive on Linux.

---

### RAID Backups

On busy servers that manage large, complex databases that are constantly changing, backing up becomes a much more serious need. After all, if your Web server database has stored 1,000 new customer orders over the last few hours, you can't afford to run the risk of losing those transactions. RAID (Redundant Array of Inexpensive Drives) is a good way to protect such critical data. With RAID, data is constantly backed up to an extra set of drives. Although this doesn't necessarily protect you from a major disaster like fire or flood, it certainly gives you a current backup to restore from in the event of a hard drive failure. If you happen to be running on a Pentium III based system, you're in luck! RAID 5 performance in Red Hat 6.2 has been substantially increased for these types of computers.

RAID is a pretty big topic in and of itself. If you're interested in pursuing a RAID backup system, the Software-RAID mini HOWTO is an excellent starting point for learning what RAID is all about. The Root-RAID HOWTO covers specific techniques for creating a RAID filesystem.

---

Exactly how to install and use your backup device depends on the type of device you get. Typically, though, after the device is installed, its disks will be available as a subdirectory in /dev, just as floppy (dev/fd0) and CD-ROM (/dev/cdrom) devices are.

## WHEN TO BACK UP

How often you back up your hard disk depends on how often it changes. Most businesses will perform a *full backup* (also called a *level 0 backup*) of the entire hard disk about once a week. On other days, they'll do an *incremental backup* (also called a *level 1 backup*, *level 2 backup*, and so on) of only the files that have changed since the last full backup. In the event of a relatively minor catastrophe, such as an accidentally deleted directory, it's easy to restore just that directory from the latest incremental backup. A more severe problem, like a hard disk crash, requires restoring the full backup, and then the various incremental backups to get the disk to where it was at the time of the last incremental backup.

PART

**II**

CH

**16**

One approach is to do a level 0 backup on a regular basis, such as every Friday afternoon. Then on subsequent days of the week, do a level 1 incremental backup, as shown here:

| | |
|---|---|
| Friday: | Level 0 backup |
| Monday: | Level 1 backup |
| Tuesday: | Level 1 backup |
| Wednesday: | Level 1 backup |
| Thursday: | Level 1 backup |

In this scenario, you need only two separate media for the backup, one tape or disk for the level 0 backup, another for the level 1 backup. (A large level 0 backup, however, might span a few tapes or disks, depending on the relative sizes of your hard disk and backup media). To recover from a minor mishap, such as deleted or overwritten files, you can restore from the level 1 backup. In the unlikely event of a hard disk crash, you can restore from the level 0 medium first, then from the level 1 medium to bring everything up-to-date to the last backup.

Another approach is to have several levels of backups, where each gets smaller because it's only backing up what's changed since the previous backup. That scenario would look something like this:

| | |
|---|---|
| Friday: | Level 0 backup |
| Monday: | Level 1 backup |
| Tuesday: | Level 2 backup |
| Wednesday: | Level 3 backup |
| Thursday: | Level 4 backup |

The advantage here is that the incremental backups are quick, small, and easily managed. But you'll need a tape or disk for each level. And in the event of a major system crash, you'll need to restore from level 0, then level 1, then level 2, and so forth, on up to the most recent incremental backup.

Regardless of the approach you use and the schedule you follow, the important thing is to stick with it. That way, you always know where you stand in terms of available backups. And, do remember to keep the media off-site when not needed. If you keep the backup media anywhere near the computer, you're likely to lose those backups in the event of fire, theft, or some other unforeseen disaster.

# BACKUP AND RESTORE UTILITIES

Just as you have a choice when it comes to selecting a backup medium, you have a choice when selecting software to manage your backups. You could, of course, just use the tar command to archive your hard disk. For example, the following simple command will create a full backup of your entire filesystem to whatever *device* you specify in the command:

```
tar -cvfzM devicename /
```

The z switch tells tar to compress while it's copying, thereby making better use of the space available on the backup medium. The M stands for "MultiVolume" and tells tar to prompt you when one tape or disk is full so that you can insert another to continue a backup.

Incremental backups are a little trickier with tar. You need to use the find command to limit the backup to files whose last modification time (mtime) was n days ago, where n is the number of days since the last backup.

```
tar -cv 'find / -mtime -1 -type f -print'
```

-mtime -1 specifies files that have been modified within the last 24 hours. The -type f option specifies that only regular files be backed up. Without this option, find would back up entire directories, even if only one file within that directory has changed. The -print option displays the full name of every file that matches the criterion, which in turn becomes the input to the tar command.

Use the -x option in tar to restore from the backup medium. For example, the command shown here restores everything from the devicename:

```
tar -xv devicename /
```

The downside to using tar is that it's a bit slow and awkward, and the commands can get pretty complicated. There are much better tools out there. Choosing the tool that's right for you and works well with your selected medium is a matter of personal taste. The sections that follow will describe some common backup and restore utilities.

## KDE KDAT

If you use the KDE desktop and magnetic tape as your backup media, the KDat utility is tough to beat. Even though it uses tar to create backups, its information-rich graphical interface makes it easy to create, and restore from, backup tapes. To use KDat from the KDE Desktop, click the K start button and choose Utilities, Tape Backup Tool. Choose Edit, Preferences to define your tape device. (You need only do that once.)

To mount/unmount a tape, click the Mount/Unmount Tape button in the toolbar. Simple Backup and Restore buttons and options on the File menu make it easy to create backups and restore from them. It even comes with its own legible instructions that you can get to by simply choosing Help, Contents from its menu bar (see Figure 16.5).

**Figure 16.5**
The KDat tape backup utility and its online help.

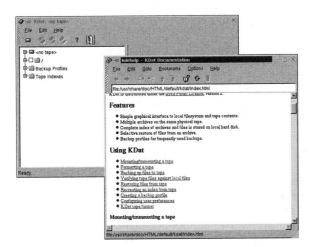

## TAPER

Taper doesn't have quite the user-friendly interface that KDat offers. But it still beats trying to manage backups manually using tar. Taper comes with Red Hat Linux, but isn't installed automatically during initial setup. So before you can use taper, you'll need to install it from your Red Hat CD-ROM #1 using RPM or GnoRPM (see Chapter 13). Once installed, you can view quick help for taper by entering the command taper -?. You'll find more extensive documentation under /usr/doc/taper-version.

Despite the word "tape" in its name, taper supports many backup devices. You need to specify your media type and device type in the startup command for taper, using the following syntax:

```
taper -T type [options] [device]
```

type refers to one of the tape types listed in the second column of Table 16.2. The device is the name of the backup device (that is, /dev/devicename) as in the examples shown in the third column of that table. The options are described in the /usr/doc/taper.txt file.

**TABLE 16.2   EXAMPLES OF DEVICE TYPES AND DEVICE NAMES USED IN THE taper STARTUP COMMAND**

| Device/Medium | Tape Type | Device Name |
| --- | --- | --- |
| File on hard disk | l | file |
| Floppy disk | r | /dev/fd0 |
| Ftape floppy tape | f | /dev/ftape |
| IDE tape drive | i | /dev/ht0 |
| SCSI tape drive | s | /dev/sdb2 |
| SCSI Zip drive | r -b | /dev/sdb1 |
| Zftape floppy tape drive | z | /def/zftape |

## DUMP AND RESTORE

dump and restore are two more command-line driven programs that come with Red Hat Linux. To use them, you must first install the dump-*version*.rpm package from the Red Hat Linux CD-ROM #1, using RPM or GnoRPM as discussed in Chapter 13. dump can handle a wide variety of backup devices and media, and has built-in support for multi-volume backups that span two or more tapes or disks. It also has built-in options for handling various levels of backups from 0 (full backup) to 9, so you need not pipe input to it from a find command.

The restore command is the opposite of dump—it copies the files or filesystem from any backup made with the dump command. restore is installed automatically when you install the dump package from the CD-ROM. When you've installed the dump package, you'll find that each command has its own man page, man dump and man restore. More extensive documentation is available, after installation, in the /usr/doc/dump-*version* directory.

### cpio

The cpio utility is a UNIX original command-line program that's just a bit easier to use than plain tar commands. But its age is apparent in that it supports many older formats that have become obsolete, and it's strictly command-driven. Like tar, it can accept a list of filenames generated from a find command as input. You can learn about cpio from its man page or documentation in the /usr/doc/cpio-*version* directory. However, unless you happen to be stuck with some really old backup hardware, it's unlikely you'll want to use this archaic beast.

## OTHER SOLUTIONS

You can also use software products that don't come with the Red Hat package that can simplify the task of managing backups. The commercial product BRU-2000 provides an easy-to-use graphical X interface and built-in support for 37 different backup devices. To learn more about BRU-2000, visit the Enhanced Software Technologies home page at www.estinc.com. To get a sense of how you'll use BRU-2000, you can peruse the online user's manual at http://www.estinc.com/manuals.html. If you use a GUI, you'll want to take a look at the documentation for the X11 Interface.

AMANDA, the *Advanced Maryland Automatic Network Disk Archiver*, is a very sophisticated backup tool that allows a network administrator to set up a single master backup server to back up multiple hosts to a large-capacity tape drive. AMANDA can back up a large number of workstations running different versions of Linux and UNIX, as well as Windows hosts that are connected via Samba (see Chapter 24). Best of all, it's free. For more information, visit www.amanda.org on the Web.

# PROJECT: BACK UP YOUR HOME DIRECTORY

For an individual user, making simple day-to-day backups of your personal files is probably the most common task. In many cases, you can get all your documents onto a single floppy disk. The task is even easier if you create a subdirectory, perhaps named mydocs, within your home directory, and use it to store all your personal documents. You can, of course, create subdirectories within that mydocs directory to organize your files by type, project, or whatever method makes the most sense for you.

Creating a quick floppy disk backup to take home or store in a safe place then becomes the simple task of backing up just your mydocs directory. Or, when that directory gets to be too large for a floppy, you can back up individual subdirectories to floppies on an as-needed basis. There's no need to use fancy backup software for such backups—you can probably accomplish the task in a matter of minutes at the end of each day, or as convenient. To get the most mileage out of the floppy disk, you can use zip to compress and archive the files before copying them to the floppy.

To do this, you'll need to ensure that the superuser has granted you mounting privileges for the floppy drive (see the Case Study in Chapter 6, "System Administration Basics"). You'll need to put that disk in the floppy drive, then mount it. In a terminal window, enter the following zip command (if you're not backing up the mydocs subdirectory of your home directory, substitute the appropriate directory name for mydocs):

```
zip /mnt/floppy/mydocs.zip ~/mydocs/*
```

When the floppy drive light goes out, you can verify the copy by double-clicking the floppy icon on your desktop, or by entering the command ls /mnt/floppy. You should see a file named mydocs.zip (or whatever name you supplied in the zip command). To view the contents of that zip file and make sure it contains the files you intended, enter this command:

```
unzip -l /mnt/floppy/*zip
```

Should you ever accidentally delete your entire mydocs subdirectory, you can easily create a new one and restore the files from the floppy to that subdirectory. At the command prompt, enter this command to create the mydocs subdirectory in your home directory:

```
mkdir ~/mydocs
```

The new subdirectory will, of course, initially be empty. To restore its contents, mount the floppy disk that contains the backup file. Then, because the unzip command will restore files relative to the current working directory, you need to first enter the command shown here to get to the root directory:

```
cd /
```

Then, enter the following command to restore the `mydocs` subdirectory, and all its files, to your home directory:

```
unzip /mnt/floppy/*zip
```

From there, you can use the GNOME or KDE file manager to verify your restoration. Or use the following commands:

```
cd ~/mydocs
ls -a
```

CHAPTER **17**

# ADVANCED SYSTEM ADMINISTRATION

## In this chapter

# MANAGING PROCESSES

In your day-to-day work with a computer, you may use only *interactive applications* like word processing and spreadsheets. These programs don't consume a whole lot of system resources. If you work in a scientific, engineering, or animation environment, however, you may use more calculation-intensive applications that take hours, or even days, to be completed. If the latter is the case, you'll definitely want to know about managing processes. Here's why. Suppose you have to run a job (program) that you know will take many hours to complete. The startup command for that hypothetical program is doit. If you just enter the doit command at the command prompt, that program will run in the foreground, and you won't see your command prompt again until that job is finished. However, if you were to enter the command doit &, the & symbol tells Linux to run the job in the background. And, you get your command prompt back immediately so that you can be doing other things during those hours that it will take to complete the large doit job. This, in a nutshell, is what Linux's *multitasking* capability is all about—the ability to have many jobs going on at the same time.

Behind the scenes, multitasking works like this: Each job that's being run consists of one or more *processes*. Because there is only one processor (in most machines), the processes have to "take turns" getting access to the processor. Linux handles the task of giving each process its own turn, or *timeslice*, automatically. So you don't have to sit there and give each process its turn on your own. You can, however, prioritize processes to determine which get the most timeslices, and which get the least. For example, if you're running the big doit program in the background, and everything else you're trying to do is running slow as molasses in winter, you can give doit a lower priority so that it gets fewer timeslices. That means it will take doit even longer to get its job done. But, you'll be able to use your computer at speeds much closer to what you're accustomed to while doit is doing its thing. This whole business of running multiple processes, prioritizing them, and so forth is called *managing processes*. And as you might expect, Linux offers several tools to help you manage processes.

## VIEWING RUNNING PROCESSES

When you first start your computer, the init procedure automatically launches several processes that are always running in the background to perform some task. Many are daemons—like the lpd (printer) daemon discussed back in Chapter 14, "Printing from Linux"—which keep an eye out for jobs waiting to be printed, and then send them off to the printer on an as-needed basis. To see all the processes that are running at any given moment, in order from the most resource-usage to least resource-usage, you can do any of the following:

- Enter the command top at the command prompt. (When you're done, type q to get back to your command prompt.)
- In GNOME, click the Main Menu button and choose Utilities, System Monitor to open GTop (see Figure 17.1).
- In KDE, click the K button and choose Utilities, Process Management to open KPM (see Figure 17.2).

**Figure 17.1**
GTop is GNOME's graphical tool for analyzing top processes.

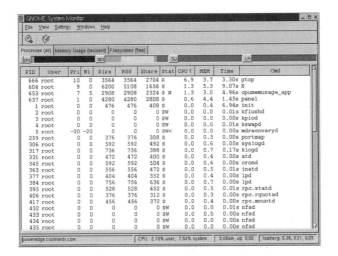

**Figure 17.2**
KPM (K Process Manager) is KDE's graphical tool for analyzing top processes.

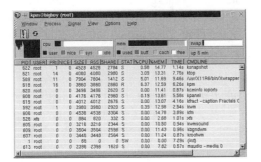

Each process is given a unique number called the Process ID (PID), which is how Linux identifies each process. In some cases, you'll need to know a process's PID if you want to change something about the process. The PID is plainly visible in the first column of whichever version of "top" you're using to view running processes. The name of the program associated with the PID appears in the last column. The columns in between give you detailed information about each and every process, and are explained here:

> **Tip**
>
> Windows NT users will notice that "top" displays much of the same information as NT's Task Manager.

- **User:** The name of the user that owns (started) the process.
- **Pri:** The maximum length of the process's next timeslice, expressed in the range of -20 (high priority, long timeslice) to 20 (low priority, small timeslice).
- **Ni:** The nice value of the task, which is its general priority setting. Will be a value in the range of -20 (high priority) to 20 (low priority).

- **Size:** The size of the process's code and any data.
- **RSS:** Total amount of physical memory used by the task, in kilobytes.
- **Share:** The total amount of shared memory used by the task.
- **Stat:** The current state of the task: S (sleeping), D (dead, though more like interruptible sleep), R (running), Z (zombie), T (traced or stopped), N (positive nice value), or W (swapped-out process).
- **CPU:** The process's share of available CPU time since last screen update.
- **MEM:** The process's share of physical memory.
- **Time:** Total CPU time that the process has been given since startup.

## PUTTING AN EXISTING PROCESS IN THE BACKGROUND

Suppose you start a lengthy program like the doit example, without using the & character to put it in the background. Your command prompt, normally, wouldn't reappear until doit has finished. But you could move doit into the background, and get your command prompt back. To do so, you first need to press Ctrl+Z to suspend the current process. The process is temporarily stopped, and you see something like this on the screen above the new command prompt that appears:

```
[1]+ Stopped    doit
```

The number 1 is the process *job number*. The message is telling you that the job, number 1, is not currently running. To move that process into the background and get your command prompt back, enter the bg command followed by a space and the job number. For example, entering the command

```
bg 1
```

gets the doit program running again, but as a background process so you still have your command prompt to work with.

To do the opposite—bring a background process into the foreground—use the fg command followed by the job number. For example, entering the command fg 1 brings the doit program back into the foreground and prevents you from getting a fresh command prompt until the doit program finishes its task.

> **Tip**
>
> Entering the command jobs at the command prompt lists all jobs you have running in the background and the number assigned to each job. Note that the job number is not the same as the PID number discussed later in this chapter.

## PRIORITIZING PROCESSES WITH NICE

You can prioritize background processes using the nice command. For regular users, a process can have a nice value of anywhere from 0 (same priority as other processes) to 20 (very "nice," and allows other processes to have a larger piece of the pie.) The superuser can assign priorities in the range of -20 (not "nice" at all, and takes quite a lot of resources from other programs) to 20 (very "nice" to other programs). By default, most processes get a nice rating of about 0, which gives them all equal access to computer resources.

> **Note** Actually, only the superuser can decrease a process's nice priority. Regular users can only increase a process's priority.

As an example of why you might want to prioritize a task, let's look at the hypothetical doit script again. Imagine a system where many users are performing work on the same computer where doit is running. If you were to run doit with a nice rating of -20, doit would be able to consume a lot of resources, and its job would be done quickly. However, all the other users on the system would notice a dramatic slowdown on their system because doit gobbles up resources. On the other hand, if you don't really need the results of the doit program until tomorrow, then it may make sense to run doit with a nice rating of 20. It will take longer that way, but other users won't notice any major slowdown on their systems.

PART
**II**

CH
**17**

The syntax for giving a background process a priority within nice's -20 to 20 scale looks like this:

```
nice -ratingcommand &
```

rating is a number in the range of -20 to 20, and the command is the program to run. The ampersand (&) at the end of the line puts the process in the background. For example, to make the doit program run in the background and be exceedingly "nice" to other programs (that is, not hog up too many resources), you'd run it with a low priority, like this:

```
nice -20 doit &
```

Note that the hyphen is part of the option, not a negative sign. If you wanted to give doit a very high priority of -20, you'd enter the following command instead:

```
nice --20 doit &
```

> **Tip** Actually, backups can take a long time. You could use nice and renice to prioritize your backups. You can also use cron, discussed later in this chapter, to schedule backups to occur each night, each week, or whenever.

To change a background process's priority, use the renice command with this syntax:

```
renice -numberPID
```

number is the rating in the range of -20 to 20, and PID is the process's ID, as shown by the ps (process status) command discussed back in Chapter 11, "Configuring Startup and

Shutdown." For example, suppose the hypothetical doit program is running in the background. Entering the ps command might display something like this:

```
PID  TTY   TIME     COMMAND
740  pts/0 00:00:00   bash
743  pts/0 00:00:00   bash
744  pts/0 00:00:00   doit
745  pts/0 00:00:00   ps
```

The third line down shows you that the Process ID (PID) to the doit process is 744. Hence, the command shown here would re-prioritize that command so that it has a nice rating of -10:

```
renice --10 744
```

**Tip**

In GNOME's System Monitor and KDE's Task Manager, you can `renice` a process by right-clicking its line and choosing Renice or Renice Task. At the command prompt, the `nice`, `renice`, and `ps` commands all have their own man pages.

## KEEPING PROCESSES ALIVE WHEN THE PARENT DIES

Just about every process running in Linux is the *child* of the process that started it. The processes that start automatically at bootup are all children of the init process (and as such, init is the parent of all those processes). Any command that you start from your command prompt is a child of your login shell. By default, whenever a parent process is "killed," all its child processes are killed along with it. This means that if you have some background processes running when you log out, you'll kill off your login shell and all the child processes you launched from that shell.

This posed an especially tricky problem when people started using modems to connect to machines and launch processes. In essence, when you "hung up" the modem, you killed off that login shell and all the child processes launched from that shell. The solution was to come up with the nohup (No Hangup) command which ignores the "hang up" signal send-to processes when you log out. The following is the syntax for the command:

```
nohup command &
```

*command* is the command or name of the program to run. For example, the following command starts the doit command as a background process. The person who started doit could log out of the system without killing off the doit program:

```
nohup doit&
```

**Tip**

Both `nohup` and `kill` (discussed next) also have their own man pages.

## STOPPING PROCESSES WITH `kill`

Normally, a process runs until its job is done (or until its parent process is stopped if the process was started without the `nohup` command). If a problem or any other situation requires terminating a process before it terminates naturally, you can use the `kill` command to stop the process. `kill` actually operates by sending a *signal* to the running process. The syntax for the `kill` command is as follows:

```
kill [-s signal] [-p] pid...
```

Optionally, to list signal names only, without killing a process, you can enter this command:

```
kill -l
```

The `-s signal` portion is optional. If omitted, the process is sent a `TERM` (terminate) signal, which simply kills the process. The `pid` can actually be the process ID (as displayed by the `ps` command), or a process name. It can also be the number zero (as in `kill 0`) to terminate all child processes under the current shell. The `-p` option, like `-l`, simply prints (displays on the screen) the PID of the named process.

The `signal` sent to the process can be any of the 30 or so signals that appears when you enter the `kill -l` command. If omitted, the process is sent a `SIGTERM` signal, which is the normal way to kill a process. For example, `kill 744` kills process number 744. If you used the `nohup` command to start the process, it will ignore the `SIGTERM` signal and keep running. To absolutely kill a process, regardless of whether you started it with `nohup` or not, use `kill -9 pid`.

> **Note**
>
> Use `kill` with the `-9` option only as a last resort, when normal killing won't work. `kill -9` terminates the process immediately and unconditionally, without letting it close any open files. This can result in corrupted data files if the command is used to kill a process that's writing data to a file.

In GNOME's System Monitor, GTop, you can kill a process by right-clicking it and choosing `SIGTERM`. The effect is the same as using the `kill` command with no signal; the process terminates normally, closing any open data files first. If the process can't be killed that way, you can right-click the process line and choose `SIGKILL`, which is the same as using -9 with the `kill` command—the process is killed immediately and unconditionally.

In KDE's Task Manager you can click any process's line, then click the Kill Task button to kill the task normally. If the task can't be closed that way, you can right-click the task's line and choose `SIGKILL` to terminate the task immediately.

# AUTOMATING TASKS

Linux comes with two programs that make it easy to start jobs at a specific date or time in the future:

- **at:** Schedule a job to run one time in the future.
- **cron:** Schedule a job to run on a regular basis (that is, daily, weekly, or monthly) in the future.

Both programs are handled by daemons, named `atd` and `crond`, that are automatically started at bootup.

**Note**

> If you have any problems with `at` or `cron`, enter the command `chkconfig—list` to look up their startup daemons `atd` and `crond`. They should both be marked "on" for runlevel 3 and runlevel 5. If not, you can use ntsysv to enable those daemons.

## SCHEDULING JOBS WITH AT

The at command lets you run a task once at some time in the future. The basic syntax for the at command is as follows:

`at timespecification`

`timespecification` can be a specific time of the day, a time and a date, or a passage of time relative to now. If only a time is given, "today" is assumed, unless that time has already passed today. If the time has already passed today, then the command is run tomorrow at the specified time. Examples of how you can express times and dates are listed in Table 17.1.

**TABLE 17.1   EXAMPLES OF SPECIFYING TIMES AND DATES WITH THE at COMMAND**

| Syntax | Example | Meaning |
|---|---|---|
| at *hh:mm* | at 13:30 | At 1:30 in the afternoon |
| at *hh:mmam/pm* | at 1 p.m. | At 1:00 in the afternoon |
| at *hh:mm month day year* | at 11:59 p.m., 12/31/99 | At 11:59 p.m. on 12/31/99 |
| at NOON | at NOON | At noon today, or tomorrow if it's past noon |
| at MIDNIGHT | at MIDNIGHT | At midnight today |
| at TEATIME | at TEATIME | At 4:00 today, or tomorrow, if it's past 4:00 |
| at *hh:mm* TOMORROW | at 6:00 TOMORROW | At 6:00 a.m. tomorrow morning |
| at *hh:mm weekday* | at 9:00 WED | At 9:00 a.m. on Wednesday |
| at now + *n time-units* | at now +2 HOUR | Two hours from now |

When using at now +*n* *time-units*, the *n* can be any number. The *time-units* specification must be one of the following words—*minutes, hours, days, weeks*. The at command has a *granularity* of one minute. This means that the at daemon checks for pending jobs once every minute. There's no point in trying to schedule a job down to the second because the daemon doesn't check every second.

After you enter an at *timespecification* command and time specification, the command prompt changes to at>. Enter the command you want executed at the specified time, just like you would if this were the normal command prompt. If you want multiple commands executed at the specified time, press Enter after typing each command. When you're done entering commands to be executed later, press Ctrl+D to indicate that you're done. The task will be assigned a job number, and you'll be returned to the normal command prompt.

> **Tip**
>
> To see the current system date and time, enter the command date.

PART
II

CH
17

As an alternative to typing in commands at the at> prompt, you can use any text editor to type a list of commands that you want executed at a specific time. Just be sure to start each command on its own line. To execute all the commands in that file at a specific time, use -f *filename* in the at command. For example, suppose you create a text file named jobstodo and store it in the /root directory. The jobstodo file contains commands that can be executed at the bash command prompt. To run the commands in the jobstodo file at 3:00 a.m., you'd enter the following command:

```
at -f /root/jobstodo 3:00
```

To view a list of pending jobs scheduled with at, enter this command:

```
atq
```

If the command returns nothing or a message tells you that you have mail waiting, then there are no pending at jobs. If there are any pending jobs, they'll be listed with a job number in the first column, like this:

```
4   2000-03-31   6:00 p
5   2000-03-31   7:30 p
```

If you want to cancel a pending job, use the atrm (at remove) command followed by a space and the job number to be removed. For example, to cancel the second job shown in the preceding example and remove it from the queue, you'd enter the following command:

```
atrm 5
```

Running atq a second time would verify that the job has been removed from the queue.

The at command assumes that you won't be sitting at the computer when the job is run. In fact, you don't even need to be logged in because the job is automatically run as a background process. Any output that the job would normally display on the screen is stored in a file instead, so that you can view the results at your leisure. Typically the results are stored in the

/var/spool/mail under the username of the person who scheduled the job. For example, if you were logged in as the superuser when you scheduled a job, when the job is executed and finished, you'd find the feedback from that job (if any) in the /var/spool/mail/root file. You can browse to that file's icon using any file manager, then right-click the file's icon and choose View or Open With (followed by any text view or text editor) to view its contents.

By default, anyone can use the at command in Red Hat Linux. To prevent certain users from using this command, you need to create either a file named /etc/at.allow or a file named /etc/at.deny. If it's easier to list users who are allowed to use the at command, create the /etc/at.allow file using any text editor, and list the usernames of those people who are allowed to schedule tasks with the at command. If it's easier for you to list users who are *not* allowed to use the at command, create the /etc/at.deny file, but this time list the usernames of people who are not allowed to use at. There's really no need to create both a /etc/at.allow and /etc/at.deny file—one or the other will do. It's just a matter of deciding which list is easier to create and maintain—the list of allowed users or the list of disallowed users.

The atd daemon must be running for your at commands to work. Typically, atd is started automatically at bootup, so this shouldn't pose a problem. If in doubt, you can enter the command chkconfig --list for a quick summary of which runlevels start atd automatically. As long as atd is marked "on" for runlevels 3 and 5, you should be fine. If not, you can use ntsysv or any of the other graphical tools discussed in Chapter 11 to ensure that atd is started automatically at bootup. For more detailed information on the at command, see its man page (man at).

## SCHEDULING A JOB WITH CRON

The cron program (also called *crontab*) is similar to at, except that rather than running the scheduled task just once, it runs the task repeatedly at specified intervals. For example, you could use cron to perform an unattended backup every day at 3:00 a.m. If your Linux machine is acting as a Web server, you could use cron to generate a report of visitor statistics every day at midnight, as well as weekly and monthly statistics.

> **Tip**  cron also goes by the name of Vixie Cron, after its creator Paul Vixie.

cron also works a little differently from at. Jobs to be performed on a regular basis are stored in a *cron table*, called *crontab* for short and stored as /etc/crontab. To create and manage the cron table, you use the crontab command with either of the following syntax:

```
crontab [-u user] file
crontab [-u user] {-e ¦ -l ¦ -r}
```

*user* is the username of the person whose cron table is being altered. If omitted, the current user (yourself) is assumed. The *file* option is used to create a new cron table, or specify one for editing. The switch options are mutually exclusive; you can use only one in a single `crontab` command. The purpose of each optional switch is summarized here:

- **-e**: (edit) Changes the current cron table
- **-l**: (list) Displays the current cron table on the screen
- **-r**: (remove) Deletes the current cron table

> **Note**
> If you use the `su` command to become another user before running crontab, be sure to use the `-u` option in the `crontab` command. Otherwise, crontab might be confused about who that actual user is at the moment.

cron only works if the cron daemon, `crond`, is loaded and running. By default, `crond` is started automatically when you boot your computer, whether you start in runlevel 3 (command prompt) or runlevel 6 (GUI). Should you have any problems, you can always verify that `crond` is being loaded at startup using the `ntsysv` command or any of the graphical tools discussed in Chapter 11. When running, `crond` has a granularity of one minute, just like the `at` command. This means that once very minute `crond` "wakes up" and checks whether there are any jobs scheduled to be launched during the previous minute. If it finds any such scheduled jobs, it runs them and then emails the result to whomever scheduled the job. As with the `at` command, the job is run in the background and requires no interaction from the user.

Each user (including the superuser, of course) can have her own *crontab file*. A crontab file is a list of scheduled tasks, which includes information about how often and when the task is to be run. The task can be any Linux command or the command needed to run a script or program.

## SPECIFYING CRON SCHEDULES AND COMMANDS

Each line in the crontab file contains six fields that define how often the job is to take place and which command needs to be executed to perform the job. Be forewarned, the syntax is a little weird and hard to get used to. (I don't make these things up, I just write about 'em.) Anyway, the first five fields define the schedule, the last field specifies the command to be executed. The fields are organized as follows, each separated by a blank space:

`Minute Hour DayOfMonth Month DayOfWeek Command`

The following are your options:

- **Minute**: Specifies the minute to run, in the range of 0-59.
- **Hour**: Specifies the hour to run, in the range of 0-23 using military hours (for example, where 13 is 1:00 in the afternoon).
- **DayOfMonth**: Specifies the day of the month to run, in the range of 0-31.
- **Month**: Specifies the month to run, as a number in the range of 0-12, or the first three letters of the month name.

- **DayOfWeek**: Specifies the day of the week to run, in the range of 0-7, where both 0 and 7 represent Sunday. The first three letters of the day name can be used instead of the number.

- **Command**: The command to run. Can include the path if the command represents a program or script.

You can specify ranges using a hyphen. For example, the range 8-5 in the Hour field means "run at 8, 9, 10, 11, 12, 1, 2, 3, 4, and 5 o'clock." The range 1-5 in the DayOfWeek field means to run on Monday, Tuesday, Wednesday, Thursday, and Friday. The range can be incremented by following it with a slash and a number specifying an increment. For example, the range 1-31/2 in the DayOfMonth field means "every other day of the month." In the Hour field, the range/increment 0-23/3 means "every three hours, throughout all 24 hours of the day."

You can use a comma to specify multiple values within a specific field. For example, 1,15 in the Month field means "on the 1st and 15th day of the month." An asterisk (*) in a field means "all." For instance, an * in the DayOfWeek field means "every day" (the same as 0-7). An * in the Month field means "every month of the year." You can increment the * as well. For instance, */5 in the Minutes field means "every five minutes." Do not leave any fields blank. Don't forget that the sixth field must be the command to run. Table 17.2 shows some examples of cron schedules using all six fields:

**TABLE 17.2 EXAMPLES OF TASK SCHEDULES FOR CRON**

| Schedule | What It Means |
|---|---|
| 0 * * * * /root/doit | Run the script/program named doit once every hour, everyday. |
| 30 18 * * 5 /home/lana/myjob | Run /home/lana/myjob at 6:30 p.m. every Friday. |
| 0 0 * * fri /usr/bin/weekwrap | Run /usr/bin/weekwrap every Friday at midnight. |
| 0 12 1,15 * * /usr/bin/biweekly | Run /usr/bin/biweekly on the 1st and 15th day of every month. |
| 0-59/5 * * * * /root/takeapeek | Run /root/takeapeek every five minutes, every hour of every day. |
| 59 23 14 apr * /root/taxdue | Run /root/taxdue at 11:59 p.m. on April 14th. |
| 15 18 * * * /usr/bin/whatever | Run /usr/bin/whatever at 6:15 p.m. every day. |

**Note**

All the hypothetical commands in Table 17.2 represent programs or scripts that don't actually exist in Red Hat Linux. You'll learn to create your own scripts and programs in Part VII of this book.

In the command portion of a crontab line, you can use percent (%) signs to represent a press of the start of text that normally would be typed in at the keyboard. You can use additional percent signs to represent pressing Enter while entering text at the keyboard. For example, when sending an email message using the simple `mail` command (see Chapter 31, "Setting Up Email Services"), you might do the following:

1. Type the command `mail -s whatever root` to send a message to the superuser.
2. Press Enter to start typing the note.
3. Type the message `test test test`, for example.
4. Press Enter twice to insert two blank lines.
5. Sign the letter "Your Pal."
6. Press Ctrl+D twice to send the message.

To simulate those three presses on the Enter key in a `cron` command, you'd use the syntax:

```
mail -s "Whatever" root%test test test&&Your Pal
```

If you wanted to send that message at 12:00 noon Monday through Friday every day of the week (perhaps just to drive root crazy—I can't think of any other reason you might want to do this), the crontab entry would look like this:

```
0 * * * * mail -s "Whatever" root%test test test&&Your Pal
```

Whenever the superuser enters a simple `mail` command to check her mail, if it's after 12:00 noon, she'll see the following message:

```
...
Subject: whatever
Test test test

Your pal
```

## SCHEDULING CRON JOBS

As mentioned previously, every user has his or her own crontab file. To create or edit your own cron file, you use the `-e` (edit) option in the `crontab` command. But be forewarned—the `-e` switch will open the file for editing in the vi editor (discussed in Chapter 6, "System Administration Basics"). Since vi is not the most intuitively obvious editor around, you might wish to use something else, such as GNOME's gEdit. To do so, you must first get to a terminal window and enter the `export EDITOR=editorname` command, where *editorname* is the command used to start your favorite editor. For example, if you're in GNOME's terminal window and want to use gEdit, you'd enter the following command:

```
export EDITOR=gedit
```

Then enter this command to edit your crontab file:

```
crontab -e
```

If this is the first time you've created a cron job, you may notice a message that tells you that there is no cron file for you. Not to worry—one will be created on the spot. Then you need to type in the six-field line that defines the schedule and task to be performed, remembering to separate each field with a blank space. If you want to try something simple for starters, you might enter the following line, as I've done in Figure 17.3.

```
* * * * date > /dev/tty2
```

**Figure 17.3**
A cron schedule typed up in gEdit, containing the mandatory six fields separated by blank spaces.

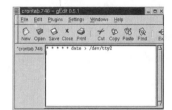

Be sure to press Enter after typing the line to complete the line. Otherwise, it won't work. I suppose I should mention that in the line, the * * * * * part means "every minute of every day." The date command displays the current system date and time. Normally, cron would email this output to whomever created the cron file. But here I've tricked cron into displaying the date on the screen by redirecting its output to tty2 (that is, virtual console 2). After typing your line and pressing Enter, choose File, Exit from your editor's menu bar, and choose Yes when asked about saving the file. Then press Ctrl+Alt+F2 to go over to virtual console 2. Log in under the same username you originally logged in under before editing your crontab file, and wait a bit. The current date and time will appear on the screen once every minute (because that's what my somewhat corny example makes it do).

To see if the command does what it's supposed to do, remember that it sends its output to tty2. So first you'll need to press Ctrl+Alt+F2 to switch to virtual console 2. Log in there under the same username you logged in with prior to creating or editing your crontab file. Then wait a minute or so. You should see the system date and time appear on the screen once every minute. When you've had enough of that, just press Ctrl+Alt+F7 to return to your GUI.

---

**Another Way to Get Cron Started**

If your chosen editor refuses to create a cron file for you, try this approach instead. Start your editor from scratch to begin with a blank document. Type your cron line(s) normally, exactly as shown in Figure 17.3. This time, after you choose File, Exit and choose Yes to save the file, give the saved file a temporary name, such as ~/crontemp. Doing so will save that text as a regular text file.

Then, pass that text file into crontab by entering the command crontab *filename*. For example, if you saved your text file as ~/crontemp, you'd enter the command crontab ~/crontemp. You won't see any feedback on the screen if the command is successful. But if you enter a crontab -l command, you should see the new line added to your crontab file. You can then delete the temporary file you created because its content has now been copied into crontab.

---

Once you've created a crontab file, the crontab -e command will open your existing crontab. Be sure to list each scheduled task on a separate line. For example, in Figure 17.4 I've added a second line to the sample crontab file. The new line simply displays the message "I'm back" every two minutes. The important point, though, is that each task is on a separate line, and each contains exactly the six fields, as required.

> **Tip**
>
> If entering `crontab -e` takes you into vi, and you want to get out without saving any changes, press the Esc key, type `:q!`, and press Enter. If you've recently edited crontab, press ~UA a few times at the command prompt to bring you back to the `export EDITOR=...` command, and press Enter to re-execute that command. Then enter your `crontab -e` command.

**Figure 17.4**
Each scheduled task in a crontab file must be on its own line and contains exactly six fields.

If you actually make this change, save the file, and press Ctrl+Alt+F2 to test it, keep in mind that the "I'm back" message appears every two minutes, not every minute.

## VIEWING THE CRONTAB FILE'S CONTENTS

To see what's in your crontab file at any time, use the `-l` (list) option, as shown here:

```
crontab -l
```

You'll see something like the following:

```
# DO NOT EDIT THIS FILE - edit the master and reinstall.
# (rootscrontab installed on Wed Jul  7 13:47:27 1999)
# (Cron version -- $Id: crontab.c,v 2.13 1994/01/17 03:20:37 vixie Exp $)
* * * * date > /dev/tty1
*/2 * * * * echo "I am here" > /dev/tty1
```

The first three lines are comments that Linux ignores. You can tell they're comments by the leading # character. Don't worry about the DO NOT EDIT THIS FILE warning—it applies only to manually editing cron files in the /var/spool directory, where the daemon looks for cron jobs. The comment should say something like, "Do not edit /var/spool/*username*-manually. Always use `crontab -e` to edit your cron file." That would be a much more accurate statement.

## DELETING THE CRONTAB FILE

To get rid of your crontab file altogether, use the `-r` (remove) switch, shown here:

```
crontab -r
```

This command removes only your personal crontab file, not the crontab file for other users. When you're tired of the corny example demonstrated earlier in this chapter, you can enter crontab -r to get rid of it.

## SUPERUSER CRON POWERS

The superuser can edit any user's crontab file using the -u switch. For example, entering the command crontab -u lana -e would allow the superuser to edit the user lana's crontab file. The superuser can also grant or deny cron privileges to users by creating an /etc/cron.allow or /etc/cron.deny file. If /etc/cron.allow exists, only users whose usernames are listed in that file will have the right to use cron. If /etc/cron.deny exists instead, all users except those whose usernames are in that file will have cron privileges. cron, crontab, and crond all have man pages. Typically terse to the point of being unintelligible, but useful when you need reminders of the details.

# PROBLEM SOLVING WITH LOGS

Linux keeps track of the activities of various programs and daemons in files called *logs* or *logfiles*. They're also called *system logs* to differentiate them from application logs, which other programs on the system create and maintain on their own. (For example, the Apache Web server creates its own application logs independently of Linux.) The information tracked in the logs is terse, perhaps to the point of being unintelligible to the casual user. However, as you learn more about administering a Linux system and what the different programs and daemons do, the log files can become a valuable source of information for tracking down the cause behind a problem. In fact, any time you come across a problem in Linux, a quick peek through the log files to see if any services failed to start is often a good starting point.

As you've no doubt seen when you first start up your computer, Linux displays a whole lot of little messages on your screen before it gets to the command prompt. Those messages are there to keep you apprised of what's going on during startup. If Linux can't start a requested service while booting up, it's flagged as "FAILED" when its message appears on the screen. If your computer is faster than, say, molasses in the dead of winter, most of these messages probably whiz by too quickly to do you any good. Fortunately, those very same messages are stored in a log file, so you can go back and review them after the computer has started.

All the log files are stored in the /var/log directory. (As you may recall, the /var directory is used to store "things that *vary*." Since log files are often updated automatically behind the scenes, their content certainly does change from time to time. Also, rather than cramming all messages from all services into a single huge log file, Linux divides the messages into several different files based on the service that created the message. The main system logs on a typical Red Hat Linux installation are summarized here:

- **/var/log/boot.log**: Messages from bootup sequence listed in date/time order. The most recent bootup's messages are listed near the end of the file.

- **/var/log/cron**: If you schedule tasks with cron, this log file keeps track of which tasks were started, and when.

- **/var/log/dmesg**: Messages from or about devices. Handy for tracking down and solving hardware problems.

- **/var/log/maillog**: Keeps track of all email messages.

- **/var/log/messages**: Keeps track of all error messages. The first place to look if some error messages whiz by on the screen too quickly for you to read.

- **/var/log/secure**: Keeps track of who logged in, and when. You can track other users' activities and look for anyone attempting to crack into the system without a password.

## VIEWING LOG FILES

All of the log files are simple text files, so there are many ways to open them and view their contents. In GNOME's file manager, gmc, viewing the contents of a log file is a snap. Just navigate to the /var/log directory, right-click the log file whose contents you want to see, and choose View from the menu. Once the log file is open in the text file viewer, as shown in the example in Figure 17.5, pressing Ctrl+End takes you right to the bottom of the file. You can also use the Search option in the menu bar to look up a particular word or phrase.

**Figure 17.5**
Viewing the contents of /var/log/ boot.log from gmc, GNOME's file manager.

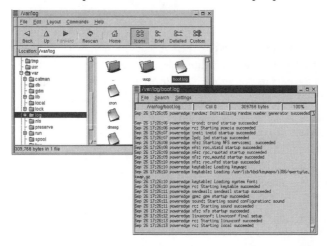

In KDE's file manager, kfm, you need to navigate to the /var/log directory and click the icon of the file you want to view. Since the log files are text files, they'll open in KDE's simple text editor program. Optionally, you can right-click the file's icon, choose Open With, then click the Browser button to select the program you want to open the file with.

From the command prompt, you can use the less program to open the log file so that you can scroll up and down with the ~UA, ~DA, PgUp, and PgDn commands. For example, to scroll through the boot.log file you'd enter the following:

```
less /var/log/boot.log
```

> **Tip**
>
> Don't forget that once you're in the `less` program, you need to type `q` to quit when you want to get back to the command prompt.

Some log files (including `boot.log`) can be very lengthy. The newest information in a log file is usually at the bottom of the file. If you just want to take a quick look at the last 10 lines of a log file, you can use the `tail` command, as shown here:

```
tail /var/log/boot.log
```

To view the first 10 lines of a file, use the `head` command, like this:

```
head /var/log/boot.log
```

Both the `head` and `tail` commands support a `-n` switch that lets you specify the number of lines you want to view. For example, to view the last 20 lines of the `boot.log` file, you'd enter the command:

```
tail -n 20 /var/log/boot.log
```

Neither the head nor the tail program provides the ability to scroll through text. So they are only useful for taking a quick look at the first or last few lines of a file.

## LOG FILES BEHIND THE SCENES

Log files are created and maintained by the `syslogd` daemon, which automatically starts when Linux boots up. Like just about everything else in Linux, even log files can be configured and customized. `Syslogd` gets its configuration information from a file named `/etc/syslog.conf`, which initially looks something like this (on most Linux systems):

```
# Log all kernel messages to the console.
# Logging much else clutters up the screen.
#kern.*                 /dev/console

# Log anything (except mail) of level info or higher.
# Don't log private authentication messages!
*.info;mail.none;authpriv.none    /var/log/messages

# The authpriv file has restricted access.
authpriv.*          /var/log/secure

# Log all the mail messages in one place.
mail.*              /var/log/maillog

# Everybody gets emergency messages, plus log them on another
# machine.
*.emerg                 *

# Save mail and news errors of level err and higher in a
# special file.
uucp,news.crit          /var/log/spooler

# Save boot messages also to boot.log
local7.*            /var/log/boot.log
```

Every message generated by the system is also given a "severity" rating, from the least critical (debug) to the most critical (emerg), as shown here:

- debug
- info
- notice
- warning
- err
- crit
- alert
- emerg

Although it's unlikely that you'd want to tweak `syslog.conf` any time soon, it certainly doesn't hurt to know what it's describing. The comments (the lines that start with # characters) pretty much describe it all, but we can flesh that out a bit to give you a better sense of what's going on behind the scenes. The line

```
#kern.*    /dev/console
```

means if the line were uncommented, kernel (`kern`) messages of all severity ratings (*) get sent to the screen (`/dev/console`). The next uncommented line starts with `*.info;mail.none;` `authpriv.none`. Each semicolon separates a `source.severity` pair, as summarized here:

- **`*.info`**: All messages rated "info" or higher.
- **`mail.none`**: No messages generated by the email system.
- **`authpriv.none`**: No messages generated by authentication logons or privileges.

Following those three pairs is `/var/log/messages`. So what that line really says is All messages of severity—"info" or higher—*excluding* messages from mail and authentication processes, get sent to the log file `/var/log/messages`.

The next lines send all messages having to do with authentication (user logons) and mail to their own separate log files named `/var/log/secure` and `/var/log/maillog`:

```
# The authpriv file has restricted access.
authpriv.*        /var/log/secure

# Log all the mail messages in one place.
mail.*           /var/log/maillog
```

The rest of the lines ensure that any message rated "emergency" is broadcast to everyone, messages having to do with uucp and news (Internet services) are logged to `/var/log/spooler`. Messages generated during bootup on the local machine are sent to `/var/log/boot.log`.

To prevent logs from growing indefinitely and eventually eating up all your disk space, Linux automatically *rotates* the logs from time to time. Exactly how and when log files are rotated is defined in yet another configuration file, named `/etc/logrotate.conf`. By default, the configuration file is set up to empty most log files weekly. However, four weeks of *backlogs* are also maintained in separate files, which you can see in the `/var/log` directory. Last week's log have the filename extension `.1`, the previous week's logs are stored in the `.2` file, and so forth. Thus, the `/var/log/messages` file contains this week's error messages, `/var/log/messages.1` contains log messages from one week ago, and so forth.

It seems unlikely that you'd need to change the `/etc/logrotate.conf` file any time soon (if ever), so I won't go into all the details of its syntax here. Of course, you can get all the details about all aspects of managing and rotating log files from the following ever-present man pages:

- `man rotatelog`
- `man syslogd`
- `man syslog.conf`
- `man klogd`
- `man logger`
- `man syslog`

# MONITORING PERFORMANCE

Linux, GNOME, and KDE all provide tools for analyzing your machine's hardware and performance. On a single-user system, it's unlikely that performance will be a major issue. But when you get into building servers (as you'll be learning later in this book), knowing your system's hardware and performance can help you get the most from your hardware and software investments. For instance, if a server is running just too darn slow, the performance tools can help you find the bottlenecks that are causing the problem. For example, if your CPU and disk input/output isn't overloaded, but your RAM memory and swap file (which carries RAM overloads) are running constantly, you know that RAM is the bottleneck. Increasing the amount of RAM and the size of the swap file could prove to be a cost-effective solution to the problem.

## GNOME INFO AND MONITORS

In GNOME, clicking the Main Menu button and choosing Utilities, System Info brings up the System Information dialog box, which provides basic information about your hardware and version of Linux. The Detailed Information button in that dialog box brings up more information about Disk, Memory (RAM), and the CPU (see Figure 17.6).

Information about memory usage and filesystems is also available from the System Monitor option. To open the System Monitor, click the GNOME Main Menu button and choose Utilities, System Monitor. Click the Memory Usage (resident) and Filesystems (free) tabs to view those statistics.

**Figure 17.6**
GNOME's System
Information and
Detailed System
Information dialog
boxes provide
quick information
about the system.

GNOME also offers a Stripchart Plotter, shown in Figure 17.7, that tracks performance as you use the system, sort of the way an EKG machine plots heartbeats over time. To open the plotter, click the GNOME Main Menu button and choose Utilities, Stripchart Plotter. To learn more about what the plotter is showing you, right-click the plotter and choose Help. To tweak its appearance or behavior, right-click the plotter and choose Params.

**Figure 17.7**
GNOMEs Strip-
chart Plotter
monitors various
aspects of system
performance as
the machine is
running.

GNOME also offers some "mini-monitors" that you can put right on the panel to keep abreast of system performance at all times. To select the monitors you'd like to place on your panel, click the GNOME Main Menu button and choose Panel, Add Applet, Monitors, and then any applet that tickles your proverbial fancy. Figure 17.8 shows examples of the CPU/MEM Usage, CPULoad, and Disk Usage mini-monitors already placed on the panel.

**Figure 17.8**
GNOME's CPU-
Load, CPU/MEM
Usage, and Disk
Usage mini-
monitors on the
panel.

CPU/MEM
Usage monitor

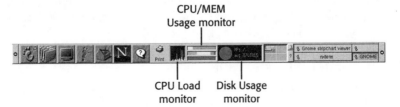

CPU Load
monitor

Disk Usage
monitor

PART
II
CH
17

> **Tip**
>
> Chapter 12, "Panel Applets," in your Red Hat Linux *Getting Started Guide* also discusses the GNOME panel mini-monitors. If you don't have that manual handy, you can find the same information at `http://www.gnome.org/users-guide/appletsmon.html`.

## KDE INFO AND MONITORS

KDE offers many graphical tools for viewing and monitoring system performance. Within KDE you can find those tools by clicking the K button and choosing Settings, Information. You'll see a menu of programs that provide information about various aspects of the system (see Figure 17.9). If both GNOME and KDE are installed, and you happen to be in GNOME at the moment, click the GNOME Main Menu button and choose KDE Menus, Settings, Information to get to that same set of options.

**Figure 17.9**
KDE offers a wide range of options for viewing your system's hardware, settings, and performance.

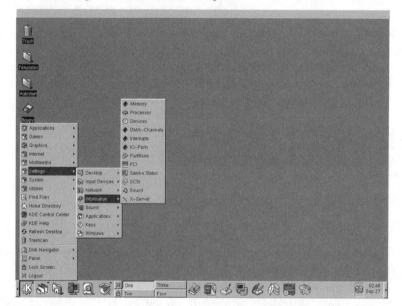

Although KDE doesn't have any "live" mini-monitors that you can put on the panel, you can easily create a button to pop up any of the programs shown on the Settings, Information menu. Just click the K button, then choose Panel, Add Application, Settings, Information, and the program you'd like one-click access to.

## COMMAND PROMPT INFO AND MONITORS

Linux also offers commands that provide information about the system and its performance. Since these are all character cell-based, you don't get the fancy, easy-to-read charts that the graphical programs offer. Instead, you get a lot of abbreviations and numbers. But generally, a high percentage value will point out which device resource is being stressed the most, and hence is likely to be a bottleneck. For example, if a server is using 98% of swapping memory most of the time, adding more memory will speed things up. The following are commands that you can use to check on hardware and performance from the command prompt:

- **du**: Estimates disk space usage (see man du).
- **free**: Displays the amount of free RAM and swap memory (see man free).
- **less /proc/cpuinfo**: Provides basic information about the computer's CPU.
- **top**: Like gTop described earlier in this chapter, shows "top processes" and general resource usage (see man top).
- **vmstat**: Reports virtual (swap) memory statistics (see man vmstat).

More information on using these tools to determine and improve system performance can be found in the following HOWTOs:

- Linux Benchmarking HOWTO
- Config HOWTO
- Large Disk HOWTO

PART

**II**

CH

**17**

As I mentioned earlier, you may not need to bother with any of these tools while using Linux on a standalone PC, or even as a network client. But as you progress through future chapters and learn more about building servers, you'll find these tools will help you get the most from your hardware. I'll refer back to this section, where appropriate, within those later chapters. For now, it's sufficient to know that such tools exist.

# TIPS FOR INSTALLING NEW HARDWARE

This book contains many instructions for installing specific kinds of commonly used hardware, including modems, printers, and Ethernet cards. But it's pretty difficult to some up with generic steps for installing all all the different types of hardware that Linux supports. There are just too many different "classes" of hardware (removable drives, graphics accelerators, CD-Rs, CD-RWs, RAID backup devices, and so forth), and too many products within each category to provide step-by-step instructions for every possibility. However, I can give you some tips that will help you install just about any type of hardware.

First and foremost is the hardware compatibility list at www.redhat.com/support/hardware. Before you buy any new piece of hardware, you'll want to make sure you're buying a product that's known to be supported by Red Hat Linux. Once you've purchased the product, your best support will probably be the written documentation that came with the product, as well as the manufacturer's online or telephone support. You'll especially want to pay particular attention to any Linux-specific information in that documentation. One thing's for certain, though: No matter what type of device you're installing, you'll want to shut down the computer first. After you install the hardware and restart the computer, you may find that the job of configuring the hardware has suddenly become easy thanks to the Kudzu program that came with your Red Hat Linux 6.2 package.

## INTRODUCING KUDZU

Kudzu is a program that's designed to make Linux hardware installation a lot easier than it has been in the past. You may not have seen the Kudzu program yet because it comes into play only after you've installed new hardware (or removed some hardware) and rebooted the computer. Essentially, here's how it works. When you first start your computer, Kudzu checks all your available hardware and compares it against a database of known, installed hardware. From that comparison, Kudzu is able to determine whether any new hardware has been installed, or if any existing hardware has been reconfigured or removed. If it finds new hardware, it gives you the ability to install and configure that new hardware on the spot. Currently Kudzu is capable of detecting and probing the following types of hardware:

- PCI cards
- SBUS cards
- Serial devices (PnP devices, mice, modems)
- Parallel port devices (printers)
- SCSI devices (provided the appropriate SCSI modules are loaded)
- IDE devices
- PS/2 mice

Other types of devices will be added as Kudzu evolves.

After you add, change, or remove hardware and turn the system back on, you'll want to keep an eye on the screen during bootup. When the message "Checking for new hardware" appears during bootup, that's when Kudzu is analyzing the hardware. If anything has changed since the last time you booted up, the main Kudzu screen will appear. You'll then have 30 seconds to press any key to launch Kudzu and make a decision about how you want to handle the new (or removed) hardware. (If you don't respond within 30 seconds, Kudzu just closes and bootup continues normally, ignoring the new, changed, or modified device.)

The options presented by Kudzu are determined on the type of change it detected. If Kudzu has detected new hardware added to the system, you can choose from the options presented in Figure 17.10 and summarized here:

- **Configure:** Adds the device to the system, and runs any programs required to configure the device.
- **Ignore:** Doesn't configure the device, but flags it as "installed" so it's not detected on subsequent bootups.
- **Do Nothing:** Doesn't register or configure the device. So you'll be given the same options on subsequent bootups.

**Figure 17.10**
Kudzu has detected a new piece of hardware—an external modem in this example—added to the system.

If Kudzu has determined that a piece of hardware has been removed, it presents these options instead:

- **Remove Configuration:** Removes the configuration information for the hardware. You might select this if you were planning to never re-install that piece of hardware in this computer.

- **Keep Configuration:** Allows you to keep the current configuration for the hardware device, even though the device is no longer installed. Kudzu will not detect the device in future startups. Handy if you plan to re-use the hardware at a future time.

- **Do Nothing:** Does neither of the above, which means that Kudzu will keep the existing configuration, and also present these options each time you reboot the computer.

As I write this chapter, there's little documentation available for Kudzu. (Kudzu is pretty self-explanatory, however, once it starts up.) You can also learn about Kudzu from its man page (man kudzu) as well as its README file in /usr/doc/kudzu-0.20/README.

## Other Hardware Installation Help

While Kudzu represents the easiest and most modern approach to installing and configuring new hardware, it doesn't work with all hardware. Sometimes, you need to do some manual configuration to get a device working. Again, any documentation that came with the product is likely to be your best bet. But you might also want to check out any HOWTOs that might be relevant to the hardware you're trying to install. HOWTOs that focus on installing specific types of hardware are available on your hard disk and/or CD-ROM, as well as at the following Web sites:

**Tip**

See "HOWTOs and FAQs" in Chapter 5, "Getting Help," if you need a reminder on how to get to HOWTOs in your Linux system.

PART
**II**

CH
**17**

- **3 Button Serial Mouse mini-HOWTO:** `www.redhat.com/mirrors/LDP/HOWTO/mini/3-Button-Mouse.html`
- **3Dfx Graphics Accelerator HOWTO:** `www.redhat.com/mirrors/LDP/HOWTO/3Dfx-HOWTO.html`
- **ADSL/DSL Modem mini-HOWTO:** `www.redhat.com/mirrors/LDP/HOWTO/mini/ADSL.html`
- **Bridge mini-HOWTO:** `www.redhat.com/mirrors/LDP/HOWTO/mini/Bridge.html`
- **Bus Mouse HOWTO:** `www.redhat.com/mirrors/LDP/HOWTO/Busmouse-HOWTO.html`
- **Cable Modem HOWTO:** `ftp://metalab.unc.edu/pub/Linux/docs/HOWTO/unmaintained/mini/Cable-Modem`
- **CD-Writing HOWTOs:** `www.redhat.com/mirrors/LDP/HOWTO/CD-Writing-HOW-TO.html` and `http://www.redhat.com/mirrors/LDP/HOWTO/mini/RedHat-CD.html`
- **CD-ROM HOWTO:** `www.redhat.com/mirrors/LDP/HOWTO/CDROM-HOWTO.html`
- **Ethernet HOWTO:** `www.redhat.com/mirrors/LDP/HOWTO/Ethernet-HOWTO.html`
- **Fax server mini-HOWTO:** `www.redhat.com/mirrors/LDP/HOWTO/mini/Fax-Server.html`
- **Ftape HOWTO:** `www.redhat.com/mirrors/LDP/HOWTO/Ftape-HOWTO.html`
- **IR (InfraRed) HOWTO:** `www.redhat.com/mirrors/LDP/HOWTO/IR-HOWTO.html`
- **ISDN HOWTO:** `ftp://metalab.unc.edu/pub/Linux/docs/HOWTO/unmaintained/mini/PPP-over-ISDN`
- **Jaz Drive HOWTO:** `www.redhat.com/mirrors/LDP/HOWTO/Jaz-Drive-HOWTO.html`
- **Large (Hard) Disk HOWTO:** `www.redhat.com/mirrors/LDP/HOWTO/Large-Disk-HOWTO.html`
- **Leased Line mini-HOWTO:** `www.redhat.com/mirrors/LDP/HOWTO/mini/Leased-Line.html`
- **MP3 HOWTO:** `www.redhat.com/mirrors/LDP/HOWTO/MP3-HOWTO.html`
- **Modem HOWTO:** `www.redhat.com/mirrors/LDP/HOWTO/Modem-HOWTO.html`
- **Modem Sharing mini-HOWTO:** `www.redhat.com/mirrors/LDP/HOWTO/mini/Linux-Modem-Sharing.html`
- **Multi Disk HOWTO:** `www.redhat.com/mirrors/LDP/HOWTO/Multi-Disk-HOWTO.html`
- **Optical Disk HOWTO:** `www.redhat.com/mirrors/LDP/HOWTO/Optical-Disk-HOWTO.html`
- **PCI HOWTO:** `www.redhat.com/mirrors/LDP/HOWTO/PCI-HOWTO.html`
- **PCMCIA HOWTO:** `http://www.redhat.com/mirrors/LDP/HOWTO/PCMCIA-HOWTO.html`
- **Plug-and-Play HOWTO:** `www.redhat.com/mirrors/LDP/HOWTO/Plug-and-Play-HOWTO.html`

- **RAID HOWTOs:** www.redhat.com/mirrors/LDP/HOWTO/mini/ DPT-Hardware-RAID.html and www.redhat.com/mirrors/LDP/HOWTO/ Root-RAID-HOWTO.html

- **Serial HOWTO:** www.redhat.com/mirrors/LDP/HOWTO/Serial-HOWTO.html

- **Sound HOWTO:** www.redhat.com/mirrors/LDP/HOWTO/Sound-HOWTO.html

- **Sound Blaster AWE 32/64 mini-HOWTO:** www.redhat.com/mirrors/LDP/HOWTO/ mini/Soundblaster-AWE.html

- **Sound Blaster 16 HOWTO:** ftp://metalab.unc.edu/pub/Linux/docs/HOWTO/ unmaintained/mini/Soundblaster-16

- **Token-Ring mini-HOWTO:** www.redhat.com/mirrors/LDP/HOWTO/mini/ Token-Ring.html

- **Ultra-DMA mini-HOWTO:** www.redhat.com/mirrors/LDP/HOWTO/mini/ Ultra-DMA.html

- **UPS HOWTO:** www.redhat.com/mirrors/LDP/HOWTO/UPS-HOWTO.html

- **Wacom TabletHOWTO:** www.redhat.com/mirrors/LDP/HOWTO/ Wacom-Tablet-HOWTO.html

- **Zip Drive mini-HOWTOs:** www.redhat.com/mirrors/LDP/HOWTO/mini/ ZIP-Drive.html and www.redhat.com/mirrors/LDP/HOWTO/mini/ZIP-Install.html

Admittedly, some the HOWTOs may be dated, and might not give you all the information you need to the particular piece of hardware you're installing. As Red Hat likes to say, "*Some documentation is better than no documentation at all.*" (Personally, however, I'm not so sure I agree with that concept.)

## PASSWORD ENCRYPTION

When you first installed Linux, you may have been given some options that you didn't pay much attention to regarding passwords. If you've forgotten what they were, you can take another look at them by entering the command **authconfig** at the command prompt or in any terminal window. The Authentication Configuration options, and the selections you made during the installation, appear in a character cell dialog box (see Figure 17.11).

**Figure 17.11**
The Authentication Configuration dialog box shows all your configuration options.

The NIS options are relevant only if this computer is currently connected to a network that's managed by NIS (Network Information Services). NIS is a server that, essentially, allows all the usernames and passwords for the entire network to exist on a single computer, which makes managing all of that a lot easier. If the computer you're sitting at is indeed a client on an NIS-managed network, you can select the Enable NIS option by pressing the spacebar. Then you'll need to provide the NIS domain name. You'll also need to either specify the IP address of the NIS server, or opt to have the computer request the NIS address via a message that's broadcast to the entire network. If you're not sure how to fill in any of these blanks, you'll need to ask your network administrator (or whoever set up NIS services on that network) for the correct information.

**Tip**

Chapter 26, "Setting Up Network Information Services (NIS)," explains how to set up and use NIS on a network.

If you don't select the option to use NIS authentication, you have two other options to choose from: Use Shadow Passwords and enable MD5 Passwords. To understand what those are about, you first need to understand what happens if you don't select either option. If you opt to use neither Shadow and/or MD5 passwords, all your users' passwords will be stored in the file /etc/passwd. The /etc/passwd file isn't protected from prying eyes. Any user can open the /etc/passwd file and take a look at its contents. The passwords will be *encoded* (though not *encrypted*). Although the encoding disguises the password well beyond recognition for the average user, there are crackers who know how to decode the passwords. Essentially, the cracker compares all the passwords in your /etc/passwd file to a database "dictionary" of common passwords. When she finds a match between a word in her dictionary and one of your encoded passwords, she can log into your system as that user, with whatever privileges that user has.

This is one of the most common methods used to break into password-protected systems that don't use password encryption. The two additional levels of password security—Shadow Passwords and MD5 Passwords—are available in Red Hat Linux 6.2. Both are essentially tools to make your passwords much less vulnerable to attack, and each has its own unique capabilities.

## SHADOW PASSWORDS

Shadow passwords are more secure than regular Linux passwords for two reasons:

■ The passwords are stored in a separate /etc/shadow file, which only the root can open.

■ The passwords are encrypted within that file.

The combination of the two prevents regular users from even viewing the contents of the encrypted passwords. Furthermore, even if someone did gain root access to the passwords, the encryption would be much tougher to decode than the encoded passwords. In fact, they would no longer be vulnerable to the commonly used dictionary attack.

If shadow passwords aren't selected in your authconfig dialog box, you can select that option now to switch to Shadow passwords. If you're interested in learning more about shadow passwords, a good starting point might be the Shadow-Password-HOWTO on your hard disk, Red Hat CD-ROM #1, and at `www.redhat.com/mirrors/LDP/HOWTO/Shadow-Password-HOWTO.html`.

---

**Tip**

If you've forgotten how to get to the HOWTOs, see "HOWTOs and FAQs" in Chapter 5.

---

PART

**II**

CH

**17**

## MD5 PASSWORDS

MD5 passwords, like shadow passwords, are more secure than regular passwords because they're encrypted. Unlike other passwords, which are often limited to eight characters or less, MD5 passwords can be up to 256 characters in length. MD5 passwords are also compatible with Pluggable Authentication Modules (PAM). PAM is a unified authentication method that makes your system more secure. For example, with PAM you can allow specific users to log in only during specific times of the day, and from specific places. You can set resource limits on users so they can't perform "denial of service" attacks on Web sites and ftp sites. PAM and M5D also support the use of shadow passwords. So you can select both Use Shadow Passwords and Enable MD5 Passwords if you like.

## PLUGGABLE AUTHENTICATION MODULES (PAM)

PAM is a service that's made available to system administrators to simplify the task of managing user accounts and passwords. Normally, a system administrator might need to recompile any program that perform authentication. With PAM, the administrator can determine how authentication is performed by managing a single configuration file. Unless you're planning to become a network administrator or security administrator on a large LAN, you may never need to mess with the configuration file. When you installed Red Hat Linux, it already set up PAM to make administration as easy as possible for you. And when you install packages using RPM or GnoRPM, they too are automatically configured to use PAM authentication.

Editing the PAM Configuration file is a complex task that goes beyond the scope of this book. It's just one of those huge topics that can't be covered in depth in a general book like this one. However, there are plenty of places where you can find more information on PAM, and the various password authentication schemes:

- **A Linux-PAM Page:** `www.kernel.org/pub/linux/libs/pam/index.html`
- **PAM Security HOWTO:** `www.kernelnotes.org/HOWTO/Security-HOWTO.html`
- **What is Linux PAM?** `www.kernel.org/pub/linux/libs/pam/whatispam.html`

- **User Authentication with PAM:** www.redhat.com/support/manuals/
  RHL-6.2-Manual/ref-guide/s1-sysadmin-auth.html

- **Shadow Password HOWTO:** www.redhat.com/mirrors/LDP/HOWTO/
  Shadow-Password-HOWTO.html

- **Authentication Configuration:** www.redhat.com/support/manuals/RHL-6.2-Manual/
  ref-guide/s1-install-authconf.html

---

**LDAP**

LDAP (Lightweight Directory Access Protocol) is yet another service for network administrators to simplify user account management. LDAP is a directory service based on a client-server model that runs on Internet transport protocols, including TCIP. For more information, see /usr/doc/pam-0.68, /usr/doc/PAM_ldap-36, and the LDAP HOWTO at www.redhat.com/mirrors/LDP/HOWTO/LDAP-HOWTO.html.

---

# USING SUID, GUID, AND STICKY BIT PERMISSIONS

While we're on the subject of security, there's another issue that hasn't been discussed yet in earlier chapters—largely because it's one of those obscure topics that tends to complicate things. This topic is somewhat related to the read (r), write (w) and execute (x) permissions that you can grant to a file's owner, group, and the rest of the world. All of that was discussed in the section "Owners, Permissions, and Groups" in Chapter 3, "Understanding the Linux Filesystem." The new set of "permissions" you're about to learn of, though, apply only to programs. They don't apply to any other kind of file, be it a document, script, configuration file—whatever.

The concepts are Set UID (or SUID), Set GID (or SGID), and sticky bits. Each of these items is a *bit* in a file that can be either turned on, or turned off, like a check box option. To understand their roles you first need to understand that usually a running program is owned by whoever ran the program. Which is to say, the program "inherits" the user's permissions, as granted by the superuser. Also, once a program has finished running, it's usually removed from memory to make room for other programs or data. The SUID, GUID, and sticky bits change all of that.

When the Set UID bit is activated on a program file, then the person running the program "inherits" the permissions granted to the program. The owner of the program remains root, who actually owns the program. The person using the program then has the *effective ID* of the program's original owner, because the User bit has been set so that the owner of the program remains the same no matter which user actually started the program. Thus, if the program has the ability to read, write, and delete files, the user running that program also has the ability to read, write, and delete files, regardless of what his normal permissions might be.

The Set GID bit works in a similar way. When the Set GID bit is turned on, effective group ID of the person running the program is the group ID that's assigned to the program file.

Hence, the person running that program automatically gets all permissions that the administrator assigned to whatever group owns the program file.

Looking at it another way, Set UID and Set GID allow the administrator to set User and Group permissions to whomever happens to be running the program. She doesn't need to tweak users' individual permissions to allow them to run the program effectively. Of course, such an action could cause a security risk. But exactly how big that risk is depends on the sophistication of the people using the program, as well as the power that the program gives its user.

## STICKY BITS

The sticky bit tells the system to save a copy of the program in memory after the program completes. This is a timesaver if the program is one that gets run often, because the program won't be need to hauled in from the hard disk every time it's called. Instead, the system will just run the "sticky" copy of the program that's already in memory.

## CHANGING SUID, GUID, AND STICKY BIT

You can set the SUID, GUID, and sticky bit of any executable program file through any file manager, or with the chmod command. To use a file manager, just locate the icon of the program on which you want to change these bits. Right-click the icon and choose Properties. Click the Permissions tab and you'll get a display like the left dialog box shown in Figure 17.12.

**Figure 17.12**
Dialog box for changing file permissions from kfm, the graphical file manager for KDE (left), and gmc, GNOME's file manager (right).

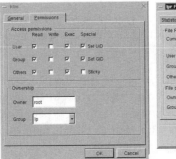

The example shows the permissions set for the /usr/bin/lpr program, which is a program any user can run to print. These are the default permissions assigned to the file when it's first installed. Note that Set UID and Set GID are both selected, meaning the SUID and GUID bits are turned on. Hence, anyone running this program does so with the effective permissions of the program itself (Read and Execute).

**Tip**

To see a listing of all programs that have their Set UID or Set GID bits turned on, enter the command find / -perm -2000 -o -perm -4000.

The sticky bit is not turned on, so the program won't remain in memory after it has completed its job. I imagine someone decided that the advantage of keeping this particular program in memory didn't outweigh the advantage of keeping tied up the memory it requires.

## USING THE COMMAND PROMPT TO CHANGE BITS

As you may recall from the section titled "How File Permissions Are Displayed" in Chapter 3, the ls command with the -l switch displays the contents of a directory, with each file's permissions displayed in a format something like the following:

`-rwxr-x---`

The - indicates that the file is just a normal file (as opposed to a directory). The first three characters after the dash, rwx in this example, summarize the owner's permission. In this case, the owner has read (r), write (w) and execute (x) permissions. The second three characters indicate the permissions granted the file's owning group. In this example the group's permissions are r-x, which means the groups can read and execute the file, but they can't read it. The last three letters represent permissions for Other—everyone else in the world. In this case, they have no permissions, as indicated by the ---).

Although I didn't mention it back in Chapter 3, the -l switch in the ls command also shows the status of the Set UID, Set GID, and sticky bits. Normally, where the letter x would appear in the owner or group's permissions, the letter s will appear to indicate that the Set UID and/ or Set GID bit is set. Thus, entering a command such as

`ls -l /usr/bin/lpr`

displays the permissions for the lpr program in ls's format (which isn't quite as easy to read as the format used by the properties dialog box.) The output of the command looks like this:

`-r-sr-sr-x  1   root  lp ... /usr/bin/lpr`

root is the owner name, and lp is the group name. What's important here, however, is that you can see that the Set UID bit is set on because the first set of permissions is r-s. The s appears where the x would normally appear. Likewise, the group's permission is r-s. And once again, the letter s where the x would normally appear (if execute permission were granted) tells you that the Set GID bit is set on too.

In this case, the sticky bit isn't set up, because that always appears as the letter t in place of the letter x at the end of the rest of the world's permissions. Thus, if the lpr program did indeed have its sticky bit set on then the ls output for the lpr program would look like this instead:

`-r-sr-sr-t  1   root  lp ... /usr/bin/lpr`

To change SUID, GUID, and the sticky bit using the chmod command, you can use the chmod relative syntax which is as follows:

`chmod [ugoa...] [+-=] [rwxXstugo...] file(s)`

The three items in square brackets define a single *mode* for the file. Each mode is one or more of the letters ugoa, one of the symbols +=-, and one or more of the letters rwxXstugo. Here's what the letters and symbols the define a mode mean:

- **u:** User (owner)
- **g:** Group
- **o:** Other (rest of world)
- **a:** All (User, Group, and Other)
- **+ :** Adds new permissions to existing permissions
- **= :** Replaces existing permissions with new permissions
- **–:** Removes specified permissions but leaves remaining permissions intact
- **r:** read
- **w:** write
- **x:** execute*
- **X:** Executes only if the file already has execute permission from a user*
- **s:** Sets UID bit on if applied to user (u); sets GID bit on if applied to group (g)
- **t:** Sets sticky bit on
- **u:** Sets specified group's permissions equal to the file's User (owner) permissions
- **g:** Sets specified group's permissions equal to the file's Group permissions
- **o:** Sets specified group's permissions equal to the file's Other permissions

*When applied to a directory rather than a file, the execute (x and X) permissions have slightly different meanings. A person with the ability to "execute" a directory actually has the right to open the directory.*

To set a program file to have the effective user be the owner of that file, use this syntax:

```
chmod u+s file(s)
```

`file(s)` is the name of the file you want to set the bit on. You can specify multiple files using wildcard characters.

To set the GID bit, use the following syntax:

```
chmod u+g file(s)
```

If you prefer to use numeric absolute permissions, you'll need to use a four-digit number rather than the usual three-digit number to set the SUID, GUID, or Sticky bit. Table 17.3 lists the numbers required to set the bits (where *xxx* represents the rest of the number in the mode). Look at the following `chmod` command:

```
chmod 4770 whatever
```

This turns on the Set User ID bit of the file named whatever. The 770 portion grants read, write, and execute permissions to the owner and group, and no permissions to the rest of the world.

PART
**II**

CH
**17**

TABLE 17.3   NUMBERS IN THE LEFT COLUMN USED IN Chmod + COMMAND TO CHANGE STICKY, GID, AND UID BITS

| Number | Meaning |
| --- | --- |
| 1*xxx* | Turn on sticky bit |
| 2*xxx* | Turn on Set Group ID bit |
| 4*xxx* | Turn on Set User ID bit |
| 3*xxx* | Turn on sticky and Set Group ID bits |
| 5*xxx* | Turn on sticky and Set User ID bits |
| 6*xxx* | Turn on Set User ID and Set Group ID bits |
| 7*xxx* | Turn on all three bits; sticky, Set Group ID, Set User ID |

# TROUBLESHOOTING: SPEEDING UP A SLOW SYSTEM

Although the character cell performance tools like vmstat don't give you an intuitively obvious view of how your system is running, the numbers alone can be useful. In particular, the numbers provided by the vmastat program can provide some quick insight into possible performance bottlenecks. When you run vmstat, you see the following information. (Yours will be different of course; the numbers here are just an example from one of my computers):

```
procs                 memory  swap    io  system
r b w swpd   free  buff cache si so bi bo  in  cs us sy id
1 0 0     0 23896 21764 24896  0   0 42 6 132 160  3  5  92
```

At first glance the information might appear to be a bunch of useless gibberish. But surprisingly, the first three columns, r, b, and w, can provide quite a bit of insight into an overworked server that's not keeping up with its workload. The three columns, and what they indicate, are summarized as follows:

- **r:** The r (run) column shows the number of processes that are waiting for the CPU to pay attention to them so they can be run. The larger the number here, the slower and more "backed up" your system is. A faster processor would likely be the best investment in getting this machine to perform better.

- **b:** The b (blocked) number shows processes that are waiting for some kind of attention, usually from a block device such as your hard disk. A large number here probably means that your hard disk is slowing down the system. A faster hard disk, or a second hard disk and more partitions, would help bring this number down in size and enhance performance.

- **w:** The w (*swapped*) value indicates the number of processes that are currently swapped out to virtual (swap) memory. A large number here indicates that RAM is the main bottleneck. Increasing the amount of RAM in the computer would help speed things along.

The remaining columns are just raw numbers that tell you more about the load the machine is carrying, rather than relative performance:

- **swpd:** The amount of swap memory currently in use (in kilobytes)
- **free:** The amount of RAM memory available but not currently in use
- **buff:** The amount of memory in the I/O buffers
- **cache:** The amount of I/O cache, in kilobytes
- **si:** Program pages that are swapped into memory
- **so:** Program pages that are swapped out of memory
- **bi:** Number of blocks in from hard disk
- **bo:** Number of blocks out to hard disk
- **in:** Number of interrupts per second
- **cs:** Number of context switches per second
- **us:** Percent of processor time used for processing user request
- **sy:** Percent of time processor has spent performing system requests
- **id:** Percent of time the processor has sat idle

# LINUX AND THE INTERNET

# CHAPTER 18

# CONNECTING TO THE INTERNET

In this chapter

# GETTING ONLINE

I'm not going to get into a big tutorial on "What is the Internet?" I'll assume you already know that the Internet is the big worldwide network that provides services like the World Wide Web, email, and others.

The question I'll focus on here is, "How do I access the Internet from my Linux computer?" In other words, this chapter focuses on connecting to the Internet as a *client* (in this case, a consumer) and not as a service provider. I'll focus on creating a *dial-up account*, where you connect to the Internet through a modem (or similar device) and an Internet service provider (ISP) on an as-needed basis. When you've finished browsing the Web, checking your email, downloading files, or whatever, you disconnect from your ISP and your PC is no longer connected to the Internet.

**Note**

A server on the Internet is generally connected 24 hours a day, seven days a week. Getting that sort of connection and setting up a server is a topic that will be discussed in Part VI of this book.

So the question this chapter attempts to answer is simply: "How do I use the Internet from my Linux computer?" For almost everyone who is looking to just browse the Web, download files, do email, and the like, the simple answer is to go through the following three-step process:

1. Get and install a modem that will work with Linux.
2. Get an account with an Internet Service Provider (ISP).
3. Set up your PPP account so you can get online.

It would be great (for both of us) if I could just leave it at that. But unfortunately, each step is fraught with challenges and details that can drive you up a wall. To try to keep it simple, I will focus on the most typical scenarios for setting up Internet access as a typical user. Later in the chapter, I'll point out some resources for dealing with less common scenarios. I'll start with step 1, choosing and installing a modem.

# INSTALLING A MODEM

The first challenge is finding a modem that will work with Linux. Just visit the Red Hat Hardware Compatibility list for Tier 1 (fully compatible) modems. Here is a brief version of it:

- External modems
- Lucent Venus-based PCI internal modems

What the list should probably say is that most external modems will work just fine, whereas most internal modems will not. The biggest bugaboo in the whole modem situation is that the market is currently filled with "Winmodems," which are not true modems. Winmodems, also called *software modems*, *HSP* (Host Signal Processor) and *HCF* (Host Controlled Family) modems, do not contain all the hardware that a "real" modem has. Instead, these modems use the CPU ( like the Pentium processor) to do some of the work normally performed by the modem hardware. The end result is that the modem is much less expensive; therefore, manufacturers like to put these modems into systems they sell because they can sell them for less. The problem is that the modem works only when Windows is installed as the operating system. Other operating systems, including Linux, don't have the appropriate drivers to make the modem work. This can be a major bummer, especially if you discover this unpleasant fact after spending countless hours trying to get your incompatible modem to work in Linux.

**Tip**

The Hardware Compatibility List is available as the Hardware HOWTO on your Red Hat Linux CD-ROM or hard disk (refer to Chapter 5, "Getting Help"). If you have Internet access through another computer, you can see the latest version of the Hardware Compatibility List at `http://www.redhat.com/support/hardware`.

As this chapter is being written, the list of modems that are *not* supported by Linux looks like this:

PART

**III**

CH

**18**

- The IBM Mwave modems
- Plug-and-Play (PNP) modems (these may be set up via isapnptools and setserial)
- Modems that require software drivers for compression, error correction, high-speed operation, and the like
- PCI Memory Mapped Modems (these do not act like serial ports)
- Internal SupraExpress 56K
- Internal SupraSonic 56K
- Newer Internal Laptop Modems
- The Multiwave Innovation CommWave V.34
- US Robotics WinModem series
- US Robotics Sportster Voice/Fax modem (X2 model 1785 internal PNP)
- Boca modem (model M336l)
- Boca Research 28.8 internal modem (model MV34AI)
- Zoltrix 33.6 Win HSP Voice/Speaker Phone modem
- Motorola ModemSURFR internal 56K
- DSVD modem
- Compaq 192 PCMCIA modem/serial card
- New Media Winsurfer PCMCIA modem/serial card

Although it may sound like rather vague advice, your best bet in selecting a modem is to find a "plain vanilla" 56K V.90 external modem. Since an external modem connects to the serial port at the back of your PC, Linux really just has to deal with the serial port. The 56K speed is about the fastest you can get on a standard phone line without getting into the added expense of ISDN or DSL. And the V.90 standard is currently supported by virtually all ISPs.

Once you've purchased a modem, you need to install it as per the manufacturer's instructions. For an external modem, this generally requires plugging the modem into the wall, then connecting the modem to the Serial 1 (or COM 1) or Serial 2 (or COM 2) plug on the back of the computer. Then you use a regular phone line to plug the modem's line port into the telephone jack. If you need to use that same telephone line for voice calls, you can connect the phone jack on the modem to a telephone. But again, follow the modem manufacturer's instructions for details.

---

### If Windows Is Installed

If you have Windows on the same computer as Linux, you might try installing the modem and setting up your ISP account in Windows first. Windows is considerably more user-friendly when it comes to installing a modem, testing it, and setting up an account with an ISP. Plus, the modem itself may come with instructions for installing via Windows 95/98 because that's the most popular operating system for SOHO (*Small Office-Home Office*) environments where modems are used most heavily.

The important point, however, is to remember that just because a modem works in Windows doesn't mean it's going to work in Linux. For example, any Winmodem will work just fine in Windows, but not at all in Linux. If you do install your modem via Windows, you can see which COM port it's connected to by clicking the Windows Start button and choosing Settings, Control Panel, Modems.

---

Installing an internal modem (if you can even find one that will work with Linux) requires taking the cover off the case and installing the modem in an available ISA or PCI slot. If the modem has dip switches that allow you to define the modem's serial port and so forth, set those switches before you install the modem into the PC. Again, you'll need to follow the manufacturer's instructions on that, as I have no way of knowing anything about the make and model of your particular modem. Assuming the modem is physically connected to the computer, is turned on, and is ready for action, you're ready to tell Linux that the modem exists.

## IF KUDZU CHIMES IN

The first step after installing a new piece of hardware on your computer is, of course, to turn the computer on. There's a good chance that Kudzu will detect the new modem during boot up, so keep your eyes peeled for the Kudzu screen. If it appears you should go ahead and chose Configure when given the option. Chances are, Kudzu won't even ask for any information. It will just briefly display a Configuring... message, then boot up normally. You'll want to keep reading, though, to make sure everything is set up correctly.

## WHERE IS YOUR MODEM CONNECTED?

Just as Red Hat Linux uses /dev/floppy to refer to your floppy drive and /dev/cdrom to refer to your CD-ROM drive, it will want to use /dev/modem to refer to your modem. You'll need to run the modemtool program to set up this association. First, you'll want to make absolutely certain that you know which serial port your modem is connected to. The most likely scenario is that your modem is connected to one of your first two serial ports. In Linux, these are referred to as /dev/cua0 and /dev/cua1. (In DOS/Windows, they're referred to as COM1 and COM2, respectively). To check /dev/cua0, enter the command:

```
statserial /dev/cua0
```

After you press Enter, look for the lines beginning with RTS, CTS, DSR. If /dev/cua0 is the correct port, their values will all be set to 1, as shown here:

| | | |
|---|---|---|
| RTS | 1 | Request To Send |
| CTS | 1 | Clear To Send |
| DSR | 1 | Data Set Ready |

To get back to a command prompt at the end of the list, press Ctrl+C. If any of those values is zero, test /dev/cua1 by entering this command:

```
statserial /dev/cua1
```

Again, look for 1 values in the RTS, CTS, and DSR rows. Make sure you jot down exactly which port is the one that your modem is connected to. And remember to press Ctrl+C to get back to the command prompt.

### DEFINING /dev/modem WITH MODEMTOOL

Next, you need to use the modemtool to tell Linux which serial port your modem is connected to. You should be in GNOME, KDE, or some other GUI to do this. You should also be logged in as root (the superuser). Then, in a terminal window enter the following command:

```
modemtool
```

You'll come to a dialog box titled Configure Modem, as shown in Figure 18.1.

**Figure 18.1**
The Configure Modem dialog box lets you tell Linux which serial port your modem is connected to.

If your modem is connected to /dev/cua0, then you want to click the ttyS0 option shown in the figure. If your modem is connected to /dev/cua1, then you want to click the ttyS1 option.

PART

**III**

CH

**18**

Click the OK button. The device name /dev/modem should now point to your modem. In fact, if you want to verify that, you can locate the icon for /dev/modem using GNOME's file manager. Right-click that icon and choose Edit Symlink. You'll see a dialog box that says "modem" points to, followed by ttyS0 if your modem is connected to serial port 1, or ttyS1 is the modem is connected to serial port 2. Don't change the settings. Just click Cancel to leave the setting as is.

> **Tip**
>
> TtyS0 or ttyS1 is actually the serial port through which modem communications will be sent. However, the number (0 or 1) should match the cua number of the device, such as cua0 or cua1.

All you've really done here is set the device name, /dev/modem, to the proper serial port for your modem. However, this is good because many of your communications programs can now refer to your modem as simply /dev/modem. (This is similar to the way you can use /dev/floppy to refer to your floppy disk and /dev/cdrom to refer to your CD-ROM drive.)

# CHOOSING AN INTERNET SERVICE PROVIDER (ISP)

The second major challenge facing you is finding an Internet service provider (ISP). The ISP is a company that has a 24/7 connection to the Internet. When you sign up, you'll typically get a *dial-up account*, where you connect to their network, which is in turn connected to the Internet. Hence, you have access to the Internet whenever you dial in with your modem.

Many ISPs have Windows and Macintosh programs that simplify setting up your account. But I haven't heard of any, yet, that have gone to any great lengths to simplify access for UNIX or Linux. Your best bet in finding an ISP might be to simply check your local Yellow Pages and start shopping around. Tell them you plan to connect with Linux to see what they can offer in terms of support. If you can get specific step-by-step instructions for connecting *your* Linux machine to *their* service, the task will probably be easier. I will present a couple of the "typical" scenarios for connecting to an ISP using common PPP (Point-to-Point Protocol) later in this chapter. But specific instructions from your ISP might be a little easier to follow, since I need to be somewhat general when presenting my instructions.

Of course, you'll want to consider the cost as well. Some ISPs offer inexpensive accounts that offer limited hours per month. Some offer unlimited access for a fixed price. Virtually all provide basic Web access and email. You'll want to make sure they have modems that match yours. For example, if you have a 56K V.90 modem, you'll want to find an ISP that offers that kind of access. And finally, you'll want to make sure you find one that has a local phone number that you can dial for free. You can check the front of your White Pages for phone number prefixes in your local (free) dialing area. Then try to find an ISP that offers a dial-in number with one of those prefixes. Otherwise, you'll be wracking up toll charges from Ma Bell whenever you're online.

Once you find an ISP, they'll give you some information about your account. You can jot that information down in a third column for Table 18.1. Note that the second column contains only hypothetical examples of what the information might look like. Using information from the second column of this table while setting up your own account will do you no good.

**TABLE 18.1    TYPES OF INFORMATION YOU'LL GET FROM AN ISP TO SET UP YOUR ACCOUNT**

| Line Item | Account Information | Example |
|-----------|---------------------|---------|
| 1. | Dial-up access number | 555-1234 |
| 2. | Authentication method | PAP |
| 3. | Username/Login name | alan |
| 4. | Login password | fatchance |
| 5. | Default domain name | whatever.com |
| 6. | Name Server (DNS 1) | 192.188.72.16 |
| 7. | Name Server (DNS 2) | 192.188.72.29 |
| 8. | IP address (unless *dynamic*) | 204.12.34.123 |
| 9. | Subnet mask | 255.255.255.240 |
| 10. | Your email address | alan@whatever.com |
| 11. | Incoming (POP3) mail server | mail.whatever.com |
| 12. | Outgoing (SMTP) mail server | smtp.whatever.com |
| 13. | Email username | alan |
| 14. | Email password | mailpassword |
| 15. | News (NNTP) server | news2@whatever.com |

PART

**III**

CH

**18**

Regarding the IP address shown in line item 5—in many cases, the ISP won't give you a *static* IP address. Instead, your computer will be automatically given a *dynamic* IP access whenever you log in. There's no disadvantage to using a dynamic IP address—you only need a permanent (static) IP address when you're planning on setting up your own Web server. If your ISP doesn't give you a static IP address, simply write *dynamic* in the third column of Table 18.1 for line item 5.

# SETTING UP, GETTING CONNECTED

After you have your modem installed and defined as /dev/modem, and you have information about your account from your ISP, the next step is to set up your PPP dial-up account. There are several ways to do this. The easiest way is to use the Red Hat Linux 6.2 Internet Connection packages.

Make sure that the following packages are installed on your computer:

```
ppp-2.3.11-4.i386.rpm
rp3-1.0.7-4.i386.rpm
usermode-1.20-1.i386.rpm
```

You can use the rpm -q <packagename> command to verify that they are installed. If they aren't, install them from your Red Hat 6.2 CD now!

## SETTING UP YOUR PPP ACCOUNT

If you've downloaded and installed the latest PPP packages, you can follow these steps to configure your PPP account:

1. Open GNOME, click the Main Menu button and choose Internet, Dialup Configuration Tool. Two windows titled Internet Connections and Add New Internet Connection appear.

2. Click the Next button in the Add New window.

3. If the next window complains that you don't have a modem installed, don't worry about it. Just click the Next button and your modem should be detected and displayed in the Modem Found page that appears. Click the Next button.

4. The next screen to appear, shown in Figure 18.2, asks about your ISP account.

**Figure 18.2**
The Add New Internet Connection program requesting information about your ISP account.

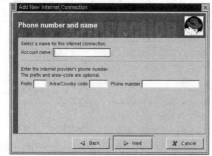

5. Next to Account Name, type in the name of your ISP, or any name that will help you identify this connection. This name can be whatever you like, you need not copy anything from the ISP exactly.

6. In the remaining boxes, type the country code, area code, and phone number you'll use to dial up to the Internet. If the number is local, you can leave the country code blank, and leave the area code blank as well unless you live in an area that requires 10-digit dialing.

7.  Click the Next button, and fill in the user name and password provided by your ISP (such as line items 3 and 4 from Table 18.1). Then click the Next button again.

8.  The next wizard screen asks about your ISP. If you see your ISP in the list provided, select that one. Otherwise, select Normal ISP. Then click the Next button.

9.  The last screen will review the information you entered. Click the Finish button.

At this point, the Internet Connections window should contain a line for the ISP you just entered, as in the example shown in Figure 18.3. Before you test the connection, a little more tweaking may be in order:

1.  Click on the new account you just created, the click on the Edit button.

2.  Click on the Advanced tab.

3.  For starters, select the first option (Let PPP Do All Authentication), and the third option (Let User Start and Stop Connection).

4.  If your ISP gave IP addresses of primary and secondary nameservers or DNS servers (line items 6 and 7 from Table 18.1), type those addresses into the First DNS Server and Second DNS Server boxes. Otherwise, leave those options blank.

5.  Click the OK button.

**Figure 18.3**

One Internet connection added to the dialog box of available Internet connections for this Linux computer.

Finally, to test the connection, select the ISP's name in the Internet Connections dialog box, then click the Debug button. If all is well, you will probably hear the modem dial out and attempt to make a connection. This Debug procedure won't actually connect you to the Internet. But it will point out any potential problems that might occur along the way. Most likely you'll end up with a message that states Starting PPPD at... followed by the date and

PART

**III**

CH

**18**

time. That's a good sign, as this means the PPP daemon is running and your connection is probably successful. The real test, however, is whether or not you can actually get connected, as discussed next. For the moment, close the test results window and the Internet Connections window, regardless of the outcome of your Debug test, to see about making a "real" connection.

## CONNECTING WITH THE RED HAT PPP DIALER

To connect to the Internet from GNOME, you can use the PPP dialer. Here's how:

1.  Click the GNOME Main Menu button and choose Internet, RH PPP Dialer.

2.  In the Choose dialog box that appears, click the name of your ISP, and then click the OK button.

3.  When asked if you really want to start that Interface, choose Yes.

4.  A progress bar will bounce back and forth as Linux tries to make the connection. You may hear some modem activity while this is taking place.

When you're connected, only a tiny dialog box remains, like the one shown in Figure 18.4. As you start interacting with the Internet, the dialog box will plot Send and Receive information in a graph form. Until you actually start using the Internet, however, the only way to know for sure whether you're connected is to rest the mouse pointer on the small dialog box. If the message "Click to disconnect from *your ISP name*" appears, as in the figure, that means you are currently connected. You are now free to browse the World Wide Web, do email, transfer files, and so forth, as discussed in Chapters 19-21. In fact, you can even skip the rest of this chapter and try some of those services now. But if you have any trouble connecting to an Internet source, you'll want to come back to this chapter and try some of the following techniques to fix any problems that might arise.

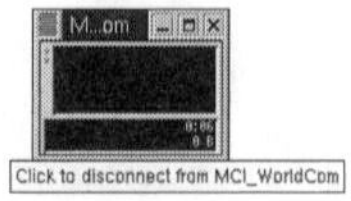

**Figure 18.4**
Once you're con-
nected to your
ISP, only a tiny
dialog box re-
mains. The tooltip
tells you you're
currently con-
nected to that ISP.

Just keep in mind that whenever you want to connect to your ISP, you need to run the RH PPP Dialer, by following the previous four steps. Whenever you want to end your connection to the Internet, click on the tiny dialog box that remains. You'll see a prompt asking if you're sure you want to disconnect. Just click its Yes button to disconnect.

## SETTING UP PPP IN LINUXCONF

Chances are the previous techniques will give you the Internet access you need from GNOME. But, since the new programs aren't exactly perfect yet, you might also want to try some of the older methods, particularly if you have any problems connecting with the procedure just described.

To set up a PPP account using LinuxConf, you must log in as root (the superuser), and get to the GNOME desktop. Then, follow these steps to get started:

1. Click the GNOME Main Menu button and choose System, LinuxConf.
2. Open the Config, Networking, Client Tasks categories.
3. Click the PPP/SLIP/PLIP option (see Figure 18.5).

**Figure 18.5**
GNOME Linux-Conf ready to create a PPP dial-up connection to your ISP.

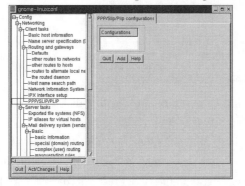

4. Click the Add button to create a new account. When prompted which type of account you want to create, choose PPP and then click the Accept button.

**Tip**

If there's already an account named ppp0 in your PPP configurations, it's most likely one you created using the &&& tool described earlier in this chapter. LinuxConf is "aware" of that other account because it gets it information from the same configuration file.

5. In the next set of options to appear, use the Phone Number field to type the number you need to dial to connect to your ISP (line item number 1), but do not use any spaces, parentheses, or hyphens (for example, 5551234). If you're inside a business where you need to dial a number to get an outside line, make that number the first digit. For example, if you need to dial 9 to get an outside number, you'd enter 95551234.

6. If your ISP uses PAP authentication (line item 2), select the Use PAP Authentication button (so it looks pushed in).

7. In the Login Name and Password fields, type in the name and password provided by your ISP (line items 3 and 4). At this point your screen shows something like Figure 18.6, with your own account data filled in, as opposed to the hypothetical data from Table 18.1.

**Figure 18.6**
The first stage of setting up a PPP account is completed.

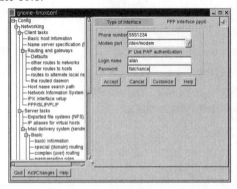

8. Click the Accept button. You're returned to the first dialog box, where you now see a connection named ppp0 or ppp1 listed.

9. In the left column of LinuxConf, click the Name Server Specification (DNS) option.

10. In the default Domain Textbox, enter your ISP's domain name (line item 5).

11. In the Nameserver1 textbox, type the IP address for your primary DNS server (line item 6).

12. If your ISP gave you a secondary DNS address (line item 7), type that into the Nameserver2 textbox. Your screen should now look something like Figure 18.7.

**Figure 18.7**
The second stage of setting up a PPP account is completed.

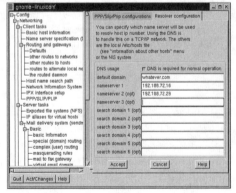

13. Click the Accept button.

Now you'll want to check your line speed, modem connection, and possibly grant the ability to connect to the Internet for regular users. Follow these steps:

1. Click the account you just created, ppp0 or ppp1, to edit that account.

2. If you want regular users to have access to the Internet through this account, select the Allow Any User (De)Activate the Interface option.

3. Set the Line Speed option to the highest speed your serial card (not your modem) can handle. Typically this will already be preset to the correct value of 115200.

4. Verify that the Modem Port option is set to /dev/modem (see Figure 18.8).

**Figure 18.8**
Granting regular users the privilege of using the PPP account to access the Internet.

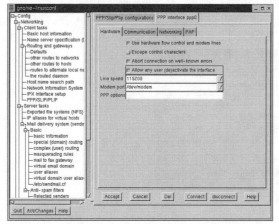

5. Click the Accept button.

6. Click the Quit button under the Configurations list (ppp0).

7. Click the Quit button near the lower-left corner of the LinuxConf window.

8. Click the Activate the Changes button that appears.

LinuxConf will close, and your connection should be ready to use.

## CONNECTING WITH USERNET

The UserNet program in GNOME will be the easiest way to make your connection. To give yourself easy access to UserNet via the panel and/or your personal menu, first follow these steps:

1. Click the GNOME Main Menu button and choose AnotherLevel Menus, Networking.

2. If you want to create a panel button for connecting to the Internet, right-click the UserNet option and choose Add This Launcher to Panel.

3. If you want to add UserNet to your personal menu, right-click the UserNet option again and choose Add This to Personal Menu.

4. Click anywhere outside the open menus to close them.

The panel button for UserNet will probably have a GNOME footprint on it. When you point to the button, its tooltip reads Control User-Controllable Network devices. If you'd like to give the button a better tooltip and icon, right-click the button and choose Properties. Then type a new tooltip in the Comment textbox, and choose a new icon. In Figure 18.9, I changed the tooltip to UserNet PPP Dial-Up Account and the icon to a globe from the /usr/share/pixmaps directory.

**Figure 18.9**
Launcher Properties dialog box for the UserNet PPP Dial-Up program.

You only have to do this procedure once. In the future, whenever you want to connect to your ISP, first make sure your modem is plugged in and turned on (if it's an external modem). Then, use whichever following technique is most convenient for you to start UserNet:

- If you created a panel button for UserNet, just click that button.

- If you added UserNet to your Personal menu, click the GNOME Main Menu button and choose UserNet.

- Click the GNOME Main Menu button and choose AnotherLevel Menus, Networking, UserNet. You'll see the UserNet dialog box appear, looking something like Figure 18.10. (Yours may show an additional ppp1 account, which is most likely the one you just created.)

**Figure 18.10**
A red button in the Status Info column indicates that you're not connected to that service at the moment.

- In a terminal window, type the command usernet & and press Enter.

**Tip**

To create a desktop icon for UserNet, simply drag the UserNet icon from the panel onto the desktop (using the left mouse button), and drop it there.

Buttons down the left side of the UserNet dialog box are titled Toggle Interface because they act like toggle switches. Clicking the button disconnects from the service if you're currently connected or connects to the service if you're currently not connected. The Status Info box to the right of each network resource in UserNet indicates the status of that service, as summarized here:

- **Green:** Connected and working
- **Yellow:** Trying to connect
- **Red:** Not connected

To make your connection, click the ppp0 button. The Status Info button should turn yellow, and perhaps you'll hear your modem make all kinds of weird sounds. When the connection is complete, the Status Info button will turn green, and you're online. If you want to browse the World Wide Web, just fire up Netscape Communicator, as discussed in Chapter 19, "Browsing the World Wide Web." To set up your email and newsgroup accounts, see Chapter 20, "Working with Email and Newsgroups."

## DISCONNECTING IN USERNET

When you've finished using the Internet, don't forget to disconnect from your ISP. Just click the ppp0 button in UserNet. The Status Info button will turn yellow as you're disconnecting, then turn red when you're no longer connected. To close the UserNet dialog box, just click its Exit button.

## CONFIGURING PPP IN KDE

There are a couple of ways you can give yourself easy access to the Internet in KDE. If you already set up your PPP account in GNOME as described in the previous section, you can just plop onto your KDE desktop a couple of shortcut icons to UserNet and Netscape. If you didn't set up an account in GNOME, you can use the kppp utility to set up your Internet access. The latter method is a bit more complicated, but if you're strictly a KDE person, it might be your best bet.

Before you use either approach, make sure you're logged in as root (the superuser) and you're at the KDE desktop. If you're currently in GNOME and you have installed KDE (as discussed in Chapter 10, "Installing and Using KDE"), you can use the Switchdesk program to switch over to KDE:

1. Open a terminal window in GNOME.
2. Enter the command `switchdesk`.
3. Select KDE from the options that appear.

4. Click the OK button.

You'll see a message indicating that you need to restart X to get to KDE. Click the OK button in that window. Then click the GNOME Main Menu button and choose Logout, Logout, Yes. If you're taken to the command prompt rather than directly to KDE, enter the command startx to restart X.

### MAKING A KDE SHORTCUT TO USERNET

If you set up UserNet in GNOME, the easiest way to give yourself access to the Internet from KDE is to simply create desktop shortcuts to the UserNet and Netscape programs. Assuming you're at the KDE desktop, just follow these steps:

1. Right-click the KDE desktop and choose New, Application.

2. Click the Clear button and then type UserNet as the new application's name.

> **Tip**
>
> Actually, in step 2 you're typing the icon's label, which can be anything you want. For example, you could type Get Online or something like that.

3. Click the OK button.

4. In the kfm dialog box that appears, click the Execute tab and type /usr/bin/usernet (all lowercase letters) as the command to execute, as in Figure 18.11.

**Figure 18.11**
Setting up a KDE desktop shortcut to launch UserNet.

5. If you want to change the icon picture, click the icon button and select an icon from the Select Icon dialog box that appears. Then click the OK button at the bottom of the Select Icon dialog box.

6. Click the OK button at the bottom of the kfm dialog box.

To test the new shortcut, just double-click it. The UserNet window should appear, looking just as it did in GNOME.

> **Tip**
>
> Here's another way to start UserNet from KDE at any time: Press Alt+F2, type the command usernet, and then press Enter.

## MAKING A KDE SHORTCUT TO NETSCAPE

Before you actually go online, you may want to give yourself quick access to Netscape Navigator as well. If UserNet is open, you can click its Exit button. Then follow these steps:

1.  Once again, right-click the KDE desktop and choose New, Application.
2.  Click the Clear button and then type `Netscape` (or whatever label you want for this new icon).
3.  Click the OK button.
4.  In the next dialog box that appears, click the Execute tab and type `/usr/bin/netscape` (all lowercase letters) as the command to execute.
5.  Once again, if you want to change the icon picture, click the icon button and select an icon from the Select Icon dialog box that appears, and then click its OK button. Figure 18.12 shows an example in which I selected the large Netscape N as the icon.

**Figure 18.12**
Setting up a KDE desktop shortcut to launch Netscape Navigator.

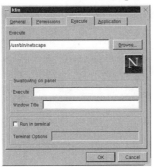

6.  Click the OK button at the bottom of the kfm dialog box.

To fully test both buttons, you need to make your Internet connection and then make sure you can open Netscape Navigator. The exact steps are as follows:

1.  Double-click your new desktop shortcut icon to UserNet.
2.  Click the ppp0 button and wait for the status indicator to turn green.
3.  Double-click the new Netscape shortcut icon on your desktop. (You may have to be patient—it can take several seconds for Netscape to load, especially the first time.)

You should now be able to browse the Web (Chapter 19), do email, participate in newsgroups (Chapter 20), and use other Internet services. Just don't forget to disconnect when you've finished—simply close the Netscape Navigator window, then click the ppp0 button in UserNet when you're ready.

**Tip**

For more information on customizing KDE's menus and panel, see its online help. Click the KDE Help button in its panel. Then view some of the help screens under "Getting the Most from KDE."

Whether or not you also want to create access via the kppp utility (described next) is a matter of personal preference. If you have any problems using your UserNet and Netscape buttons, perhaps setting up a kppp account will provide a solution. Also, kppp does have a handful of bells and whistles that UserNet doesn't, such as connection statistics, load monitoring, and so forth. To decide whether those items are worth your effort is, again, something you'll need to decide for yourself.

### CONFIGURING KPPP

kppp is automatically installed when you install KDE. However, its permissions are locked down pretty tight to prevent anyone but the superuser from setting it up, and even using it. So before you do anything else, you'll need to follow these steps:

1. Open a terminal window in KDE and enter the command `chmod 4711 /usr/bin/kppp` to extend the permissions of kppp.

2. Use your favorite text editor to open the `/etc/ppp/options` configuration file and remove the word *lock* from the file. Don't worry if the file ends up being empty.

> **Tip**
> From the KDE terminal window you can enter the command `kedit /etc/ppp/options` to complete step 2.

3. Close and save the modified `/etc/ppp/options` file.

These steps will give you the permissions you need as superuser to make changes to the kppp configuration. It will also allow regular users to gain access to the Internet through the PPP account you set up in the steps that follow.

Next it's time to set up the PPP account. You should have already installed your modem, set up an account with an ISP, and filled in as many blanks as possible in the third column of Table 18.1. Then, to get started in configuring kppp, follow these steps:

1. Click the K Start button and choose Internet, kppp.

2. You might see a brief message telling you that you can right-click a control to see a tooltip containing more information. If you don't want to be reminded anymore about that in the future, select the check box. Click the OK button.

3. In the kppp dialog box that appears, click the Setup button.

4. In the kppp Configuration dialog box that appears, click the New button to define a new account. The New Account dialog box appears.

5. In the Connection Name text box, type a name of your choosing to describe this account. You can type the ISP's name if you want.

6. In the Phone Number field, type the dial-up number provided by your ISP, (see line item 1 from Table 18.1). You can include the hyphen if you like (555-1234) or omit it (5551234).

7. Choose your authentication method (line item 2 from Table 18.1) from the Authentication drop-down list (see Figure 18.13).

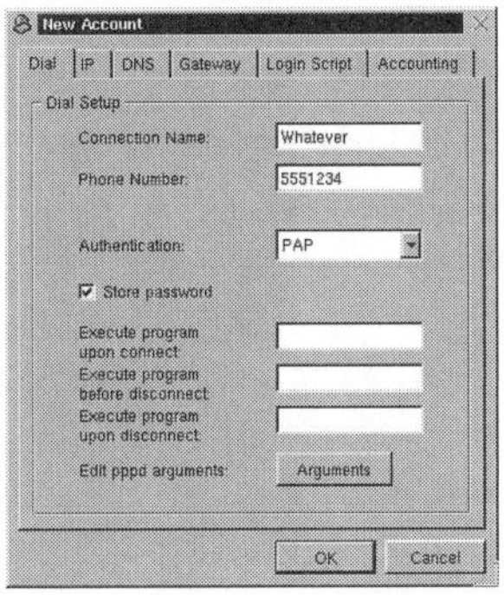

**Figure 18.13**
Sample kppp account name, dial-up number, and authentication type for a PPP Internet account.

8. Click the IP tab. If your ISP will be assigning your connection an IP address dynamically (the most likely scenario), choose the Dynamic IP Address option. Otherwise, choose the Static IP Address option and enter the IP Address and Subnet Mask provided by your ISP (line items 8 and 9).

9. Click the DNS tab. Next to Domain Name, type the default domain name provided by your ISP (line item 5).

10. In the DNS IP Address text box, type the primary nameserver IP address provided by your ISP (line item 6). Then click the Add button.

11. If your ISP gave you a secondary name server IP address (line item 7), type that into the DNS IP Address box and click the Add button again. The nameserver addresses should be listed in the DNS Address List box as shown in Figure 18.14.

**Figure 18.14**
The ISP domain name and primary and secondary nameservers have now been added to the DNS tab of kppp's New Account dialog box.

12. Click the OK button at the bottom of the New Account dialog box.

13. Click the OK button at the bottom of the kppp Configuration dialog box.

14. Click the Quit button at the bottom of the kppp dialog box.

That should be all you need to set up your PPP account in kppp. Now you're ready to take it for a spin.

PART
**III**

CH
**18**

### MAKING THE CONNECTION WITH KPPP

To test your new connection, as well as use it at any time in the future, follow these steps:

1. Click the K Start button.

2. Choose Internet, kppp from the menus. The kppp dialog box appears.

3. The account you just created should appear in the Connect To drop-down list (see Figure 18.15). If you've created several PPP accounts, choose the one you want to use from the list.

**Figure 18.15**
About to dial into an ISP using kppp.

4. Type your Login name (username) and password in the text boxes provided.

5. If you want to see a log of activity as the modem makes the connection to your ISP, choose the Show Log Window option.

6. Click the Connect button and wait for the connection to be made.

Once connected, you can browse the Web, do your email, and have access to other services as described in Chapters 19-20. If you haven't created a desktop shortcut to the Netscape program yet, you may want to read the section "Making a KDE Shortcut to Netscape" earlier in this chapter to give yourself easy access to that program.

### PROJECT: MORE RESOURCES

Modem communications can be a large and complex subject. In fact, one could probably write a book nearly the size of this one that deals strictly with modem communications in Linux. In this chapter I've tried to simplify things by focusing on the type of connection that the vast majority of you will want to make—namely, your basic PPP connection to an Internet service provider through a standard modem.

If you have any problems, or if you have some expertise in hardware and want to get deep into all the technical details and options available to you, here are some resources to consider. If you need reminders on accessing HOWTOs and other sources of information, please refer to Chapter 5. Otherwise, check out the following additional resources:

- ADSL mini-HOWTO (for Digital Subscriber Line accounts)
- Cable-Modem mini-HOWTO (for cable modems)
- Hardware HOWTO
- Linux Modem-Sharing mini-HOWTO at `www.linuxhq.com/HOWTO/mini/Windows-Modem-Sharing.html`
- Modem HOWTO
- PCMCIA HOWTO (for PC-Card modems used on laptops)

- Plug-and-Play HOWTO (for PnP modems and the isapnp program)
- Serial HOWTO
- PPP Daemon man page (man pppd)
- Chat program man page (man chat)
- Minicom man page (man minicom)
- Dip Program man page (man dip)
- If you have any problems with kppp, read through its built-in help screens. Just start kppp and click the Help button.

Also, do keep in mind that modem communications are a form of networking. You should be able to set up a basic dial-up account by following the steps provided in this chapter, without getting into all the thorny details of Linux network administration and the TCP/IP protocol used by the Internet. But on the other hand, a deeper understanding of general networking in Linux will make it easier to understand some of the topics you're bound to come across when viewing the resources described previously. Part IV of this book covers all the networking concepts. And Part V covers using Linux as an Internet server rather than purely as a client.

# CHAPTER 19

# BROWSING THE WORLD WIDE WEB

## In this chapter

# SURFING THE WEB

If you have any experience browsing the World Wide Web using Microsoft Internet Explorer or Netscape Navigator, you'll find that the process is pretty much the same in Linux. If you have a dial-up account, like the kind discussed in Chapter 18, "Connecting to the Internet," you first need to connect to the Internet using the Usernet or kppp program, whichever you prefer. Wait a moment for the connection to complete. If your computer is connected to the Internet through a LAN or some form of dedicated account, where you're connected 24 hours a day, seven days a week, you probably don't need to do anything to connect. To start browsing the Web, just fire up Netscape Navigator using whichever technique is most convenient for you at the moment:

- In GNOME, click the Netscape Communicator button in the Panel.
- Click the GNOME Main Menu button and choose Internet, Netscape Communicator.
- If you created a desktop shortcut in KDE, click that shortcut icon.
- Type the command netscape in a terminal window and press Enter.

The first time you start Netscape you'll need to need to accept its license agreement by clicking an Accept button. You'll also see one or more dialog boxes titled Netscape Error that tell you that Netscape has created a directory to be used as a cache (a place for storing Web pages and graphics that you view on your system). This is actually a normal event that occurs the first time a new user starts Netscape, and not an indication of a problem. You can click the OK button at the bottom of that dialog box to close the dialog box whenever you wish.

> **Note**
>
> Technically, the product you'll be using is called Netscape Communicator. But since everyone seems to call it just "Netscape," I'll do the same in this chapter.

When Netscape opens you may be shown a local Web page (one that's on your computer). The URL (Uniform Resource Locator) for that page will appear in the Location drop-down list, perhaps looking something like this:

```
file:/usr/doc/HTML/index.html
```

The file: part at the beginning of that URL tells you that you're currently viewing a file that's on your own system. To visit any Web page, just type its URL into the Location drop-down list and press Enter. If the site's URL starts with http://www: (as most do), you don't need to type that part. So for example, if you want to visit Red Hat's Web site, follow these steps:

1. Drag the mouse pointer through the URL currently shown in the Location drop-down list to select it.

2. Type the URL of the page you want to visit (redhat.com, for example).

3. Press Enter, and then wait.

Exactly how long it takes for the page to appear depends on the speed of your Internet connection, so you might need to be patient. Figure 19.1 shows Red Hat's home page at http://www.redhat.com on the day I visited. Of course, Web pages change all the time, so there's no telling how the page will look when you visit. Labels in the figure point out various components of the program that will be discussed in this chapter.

**Figure 19.1**
Red Hat's home page in Netscape Navigator.

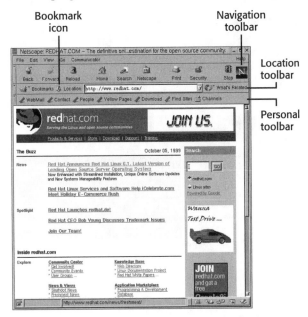

Bookmark icon

Navigation toolbar

Location toolbar

Personal toolbar

The first time you visit a page, it may take quite a while for the entire page to appear. However, when you do, portions of the page will be stored in your Internet disk cache on your hard disk. So future visits to that same site will go more quickly because Netscape will need to download only things that have changed since your last visit.

As you probably know, any underlined text in the page is likely to be a *hyperlink*—a link to some other page. Graphic images often act as links too. You can tell whether something is a link by resting the mouse pointer on it. If the mouse pointer changes to a small hand with the index finger pointing, the mouse pointer is resting on a link. To follow the link, just click it once using your left mouse button.

After you follow a link to a new page, you can use the Back button in Netscape's Navigation toolbar to return to the page you just came from. After you back up from one or more pages, the Forward button will become available. You can click that button to return to the page you just backed out of. Of course, at any time, you can go to a specific site simply by entering the site's URL into the Location drop-down list.

Netscape automatically keeps track of URLs that you type into the Location box. So it's not always necessary to retype the entire URL to return to a recently visited site. Instead, click the drop-down list button, as in Figure 19.2, and then click the URL of the site you want to revisit. You can also find a list of recently visited pages on the Go menu. Just click Go in Netscape's menu bar, then click on the URL of the site you want to visit.

**Figure 19.2**
Netscape's History list keeps track of URLs you typed into the Location drop-down list.

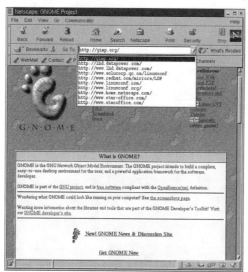

## SEARCHING THE WEB

Searching the Web via Linux and Netscape is a simple matter of going to your favorite *search engine* and looking for any word or phrase that interests you. You can also look up definitions of terms in dictionaries and glossaries. Some of the more popular resources for finding information on the Web are listed in Table 19.1.

TABLE 19.1    SOME POPULAR SEARCH ENGINES AND THEIR URLS

| Site | URL |
| --- | --- |
| About.com | `http://www.about.com` |
| Acronyms and Abbreviations | `http://www.ucc.ie/cgi-bin/acronym` |
| AltaVista | `http://www.altavista.com` |
| Ask Jeeves | `http://www.aj.com` |
| C\|Net | `http://www.cnet.com` |
| C\|Net Tech Glossary | `http://www.cnet.com/Resources/Info/Glossary` |
| Dogpile | `http://www.dogpile.com` |
| Excite | `http://www.excite.com` |
| GoTo | `http://www.goto.com` |
| HotBot | `http://www.hotbot.com` |
| Infoseek | `http://infoseek.go.com` |
| LookSmart | `http://www.looksmart.com` |
| Lycos | `http://www.lycos.com` |
| Netscape Search | `http://search.netscape.com` |
| Snap | `http://www.snap.com` |
| WebCrawler | `http://www.webcrawler.com` |
| Yahoo! | `http://www.yahoo.com` |

If you're specifically looking for information and documentation for Linux, or even Red Hat Linux, Red Hat's Support site will probably be your best bet. The URL for that page is `http://support.redhat.com`. On most of Red Hat's Web pages you'll also find a search bar, as in Figure 19.3, where you can enter any word or phrase to search for. Then you can opt to search just `redhat.com` or a wider range of sites devoted to Linux. Click the Go button, and your search begins.

**Tip**    My own Web site at www.coolnerds.com offers a handy tool for quickly searching multiple engines and dictionaries for a word or phrase.

Clicking the Search button in Netscape's Navigation toolbar takes you directly to Netscape's search site. The People, Yellow Pages, Download, Find Sites, and Channels buttons in the Personal Toolbar offer handy tools for finding people, businesses, and Web sites. The What's Related button in Netscape provides a drop-down list of search engines, stock quotes, news stories, and more. Definitely worth a click!

**Figure 19.3**
Red Hat's search bar makes it easy to search their site, or several Linux sites, for Linux-specific information.

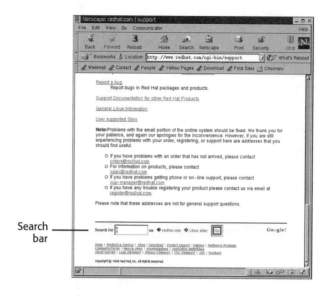

Search bar ————

When you get to a Web page, you can search for any word or phrase within that page only. This technique is helpful when you're viewing a lengthy page or list of links and don't want to read through everything to find a specific topic. To search the current page, choose Edit, Find in Page from Netscape's menu bar, or press Alt+F. The Netscape:Find dialog box will appear. Type the word or phrase you're looking for. If you want to find only text that matches the upper/lowercase letters you typed, choose Case Sensitive. If you want to search backward (above the cursor), choose Find Backwards. Then click the Find button to start the search.

If your desired word or phrase is found, it will be highlighted on the page. (You may need to move the Find dialog box around to see what's behind it.) You can click the Find button repeatedly to find each occurrence of your word or phrase. When you get to the end of the document and no more text matches your search, you'll see a message to that effect and be given the option to start searching from the top again. When you've finished searching the current page, click the Close button in the Find dialog box.

# KEEPING TRACK OF FAVORITE PAGES

As you gain experience using the Web, you'll no doubt find pages that you want to visit on a regular basis. For example, news sites, stock market sites, auctions, and others might be on your daily or weekly visit schedule. Rather than memorizing all the necessary URLs and typing them in each time, you can create a collection of *bookmarks*. As in a real book, each bookmark is a link to a specific page on the Web.

Netscape comes with many sample bookmarks already set up for you. To view them, click the Bookmarks button on the Location toolbar. You'll see several categories of bookmarks, such as Business and Finance, Computers and Internet, and so forth already on the menu. Clicking any category displays links to specific pages within that category (see Figure 19.4). Clicking on any option within a category takes you straight to the appropriate Web page.

**Figure 19.4**
Sample book-marks within the Business and Finance category in Netscape.

Use the textured button at the left side of any toolbar to open, close, or move the toolbar. You can also show/hide toolbars by choosing options from Netscape's View menu.

When you're browsing on your own and come to a site that you think you'd like to revisit in the future, you can do whichever of the following is most convenient to bookmark the site:

- Click the Bookmarks button in the Location toolbar and choose Add Bookmark.
- Press Alt+K on the keyboard.

Nothing special will happen on the screen. However, the next time you open the Bookmarks menu, you'll see the page's title at the bottom of the Bookmarks menu. You can just click that item to return to the site at any time in the future.

To create a quick desktop shortcut to a favorite Web page, drag the green icon to the left of the Location label in the Location toolbar onto your desktop, and drop it there. You can also put such shortcuts in folders by dragging the same icon into a folder in your file manager.

## ORGANIZING BOOKMARKS

As your collection of bookmarks grows, you'll probably want to categorize links for easier access. To organize your bookmarks, click the Bookmarks button and choose Edit Bookmarks. Or just press Ctrl+B. The Communicator Bookmarks dialog box shown in Figure 19.5 appears. Each folder in the list represents a category. You can expand a folder to see its contents by clicking the plus sign (+) to the left of the category name. To hide the contents of the folder once again, click the minus sign (-) to the left of the category name.

PART

**III**

CH

**19**

**Figure 19.5**

The Communicator Bookmarks dialog box for editing Netscape bookmarks.

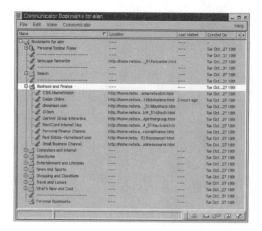

To reorganize bookmarks, just drag them. For example, if you wanted to move a bookmark from the bottom of the menu into the Personal Bookmarks folder, you'd simply drag that bookmark to the appropriate folder and drop it there. To arrange bookmarks within a category, such as when you want to put them into alphabetical order, just drag the bookmark within its category to its new position.

**Tip**

To move a bunch of bookmarks into a folder, click the first bookmark that you want to move. Then Shift+Click the last bookmark that you want to move. Ctrl+Click individual bookmarks to select/de-select them. Then drag any highlighted bookmarks into the desired folder.

You can also rearrange bookmarks and folders using menus or the keyboard. Just click the item you want to move, so that it's highlighted. Then do one of the following:

■ Choose View, Move Up, or press Shift+~UA to move the item up.

■ Choose View, Move Down, or press Shift+~DA to move the item down.

## RENAMING AND DELETING BOOKMARKS

If you don't like a bookmark's description, right-click the bookmark and choose Bookmark Properties from the pop-up menu. Change the Name entry for the bookmark to anything you like. You can also enter a description of the site, for your own future reference.

To delete a bookmark, just right-click it and choose Delete from the pop-up menu.

**Tip**

Whenever you need a reminder of the basic skills described in this chapter or want to learn about some other feature, choose Help, Help Contents from Netscape's menu bar. Or press the Help (F1) key.

### CREATING BOOKMARK FOLDERS

You can also create your own folders for storing personal bookmarks. To create a new folder, follow these steps:

1. Click the folder beneath which you want to place the new folder. (In other words, the new folder will appear below whatever folder you click on.)

2. Choose File, New Folder from the Communicator Bookmarks menu bar. Type in a name for the folder and then click the OK button.

Once the folder exists, you can drag any bookmark onto the folder's icon to move that bookmark into the new folder.

### SEARCHING BOOKMARKS

If your collection of bookmarks gets really big and you start forgetting what's where, you can actually search your collection of bookmarks for any word or phrase. In the Communicator Bookmarks dialog box, choose Edit, Find in Bookmarks. Type the word or phrase that you want to search for. You can also choose options to broaden or narrow your search. For instance, you can search bookmark names, URLs (Location), Descriptions, or any combination thereof. You can make the search case-sensitive or limit the search to only whole words that match your text. Click the Find button to begin your search.

## SAVING AND SHARING BOOKMARKS

As time goes by and you put effort into collecting and organizing bookmarks, that collection of bookmarks will become increasingly valuable to you. You can store bookmarks in separate files for safe-keeping on floppy disks and such. You can also maintain multiple bookmark collections by saving each collection to its own file. And you can also share your collection of favorites with other users. To get started, save your current bookmark collection by following these steps:

1. In the Communicator Bookmarks dialog box choose File, Save As.

2. Type in a filename, such as *myBookmarks*, then choose OK.

If you want to create a backup copy of those bookmarks to a floppy disk, just copy the file you created (*myBookmarks*, in this example) onto a floppy disk. If you want to send your bookmark collection to another user over the Internet, you can attach the bookmark file to an email message, as discussed in Chapter 20, "Working with Email and Newsgroups."

To open a saved bookmark list, follow these steps:

1. In the Communicator Bookmarks dialog box choose File, Open Bookmarks File.

2. In the left column of the Open Bookmark File dialog box that appears, work your way to the directory that contains the bookmark file you want to open.

3. In the right column, click on the name of the bookmark file you want to open, then click the OK button.

PART
III

CH
19

## CHECKING WHETHER FAVORITE PAGES HAVE CHANGED

Besides helping you keep track of favorite pages, bookmarks can let you see, at a glance, which sites have changed since your last visit. To use this feature, first get to the Communicator Bookmarks dialog box. Then follow these steps:

1. If you want to check only one or a few bookmarks, select the ones you want to check. Click the first one that you want to check, and Ctrl+Click additional bookmarks to check.

2. Choose View, Update Bookmarks.

3. In the dialog box that appears, choose All Bookmarks to check all of your bookmarks, or Selected Bookmarks to check only those bookmarks you selected in step 1 (if any).

4. Click the Start button.

It will take a little while for Navigator to check all the bookmarked sites to see if they've changed since your last visit. When done, you'll see a message telling you how many bookmarks were checked and how many have changed since your last visit.

If a page has changed, Navigator puts a special mark on the page's bookmark icon. If Netscape wasn't able to reach the site, for whatever reason, a question mark will appear on that site's bookmark icon.

## PUTTING BOOKMARKS ON YOUR PERSONAL TOOLBAR

The Personal toolbar is highly customizable. The buttons on it are really just examples of what you might want to put on the toolbar. You can add buttons to that toolbar—or replace existing buttons—to suit your own tastes.

There are a couple of ways you can add a bookmark to the Personal toolbar. If you're currently viewing a page for which you'd like to create a toolbar bookmark, just drag the bookmark icon onto the Personal toolbar, and drop it there.

> **Note**     The Bookmark icon is just to the left of the label Location in the Location toolbar.

If you've already bookmarked a page, you can copy that existing bookmark onto your Personal toolbar. In fact, you can copy an entire bookmark category onto the Personal toolbar to give yourself easier access to those sites. To do this, follow these steps:

1. Click the Bookmarks option in the Location toolbar and choose Edit Bookmarks.

2. Select a bookmark or bookmark category by clicking it once.

3. Choose File, Add Selection to Toolbar from the Bookmarks window's menu bar.

If you add too many buttons to your Personal toolbar, there won't be room to display them all across the screen. You can, of course, delete any buttons you don't need. Or rename existing buttons to make their titles smaller. Follow these steps to customize the Personal toolbar in this manner:

1. If you aren't already in the Bookmarks window, click the Bookmarks option in the Location toolbar and choose Edit Bookmarks.

2. Expand the Personal toolbar folder category if it's currently collapsed. Each item listed in that folder represents a button on the Personal toolbar:

   - To delete a button, right-click its name in the list, and choose Delete.
   - To retitle a button, right-click its name, choose Bookmark Properties, and type a new label in the Name textbox.
   - To rearrange buttons on the Personal toolbar, drag and drop the item's icon to some new location within the list.

3. Click the OK button.

You can even designate any existing category of bookmarks to be your Personal toolbar buttons. Again, if you're not already in the Communicator Bookmarks window, click the Bookmarks option in the Location toolbar and choose Edit Bookmarks. Select the bookmark folder whose items you want to appear on the Personal toolbar. Then choose View, Set as Toolbar Folder from the menu bar within the Communicator Bookmarks window.

# PERSONALIZING NETSCAPE

There are many other ways to personalize how Netscape Navigator looks and acts on your computer. However, to cover them all here would get us too far off the topic that's at the heart of this book (namely, Linux). To view your options, though, choose Edit, Preferences from Netscape's menu bar. The Netscape: Preferences dialog box appears (see Figure 19.6). The left column represents categories of options. You can expand and contract a category by clicking on the triangle to the left of the category name.

**Figure 19.6**
Choosing Edit, Preferences from Netscape's menu bar displays the dialog box shown here.

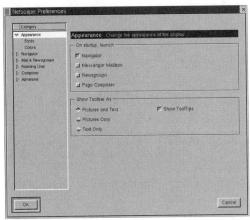

Many of the items are self-explanatory. But there's also plenty of help available to you. To view the help screens for customizing Netscape, you'll need to close the Preferences dialog box. Then choose Help, Help from Netscape's menu bar. In the left column of the help window that appears, choose Browsing the Web. Then scroll down though the right column until you get to the heading titled "Customizing Your Browser."

# CASE STUDY: CREATING A LIBRARY OF LINKS

If there's anything a Linux user needs—be it a newbie or an old pro—it's access to information. Linux is so "huge" in its scope, so highly configurable, and evolving at such a rapid rate, I doubt one could ever get to a point where they "know it all." The Web, of course, is always a repository of information on virtually all subjects known to humankind.

One thing you can do to expand your own information horizons is to create a bookmark folder in Netscape that contains links to all your favorite Linux Web sites. As you may recall, to add a site to your bookmarks collection, you just need to visit the site and choose Bookmarks, Add Bookmark from the Personal toolbar. Or you can just press Alt+K. Table 19.2 lists some sites that you might want to visit and bookmark to get your own collection started.

**TABLE 19.2   MY FAVORITE LINUX WEB SITES**

| Site Name | URL |
| --- | --- |
| Filewatcher.org | http://filewatcher.org |
| FreshMeat.net | http://www.freshmeat.net |
| GNOME Home Page | http://www.gnome.org |
| GNU Project Home Page | http://www.gnu.org |
| Informit | http://www.informit.com |
| KDE Home Page | http://www.kde.org |
| Lilo.org | http://www.lilo.org |
| Linux Documentation Project | http://www.redhat.com/mirrors/LDP |
| Linux Newbie Administrator Guide | http://www.magma.ca/~bklimas |
| Linux Online (Linux.org) | http://www.linux.org |
| Linuxberg Software Downloads | http://www.linuxberg.com |
| LinuxCare | http://www.linuxcare.com |
| LinuxConf Home Page | http://www.solucorp.qc.ca/linuxconf |
| Macmillan USA | http://www.mcp.com |
| Man pages, FAQs, HOWTOs | http://www.redhat.com/mirrors/LDP/docs.html |
| Netscape | http://home.netscape.com |
| Netscape Plugins | http://home.netscape.com/plugins/by_platform.html |

**TABLE 19.2    CONTINUED**

| Site Name | URL |
|---|---|
| Que Publishing | `http://www.quecorp.com` |
| Red Hat Knowledge Base | `http://www.redhat.com/knowledgebase` |
| Red Hat Linux User's FAQ | `http://www.best.com/~aturner/RedHat-FAQ` |
| Red Hat Support | `http://www.redhat.com/support` |
| RPM.org | `http://www.rpm.org/` |
| Slashdot News | `http://www.slashdot.org` |

When you've finished building your collection, you can organize the Web sites into a new folder called Linux. Click the Bookmarks button in Netscape's Location toolbar, and choose Edit Bookmarks. In the list, click the category that will be above the new category you're about to create (that is, click on Entertainment and Lifestyles to keep categories in alphabetical order). Then, in the Communicator Bookmarks dialog box choose File, New Folder, name the folder Linux, then click the OK button.

Down at the bottom of the list, click the first of the bookmarks you added. Then hold down the Shift key and click the last item in the list. The entire range of bookmarks will be selected. You can then drag the selection to the new Linux folder and drop the items into that category. Once the items are in the folder, you can right-click any item and choose Bookmark Properties to change its name. You can then arrange the bookmarks into alphabetical order, if you like, by dragging them up and down the list. It may take a few minutes, but it's a handy set of links to have organized. Figure 19.7 shows how my list looked after spending a few minutes getting it organized.

**Figure 19.7**
A new bookmark category named Linux with some bookmarks in it.

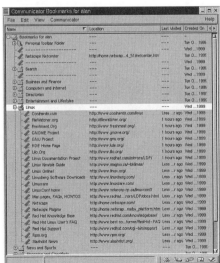

When you've finished organizing, you can click on the new Linux category folder again to select it. Then choose File, Add Selection to Toolbar from the Communicator Bookmarks window. Then choose File, Exit to close the Communicator Bookmarks dialog box. Your Personal toolbar will now contain a button labeled Linux. Clicking the button will give you instant one-click access to all those Web sites (see Figure 19.8).

**Figure 19.8**
Collection of Linux-related bookmarks added to the Personal toolbar in Netscape.

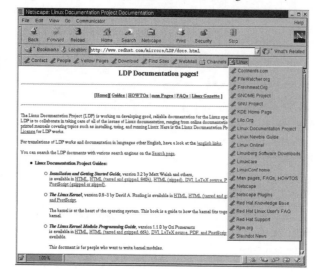

# CHAPTER 20

# WORKING WITH EMAIL AND NEWSGROUPS

**I**n this chapter

# Setting Up Your Accounts

Netscape Communicator is a real "one-tool-fits-all" kind of application. And, as you'll learn in this chapter, you can use Netscape to send and receive email, as well as to participate in Usenet newsgroups. I suppose anyone buying this book already knows what Internet email and newsgroups are about. So I won't go into any long explanations about those services. Instead, we'll start out with configuring Netscape Communicator to use those services.

Before you proceed, though, make sure you've installed a modem and set up an account with an Internet service provider, as discussed in Chapter 18, "Connecting to the Internet." You should also have filled in line items 10 through 14 of Table 18.1 in that chapter. If your ISP offers a direct *newsfeed*, you should have gotten a NNTP server address as well. However, it's not entirely necessary to have an NNTP server to access newsgroups. As you'll learn later in this chapter, you can also access newsgroups through the World Wide Web and Netscape Navigator.

## Setting Up Your Email Account

To set up your email and newsgroup account services in Netscape, follow these steps:

1. Start Netscape Communicator, as discussed in Chapter 19, "Browsing the World Wide Web."
2. Choose Edit, Preferences from Netscape's menu bar.
3. Expand the Mail & Newsgroups category.
4. Click the Identify option.
5. Type your name, as you want it to appear in the header section of email messages you send out, under Your Name.
6. Type your email address (line item 10 from Table 18.1) under Email Address.
7. If your return email address is different from the email address you just entered, type that other email address under Reply-To Address.
8. If you'd like to include a company or organization affiliation in your return address, type that under Organization.
9. You can leave the Signature File entry as is, pointing to a file named .signature in your home directory. Later in this chapter, you'll learn how to set up that signature file.

At this point your dialog box should look something like the example shown in Figure 20.1. Obviously, yours should contain information that's relevant to your email account rather than my hypothetical account.

Next, you need to fill in information about the mail servers provided by your ISP account. Here's how:

1. Click the Mail Servers option in the left pane of the Netscape Preferences dialog box.
2. Under Incoming Mail Servers, click on pop to select it, then click the Edit button.

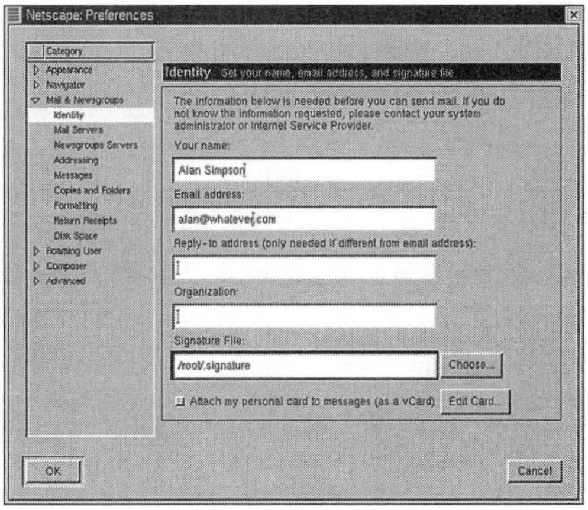

**Figure 20.1**
Sample Identity dialog box filled out for hypothetical email account.

3. At Server Name, type the address of your incoming (pop3) mail server, line item 11 from Table 18.1.

4. Leave the Server Type button set to POP (unless your ISP told you to use MoveMail or IMAP instead).

5. At User Name, type the email username provided by your ISP (line item 13 from Table 18.1).

6. If you don't want to type in your password each time you check your email, select the Remember Password option.

**Caution**

If you share this computer with other users and select Remember Password, it's possible that those other users could download and view your email. Don't select the Remember Password option if privacy is important.

7. If you want Netscape to check for mail automatically on a regular schedule, choose the Check for Mail option, and specify how often you want Netscape to check for mail.

8. You'll probably want to have Netscape download messages from your mail server automatically, so leave that last option, Automatically Download Any New Messages selected. Figure 20.2 shows some data filled in for my hypothetical account.

**Figure 20.2**
The General tab filled out for defining an incoming mail server.

9. Click the POP tab.

10. If you want to leave your email messages on the server after downloading them, select the first option on the POP tab.

---

**To Leave or Not to Leave Messages on the Server**

If you choose the option to leave messages on your email server, your collection of messages will grow indefinitely. Many ISPs charge for storage space. So as a rule, you don't want to leave copies of messages on their server.

There are situations, though, where you may want to leave copies of messages on the server. For example, let's say you have a laptop or home computer that you can use to access your email account, but you want to keep all your messages on your "main" computer in the office. If you select Leave Messages on Server on your home or laptop computer, you can view your email messages without removing them from the server.

Later, when you access your email from your main computer in the office, the messages will be downloaded once again. That way, you can still store email messages in special files for future reference on that computer. If you *didn't* select Leave Messages on Server on your laptop or home computer, you'll end up with some messages stored on those computers and other messages stored on your main computer. This can make it difficult to find messages that you need to save and reply to at some point in the future because you need to remember which machine each message is stored in.

If you also select the second option on the POP tab, you'll have the option of leaving a message on the server or deleting it on the spot. For example, while reading your email from your home or laptop computer, you could delete any junk mail messages right then and there. When you get to your main computer and download your email messages, the junk mail will already be gone.

---

11. If you selected the first option in the POP tab, you can select the second option to select email messages to delete on a case-by-case basis.

12. Click the OK button to save your settings.

Next, you need to define your Outgoing (SMTP) Mail Server as follows:

1. Next to Outgoing (SMTP) Mail Server, enter the server name provided by your ISP (line item 12 from Table 18.1).

2. If your ISP requires a username for outgoing mail, type that name into the Outgoing Mail Server User Name textbox. Most ISPs don't require such a name, so you can probably leave that option empty. Figure 20.3 shows the Mail Servers dialog box filled in with some hypothetical data.

## SETTING UP YOUR NEWSGROUP ACCOUNT

If your ISP gave you a news server or NNTP account address, you can follow these steps to set up your local newsfeed account:

1. Click the Newsgroup Servers option in the left pane of the Netscape Properties dialog box.

2. Click the Add button to define a new account.

3. Type the news server account name provided by your ISP (line item 15 from Table 18.1) next to the Server label.

4. If you want to prevent other users (including kids) from accessing newsgroups through this account, select the Always Use Name and Password option (see Figure 20.4).

**Figure 20.3**
The Mail Servers dialog box in Netscape Preferences with some hypothetical data filled in.

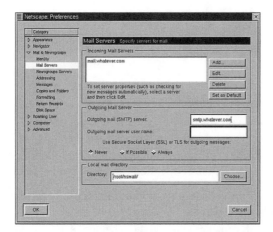

If your news server requires that you always log on with that user name and password, you also want to select the Always Use Name and Password option as well.

**Figure 20.4**
Hypothetical news server and options filled in.

5.  Click the OK button to save your settings.

There are other options you can experiment with later, after you're sure your accounts are working. For now, we'll stick with the basics to try to keep things as simple as possible. That way, if you have any problems later, it will be easier to track them down and correct them.

To save all your settings and exit Netscape for the time being, follow these steps:

1.  Click the OK button in the Netscape Preferences dialog box.
2.  Close Netscape by clicking its Close (X) button or by choosing File, Exit from its menu bar.

## CREATING YOUR SIGNATURE FILE

A signature file contains the text that you want to appear at the end of every message you send. Creating the signature file saves you the trouble of having to type all that information at the end of every message you write. Each user's signature file is stored in a hidden file named .signature on the user's home directory. So, if you're the superuser (root), your signature file will be stored in /root/.signature.

PART
III

CH
20

To see if you already have a signature file, open a terminal window and enter the `ls` command with the `-a` (all) option to view the contents of your home directory, as in the following example:

```
ls -a ~
```

You can create or edit your signature file using any text editor. For example, in GNOME you can use gEdit (click the Main Menu button, choose Applications, gEdit). In KDE you can use kedit (K button, Applications, Text Editor). If you already have a signature file that you want to edit, choose File, Open from your editor's menu bar, and open the `.signature` file on your home directory. To create a new signature file, don't open anything.

You can type any text you like into your signature file, there's nothing technical here. At the very least you'll probably want to type your name and return email address. Some people like to add in a little saying or graphic images composed of characters like this (a guy peeking over a fence):

```
              o o
- - - - - - - - - - - - -U- - - - - - - - - - - - -
```

In Figure 20.5 I've inserted a blank line (by pressing the Enter key) and typed in my name, email address, and Web site URL. Not terribly amusing, but useful.

> **Tip**
>
> Keep your signature lines to fewer than 80 characters, so the lines don't wrap and mess up the effect.

**Figure 20.5**

A sample signature file. This text will automatically appear at the end of messages you send out.

When you've finished typing your signature file, close your text editor program. When asked about saving the file, choose Yes. If this is a new file and you're logged in as the superuser, save it to your home directory as `.signature` by entering the filename as in either of the following:

```
~/.signature
```

```
/root/signature
```

# DOING INTERNET EMAIL

You can use Netscape Communicator to compose, send, and receive email messages. If you have a dial-up account, connect to your ISP as discussed in Chapter 18. Once you're online, start up Netscape and choose Communicator, Messenger from its menu bar (or just press Alt+2). The Netscape Mail & Newsgroups component opens (see Figure 20.6).

**Figure 20.6**

The Netscape Mail & Newsgroups components lets you compose, send, and read email messages.

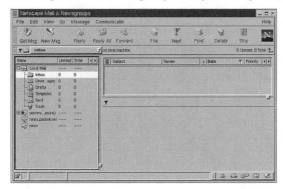

## COMPOSING AND SENDING EMAIL

Composing and sending an email message is pretty easy in Netscape. I'll cover the basics here, but again, since this is a book on Linux, I don't want to get into all the Netscape options and details. Once you've learned the basics, you can expand your knowledge by choosing Help, Help from the Mail & Newsgroups menu bar. Then click Using Email in the left column of the NetHelp window that appears. For starters, though, here's how you compose and send an email message:

1. Click the New Msg button in the toolbar. A window titled Compose appears.
2. Type the email address of the recipient in the To box.

> **Tip**
>
> To test your email, send a message to your own email address.

PART

**III**

CH

**20**

3. Press Tab or click in the Subject textbox. Then type a brief description of your message. This will appear in the header (one-line description) of the recipient's email program.
4. Press Tab or click within the body of the message.
5. Type the body of the message. You can use the Backspace and Delete keys, as well as standard editing techniques used in most text editors, to make changes and corrections.

6. If you want to check your spelling before sending off the message, click the Spelling button in the toolbar. Each "suspect" word will be highlighted, and you can choose to replace that word with a word listed under Suggestions or ignore the suspect word if it's already correct. Click Done when the spelling-checker reaches the end of the message.

7. Figure 20.7 shows a sample email message I addressed to myself (my real email address). When you're ready to send your message, click the Send button near the upper left corner of the Compose window.

**Figure 20.7**
Sample email message, ready to be sent to me at alan@coolnerds.com.

You may see a message indicating that some recipients may not be able to receive mail that's formatted with HTML. If you don't use any HTML formatting in your message, this is a non-issue. So you can choose Send in Plain Text Only, then click the Send button. You may see a brief message in the status bar of the Compose window as the message is sent. Then the Compose window will disappear, and you'll be returned to the Mail & Newsgroups component.

> **Note**
> HTML is a formatting language mainly used to design Web pages. You can learn more about that from the Sending Messages section of the NetHelp window for the Mail & Newsgroups component.

Depending on how your email is configured, the message might be placed in your Unsent Messages folder rather than being sent out to the Internet immediately. If so, you'll see the number of messages that are waiting to be sent in the left column of the Mail & Newsgroups component. If the total number of messages waiting to be sent is greater than zero and you want to send those messages now, choose File, Send Unsent Messages from the menu bar. If a message indicates that you're not online, connect to your ISP through User net or the kppp program, as described in Chapter 18. Then choose File, Send Unsent Messages again.

## READING AND REPLYING TO EMAIL

To check your email, you need to first download to your own computer any messages that are waiting on your Internet mail server. That's simple to do:

1. Click the Get Msg button in the upper left corner of the Mail & Newsgroups component.

2. If prompted, enter your email password (line item 14 from Table 18.1), and then click the OK button. You'll see a progress indicator as new messages are retrieved from the server.

When all the messages have been downloaded to your computer, you'll see the message headers in the top-right pane of the Mail & Newsgroups component. To read a message, just click its header. The full content of the message appears in the lower pane, as shown in the example in Figure 20.8.

**Figure 20.8**
Reading a sample email message I sent to myself.

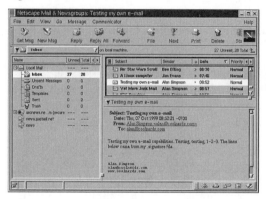

After reading the message, you can do any of the following:

- To reply to the message, click the Reply button in the toolbar. Type your reply, then click the Send button in the upper-left corner of the Compose window.

- If you want to pass the message onto someone else, click the Forward button in the toolbar. Type the new recipient's email address in the To box, and then click the Send button.

- To delete the message, click the Delete message in the Mail & Newsgroups component toolbar.

- To keep the message in your Inbox (perhaps to deal with it later), simply do nothing.

You can also create subfolders under your Inbox folder to store messages that you don't want to deal with right away, but don't want to keep in your Inbox either. Just right-click the Inbox folder name and choose New Subfolder. Type in a folder name (such as Pending or whatever). To place the folder beneath your Inbox, choose Inbox from the drop-down list. Then click the OK button. You can create as many subfolders as you wish to organize your messages into whatever categories are appropriate for you.

To move a message from your Inbox into a subfolder, right-click the message header and choose Move Message. Then choose the appropriate folder and subfolder. To view messages in a subfolder, just click the subfolder name in the left column of the Mail & Newsgroups component window.

And that pretty much covers all the basics of sending and receiving email. Again, you can learn a lot more from Netscape's built-in Help screens. In this book, however, it's time to cover the basics of participating in Usenet newsgroups.

# PARTICIPATING IN USENET NEWSGROUPS

Usenet newsgroups are a great resource of information on virtually any topic you can think of. Unlike the Web, where people post pages of information, newsgroups are more like an open, public email service. When you *post* a message to a newsgroup, everyone in the newsgroup can read your message. This is a great way to ask a question to a whole bunch of experts in two seconds flat. There's a good chance someone will answer your question within the next 24 hours.

Newsgroup messages are also *archived*, meaning that old questions and answers are kept on the server for several months, perhaps longer. So often, you don't even need to post a question to get an answer. If you just browse through the archived messages, you may find that someone else has already asked the same question. And perhaps some expert has already answered that question.

There are a couple of ways to participate in newsgroups. If your ISP gave you an account for accessing Usenet newsgroups, this means you have a *direct newsfeed*, and you can handle newsgroup messages using the same basic techniques that you use to handle email. If your ISP doesn't offer a direct newsfeed, you can browse through newsgroups via the World Wide Web and Netscape Navigator. Using the techniques described in Chapter 19, just go to www.deja.com. Once you get to the Deja.com home page, you can choose the Help and User Tour options on that page to learn more about participating in newsgroups through your Web browser.

First, you'll be bombarded with a fair amount of jargon when you start getting into newsgroups. The following list covers the main buzzwords you'll encounter while participating in newsgroups:

- Each message in a newsgroup is called an *article*, a *post*, or a *message*.
- A series of posts launched from a single question or other message is called a *thread*.
- *Lurking* is hanging around a newsgroup to see what's being discussed, without actually participating in the group. It's OK to lurk because you'll want to know what's going on in a newsgroup before you get involved.
- A *moderated* newsgroup is one where editorial people weed out posts that are obnoxious or irrelevant to the newsgroup, improving the overall quality of information that the group offers.

- An *unmoderated* newsgroup is one where nobody oversees the content, and anything goes.

- A *poster* is a person who posts articles to the group.

- *Spamming* is posting advertisements or any other junk mail and trying to disguise it as a valid post. Spamming is *heavily* frowned upon.

- *Flaming* is sending nasty messages to someone in a newsgroup. If you spam a group, you will get flamed!

There are thousands (if not tens of thousands) of newsgroups on the Internet. The name of the group gives you some indication of the topic that the group discusses. Newsgroup names generally follow the pattern:

`category.subcategory.sub-subcategory`

The first category name is the broadest description of the group. Subsequent category names narrow down the subject to a specific topic. Common category names, the subjects they encompass, and examples are listed in Table 20.1.

**TABLE 20.1   EXAMPLES OF COMMON NEWSGROUP CATEGORIES**

| Main Category | Subjects | Example |
| --- | --- | --- |
| alt | Alternative lifestyles and topics | `alt.alien.visitors` |
| bionet | Biology | `bionet.biophysics` |
| biz | Business | `biz.marketplace.jobs` |
| comp | Computers | `comp.os.linux.answers` |
| law | Legal issues | `law.library` |
| misc | Miscellaneous | `misc.creativity` |
| news | Usenet news | `news.newusers.questions` |
| rec | Recreation | `rec.pets.dogs` |
| sci | Science | `sci.physics` |
| soc | Social issues | `soc.feminism` |
| talk | Discussions and opinions | `talk.philosophy` |

PART

**III**

CH

**20**

For the rest of this chapter, I'll assume you do have a direct newsfeed and that you've already set up your modem and know how to connect to the Internet as discussed in Chapter 18. Also, you should have already specified your news server name as discussed under "Setting Up Your Newsgroup Account" earlier in this chapter.

## EXPLORING THE NEWSGROUPS

The first step in exploring the newsgroups is to determine exactly which newsgroups are available from your local news server. Here's how you do that:

1. Start Netscape Communicator.

2. Choose Communicator, Messenger from its menu bar, or press Alt+2 to open the Mail & Newsgroups component.

3. Click the name of your local news server in the left column.

4. Right-click the name of that news server and choose Subscribe to Newsgroups.

A new dialog box will appear. If this is the first time you've ever visited your local news server, it may take several minutes for the names of all the available newsgroups to be downloaded to your computer. A progress indicator at the bottom of that dialog box will keep you informed of how the download is going. When the download is finished, a list of newsgroups that are available on your news server will appear.

Some of the newsgroup names will have a + sign to the left. The + sign indicates that there are multiple categories within that group. Clicking the + sign expands the category so that you can see the groups within that category. For example, in Figure 20.9 I've clicked the + sign next to the news.* category to see all the newsgroups with the news as their main category name. Some of those categories have subcategories within them. For example, news.admin.* contains 14 groups. Expanding that category would reveal all the newsgroups that start with news.admin, such as news.admin.announce, news.admin.censorship, and so forth. Newsgroups that contain messages that you haven't read yet are shown in boldface with the number of unread messages off to the right. If this is your first visit, any newsgroup that has one or more messages in it will be boldfaced in your list because you haven't read any messages yet.

**Figure 20.9**
Names of newsgroups that are available on your local news server.

There are likely to be thousands of newsgroups in your list, and you might not be interested in reading through all their names. You can limit the list to newsgroup names that contain some word you're interested in. For example, you might want to view all newsgroups that contain the word "linux." Or you may want to take a look at all the newsgroup names that contain the word "newbie" or "answers," which are good for beginners. To search the newsgroup names and narrow your list down, follow these steps:

1. Click the Search tab.

2. Type the word that describes your interest into the Search textbox.

3. Click the Search Now button.

The list of newsgroup names that appears all contain the word you entered in the Search textbox, as in Figure 20.10 where I've searched for newsgroups that contain the word "linux."

**Figure 20.10**
Newsgroup names that contain the word "linux."

## SUBSCRIBING TO A NEWSGROUP

To see the messages in a newsgroup, whether just to lurk or to participate, you need to *subscribe* to the newsgroup. No, it doesn't cost any money, and you can unsubscribe at any time. Subscribing is simply a way of telling Netscape which newsgroups you're interested in. That way, Netscape will know which newsgroups you want to explore in more detail and/or keep track of. And it will download individual messages only for those newsgroups you've subscribed to, which in turn will prevent a lot of irrelevant messages from being downloaded to your computer and eating up disk space.

Subscribing to newsgroups is easy. On the Search tab, do the following:

1. Click the name of the newsgroup to which you want to subscribe.

2. Click the Subscribe button to the right of the list of newsgroup names.

You can subscribe to as many newsgroups as you wish. Each newsgroup that you subscribe to will be indicated by a check mark to the right of the newsgroup name. You can also change the word in the Search textbox to view newsgroup names that contain some other word and subscribe to those newsgroups in the same manner. Click the OK button when you've finished. A list of all the newsgroups that you subscribed to will appear beneath your news server name in the left panel of the Mail & Newsgroups component window. For example, in Figure 20.11 you can see I've subscribed to the newsgroups named comp.os.linux.answers, comp.os.linux.help, comp.os.linux.networking, linux.redhat, and news.answers.

---

**Tip**

news.newusers.questions and comp.os.linux.answers are good groups for newsgroup and Linux newbies.

PART
**III**

CH
**20**

**Figure 20.11**
Newsgroups to which you've subscribed appear beneath the news server's name in the left column of the Netscape Mail & Newsgroups window.

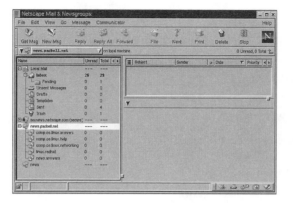

## READING NEWSGROUP MESSAGES

To view the messages in a newsgroup to which you've subscribed, just click the name of the newsgroup. Messages within that group will start downloading to your computer automatically. If a newsgroup contains more than 500 messages, you'll be given the option to download them all or just the most recent ones. Limiting the download to the most recent messages will save some time.

> **Tip**
>
> In the Mail & Newsgroups window, you can drag the lines that separate column headings to narrow and widen columns. Drag the button near the lower right corner of the left pane to adjust its width.

Once the message headers are downloaded, they'll be listed in the right pane in the same manner that email messages are listed in your Inbox. Messages you've never read are displayed in boldface. Most of the messages are questions. If the message has a reply, you'll see a tiny icon with a green arrow to the left of that message. Click that little icon to expand the message so you can see the replies. For example, in Figure 20.12 I've clicked a message that has such an icon to the left. I can now view the original message and the replies just by clicking their headers. As with email, the body of the message appears in the pane below the message header.

## POSTING QUESTIONS TO A NEWSGROUP

To post a question to a newsgroup, first make sure the name of the newsgroup you want to post to is selected in the left column of the Mail & Newsgroups window. Then click the New Msg button in the toolbar. The Compose window will open, just as though you were about to write an email. The message will be pre-addressed to the selected newsgroup. Be sure to type a brief subject that explains the exact purpose of your message because people who do answer questions will often decide which messages to read based on the subject. Type your message and press the Send button in the upper-left corner of the Compose window.

**Figure 20.12**
Reading a message that's been posted to a newsgroup.

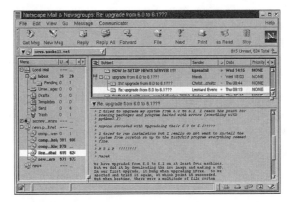

 **Caution**

Newsgroups don't handle HTML well, so make sure you send all newsgroup messages as "plain text."

While you're cruising a newsgroup, you may want to read through some questions to see if there are any you can answer. When you find such a question, click the Reply button in the toolbar. Then just type your answer and click the Send button.

## MORE ON NEWSGROUPS

As mentioned earlier in this chapter, I only have enough space to get you up and running on newsgroups, given that the real topic of this book is Linux. You can learn a lot more about newsgroups in general, and about accessing newsgroups with Netscape's Mail & Newsgroups component, from the following sources:

- Choose Help, Help from Netscape's menu bar and click Newsgroups in the left column of the NetHelp window that appears.

- Use your Web browser, Netscape Navigator, to visit Netscape's Support site at home.netscape.com/support.

- Newsgroup categories that start with the word "news" are about Usenet newsgroups in general. Consider subscribing to some of those newsgroups to see what you can learn, or to post questions.

- Deja, a Web-based newsgroup service, at www.deja.com provides access to many newsgroups through your Web browser.

### PROJECT: GET INVOLVED

Newsgroups work best when everyone can give a little and take a little. Even if you're fairly new to Linux, you may have knowledge of Windows, the Macintosh, or some specific program that would be useful to other people who are beginners in your area of expertise. Why not join a newsgroup where you're already an expert? Use the Search tab shown previously in Figure 20.10 to locate groups that contain the word "newbie" or "questions" or

PART
**III**

CH
**20**

"answers," or some topic in which you have some expertise. Then subscribe to a group or two.

Whenever you visit newsgroups to post a question or to look to see if your question has been answered, take a minute to stop by the newsgroups where you already have some expertise. Look through the messages and answer whatever questions you can. Consider it "payment" for the answers you get to your own questions. If everybody asks some questions, and answers some, the newsgroups become a better repository of expert information for everyone to enjoy.

# CHAPTER 21

# Using FTP, Update Agent, and Telnet

## In this chapter

# USING THE UPDATE AGENT

In the ever-evolving world of Linux, bug fixes, changes, and improvements to existing programs are frequent. Red Hat 6.2 includes a new program named Update Agent that makes it easy for you to locate, download, and install new packages as they become available. To use the Update Agent, you must first register your copy of Red Hat Linux 6.2. If you haven't already done so, please see Appendix B, "Installing Red Hat Linux," for specific instructions. You'll also need some kind of connection to the Internet because the updates will all come from Red Hat's own priority FTP server. Finally, you'll need to be logged in as the superuser (root). Assuming you've met those conditions, here's how to start the Update Agent:

- In GNOME, click the Main Menu button and choose System, Update Agent.
- In KDE, click the K button and choosing Red Hat, System, Update Agent.
- In a terminal window, enter the command up2date.

A new window titled Red Hat Update Agent will appear, as in Figure 21.1. Before you can use Update Agent, you'll need to configure it. You only need to configure the program once, not each time you plan to use it in the future.

**Figure 21.1**
The Update Agent program's window on the screen.

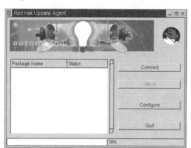

## CONFIGURING UPDATE AGENT

Configuring Update Agent is a pretty simple task. Just click the Configure button in the main window, and you'll come to the User tab of the configuration options, as shown in Figure 21.2. Initially, they may all be blank. You need to fill in the blanks as follows:

- **User ID:** Fill in the same username you used when registering your Red Hat 6.2 product.
- **Password:** Type in the same password you entered when registering your Red Hat 6.2 product.
- **EMail Addresses:** Fill in (at least) your primary email address in the Add New prompt. Then click the Add button to add it to the list.

Figure 21.2 shows an example (using a fake password, of course—don't bother trying to log in as me). If you want to get rid of any extraneous email addresses in the list near the bottom of the dialog box, just click the address you want to remove, and then click the Remove button.

**Figure 21.2**
An example of the User tab of Update Agent's configuration options filled in.

Next, click the Retrieval tab to get to the options shown in Figure 21.3. In the Server option, type `priority.redhat.com` as shown in the figure, since that's the server that stores the packages that you most likely will want to update. The Program option is automatically set to the correct program name and can't be changed. In the center of the dialog box, you can choose from the following options:

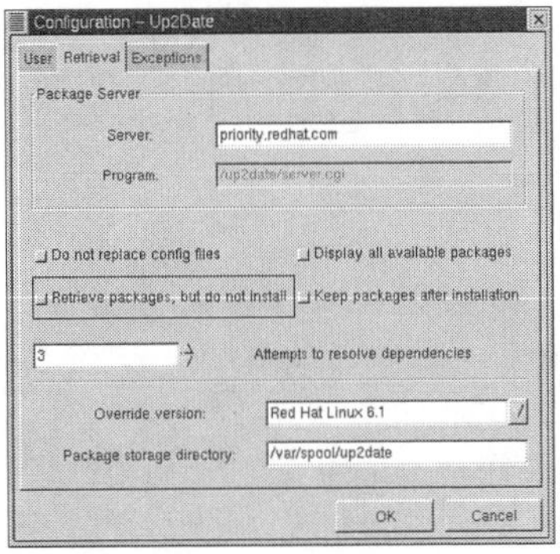

**Figure 21.3**
The Retrieval tab of Update Agent's configuration dialog box.

- **Do Not Replace Config Files:** If selected, ensures that your own configuration files are never replaced with updated files.

- **Retrieve Packages, But Do Not Install:** If selected, downloaded packages will be stored in the Package Storage Directory specified near the bottom of the dialog box, but they won't be installed. You'll need to perform the installation separately. If you want to take the easiest approach, leave this option unselected.

- **Display All Available Packages:** If selected, Update Agent displays all of the packages that are available for download. If deselected, Update Agent limits its display to packages that need updating on your system.

PART

**III**

CH

**21**

- **Keep Packages After Installation:** If selected, the package (.rpm) file is not erased after the package has been installed.
- **Attempts to Resolve Dependencies:** Determines how many times Update Agent will attempt to resolve dependencies among the packages to be downloaded. The default (3) is usually sufficient.

**Tip**

> Packages and package dependencies are discussed at length in Chapter 13, "Managing Packages with RPM." However, it's not necessary to know all the details at this point.

- **Override Version:** This should be set to Red Hat Linux 6.2 because that's the version you're using.
- **Package Storage Directory:** The directory where downloaded packages will be stored, /var/spool/up2date by default.

The Exceptions tab lets you specify packages and files that should never be updated. You can use wildcard characters to specify files to exclude. For example, under Skip Packages on that tab you'll see kernel* as one of the items listed. That will prevent your sensitive Linux kernel files from being downloaded and updated while Linux is running. When you've finished filling in the blanks in the Configuration dialog box, click the OK button to return to the main window.

## PERFORMING THE UPDATE

Once you've configured Update Agent, you can use it at any time to bring your Linux machine up to date with all the latest software releases. If you have a dial-up connection to the Internet, you can use the RH PPP Dialer discussed back in Chapter 18, "Connecting to the Internet," to get online. Then just open up the program as described earlier in this chapter, and click the Connect button. In the status bar, the Update Agent will keep you informed of its progress and what it's doing at the moment. Eventually, it will open Netscape Navigator on your system and show you a Web page listing all the files for Red Hat 6.2 that have been released since the product was released, as in the example shown in Figure 21.4.

**Note**

> If you selected the Display All Available Packages option in Update Agent's configuration options, then the Web page *will* show all available packages—even those you're already up to date with.

**Figure 21.4**
Web page showing updated packages and files that you can download to your own computer to bring all your software up-to-date.

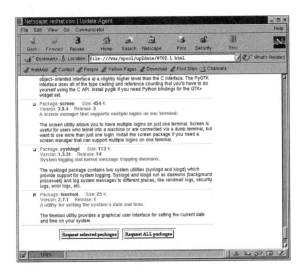

To choose a package to download and install, click the check box to the left of the package name. The button will appear pushed in on packages you've selected to download. At the bottom of the list you'll see two buttons—one titled Request Selected Packages. Clicking that button will begin downloading the packages you selected while scrolling down the page. If you click the Request ALL packages option, then every package listed on the page will be downloaded to your computer.

A new window will appear to keep you posted on how the download is going. Once a file has been downloaded, a red arrow will appear next to its name in the list. As each package is installed, its red arrow changes to a check mark, indicating that the latest package is now installed on your system. In Figure 21.5, all selected packages have been downloaded and installed to my system.

**Figure 21.5**
Check marks indicate that all selected packages have been downloaded and installed.

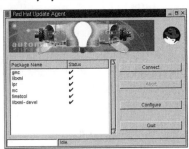

If you did opt to Retrieve Packages, But Do Not Install, then you'll need to install them manually using the rpm command or GnoRPM discussed in Chapter 13. For example, if you downloaded the timetool package to your system into the /var/spool/up2date directory, you could install that package simply by entering the following command in any terminal window or at any command prompt:

```
rpm -Uvh /var/spool/up2date/time*.rpm
```

> **Tip** For more information on using the `rpm` command, refer to Chapter 13.

And that's all there is to it. All you need to do is remember to occasionally check to see which new packages are available. Definitely do so whenever you're having a problem with a program. To learn more about any package, you can read through the errata sheet at www.redhat.com/errata and the links available from that page to get the latest information on what's been fixed or improved since the original release of Red Hat Linux 6.2. Or check the solutions database, FAQs, and gotchas available from www.redhat.com/support.

# WHAT IS FTP?

FTP is an acronym for *File Transfer Protocol*, and is yet another service of the Internet. As the name implies, FTP is all about transferring files from one to computer to another, via the Internet. You can use FTP to *download* files from some remote computer on the Internet to your own local computer. Some FTP sites will also let you *upload* files from your computer to a remote computer on the Internet. In a sense, the whole procedure is like copying files from your hard disk to a floppy disk or some other type of removable disk. The difference is that the transfer usually takes place between your own computer's hard disk and the remote computer's hard disk.

By far and away, the most common use of FTP is to download files to your own computer via the Internet. Members of the GNU project who offer free software often post their files on FTP sites so that people can download and use those files. Such sites generally offer *anonymous FTP*. The term "anonymous" in this case means that you can get onto the site and download files even if you don't have a user account on that remote computer. Typically, you log in to such a site with the username anonymous and your email address as your password. That way, *anyone* who's interested in the program or files that the FTP site has to offer can easily download those files at their own convenience.

Just as Web sites have addresses (such as www.redhat.com), so do FTP sites. The format of an FTP site's name is similar to a Web site's address with the letters *www* (World Wide Web) replaced by the letters *ftp*. In some cases you'll see an FTP site address preceded with *ftp://* such as ftp://ftp.redhat.com. But you rarely, if ever, need to type the ftp:// part of the name. Most programs can figure out that the site you're trying to get to uses FTP because the address starts with the letters *ftp*.

# DOING FTP THE EASY WAY

You can do FTP from the command prompt. And you can even do FTP using Netscape Navigator. But the easiest and most efficient way to do FTP is with the gftp program from GNOME or the KDE desktop. If you have a dial-up connection, connect to your ISP in the usual manner. Then, do one of the following:

■ In GNOME, click the GNOME Main Menu button and choose Internet, gftp.

■ In KDE, press Alt+F2, type gftp, and then press Enter.

> **Tip**
>
> To create a KDE desktop shortcut to gftp, right-click the KDE desktop and choose New, Application. Click the Clear button and type gftp and then click OK. Click the Execute tab in the dialog box that appears, type gftp as the command to execute, and then click the icon button if you'd like to choose a custom icon for this shortcut.

When gftp first opens, you're greeted with the window shown in Figure 21.6. The left pane, titled Local, shows the contents of a directory on your own local hard disk. You can navigate down into subdirectories by double-clicking the directory's name or folder icon in the left column. To navigate up to the parent directory of the current directory, double-click the bent arrow at the top of the directory list. The complete path to the directory you're currently viewing is shown above the list. You can also create a new directory for the files you plan to download. For example, in this figure I started at the /root directory. From there I chose Local, Make Directory from the menu bar, and typed in the new name ftpDownloads. After saving the new directory, I double-clicked its name in the left column of gftp to switch to it. So now, any files I download will go into the new /root/ftpDownloads. That'll make it easy to find them later.

**Figure 21.6**
Local files and directories will be listed in the left pane of the gftp program. Remote files and directories are in the right pane.

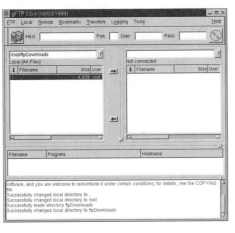

The right pane works exactly like the left pane except that it shows you the directories and files of the FTP site you're logged into at the moment. When you're not logged into a specific FTP site, that list is empty and is titled Not Connected. The columns titled Filename, Progress, and Hostname will show you the progress of files as they're being downloaded to your computer (or uploaded to a remote computer). The wide pane at the bottom of the window will show other general messages reflecting the success or failure of various activities you try.

---

**Tip**

The official home page of gftp is http://gftp.seul.org.

---

## Configuring gftp

Configuring gftp is pretty easy. The only thing you really need to do is choose FTP, Options from gftp's menu bar. In the General tab of the dialog box that appears, you should type in your actual address next to the Email Address option. You don't have to bother with settings on the Proxy Server tab, unless you work in an environment where you must go through a proxy server to access the Internet. In this case, you (or your network administrator) will need to fill in the blanks on the Proxy Server tab so you can gain access to the Internet via gftp.

## Connecting to an FTP Site

There are thousands of FTP sites on the Internet. And you'll learn about them as you gain experience. Three anonymous FTP sites that are of particular interest to Red Hat Linux 6.2 users are ftp.redhat.com, rawhide.redhat.com, and www.rpmfind.net. But no matter what the address of the site you want to visit, you always go about it by following these simple steps:

1. If you're currently connected to a site, choose Remote, Disconnect from gftp's menu bar.

2. Next to Host in gftp's toolbar, type the address of the FTP site you want to visit (such as ftp.redhat.com).

3. If you know for certain that the Port Number option to the right of the Host option is wrong, type in the correct port number.

4. If you're logging into an anonymous site, you can leave the User and Pass option as they are (anonymous as the username and the password as a bunch of asterisks). Then skip to step 6.

5. If you're logging into a site that doesn't allow anonymous logins, like priority.redhat.com, then type your username and passwords into the appropriate blanks. Use the name and password you made up when registering your Red Hat 6.2 product at www.redhat.com/now.

6. Click the button showing two monitors that are located at the left side of gftp's toolbar.

Messages will fly by in the bottom window of the screen. Assuming you performed all the preceding steps correctly and the site you're visiting isn't already overloaded with users, you should end up with a successful connection. The right pane will then show the directories and files available for download from the FTP site you're connected to. For example, in Figure 21.7 I've connected to priority.redhat.com, and the right pane initially shows folders containing downloaded files for various versions of Red Hat Linux.

**Figure 21.7**
Successful connection to priority. redhat.com via gftp and my personal username and password.

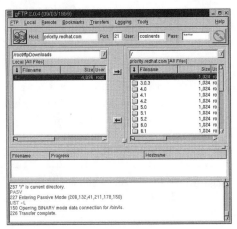

As with any file listing, you can navigate through directories in the right pane (on the remote computer) by double-clicking directory names to open them and by clicking the bent arrow at the top of the list to go back up to the parent directory. For example, to get the appropriate files for version 6.2 displayed in the right column of Figure 21.7, you'd double-click the 6.2 directory to open it. Then you'd double-click the i386 (or whatever folder) to view PC files that are available for download. Optionally, you could open the SRPMS directory if you're looking for source code to download, or images if you're looking for disk images (.img files)—or noarch if you're looking for packages that aren't written for a specific architecture.

> **Tip**
>
> Packages that aren't written for a particular hardware platform often have the word *noarch* in their filename, although you'll also find packages that don't have that word in their filenames. So if you don't find a particular package in the i386 folder, check the noarch folder.

## DOWNLOADING FILES WITH GFTP

After you have the left column pointing to the directory on your local computer in which you want to store the downloaded files, and you have the right column showing files that are available for download in the right column, the rest is easy. Follow these steps:

1. In the right column again, select the file(s) you want to download. You can click a file's name to select it. You can also use Ctrl+click to select (and deselect) additional files to download. You can also use Shift+click to extend the selection through several file names to select them.

2. Click the left-pointing arrow button between the two panes.

As files are copied from the remote computer to your own, you'll see messages displaying progress in the lower pane of gftp. The left column may not show each downloaded file automatically. But you can always choose Local, Refresh from gftp's menu bar to get an updated list of files in that left column.

> **Tip**
>
> If you see a message indicating that a connection has "timed out" and you're no longer connected, just click the button with the two monitors in gftp's toolbar to immediately reconnect.

When the download is complete you'll see the message Transfer complete in the scrolling text pane at the bottom of gftp's window. If you downloaded packages (.rpm files) and want to install them, refer to Chapter 13 for information on installing packages with GnoRPM and the rpm command.

## UPLOADING FILES WITH GFTP

The process of uploading files from your computer to a remote FTP site is pretty much the same as the process for downloading. However, not all sites accept uploads, so first make sure you know you can perform an upload. Also, you'll need to know which directory on the remote FTP site will accept your incoming files. Typically that directory is named *incoming* or perhaps *dropbox*. But only the owner of the FTP site can give you the specifics.

To upload, first log in to the remote site using `gftp` as described earlier in this chapter. In the left pane, navigate to the directory on your computer that contains the files you want to upload. In the right pane, navigate to the directory on the FTP site that's capable of accepting your uploaded files. Then click the right-pointing arrow button to copy files from your local directory to the remote computer. Wait for the transfer to be completed, and you're done.

# USING TELNET

Last (and perhaps least) among the Internet tools built in to Red Hat Linux 6.2 is Telnet. Telnet is a protocol that allows a remote machine to connect to and control a remote computer through a text interface. For example, a computer in the office might act as a Telnet server allowing people at remote locations to access the computer's resources.

> **Note**
>
> Setting up a Linux computer to act as a Telnet *server* is a topic that Chapter 32, "Setting Up Telnet and FTP Services," covers. In this chapter we're looking at Telnet from the client side—your accessing some remote Telnet computer from your own local computer.

With Telnet installed, any computer that has a Telnet client can log into the Linux computer and interact with the command prompt—exactly as if you were sitting in front of the machine in text-only mode. Windows users can access Telnet just by typing `telnet` at a command or run prompt. Macintosh users should download BetterTelnet from `http://www.cstone.net/~rbraun/mac/telnet/`.

Telnet is a command-driven program—there are no fancy interfaces involved. To start a `telnet` session, you'll typically go to a command prompt and enter the following command:

```
telnet someserver.someplace.com
```

`someserver.someplace.com` is the hostname or IP address of a Telnet server that you know of and have permission to use. Once you've entered the Telnet command just shown, you'll get some sort of feedback letting you know when you're successfully connected. Typically you'll be asked to log in as well, as in the following example:

```
Trying 123.123.123.123...
Connected to someserver.someplace.com
login:
```

> **Tip**
>
> If the Telnet program isn't available on your computer, you install it from the Red Hat CD-ROM number 1. If you use GnoRPM, you'll find it under Packages, Applications, Internet.

At the login prompt, enter your username and press Enter. You'll then be prompted for your password, which you'll need to enter as well. From that point on, you can essentially enter any Linux command or launch any program just as you would on your local computer. However, you'll need to keep in mind that your local computer is sort of out of the picture at the moment, and your monitor and keyboard are interacting with the remote computer you've connected to.

When you've finished a Telnet session, enter the command logout. You should see a message stating that the session was terminated by the foreign computer (that's your computer from the Telnet server's point of view). You'll then be returned to the normal operation of your own local computer.

Places that allow people to telnet into their computers and fool around anonymously are few and far between. So I can't give you much more specific information than what I've provided. Typically, if you need Telnet access to a computer in the office from your home or laptop computer, the company network administrator will set up an account for you. He or she can provide the specifics of connecting and what you can and should do once you are connected.

## PROJECT: GET YOUR COMPUTER UP-TO-DATE

Probably the smartest thing you can do with the information you've learned in this chapter, right now, would be to start bringing your Red Hat Linux 6.2 packages up-to-date. If you have a simple 56KB dial-up connection, it might take a really long time to download and install *all* the packages, so you may want to do just a few each day. Also, some packages you might want to avoid if you're not a programmer/software developer are the SRPMs (Source Code RPMs). Also, avoid packages that have the word "devel" in their names because these too are packages that are put together specifically for programmers.

> **Tip**
>
> At the time of this writing, there were no upgrades available for 6.2, but by the time you read this, there almost certainly will be!

To get started, connect to the Internet in the usual manner on your computer, and start the Update Agent as discussed at the beginning of this chapter. You can learn more about the various packages, and why you might want to upgrade them, from Red Hat's Errata site at www.redhat.com/errata.

Only packages that need to be updated will appear in the Update Agent display.

You can also download these packages using the gftp program described earlier in this chapter. You'll find them at the address updates.redhat.com in the /6.2 directory. Filenames that contain *i386* are in the /i386 subdirectory; files that contain *noarch* are in the /noarch subdirectory.

# PART IV

# LINUX NETWORK ADMINISTRATION

# CHAPTER 22

# CREATING A LOCAL AREA NETWORK

**I**n this chapter

# TCP/IP CRASH COURSE

In Part III of this book, "Linux and the Internet," you learned how to connect a single Linux computer to the Internet, via a PPP dial-up connection. Starting here in Part IV, "Linux Network Administration," you'll begin learning how to put together a *local area network* (*LAN*) consisting of two or more computers. There are no modems and phone lines involved in a LAN—presumably the computers are close enough to one another that you can run a cable from one computer to the next. Each computer in the LAN will also need to have a *network interface card* (*NIC*) installed in it, to which the LAN cable connects. Each computer in the LAN must also have a unique *hostname* and *IP address*. To assign hostnames and IP addresses to your computers, you'll first need to understand a little about TCP/IP (Transmission Control Protocol/Internet Protocol), the protocol used by the Internet and the vast majority of LANs throughout the world.

> **Tip**
>
> The term *intranet* is often used to describe a LAN that's built around the TCP/IP protocol because the LAN can act like a small, private version of the Internet with common Internet services such as Web browsing, FTP, and email.

In TCP/IP, every *host* (computer or other device) that's connected to the network has a unique *IP address*. That address is composed of four *octets* (basically, numbers in the range of 0 to 255) separated by decimal points (also called *dotted decimal notation*). For example, the *loopback address* (often abbreviated *lo*) of a host might be `127.0.0.0`. My Web site at www. coolnerds.com is actually at the IP address `208.55.30.20`. This perhaps brings up the question, "How do you avoid giving a computer on your LAN the same IP address as some computer on the Internet?" The answer to that is fairly simple. You just use the range of IP addresses that are reserved for private, local area networks. In most smaller LANs (254 or fewer computers), those addresses begin with the octets `192.168`, as discussed in the following section.

## LAN NETWORK ADDRESS

All computers in a single LAN should have all three of the first octets be the same. For example, you could have 254 hosts in a single LAN by assigning the addresses `192.168.1.x` to each computer in the LAN, where *x* is some number in the range of 1 to 254. You could create a second LAN within the same company, consisting of up to another 254 computers, that uses addresses in the range of `192.168.2.x`, a third LAN that uses addresses in the range of `192.168.3.x`, and so forth. My guess, though, is that you're most likely to start by building a single LAN that has 254 or fewer computers in it.

You aren't limited to 254 computers per LAN. There are other ranges of addresses that allow you to create even larger networks. For example, a single class A network can have over 16 million unique addresses. A class B LAN can have more than 65,000 unique addresses. Exactly how big you go depends on which reserved address range you use and the subnet mask associated with that range. Table 22.1 summarizes the address ranges and capabilities of class A, B, and C networks.

**TABLE 22.1    RANGES OF PRIVATE ADDRESSES RESERVED FOR CLASS A, B, AND C LOCAL AREA NETWORKS**

| Address Range | Subnet Mask | Provides | Addresses per LAN |
|---|---|---|---|
| 10.0.0.0-10.255.255.255 | 255.0.0.0 | 1 class A LAN | 16,777,216 |
| 172.16.0.0-172.31.255.255 | 255.255.0.0 | 16 class B LANs | 65,536 |
| 192.168.0.0-192.168.255.255 | 255.255.255.0 | 256 class C LANs | 256 |

**Note**

There are many books that are entirely dedicated to the subject of TCP/IP, which describe the overall scheme of things in more detail. In this book, of course, I can only introduce the general topic, and focus on those aspects of TCP/IP that you need to know to build a LAN.

**Windows IP Addresses**

If the computers you're working with are connected to one another via a LAN you created in Windows, you can easily find out which IP address has been assigned to each machine. First, click the Start button, choose Run, type winipcfg, and press Enter. A dialog box titled IP Configuration appears.

You'll see a drop-down list near the top of that dialog box. Be sure to select the name of your NIC card from the list (*not* the PPP Adapter option). The computer's IP address will appear just below that drop-down list. Jot that down. If the current computer will dual-boot between Windows and Linux, use that same IP address when giving the host its unique IP address in Linux.

## NETWORK AND BROADCAST ADDRESSES

Focusing again on our relatively small LAN, you need to be aware that the addresses at the two extreme ends of the range are reserved for use as the LAN's *network address* and *broadcast address*. For example, if you use addresses in the range of 192.168.1.0 to 192.168.1.255, the first address is reserved as the network address, and the last address is reserved as the broadcast address. Thus, you can only assign individual computers on the LAN IP addresses in the range of 192.168.1.1 to 192.168.1.254 as summarized here:

```
Network Address:  192.168.1.0
                  Individual hosts: 192.168.1.1 to 192.168.1.254
                  Broadcast Address: 192.168.1.255
```

The network address is used by some processes to refer to the network as a whole. As the name implies, the broadcast address is used by some processes to send the same message to every computer in the LAN.

## SUBNET MASKS

Each host in the LAN has a *subnet mask*. The mask is simply a octet that uses the number 255 to represent the network address portion of the IP address, and a zero to identify the host portion of the address. In a class C LAN (such as the one we're using as an example in this chapter), each host will have the same first three octets 192.168.1. Only the fourth digit will be unique to each host. To "tell" various processes that they are currently in a class C network, each host will use a subnet mask of 255.255.255.0. That's the "machine way" of saying "you're in the LAN 192.168.1." The zero at the end of the subnet mask says "the last digit will be a unique host within this LAN."

## DOMAIN NAME

Your entire network can also have a name called a *network name* or *domain name*. The domain name is generally some name followed by one of the well-known Internet suffixes like .com, .org, .mil, .edu, .net, and so forth. If the network you're creating is already connected to the Internet as a server, chances are your LAN already has a domain name, such as yourBusinessNameHere.com. To get an "official" domain name like that, you need to register through InterNIC. Your best bet these days is to go through one of the registration services like Network Solutions (www.networksolutions.com) or Register.com (www.register.com).

If you have a simple dial-up connection to the LAN and don't really serve the Internet directly from your LAN, then you can pretty much name your LAN anything you want. If you have a domain name of your own already, you can use that for your private LAN. For example, I named my private LAN coolnerds.com, which also happens to be the domain name of my Web site. Even though my Web page isn't actually served from the network I'm using right now, I can still name my private LAN coolnerds.com without fear of it being confused with the site at www.coolnerds.com. Because this network uses IP addresses in the range of 192.168.1.1 to 192.168.1.x, it's private, so its domain name won't be accessible from the Internet.

## HOSTNAMES

Each computer in the LAN needs a unique *hostname*. This is simply a name that you make up on your own and give to each computer. The name should not contain any blank spaces or punctuation. Just to minimize your own typing, you may want to keep the name short as well. Try to think of a name that will be easy to remember. In the LAN I built to write this book, I named two of the machines P300 and K63 (after the processor I used to build each machine). Two others are named BigBoy and PowerEdge. You can, of course, name your own machines whatever you like. Just make sure that no two hosts have the same name.

Table 22.2 summarizes what we've covered so far in this chapter, using 192.168.1.0 as the network address. As you can see, every host in the LAN will have the same network address, broadcast address, subnet mask, and domain name because those addresses identify the network as a whole. Within the network, each machine will have a unique hostname and IP address to identify that specific host. Since I've assigned the network address 192.168.1.0 to the network as a whole, each host must have a unique IP address in the range of 192.168.1.1 to 192.168.1.254. The very last number, 192.168.1.255, is reserved for the broadcast address.

**TABLE 22.2    SAMPLE IP ADDRESSES FOR A LAN WITH 254 OR FEWER INTERCONNECTED COMPUTERS**

| IP Address | Example | Same/Unique |
|---|---|---|
| Network address | 192.168.1.0 | Same for all hosts |
| Domain name | coolnerds.com | Same for all hosts |
| Broadcast address | 192.168.1.255 | Same for all hosts |
| Subnet mask | 255.255.255.0 | Same for all hosts |
| Hostname | *whatever* | Unique to each host |
| Host addresses | 192.168.1.*x* | *x* must be unique to each host |

*The x value must be unique to each computer and must be a value between 1 and 254 (inclusive).*

## ASSIGNING IP ADDRESSES IN A LAN

So now we know that each host in a LAN will have a unique IP address. This brings up the question, "Just *how* does each host *get* its own unique address?" There are two possibilities. Either you (or the network administrator) assigns a *static IP address* to each computer in the LAN, and that address never changes. Or, some kind of server automatically assigns a *dynamic address* to each computer as it logs into the network.

### STATIC IP ADDRESSING

If you're building your LAN from scratch, and you don't have a DHCP or BootP server anywhere in the LAN, you'll need to manually assign a *static IP address* to each computer in the LAN. Just remember that the first three octets must be the same for each host, and the last digit must be unique to each host. Thus, in a LAN consisting of five computers, you could assign the IP address 192.168.1.2 to one computer, 192.168.1.3 to another computer, 192.168.1.4 to a third computer, and so forth. Each host will also need a unique hostname, which you can make up on your own. As summarized in Table 22.2, each host will have the same network address (192.168.1.0, in this example), the same broadcast address (192.168.1.255, in this example), subnet mask (255.255.255.0), and the same domain name.

Figure 22.1 shows a small sample network that uses static IP addresses. This figure shows the IP address and hostname to be assigned to each computer. A good starting point in setting up your own LAN might be to simply go from one computer to the next and jot down the IP address and hostname of each computer on a Post-It note, so that you can refer to it later when you start actually configuring the LAN hardware and software. You can assign the host number (the last digit in the IP address) arbitrarily; just make sure you keep the first three octets the same on each computer (such as 192.168.1.*x*).

**Figure 22.1**
Each host in this soon-to-be LAN is assigned a unique hostname and IP address. Information that's the same for each computer is also defined.

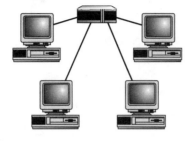

## DYNAMIC IP ADDRESSING

If the LAN you're building, or adding to, has a *DHCP* (Dynamic Host Configuration Program) server, then each computer will automatically be assigned a unique IP address as it joins the LAN. BootP is a similar service that can automatically assign unique IP addresses to each host on the LAN. However, neither DHCP nor BootP "just happen" in a LAN. Somebody has to add a program or device that offers that capability, and that device will act as a host with an IP address of its own. A fairly typical example of a DHCP device might be a router that acts as an Ethernet hub on one side and a connection to the Internet on the other side, as illustrated in Figure 22.2. (WebRamp at www.webramp.com and Cisco at www.cisco.com both make such devices.)

> **Tip**
> The role played by the Ethernet hub/router in a LAN is discussed in the section "The LAN Hardware" later in this chapter.

**Figure 22.2**
This LAN includes a router that provides DHCP services, and also connects all computers in the LAN to an ISP and the Internet.

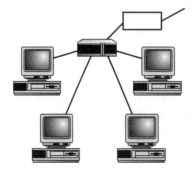

In the LAN shown in Figure 22.2, it's not necessary to assign each host its own unique IP address because the DHCP server will automatically give each host an IP address as soon as it becomes part of the LAN. The network and broadcast addresses will also be assigned by the DHCP server. So you really need concern yourself only with giving the LAN a domain name and giving each host a unique hostname.

I should mention that Figure 22.2 is *only* an example. It's possible that any regular computer in the LAN could act as a DHCP server. If you're adding a computer to an existing LAN, the only way to know for sure whether the LAN offers DHCP or BootP services is to check with the person in charge of the LAN, who typically goes by the title of *network administrator*.

---

**Ask Your Network Administrator**

I hate to offer the phrase "ask your network administrator" as a solution to a problem because I know many of you are aspiring to be the network administrator, and really have no such person around to ask. However, if you're working in a company that's large enough to have a network administrator, you probably will have to consult that person from time to time if you're adding computers to an existing LAN.

My real focus here, though, is to help you build a working LAN from scratch. For that reason, my goal is to explain everything you need to know to build a LAN, without the support of a local expert—and, without confusing things by getting into all the "theory" of TCP/IP and such.

---

# THE LAN HARDWARE

A LAN isn't truly a LAN until there's some hardware connecting all the computers together. There are different types of hardware schemes available, including Token Ring, ARCnet, and Ethernet. But by far and away, the popular hardware used for building modern networks is Ethernet. Ethernet hardware is available at virtually all computer stores and is fairly inexpensive.

To create an Ethernet LAN you'll need an Ethernet Network Interface Card (NIC) for each computer in the LAN. You'll also need at least one *Ethernet Hub* with at least as many available jacks as there are computers in the LAN. And finally, you'll need an Ethernet cable (also called a 10BaseT cable) to connect each computer's NIC to the Ethernet hub (see Figure 22.3). (Figures 22.1 and 22.2 show examples of hubs and the cables as well.)

When choosing Ethernet hardware, the most important step is choosing Ethernet cards that are compatible with Linux. Appendix D, "Linux-Compatible Ethernet Cards," lists those cards, as well as the Linux *module* (also called the *driver*) that each card requires. You can often save some money by buying a package of LAN cards. For example, to set up the LAN I created for writing this book, I purchased a five-pack of SMC's EtherPower II 10/100 cards from one of the online computer stores. They were a snap to install and configure, even on my heterogeneous LAN containing both Windows and Linux computers.

For a simple LAN, choosing an Ethernet hub is simply a matter of finding one that has at least as many jacks as necessary to accommodate all the computers you want to add to the LAN. Obviously, it's better to have too many, rather than too few, jacks because the empty jacks won't hurt anything and will give you room to grow. In larger networks, you may need to buy several hubs and interconnect them together, according to the manufacturer's instructions, in order to end up with enough jacks for your LAN.

If you want all the computers in the LAN to have access to the Internet through a single account with an ISP, the router/Ethernet hub combo illustrated in Figure 22.3 is a great solution. Be aware, however, that such devices generally need to be configured by one of the computers in the LAN. And some devices might offer only Windows and Macintosh configuration programs. That's not a problem if you have Windows PCs and/or Macintosh computers in the LAN. But if you have only Linux computers in the LAN, you'll need a router that can be configured using some kind of Linux-based configuration program.

**Figure 22.3**
Each computer in an Ethernet LAN must have a Network Interface Card installed and a cable that connects that card to an Ethernet hub.

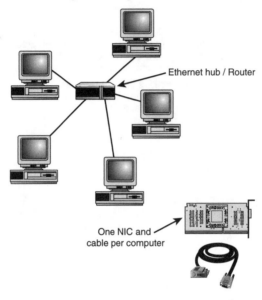

Ethernet hub / Router

One NIC and cable per computer

> **Tip**
>
> Ascend (www.ascend.com) and Cisco (www.cisco.com) both offer very Linux-friendly hardware. If you're comfortable with configuring ethernet cards in Linux, and happen to have a spare computer (an old 486 will do), you can actually use Linux to connect your LAN to the Internet. Read the included "IP-Masquerade" HOWTO for more information.

Choosing cables is pretty straightforward as well. Most Ethernet networks use 10BaseT cable with RJ45 plugs at each end. And such cables are readily available wherever Ethernet hardware is sold. You just want to make sure to get appropriate lengths of cable so that each host can reach the Ethernet hub.

## INSTALLING THE HARDWARE

After you've acquired all the hardware, you need to install it. The first step, of course, is to power down every computer in the LAN and remove its power cord. You don't want the machine to be on, or come on accidentally, while you're installing the Ethernet cards. At this stage it's simply a matter of plugging the Ethernet card into the appropriate slot on the computer's motherboard, as per the manufacturer's instructions. Then find a place for the hub and run a cable from each computer's NIC card to the Ethernet hub.

Make sure you follow all the instructions that came with the LAN hardware before you start up any computers in the LAN. If you buy a router that connects the LAN to the Internet, or one that provides DHCP services, you'll probably have to do some configuration on that, again following the manufacturer's instructions. But essentially, after every computer is connected to the hub via a cable and NIC card, you're ready to start firing up the computers and configuring their Ethernet cards to get the LAN working.

# CONFIGURING THE LAN

If you install your Ethernet cards, cables, and hub before you install Linux, you'll be prompted for network configuration during the Linux installation process. In fact, you may have already done all of that, but left the network information blank (or guessed at addresses incorrectly) during the installation process. If you install the Ethernet card *after* you've installed Linux, the next time you turn on the computer, the Kudzu program may detect the Ethernet card and configure it for you. Follow these steps to watch for, and use, Kudzu to configure your Ethernet card:

1. Watch the screen closely during the entire bootup process. If you see a dialog box titled Welcome to Kudzu, press Enter to start the configuration process.

2. Near the top of the next dialog box to appear, you should see the brand name of your Ethernet card. Press the Enter key to continue with the configuration.

3. After a brief delay, you'll see the prompt Would You Like to Set Up Networking?.

4. For now, press Tab, and then press Enter to choose No. Later in this chapter you'll use LinuxConf to set up networking.

At this point, the bootup should continue normally. You should log in as root to give yourself the power to set up networking via LinuxConf, as discussed next.

## USING LINUXCONF TO CONFIGURE YOUR ETHERNET CARD

You can use LinuxConf at any time to configure, or re-configure, your Ethernet card. As you may recall, you can start LinuxConf from GNOME by clicking the Main Menu button and choosing System, LinuxConf. Optionally, you can also enter the command linuxconf in any terminal window. Then, follow these steps:

1. Open Config, Networking, Client Tasks, Basic Host Information.

2. On the Host name tab, type the fully qualified hostname you've decided to give the computer you're sitting at. By "fully qualified," I mean the hostname followed by a period and the domain name for the network. For example, in Figure 22.4 I'm configuring the Ethernet card in the computer I've named P300, so I've named that machine P300.coolnerds.com.

3. Next, click the Adaptor 1 tab, which represents your Ethernet card settings.

4. Make sure the Enabled button is pushed in. (This is critical—the card won't work at all if it's disabled!)

**Figure 22.4**
Type the current computer's hostname into the first tab of Linux-Conf's This Host Basic Configuration.

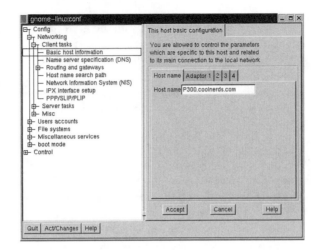

5.  If you don't have a DHCP or BootP server on your LAN to automatically assign IP addresses to clients, choose Manual, and then continue with the following steps. If you do have DCHP or BootP services in your LAN, choose either DHCP or BootP as appropriate, and then skip to step 12.

6.  Under Primary Name + Domain, type this computer's hostname followed by a dot and the LAN's domain name (such as `P300.coolnerds.com`).

7.  Under Aliases, enter this computer's hostname. Optionally, you can give this computer other "nicknames" if you like. Just be sure to separate each name with a blank space.

8.  Next to IP Address, type the IP address you've chosen for this computer (such as `192.168.1.3`).

9.  Next to Netmask, type `255.255.255.0`.

10. Under Net Device, choose eth0 (which represents the first Ethernet card in your computer).

11. The Kernel Module option will usually fill in automatically. It should be the name of the driver for your Ethernet card, as listed in Appendix D. Typically, if you leave it blank, the correct module name will be entered automatically when you exit LinuxConf.

12. Click the Accept button.

Figure 22.5 shows an example where I've configured the Ethernet card in the host I named P300 in my LAN. Be aware that you must repeat the preceding steps 1-11 for every computer in the LAN, making sure to enter the correct hostname and IP address for each computer that you sit at. You'll also want to set up the `/etc/hosts` file on every computer in the LAN, as discussed later in this chapter.

**Figure 22.5**
Example of configuring an Ethernet card via LinuxConf. Here I've configured the computer named P300.

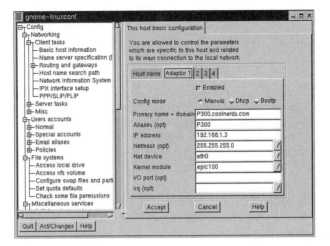

## NAMESERVER SPECIFICATION

The next step in setting up a LAN is to tell Linux where to look for IP addresses when only a computer's hostname is given. There are a couple of ways that Linux can find that information, one being through DNS (Domain Name Services) and the other through a local file at /etc/hosts on the computer. Actually, there are other ways, such as NIS (Network Information Systems), but let's not overcomplicate things right now. Chances are, at this point, you'll have DNS from your ISP whenever you connect to the Internet. But resolving local hostnames (such as BigBoy and P300) into IP addresses will have to be done through the local /etc/hosts file. So I suggest you do the following:

1. Open the Name Server Specification (DNS) category in the left column of LinuxConf.

2. Select DNS Usage (its button is pushed in).

3. Next to Search Domain 1, type localdomain as in Figure 22.6.

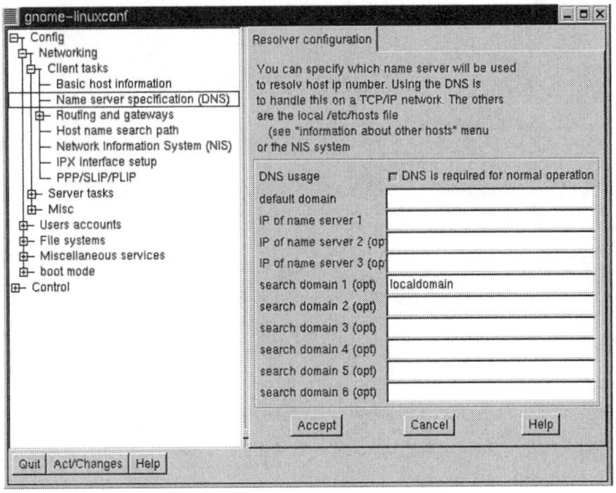

**Figure 22.6**
Allowing DNS services and the local network to be used for resolving hostnames into IP addresses.

4. If you know for certain that you have a primary and secondary nameserver available from this Ethernet card and know their IP addresses, you can fill those in as IP of nameserver 1 and IP of nameserver 2. If you're unsure of those IP addresses, leave both those options blank as in Figure 22.6.

**Note**

If you have a PPP/modem connection to the Internet, as discussed in Part III of this book, the nameservers provided by your ISP are *not* relevant to the Ethernet interface. Those addresses are relevant only to the PPP interface, and should not be entered in the Resolver Configuration tab of LinuxConf.

5. Click the Accept button.

## HOSTNAME SEARCH PATH

Next, you need to tell Linux the order in which to go looking for IP addresses assigned to hostnames. The most likely scenario is that you'll use the local hosts file to resolve local hostnames and an ISP's domain name services to resolve Internet domain names. So follow these steps:

1. Open the Routing and Gateways category in the left column of LinuxConf.
2. Open the Host Name Search Path option.
3. Choose the Multiple IPs for One Host option.
4. Unless you know for certain that you have NIS services in this LAN, I suggest you choose the Hosts, DNS option (see Figure 22.7).

**Figure 22.7**
Specify Hosts as the first name service, DNS as the second service.

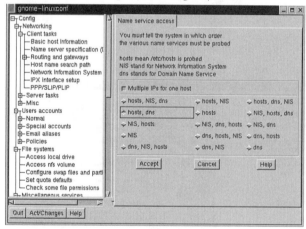

5. Click the Accept button.

## SETTING UP /etc/hosts

In order for Linux to find a computer within your LAN based on the computer's hostname, it needs some way to find the IP address of that host. There are several techniques that allow these lookups. For example, if your computer has DNS (Domain Name Service) or NIS (Network Information Service) installed already, then all the hostnames and IP addresses are already listed in a nameserver. You simply have to ask the network administrator for the IP addresses of those nameservers (unless you already created them yourself, in which case you already know those IP addresses).

In a relatively small and simple LAN, like the example shown in Figure 22.1, where there is no centralized nameserver, you need to set up a hostsfile on each PC that lists the hostname, IP address, and aliases (nicknames) associated with every host in the LAN. This information is stored in a simple text file named /etc/hosts. This step can be tedious, particularly if there are many computers in the LAN. But as I'll discuss in a moment, you can use a little cut and paste to help speed things along. For starters, though, you'll need to go to any one of the computers on the LAN and follow these steps to create your /etc/hosts file using LinuxConf:

1. Open the Misc category in the left column of LinuxConf.

2. Open the Information About Other Hosts category. Initially, you'll see one or two entries for the current computer only.

3. Click the Add button to add an entry for one other host in your LAN.

4. In the dialog box that appears, type the Primary+Domain Name of one other computer in the LAN (such as Athlon.coolnerds.com).

5. Next to Alias, you can type one or more "nicknames" for that computer. Typically, the hostname alone (such as *Athlon*) makes a good nickname.

6. Next to IP number, type the IP address of the computer to which you've assigned that hostname.

7. Click the Accept button.

8. Repeat steps 3-7 one for each host in the LAN.

When you've finished, the /etc/hosts tab of LinuxConf should include one entry for every host in your LAN, plus one extra entry for the local machine's loopback (localhost) interface, as in the example shown in Figure 22.8. Now you can save the changes and exit LinuxConf by following these steps:

1. Click the Quit button at the bottom of the list after you've typed in all the IP addresses and hostnames.

2. Click the Quit button at the bottom of the LinuxConf dialog box to close LinuxConf.

3. When prompted, click the Activate the Changes button to activate your changes and close LinuxConf.

## REPEAT FOR EVERY HOST

At this point you've configured one computer in your LAN. You need to go to each and every computer in the LAN and repeat all the steps starting at the section titled "Configuring the LAN." However, if you have a lot of hosts in the computer and don't feel like manually entering each host's IP address and name as in steps 27-34, you can edit the /etc/hosts file on each computer manually, using cut and paste to copy information from the one file you created manually.

**Figure 22.8**
Using LinuxConf to set up `/etc/hosts` on one computer in our sample `coolnerds.com` LAN.

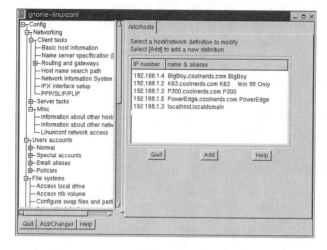

Copy the completed `/etc/hosts` file to a floppy disk. At each computer in the LAN, open its `/etc/hosts` file in your favorite text editor. Then open the hosts file from the floppy in a text editor. Then just copy and paste information from all hosts other than the local computer into the local computer's `/etc/hosts` file.

As you can see in Figure 22.9, the `/etc/hosts` file is just a list of IP addresses and hostnames divided into three columns. The first column is an IP address, and the second column (created by adding spaces or tabs) is the fully qualified hostname of that computer. The third column, again separated by spaces or tabs, is the alias (nickname) for that computer. A computer can have multiple nicknames, provided you separate each with a blank space.

For example, in Figure 22.9 I've given the machine named `PowerEdge.coolnerds.com` two nicknames: *PowerEdge* and *Server*. I plan to use that computer as a server for various services as this LAN grows, and hence the easy-to-remember nickname "Server."

> **Tip**
>
> For reminders on copying files to a floppy disk, see "Moving and Copying Files in File Manager" in Chapter 3.

Of course, if, for whatever reason, you're not comfortable using the cut and paste method to manually build a `/etc/hosts` file on each computer, you can just set up the /etc/hosts file using LinuxConf on each computer. The main point to remember is that the local computer is listed twice, and every other computer in the LAN is listed once.

**Figure 22.9**
You can edit /etc/hosts using any text editor. Copying and pasting information from one computer's hosts file to another is less tedious than manually defining each host at each machine.

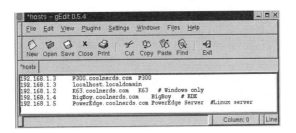

# TESTING THE LAN

After you've completed all the previous steps on each computer in the LAN, it's time to give it the acid test. The main question is whether the computers will be able to communicate with one another immediately after booting up. The best way to find out for sure is to first go to each computer and reboot it using the Logout option in your favorite GUI or the `reboot` command at the command prompt.

As each computer starts booting up, you can watch the screen as various test are performed. In particular, watch for the Setting Hostname, Bringing Up Interface lo, and Bringing Up Interface eth0 prompts. The hostname should be the name that you assigned this machine in LinuxConf (as opposed to the old `localhost.localdomain` name). The lo and eth0 interfaces should both register "OK" as in the following example:

```
Setting hostname P300
...
Bringing up interface lo     [OK]
Bringing up interface eth0    [OK]
```

To test whether the computers can communicate with one another in the LAN, use the trusty `ping` command. Just get to a terminal window or command prompt and enter the command `ping` followed by a blank space and the IP address, fully qualified hostname, or alias (nickname) of any computer on the LAN other than the one you're sitting at. (It really makes no sense to ping the computer in front of you.) For example, suppose I'm sitting at the computer I've named Athlon. To test the connection to the computer named PowerEdge, I could enter any one of the following commands:

```
ping 192.168.1.5
```

```
ping poweredge.Coolnerds.com
```

```
ping poweredge
```

```
ping server
```

The computer will start sending messages to whichever computer you specified. If the two computers are able to communicate, you'll see a list of messages something like the following, as packets are sent back and forth between the computers:

```
64 bytes from 192.168.1.5: icmp_seq=0 ttl=255 time=0.8ms
64 bytes from 192.168.1.5: icmp_seq=2 ttl=255 time=0.3ms
64 bytes from 192.168.1.5: icmp_seq=3 ttl=255 time=0.3ms
...
```

Press Ctrl+C at any time to stop the test. Some basic information about the entire test will appear, as in the following example:

```
... PowerEdge.Coolnerds.com ping statistics ...
4 packets transmitted, 4 packets received, 0% packet loss
round-trip min/avg/max = 0.3/0.4/0.8 ms
```

All of this information indicates that the test was totally successful. In particular, the 0% packet loss tells you that the test went perfectly, which is what you want.

If entering the ping command results in something like this instead

```
From P300.Coolnerds.com (192.168.1.3): Destination Host Unreachable
```

then the two computers are not communicating. When you press Ctrl+C to stop the test, you'll get some feedback including a message indicating a 100% packet loss. In that case, see the "Troubleshooting a LAN" section near the end of this chapter for some help. You might try pinging several different machines from the current computer first. If you can successfully ping any other computer in the LAN, then the problem probably lies in the computer that you cannot ping. If you can't ping any computer in the LAN, then the problem is most likely centered in the computer you're sitting at.

## YOU'RE DONE

When you can successfully ping all the computers in the LAN, the basic infrastructure of this LAN is intact, and you can start installing and configuring various network services, as described in the next two chapters. Do keep in mind that in this chapter and the next two, we'll be focused on the type of small, relatively simple LAN created in this chapter. Chapters 25-27 will discuss techniques for accessing other networks.

# TROUBLESHOOTING A LAN

If, for whatever reason, you're unable to ping another computer in the LAN, there are several steps you can take to get to the root of the problem and get things working. For starters, you might want to consider shutting down every computer in the LAN (using halt). While the machines are down, check the cable connection between every computer and the hub very carefully, making sure all plugs are in nice and snug.

> **Tip**
>
> You can check and fix loose cables while the computers are running. The only reason for shutting everything down here is so you can watch for feedback on the screen during bootup.

As you bring up each computer, watch for the following feedback while the computer is booting up. If you type the letter I when given the opportunity to do an interactive startup, you'll be able to slow things down and watch more closely, although the actual interactive part won't start immediately. Before the interactive part begins, look for the line that reads:

```
Setting hostname: xxx.networkname    [OK]
```

Make sure the hostname and network name you assigned to this host are spelled correctly. If not, you'll need to return to the Basic Host Information portion of LinuxConf (refer to Figure 22.4) and correct the spelling, after the computer is fully booted.

If you opted to do an interactive startup, the screen will start prompting you, asking if you want to start various services. Always answer Yes, and watch for the results of particular tests. If Kudzu detects your Ethernet card, then the card wasn't configured properly the first time through. Go ahead and let Kudzu configure the card. And when asked about configuring the network, answer Yes and make sure you type in the correct IP address and other information for the computer you're sitting at.

The following line is an important one, too:

```
Bringing up interface eth0    [OK]
```

This tells you whether your first (or only) Ethernet card is working. If this fails, you should check all the network settings in LinuxConf, as discussed throughout this chapter, to ensure that the card is configured correctly.

---

**Tip**

You can also bring the Ethernet interface up, or down, using the `ifup` (*interface up*) and `ifdown` (*interface down*) commands and watch for error messages that might prove useful. The command `ifdown eth0` shuts down the eth0 interface. The command `ifup eth0` brings it back up.

# CHAPTER 23

# SHARING FILES WITH NFS

In this chapter

# SHARING RESOURCES ON A LAN

Probably the most common use of a local area network is to allow users on different machines access to the same files on one centralized computer. For example, if a company maintains a database of customers, parts, and so forth, it's much more efficient for all users to access the same database, rather than for each user to have his own copy of the database, because changes that are made to the centralized database are immediately available to all users.

Similarly, it's often useful to create a single shared directory on a computer for storing all files related to a given project. That way, everyone working on the project has access to all its files. Backing up and managing all those files is greatly simplified as well. One of the tools that Linux (and UNIX) uses to share directories in a LAN is called Network File System, or NFS. Typically, NFS is installed automatically whenever you install Red Hat Linux. So long as you have your network up and running, as discussed in Chapter 22, "Creating a Local Area Network," setting up shared directories is pretty easy.

There are two sides to the NFS equation: the *server* and the *client*. The server is the computer that actually houses the shared directory. Any computer in the LAN can act as an NFS server. Every single computer in the LAN could share some of its directories with all other computers in the LAN. File and directory sharing is often done this way in small *peer-to-peer networks*. The only problem with this approach is its lack of centralization. Users generally share directories on an as-needed basis, and things eventually become pretty haphazard. Most organizations prefer a *client-server* approach where shared directories are placed on a single computer, often called the *file server*. This approach makes it easier to maintain security for the shared files, as well as to perform backups and other routine maintenance tasks.

The client side of the equation, as you may have guessed, is any computer that can gain access to the shared directory. Simply creating a shared directory and/or fileserver doesn't automatically give everyone in the LAN access to that directory. Instead, the network administrator can control exactly which clients do and don't have access, and also control how much access they have (such as read-only, or read/write access).

# AWAKENING THE NFS SERVER

For NFS to work, the computer that's sharing a directory must have the NFS software already installed. As mentioned, this is usually a given in Red Hat Linux. But just to play it safe, you can sit down at the computer that will be sharing a directory and run a couple of tests to ensure that the machine is ready. First, at the command prompt (or in any terminal window) enter this command:

```
rpcinfo -p
```

You should see something like this, indicating that the NFS portmapper is ready:

```
program     vers  proto  port
100000      2    tcp    111   portmapper
100000      2    udp    111   portmapper
```

**Note** The portmapper is one component of NFS. Its job is to map calls made from clients to the correct NFS daemons on the server.

NFS relies on several daemons to perform its task. Before attempting to share a directory or device, enter the following command to check the status of NFS:

```
/etc/rc.d/init.d/nfs status
```

If the command returns no feedback, or you see messages indicating that the services are stopped, you should stop, and then restart NFS by entering this command:

```
/etc/rc.d/init.d/nfs stop
```

When all services have been stopped, you're returned to the command prompt. To restart the services, enter the following command (press the ~UA key, change `stop` to `start`, and then press Enter):

```
/etc/rc.d/init/d/nfs start
```

You should see several messages indicating that various daemons have started, each followed by an [OK] to indicate success.

## NO SUCH FILE OR DIRECTORY

If your screen reports that there's no such file or directory as NFS, you'll need to install the `knfsd` (Kernel NFS Server Daemon) package from the Red Hat CD-ROM #1. You can insert and mount (if necessary) the Red Hat Linux CD-ROM #1 into your CD-ROM drive. Then use GnoRPM to install `knfsd-1.4.7-7.i386.rpm`. Or just enter the following command:

```
rpm -ivh /mnt/cdrom/RedHat/RPMS/knfsd-1*.rpm
```

Try entering the `/etc/rc.d/init.d/nfs stop` and `/etc/rc.d/init/d/nfs start` commands when the installation is complete, to make sure you can get the NFS server running. You won't get any feedback from the commands, but in this case, no feedback is good feedback.

## ENSURING NFS IS AVAILABLE AT STARTUP

On any computer that will be sharing devices or volumes, you'll want to ensure that NFS is one of the system services that's started up automatically. To do so, follow these steps:

1. Enter the command `setup` at any command prompt.
2. Using the ~DA key, scroll down to System Services, and then press Enter.
3. Use the ~DA key to scroll down to the NFS service.
4. If the NFS option is *not* selected (its brackets don't contain an asterisk), press the spacebar to select that service.
5. Press Tab and then press Enter to choose OK.
6. Press Tab twice and then press Enter to choose Quit.

That should do it. To make doubly sure, you can enter a `reboot` command to reboot the system, providing that no users are currently accessing the server. As startup messages scroll by you should see [OK] indicators for all services, including NFS services.

# SHARING A DIRECTORY (SERVER SIDE)

You can share any existing directory on any computer in the LAN. Of course, you can create a new directory to share as well. In fact, it's a fairly common practice to put all shared directories within a single directory named /exports. Or, if you haven't partitioned the / directory with lots of room, make /exports a subdirectory of /usr or some other directory. Either way, it's easier to identify and manage all the shared directories in the future because you know they're all defined within a single directory.

For example, let's say you plan to create a directory named projectx that will be shared by several users in the LAN. Putting that new directory inside the /usr/exports directory will make it clear that the directory is shared. You can create the /usr/exports and /usr/exports/projectx directories in the usual manner using a file manager. Or, at any command prompt just enter these commands:

```
mkdir /usr/exports
mkdir /usr/exports/projectx
```

Either way, you should now have a directory named /usr/exports/projectx in your filesystem as in Figure 23.1. (I added a few files to mine, but yours can start out empty.)

**Figure 23.1**
A new directory named /usr /exports, and subdirectory named projectx, added to the filesystem on my PowerEdge host.

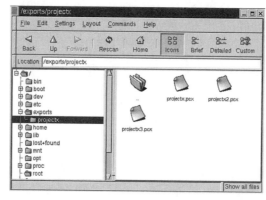

Now that the directory exists, you can use LinuxConf to share it with other computers in the LAN. Start LinuxConf in the usual manner (click the Start button and choose System, LinuxConf, or enter the command `linuxconf` at a command prompt). Then follow these steps:

1. In the left column of LinuxConf, open Config, Networking, Server Tasks, Exported File Systems (NFS).

2. Click the Add button. A tab titled One Exported File System appears.

3. In the Path to export box, type the complete path to the directory to be shared (/usr/ exports/projectx in my example).

4. If you like, you can type a descriptive comment of your own wording into the optional Comment box.

5. Next to Client Name(s), list at least one client that can have access to this shared directory. If several clients will all have the same permissions, you can list each client separated by a blank space. (The LinuxConf Help says to use commas, but that doesn't appear to work.) For example, in Figure 23.2 I've given the computers named BigBoy, P300, and K63 all the same permissions to access the shared directory.

**Figure 23.2**
The directory
/usr/exports/
projectx will be
accessible from
clients BigBoy,
P300, and K63.

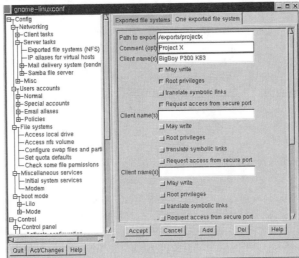

6. To assign more clients, with different privileges, use the second Client Name(s) entry box on the panel. (Click Help for information about privileges, or see the next section, "Server-Side Privileges.")

**Tip**  You can use the wildcard character to represent groups of clients. For example, entering *.mylan.com as the client name would grant permission to all clients on the mylan.com network.

7. Click the Accept button.

8. You'll see the exported directory listed on the Exported File Systems tab (see Figure 23.3). Click the Quit button beneath the list.

9. Click the Quit button at the lower-left corner of the LinuxConf window, and then click Accept the Changes when prompted.

Before we get into accessing the shared directory from a client computer, let's take a moment to review some of the options presented to you while setting up a directory to share.

**Figure 23.3**
One shared directory defined in LinuxConf.

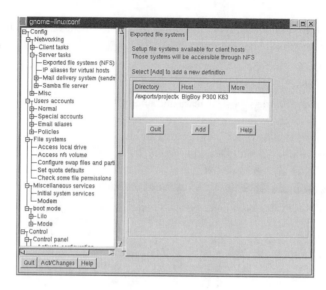

## SERVER-SIDE PRIVILEGES

You can tweak privileges granted to the shared directory while you're defining the share, or afterwards. If you've already defined a shared directory and closed LinuxConf, and then need to go back and make changes, simply reopen LinuxConf. In the left column of LinuxConf, open Config, Networking, Server Tasks, Exported File Systems (NFS) once again. Then click the shared directory you want to change. The One Exported File System tab for that shared directory will reappear. You can add or delete client names, and change permissions for clients. Here's a quick summary of the privileges you can grant to clients:

- **May Write:** If selected, the client can read from, and write to, the shared directory. If not selected, the client can only read from the shared directory, but neither write to it nor make any changes to its contents.

- **Root Privileges:** If selected, a user who is logged in as root at a client computer retains root permissions on the shared directory. If de-selected, then root has only normal user privileges on the shared directory.

- **Translate Symbolic Links:** Supposedly converts absolute symbolic links into relative links to ensure that links work correctly when accessed from a client computer. However, selecting this option in Red Hat 6.2 results in an error message stating that `link_relative` isn't supported in the `/etc/exports` file. So don't select it.

- **Request Access from Secure Port:** If selected, only requests from secure ports will be allowed to access the shared directory. All other requests will be ignored.

## THE /etc/exports FILE

All information about shared directories on the current computer is actually stored in a simple text file named `/etc/exports`. LinuxConf just provides a graphical approach to editing that file. But as with any configuration file, you can also make changes manually using any text editor. Figure 23.4 shows a sample /etc/exports file in gEdit.

**Figure 23.4**
A sample /etc/exports file open in gEdit.

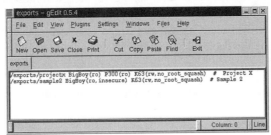

The format of /etc/exports is as follows: Each line represents a single shared directory. Each line is divided into three columns separated by one or more blank spaces. The first column is the path to the shared directory. For the sake of example, I added a second shared directory named /usr/exports/sample2.

The second column has one or more names of clients that have access to the shared directory, followed by the clients' permissions in parentheses. If multiple clients have the same set of permissions, their names are separated by spaces. For example, the /usr/exports/projectx directory grants equal permissions to clients BigBoy, P300, and K63. The permissions granted to a client (or group of clients) follows the last client name (without any spaces), and are enclosed in parentheses. The following are possible permissions:

- **ro:** Read-Only. The client can read, but not write to, the shared directory.
- **rw:** Read/Write. The client can read the directory as well as write to it.
- **no_root_squash:** If included, allows a user logged in as root to retain root permissions in the shared directory.
- **link_relative:** This is the one that Red Hat 6.2 apparently doesn't support, even though LinuxConf offers it as the Translate Symbolic Links option. Should not be included in your /etc/exports file.
- **insecure:** If included, allows connections from nonsecure ports.

Notice that in the second line, where a directory named /usr/exports/sample2 is being shared, two different clients are granted permission, but each has its own unique set of permission. BigBoy, for that shared directory, has Read-Only (ro) privileges, and can log in from an insecure port. Client K63 has Read/Write (rw) permissions, and root privileges when its user is logged in as root (no_root_squash). The # symbol and text to the right of it are comments for human consumption only. Linux ignores the # sign and everything to the right of it.

**Note**

For even more information on the /etc/exports file, enter the command man exports to view its man page.

### WHENEVER YOU CHANGE THE EXPORTS TABLE

Whenever you change the /etc/exports table on a computer, it's important to stop, then restart, the NFS daemons. Doing so tells the appropriate daemons (rpc.nfsd and rpc.mountd) that the table has been changed, and triggers them to update their own internal tables. To stop and restart the daemons, enter the following command:

```
/etc/rc.d/init.d/nfs restart
```

or to see each service start and stop individually and get more feedback on the screen, enter these commands:

```
/etc/rc.d/init.d/nfs stop
/etc/rc.d/init.d/nfs start
```

You should also enter the following command to see if the internal tables now held by the daemons contain any errors:

```
exportfs -a
```

If the command returns nothing that means there are no errors in the file.

**Tip**

The command exportfs -v shows a verbose list of shares defined on the current computer. You can learn more about exportfs by viewing its man page, man exportfs.

## ACCESSING A SHARED DIRECTORY

To access the shared directory, go to any computer to which you've granted access privileges. Create a mount point that you'll use to represent the shared directory on your own computer. For example, you might want to use a file manager or use the mkdir command to create a directory named /mnt/projectx as in the example shown in Figure 23.5. Always leave this directory empty because it's only a placeholder for the shared directory, in much the same way that /mnt/cdrom and /mnt/floppy are placeholders for whatever disks you mount in those drives.

There are a couple of ways you can access the shared directory now. If you want to do it on-the-fly, on an as-needed basis, you can enter a mount command using the following syntax:

```
mount servername:/shareddirectorylocalmountpoint
```

servername is the hostname of the computer that's housing the shared directory (such as PowerEdge in my example), shareddirectory is the name of the exported directory (/usr/exports/projectx), and localmountpoint is the name of the directory on the client computer that you've created as a placeholder. For example, to mount the sample directory described in this chapter, from any client that has access privileges to that directory, you could enter the command:

```
mount PowerEdge:/usr/exports/projectx /mnt/projectx
```

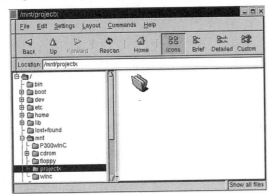

**Figure 23.5**
In this example I've created an empty directory named /mnt/ projectx on a client computer to act as a place-holder for the shared directory.

When the shared directory has some files in it, you can always verify that you've made a connection simply by viewing the contents of the placeholder directory. For example, you could open /mnt/projectx in a file manager, or enter the command ls /mnt/projectx to view that directory's contents.

> **Tip**
> Entering the command mount with no arguments will show you all currently mounted directories, including mounted NFS shares.

> **Tip**
> If the mount command leads to an error message indicating that RPC isn't registered, or something to that effect, stop and restart NFS on the current computer by entering the commands /etc/rc.d/init.d/nfs stop and /etc/rc.d/init.d/nfs start.

## AUTO-MOUNTING THE SHARED DIRECTORY

Perhaps an even more convenient way to access the shared directory from a client machine would be to have the connection made automatically at startup. This would be particularly handy if you shut down your machine often. You can use LinuxConf to set up such an auto mount. Just start LinuxConf on the client computer of your choosing. Then follow these steps:

1. Open Config, File Systems, Access NFS volume.

2. In the Server box, type the name of the server computer that houses the shared directory (PowerEdge in my example).

> **Tip**
>
> The term *volume* simply refers to any chunk of disk storage. An entire hard disk is a volume, as is a single directory on the hard disk. A shared directory might also be called an *NFS share*, a *shared volume*, a *shared device*, a *share*, or even an *export* or *exported volume*.

3. Next to Volume, type the full path to the shared directory (/usr/exports/projectx in my example).

4. Next to mount Point, type the full path to the placeholder directory you created on the current computer, as in Figure 23.6.

**Figure 23.6**
The Volume Specification tab in LinuxConf lets you auto-mount a shared directory at startup.

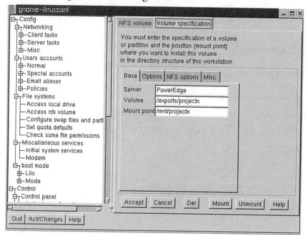

5. Optionally, select options from the Options, NFS Options, and Misc tabs as described in the later section "Options on the Client Side." However, the defaults will work fine for most people, so you can move on to step 6 now if you like. Then make adjustments later, if necessary.

6. Click the Mount button to mount the shared directory. (If you already mounted it using the mount command, you can click Unmount and then click Mount to test this connection.)

7. Click the Accept button. You'll see the new mount listed in the NFS Volume tab (see Figure 23.7).

8. Click the Quit button below the list.

9. Click the Quit button at the lower-left corner of LinuxConf, and then click Activate the Changes when prompted.

## THE /etc/fstab FILE

As you may recall from Chapter 6, "System Administration Basics," information about filesystems that are mounted automatically as the computer boots up is stored in a file named /etc/fstab (*file*system *tab*le). The same is true for connections to shared directories defined in LinuxConf. For example, after defining access to the shared `PowerEdge:/usr/exports/projectx` directory on a client computer, opening that client computer's `/etc/fstab` file will reveal a new line, as in Figure 23.8.

**Figure 23.7**
The NFS Volume tab in LinuxConf lists shared NFS volumes that will be automatically mounted at startup.

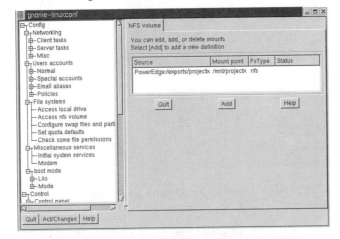

**Figure 23.8**
The last line in this `/etc/fstab` file sets up the connection to a shared directory on the computer PowerEdge.

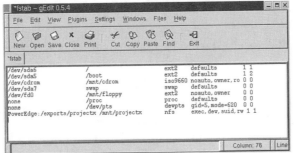

As always, you can edit the `/etc/fstab` file manually at any time using any text editor. Note that the first column shows the hostname of the computer that holds the shared directory, followed by a colon and the complete path to the shared directory (such as `PowerEdge:/usr/exports/projectx`). The second column, which must be preceded by at least one blank space, indicates the placeholder directory on the current computer that will represent the share when mounted (such as `/mnt/projectx`). The third column indicates the file system's type, which will always be nfs when connecting to a directory that's been shared via nfs. The last three columns indicate permissions, as discussed in the sections that follow.

## OPTIONS ON THE CLIENT SIDE

On the client side of a shared directory, you have a whole lot of options and permissions to choose from. As you may recall from earlier in the chapter, when defining the client side of the connection in LinuxConf, the Volume Specification tab provides several additional tabs of options that we didn't delve into at the time. Most are general options that apply to all types of mounted devices. But we'll take a look at them individually starting with the ones on the Options tab shown in Figure 23.9.

**Figure 23.9**
The Options tab in the Volume Specification tab of LinuxConf presents many options for defining a client's access to a shared directory.

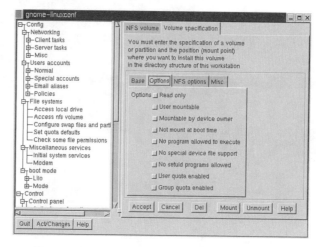

Note that in the list, letters shown in parentheses indicate the code used within the /etc/fstab file to indicate that the option is turned on:

- **Read Only (ro):** If selected, the device is mounted as Read-Only so the client can read, but not write to or change the shared directory. If not selected, the device is mounted Read/Write (rw).

- **User Mountable (user):** If selected, any user can mount the shared directory. If not selected, only root has mounting privileges.

- **Mountable by Device Owner (owner):** If selected, only the owner of the device, as defined in the device's properties, can mount the device.

- **Not Mount at Boot Time (noauto):** If selected, the shared directory will not be mounted automatically when the computer first starts. (Required when the shared device is a removable drive, such as a CD-ROM drive.)

- **No Program Allowed to Execute (noexec):** If selected, users cannot run programs from the shared directory.

- **No Special Device Support (nodev):** To increase security, you can choose this option so that any special access privileges defined in /dev on the client are ignored.

- **No Setuid Programs Allowed (nosuid):** When selected, this option tightens security by preventing users from running programs as some other user (typically root).

- **User Quota Enabled (usrquota):** When selected, user quotas defined in the quota.user file (see Chapter 25, "Gateways, Routers, Switches, and Other TCP/IP Mysteries Explained") are enforced.

- **Group Quota Enabled (grpquota):** When selected, group quotas defined in the quota.group file (Chapter 25) are enforced.

The NFS Options tab lets you define nfs-specific mounting options (see Figure 23.10). These will also be listed in /etc/fstab, if selected.

**Figure 23.10**
The NFS Options tab provides options that are unique to mounting nfs shares.

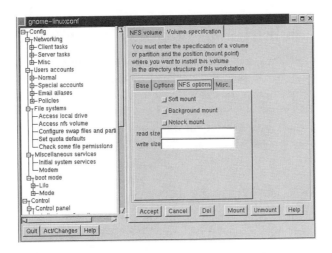

The letters shown in parentheses indicate how the option appears in /etc/fstab if selected in LinuxConf:

- **Soft Mount (soft):** If selected, Linux will try repeatedly to access the share if it's not accessible immediately. The Retrans option, accessible on the Misc tab, specifies how many times the attempt will be made before returning a failure.

- **Background Mount (bg):** Should the initial attempt at mounting fail, this option will place the process in the background, and keep trying to connect until the shared volume becomes accessible. A good choice if there's any chance the server won't be available when the client starts up.

- **Nolock Mount (nolock):** Do not use locking, do not start the locking daemon (lockd).

- **Read Size (rsize):** The number of bytes to be read across the network at once. Leave this option blank to accept the default of 8192 bytes, unless there's something unusual about your drive or network that requires a different setting.

- **Write Size (wsize):** The number of bytes to be written across the network at once. As with Read Size, this should be left blank to accept the default of 8192 bytes. Otherwise, the performance of your network could be impaired.

The last tab, titled Misc, simply allows you to enter any other options that might be unique to your network, as well as a comment placed at the end of the line in /etc/fstab. If you opted for a soft mount, the Other options box will contain Retrans=5, which indicates the number of times that the transmission will be attempted before failing. There are also quite a few other options that you can enter into the Other options box. Most are pretty esoteric. But if you want to learn more, see the man page for mount (such as man mount). The man pages for nfs, nfsd, and mountd also contain detailed technical information.

# CASE STUDY: SHARING A "HIDDEN" WINDOWS DRIVE

As you learned in earlier chapters, you can set up your computer so that you have the choice of booting up in either Windows or Linux. When booted up in Linux, you can still access the Windows C: drive if you set up your /etc/fstab file correctly, as discussed back in Chapter 12, "Using DOS and Windows." Suppose you'd also like to access that nonbooted Windows C drive from other computers in the network as well. That can certainly be done. You just need to set up that nonbooted Windows disk as an NFS shared directory, as you'll learn in this case study.

## MOUNTING THE WINDOWS DRIVE

The first step to sharing a nonbooted Windows drive is to make sure that the drive is automatically mounted at boot time. First, you need to create a mount point for the drive. If you haven't already done that, you can just enter a command like mkdir /mnt/winc to create an empty placeholder directory for the Windows drive.

Then, if you haven't already done so, you need to set up the /etc/fstab file to mount the Windows drive automatically at bootup. You'll need to know the drive's device name (such as /dev/sda1), and then add it to /etc/fstab as discussed in the section "Mounting Windows/DOS Partitions" in Chapter 12. Reboot to verify that the drive will be mounted automatically at startup. When you can open your favorite file manager, open the /mnt/winc mount point and see the contents of the Windows drive, then you know the directory is ready to be set up as an NFS share (see Figure 23.11).

**Figure 23.11**
Opening /mnt/ winc on this computer shows the contents of Windows drive C:, even though I'm booted up in Linux at the moment.

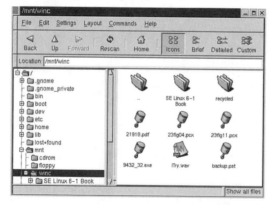

Earlier I said it's good practice to put all the shared directories from a single machine into a directory named /usr/exports. In this way, you can always see, at a glance, exactly what's being exported via NFS from the current computer. In this example, however, our shared directory already has a mount point, /mnt/winc. To stay with our sense of good style, you can still create a /usr/exports directory. Then, just put a symbolic link to the /mnt/winc directory inside the /usr/exports directory. That way, you still have a record of the share, but you don't have to change the /mnt/winc mount point. To create the symbolic link, you'll first have to create the /usr/exports directory on the current computer (if you haven't already done so). The command `mkdir /usr/exports` will do the trick, although you can do it just as easily from within your favorite file manager.

An easy way to create the symbolic link is to open two file manager windows (in GNOME's file manager, choose File, Create New Window from the menu bar). In the left pane of one of the windows, select `/mnt` as the directory to view. In the other window, select `/usr/exports` as the directory to view. Then, using the middle mouse button, drag the icon for the `winc` directory from the right pane of the `/mnt` directory contents into the right pane of the file manager window displaying the contents of `/usr/exports`. Release the middle mouse button and choose Link Here. You should see a symbolic link (a.k.a. a shortcut icon) with a little curved arrow in its lower-right corner within the `/usr/exports` directory now (see Figure 23.12). That icon will become the very thing you want to share via NFS.

> **Tip**
>
> You can also use the `ln` command with the -s switch to create a shortcut. For example, to create a shortcut to `/mnt/winc` in the `/usr/exports` directory you'd enter the command `ln -s /mnt/winc usr//exports/winc`.

**Figure 23.12**
The /usr/
exports direc-
tory now contains
a symbolic link to
the /mnt/winc
directory on the
same computer.

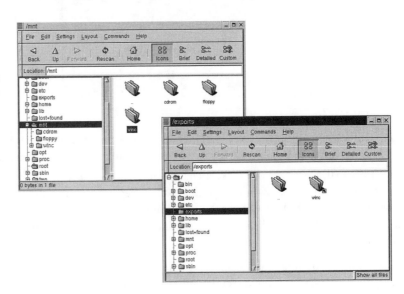

You can then close the File Manager windows, and share the `/usr/exports/winc` icon using LinuxConf, as discussed next.

## SHARING THE SYMBOLIC LINK

Even though the `/usr/exports/winc` icon is just a symbolic link to `/mnt/winc`, you can still make it into an NFS share just as you would a real directory. Open LinuxConf and in the left column, follow these steps:

1. Open Config, Networking, Server Tasks, Exported File Systems (NFS).

2. Click the Add button. A tab titled One Exported File System appears.

3. In the Path To Export box, type the complete path to the directory to be shared (/usr/exports/winc in this example).

4. If you like, you can type a descriptive comment of your own wording into the optional Comment box.

5. Next to Client Name(s), list the clients that have permission to access the shared drive.

6. Choose options for those clients, such as May Write, as shown in Figure 23.13.

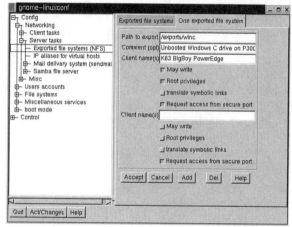

**Figure 23.13**
Setting up /usr/ exports/winc as an NFS share in LinuxConf.

7. Click the Accept button.

8. Click Quit beneath the list of shares, click Quit near the lower-left corner of LinuxConf, and then click the Activate the Changes button if prompted.

Remember that, whenever you make a change to the /etc/exports file, you'll want to go through the ritual described in the section "Whenever You Change the Exports Table" earlier in this chapter. To make absolutely certain the drive is now shared, you may want to open /etc/exports and make sure there's a line for the /usr/exports/winc directory listed within that file.

You should now be able to go to any client computer in the network that has permission to access the /usr/exports/winc directory, and mount that directory using techniques described under "Accessing a Shared Directory" earlier in this chapter. Remember to create a mount point on the client first. For example, you might enter a command like mkdir /mnt/P300WinC if the shared Windows drive is on a client named P300. Then to mount the shared directory manually, you could enter a command like the following:

```
mount P300:/usr/exports/winc /mnt/P300WinC
```

If, instead of a clean mount, you get an error message indicating that the RPC program isn't registered, you'll want to ensure that nfs is auto-started on the computer that's sharing the Windows drive. Follow the steps in the section "Awakening the NFS Server" earlier in this chapter on that computer to make sure the computer is capable of sharing the directory via NFS. You may want to reboot both the computer serving the `/usr/exports/winc` and any clients from which you want to connect, just to make sure things will work normally each time you start the computers in the future.

Remember, too, that once you can mount the share manually with the `mount` command, you can automate the mount by updating your `/etc/fstab` file, as discussed in "Auto-Mounting the Shared Directory" earlier in this chapter.

# CHAPTER 24

# SHARING WINDOWS/LINUX RESOURCES WITH SAMBA

## In this chapter

# SHARING WINDOWS RESOURCES

To access Windows resources from Linux computers, the Windows computers, of course, need to be connected to the same network and should use the TCP/IP protocol. If you haven't yet connected the Windows computer to the LAN, you'll need to do so using whatever techniques are appropriate for your particular version of Windows. You'll want to know the domain name (NT) or workgroup name (Windows 95/98) that the computer belongs to. Typically, this will be the same as the domain name used by the Linux computers in the same LAN. For example, to view or change the workgroup name in a Windows 98 computer, you can right-click the Network Neighborhood icon on the Windows 98 desktop and choose Properties. The computer name (a.k.a., hostname) and workgroup name appear on the Identification tab of the Network dialog that appears (see Figure 24.1).

**Figure 24.1**

The Identification tab of the Network properties dialog box shows the computer name and workgroup name in Windows 98.

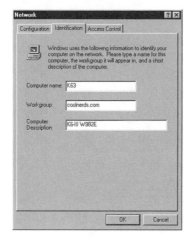

In the Configuration tab of that same dialog box, you should see a TCP/IP protocol linked to your Ethernet card (such as `TCP/IP -> SMC EtherPower II 10/100 Ethernet Adapter` shown in Figure 24.2). If that protocol isn't set up, you can use the Add button on the Configuration tab to add Microsoft TCP/IP protocol to your list of installed network components. If you want the current computer to share its printer or share files, you need to also click the File and Print Sharing button, and make sure you select the appropriate options.

Lastly, you can choose between Share-Level Access Control and User-Level Access Control on the Access Control tab of the Network properties dialog box. When you're creating a new LAN, it's easiest to choose Share-Level Access Control, where you can supply a password for each shared device. Although later down the road, after you get everything working you might want User-Level Access Control where you specify users and groups who have access to each shared resource. That all depends on how tight you need to make your overall security scheme once the network is fully up and running.

Finally, you need to specifically share the devices that you want other LAN clients to access. In most versions of Windows this is a simple matter of right-clicking the item's icon; choosing Sharing, Shared As; and giving the device a Share Name. For example, in

Figure 24.3 I right-clicked the icon for the My Documents folder on the K63 computer, chose Sharing, and selected Shared As. I gave the folder a share name (K63_MYDOCS), a comment, and Full access. I set virtually no restrictions on accessing the folder in this example, and hence haven't assigned a password.

**Figure 24.2**
File and print sharing capabilities enabled on this Windows 98 PC.

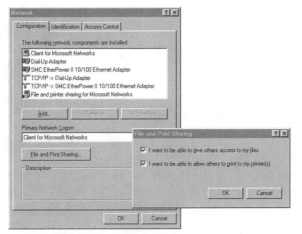

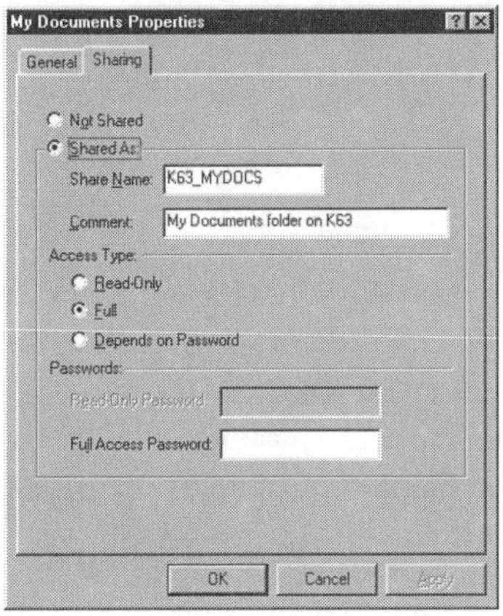

**Figure 24.3**
Windows dialog box where I've shared the My Documents folder on the computer named K63.

Once a device has been shared, a hand appears beneath its icon. For the sake of example, I've shared three resources on the K63 computer by right-clicking each resource's icon and choosing Sharing. If you look closely at Figure 24.4 you can see that the printer, CD-ROM drive (D:), and My Documents folder on drive C: have all been shared on the computer named K63. In each case I didn't require a password to access the share, just to keep things simple for the time being.

**Note**

There are lots of versions of Windows around nowadays, and the exact steps you follow to share a resource may vary from one version to the next. I can only present some examples here. Refer to your Windows documentation if you need any help setting up a network and sharing devices on a computer.

**Figure 24.4**
The printer, CD-ROM drive, and My Documents folder on this Windows 98 PC have all been shared.

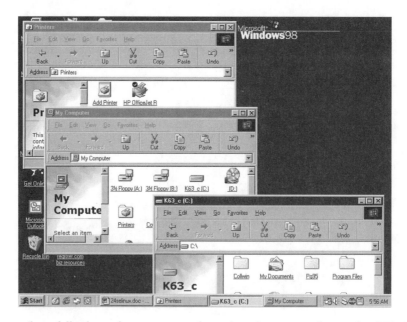

So now, you (hopefully) know how to access these shared resources from other Windows computers in the LAN. (Hint: You go through the Network Neighborhood icon.) Now you'll learn to access those resources from Linux computers on the same LAN, using Samba.

## UNDERSTANDING SAMBA

To gain access to shared resources that are on a Windows computer, you need to install and activate the *Samba client* package. Samba gets its name from the networking protocol it translates to and from TCP/IP, the *System Message Block* (SMB) protocol used by Windows. In fact, the terms *Samba* and *SMB* are sometimes used interchangeably. However, technically speaking, SMB is a Windows protocol, and Samba is a suite of programs that allow Linux computers to interact with computers that use the SMB protocol.

Samba can also act as a server, offering up resources on a Linux computer for other network clients (both Linux and Windows clients). For example, if you have a printer or directory on a Linux computer that you want to share, Samba can do the job. To share resources, you need to install the *Samba server* software. Of course, any Linux computer can have both the Samba server and Samba client software installed. This means that any Linux computer in the network can share some of its resources with other computers and also use resources that are being shared by other computers.

## INSTALLING THE SAMBA CLIENT SOFTWARE

As mentioned, there are two sides to Samba. There's the Samba client (the `samba-client*.rpm` package), which can access shared SMB resources. Typically, the Samba client is installed automatically whenever you install Linux on a computer. But there's an easy way to find out whether or not the Samba client is already installed. Just enter the following command:

```
rpm -q samba-client
```

**Tip**

Remember, you don't need to install Samba or anything else special on the Windows computers. Samba interacts directly with the SMB networking protocol that's built into Windows.

For Samba to work correctly, you also need to have the `samba-common*.rpm` package installed. Again, to make sure that package is installed, enter this command:

```
rpm -q samba-common
```

If either package isn't installed, you can install it from the Red Hat Linux CD #1 in the usual manner. That is, put the CD in the CD-ROM drive, and mount it if it doesn't mount automatically. Then, to install the Samba client enter the following command:

```
rpm -ivh /mnt/cdrom/RedHat/RPMS/samba-client*.rpm
```

If you need to install the `samba-common` package, enter this command:

```
rpm -ivh /mnt/cdrom/RedHat/RPMS/samba-common*.rpm
```

Remember that all of the previous steps install Samba client services on only one computer, not the entire LAN. If you want other computers in the network to serve or access Samba shares, you'll need to repeat all the steps on those other computers. But once you've installed the Samba client software on a Linux computer, you'll be able to access shared Windows resources from that Linux computer.

## ACCESSING WINDOWS RESOURCES FROM A LINUX COMPUTER

Accessing Windows resources from a Linux computer isn't quite as easy as accessing resources through the Windows Network Neighborhood icon. But, at least it's do-able. To see what shared resources are available on a Windows client, you can enter the `smbclient` command with the `-L` (list) option, followed by the hostname of the computer that contains those resources. For example, I shared a printer, a folder (My Documents), and a CD-ROM drive on my Windows computer named K63. Entering the following command on a Linux computer will first ask for a password:

```
smbclient -L K63
```

If the shares are password-protected, you'll need to enter an appropriate password. But if the shares aren't password-protected, you can just press Enter. The screen then displays a list of available resources on the K63 computer, as follows. The names and comments shown here are the ones I entered on the Windows computer while sharing the devices:

```
Sharename     Type      Comment
K63_CD        Disk      CD-ROM drive on K63 Windows computer
K63_MYDOCS    Disk      My Documents folder on K63
PRINTER$      Disk
HP_R80        Printer   HP OfficeJet R80 on K63
IPC$          IPC       Remote Inter Process Communication
Server        Comment
K63           K6-III W982E
Workgroup     Master
COOLNERDS.COM K63
```

Neither PRINTER$ nor IPC$ are resources I specifically shared. Rather, they're resources created automatically by Samba to allow the connection between resources. What's mainly important is the exact spelling (including case) of the Server (such as K63) and the shared devices (such as K63_CD, K63_MYDOCS, and HP_R80, the printer in my example).

## ACCESSING WINDOWS DRIVES AND DIRECTORIES

There are a couple of ways to access shared drives and directories on the Windows computer from a Linux machine. Probably your leastfavorite will be to connect to the resource using the smbclient command. This approach is similar to connecting to an FTP site in that you then get a special command prompt that, in turn, provides its own unique set of commands for transferring files to and from and the Windows resource. The syntax for this type of connection is simply smbclient //hostname/sharename. For example, to connect to the K63_MYDOCS directory from my Linux computer, I'd enter the following command:

```
smbclient //K63/K63_MYDOCS
```

When prompted for a password, you can simply press Enter if the shared resource requires no password. The command prompt changes to this:

```
smb:\>
```

The new prompt tells you that you can now use the DOS-like commands summarized in Table 24.1 to view and interact with the connected My Documents folder.

### TABLE 24.1  SOME COMMANDS YOU CAN USE WITH smbclient TO ACCESS RESOURCES AND COPY FILES

| SMB Prompt Command | Description |
| --- | --- |
| cd directory | Changes to the specified directory on the remote computer. (For example, cd.) |
| dir or ls | Shows directory contents on the remote computer. You can add a mask (as in dir m*). |
| cd dosdirectory | Changes to the specified *directory* on the remote computer (cd mypix*, for example). |

TABLE 24.1    CONTINUED

| SMB Prompt Command | Description |
| --- | --- |
| lcd *directory* | Changes to the specified directory on the local Linux computer (lcd /home, for example). |
| del *file(s)* | Deletes specified file(s) on the remote computer (as in del *.bak). |
| get *remotename localname* | Copies specified remote file to current directory, giving it the name specified in *localname* (as in get mystuff.txt K63mystuff.txt). |
| mget *file(s)* | Copies multiple files matching *file(s)* from the remote machine to the local machine (mget mytstuff.*, for instance). |
| md or mkdir *directory* | Creates the specified directory on the remote computer (as in md newstuff). |
| rd or rmdir *directory* | Deletes the specified directory on the remote computer (rd oldstuff, for example). |
| put *filename remotename* | Copies specified *filename* from the local machine to the remote machine, giving copied file *remotename* (as in put mystuff.txt linuxmystuff.txt). |
| mput *file(s)* | Copies specified file(s) from the local computer to the remote computer (mput mystuf*.*, for instance). |
| ! *shellcommand* | Executes a bash shell command specified (such as ! ls). |
| ? *command* or help command | Provides help for an smbclient command (such as ? mput). |
| exit or quit | Closes the connection and the smbclient program, returning you to the normal command prompt. |

*Long directory names need to be shortened to the old DOS 8.3 equivalent. Usually this is just the first six characters (excluding any spaces), followed by ~1. For example, to switch to the subdirectory named My Pictures in the My Documents folder, I'd enter the command cd mypict~1. Using smbmount, as described in the following paragraphs, gets around this problem of having to translate long filenames to DOS 8.3 names.*

Clearly, if you're not a big fan of typing commands, that first alternative may not appear too attractive. The second approach offers a more visual drag-and-drop approach, where you can mount the shared Windows directory as a directory on your current Linux machine. Then you can use a graphical file manager to view and transfer files.

To mount a remote Windows drive or directory so that it acts like a directory on the local computer, you first need to create a blank directory on your local computer to act as a placeholder. (You need only do that part once, not every time you want to connect.) For example, let's say I want to create a directory named /mnt/k63mydocs on my local Linux computer to display the contents of the My Documents folder on the K63 Windows computer. To create that directory, just enter the following command at the regular Linux command prompt, as shown here:

```
mkdir /mnt/k63mydocs
```

If you're still at the `smb:\>` prompt on the Linux computer, make sure you enter `exit` or `quit` to return to the regular command prompt before entering regular commands like the ones that follow.

To mount the remote directory to that placeholder directory, use the `smbmount` command with the syntax `smbmount` *remote resource local placeholder*. For example, entering the following command mounts the My Documents folder on the K63 computer as `/mnt/k63docs` on the current Linux computer:

```
smbmount '//K63/K63_MYDOCS' '/mnt/k63mydocs'
```

You need to be logged in as root to use the smbmount command.

In some situations, such as when you're connecting to an NT computer, you may have to provide a username with the `smbmount` command. If that's the case, just add `-U` followed by a blank space and your username to the end of the command, as shown here:

```
smbmount '//K63/K63_MYDOCS' '/mnt/k63mydocs' -U alan
```

Once again you'll be prompted for a password. But if the shared resource doesn't require a password, you can just press Enter. You'll be returned to the regular command prompt. At this point, you may want to use the GNOME or KDE file manager to work with the contents of the remote Windows directory. For example, in Figure 24.5 I've opened up GNOME's file manager and worked my way to the `/mnt/k63mydocs` directory. The right pane is actually showing the contents of the My Documents folder on the K63 computer. By opening a second file manager window, I can transfer files across computers simply by dragging and dropping their icons in the usual manner.

**Figure 24.5**
The GNOME file manager displaying the contents of `/mnt/k63mydocs`, which is actually the My Documents folder on a Windows computer named K63.

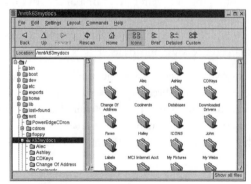

> **Tip**
>
> If the /mnt directory in your file manager doesn't initially show the new subdirectory, collapse the /mnt directory by clicking the minus sign (-) to its left. Click the Rescan button in the toolbar, and then reopen the /mnt directory to view its subdirectories.

Use the same procedure to mount a shared CD-ROM drive from the Windows machine to a local directory on the Linux computer. First, create a placeholder directory on the Linuxcomputer. For example, to create a placeholder named /mnt/k63cdrom on my Linux computer, I'd enter this command at the Linux command prompt:

```
mkdir /mnt/k63cdrom
```

After placing a CD in that CD-ROM drive on the Windows computer, I'd enter the following command to mount it as a directory on my local Linux computer:

```
smbmount '//K63/K63_CD' '/mnt/k63cdrom'
```

Once again, I could press Enter to bypass the Password prompt. Opening a file manager and then opening the /mnt/k63cdrom directory within that file manager would then show the contents of the CD in the Window CD-ROM drive.

To unmount a mounted Samba share, use the smbumount command with the following syntax:

```
smbumount placeholder
```

For example, the following commands would dismount the mounted /mnt/k63mydocs and /mnt/k63cdrom directories:

```
smbumount /mnt/k63mydocs
smbumount /mnt/k63cdrom
```

If you get a device busy error when trying to dismount an SMB share, you're probably "on" that device in a file manager or the command prompt. Close the file manager or switch to some other directory on the Linux computer, and then try again.

## ACCESSING A WINDOWS PRINTER

There are a couple of ways to access a printer that you've shared from a Windows computer as well. For simple printing of text files, you can connect to the printer using the smbclient command with the usual syntax smbclient //hostname/sharename. So, for example, to connect to the printer shared as HP_R80 on my K63 machine, I'd enter this command at the Linux command prompt on a Linux computer:

```
smbclient //K63/HP_R80
```

Once again, I can bypass the Password prompt, since I didn't put any password restriction on the printer when sharing it from Windows. The smb:/> prompt replaces the regular Linux command prompt. Printing-related commands accessible from the smb:\> prompt are summarized in Table 24.2.

**TABLE 24.2   PRINTING-RELATED COMMANDS ACCESSIBLE FROM** smb:\> **PROMPT**

| SMB Prompt Command | Description |
| --- | --- |
| print file | Prints the specified file to the remote printer |
| queue | Displays all print jobs queued up on the remote printer |
| exit or quit | Returns to the normal Linux command prompt |

For example, to print a file named `sample.txt` from the `/root` directory of the local Linux computer, I'd enter this command:

`print /root/sample.txt`

To disconnect from the printer and return to the normal command prompt, I'd enter the `exit` or `quit` command.

That approach is fine for printing simple text files from the `smb:\>` prompt. But if you really want to take advantage of the Windows printer, you'll probably want to use the `smbprint` command, which makes printing to a Windows printer relatively seamless (that is, you can access the printer as though it were connected to your local Linux computer). Using `smbprint` takes a little configuration though. You can use the `printtool` program to simplify the configuration. As you may recall from Chapter 14, "Printing from Linux," you can run that tool by entering `printtool &` in any terminal window. Then, follow these steps:

1. Click the Add button.

2. Choose SMB/Windows 95/NT Printer and click OK.

3. Read the warning, and then click OK.

4. Fill in the blanks, as in the example shown in Figure 24.6, using information that's relevant to your own shared Windows printer. Here's a quick summary of why I filled in the blanks as shown in the example:

**Figure 24.6**

Using `printtool` to define a remote printer that's been shared by a Windows computer named K63.

- **Names:** This can be any name you want to give the printer.

- **Spool Directory:** It's common practice to use the directory `/var/spool/samba` for Samba print jobs.

- **File Limit in Kb:** Zero (0) indicates no file size limit.

- **Hostname of Printer Server:** Hostname of the computer that the printer is shared from—K63 in my example.

- **IP Number of Server:** The host computer's IP address.
- **Printer Name:** The name of the printer as shown by the `smbclient -L` command, `HP_R80` in my example.
- **User**: None (my setup requires no username).
- **Password:** None (my setup requires no password).
- **Workgroup:** The workgroup/domain to which the Windows computer belongs.
- **Input Filter:** Click the Select button and choose the printer driver that best matches your printer.
- **Suppress Headers:** Select to avoid printing job information at the start of each print job.

5. Click the OK button after filling in the blanks.

6. Choose PrintTool, Quit from `printtool`'s menu bar.

Once you set up the printer in this manner, it should be easy to print from any program's Print dialog box. For example, let's say you're viewing a Web page in Netscape Navigator and want to print a copy of it on the Windows printer. After choosing File, Print from Navigator's menu bar, you're asked for a print command to use (see Figure 24.7). The print command default is typically something like `lpr`. To print to your remote Windows printer, use this syntax as your print command:

```
lpr -printername -l
```

`printername` is the name that you gave to the printer at the top of the list of `printtool` options. For example, I would enter the following as the printer command:

```
lpr -Phpr80 -l
```

That's a hyphen and lowercase *L* at the end of the command—this is an `lpr` command switch that lets the printer's filter control the print job.

**Figure 24.7**
Selecting the shared Windows Hewlett-Packard R80 printer to print a document from a Linux program.

In many Linux programs, you won't even have to go to that much trouble. When you get to the program's Print dialog box, you'll be able to choose the HP R80 printer from a simple drop-down list, and then click the Print button.

# INSTALLING SAMBA TO SHARE LINUX RESOURCES

So far you've seen how Samba can be used as a client to shared resources provided by Windows computers. But Samba can also play the role of server, offering shared resources from one computer that other network clients—both Linux and Windows clients—can access. Using Samba as a server is one of those huge topics that could take up an entire book. So in this chapter, our goal is to set up a basic server that's accessible from both Windows and Linux clients. References to the more esoteric capabilities are provided near the end of the chapter.

The first step in setting up a Samba server is, of course, to decide which Linux resources you want to share. For example, if you want to share a printer, and perhaps some directories, from a particular Linux computer, you need to set up the Samba server on *that* specific computer only (not all the computers in the network). For the sake of example, let's say my PowerEdge computer (IP address 192.168.1.5) has a printer attached to it that I want to share. I would need to first install the Samba server package on that computer.

Typically, the server side of Samba's capabilities is not installed with a standard Red Hat Linux 6.2 installation. But just to make sure you're not reinstalling software that's already there, you can go to the machine on which you plan to install the Samba server, and enter this command to see if the server is already installed:

```
rpm -q samba
```

Most likely you'll discover that Samba is not installed. You can install it from a mounted Red Hat Linux CD #1 by entering the following command:

```
rpm -ivh /mnt/cdrom/RedHat/RPMS/samba-2*.rpm
```

You should also have the samba-common package installed on that same computer. Again, to see if that's installed, enter this command:

```
rpm -q samba-common
```

If that package isn't installed, you can install it from the Red Hat CD-ROM with this command:

```
rpm -ivh /mnt/cdrom/RedHat/RPMS/samba-common*.rpm
```

So far, so good. Next, you'll want to ensure that the Samba server is automatically started whenever you boot up that computer, as discussed next.

## AUTO-STARTING SAMBA SERVER

Once installed, you'll want make sure Samba services start up automatically each time the computer is booted. Otherwise, you'll need to remember to start those packages manually whenever you want to use Samba. To start Samba services automatically, follow these steps:

1. Enter the command setup at the Linux command prompt.
2. Choose System Services, and scroll down to the smb option.

3. If smb is not already selected, move the highlight bar to it (using the ~DA arrow key), and press Enter to select that service. In Figure 24.8, you can see that smb is now selected.

4. Press Tab, and then Enter to choose OK.

5. Press Tab twice, and then Enter to choose Quit.

To verify that the Samba server starts at bootup, you can reboot the computer and watch the feedback messages on the screen as Linux loads services. The following two lines should appear within the list of services:

```
Starting SMB services    [OK]
Starting NMB services    [OK]
```

**Figure 24.8**

Samba (smb) is selected as a service to start up automatically when the computer starts.

PART

**IV**

CH

**24**

If, for whatever reason, you need to start or stop Samba on a computer, you can enter either of the following commands to do so:

```
/usr/sbin/samba stop
/usr/sbin/samba start
```

You can verify that Samba is running on a Linux machine by entering this command:

```
/usr/sbin/samba status
```

You should see some feedback such as the following (although your pid numbers will probably be different):

```
smbd (pid 598) is running...
nmbd (pid 609) is running...
```

Finally, you'll want to make sure your basic network infrastructure is still working correctly. Samba won't work if the network isn't working. And you could drive yourself nuts trying to get it to work if you didn't realize that the problem lay elsewhere. To make sure you can connect, just go to any other Linux computer in the network and ping the computer that you installed the Samba server software on. For example, I would enter the command ping 192.168.1.5 because that's the IP address of the computer I installed the Samba server on.

To test the connection from a Windows computer, you'll first need to get to the DOS command prompt (typically, you just have to click the Start button and choose Programs, MS-DOS Prompt). Use the ping command again to try to reach the Samba server computer once again (ping 192.168.1.5, in my example) to verify that the server is reachable from that computer. If your ping fails, there's no sense in trying to configure Samba because it won't work until you can successfully ping the computer on which you installed the Samba server.

## DEFINING SAMBA USERS

The Samba server is reasonably secure, and you have to define usernames and passwords of people who are allowed to access shared resources on the server. In fact, you have to create user accounts and passwords in both the /etc/passwd file, as well as the new /etc/smbpasswd file that the Samba server has installed. The easiest way to do so is through LinuxConf, which will kill two birds with one stone by entering each new user in both files. On the computer on which you've installed the Samba server, start LinuxConf, and then open the Config, UsersAccounts, Normal, User Accounts options. Then use the Add button in the right pane to enter the username and password of each user who will be allowed access to the server. You need only fill in the Login Name and Full Name boxes for any given user. Then click the Accept button and enter the password for that user, twice, as prompted on the screen.

For maximum flexibility (which is always good when you're first trying to get something to work), you can also create a user named pcguest, with some easy-to-remember password such as "guest". Figure 24.9 shows an example, where I've added users named alan, afraser, amarie, and pcguest to the list of users on the computer that now houses the Samba server (PowerEdge, in my example).

**Figure 24.9**
Each user who will have access to the Samba server should be added to the list of users for the computer on which the Samba server is installed.

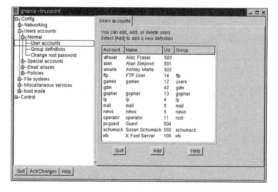

If you want to be able to log in to the Samba server with the username root, you should add that username to the smbpasswd file *only*. To accomplish that, get out of LinuxConf altogether, saving and activating any changes. Then get to a command prompt and enter the following command:

```
smbpasswd -a root
```

When prompted, enter a password for the root username twice.

**Note**  Accessing a Samba server as root does pose some security risks. The password can be intercepted via the SMB logon, and Windows users could gain root access to the server. So you'll definitely want to use this capability with caution!

## BACKING UP /etc/smb.conf

The technique for sharing Linux resources from Samba is radically different from sharing resources in Windows. Rather than right-clicking icons, you need to define all shared resources in a single file named /etc/smb.conf. When you installed the Samba server, that file was automatically created for you. It already contains some basic configuration stuff you'll need to share resources. However, you'll probably need to tweak it a bit depending on your network. As always, you'll want to make a backup of the original smb.conf file before you begin, in case you inadvertently make matters worse, rather than better, while tweaking. Entering the simple command cp /etc/smb.conf /etc/smb.orig will store a copy of the original file in /etc/smb.orig.

## OPENING /etc/smb.conf

Since /etc/smb.conf is just a text file, you can open it with any text editor. Figure 24.10 shows how it looks in gEdit. Note that any line starting with a hash mark (#) or semicolon (;) is a comment that will be ignored by the Samba server. Hash marks are used to comment out plain-English descriptions of options, and you never want to remove the hash mark at the beginning of any such line. Semicolons are used to comment out actual commands in the configuration file that you may, or may not, want to use. If you want to activate a command within the configuration file, simply delete the semicolon. I'll tell you, specifically, which lines you want to comment out to get your Samba server going in the sections that follow.

PART
**IV**
CH
**24**

**Note**     You must be logged in as root to edit the /etc/smb.conf file.

**Figure 24.10**
The /etc/
smb.conf file
open in GNOME's
gEdit text editor.

**Tip**     You can edit /etc/smb.conf via LinuxConf's Config, Networking, Server Tasks, Samba File Server options. However, since LinuxConf offers access to the entire

bewildering array of Samba options, I think it might be easier to just edit /etc/
smb.conf directly on your first time through.

Although it's difficult to tell from your first glance, the smb.conf file is divided into three major sections: [global], [homes], and [printers]. The [global] section configures the Samba server as a whole. The [homes] section allows for each registered user to have their own home directory on the server. And the [printers] section lets you share specific printers attached to the computer. You can add still more sections to share specific resources, as you'll learn later in this chapter. For the moment, however, you only need to make a few changes to the [global] section of the file to get a decent Samba server working on your network.

First, the line that reads

```
workgroup = MYGROUP
```

defines how the Samba server appears in the Windows Network Neighborhood window. Since MYGROUP isn't terribly informative, you might want to change that to something like the following:

```
workgroup = SAMBA
```

Whatever name you decide to use, try to keep it short (eight characters or fewer), use all uppercase letters, and don't include any blank space or punctuation marks.

To allow guest accounts, uncomment the following line:

```
guest account = pcguest
```

To simplify access from Windows clients, you should uncomment the following two lines. If any of your Windows users have a username or password that is more than eight characters in length, you should increase 8 to whatever the longest username and password will be. These lines, essentially, relax restrictions on usernames and passwords passed to the Samba server by specifying how many non-case-sensitive letters are allowed in the username and password:

```
password level = 8
username level = 8
```

If any of your clients are Windows 95 OSR2 or later, Windows 98, Windows 2000, or Windows NT Service Pack 3 or later, the following lines should also be uncommented. All of those more recent versions of Windows use encrypted passwords, and won't be able to access the Samba server's resources if you leave those lines commented out:

```
encrypt passwords = yes
smb passwd file = /etc/smbpasswd
```

Of course, encrypted passwords would pose a problem for any computers using the old original Windows 95. A simple alternative would be to update the operating systems on those machines to Windows 98, NT with Service Pack 3, or any other more recent version of Windows. The other, more complex approach is to leave the encrypted passwords disabled (commented out) in Samba. Then turn off encrypted passwords in all post-Windows 95

OSR2 operating systems. Doing so requires editing the system Registry on the Windows computers, which itself is risky business. But if you need to disable encrypted passwords in Windows 98, NT, or 2000, the Samba documentation in /usr/doc/samba-2.0.5a will show you what needs to be done.

By default, the /etc/smb.conf file is already set up to share any printers that are installed on the computer. So if you do have one or more working printers on that machine, they will be shared automatically. Although you don't need to make any changes, I suppose I should point out that these two lines in the [global] section are the ones that share all printers connected to the computer:

```
printcap name = /etc/printcap
load printers = yes
```

> **Tip**
>
> The /etc/printcap file mentioned in the preceding configuration lines is the file that holds information about the printers you've installed on the current computer using the printtool program discussed in Chapter 14.

It just so happens that the PowerEdge computer that I'm using as my Samba server has a printer named Epson installed on it (with the nickname lp). So I would expect that to show up later when testing my connections to the Samba server.

That should be enough to allow other computers to access any printers that are attached to the Samba server computer. Also, each user will have access to his own home directory on the server. You can now close and save the /etc/smb.conf file. Before you try it out, however, there are a couple of things you need to do as discussed in the following sections.

### TESTING /etc/smb.conf

Any time you edit the /etc/smb.conf file, you should run the testparm program. testparm will check to see if there are any obvious errors in the file, and report those errors to you. If there are no errors, you'll see a message that states Loaded services file OK, followed by a prompt to press Enter to see a dump of the /etc/smb.conf file with all comments removed. It's a rather daunting list that, for the time being, you can ignore.

### ACTIVATING A NEW /etc/smb.conf FILE

It's important to understand that any changes you make to /etc/smb.conf will be totally ignored until you restart the Samba server. The server program only reads the configuration file once, when it first starts. So if you don't restart Samba, your changes won't take effect until the next time you reboot the machine! To avoid rebooting, you can just enter the following command to stop and restart the Samba server:

```
/etc/rc.d/init.d/smb restart
```

You should just see four brief messages about stopping, then starting the Samba SMB and NMB services, followed by [OK] indicators. Now your Samba server is in sync with the settings defined in /etc/samba.conf, and you can run the following "acid" tests:

- Can you access the shared resources from other Linux computers?
- Can you access those resources from Windows computers?

> **Tip**
>
> If manually configuring Samba makes you a bit uneasy, don't worry—let SWAT do the work for you! The Samba team is now advocating the use of the SWAT configuration tool that comes with Samba as the preferred configuration method. Just make sure that the line beginning with "swat" in your /etc/inetd.conf file is uncommented, then open a Web browser on your Linux computer and point it to http:// localhost:901. A Web page will appear that lets you graphically set up your Samba options! Type man swat at a command line for more information.

## TESTING SAMBA FROM A LINUX COMPUTER

To test the Samba from a Linux computer, use the smbclient command. To just see which shared resources are available, use the following syntax:

```
smbclient -L //host -U username
```

host is the hostname or IP address of the Samba server computer, and username is any valid username you entered on that computer. For example, if the name of the computer that's sharing resources is PowerEdge, with an IP address of 192.168.1.5, and amarie is the name of a valid user on that computer, then entering either command here would do the trick:

```
smbclient -L //PowerEdge -U amarie
smbclient -L //192.168.1.5 -U amarie
```

When prompted for a password, you must enter the correct password for the user specified in the command. After you press Enter, you'll see something like this:

```
Sharename      Type      Comment
IPC$           IPC       IPC Service (Samba Server)
epson          Printer   lp
amarie         Disk      Home directories
Server             Comment
POWEREDGE          Samba Server
Workgroup          Master
COOLNERDS.COM      K63
SAMBA              POWEREDGE
```

The actual shared resources on the server are a printer named Epson (nicknamed lp). Because I set up the smb.conf file to show the user's home directory, a directory named amarie is also available. At the bottom of the list you can see there are actually two workgroups defined on my network now. There's COOLNERDS.COM, and the computer named K63 is the "master" of that workgroup. And there's a new workgroup named SAMBA, and the computer named POWEREDGE is the "master" (owner) of that workgroup.

To actually log in to a resource, you need to use the smbclient command with the following slightly weird syntax:

```
smbclient '//host/section' -U userid
```

host is the IP address or hostname of the computer that the Samba server is installed on, section is the name of the section within /etc/smb.conf that defines the shared resource, and userid is any valid username that you added to the user list on the Samba server computer. Currently, the only shared disk resource on the Samba server is in the section titled [homes] of that file. But as you'll learn momentarily, you can share other directories and replace section with those directory names. But for the moment, since [homes] is the only shared directory, either of the following commands will allow me to log in to amarie's home directory on the Samba server:

```
smbclient '//192.168.1.5/homes' -U amarie
```

```
smbclient '//PowerEdge/homes' -U amarie
```

PART

**IV**

CH

**24**

Either way, a successful connection would first request a password. You must type in the password you gave to this user on the Samba server (which may or may not be the same as the password the user logs in with). After you press Enter, you'll get a little feedback about the connection, and the command prompt will change to the following:

```
smb: \>
```

That means you have made a successful connection. You can now enter any valid SMB prompt command, as listed in Table 24.1, to further test the connection. For example, entering a simple dir command will display the contents of the user's home directory on the server. Initially you'll just see the default files like .Xdefaults, .bash_profile, and so forth. But at least you know the connection is working.

To get back to your normal command prompt, enter the command quit or exit.

If the connection fails, you may have simply typed the wrong username or password, or mistyped one or the other. You might try logging in with the username pcguest and whatever password you created for that guest account.

## TESTING SAMBA FROM A WINDOWS COMPUTER

The acid test for checking your connection from a Windows computer is to open the Network Neighborhood icon. Within Network Neighborhood, open the Entire Network icon. If your connection is successful, you'll see an icon for the connection to the Samba server. The icon's label will be whatever you typed next to workgroup = in the /etc/smb.conf file. Opening that icon will reveal an icon for the computer that the Samba server is installed on. Opening *that* icon will reveal the shared resources available to you from that machine.

---

**Tip**

If an expected Samba share doesn't appear in Network Neighborhood, choose View, and then Refresh (or press the F5 key) to rescan the network. You might try doing it a couple of times, at different levels within Network Neighborhood.

If you continue to have difficulty accessing the Samba share, try using the Windows Find option to locate the host. Click the Windows Start button and choose Find, Computer. In the dialog box that appears, enter the hostname of the computer you're looking for.

In my example, where I logged into the Windows computer with the username *alan*, I'd see an icon for my home directory on the Samba server, which is labeled simply alan, as well as an icon for the printer attached to that computer, which is named epson, as in Figure 24.11.

**Figure 24.11**
The Samba server's resources on the PowerEdge computer through the Windows 98 Network Neighborhood icon.

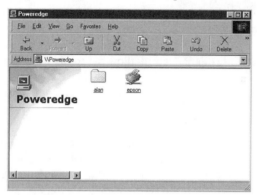

Granted, this isn't the most thrilling little test in the world. But the important point is that the basic connectivity is in place and working. Next, we'll look at how you can access the shared printer (if any) that's connected to your Samba server.

# ACCESSING A SHARED LINUX PRINTER FROM WINDOWS

To make access to the shared Linux printer as easy as possible, you can add an icon for it to your Printers folder. The procedure is almost identical to installing a local printer on a Windows computer. You'll need your original Windows CD-ROM or a printer driver disk for the printer. Insert that into the appropriate drive. If the Windows Auto Start window pops up on the screen, just close it. Then follow these steps:

1. Open your My Computer icon, and then open the Printers folder.

2. Open the Add Printer icon, click Next, and choose Network Printer when given the option. Then click the Next button.

3. When prompted for the network path or queue name, browse through Network Neighborhood, Entire Network, your Samba server, the name of the machine to which the printer is connected, and finally the printer's icon, as in Figure 24.12.

4. Click the OK button, answer additional wizard questions, and then click Next.

5. When you get to the list of printers, choose your printer make and model. Or, if you'll be installing the printer driver from a floppy disk, click Have Disk and browse to the drive and directory that contains the printer driver.

6. Install the printer driver as you normally would in Windows.

**Figure 24.12**
Creating a local printer icon for Windows that provides access to a remote Linux printer shared by Samba.

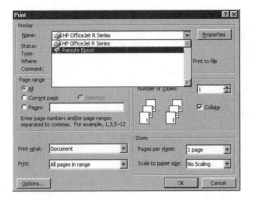

7. When prompted for a printer name, enter any name that will describe the printer. In my example, I named the printer *Remote Epson*.

8. You can choose Yes when asked if you want to print a test page.

9. The printer driver program should now load from the CD or floppy disk, after which the test page should be printed on the remote printer. The Printers folder will also contain a new icon representing the remote printer.

To access the printer from most Windows programs, just choose File, Print from whatever program you happen to be working in. Choose the remote printer from the drop-down list and click OK (see Figure 24.13).

**Figure 24.13**
The Remote Epson printer here is actually the Epson printer that's being shared by Samba on a Linux computer.

# ACCESSING A SHARED LINUX PRINTER FROM LINUX

If you want easy access to the shared Linux printer from other Linux computers in the network, you can install the printer as a network printer using the `printtool` program. Go to any Linux client computer and start the `printtool` program as root (enter `su -c printtool &` from a terminal window if you're not currently logged in as root). Click the Add button, choose `SMB/Windows 95/NT Printer`, and then fill in the blanks as appropriate. For example, in Figure 24.14 I've filled in the blanks to access the remote printer named *Epson* on my PowerEdge computer.

**Figure 24.14**
Setting up access to a remote Linux printer being shared by Samba.

Save your settings and when you get back to PrintTool's main window, you can test the connection. Click on the line representing the printer you just installed. Then choose the first two options from the Tests menu option in PrintTool. When everything seems to be working properly, you can close the PrintTool program.

In all other respects, using the shared Linux printer is just like using a shared Windows printer, as discussed earlier in this chapter. For example, if you choose File, Print from a program's menu bar, you'll usually see some print command, such as lpr in the Print dialog box. To specify the remote printer, add -P and the name of the printer. For example, in Figure 24.15 I changed the Print command to lpr -Pepson to have the printed page print on the remote Epson printer.

**Figure 24.15**
The command lpr -Pepson directs the print job to the shared Epson printer on this network.

# SHARING DIRECTORIES WITH SAMBA

The default /etc/smb.conf configuration file is set up to give users their own home directories on the server. But of course, you may well want to create a shared directory to house all the folders that go with a given project, say Project Y. More specifically, you want to create a shared directory, named ProjectY, on the Samba server computer. Furthermore, you specifically want to grant access privileges to the users afraser, alan, and amarie, as they are the three people working together on that project.

First and foremost, you have to create that directory on the server computer. You might want to create a parent directory, perhaps named sambaShares, to house all your Samba shared directories, just to keep them organized, although that's entirely optional. For our example, however, let's suppose we plan to create a /sambaShares/ProjectY directory to share from the PowerEdge computer which, as you know, is the computer in my network that I installed the

Samba server on. To create the directory, use any file manager. Or, just enter the following commands:

```
cd /
mkdir /sambaShares
mkdir /sambaShares/ProjectY
```

Just for the sake of example, I'll throw a few files in that directory. Figure 24.16 shows how the directory looks through GNOME's file manager.

**Figure 24.16**
A directory named `ProjectY` contained within a directory named `sambaShares` is what I'll use to demonstrate how to create a shared Samba server directory.

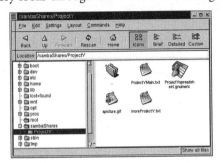

As mentioned earlier, to share a directory through the Samba server, you need to create a section within `/etc/smb.conf` that represents that share. Open `/etc/smb.conf` using any text editor, then scroll down to the bottom of the file. Along the way, you'll notice many examples of shares, all commented out with semicolons. Those examples are *just* examples, and don't actually share anything. But they do show the basic structure of a section that defines a shared directory, as shown here:

```
[sharename]
    comment = whatever_you_like
    path = fullpath
    writable = yes¦no
    public = yes¦no
    browseable = yes¦no
    valid users = username1username2 ...
    create mode = number
```

In this section, the following corresponds to the syntax:

- *sharename* is the name of the share as it will appear in Network Neighborhood and Linux clients. The limit is up to nine characters, no spaces or punctuation marks.

- *whatever_you_like* is any plain-English comment that describes the shared resource.

- *fullpath* is the full path to the shared directory.

- writable= is yes if users can write to the directory, or no if you want it to be read-only.

- public= is yes if you want people who can't log in to the Samba server to still have access to the directory, or no if you want only validated users to access the share.

- browseable=is yes if you want the share to be visible to all users, even those who can't open it, or no if you want the share to be visible only to users who can access the share.

- valid users= is followed by a list of usernames, separated by blank spaces, specifying who can access the share.

- read list= *username1 username2* ... lets you define a list of users (separated by blank spaces) that are granted Read-Only permission to files on the share, even if the share itself is writable. This command is optional and can be omitted.

- write list= *username1 username2* ... lets you define a list of users (separated by blank spaces) that are granted Read/Write permission to files on the share, even if the share itself is not writable. This command is optional and can be omitted.

- number is the number that reflects the permissions assigned to any newly created files on the directory. The default (if you omit the option) is 0744, which specifies that each new file grants Read, Write, and Execute permissions to the file's owner, whereas other members of the owner's group get Read-Only permissions. A create mask of 0775 would grant the owner and all group members Read, Write, and Execute permissions, and everyone else Read and Execute permissions.

Amazingly, there are even more parameters that you can use to define privileges and such, but the list above should cover everything that just about everybody needs. Using our ProjectY directory as our example, let's suppose we want the share to be named *projecty*. We'll give alan, afraser, and amarie permission to read and write files to the directory, we'll make the directory public and browseable, and we'll use a create mode of 0775 so that all group members have access to the files. Here's the exact text you'd need to add to /etc/smb.conf to make that happen:

```
[projecty]
  comment = Shared Project Y Files on PowerEdge
  path = /sambaShares/ProjectY
  valid users =alan afraser amarie
  public = yes
  writable = yes
  browseable = yes
  create mask = 0775
```

Figure 24.17 shows that as it appears after typing it into /etc/smb.conf using GNOME's gEdit editor.

**Figure 24.17**
Entry to share
/sambaShares/
ProjectY from
Samba server,
giving access per-
mission to users
alan, afraser, and
amarie.

Don't forget that any time you change the /etc/smb.conf file, you want to test the new version and restart the Samba server. Open a terminal window and enter the following commands:

```
testparm
/etc/rc.d/init.d/smb restart
```

Don't forget, too, that initially Linux makes each new user a member of his or her own group only (the group name being the same as the username). To ensure that users alan, afraser, and amarie can change each others' files, you'll want to make all those users members of the ProjectY group.

## ACCESSING THE NEW SHARE FROM WINDOWS

To access the new directory on a Windows computer (assuming you're logged in with one of the valid usernames for that share), open Network Neighborhood. Then follow the same path you followed to access other stuff on that share—Entire Network, Samba (or whatever you named your Samba server workgroup), and PowerEdge (or whatever host you installed the Samba server on). You should see an icon named *ProjectY* representing the newly shared directory. To create a quick desktop shortcut to that directory from your desktop, drag the icon onto the desktop and drop it there. When asked if you want to create a shortcut, choose Yes. In the future, just opening that desktop icon will display the contents of that shared directory, as in the example shown in Figure 24.18.

**Figure 24.18**
The contents of the shared Project Y directory plainly visible from a Windows computer on the same network.

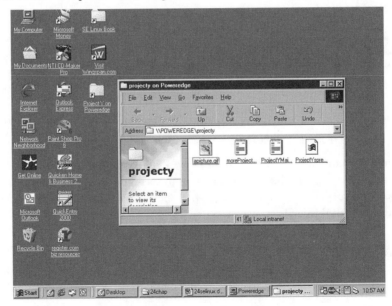

## ACCESSING THE NEW SHARE FROM LINUX

To access the new share from Linux, use the exact same procedures you used to access a shared Windows directory, as described under "Accessing Windows Drives and Directories" earlier in this chapter. For example, to check for the existence of the share and make sure you know the exact spelling of the resource, you could enter this command to list the shared resources on the PowerEdge computer:

```
smbclient -L PowerEdge
```

After pressing Enter to bypass the password prompt, your list of PowerEdge computers should include the new share, as in the following example:

```
Sharename    Type       Comment
projecty     Disk       Shared Project Y Files on PowerEdge
epson        Printer    lp
...
```

To actually mount the shared directory so that you could treat it as a local directory, you'd first want to create a local mount point. For example, let's say I want to use /mnt/projecty as the mount point for the shared directory. Entering this command creates an appropriate, empty directory:

```
mkdir /mnt/projecty
```

Then, to mount the remote directory you'd enter the following command (in this example):

```
smbmount '//PowerEdge/projecty' '/mnt/projecty' -U amarie
```

You'll need to enter the user's valid password when prompted, and then press Enter. Now you can interact with the remote directory just as though it were a local directory named /mnt/projecty. For example, Figure 24.19 shows how /mnt/projecty looks when viewed through GNOME's file manager.

**Figure 24.19**
After using smbmount to mount the remote Project Y directory, you can easily access that directory through its local mount point.

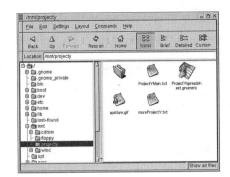

## MORE ON SAMBA

As I said earlier in this chapter, Samba offers a bewildering array of options and capabilities—far more than I can hope to cover in a single chapter. There are, of course, entire books written about Samba. However, you'll also find plenty of documentation right on your own computer, including the following:

```
man smbclient
man smbmount
man smbumount
man smb.conf
man testparm
```

On any computer on which you install the Samba server, you'll find even more documentation, as summarized here:

```
man smbd
man nmbd
man smbstatus
man smbpasswd
man smbtar
```

Also on the computer that you've installed the Samba server on, you'll find pages and pages of FAQs, READMEs, information about interacting with specific versions of Windows, and more under /usr/docs/samba-2.0.5a. And, of course, for the latest and greatest of everything online, there's www.samba.org.

# CASE STUDY: SHARING A WINDOWS CD-ROM DRIVE

If there's anything that'll drive you batty in the computer world, it's a computer that doesn't have its own CD-ROM drive—unless, of course, that computer is part of a network, in which case the computer can just use any shared CD-ROM on the network. Sharing a CD-ROM drive is pretty much the same as sharing a printer or directory. Things do get a little tricky, though, because there's the whole business of mounting and unmounting CDs each time you change the disk in the drive. For example in Linux, once you mount a CD-ROM drive, the Eject button for that drive doesn't work. You have to unmount the disk before you can eject it. And if several people on the network all have the same CD mounted, they all have to unmount before the CD can be removed from its drive. It gets even more complicated than that. So if at all possible, use a CD-ROM drive from a Windows computer as a shared CD-ROM drive accessible to all computers in the network.

> **Tip**
>
> To connect a laptop to a network, you usually need to purchase a PC Card (or PCMCIA) Ethernet card that allows you to plug the laptop right into the Ethernet hub.

We've looked at examples of sharing devices on Windows computers earlier in this chapter. But let's review the procedure in detail, with special emphasis on using the shared CD-ROM drive on Linux computers that are in the same network. As you may recall, sharing a CD-ROM drive on a Windows computer is as easy as opening My Computer, right-clicking the icon for the CD-ROM drive you want to share, and choosing the Sharing option. Choose Shared As, give the device a share name and descriptive comment, and choose Read-Only as the access type (since all CD-ROM drives are Read-Only). Figure 24.20 shows an example where I've shared the CD-ROM drive from my Windows computer named K63.

**Figure 24.20**
Sharing the CD-ROM drive from my Windows computer named K63.

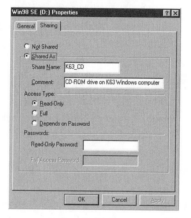

To verify that the CD-ROM can be reached from a Linux computer, use the smbclient command with the -L switch. For example, if you shared the CD-ROM from a computer named K63, then you'd enter the command smbclient -L K63. Press Enter when asked for a password, and you should see the CD-ROM drive listed along with any other shares that are available from that computer.

To mount the CD-ROM drive from a Linux computer, you'd first need to create a mount point for it. For example, you might enter the command mkdir /mnt/wincdrom to create a mount point for a CD-ROM drive that's shared from a Windows computer. You can name the mount points anything you want. Just try to come up with a name that will be easy to remember in the future.

Next, you'll need to put a CD into the CD-ROM drive you plan to mount. Then, use the `smbmount` command to mount the drive. For example, to mount the shared CD-ROM drive from the K63 computer to my local `/mnt/wincdrom` mount point, I'd enter the following command:

```
smbmount '//K63/K63_CD' '/mnt/wincdrom'
```

Since I've put virtually no restrictions on that CD-ROM drive, there's no need to specify a user name with `-U`. And you can simply press Enter when asked for a password. Entering the following commands then takes you to the drive's mount point and displays a list of directories and files on the CD that's currently in that drive:

```
cd /mnt/wincdrom
ls
```

Obviously, you could also view the contents of the CD by opening any File Manager, and then opening the `/mnt/wincdrom` directory.

Suppose you need to run some kind of program on the CD-ROM, or you want to install a Red Hat package. All you need to do is make sure you put the right mount point in the command. For example, to run a Linux program that's on the CD-ROM, you'd enter a command like the following:

```
/mnt/wincdrom/programpath
```

*programpath* is the path and filename of the program you want to run.

As another example, suppose the CD in the Windows CD-ROM drive includes some Red Hat packages (`.rpm` files) that you want to install or upgrade. The plain old `rpm` command would work fine. Just make sure you reference the mount point for the shared CD-ROM drive. For example, to install the `efax` package from `/RedHat/RPMS/` on the Red Hat CD-ROM #1, you'd enter the command:

```
rpm -ivh /mnt/wincdrom/RedHat/RPMS/efax*.rpm
```

The fact that the Red Hat Linux CD happens to be in a shared Windows CD-ROM drive does not, in any way, compromise your ability to use that CD. To Linux, a CD-ROM drive is a CD-ROM drive, whether it's local, or shared from a Windows computer.

**PART**

**IV**

**CH**

**24**

---

**Tip**

You could also use `gnorpm` to install packages from the shared CD-ROM drive. After you select Install and Add from `gnorpm`'s options, just browse to the mount point that represents the mounted, shared CD-ROM drive (`/mnt/wincdrom` in my example).

Before you remove the CD from its drive on the Windows computer, you'll want to remember to unmount the drive. Switch to any directory other than /mnt/wincdrom (so you don't get a `Device is busy` error message when you try to unmount). Then enter the following command:

```
smbumount /mnt/wincdrom
```

Now you can remove the CD from the Windows computer's CD-ROM drive if you like.

# CHAPTER 25

# GATEWAYS, ROUTERS, SWITCHES, AND OTHER TCP/IP MYSTERIES EXPLAINED

In this chapter

# UNDERSTANDING NETWORKS

The more you work with Linux and security, the more you're going to find that a background in networking, and TCP/IP specifically, is needed to fully understand what is going on. Networks are complex beasts with a great deal of support hardware that manages them. Routers, bridges, switchesare all part of the wonderful world of networking. This chapter introduces you to networking and provides you with a solid background on the TCP/IP protocol.

The easiest way to discuss something as complex as a network is to break it up into abstract pieces. There have been several attempts at providing such a model, but most have failed to cover all the aspects of defining the components that can be considered part of a network. Luckily for us, there is one model that has been widely accepted internationally, and can be used to describe both present and future network models in an abstract manner.

## OSI BY THE ISO

**What Is the ISO?**
The ISO, or *International Standards Organization* is a group comprised of members from over 75 countries who work together to compile and maintain engineering standards from around the world. Interestingly enough, ISO is not an acronym; the ISO was named for the Greek word *iso*, which means "equal." The ISO created the network model we will use for examining TCP/IP.

The International Standards Organization (ISO) recognized the need for a model that could be used when designing networking protocols. The *Open Systems Interconnect* (OSI) network model provides us with an abstract view of how a network functions from the wiring that connects the computers to the programs that we use to communicate. *Layers* are the key component to the OSI model. A layer in the network model is simply a functional piece of the whole network. Breaking the network down into layers provides us with a starting point for our definition of a network, and allows us to build up the components we need to create a network that does what we want. From a development standpoint, defining networking based on a layered model allows for the development of new technologies that take advantage of existing hardware and software by using underlying layers that are already in place. As you read about the OSI model, try to picture the relationship between the components. Each layer has a distinct and necessary purpose. Together, the whole truly is greater than the sum of its parts.

## OSI NETWORK MODEL OVERVIEW

A total of seven layers is used in the OSI model to describe a network from the ground up. These layers, in order, are the *physical, data link, network, transport, session, presentation*, and *application* layers. Each layer builds upon the next and would be completely useless by itself, or if one of the preceding layers were missing. It follows that each layer cannot exist in a vacuum; it must possess some knowledge of the layers that surround it and have a method of communicating to those layers. In its specification of the OSI model, the ISO does not bind any particular network standard, such as TCP/IP, to the model. By basing the layers on their function, rather than specific existing network standards, the ISO has provided a model that is robust, open, and can be used to explore existing network specifications and design the standards of the future.

## THE HARDWARE/PHYSICAL LAYER

This is the first layer, which provides the foundation that the following layers will build upon. *Hardware* refers to the computer, network cable, satellite dishes, or any other devices that you choose to use when linking two or more computers. This includes the actual physical wiring and the electrical signals that travel through them. For satellite hardware, this would include the radio waves that pass to and from the satellites. The hardware must also have the capability to determine when a signaling problem has occurred and to notify upper levels of the trouble.

These tasks may sound a bit daunting, but they happen at a level that most of us need not worry about. The signaling properties are handled by the hardware we choose to link the computers with, so we don't need to design our signaling methods each time we setup a network.

## THE DATA LINK LAYER

Once we have made a physical connection at the hardware layer, we need to be able to move data over the connection. This is the purpose of the *data link* layer. A unit of data, called a *frame* or *packet*, is to be transmitted over our hardware layer. The data link layer must be capable of creating the packet holding our information, identifying the destination of the remote machine, or node, which will receive the data, providing low-level error checking to identify any problems that may have occurred, and acting on those problems. It is also the responsibility of the data link layer to regulate the transmission of data from the hardware layer. Depending on the type of network you are setting up, there are certain conditions during which the machine must either wait its turn to transmit data, or wait for a certain length of time to pass before it can transmit again. An example of this behavior would be if two nodes on an Ethernet network attempted to send data at the same time. The result is a *collision*, in which the information from the two nodes overlap, and is unintelligible.

When a collision occurs, the data link layer must make a decision on how to handle the problem. Should it retransmit the data immediately? If it does and the data link layer on the other node makes the same decision, the result would be another collision...and another...and another, and so on. Later in the chapter, we'll look at the data link layer in relation to TCP/IP. You will learn how this event has been well thought out, and precisely how the situation is handled. For now, just be aware that such problems can and do occur, and the data link layer is responsible for keeping them to a minimum. The data link layer provides the bridge between hardware and software. It must communicate directly with the hardware layer, prepare data to be sent, and receive incoming data; then, after verifying the correctness of the data, it must make it available to the next layer.

On your computer system, the data link layer is typically represented by your network driver—in the case of Linux, it's a kernel module.

## THE NETWORK LAYER

With the data link layer in place, we have the necessary logic to transmit information to different nodes on our network. Networks are, however, not isolated entities. A network can consist of many different nodes, using many different hardware layers and data link layers.

---

**What Is a Node?**
A *node* is any device that is connected to a network. For our purposes, it usually refers to a computer.

---

That being the case, how can one network communicate with another? At the data link layer, there is a low-level addressing scheme that identifies individual nodes, and is specific to the hardware underneath it. In order for heterogeneous networks to exist, there must be a common way of identifying nodes at a higher level. The *network* layer provides this addressing scheme. Once a common addressing method is available, then we need to worry about the most efficient way to communicate between our different networks. Once again, this is the responsibility of the network layer.

The network layer must provide alternate paths between nodes if failures occur and constantly be "aware" of the layout of the network. On the Internet there are literally millions of subnets to take into account. Moving data efficiently and reliably between them is a monumental task, and is referred to as *routing*.

## THE TRANSPORT LAYER

Our model is now to the point where we can send information and it will be able to find its way from one node to another node sharing the same network layer; things become significantly easier at this level and throughout the remaining layers. The primary concern of the *transport* layer is that the data we receive is actually what we're supposed to be receiving. The amount of data that can be transmitted on a network at a time is finite. The transport layer takes the information to be sent and breaks it into individual *datagrams* that are sent and reassembled into a complete message by the transport layer at the receiving node. The transport layer may also provide a signaling service for the remote node so that it is notified when its data has been received successfully.

Unfortunately, networks are dynamic, and things do go wrong on a regular basis. Packets are lost on bad wiring, connections are broken when people decide to rewire the network in their office, and messages are scrambled as they are routed through different subnets. Because of these sorts of problems, datagrams are not guaranteed to arrive in a specific order. If an error does occur during transmission, it is up to the transport layer to reliably correct the error. Depending on the network protocol in use, this does not necessarily mean that it will ensure that the data is exactly the same as when it was sent. What it does mean is that there is no ambiguity in what happens to the data. A set of rules is followed that details the handling of the error and how to correct it. This may mean resending just the damaged data or restarting from the beginning, but even if this involves discarding the erroneous data and continuing, it is still considered error correction. However, if an email is sent from your supervisor over a TCP/IP network with the message "You will never be fired" and arrives as "You will be fired," you can be assured that the transport layer is not doing its job.

## THE SESSION LAYER

Most data transmitted over a network is not in the form of a single packet. Typically two or more nodes open *connections* between themselves and exchange multiple packets back and forth. When they are done communicating, the connections are closed. It is also possible for multiple connections to be made to a single machine (think of how long you'd have to wait to download your favorite Web pages if the computer serving them to you could only serve one page to one person at a time). The *session* layer manages the opening and closing of connections, and assures the layers above it that each connection has its chance to send and receive data. If you ever open multiple connections to multiple Web sites, you are putting the session layer to use. Most of today's computers are capable of multitasking and providing many sorts of services over the Internet. They must call upon the session layer of the network in order to serve their data to other machines in an efficient manner. You can think of the session layer as the dividing lines on a highway—they define starting and ending points, and allow multiple lanes of traffic to flow along concurrently.

## THE PRESENTATION LAYER

With so many layers already in place, it may seem difficult to imagine that we still need two more before our model is complete. The *presentation* layer provides a simple service to the network model. It prepares data for its trip across the network, and readies it for use in an end user application when the journey is complete. Syntax for communicating with a remote machine may also be defined in the presentation layer. The presentation layer serves as a translator for the data that the application layer wants to send.

A growing use for the presentation layer is to provide secure communications over a network. Data can be encrypted in the presentation layer before it is passed down to the lower layers for transmission. Similarly, data can be compressed in this layer. Compressing the data before sending it can result in significant speed increases in transmitting and receiving. Why isn't all data encrypted and compressed before it is sent? Keep in mind that compressing and encrypting data is a time-consuming task, and a balance must be maintained between network speed and the rate at which the local and remote nodes can process the incoming data within the presentation layer.

## THE APPLICATION LAYER

Now we arrive at the last part of the OSI model, the *application* layer. This layer provides the final interface to the network that we, the end users, use to access network services. You've probably interacted with the application layer of the TCP/IP protocol if you've used a Web browser, a mail reader, or anything else over the Internet.

PART

**IV**

CH

**25**

# UNDERSTANDING TCP/IP

### Why Is TCP/IP Called a "Suite"?

TCP/IP is often referred to as a *suite*. This is because it can be broken down into individual subprotocols, with these lower level protocols making up a "suite" of protocols. Syntactically, you may refer to TCP/IP as a protocol suite, or as a singular protocol.

Now that we know what the OSI network layers do from a general functionality standpoint, let's integrate our knowledge of the network model with TCP/IP. This will enable you to see exactly how the various pieces of network hardware fit into the big scheme of things.

## THE HARDWARE LAYER

The hardware, or physical layer, as we learned earlier, makes up the basic underlying connection of the network. In most TCP/IP networks, this will be a form of wiring. It is also possible to build a TCP/IP network with things such as microwave and radio transmitters, but these are generally used in highly specialized situations where buildings must be linked over large distances.

### THINNET

The most common Ethernet wiring is generally coax cable or *thinnet*. This cable is usually found in buildings that were wired 10 to 15 years ago. It is very similar to the wiring that your cable box uses. Although this is the most common form of wiring, it is also the most problematic. Coax cable is laid out in a string, and network devices are connected to it in series. The loose ends at each end of the string are "terminated" by placing a 50ohm resister on each end. This assures that there won't be signal reflection on the line, which would make data transmission unstable, or more likely, impossible. To imagine what signal reflection does, you can see the results by finding a friend and a piece of rope. Ask your friend to hold the end of the rope tightly, and then take the other end of the rope and give it a shake. You'll see a wave travel down the length of rope, and, upon reaching your friend, it bounces back along the length of the rope. On a computer network, this reflection happens at the speed of light. Packets that your own computer creates are themselves reflected, and that reflection in turn creates a collision with the original packet. This situation can bring an entire network, consisting of hundreds of computers, to its knees in seconds. The 50ohm terminators absorb the signal at the end of the wire and prevent the reflection problem from occurring. This type of network is called a *bus* topology.

### TWISTED PAIR

The increasingly common—and thankfully so—standard in wiring is *twisted pair*. Twisted pair resembles a very fat phone line, and does not suffer from the problems of thinnet. In a twisted pair network each device has its own strand of wire that runs between the machine and a central point called a *hub*. The hub has several ports, and each port can feed a network device, or perhaps even another hub. The network layout for twisted pair networks is called a *star topology* because the physical layout of the wiring looks somewhat like a star.

There is no need for termination on a twisted pair network because it is handled internally by the hub and the computer's network card. In addition, most hubs have the capability to detect excessive or unusual activity on a port and isolate it from the rest of the network. This keeps a single computer from bringing down the rest of the network. Each piece of twisted pair can be up to 100 meters long, so the potential distance between the farthest connections on the network is about 680 feet. While this is the same as thinnet, the star topology allows machines to be placed anywhere within 100 meters of the hub, which allows a single hub 10BaseT network far greater reach than a single strand thinnet network.

## THE DATA LINK LAYER

Data is transmitted across an Ethernet network in the form of discreet "pieces" of information. These pieces are known as packets, or frames. A frame has a structure which identifies where the information is going, where it is headed, the type of information contained in the frame, the data to be transmitted, and a *cyclic redundancy check* (CRC) which helps detect errors that occur in transmission.

The amount of data transmitted in each frame is extremely small. In order to transmit a file of 100KB, it would take over 68 packets of the maximum size of 1,500 bytes. As we move up through the network layers there will be more and more information that each layer must add to each frame that is sent. You will find that there is quite a bit of overhead created by the other layers, and that it will actually take quite a few more than 68 packets to send our 100k file.

With such a large number of packets being sent back and forth, it is extremely likely that data will, at some point, be corrupted. This is where the CRC comes into play. A cyclic redundancy check is often used to determine if data has arrived at its destination unharmed. A CRC is a unique number that is generated from the data stored in the frame. It is unique for each sequence of data. Upon receiving the data, the receiving computer calculates a CRC based on the data in the frame and compares it to the CRC information that is sent with the frame. If there is a match, the data is assumed to be correct. If not, there has been an error in transmission and the data will need to be retransmitted.

### GETTING DATA TO ITS DESTINATION

In each frame, there is a source and destination address. Every Ethernet device on a network has a unique identifying address called a *hardware address*, or *MAC address*. This address is 48 bits long, and is assigned by the manufacturer of the network device. It is *the* defining address for the basis of Ethernet network communications. You can usually find the address for your network hardware silk-screened onto the network card or labeled on the outside of the device. The address is most likely displayed as a six-part hex number, sometimes separated by colons. For example, the address of the machine I'm currently using is:

```
00 00 94 7b 75 7f
```

There doesn't exist, anywhere, an Ethernet device with the same address. This address is mine, and mine alone.

When data is transmitted over the Ethernet, it travels along the line, and the individual network devices examine each frame as it passes. If a device's hardware address matches the destination address on the frame, it reads the rest of the information from the frame and passes the information up through the network layers so that it can be processed by whatever software is appropriate.

You can use the ifconfig command to display all sorts of information about your network interfaces, including the hardware addresses (Hwaddr) as shown here:

```
[jray@pointy jray]$ ifconfig
eth0    Link encap:Ethernet HWaddr 00:90:27:9A:4C:C1
        inet addr:204.210.234.197 Bcast:204.210.234.255 Mask:255.255.255.0
        UP BROADCAST RUNNING MTU:1500 Metric:1
        RX packets:77521 errors:1 dropped:0 overruns:0 frame:0
        TX packets:47915 errors:0 dropped:0 overruns:0 carrier:0
        collisions:10222

eth1    Link encap:Ethernet HWaddr 00:A0:C9:B3:5B:A2
        inet addr:192.168.0.1 Bcast:192.168.0.255 Mask:255.255.255.0
        UP BROADCAST RUNNING MULTICAST MTU:1500 Metric:1
        RX packets:28973 errors:0 dropped:0 overruns:0 frame:0
        TX packets:58616 errors:0 dropped:0 overruns:0 carrier:0
        collisions:19708

lo      Link encap:Local Loopback
        inet addr:127.0.0.1 Mask:255.0.0.0
        UP LOOPBACK RUNNING MTU:3924 Metric:1
        RX packets:311 errors:0 dropped:0 overruns:0 frame:0
        TX packets:311 errors:0 dropped:0 overruns:0 carrier:0
        collisions:0
```

## COLLISION RECOVERY

As I mentioned earlier, there are special circumstances that can and do occur that are the data link layer's responsibility to deal with cleanly. Collisions happen when frames of data are transmitted simultaneously on the network. Transmitting machines monitor the Ethernet line and send their frames only when they see that the line is inactive. Unfortunately, if more than one station sees the network as being inactive and both need to send data, it is likely that they will both send the data at the same time and cause a collision. Collisions are part of the design of Ethernet and are not indicative of an error in the network. They are a common occurrence on an Ethernet network, and must be handled in a manner that reduces the likelihood that they will reoccur.

Ethernet uses what is called a *backoff* algorithm to determine what it will do when a collision takes place. The name "backoff" is descriptive of the action that is taken to eliminate the problem. The devices that were involved in creating the collision "back off" from sending data and wait a random number of microseconds, and then attempt to retransmit their data.

If consecutive collisions take place, the amount of time each device waits before retransmitting is increased. If the failures continue, the frames may eventually be discarded, and it is left to the software at upper layers to deal with the error that has taken place.

## THE NETWORK LAYER

The network layer implements the "IP" in TCP/IP. It is the *Internet protocol* that allows packets to be routed across different types of hardware and data link layers. It allows SLIP connections to talk to PPP connections and PPP connections to talk to Ethernet devices. The protocol does not take into account data reliability, ordering of data, or other necessities of networking. It provides an addressing scheme and a mechanism to fragment packets for transmission across networks that allow very limited frame sizes.

Each frame of information that is processed by this layer of the network is considered a separate and unique item. There is no concept of a continuous connection. The IP module takes data from the TCP module, applies the appropriate addressing information to the data, and delivers it to the data link layer. The concept of a connection will be introduced later in the sections "TCP/IP and the Transport Layer" and "TCP and the Session Layer." As data moves along a TCP/IP network that is comprised of several smaller networks, decisions must be made about the path that the data takes along its trip. It will travel through devices called *routers* or *gateways* that provide the necessary links to the other networks.

Included in the IP data is a parameter called the *Time to Live* or *TTL*. This is a time limit that is set for the data to reach its destination. As the data passes through each gateway the TTL is reduced. When the time reaches zero, the data is discarded. Since an electrical signal cannot be destroyed, it is simply no longer transmitted to other networks, and its journey stops when the signals reach the network's termination. If the TTL did not exist, it would be possible for a packet to "live" forever, travelling in loops around a network.

Lastly, the IP module provides its own error checking with a checksum of the data that it sends with each packet. A *checksum* is simply a numeric sum of the data that needs to be verified. If a receiving device, such as a remote computer or a gateway, notices that the checksum it calculates differs from the one that is contained in the frame, it will discard the frame.

### IP ADDRESSING

As you know, addresses are currently 32 bits long, and are commonly refereed to as *IP addresses*. They are most commonly represented as four eight-bit numbers separated by periods. An example of such an address is as follows:

```
140.254.85.2
```

It is possible for a single host to have multiple IP addresses for a single network connection. This is commonly called *virtual hosting* since the machine is acting as several "virtual" devices, although it is only one. Similarly, it is also possible for a single host machine to have multiple real connections to a network, such as multiple Ethernet cards. Each of these connections must have a unique address, despite the fact that all the connections belong to the same machine. This practice is called *multihoming*.

## FRAGMENTATION

The IP module handles *fragmentation* of packets as it sees necessary. Although causing fragmentation seems like something that should be avoided, it is a common occurrence and is needed for TCP/IP to be effectively implemented across a variety of networks.

Fragmentation must take place as packets move from a network that allows large packet sizes to one which has a lower limit on the size of the data. Packets are split into a number of pieces that are flagged as being fragmented. When the fragmentation takes place, information about the source and destination addresses is copied to each of the newly created packets. Information is also stored with each packet that allows the receiving device to reassemble the fragmented packets into their original sequence. It is possible for data to be sent with a Don't Fragment flag set. In these cases, the data will be discarded before it is forced to be fragmented.

## COMMUNICATION PROBLEMS

The IP layer provides a basic mechanism for allowing information about errors and routing to be communicated between devices. This is called *ICMP*, or the *Internet Control Message Protocol*.

If a gateway cannot forward a packet to its destination network, or for some reason a packet cannot reach its destination, an ICMP message may be sent. Gateways may also send ICMP messages to hosts to inform them of a shorter route that they can use to send data to their destination. In the event of an error, a typical ICMP message that might be sent is Destination Unreachable—or, if the Time To Live for a packet expires, a Time Exceeded message may be sent. This does not, however, ensure reliable communications. There is no guarantee that every error that occurs will be reported with a corresponding ICMP message. It is left to the next layer to provide a method for ensuring that data reaches its destination in its original form.

# TCP/UDP AND THE TRANSPORT LAYER

Although we are discussing TCP/IP networks, let's first take a look at the transport protocol known as *UDP, or User Datagram Protocol*. UDP is important because it is used extensively on TCP/IP networks, and is generally considered part of the TCP/IP protocol. The primary difference between UDP and TCP is that UDP does not provide for reliable data transmission. In fact, there is no guarantee by the protocol that data will even arrive at its destination. Although this may seem like a strange "requirement" for a protocol, it is actually quite useful. When the goal of a program is to transmit as much information as quickly as possible where any given piece of the data is relatively unimportant, UDP is used. Applications that transmit video, for example, are interested in getting the video stream to its destination as quickly as it can. It doesn't matter if a pixel or two are scrambled, just that the video is as smooth and fluid as possible. This sort of communication is also used in many

Internet games. When playing a multiplayer game over the Internet, it is unlikely that every single piece of position information is necessary for the game to function properly—therefore data is sent out as quickly as possible, and what doesn't arrive in its original form is discarded. Many programs will use a separate TCP connection as well as a UDP connection. Important status information is sent along the reliable TCP connection, whereas the main data stream is sent via UDP.

The purpose of TCP is to provide data transmission that can be considered reliable and to maintain a virtual connection between devices or services that are "speaking" to each other. TCP is responsible for data recovery in the event that packets are received out of sequence, lost, or otherwise corrupted during delivery.

TCP and UDP introduce the concept of ports. A *port* is a virtual *outlet* that can be opened on a network device. Ports are generally predetermined and are related to a particular service that is running on a machine. By specifying ports and including port numbers with TCP/UDP data, the process of *multiplexing* is achieved. Multiplexing allows multiple network connections to take place simultaneously.

The port numbers, along with the source and destination addresses for the data, determine a *socket*. Each machine that communicates using TCP will open a socket to the receiving machine. Once the sockets are connected, the machines may speak across the connection reliably. A single machine may open multiple sockets and handle many incoming or outgoing connections at once.

## TCP AND THE SESSION LAYER

As we defined earlier, the session layer is responsible for maintaining point-to-point communications within the network model. TCP provides this connection functionality in the form of sockets, as we have seen in the previous section. Two sockets connect to provide our "virtual" circuit between two devices, and thus a *session*. This is an example of how it is sometimes difficult to fully expand a network standard to the OSI network model. In the case of TCP/IP, TCP extends across both the transport layer and the session layer, providing a full range of services. We have already covered TCP and its capabilities, so we've inadvertently covered the session layer without even knowing it. That was rather quick and painless, wasn't it?

## THE PRESENTATION LAYER

The presentation layer is simple to understand, but provides so many services that it may be a bit surprising how much variation exists in this layer. If you have email, you may have seen acronyms such as POP or SMTP server in your configuration files. These are essentially languages, or TCP/IP protocols, that your computer can speak in order to send and receive email information to and from other machines. Each one of these languages usually operates on a uniquely defined port number.

## THE APPLICATION LAYER

Finally we reach the top of the network model with TCP/IP fully implemented underneath. The application layer provides the friendly face that we are used to seeing when we use our computers. Programs running in the application layer will usually extend into the presentation layer as well. They implement both the user interface and the language into which the interface must translate its data in in order to speak on the network.

# THE HARDWARE BEHIND NETWORK TRAFFIC

By this point in time, you probably have a good idea of what the various pieces of network hardware do just from reading about TCP/IP. We've discussed the idea of subnets and how they can be combined into a larger TCP/IP network. The devices that accomplish combining these networks into one larger network are known by a variety of names, such as routers, bridges, or gateways. Generally, if you hear someone refer to a device as a gateway and another person refers to it as a bridge, they're both probably right. The distinctions between these different pieces of hardware have blurred in the past few years, and it isn't at all easy to come up with a good explanation as to how to really tell them apart. We are concerned with devices that interconnect different subnets no matter what the name, and will now take a look at the traditional definitions of these devices.

## REPEATERS

The simplest network linking device is a *repeater*. Repeaters work entirely at the hardware level and provide a simple service to the networks they connect. As the name implies, a repeater "repeats" packets across two or more networks, effectively linking them. It has no capability to process the information that it moves; it simply copies a signal from wire to wire. This allows networks to be extended beyond the length of the wiring.

Repeaters and hubs are essentially the same device. A repeater will take an incoming line and repeat the signal across several outgoing lines, in the same way as a hub. The naming convention that seems to be used the most is that hubs seem to be associated with twisted pair/10BaseT wiring, whereas repeaters are used with thinnet. In both cases, the end result is the same.

## SWITCHES

*Switches* are a type of connecting device that can be deployed to help reduce traffic on a network. With regard to Ethernet, this is called "switched" Ethernet. Switches work by segmenting local networks. The main network feeds the switch, and then several subnets plug into it. As a packet arrives at the switch, the switch looks up the destination device from an internal ARP cache and "switches" the packet to the appropriate port. This device is similar to a bridge, and also operates on the data link layer, making it useful for segmenting LANs running any protocol. Switching is generally used on a smaller workgroup level to divide individual networks within a building or department. With recent drops in the price of switch equipment, it is becoming very common for switches to be used in the place of hubs.

Switches use two different technologies to provide their services. *Cut-through* switching analyzes incoming frames for the hardware address and then immediately sends the frame to the appropriate destination. This is essentially offering the functionality of a slightly more advanced repeater. *Store and forward* is the other type of switching technology, which stores the entire incoming frame before resending it. This allows the switch the chance to look for errors and other problems with the packet, and discard it if it finds a problem.

In cases where there are thousands of interconnected network devices, it is likely that from time to time a device will fail and send up a broadcast storm. A year ago, a network printer took down the computers in several campus buildings when it decided to send out garbage packets as quickly as it could. In some cases, computers had to be physically removed from the network cable before they became usable again. The campus network had originally been designed to act as one gigantic subnet, so all packets were broadcast everywhere. With appropriately configured bridges or store and forward switches, this problem wouldn't have affected anything but the local network of the printer. Instead it brought several hundred machines to a screeching halt.

## BRIDGES

*Bridges* operate at the data link layer of the network. This means that they do not have any information on the upper-level protocols that are running across them. A bridge links two or more networks at the lowest possible level. If a bridge is connecting to two Ethernet networks, it is concerned solely with transmitting Ethernet frames between the two networks. Bridges make all of their routing decisions based on the information contained in the Ethernet frame header, which in turn is based on hardware addresses, rather than on the IP address or any other protocol-based data.

Bridges also provide the capability to filter packets based on source information and other parameters in each frame. They can be used to reduce traffic from broadcast packets (packets sent out to the entire network) and multicasting, which we will discuss shortly. Because of this, bridges are commonly used to isolate high traffic networks from one another.

## ROUTERS/GATEWAYS

*Routers* and *gateways* are the same device, and may be used interchangeably, as undoubtedly you've noticed me do in what you've read so far. The router is a much more sophisticated device than either the repeater or the bridge, yet can also perform the same services that either of the lower level tools provide. Routers operate on the upper layers of the network, providing services that are specific to TCP/IP networks. Since routers understand the upper-level protocols, they can be used to combine subnets with different physical layers into a common TCP/IP network. Bridges and repeaters are generally used to move data between subnets that are based on a similar hardware layer. Routers, on the other hand, are concerned with the information that is contained in each packet, and have the capability to examine it in order to make decisions. This allows TCP/IP addresses to be used to move the packet towards its destination. It also allows very specific traffic to be screened out or routed in an extremely configurable manner. IP addresses, ports, and so forth can all be looked at by the router and used to filter data.

---

**Are Gateways and Routers Really the Same Thing?**
For all intents and purposes, yes. Gateways, however, have traditionally been used to link networks that are dissimilar, whereas routers are used to link networks based on the same protocol.

---

# GETTING INFORMATION TO ITS DESTINATION

As data moves from network to network, it is said to make a *hop*. Hops can occur at the hardware level for devices being linked by bridges, or at a higher level with a gateway/router. If we look at the number of hops being made across a TCP/IP network, be aware that there may be several smaller "hops" across bridges that take place in order for data to reach each gateway.

Your network may have one or more gateways, depending on its configuration. There will be a gateway designated as your network's primary route or gateway; the IP address of this device is used when setting up client devices so they know where to send TCP/IP packets if the destination IP address is not on the local network.

Let's look at how decisions are made as to where data will go. We'll start with bridges and then look at gateways/routers. Repeaters are omitted because they do not apply logic when making their decisions—they are purely hardware devices, whereas bridges and routers have some programming to control how they process packets.

## BRIDGES

To begin to get an understanding of how packets reach their destination, let's look at how a bridge does the job of locating its destination. Remember that a bridge does not have knowledge of the TCP/IP protocol, so we will be working strictly at the data link level with Ethernet. The type of bridging that is used in an Ethernet network is called *transparent bridging*.

### TRANSPARENT BRIDGING

Transparent bridging uses an idea called a *spanning tree*. You may picture this quite literally as a branching tree, with bridges located at the joints of branches and individual networks located in-between. The base of the network spanning tree is referred to as the *root*. The root is either determined automatically based on the hardware address, or is chosen by the person designing the network layout. If there are bridges that form circular routes in the network, these are detected and deactivated. The removal of routes will lead to conditions where it is possible to remove more than one route to solve the problem. In these cases, the route that is the greatest number of hops away from the "root" is deactivated.

Once the spanning tree is constructed and loops are removed, the network begins operating by broadcasting packets that it receives to all of the bridges that are connected to it. As hosts receive and send data, the bridges build a table of the hardware addresses that are communicating with each of its interfaces—in essence, it "learns" about its surroundings. This table is then used to determine where the bridge will send data. The larger the table gets, the more specific a route the bridge can choose for each frame. After enough time passes, the bridge will contain information that allows it to successfully route any frames it receives to the appropriate destination without broadcasting extraneous information anywhere.

A drawback to this approach is that the bridged network, once it builds its tables, cannot be reconfigured without the same process happening again. If a subnet is attached to the network, the spanning tree is changed, and the broadcasting of all data on the network must reoccur. This is potentially a concern for a dynamic network environment because changes in topology may happen on a very regular basis. The good news is that transparent bridging is precisely what its name implies—transparent. As a network administrator, you only need to deal with configuring your subnets and attaching the bridge hardware between them. The bridge itself takes care of determining the correct routes to take and reconfigures itself to fit the network. All bridge operations are transparent to the administrator and user.

## ROUTERS/GATEWAYS

Routers and gateways, which "know" about particular protocols, are used to link different subnets (which, as you now know, are internally linked by bridges) to form large TCP/IP networks. Routers must be able to determine the physical address of devices on the local network to which they are attached, as well as have a knowledge of the outside network in order to move outgoing data to the correct destination. Computers that are sending data also need to be able to determine the hardware addresses of the devices to which they are sending data for inclusion in the generated frames. However, if a computer on a local network wants to send data to a remote IP address, it does not need to determine the remote machine's hardware address. Instead it uses the address of the network's router in the frame that it sends. Upon receiving this data, the router will follow the exact same process of the computer originating the transmission. It will determine the appropriate next "hop" for the data, replace its hardware address in the frame with the address of the next appropriate router (we will soon see how it determines what the appropriate router is), and then transmit the frame.

You may be wondering how computers can locate the hardware addresses of devices on its local network—the answer is called an *ARP* request.

### ARP REQUESTS

*ARP*, or *Address Resolution Protocol*, is used by devices to ask for another device's hardware address. Each network device maintains an ARP cache. This cache contains a list of devices that it is communicating with or has communicated with recently. It eliminates the need to send an ARP request every time a frame is sent. We can display the contents of a computer's ARP cache by using the /sbin/arp command shown here:

```
[root@contempt /root]# /sbin/arp
Address         HWtype HWaddress       Flags Mask     Iface
kh1-eth1-5.net.ohio-sta ether  00:90:6F:8C:74:00  C            eth0
primal.ag.ohio-state.ed ether  00:50:E4:85:20:03  C            eth0
```

ARP cache entries eventually timeout and are removed from the cache after a short period of time. If you are using a machine that has dialed into a network and has no local Ethernet connection, your ARP cache will be empty. This is because the dial-in network interface does not use Ethernet hardware addresses for its communications. It is up to the device handling the dial-in to provide the Ethernet connectivity and maintain ARP information.

## CHOOSING A ROUTE

Now we will take a look at how the router actually determines the most appropriate path for a packet to take. Each router and each computer maintains a table that identifies the IP address of a destination, the address of a gateway (or, in the case of data being sent the same network, the same address as the destination), and information about whether the route is up or not. When a packet comes into the router, this table is consulted, the appropriate router for the destination is chosen, and the packet is forwarded. The size of this routing table can be many megabytes in size—keeping track of where information needs to travel is not a trivial task.

In order for routers to keep their routing tables current, they can communicate with other routers and exchange routing information. By doing this on a frequent basis, routing information is propagated and new routes are added on a continuing basis. One of the most common protocols for communicating this information is the *RIP*, or *Router Information Protocol*. RIP information is broadcast between routers every 30 seconds. A broadcast can contain information on whether a route is currently up and the number of hops needed to reach a destination. There can be many redundant routes that a packet can take, so this information is used by the router to figure out what the best possible route is at that given point in time. When a router updates its tables based on a RIP broadcast, it will then broadcast the changes down the network. The changes propagate throughout the entire network.

Another protocol used by routers is the *Open Link State Protocol* (*OLSP*). The OLSP is a transaction-based communication protocol for routers as opposed to RIP, which is a simple broadcast of information. OLSP connections can allow routers to exchange configuration information and can even build its routing tables from scratch by downloading an entire database about the existing router's database.

## TUNNELING WITH ROUTERS

Another function of a router can be *tunneling*. Tunneling is the process of encapsulating data within the packets of one network protocol, transmitting them using that protocol, and then unencapsulating them upon reaching their destination. For example, AppleTalk originally was not a TCP/IP-based protocol, which means that AppleTalk services stop wherever the local subnet stops. AppleTalk offers extremely easy-to-use file and printer sharing and browsing, and it is nice to be able to use these features from a remote site. To do this, we must tunnel AppleTalk through a protocol that can be transmitted between each site. The obvious tunneling choice is TCP/IP. By placing a router on a local AppleTalk network and a similarly configured router on a remote network, they can communicate with each other and pass AppleTalk packets between the networks using TCP/IP as the carrier of the information. When the router on the local network sees an AppleTalk packet, it creates a TCP/IP packet that contains the AppleTalk data. This packet is then transmitted to the remote router. The remote machine decodes the AppleTalk data from the TCP/IP data, and re-broadcasts the AppleTalk packet. To local and remote networks, this is transparent. It simply appears that it is one big AppleTalk network. Using the same tunneling process, we can transmit any protocol we want over the network, even if it is only designed to operate on a local network.

A benefit to doing this sort of tunneling is that the router can modify packets before they are sent to the remote destination. The most common use for this is encryption of packets in order to form a secure network. If there is sensitive data that must be transmitted between local and remote destinations, it is entirely possible for that information to be "sniffed" or read from the network as it is being passed. If we are dealing with data being sent over a TCP/IP connection, we can create a tunnel using TCP/IP that *carries* TCP/IP. Although this may sound a bit strange, it isn't. We are simply extending our TCP/IP subnet to a remote destination and securing the communications in the process.

# PROJECT: PERUSING YOUR OPTIONS

PART

**IV**

CH

**25**

Once you understand the roles played by routers, bridges, and other internetworking products, the challenge becomes finding the appropriate hardware to fit your needs. It helps to take a look around and see what's available for Linux. Both Cisco and Lucent offer a wide range of such devices. And just viewing their offerings would no doubt give you a better sense of what's available.

To see Cisco's offerings, use your Web browser to visit their site at www.cisco.com. Their site offers product descriptions broken down into categories based on the size of the network you're building, ranging from large corporations to small home and office networks.

To check out Lucent's offerings, visit their home page at www.lucent.com. From there, you'll be able to view their product offerings for large corporations, small to medium businesses, as well as for Internet service providers. While many of their products are geared toward voice communications, you'll find routers, bridges, and switches as well.

Once you purchase a product, integrating it into your network and configuring the device is generally something you have to do by following the instructions that come with that particular device. However, LinuxConf does offer some fairly simple options for setting up routes and gateways once you've installed the appropriate hardware. You'll find those options under Config, Networking, Client Tasks, Routing and Gateways in the left column of LinuxConf.

# CHAPTER 26

# SETTING UP NETWORK INFORMATION SERVICES (NIS)

In this chapter

# INTRODUCTION TO NIS

How big is your Linux network? One or two computers—or two hundred? No matter what the size of your network, you may have experienced a bit of frustration when you go from machine to machine and run adduser over and over. On a network with more than a handful of machines, this process quickly becomes a nightmare.

In Chapter 23, "Sharing Files with NFS," you learned about using the NFS capabilities of your system to share and mount remote directories. This lets you access files on remote systems as if they were local to your computer. Unlike other operating systems, the NFS file system behaves identically to local file systems—Linux doesn't really care if your files are sitting on your local drive or on a computer sitting in another country.

One of the most common uses for NFS is to share the home directories of users among different machines. By doing this, you enable a user to log in to any machine and have his files and desktop show up exactly as it would on any other machine. If you're familiar with Windows NT, this is given the fancy name of *roaming profiles*. If you're a Linux user, however, you can just consider this business as usual. Unfortunately, getting your Linux machine to work like this isn't as easy as sharing your home directory between different machines.

Linux assigns each user on the system a specific UID and GID, or user/group ID—these are used to identify the owner of files, directories, and the like. Despite the fact that common commands display user information symbolically (owner jray; group jray), behind the scenes it's just a bunch of numbers. You can see the currently assigned numbers by looking at the third and fourth fields in your /etc/passwd file shown here:

```
root:x:0:0:root:/root:/bin/bash
bin:x:1:1:bin:/bin:
daemon:x:2:2:daemon:/sbin:
adm:x:3:4:adm:/var/adm:
lp:x:4:7:lp:/var/spool/lpd:
sync:x:5:0:sync:/sbin:/bin/sync
shutdown:x:6:0:shutdown:/sbin:/sbin/shutdown
halt:x:7:0:halt:/sbin:/sbin/halt
mail:x:8:12:mail:/var/spool/mail:
...
nobody:x:99:99:Nobody:/:
xfs:x:100:102:X Font Server:/etc/X11/fs:/bin/false
gdm:x:42:42::/home/gdm:/bin/bash
postgres:x:101:233:PostgreSQL Server:/var/lib/pgsql:/bin/bash
squid:x:102:234::/var/spool/squid:/dev/null
jray:x:500:500::/home/jray:/bin/bash
jackd:x:501:501::/home/jackd:/bin/bash
agroves:x:502:503::/home/agroves:/bin/bash
```

This UID is what causes the problem on NFS mounted volumes. For example, let's say that I have a system at work that's sharing my home directory to a newly installed Linux machine in my home. If I log in to the new system and list the files in what I *think* is my home directory, I might see something like this:

```
[jray@contempt jray]$ ls -l
total 1100
drwxr-xr-x  5 501    501       4096    Nov  9 06:08 Desktop
-rwxrwxr-x  1 501    501        200    Jan 13 23:34 crap
drwx------  2 501    501       4096    Nov  9 11:49 nsmail
-rw-rw-r--  1 501    501          4    Jan 17 15:42 perl_e1.pl
drwxr-xr-x  2 501    501       4096    Jan 28 01:18 public_html
-rw-rw-r--  1 501    501       2962    Jan 13 23:26 rpms
-rw-r--r--  1 501    501        333    Jan 28 01:18 savebutton.gif
drwxr-xr-x  4 501    501       4096    Jan 15 23:15 ssh-1.2.27
-rw-rw-r--  1 501    501    1022546    May 13  1999 ssh-1.2.27.tar.gz
drwxr-xr-x  2 501    501       4096    Nov 29 22:38 urstables
-rw-r--r--  1 501    501      56375    Jan 21 11:25 voltconf99.htm
```

Instead of the usual username jray and group jray, I see the UID and GID of my account on the old machine. I am bound to the read/write/execute permissions set for world access because I no longer own my files!

As you add users to the system, they're usually assigned sequential UIDs starting at 500—unless you manually enter the ID. Unless the UIDs match up between different systems, the ownership of files won't match up either. There are a few different ways to deal with this, which we'll talk about next.

### MAINTAIN A CONSISTENT PASSWORD FILE

If you only have a few machines and a few users, the easiest thing to do is maintain consistency between the password files on these machines. This works best in settings with very static configurations; if you have to add users every other day, it will be a bit of a pain to update files on all of the systems. Furthermore, if a user changes her password on one of the machines, it won't change on the other machines. If you or your users perform relatively frequent updates to the user configuration, you may want to consider the second option.

### SCRIPT UPDATES FROM A MASTER MACHINE

Another simple solution is to designate a "master" machine and write a script to periodically copy the updated user files to each machine on the network. The drawback to this approach is that the only place updates can take place are on the master machine. If a user were to try to change her password while logged into a machine other than the master, it would only persist until the script copied an update from the master. If you'd like a solution with none of these drawbacks, the next option, NIS, is for you.

## NIS

If the other potential solutions don't sound like the right thing for you, then perhaps you need a *Network Information Services* (*NIS*) server. NIS is typically used on existing UNIX networks and is often a necessity on Linux computers that are being integrated into a legacy network. NIS allows machines to look up user information from a centralized location. If a user changes her password on one machine, it gets changed on another. There is no need to copy files between different computers or create any customized scripts. If you are connecting to an existing UNIX network, this will enable all existing accounts to be used to gain access to your system. If you want to maintain local accounts on your computer that are not synchronized across the network, NIS can do that too. NIS will distribute only the information that you want.

NIS is not strictly a mechanism for distributing the password file across a network; it can actually maintain a synchronized repository of any information. This chapter will focus on the basic configuration files, however.

There are two parts to the NIS software: the server and the client. The server software is needed if you are going to be starting your own NIS services from scratch. If you're planning on joining an existing UNIX network that already has an NIS server, you simply need to run the client software. Let's take a look at how to create your own NIS server now.

**Tip** As you may have guessed, you need superuser privileges to set up NIS services.

## SETTING UP AN NIS SERVER

Getting your NIS-based network up and running might take a bit of tinkering. You'll need to edit several configuration files and install a few NIS-specific packages before you can test anything. To begin with, you need to have the portmapper software installed. If you're running NFS, the portmapper is already on your system. If not, be sure to check for it using `rpm -q portmap` before continuing, like this:

```
[jray@contempt jray]$ rpm -q portmap
portmap-4.0-17
```

If not, install it from your Red Hat Linux CD now. Once you've added it to your system, you need to make sure that it is turned on for your runlevel. Do this by typing `chkconfig –add portmap`.

Next, make sure that `time` services are enabled for the `inetd` process by editing your `/etc/inetd.conf` file and uncommenting the following two lines:

```
time  stream tcp   nowait root  internal
time  dgram  udp   wait  root   internal
```

Now restart `inetd` so that it will reread its configuration file. Do this with `killall -1 inetd`.

Now you're ready to install the server. You'll need to verify that the `ypserv` package is installed. Most of the packages that you'll be using begin with *YP*—this is an acronym for "Yellow Pages"—or "the place where you can find everything at your fingertips" (including your account information). Check to see if `ypserv` is installed by typing `rpm -q ypserv`. If it isn't, install it from your Red Hat Linux CD-ROM #1 now. To begin the installation of `ypserv`, be sure to mount the Red Hat CD-ROM. Then enter the following command:

```
rpm -ivh /mnt/cdrom/RedHat/RPMS/ypserv*.rpm
```

To finish the installation of ypserv, add this to your runlevel: `chkconfig --add ypserv`.

With ypserv installed, it's time to get back to editing configuration files, namely `/var/yp/securenets` and `/etc/ypserv.conf`.

## EDITING THE /VAR/YP/SECURENETS FILE

The securenets file provides access information to the server. You can enable hosts on a network or IP basis. Open the file in your favorite text editor now. It looks something like this:

```
#
# securenets  This file defines the access rights to your NIS server
#       for NIS clients. This file contains netmask/network
#       pairs. A client's IP address needs to match with at least
#       one of those.
#
#       One can use the word "host" instead of a netmask of
#       255.255.255.255. Only IP addresses are allowed in this
#       file, not hostnames.
#
# Always allow access for localhost
225.0.0.1  127.0.0.0

# The local networks
255.255.255.0  192.168.1.0
255.255.255.0    192.168.2.0
255.255.255.0    192.168.3.0

# A few remote hosts that need access
host       140.254.85.2
host       140.254.85.225
host       140.254.85.226
```

Each entry in the file is composed as a line with a subnet mask and an IP address on it. The word "host" can be used in place of a subnet of `255.255.255.255` to denote a single computer. This will enable access to the NIS server from any of the named networks or hosts. Be sure that you set this up correctly—allowing the world to be a client to your NIS server is not exactly a good idea. With securenets now out of the way, let's take a look at the file that tells ypserv how to work.

## EDITING THE /etc/ypserv.conf FILE

The `ypserv.conf` file controls how different hosts access the shared information from your ypserv process. A very basic configuration that does not impose any restrictions on access is defined here. This should be very compatible with other UNIX NIS-based systems. If you have a Linux-only network, you may want to check out the `ypserv.conf` manpage for directions on how to enable specific security settings for your system. Here is a basic configuration to edit the `/etc/ypserv.conf` file:

```
#
# ypserv.conf  In this file you can set certain options for the NIS server,
#       and you can deny or restrict access to certain maps based
```

```
#          on the originating host.
#
#          See ypserv.conf(5) for a description of the syntax.
#


# Some options for ypserv. These things are all not needed, if
# you have a Linux net.

dns: yes


# Host           : Map        : Security  : Passwd_mangle

*                : *          : none
```

## STARTING THE ypserv PROCESS

With your configuration files in place, you can start the NIS server. To do this, you must first make sure that the portmapper is running by entering /etc/rc.d/init.d/portmap start. Then, proceed with starting ypserv by entering /etc/rc.d/init.d/ypserv start. You can verify that the process is running by taking a look at the output of pmap_dump—this command lists the current programs that are registered with the portmapper program and the ports/ protocols that they are using. It should look something like this:

```
[root@pointy /etc]# pmap_dump
  100000  2  tcp  111 portmapper
  100000  2  udp  111 portmapper
  100004  2  udp  856 ypserv
  100004  1  udp  856 ypserv
  100004  2  tcp  859 ypserv
  100004  1  tcp  859 ypserv
```

As you can see, the ypserv process is up and running and is pointing to ports 856 and 859 using both UDP and TCP. You're very close to being done now!

Now that the server is running, you need to generate the initial databases that it will use. First, however, set up a domain name for the server to use. This should be a name that isn't a registered DNS name. Use the /bin/domainname command to set your domain, as shown here:

```
[root@pointy yp]# /bin/domainname poisonous
```

With a properly configured domain name, you can use /usr/lib/yp/ypinit -mto create your initial database. This program will ask you to input the names of the hosts that you want to use as servers, and will then create the database files for your system like this:

```
[root@pointy yp]# /usr/lib/yp/ypinit -m
```

```
At this point, we have to construct a list of the hosts which will run NIS
servers. pointy is in the list of NIS server hosts. Please continue to add
the names for the other hosts, one per line. When you are done with the
list, type a <control D>.
    next host to add: pointy
    next host to add:
The current list of NIS servers looks like this:
```

```
pointy

Is this correct? [y/n: y] y
We need some minutes to build the databases...
Building /var/yp/poisonous/ypservers...
Running /var/yp/Makefile...
gmake[1]: Entering directory '/var/yp/poisonous'
Updating passwd.byname...
Updating passwd.byuid...
...

pointy has been set up as a NIS master server.

Now you can run ypinit -s pointy on all slave servers.
```

Your ypserv process is now ready to be used. In order to make your user's life a bit easier, however, there's still one more process that you need to start—the rpc.yppasswdd server. This program will accept and process incoming password change requests. It should always be installed on the master NIS domain server. Add it to your runlevel with chkconfig -add yppasswdd, and then start it by typing /etc/rc.d/init.d/yppasswd start or by rebooting your computer.

> **Tip**
>
> There are quite a few processes and configuration files that need to be set up in order for NIS (and other processes to run). Although it's usually not necessary to reboot, sometimes rebooting your system is helpful. If you accidentally didn't start a process, a reboot will obviously take care of the problem. If you forgot to add something to your runlevel, it should become clear upon rebooting. After installing a server package, never assume it has been done correctly unless you can successfully restart your machine and have it come up as you would expect.

PART

**IV**

CH

**26**

Your NIS server is ready to go! Now let's take a look at setting up a client to the NIS network. After all, it's not very useful unless you have other computers on your network that can access it.

# SETTING UP AN NIS CLIENT

Setting up a client to your NIS domain is just about as exciting as setting up a server—lots of different setup files and other goodies to configure. Let's start with the most simple and crucial part of the client—the ypbind daemon. This program connects to the server and enables the exchange of information with the primary NIS domain server.

First, check to see if you have the ypbind package installed on your client workstation by using rpm -q ypbind, as shown here:

```
[root@pointy poisonous]# rpm -q ypbind
ypbind-3.3-24
```

If you don't have the software, install it from your Red Hat Linux CD before continuing. You'll also want to add the software to your runlevel by typing `chkconfig -add ypbind`. You can also configure an NIS client through LinuxConf.

## EDITING THE /etc/yp.conf FILE

Next, you need to tell the ypbind software which server it is going to bind to. To do this, you need to edit the `/etc/yp.conf` file to include a list of the servers on your network. For example, here is a very simple version of that file:

```
[root@pointy poisonous]# more /etc/yp.conf
# /etc/yp.conf - ypbind configuration file
# Valid entries are
#
#domain NISDOMAIN server HOSTNAME
#     Use server HOSTNAME for the domain NISDOMAIN.
#
#domain NISDOMAIN broadcast
#     Use broadcast on the local net for domain NISDOMAIN
#
#ypserver HOSTNAME
#     Use server HOSTNAME for the local domain. The
#     IP-address of server must be listed in /etc/hosts.
#

ypserver 192.168.0.1
```

This is a configuration file for a private subnet that I run. The master server is at the IP address `192.168.0.1`. You can include multiple lines for any other servers that you need to connect to—including slave servers. (We'll take a look at slave servers in a little bit.)

Once you've edited the file to point to your NIS server, you can start the ypbind process by typing `/etc/rc.d/init.d/ypbind start`. If everything is working as it should, your screen should look something like this:

```
[root@pointy poisonous]# /etc/rc.d/init.d/ypbind start
Binding to the NIS domain...                [ OK ]
Listening for an NIS domain server: pointy
```

With they pbind software connected to your master NIS server, you can immediately make requests from the server. The easiest way to check to see if everything is running is to use the ypcat command to see if one of the NIS-served databases is actually accessible. For example, to see the contents of my services file, I'd use `ypcat services`, as shown here:

```
[root@pointy poisonous]# ypcat services
finger          79/tcp
ntp             123/udp
npmp-gui        611/udp        dqs313_execd
bbs             7000/tcp
kerberos4       750/udp        kerberos-iv kdc
cmip-agent      164/udp
qmtp            209/tcp
who             513/udp        whod
snews           563/tcp
```

```
mailq           174/tcp
omirr           808/udp             omirrd
ssmtp           465/tcp
prospero-np     1525/udp
rtelnet         107/tcp
https           443/tcp
tcpmux          1/tcp
fsp             21/udp              fspd
...
```

Sure enough, there it is! Unfortunately, however, being able to use ypcat doesn't exactly mean that everything is ready for use. The system will still query the traditional configuration files rather than look at the NIS server.

---

**I've Read the Online Docs and I Keep Seeing References to "maps"—What Are They?**
Think of a map as the NIS database that holds a specific type of information—the passwd file data, hosts data, and so on. Maps are not necessarily named the same thing as their plain-file brethren. The file /var/yp/ nicknames contains a list of mappings between traditional names and the names of the NIS server maps.

---

## EDITING THE /etc/nsswitch.conf FILE

The easiest way to get the NIS client computer to recognize your NIS server for its lookups is to edit the file /etc/nsswitch.conf file. This file contains a list of all of the places your computer should look for information. By including NIS in this file, you can stop querying local files and start looking at your NIS server. Here is a sample nsswitch file that is configured to use an NIS server:

```
#
# /etc/nsswitch.conf
#
# An example Name Service Switch config file. This file should be
# sorted with the most-used services at the beginning.
#
# The entry '[NOTFOUND=return]' means that the search for an
# entry should stop if the search in the previous entry turned
# up nothing. Note that if the search failed due to some other reason
# (like no NIS server responding) then the search continues with the
# next entry.
#
# Legal entries are:
#
#     nisplus or nis+      Use NIS+ (NIS version 3)
#     nis or yp            Use NIS (NIS version 2), also called YP
#     dns                  Use DNS (Domain Name Service)
#     files                Use the local files
#     db                   Use the local database (.db) files
#     compat               Use NIS on compat mode
#     hesiod               Use Hesiod for user lookups
#     [NOTFOUND=return]    Stop searching if not found so far
#

passwd:   nis files
shadow:   nis files
```

```
group:       nis files

hosts:       nis files dns

bootparams: nis [NOTFOUND=return] files

ethers:      files
netmasks:    files
networks:    files
protocols:   files
rpc:         files
services:    nis files

netgroup:    nis

publickey:   nis

automount:   files
aliases:     files
```

Each of the service names (password, shadow, group, and so on) can be configured to look for information from an NIS server or a variety of different places. Typically, these lines are set to files—which refers to local configuration files. Since you're now setting up your system to use NIS, you want the computer to first check the NIS server that it is bound to; then, if that fails, to check the local files.

The ordering here is important! If you have a value defined locally but also have it defined in an NIS-served database, the NIS value will override the local value. If you have a local user named "Bob" and a network user named "Bob," the local user will no longer be able to log into the system.

After you've made the changes to your nsswitch.conf file, you should be in business. You can easily test this by logging into a client machine and seeing if it automatically recognizes settings (such as hosts, users, and so on) that previously were only accessible on the master server.

Using NIS is a wonderful way to manage the large number of configuration files that normally have to be maintained on each individual Linux computer. It can be, however, a pain to initially get up and running. If you have a need for NIS, go for it. If not, don't set it up just "for the heck of it." NIS and NFS are both known security risks. In fact, some of the worst UNIX exploits have been caused by bugs in the portmapper software, which both of these servers rely on. As with any other server, only run it if you need it—the less accessible your computer is to the outside world, the better!

# CASE STUDY: SETTING UP AN NIS SLAVE SERVER

If you're planning a large network that requires consistent and reliable service (as opposed to planning a network that will be down most of the time), you'll probably want to set up a slave NIS server in addition to your master server.

To see why it is necessary to have a slave server, try disconnecting your master server from the network, and then try to use one of your client computers. Unless all of the information from the server is duplicated in local files and these local files are made accessible in /etc/nsswitch.conf,the machine will be mostly useless. The ypbind client does not maintain a local cache of information that has been retrieved from the server. Each time a lookup is made, the master server is contacted. If the master server goes down, the client machine is left helpless and unable to perform its lookup request.

You should also install slave servers if you have a master server that is not on the same subnet with some of the clients. If you are relying on the stability of the Internet to provide connectivity between an NIS server and its clients, you're placing a great deal of trust in something you don't control. Having a slave server around to pick up the slack in case there is a failure will greatly improve the overall stability of the network.

Setting up a slave server is actually pretty simple. If you've already set up the master server and a client, you've completed most of the steps that are necessary in setting up a slave. Refer to the "Setting Up an NIS Server" section for more information. Follow these steps to get your slave server ready:

1. Install the portmapper and ypserv software.
2. Add portmap and ypserver to your runlevel by typing chkconfig -add portmap and chkconfig -add ypserv.
3. Start the portmapper with /etc/rc.d/init.d/portmap start.
4. Edit the /var/yp/securenets and /etc/ypserv.conf files.
5. Start ypserv with this: /etc/rc.d/init.d/ypserv start.
6. Install the ypbind software.
7. Add ypbind to your runlevel with chkconfig -add ypbind.
8. Edit the /etc/yp.conf file.
9. Start ypbind with /etc/rc.d/init.d/ypbind start.

Now things change—but only very slightly. Instead of using ypinit to create the default master database, you need to create a backup of the existing master database. To verify that your slave server knows where it should retrieve its files, use the following ypwhich -m command to show a list of the available maps and which machine is serving them:

```
[root@pointy /etc]# ypwhich -m
services.byname pointy
hosts.byaddr pointy
hosts.byname pointy
passwd.byname pointy
...
ypservers pointy
passwd.byuid pointy
```

You should be ready to start the slave server now. You do this with ypinit -s pointy. Once the server is ready, you can add it to your /etc/yp.conf file on other client computers on your network. If the master server is, for some reason, inaccessible, the slaver server will respond to queries in its place.

One final step in setting up a slave is to schedule the slave computer to retrieve updates from the master server. Normally updates are automatic, but, in the event that an update is made while a slave is inaccessible, it is wise to have the slave poll the server for information on a regular basis. The following are three scripts in the /var/yp directory that update the maps on the slave servers if they are out of sync: ypxfr_1perhour, ypxfr_1perday, and ypxfr_2perday. You should add these scripts to your system /etc/crontab. Edit your /etc/ crontab file and add these lines:

```
01   *   *   *   *    root    ypxfr_1perhour
02   0   *   *   *    root    ypxfr_1perday
03   0,12   *   *   *    root    ypxfr_2perday
```

With these lines added to your crontab file, your slave server is ready for action. You should now be able to take your master server offline without having any disastrous consequences.

NIS services can be a bit bizarre at first. Determining where problems are occurring is often difficult for the administrator, and, if an NIS server fails during a user's work session, it could be extremely problematic for the user.

Many people push centralized networks for the purpose of control and ease of maintenance. I've seen NT administrators running a domain with roaming profiles among three or four users—simply for the power trip. I've also seen the same administrators complaining because of the amount of time they have to spend helping each user when something on the network fails. You need to decide when implementing something like NIS is a means by which you can create a more efficient network and when it is just another extraneous server process.

CHAPTER **27**

# BEEFING UP NETWORK SECURITY

**In this chapter**

# SECURITY PROBLEMS

Security is an issue for anyone who has a computer connected to a network. If you are plugging your computer into a network just to browse the Web, you still need to make sure that your operating system is secure from attack. Red Hat Linux is not known for shipping in a secure condition., although this has been partially corrected in version 6.2. To get the maximum security for a desktop system, be sure to use the Workstation installation option. If you're running a server, however, there are two types of attacks that you should be worried about, each with different goals.

## INTRUSION

The most common type of attack that you should be worried about is an intrusion attempt. This is a very straightforward attack—someone wants to gain access to your computer. Surprisingly, most people who are trying to hack their way into your computer are not really after anything you have (unless you happen to be running a high profile Web site or something else that would attract attention). Instead, most hackers just want to *use* your computer. If they have access to a Linux machine, they can use it as a springboard for their *big* targets. Because of this, most intrusions are designed to be very "quiet." The longer it takes you to figure out that your machine has been compromised, the longer the intruder has to hack on other machines.

What makes this even more scary is that you may eventually be held accountable for damages that occur because of someone hacking a computer by way of your machine. Computer security laws are being proposed that hold a computer owner responsible for actions that are performed with their computer—regardless of who initiated them. The future almost certainly will be one where users *must* understand how to secure their systems—or face criminal negligence charges.

If you have a computer that becomes compromised, you will also face potential downtime while the problem is corrected. When a Linux machine is hacked, the hacker often installs a *rootkit*. The rootkit installs modified copies of existing software on your computer. For example, the who and ps commands are usually changed so that they filter out any logging sessions of processes that are being run by the hacker. The new binaries are typically changed in a way that makes them appear to be identical to the old binaries: same size, same dates, same attributes. Even worse, a packet sniffer might be installed on your computer that watches the network for email, Telnet, or FTP connections and records the passwords.

It's usually not worth trying to fix a hacked machine. The assumption must be made that nothing is safe. The only "pure" recovery is to wipe your hard drives and reload Red Hat Linux. Since I'm quite sure this doesn't sound like fun to most people, there is a much better solution: Make sure that your computer is not compromised to begin with. This chapter helps ensure that your computer is safe from intrusion.

# DENIAL OF SERVICE ATTACKS (DoS)

Another type of attack that you might face is a denial of service attack. As the name suggests, a *denial of service (DoS)* attack creates a condition where a specific service or all services are disrupted on your computer. DoS attacks are malicious in nature and target you specifically. This type of attack is difficult, if not impossible, to stop. In order to understand why a DoS attack is so dangerous, you need to first understand how it works.

## STANDARD DoS ATTACKS

A denial of service attack is not an attempt to gain access to your computer: It is an attempt to shut it down. While you can block an intrusion attempt at your computer, a denial of service attack keeps coming. Your computer has several states that it goes through while trying to establish a connection with an outside host. Once in a particular state, the computer that is waiting for a connection must wait a certain length of time for a response from the connecting machine or for a timeout to occur. This is the point in time that the attacker exploits.

The attacker in a DoS attack sends thousands of simultaneous requests to its victim. Each connection that is currently open or opening uses more and more resources. After a while, the computer that is being attacked can no longer keep up with servicing the requests from the attacker. The problem is that the computer being attacked can no longer keep up with *any* service requests. It is effectively shut down without anything physical ever occurring, or anyone ever breaking into the system.

Some denial of service attacks exploit bugs in the networking code of the operating system being targeted. In these cases, simply updating the operating system to the latest patches will probably take care of the problem. There are, however, DoS attacks that cannot be stopped in this way. Another means of stopping an attack is to take away access to the machine being attacked. To do this, you need to block the attack from ever reaching the wire that the target is connected to. A network *firewall* can accomplish this task.

If your network is firewalled, you can block traffic before it gets to your computers. Unfortunately, firewalls cannot stop the attack from happening. The traffic of a DoS attack will still eat up bandwidth on your network. The best way to stop a DoS attack is to determine where the attack is coming from and report it to your ISP. Sadly, a new type of DoS attack is making this almost impossible.

## DISTRIBUTED DENIAL OF SERVICE ATTACKS (DDoS)

There is a far more insidious type of DoS attack that can be even more troublesome—the *distributed denial of service* attack, or DDoS. Rather than the attack coming from a single computer, the attack is distributed among potentially thousands of attackers. Worse still, many of these attackers are probably unaware that they are attacking you!

A DDoS works a little bit differently from the standard DoS. Instead of the attacking machine sending requests to the remote target, it sends echo packets to other machines that are known to have a large amount of bandwidth. Instead of asking the machines to respond to it, the attacker does a bit of creative modification of the TCP/IP packet. The attacker modifies the request packets to appear as though they came from the machine that was attacked. All responses to these packets go to the target machine. By sending out thousands of response requests simultaneously to high bandwidth hosts around the Internet, an attacker can turn innocuous machines into a threat.

Obviously, it becomes much harder to ward off this sort of attack. You can't block traffic from thousands of hosts (well, you can, but it's gonna be a pain). System administrators need to pay close attention to their systems to make sure that they aren't being used in DDoS attacks. If you notice a large amount traffic on your network from one of your computers that you can't account for, it is possible that it is being used in a distributed denial of service attack.

# Monitoring Your Network

The first step in understanding how to protect the machines on your network is to get a handle on which services are being run. The easiest way to do this is run port scans on your network (including yourself!).

## Ports

Each service on your computer operates on a *port*. Think of these ports as the different ports on the back of your computer. If you want to use your printer, you plug into the printer port. If you want to use your joystick, it goes into the joystick port...and so on. The same thing goes for network services. If you want to use a Web site, you connect to the HTTP protocol port (80). Here are a few other common services and their ports:

| | |
|---|---|
| **FTP** | Ports 20, 21 |
| **Telnet** | Port 23 |
| **Gopher** | Port 70 |
| **Finger** | Port 79 |
| **HTTP** | Port 80 |
| **POP3** | Port 110 |
| **NTP** | Port 123 |
| **IMAP** | Port 143 |

You can find other ports that your computer knows about (but isn't necessarily servicing) by looking in the /etc/services file on your computer. A good rule of thumb is that the fewer services you're running, the more secure your system will be. Furthermore, since other machines on your local network could be used to find your passwords and gain access to your computer, you need to be aware of what everyone else is running.

If you are walking into a network administrator position on a cross-platform network, you're probably going to be surprised at what you see. With Windows and Macintosh OS now offering personal Web servers "out of the box" and Linux installing full email, FTP, and

Web services, you're likely to find that most computers on your network are acting as some type of server.

A good way to check the systems on your network to determine which services are active is to use the same tools that hackers use—namely, a port scanner. A port scanner checks to determine which ports are in a state of "open"—then matches these ports to the standard services. Within a few seconds, you can determine which servers each machine on your network is running. One of the best port scanners is *NMAP*—its use is documented here.

**Tip**

> If you are in a position where you have authoritative control over your network, you can make changes beyond the configuration of machines that will have an impact on security. The most important thing you can do is educate your users. If the clients on your network understand the security implications that many pieces of software have, they can probably be persuaded to stop using them. It's always better to control people through education, not through force.

## DOWNLOADING AND USING NMAP

NMAP is a wonderful network scanning tool. It can scan entire networks from a single command and return easy-to-interpret information about the active hosts. It supports a wide variety of different scanning techniques that can be used to scan protected hosts. Another interesting use for NMAP is to identify operating systems being used by remote computers. This functionality might not work on all computers, but it's generally right and quite incredible to see in action.

The NMAP homepage is located at http://www.insecure.org/nmap/. The software is downloadable in RPM format as well as source code. After downloading the RPM, install it as shown here:

```
[root@pointy /root]# rpm -Uvh nmap-2.3BETA12-1.i386.rpm
nmap                      ###############################################
```

Now you're ready to try scanning a host or two. First, try a machine that you know is running a few services. To scan, just use nmap followed by the name or IP address of the machine. Here is the scan of a rather heavily loaded server:

```
[root@pointy /root]# nmap poisontooth.com

Starting nmap V. 2.3BETA12 by Fyodor (fyodor@dhp.com, www.insecure.org/hmap/)
Interesting ports on dub234197.columbus.rr.com (204.210.234.197):
Port    State      Protocol  Service
21      open       tcp       ftp
22      open       tcp       ssh
23      open       tcp       telnet
25      open       tcp       smtp
53      open       tcp       domain
80      open       tcp       http
98      open       tcp       linuxconf
106     open       tcp       pop3pw
```

PART

**IV**

CH

**27**

```
110       open       tcp        pop-3
139       open       tcp        netbios-ssn
143       open       tcp        imap2
548       open       tcp        afpovertcp
600       open       tcp        ipcserver
901       open       tcp        unknown
993       open       tcp        imaps
5432      open       tcp        postgres
```

```
Nmap run completed -- 1 IP address (1 host up) scanned in 0 seconds
```

You can see that there is quite a bit going on here. Typically, this is what you *don't* want your machines to look like, unless you're sure that the services being run are secure. The less you're running, the less information the potential hacker can pick up from your computer and the fewer potential holes there are to exploit. You'll see how to shut off services in a few minutes.

Using nmap on a host-by-host basis can quickly get a bit tiring. To get around this problem, you can simply scan an entire subnet at a time. Use nmap in the exact same manner as before, just following the IP address with the "bittage" of the subnet mask (24 bits in a class C address, etc.). For example, to scan the entire class C 192.168.0.0 subnet, use nmap 192.168.0.0/24. Before you do, however, this is a good time to introduce the -O option to perform operating system fingerprinting. Just use the option with your command like this:

```
Starting nmap V. 2.3BETA12 by Fyodor (fyodor@dhp.com, www.insecure.org/nmap/)

Interesting ports on theotormon.ag.ohio-state.edu (140.254.85.8):
Port      State      Protocol   Service
139       open       tcp        netbios-ssn

TCP Sequence Prediction: Class=trivial time dependency
                         Difficulty=53 (Easy)
Remote operating system guess: Windows NT4 / Win95 / Win98

Interesting ports on rintrah.ag.ohio-state.edu (140.254.85.9):
Port      State      Protocol   Service
139       open       tcp        netbios-ssn

TCP Sequence Prediction: Class=trivial time dependency
                         Difficulty=49 (Easy)
Remote operating system guess: Windows NT4 / Win95 / Win98

Interesting ports on postoffice.ag.ohio-state.edu (140.254.85.38):
Port      State      Protocol Service
22        open       tcp        ssh
25        open       tcp        smtp
106       open       tcp        pop3pw
110       open       tcp        pop-3

TCP Sequence Prediction: Class=random positive increments
                         Difficulty=54266 (Worthy challenge)
Remote operating system guess: Mac OS X (Rhapsody 5.5) on a G3
```

As you can see, it does a pretty nifty job. The software has correctly identified two Windows computers and a Macintosh OS X server on the network. Don't worry, I cut off the display before it reached the plethora of Linux boxes.

Depending on the configuration of computers that are on your network, you might be able to use an additional feature of NMAP to determine who is running the services a computer. If an attacker can identify which user has control over a process, he or she will target the ports that have privileged access. Why try to crack into the "nobody" account, when you can go for root access? The -I option turns on the owner identification option as shown here:

```
[root@pointy /etc]# nmap -I poisontooth.com

Starting nmap V. 2.3BETA12 by Fyodor (fyodor@dhp.com, www.insecure.org/nmap/)
Interesting ports on lumpy.poisontooth.com (192.168.234.197):
Port    State       Protocol  Service         Owner
22      open        tcp       ssh             root
23      open        tcp       telnet          root
80      open        tcp       http            nobody
98      open        tcp       linuxconf       root
548     open        tcp       afpovertcp      root
5432    open        tcp       postgres        postgres

Nmap run completed -- 1 IP address (1 host up) scanned in 15 seconds
```

On this example machine, the obvious attack points are ssh, telnet, linuxconf, and afpovertcp. Eliminating any services run by root will protect your machine.

You can see what a valuable tool a program like NMAP is, but it should also be obvious what an incredible hacking tool it is as well. You should be very careful with NMAP yourself—if you use it to scan remote networks, you might find that the administrators are watching and think you are attacking. A potential intruder can have nmap search thousands of computers for easy targets, and then plan their attack accordingly. So, how do you guard against this? A piece of software called PortSentry does the job nicely.

## DOWNLOADING AND USING PORTSENTRY

PortSentry is a program that can detect and actively block port scanning programs. The software is very easy to set up and install, and eliminates much of the necessity to actively monitor your server.

PortSentry is capable of detecting almost any kind of port scan. Once it has determined that your computer is being scanned, it has several options to proactively guard against an intrusion attempt. Scans themselves are usually harmless—but they are usually performed with the intent of discovering vulnerabilities in the machines being scanned. PortScan can immediately modify your /etc/hosts.deny file to block the intruder from attempting to access inetd-controlled processes. Better yet, it can also completely block the traffic by writing firewalling IPchain rules on-the-fly. Blocking all traffic will eliminate the capability for the remote machine to talk to your computer in any way.

You can download the latest source code to PortSentry from the Psionic Web site at `http://www.psionic.com/download/`. The program is only available as source code, so you'll need to install it and do a bit of basic configuration:

1. Untar and ungzip the PortSentry archive:

```
tar -zxf portsentry-1.0.tar.gz
```

2. Change your working directory to be in the root directory of the PortSentry source code.

3. Next, you're going to have to make some changes to the `portsentry_config.h` file. Edit the definitions for `SYSLOG_FACILITY` and `SYSLOG_LEVEL` so that they look like this:

```
/* The default syslog is as daemon.notice. You can also use */
/* any of the facilities from syslog.h to send messages to (LOCAL0, etc) */
#define SYSLOG_FACILITY LOG_AUTHPRIV
#define SYSLOG_LEVEL LOG_CRIT
```

4. Now, you're ready to compile and install the software. Type `make linux install` and sit back for a few minutes. You should see something that looks like this:

```
[root@pointy portsentry-1.0]# make linux install
SYSTYPE=linux
Making
cc -O -Wall -DLINUX -DSUPPORT_STEALTH -o ./portsentry ./portsentry.c \
        ./portsentry_io.c ./portsentry_util.c
Creating psionic directory /usr/local/psionic
...
```

There is actually very little configuration that needs to be done before PortSentry can go to work for you. You'll want to configure the file `/usr/local/psionic/portsentry/portsentry.conf` to be specific to your system. By default, PortSentry will block hosts by adding them to `/etc/hosts.deny`, but it can be configured to be far more secure by denying access using IPchains and advanced scan detection. Here is a bare bones but fully functional configuration file for PortSentry:

```
ADVANCED_PORTS_TCP="1023"
ADVANCED_PORTS_UDP="1023"
IGNORE_FILE="/usr/local/psionic/portsentry/portsentry.ignore"
HISTORY_FILE="/usr/local/psionic/portsentry/portsentry.history"
BLOCKED_FILE="/usr/local/psionic/portsentry/portsentry.blocked"
BLOCK_UDP="1"
BLOCK_TCP="1"
KILL_ROUTE="/sbin/ipchains -I input -s $TARGET$ -j DENY -l"
SCAN_TRIGGER="0"
```

These options are fully documented in the sample configuration file, but are summarized here for clarity:

- **ADVANCED_PORTS_TCP**—The highest numbered TCP port to watch in advanced monitor mode. All ports under this number are monitored.

- **ADVANCED_PORTS_UDP**—The highest numbered UDP port to watch in advanced monitor mode.

- **IGNORE_FILE**—The full pathname of a file that contains a list of computers that should be ignored if they perform a port scan.

- **HISTORY_FILE**—The pathname of a file that will contain all of the actions that PortSentry has made.

- **BLOCKED_FILE**—Another filename—this time it will be used to store the names of machines that are currently blocked.

- **BLOCK_UDP**—If this is set to 1, automatic actions will be taken to block UDP scans.

- **BLOCK_TCP**—Like the previous option, setting this to 1 lets PortSentry react to a scan attempt.

- **KILL_ROUTE**—The command to run in order to filter traffic from the host.

- **SCAN_TRIGGER**—The number of scans it takes to trigger a response from PortSentry. Setting this to zero means that there will be an immediate response.

The only changes between this deployment and the sample is the inclusion of the KILL_ROUTE options and the exclusion of the KILL_HOSTS_DENY function. I use this configuration on my system with excellent results. If you have any hosts that you *never* want to be blocked, you can add them to the file /usr/local/psionic/portsentry/portsentry.ignore.

As a final step, it's useful to enable portsentry to start at bootup. You can easily do this by creating a shell script like this in your /etc/rc.d/init.d directory:

```
#!/bin/sh
#
# chkconfig: 345 91 35
# description: Starts and stops port scan monitoring
#


# Source function library.
. /etc/rc.d/init.d/functions

# Source networking configuration.
. /etc/sysconfig/network

# Check that networking is up.
[ ${NETWORKING} = "no" ] && exit 0


# See how we were called.
case "$1" in
  start)
        echo -n "Starting port monitoring services:"
        /usr/local/psionic/portsentry/portsentry -atcp
        echo "Done."
        ;;
  stop)
        echo -n "Shutting port monitoring services: "
        /usr/bin/killall -9 portsentry
        echo "Done."
        ;;
```

```
   restart)
        $0 stop
        $0 start
        ;;
  *)
        echo "Usage: portsentry {start¦stop¦restart}"
        exit 1
esac
```

Once you've added the starting and stopping script, you should add the `portsentry` service to your runlevel. Do this by running the command `chkconfig --add portsentry`. That's it! Start `portsentry` by typing `/etc/rc.d/init.d/portsentry start`. You're now guarded (rather heavily) against intrusion by individuals who might be running port scans on your network. You can test this by logging into a remote machine and trying to `nmap` your newly protected machine. You'll find that `nmap` will actually never complete. As soon as PortSentry detects the scan, it will block the remote host completely. You won't even be able to ping it!

The only drawback to this is that the "blockage" will be lost as soon as the computer is rebooted or PortSentry is restarted. You'll want to pay attention to the file `/usr/local/psionic/portsentry/portsentry.blocked.atcp` where blocked hosts are listed.

You can permanently block a host by using IPchains to block it at startup. Use the following format to forbid the remote computer from contacting your host:

```
/sbin/ipchains -I input -s <remote ip> -j DENY -l
```

You can add lines like this to the `/etc/rc.d/init.d/portsentry` file that you created earlier. Add your blocking lines to the `start` section of the file. When your computer starts, these lines will be evaluated and the hosts will be blocked.

Another option for restoring previously blocked connections is this short Perl script. I use it on my machine to read the PortSentry history file and reblock any connections that were previously blocked. In order to eliminate a host from being blocked, you'll need to remove any reference to it from the file `/usr/local/psionic/portsentry/portsentry.history`. You can feel free to modify and distribute this program as you see fit:

```perl
#!/usr/bin/perl

$blockhistory="/usr/local/psionic/portsentry/portsentry.history";

open BLOCKS,"$blockhistory";

# Read the history file
while (!(eof(BLOCKS))) {
        $in=<BLOCKS>;

        # Look for an IP address
        if ($in=~/([0-9]{1,3}\.[0-9]{1,3}\.[0-9]{1,3}\.[0-9]{1,3})/) {
            $blockme=$1;

            # If it isn't already blocked, block it now.
            if ($blockme{$blockme}!=1) {
                print "Blocking $blockme...\n";
                ·/sbin/ipchains -I input -s $blockme -j DENY -l;
```

```
        $blockme{$blockme}=1;
      }
    }
}

close (BLOCKS);
```

You can add an invocation of this script to `/etc/rc.d/init.d/portsentry`. This will automate the blocking process and give you even more peace of mind.

---

**Be Careful with IPchains!**
You can very easily disable access to your computer from remotely using the IPchains traffic blocking features of PortSentry. If you start playing with installing PortSentry on a remote machine, and then decide to test it, make sure you have an alternate path to the machine. For all intents and purposes, the PortSentry-protected machine will vanish from the network. You won't even be able to ping the remote machine!

---

You can check the extensively logged attack information by looking in the `/var/log/secure` logfile. PortSentry stores very verbose information about what the remote host is doing to your computer—for example:

```
Jan 29 23:38:32 pointy portsentry[3175]: adminalert: PortSentry is now active
and listening.
Jan 29 23:39:46 pointy portsentry[3175]: attackalert: SYN/Normal scan from
host: contempt.ag.ohio-state.edu/140.254.85.226 to TCP port: 981
Jan 29 23:39:46 pointy portsentry[3175]: attackalert: Host 140.254.85.226 has
been blocked via dropped route using command: "/sbin/
ipchains -I input -s 140.254.85.226 -j DENY -l"
Jan 29 23:39:46 pointy portsentry[3175]: attackalert: SYN/Normal scan from
host: contempt.ag.ohio-state.edu/140.254.85.226 to TCP port: 615
Jan 29 23:39:46 pointy portsentry[3175]: attackalert: Host: contempt.ag.
ohio-state.edu/140.254.85.226 is already blocked Ignoring
Jan 29 23:39:46 pointy portsentry[3175]: attackalert: SYN/Normal scan from
host: contempt.ag.ohio-state.edu/140.254.85.226 to TCP port: 435
Jan 29 23:39:46 pointy portsentry[3175]: attackalert: Host: contempt.ag.
ohio-state.edu/140.254.85.226 is already blocked Ignoring
Jan 29 23:39:46 pointy portsentry[3175]: attackalert: SYN/Normal scan from
host: contempt.ag.ohio-state.edu/140.254.85.226 to TCP port: 915
...
```

# LIMITING SERVICES

Rather than reacting to security threats, you can be a bit more proactive. There is no reason to have every known service running on your Red Hat Linux computer. The first and easiest way to disable software is by using >> `chkconfig --del <service name>` or interactively through the menu-driven `ntsysv` utility. This will stop programs from starting when you boot your computer. Much of the threat can be eliminated here.

For the sake of making things simple, Table 27.1 contains most of the network-related services that you could be running.

## TABLE 27.1 COMMON SERVICES AND HOW TO REMOVE THEM

| Service Name | Service Description |
| --- | --- |
| amd | Automatically mounts NFS volumes on demand. Not needed unless you're using NFS. |
| anacron | Like cron, anacron automatically executes commands, periodically. Unlike cron, however, it doesn't expect your machine to be on constantly. If you're running a server, you should stick with cron. |
| arpwatch | Detects changes in IP address/hardware address pairings. Useful if people have a tendency to install hardware on your network without telling you. Not needed for most installations. |
| dhcpd | Automatically supplies IP addresses and other network configuration information to client computers on the network. If you maintain your own database of static IP addresses, you probably don't need this. |
| httpd | The Apache Web server. If you're serving Web sites, keep it. If not, disable it. |
| innd | The INN news server. It is unlikely that most people need or want to run their own news server. |
| ldap | Lightweight Directory Access Protocol. The OpenLDAP server is included with Red Hat Linux but isn't needed for casual users. |
| linuxconf | LinuxConf provides a variety of configuration tools for your system. For a server that is set up and ready to go, you're probably safe to disable it. |
| lpd | The printer daemon. Not hosting a print spool on your computer? Then you don't need it. |
| mars-nwe | A NetWare-compatible server. Useful only to those who are supporting legacy or (new??!) NetWare installations. |
| mcserv | The midnight commander server. Allows remote users to connect and manipulate their files through an easy-to-use interface. |
| named | The DNS server. If you're planning to use your Linux server as a caching or authoritative nameserver, keep this. If you're not sure what that means, get rid of it! |
| nfs | NFS file services. You probably don't need this unless you are sharing file systems between different Linux computers. |
| portmap | You won't need the portmapper to run unless you're using NFS or NIS. |
| postgresql | The PostgreSQL database server. Postgres will enable you to serve SQL databases for Web or desktop use. |
| rstatd | Allows network users to request stats for your computer. Not needed. |
| rwalld | Allows network users to send messages to all the active terminals on a system. This is only useful if you like being annoyed. |
| rwhod | Enables remote users to get a list of the people who are currently logged in to a system. |
| sendmail | *The* Internet mailserver. If you just want to read email on your system, you don't need to have Sendmail running. |

**TABLE 27.1    CONTINUED**

| Service Name | Service Description |
| --- | --- |
| smb | The Samba server enables Windows file and print sharing from your Linux computer. Not needed unless you're planning to serve a Windows network. |
| snmpd | The simple network management protocol daemon. This enables remote sites to monitor your machine. Not needed. |
| squid | A high-performance Web caching engine. Usually not necessary. |
| xfs | The X Window font server. You'll probably want this if you're using X Window. If you're just running a server machine, don't bother. |
| xntpd | The network time daemon. Used to maintain a consistent time between different machines. Usually not needed. |
| ypbind | Used to bind a machine to an NIS domain. This is used in Linux/UNIX clusters, but very rarely by individuals. This should be off. |
| yppasswdd | Used with NIS, this is the network password daemon that will propagate password changes across the network. Once again, this shouldn't be needed. |
| ypserv | An NIS server. This is used to create a cluster of UNIX/Linux machines. Not useful for anyone but a server operator. |

To disable any of these services, you can use `chkconfig --del <servicename>`. This will not actually delete anything from your computer, it will remove a link from the startup file to your runlevel directory. If you later want to use one of the services that you've removed, reverse the process with `chkconfig --add <servicename>`.

# LIMITING INCOMING ACCESS

There is a completely different means by which a server process can start on your computer, rather than just at startup. The Internet daemon `inetd` enables incoming connections to trigger the start of processes on the system. This is typically used for low-volume activities. Starting and stopping processes takes more time than just starting and running a server, so these tend to be things that can have a bit of latency without causing much of a problem.

The file that contains all of the information about these processes is `/etc/inetd.conf`. Each line of this file describes the service and which program should be run when a connection attempt is made. Unfortunately, by default there are a lot of services that are left open. You can safely shut down most of the incoming services by commenting out the lines in the file. Do this by placing a # in front of each line that you'd like to remove.

As with the startup services, it's easier to determine what you need to turn on or off if you know what is available. Table 27.2 lists the default `inetd`-controlled processes.

PART

**IV**

CH

**27**

**TABLE 27.2** DEFAULT `inetd`-CONTROLLED PROCESSES

| Service Name | Service Description |
| --- | --- |
| echo | Handled internally by `inetd`, echoes characters. Not needed. |
| discard | Handled internally by `inetd`, discards all input. Not needed. |
| daytime | Handled internally by `inetd`, returns day and time information. Not needed. |
| chargen | Character generator, handled internally by `inetd`, not needed. |
| time | Handled internally by `inetd`. Returns time information, not needed. |
| ftp | Incoming `ftp` service, not needed unless you want to transfer information to computer from remote hosts using FTP. |
| telnet | Incoming `telnet` service. Telnet is historically very insecure. If you need to remotely log in to your system, read the instructions on installing ssh in Chapter 28. |
| shell | Remote shell. Used to run applications in a shell remotely. Can also be replaced by the functionality of ssh. |
| login | Remote login daemon. Similar to a Telnet server. Again, it's best to replace this with a secure alternative like ssh. |
| exec | Remote command execution. You shouldn't need this to be turned on. |
| comsat | A mail notification system. Alerts a user to new messages. This is rarely used and should be disabled. |
| talk | The UNIX Talk protocol for realtime chats. Rarely used anymore. |
| ntalk | A newer version of `talk`. Rarely used. |
| dtalk | Another version of `talk`. The Talk protocols are largely obsolete due to the popularity of instant messaging systems such as ICQ. |
| pop-2 | A POP2 mail server. POP3 has been the standard for over five years; there is no need to respond to POP2 requests. |
| pop-3 | A POP3 mail server. Unless you're running a mail server, none of the mail-related services are necessary. |
| imap | An IMAP mail server. More functional than POP3, but largely unknown to the public. IMAP is rarely needed. |
| uucp | UNIX-to-UNIX Copy. An old system for moving data between UNIX machines. Rarely used today. |
| tftp | Trivial FTP daemon. `tftp` is usually used to boot diskless workstations over a network. It is not needed by most people. |
| bootps | A `bootp` server. The included ISC `dhcp/bootp` makes this entry obsolete. Do not enable it. |
| finger | The finger daemon. Returns information about users on your computer. This is generally seen as a security risk and disabled. |
| systat | `systat` invokes the `ps` command to return information about the active processes on the computer. Do not enable this; it is a security risk. |

**TABLE 27.2    CONTINUED**

| Service Name | Service Description |
| --- | --- |
| netstat | Like systat, netstat returns information about the network by running netstat. This is another security risk and should remain disabled. |
| auth | The auth daemon will allow outside users to learn a great deal about your system, including who is running various processes on the server. This is a high-risk item and should be disabled. |
| linuxconf | The LinuxConf program lets you configure many aspects of your computer. It's very useful, but allowing remote access could be very dangerous. Disable this if you can. |
| swat | The swat tool is used to configure Samba. Although the Web interface is a wonderful tool, it does present yet another entry point for attackers. Disable this if you can live without it. |

After you've commented out the lines that you don't want running, you need to force inetd to reread its configuration file. Do this with killall -1 inetd or, if you'd like, reboot your computer.

# LIMITING BY USER

Sometimes you want to provide services to some people, but not to others. By disabling things in inetd, you disable them completely. For startup controlled processes, you can eliminate the capability of a computer to contact your computer by filtering it with IPchains. There are some advantages and disadvantages to both of these techniques.

## FILTERING WITH IPCHAINS

First, disabling access with IPchains is incredibly simple. To completely stop a remote system from contacting your computer, you can just use this command:

```
/sbin/ipchains -I input -s <remote ip> -j DENY -l
```

This will filter all traffic from the remote IP address until the computer is rebooted or IPchains is flushed. You won't be able to contact this computer and it won't be able to contact you. If you're being spammed by a user on spammail.com and you filter its IP address, you won't be able to directly send messages from your computer to it. Be sure that you understand the consequences of blocking an IP address before you actually do it.

You can insert as many of the filtering commands as you'd like into any file that is started when your computer starts. If you have created the /etc/rc.d/init.d/portsentry file that we discussed earlier, you can insert the ipchains commands into the file next to the start keyword. Otherwise, the file /etc/rc.d/rc.local will do very nicely.

Unfortunately, suppose you want the remote computer to be able to access your system by some means. Filtering in this way makes it difficult. Also, depending on the speed of your computer, IPchains may prove to be too processor intensive for your system.  There is

PART

**IV**

Cʜ

**27**

another means by which you can limit the capability of remote hosts to access inetd-controlled services—through the use of TCP wrappers.

# CASE STUDY: STOPPING ACCESS WITH TCP WRAPPERS

As you were going through the inetd.conf file, you may have noticed that the program path /usr/sbin/tcpd is repeated many times right before the name of the server that is to be run. This is a call to the TCP wrapper package. *TCP wrappers* intercept incoming connection requests to these services and check to see if the connection is allowed. If it is, the connection proceeds as it would normally. If the host trying to connect is blocked, the connection will be dropped. Unfortunately, TCP wrappers only work with the inetd-controlled processes, whereas IPchains can block anything.

The easiest way to configure TCP wrappers is to eliminate all incoming services, and then enable any hosts that you want to have access to the system. This is covered in depth in Chapter 31, "Setting Up Email Services." If you're new to any of this information, refer to the section about protection in Chapter 31 for an overview of how TCP wrappers work.

TCP wrappers are configured by editing two files: /etc/hosts.allow and /etc/hosts.deny. The most basic configuration denies access to everyone and enables access to a select few. For example, one of the first things you probably want to put on your computer is a /etc/hosts.deny file that will deny access to everyone trying to connect. This will keep your machine from being attacked through FTP and Telnet ports—the most common means of remotely accessing a computer. Here's a perfectly usable sample file:

```
#
# hosts.deny    This file describes the names of the hosts which are
#               *not* allowed to use the local INET services, as decided
#               by the '/usr/sbin/tcpd' server.
#
# The portmap line is redundant, but it is left to remind you that
# the new secure portmap uses hosts.deny and hosts.allow.  In particular
# you should know that NFS uses portmap!
ALL:ALL
```

After this file is installed, any protected service in the /etc/inetd.conf file will be inaccessible from the outside world. You can enable remote access on a machine or network basis by adding it to /etc/hosts.allow. Portions of domain names or IP addresses are matched when possible. This means that you can enter goodplace.com and enable access from any machine on the goodplace.com subnet or use 192.168.0 to enable access from the 192.168.0 subnet. This is my /etc/hosts.allow file:

```
#
# hosts.allow   This file describes the names of the hosts which are
#               allowed to use the local INET services, as decided
#               by the '/usr/sbin/tcpd' server.
#
ALL: LOCAL, 192.168.0. , .erienet.net, 24.93.121.242
```

If you'd like to have a bit more control, TCP wrappers let you enable services on a service-by-service basis. As you've probably guessed, the ALL keyword refers to *all* the services. The following are a few keywords that TCP wrappers define that you can use in place of IPs, hostnames, or service names:

- **ALL**—Matches any service or any hostname. The line ALL:ALL matches all services being accessed by all hostnames.

- **LOCAL**—Matches hosts in the same domain.

- **UNKNOWN**—Matches any machine whose hostname or IP address cannot be determined due to network or DNS problems.

- **KNOWN**—Matches computers whose hostname and IP are both accessible.

- **PARANOID**—The paranoid option matches hosts whose hostname doesn't match its IP address.

- **EXCEPT**—Used to provide exceptions to a rule. For example, to match all hosts except barney and enable all services except telnet, you'd use ALL EXCEPT barney: ALL except in.telnetd.

Every process that is blocked with TCP wrappers can be blocked specifically. Instead of using the ALL keyword, you can use the name of the server program that is started in order to block or enable it specifically. You must make sure you use the name of actual program that starts, not the service. You do not need to include the entire path of the file.

TCP wrappers are an excellent way to limit access to your system. More and more server programs are paying attention to the hosts.allow and hosts.deny ACL files. This means that depending on the software you install, regardless of whether it is started in /etc/inetd.conf, it might be protected by these files. The ssh software and AppleTalk daemon are examples of this.

If you installed PortSentry earlier, you can also configure it to automatically add hosts that have performed port scans to the /etc/hosts.deny file by adding this line to its configuration file:

```
KILL_HOSTS_DENY="ALL: $TARGET$"
```

Remember, this does not limit the capability of the remote computers to connect to other non-inetd services on your computer. The only way to do this is to actually filter traffic using IPchains.

The best possible security is to block all access to your computer and only allow connections to the outside to be made. This, however, usually turns out to be an impractical solution for most installations. The best real world installations will use a combination of filtering and connection-blocking to ward off attack. Despite employing software like PortSentry to automate the protection of your system, you will still need to periodically check your system to see if it is being abused. Both TCP wrappers and the version of PortSentry that we configured here will log to the /var/log/secure logfile. Check this file regularly and report repeated abuses to the ISPs of the would-be intruders. Protecting your system is good, but eliminating the threat is even better!

I'll leave you with a snippet from my security logfile. This is a three-day period on my home machine. This is *not* by any means a high profile Web site or workhorse of a machine. It just goes to show you that if you're online, you'll be a target—guaranteed:

```
Jan 12 00:43:57 pointy noconnect[8908]: refused connect from c2-1d055.neo.rr.com
Jan 12 10:57:42 pointy noconnect[10475]: refused connect from 170.183.40.173
Jan 12 15:02:05 pointy noconnect[11077]: refused connect from dhcp9397021.
↪columbus.rr.com
Jan 12 21:13:29 pointy noconnect[12081]: refused connect from c2-1d055.neo.rr.com
Jan 13 12:49:40 pointy noconnect[14375]: refused connect from 205.183.48.9
Jan 13 12:50:09 pointy noconnect[14384]: refused connect from pool223.chicago.
↪cohesive.com
Jan 13 12:58:16 pointy swat[14391]: refused connect from dhcp93121242.columbus.
↪rr.com
Jan 13 12:58:50 pointy swat[14392]: refused connect from dhcp93121242.columbus.rr.
↪com
Jan 13 12:59:09 pointy swat[14393]: refused connect from dhcp93121242.columbus.rr.
↪com
Jan 13 12:59:16 pointy swat[14394]: refused connect from dhcp93121242.columbus.rr.
↪com
Jan 13 23:15:29 pointy in.ftpd[6658]: refused connect from dhcp9397021.
↪columbus.rr.com
Jan 14 11:39:44 pointy noconnect[8549]: refused connect from 170.183.40.173
Jan 14 16:52:02 pointy noconnect[12776]: refused connect from 98A89858.ipt.aol.com
```

# PART V

# SERVING THE INTERNET WITH LINUX

# CHAPTER 28

# BUILDING AN INTERNET SERVER

**I**n this chapter

# WHAT IS A SERVER?

A server is simply a machine that makes information available to other "client" machines via a transmission medium—in this case, the Internet. Unlike other operating systems, Linux is both a server and a desktop in one package. During your installation of Red Hat Linux, you were offered the option of installing software for a desktop or for a server. If you happened to choose "desktop," this doesn't mean you need to reinstall—you may need to install a few of the server add-ons, but that's it.

Many traditional server packages also offer their services on a "per client" basis. This means that for each user that accesses the system, a separate license is needed. If you have 25 email clients, on some systems you may need to purchase 25 client licenses. This can quickly add up to major expenses for the server operator. Red Hat Linux does not restrict the number of users that can connect to a system. Although there are commercial "add-on" packages that do require licenses to be purchased, you can easily create a full-featured email/Web/ server without spending a dime.

# DO I NEED A SERVER?

While this may seem like a silly question to be asking, in truth it is very important. There is often very little need to operate your own full-time server. ISPs offer a variety of plans for serving Web and email for individuals and small businesses. Generally, operating a server is necessary for individuals who require absolute control over their services. If you plan to offer customized Web programming options, you'll want your own server. On the other hand, if your only interest in a server is making a few static Web pages available, you'll probably be better off serving through an ISP.

## RESPONSIBILITY

The responsibility of running a server is one big reason that individuals may choose not to run their own. ISPs typically offer backup services for their servers and will replace faulty equipment before it becomes a problem. Depending on the nature of your services, this may not be an issue, but if you're serving a few hundred users, suffer a crash, and haven't been maintaining backups, you're going to feel some heat. You may also want to consider "farming out" some of your services to an ISP. ISPs typically offer high-bandwidth connectivity. Using an ISP for Web serving, and maintaining your own lower-bandwidth services, such as email, may be the best option for your server operations.

Maintaining consistent server uptime and ensuring the data is safe is the cornerstone of producing a successful Internet business. Remember that if you promise your customers a service and don't deliver, at best you lose a customer; at worst, you end up in court.

## SECURITY

Beyond the responsibility of maintaining an operational system, you must also maintain the integrity of your system. Linux is now one of the "hot" operating systems, and has come under attack from crackers around the world. A poorly managed server will soon find that a "root kit" has been installed and that users from countries they've never even heard of are using their computer to trade software, pictures, and other not-so-goodies. To make matters worse, if the crackers use your system to commit further crimes, you may be held legally responsible.

The extent of remote cracking is well beyond what many people think. It is not unlikely that a computer left unprotected will be compromised within a matter of hours. For example—this is a sample of the security log file from my home server (poisontooth.com), which is connected via a cable modem:

```
Dec 26 18:33:52 pointy noconnect[22512]: refused connect from someone
Dec 26 18:34:04 pointy noconnect[22513]: refused connect from someone
Dec 26 18:40:55 pointy noconnect[22528]: refused connect from someone
Dec 26 18:41:08 pointy noconnect[22529]: refused connect from someone
Dec 27 03:37:13 pointy noconnect[23764]: refused connect from someone
```

> **Tip**
>
> A *hacker* is just about anyone who messes around with computers and programs, without the intent of doing anything harmful. A *cracker* on the other hand is one who attempts to break into other people's systems, often with the intent of doing some harm.

As you can see, there have been multiple attempts to connect to the machine within a short period of time. Without the appropriate security measures in place, there is little doubt your machine will meet with a cracker. To make matters worse, there are often multiple points of entry that crackers can use.

## UPDATES

Besides connecting to your machine directly using Telnet and the like, a cracker can take advantage of the software that is running on your system. Exploitable software bugs are found quite frequently on most multiuser operating systems, and patches are issued just as frequently. In order to keep your system secure, you need to remain abreast of the current security risks, and keep your system up to date with the latest versions of your software. Red Hat software maintains a Web site at http://www.redhat.com/support/errata/ that lists the current security advisories for its operating system releases. Be sure to keep track of what updates are relevant to your system and install them to prevent potential security breaches on your system. If you purchase and register the commercial version of Red Hat Linux, you can use the Red Hat Update Agent to gain access to the priority.redhat.com update site to quickly and easily get your system up to date.

PART
**V**

CH
**28**

For those who have downloaded Red Hat Linux and aren't able to use the update agent, I am including a short Perl script to automate the update procedure. Just enter a mirror FTP site for the Red Hat errata, and you're ready to go:

```perl
#!/usr/bin/perl

# (c) 2000 by John Ray
# This software may be modified, distributed, etc. as long as the original
# author's name remains somewhere in the code listing.

# $filter contains a comma separated list of package names that need to be
# filtered from the installation.  Kernel updates are best installed manually!

$filter="kernel,kde";

print "\nJohn's little update helper v.1\n";
$|=1;
@filters=split(/\,/,$filter);

if (!(-f ".updateinfo")) {
        print "Enter your update mirror hostname: ";
        $hostname=<STDIN>;
        print "Enter your update mirror path: ";
        $path=<STDIN>;
        open UPDATEINFO, "> .updateinfo";
        print UPDATEINFO $hostname,$path;
        close UPDATEINFO;
} else {
        open UPDATEINFO, ".updateinfo";
        $hostname=<UPDATEINFO>;
        $path=<UPDATEINFO>;
        close UPDATEINFO;
}
chomp($hostname,$path);

# Fix paths missing "/"'s on the ends.
if ($path=~/^[^\/]/) { $path="/".$path; }
if ($path=~/[^\/]$/) { $path=$path."/"; }

# Get the file listing using Lynx.
print "Retrieving listing from ftp://$hostname$path...";
$filelist=`lynx -source "ftp://$hostname$path"`;
print "Done!\n";
while ($filelist=~s/([^\/]*?\.rpm)\"//i) {
    $filelist[$x++]=$1;
}

# Cycle through the available files and check to see if they are installed or
# or filtered.
for ($x=0;$x<@filelist;$x++) {
    $packagename=$filelist[$x];
    $packagename=~s/\.[^\.]*\.rpm//gi;
    $rpmout=`rpm -q $packagename`;
    for ($y=0;$y<@filters;$y++) {
        if ($packagename=~/$filters[$y]/i) {
            $rpmout="filtered";
        }
    }
}
```

```
    if (!($rpmout=~/not installed/i)) {
        print $packagename," not installed.  Install now? (Y/N): ";
        $install=<STDIN>;
        if ($install=~/y/i) {
            $packagepath="ftp://$hostname$path$filelist[$x]";
            $rpmout=`rpm -Uvh $packagepath`;
            print $rpmout;
        }
    }
}

print "Done processing!\n";
```

**Tip**    Shell scripting is discussed in Chapter 34, "Shell Programming and Scripting."

The first time the program is run, it will ask you for the hostname and path to a mirror of the Red Hat update site. Subsequent invocations will not require this information. A list of available updates is then downloaded, and you are prompted to install packages that are not currently up to date on your system. You can easily include this program in your crontab file in order to fully automate the updating of your system:

```
[root@pointy jray]# ./install_updates

John's little update helper v.1
Enter your update mirror hostname: ftp.cis.ohio-state.edu
Enter your update mirror path: /mirror/redhat-updates/current/i386/
Retrieving listing from ftp://ftp.cis.ohio-state.edu...Done!
package ORBit-0.5.0-2 is not installed
ORBit-0.5.0-2 not installed.  Install now? (Y/N): Y
. .
```

This is not a perfect solution, but hopefully it will help those of you without the official Red Hat CD-ROM keep your system patched and up to date.

## MISCONFIGURATION

Misconfiguration is the final hurdle that must be overcome in order to successfully administrate a computer. For example, if your email server is configured as an *open relay* (it will accept and process mail for anyone), spammers can easily use your computer to send junk mail to thousands of soon-to-be-angry recipients around the world. This book cannot be considered a complete reference to setting up the services that you need. Complete volumes have been written about the sendmail email server that is included with every copy of Red Hat Linux. This text should get you up and running, but it is up to the reader to research their software and provide a knowledgable configuration that is appropriate for his network environment.

In short, if you decide to set up your own server, be aware of the responsibilities that come with it. It's simple to install Red Hat Linux and get Apache up and running, but keeping it up, running and secure, is an entirely different matter.

PART

**V**

CH

**28**

# NETWORK CONNECTIVITY

If you've made it this far, you've probably decided that you do indeed want to take on the task of creating your own Internet server. Now you need to get connected, which can be more difficult than it sounds. There are two basic options for the nature of the connection: Bring the connection to your server, or bring your server to the connection.

## CO-LOCATION

Many ISPs offer a service called *co-location*. Co-location allows you to set up a server machine and plug it in at your local ISP. You maintain complete control over your server, the software it runs, and the people who use it. Many ISPs offer 24-hour on-site security access that grants you physical access to your machine any time you need to service it. Choosing this method of operating a server can be very cost-effective for a small business that wants to build an Internet presence. The ISP maintains the full-time Internet connectivity, and the server operator and users connect to the machine remotely. Since you're using a Linux computer, you can use Telnet, ssh, or X to remotely manage your machine; its location is rarely of much concern!

> **Tip**
>
> ISPs that allow you to place your Internet server at their location are sometimes called *server farms*.

If you think co-location is indeed for you, be sure to check out the costs imposed by your ISP. There is typically a setup charge as well as monthly fees. For a typical setup here in Columbus, Ohio, I can gain T3 level co-location access for $200 setup and $200 a month access fee. Beyond these fees, there may be additional costs for bandwidth usage or access to support staff (for things as trivial as rebooting your computer). At the same time, there may be benefits to co-location that make additional costs worthwhile. Many ISPs run firewalls that can filter "bad" network traffic before it even reaches your computer.

> **Tip**
>
> Just because a server isn't on your property doesn't mean you don't control it. Co-location services are often very nice, including emergency power backup and air-conditioned, humidity-controlled environments. While some operating systems need to be baby-sat, Linux's remote administration makes it an excellent candidate for co-location service.

## DEDICATED CONNECTIONS

Choosing a dedicated connection means that you bring the network connection to your home or office and keep the server on your own property. Depending on your needs, this could be an extremely cost-effective method of getting a server online. The technology of bringing the network to the individual is getting better by the moment. The only stumbling point may be availability in your area. Let's take a look at some of the popular network connections and what they may cost you.

## PHONE LINES

Phone lines are still the most popular method of connecting to the Internet. They are also the slowest. Even so, with a dedicated line and a fast modem, it is entirely possible to serve a Web site (hopefully text-only) over a standard phone line. This is not recommended, but can be useful for testing purposes and can be up and running in a snap. Typical costs for a phone line are roughly $15 a month, $20 for ISP service, and $75 for a reasonable modem.

## ISDN

One step above a phone line is ISDN, or *Integrated Services Digital Network*. This service has been around for many years, but has been priced out of reach for the general public. Because of its relatively low adoption rate, ISDN is also known as "It Still Does Nothing." If you've exhausted other connection methods and ISDN is offered in your area, it may be able to provide connectivity for your network.

ISDN requires special hardware that is different from a typical modem. ISDN "modems" are more appropriately called "ISDN terminal adapters" and are priced from $150-$350. Once connected to your computer, the ISDN terminal adapter is used very similarly to a modem, but with faster throughput. The ISP service costs $30-$50 a month (on top of a $40/month connection fee), depending on the speed of your connection. Typically you have two 64Kb channels that can be combined for an uncompressed throughput of around 13Kb a second. If you choose to use a single 64Kb channel, you can use the second channel as a voice channel. This, in some cases, eliminates the need for a separate phone line, and may make ISDN seem a bit more reasonable for some installations.

## xDSL

Usually called ADSL, or *Asymmetric Digital Subscriber Line*, is a high-speed connection that is finally catching on around the country. DSL technology has been around for quite a while, but, as with ISDN, was priced out of reach of the consumer. DSL lines maintain a constant connection to the Internet and are available in a range of speeds. Rather than investing in the fastest line, you can choose slower service, and then later upgrade without altering any of your existing equipment. The scalability of xDSL up to speeds of 1.5Mb on both uplink and downlink directions make it extremely appealing for people wanting to run servers from their residence or for small businesses. DSL requires a one-time installation fee of $150, and a monthly fee ranging from $50-$500, depending on your speed requirements.

## CABLE MODEMS

Currently, cable modems are the most widely available form of high-bandwidth access available to the consumer. Cable modems offer speeds similar to xDSL, but usually not in both directions. Cable modems also share bandwidth among customers on a local circuit. As more people get cable modems in your area, the slower your throughput will be. Even so, they offer a very impressive Internet connection for around $50 a month. If you'd like to see an example of a Web site that is host on a cable-modem based service, check out `http://www.brevardmpo.com/`. It is running on a Red Hat Linux 6.2 machine located in my basement, next to a 115-gallon saltwater aquarium! I highly recommend cable-based service if DSL is not available in your area.

> **Tip**
>
> If you have a cable connection, don't assume that you can use it to serve the Internet. Many cable companies do not allow servers on their networks.

### T1 LINES

You may hear people throw around the terms T1 or T3 to describe their connection. T1 refers to a "Trunk Line Level One." This is a dedicated high-speed connection that can be used to carry voice or data communications. A T1 line carries 24 channels running at 64Kbps each. The use of a T1 line can cost upward of $4,000 a month. It's possible to buy the use of only a few channels out of the 24 available. In this case, you're buying a fractional T1 line. Higher-capacity lines that carry more channels, such as a T3, are available—but at a much higher cost. If you are sharing an office building with other companies, you may want to consider sharing the cost of a single connection for the building. For the most part, small businesses are better off investigating the emerging consumer connectivity solutions, such as DSL and cable modems before committing to a high-priced option.

## MAKING A CHOICE

Finding the right option for your Internet connectivity will require a bit of work on your part. Once you have chosen a method of connection, you'll need to make sure that the ISP offering that connection can give you a few things:

- **Dedicated connectivity**—Some ISPs limit the amount of bandwidth or connection time you can use during a day. My first ISDN provider limited the length of a connection arbitrarily, but did not include this information in their service agreement. After being connected for more than a few hours, they would manually force the connection to terminate. If they didn't catch the "long" connection, they would charge additional costs beyond the original $40/month agreement. I didn't like them very much.

- **Static IP addresses**—Since you want to run Internet services on your computer, you'll almost certainly need a static IP address. There are ways around this, including dynamic DNS. Be sure to ask the ISP for your available options. Without a static IP address, your machine may become inaccessible to the world if your ISP issues a new address.

- **Non-filtered service**—Some cable modem services filter the network traffic so that only certain services are allowed on their lines. If the services you need are being filtered, incoming connections may not be allowed to your machine. This can be a bit troublesome to debug, since everything will appear okay on your end, but the client will be refused connection. Be sure that your ISP does not filter, and has no future plans that include filtering.

- **Guaranteed uptime**—The service that you're providing to your business or your customers is only as good as the company supplying Internet access to you. If you're buying T1 access from the phone company, you can bet that for $2,000 a month, you're going to get decent service. If you're paying $40 a month to the local cable company, that may not be the case. Ask the ISP what their average monthly uptime and response time is. An average uptime of 95% still means that your Web site can be offline for a day and a half each month—not including any off-time on your end! In many cases, this is unacceptable. Be sure to choose an ISP that will enable you to make reasonable service guarantees to your customers, or your boss.

> **Tip**
>
> Most consumer-oriented services (including ADSL) do not provide guaranteed uptime. One of the reasons T1 connections are so expensive is that they do assume your Internet connection is mission-critical, and they do maintain a staff of qualified personnel who can bring a downed service back to life any time, and any day of the week.

# HARDWARE CONSIDERATIONS

Although any Linux machine can be a server, you may want to consider modifying your system to provide high-performance server capabilities. Unlike a desktop system, you don't need to worry about high performance video, sound, or even a monitor. Rather than spend your money on items that will likely never be used, consider the following:

- **RAM**—If you plan to host a large number of simultaneous connections, or are running high-volume data processing tasks, such as a database server, you'll want to load your computer up on RAM. Each connection to your machine requires memory: the more people who will be connected at once, the more memory you need. Linux is infamous for requiring an incredibly small amount of memory to do its job, but, like most other operating systems, it is always happy to have more memory. A 128MB machine should easily be able to handle a moderate Web and email load.

- **SCSI**—SCSI drives are an alternative to the IDE drives found on most systems. The SCSI standard offers increased error protection, command queuing, and other features that increase performance on server machines. With SCSI, upgrading storage space is also as simple as plugging a new drive into the back of your computer. The most important capability for a server is the ability to provide fast I/O, and SCSI helps deliver data faster than IDE drives.

- **DAT/CDR**—Invest in a reliable backup mechanism. DAT drives are cheap and extremely high capacity. CDRs offer a very reliable and error-resistant form of backup, but are limited in size. DVD-RAM drives are another option, but are currently a bit on the expensive side.

- **RAID**—For fault tolerance and a speed boost, you may wish to use RAID (Redundant Array of Inexpensive Disks) level 5 capabilities built into Linux. If you're lucky enough to be using a Pentium III, the performance of RAID 5 in Linux will be greatly enhanced. Some SCSI cards offer this in hardware, but at a significant increase in cost. To get started using RAID on your system, check out the file: `/usr/doc/HOWTO/mini/ Software-RAID` on your Red Hat Linux system.

- **SMP**—Red Hat Linux, as of Version 6.0, now ships with multiple processor support (symmetric multiprocessing) built into the kernel. Having more than one processor enables the system to take advantage of multithreaded applications by dividing processing time between the different processors. If you're mainly going to be hosting static Web sites, this won't do much for your performance. If you plan to run data analysis or computing tools on the server, SMP can come in very handy.

- **UPS**—Any computer, regardless of its "server" status, should have an appropriate power protection device on it. At the very least, a surge suppressor is a must-have. More useful is a UPS, or uninterruptable power supply. A UPS provides power to the system during a brownout or blackout. Most UPSs can also signal your computer that a power failure has occurred and shut the computer down, potentially preventing your computer from shutting off in the middle of writing to its hard drive.

- **Ethernet**—Don't just slap an Ethernet card into your new server; choose one that is well supported under Linux. Many cards have experimental support, but are not production-quality drivers. Purchasing a 10/100Mb PCI-based card is a good investment, and gives you the ability to upgrade to a higher speed network if you start with a standard 10Mb connection.

---

**Do I Really Need This Stuff?**
No. Not at all. These are components that will make your system faster and more reliable but can certainly be added over time, or not at all if you're happy with what you have! If you have a computer that Linux runs, you have a server plain and simple.

---

As you know, Red Hat maintains a very extensive list of supported hardware on its Web site. You should consult their compatibility listings before purchasing any hardware. The current hardware list is found at `http://www.redhat.com/support/hardware/`.

If you're planning to run a large server operation for a group of people, you should be aware that redundancy in systems is a very good thing. The moment that you have a server fail and a backup server is not ready, you'll understand this fully. Redundancy of equipment is also very handy if you plan on doing software development on your server. For example, if you are offering custom Web programming solutions, you do not want to be programming and debugging from the root account on your primary Web server. Keeping a redundant machine up and running for test purposes comes in very handy.

## SOFTWARE CONSIDERATIONS

Red Hat Linux ships with a lot of software. Everything you need to run a full-featured server is included "in the box." This doesn't mean, however, that there isn't better software available. Linux is gaining new users and new developers every day. Packages such as Lotus Notes and Oracle are becoming available. Many businesses are more inclined to purchase big-name traditional software packages that have a known support system, rather than relying on the open-source community to explain and fix problems as they occur. This is understandable, and it is important to know that you don't have to switch to another operating system to get this level of support.

You may also want to look at other software packages for security reasons. The sendmail email server package is capable of performing about any task you can throw at it—but it is also a mammoth software package and is difficult to grasp for the first-time administrator. Other email servers, such as qmail were designed to be small, secure, and easy for anyone to use.

> **Tip**
>
> If you are not in a position where you are being requested to use a commercial package, be sure to look at Open Source alternatives. I often find that support from the Open Source community is faster and more thorough than pay-for support packages from commercial vendors.

## CASE STUDY: MANAGING A SERVER REMOTELY

Whether you co-locate your server on a server farm or find some way to get a full-time Internet connection to your own site, you'll probably want to manage the server remotely from a desktop machine. If you're used to the command line, Telnet or ssh will be your administration tools. If you've grown accustomed to point and clicking your way through Linux, there are a few fast and easy ways to do that as well.

### VIEWING AN X APPLICATION REMOTELY

Traditionally, UNIX machines have remotely executed graphic software through remote X Window displays. This, however, requires that the remote computer have an XServer installed on it. X Window Server software is not extremely fast over remote links, and is a bit flaky in its public domain implementations that are available for the Windows and Macintosh OS. If you're using Linux, however, it is a quick and dirty way of running a graphical application remotely.

Imagine that you have two computers: your server, named *Big*, and a client machine named *Little*—and you want to run LinuxConf directly on *Big*. Follow these steps:

1. Collect the IP addresses or hostnames of Big and Little. For this example, assume they have the hostnames `big.mycompany.com` and `little.mycompany.com`.

2. From within X Window on Little, type the command `xhost +big.mycompany.com`. This tells your client computer that Big is allowed to access your X Window server and display things on your screen.

3. `telnet` into Big from your client computer. From the command prompt, type `export DISPLAY=little.mycompany.com:0`. The server Big will now know that it should display subsequent X Window applications on your remote X Window server.

4. Start the X Window application you want to run: `linuxconf`.

5. The application should start and be displayed on the screen of Little as if it were running locally.

## REMOTE DESKTOPS USING VNC

A new alternative to X Window is the VNC (*Virtual Network Computing*) server system. VNC is a freely available program that is under active development by AT&T. Server software is available for Linux, Macintosh, and Windows machines. Viewer/Control software is available for many different computers, including PalmPilots! VNC allows multiple desktops to be shared from a single Linux computer. For example, if two users have accounts, each can access her desktop simultaneously over VNC, which is much faster than by using X Window. You can download VNC from its Web site at: `http://www.uk.research.att.com/vnc/download.html`.

Once downloaded, follow these steps to get VNC up and running on your system:

1. Decompress and unarchive the software `tar -zvxf vnc-3.3.3_x86_linux_2.0.tgz`:

```
[root@pointy vnc]# tar -vzxf vnc-3.3.3_x86_linux_2.0.tgz
vnc_x86_linux_2.0/LICENCE.TXT
vnc_x86_linux_2.0/README
vnc_x86_linux_2.0/Vncviewer
vnc_x86_linux_2.0/Xvnc
vnc_x86_linux_2.0/classes/
vnc_x86_linux_2.0/classes/DesCipher.class
vnc_x86_linux_2.0/classes/animatedMemoryImageSource.class
vnc_x86_linux_2.0/classes/authenticationPanel.class
vnc_x86_linux_2.0/classes/clipboardFrame.class
vnc_x86_linux_2.0/classes/index.vnc
vnc_x86_linux_2.0/classes/optionsFrame.class
vnc_x86_linux_2.0/classes/rfbProto.class
vnc_x86_linux_2.0/classes/shared.vnc
vnc_x86_linux_2.0/classes/vncCanvas.class
```

```
vnc_x86_linux_2.0/classes/vncviewer.class
vnc_x86_linux_2.0/classes/vncviewer.jar
vnc_x86_linux_2.0/vncpasswd
vnc_x86_linux_2.0/vncserver
vnc_x86_linux_2.0/vncviewer
```

2. Copy the VNC server/viewer files to a publicly accessible location:

```
cp vnc_x86_linux_2.0/*vnc* /usr/local/bin
```

3. Run VNC:

```
vncserver
```

The first time that the server is run, it will ask you for a password to connect to your desktop. For security's sake, make this something different from your account password. It will look something like this:

```
[jray@pointy jray]$ vncserver

You will require a password to access your desktops.

Password:
Verify:

New 'X' desktop is pointy.poisontooth.com:1

Creating default startup script /home/jray/.vnc/xstartup
Starting applications specified in /home/jray/.vnc/xstartup
Log file is /home/jray/.vnc/pointy.poisontooth.com:1.log
```

Each VNC server runs on a different "display"—denoted by the number following the colon in the line New 'X' desktop is pointy.poisontooth.com:1. The desktop that was just created is desktop 1. To share that desktop so you can access it remotely, follow these steps:

1. With VNC up and running for the first time, you're going to want to stop it immediately in order to configure a few other things. To do this, enter the vncserver command with the -kill option, and the number of the desktop to kill (1 in our example) as below:

```
vncserver -kill :1
 [jray@pointy jray]$ vncserver -kill :1
Killing Xvnc process ID 7464
```

2. With VNC server stopped, you'll want to edit the file .vnc/xstartup that has been created in your home directory. By default, a generic desktop is started. If you're running KDE or GNOME, you'll want to start the appropriate desktop system for your account.

3. For example, if you're used to running KDE, you'll want the xstartup file to look like this:

```
#!/bin/sh
xrdb $HOME/.Xresources
startkde &
```

PART

**V**

CH

**28**

4. GNOME users will need the file to be edited as follows:

```
#!/bin/sh
xrdb $HOME/.Xresources
gnome-session &
```

5. You can now start VNC server again, and it will load the window manager you've configured, which is vncserver:

```
[jray@pointy jray]$ vncserver

New 'X' desktop is pointy.poisontooth.com:1

Starting applications specified in /home/jray/.vnc/xstartup
Log file is /home/jray/.vnc/pointy.poisontooth.com:1.log
```

That's it! You're now serving your desktop so that it can be connected to remotely. To connect under Linux, you can use the vncviewer command from within X Window: vncviewer <ip address:display name>. If you prefer, just type vncviewer and the system will prompt you for a IP address and display number to connect to. One of the greatest features of VNC is that it is completely cross-platform. This means that you can now access your desktop from anywhere on the Internet from just about any type of computer. For example, I can access my in-house server from my Powerbook as I type this chapter as shown in Figure 28.1.

**Figure 28.1**
VNC allows you to administrate your server remotely from a wide variety of computers. Here a Macintosh controls a remote KDE desktop.

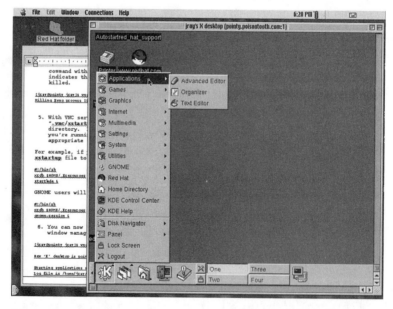

There are additional options of VNC that you may want to configure—including color and bit depth. There are two commands to change these settings from the command line:

- **-depth <value>**—The depth option lets you set a pixel depth for the display. Typical values are 8 (256 colors), 16 (65,535 colors), and 24 (true color). The lower the bit depth, the faster the display will update remotely.

- **-geometry <width>x<height>**—The size of your virtual screen. If you'd like a small screen, try 640 × 480. You can, however, specify much larger values. The virtual display geometry is not bound by your physical display. The vncviewer software will scroll the displayed screen if it exceeds the limits of your screen.

The second (and my preferred method) to permanently make these changes is to edit the vncserver file that you earlier copied to /usr/local/bin/vncserver.

Open the file in your favorite text editor, looking for this section, located near the top:

```
#
# Global variables.  You may want to configure some of these for your site.
#

$geometry = "800x600";
$depth = 16;
$desktopName = "X";
```

You can change the $geometry and $depth variables to values that you prefer. Each time you start vncserver after the edit, it will automatically start with your preferred bit depth and geometry. I find it easier than typing the command-line options repeatedly.

As you move further along in the process of establishing your server, you will appreciate the control that you gain from installing VNC. Besides remote administration, it is also extremely useful if you want to maintain your current desktop operating system and still have full access to Linux applications.

The subsequent chapters of this section will assume that you've made your choices about your server and have made the necessary arrangements to connect to the Internet. If you aren't online, I suggest exploring your options while configuring your Linux computer as an Internet server in the chapters that follow.

# CHAPTER 29

# SETTING UP DOMAIN NAME SERVICES (DNS)

In this chapter

# INTRODUCTION TO DNS

Earlier in this book, you may have configured your TCP/IP settings so that you can access the Internet on your Red Hat Linux computer. In doing so, you may have defined one or more Domain Name Servers in your `/etc/resolv.conf` file. Domain Name Servers contain the information that is necessary to translate back and forth between numeric network IP addresses such as `192.168.0.1` and symbolic addresses that you see every day, like `www.symbolicaddress.com`. Symbolic addresses are much easier for humans to remember, and also give server operators the flexibility of moving services between different IP addresses transparently to the end user.

## DOMAIN NAMES

There are different parts to each hostname that you use; you're probably familiar with addresses such as `www.poisontooth.com`. In these addresses, the *www* is the name of an individual host on the Internet. The domain name is `poisontooth.com`—it doesn't necessarily have to be associated with any machine at all. The *.com* itself is called the TLD, or *Top Level Domain*. The common TLDs are as follows:

- `.com`—Commercial domains
- `.edu`—Educational institutions
- `.org`—Nonprofit organizations
- `.gov`—U.S. Government
- `.mil`—U.S. Military
- `.net`—Commercial domains

Recent additions that are a bit less popular include the following:

- `.firm`—Businesses
- `.shop`—Sites selling goods online
- `.web`—Web groups
- `.arts`—Cultural and entertainment information
- `.rec`—Recreation and entertainment activities
- `.info`—Informational sites
- `.nom`—Personal Web sites

TLDs also identify hosts in countries other than the United States. You're probably familiar with names like the following:

- `.jp`—Japan
- `.uk`—United Kingdom
- `.nz`—New Zealand

- ■ .ca—Canada
- ■ .nl—Netherlands

Domain name servers make up a very important part of the Internet, but are usually not mentioned by texts discussing Internet servers. The Internet's DNS system is a complex hierarchy of databases, with each DNS server given authority to dictate domain names for a range of computers. Servers must also be able to query other downstream servers in order to find a hostname or IP address that they do not have authority over.

## DNS Servers

There are several different kinds of DNS servers. In order to make the process of server domain names efficient, it is necessary to divide the serving tasks among different types of servers:

- ■ **Primary Master Server**—The authoritative server for a domain.
- ■ **Secondary Master Server**—Backs up the primary server. This server is also authoritative for a domain, but instead of maintaining DNS records locally, it downloads them periodically from the primary server.
- ■ **Slave Server**—A slave server forwards queries to a known list of forwarder servers, but does not hold data of its own.
- ■ **Forwarder Server**—Forwards queries to remote outside servers. If a network limits access to the outside world except for a few machines, the forwarder would need to make DNS requests to the Internet on behalf of the machines on its network.
- ■ **Caching Server**—Responds to requests using data that it has collected from previous DNS queries.

This chapter will examine manually configuring a caching server (since it is one of the simplest types of servers), and using LinuxConf to set up a simple primary master server.

### The Reason for DNS Caching

If a master server is considered *authoritative* for a domain, then all requests for hostnames or IPs in that domain obviously must go to that server. Unfortunately, if the DNS system followed this model, DNS traffic would be enormous. Instead of constantly passing DNS lookup requests to an authoritative server, a local DNS server will cache a remote server's information after it is looked up. That local server can then answer requests for information about the remote domain without querying the distant server. In this case, the DNS server is answering without authority and is considered *non-authoritative*.

If a server is caching information, it must also make sure that the information it has stored is still good. DNS servers accomplish this by assigning each record in the DNS database a TTL (Time To Live) value in seconds. Once the TTL for a remote hostname has expired, it is erased from the caching server. The next time the remote host is queried on the local DNS server, it must connect to the remote DNS for the information.

## DNS RECORDS

The information stored in DNS servers is more than just a hostname and an IP address: There are several types of records that a remote computer can retrieve from a DNS server. You'll learn how to create some of these records when you set up your own DNS server later in the chapter. Here are some of the more commonly used DNS records:

- **Address Records**—An address record is the IP address of a particular hostname. This record is used to relate a symbolic address to a numeric address.

- **Canonical Name (CNAME)**—A CNAME record is an alias to an already existing hostname. For example, if I have defined an address record for www.poisontooth.com and I want to have ftp.poisontooth.com point to the same machine, I can add a CNAME record that points ftp.poisontooth.com at www.poisontooth.com. Any subsequent lookups on either name will report the same IP address.

- **Mail Exchanger (MX)**—MX records enable you to have mail that is sent to a particular hostname automatically sent to a different machine. You'll learn a bit more about this record later.

- **Name Server (NS)**—The nameserver records contain the nameservers for a given domain, pretty simple!

- **Start of Authority (SOA)**—The SOA information returned for a hostname contains the authoritative nameserver for the host and all machines in the same subdomain as the name. Contact information for the domain is also returned.

There are more records that can be used beyond these five. The information presented here is only a sampling of the complex beast known as the DNS.

If you are setting up your own Internet server, you will almost certainly want to be registered in a DNS server. There are two parts to this process: registering a domain name and setting up a DNS server. If you are planning to run your own DNS server, you should read the second half of this chapter first. I have chosen to present material on registering for a domain name first because it also contains information that may make running your own DNS unnecessary. There's no need to set up services when you don't have to!

# REGISTERING A DOMAIN NAME

In order to create your own Internet presence, you need to have your own domain name. Giving customers an IP address so that they can connect to your machine is not likely to go over very well. Getting a domain name is like laying claim to your piece of the Internet: It uniquely identifies your computers amid the masses on the Net. Depending on your needs, there are two options for domain names that you might want to explore:

- **Free Domain Names**—There are two primary providers of free Domain Name Service: dyndns.org and dhs.org. These companies will give you a customized hostname that you are free to use and assign to any computer you want, at any time.

The only drawback is that your hostnames take on the form of `mycomputer.dyndns.org` or `mycomputer.dhs.org`, which can leave a bit to be desired for those wanting their own corporate identity.

- **Commercial Registration**—The primary provider of domain names is Network Solutions. For a cost of $70 every two years, you can claim any available address for your own personal use. After a few clicks, `www.IloveGravy.com` could easily be yours!

Now that you know your options, let's go through the procedure of actually getting a domain name. First, we'll take a look at one of the free services: `dhs.org`.

## USING THE `dhs.org` SERVICE

Getting your own `dhs.org` hostname is relatively painless. There is absolutely no cost for the service, but donations are appreciated. Since this is a free service, there are also no guarantees. Previously, much of the free DNS service was supplied by a company called Monolith at `ml.org`. This service was terminated rather abruptly and with no notice to its users. There is no guarantee that `dhs.org` will always be around, so it's best not to base your business around one of these addresses. For casual users, however, it's fast, free, and (for now) it works! To sign up for service, visit the `dhs.org` sign-up page at `http://members.dhs.org/signup` (see Figure 29.1). All that is required on this page is a user ID that will be used to log into the system, your real name, and a valid email address. Fill this information out, and then click Signup.

**Figure 29.1**
The `dhs.org` signup procedure is amazingly quick and simple.

Next you'll be taken to a service agreement screen. Read this carefully if you have any questions or concerns about the service. Remember, you get what you pay for! Click Agree with Terms of Service to continue. Within a few minutes, you should receive a piece of email (in the account that you used to subscribe) that looks similar to this:

```
Hi,

According to our information, you just requested an account at
http://members.dhs.org/signup.
If this was not you, just delete this email and you will not hear
further from us.

To activate your account, simply go to the following url and insert
your login id and activation code: http://members.dhs.org/activate

Login id: johnray
Activation code: 15-38-8


Regards,
  DHS Support
  support@dhs.org
```

Make a note of your login ID and the activation code, and then point your Web browser at the activation Web site `http://members.dhs.org/activate` (see Figure 29.2). Click the Activate button to activate your `dhs.org` account.

**Figure 29.2**
Activate your
`dhs.org` account
using the infor-
mation provided
to you by email.

Now that your account is activated, you're immediately prompted to enter a new password, as shown in Figure 29.3. Pick a good password here. If someone can guess your user ID and password, they can point your hostname toward their computers, effectively stealing your Internet identity! Click Set when you are ready to continue.

You're ready to start using your new account. Point your browser at `http://members.dhs.org/nic` and enter your user ID and newly created password in the authentication dialog box. Now the fun begins!

**Figure 29.3**
Choose a password for your new account.

Once logged into the system, you are presented with the menu shown in Figure 29.4. From here, you can choose ID Maintenance, which enables you to change the email address and password that is associated with the account.

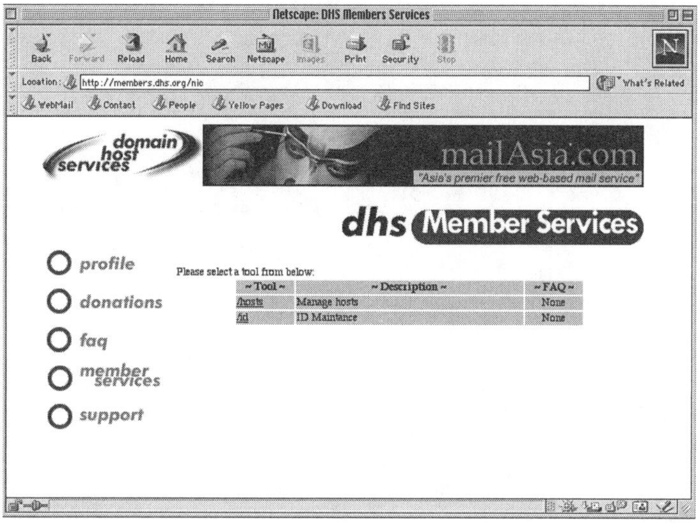

**Figure 29.4**
The main
`dhs.org` menu is rather sparse.

The other available option, Manage Hosts, allows you to add and delete hostnames that you've registered with the service. Click the Manage Hosts link now.

Available hosts are shown in a list under the Host Maintenance heading. In Figure 29.5, you can see that one host, `poisontooth.dhs.org`, has already been defined. Selecting the button to the left of the hostname and clicking delete allows the administrator to remove that entry from the system. Clicking Edit allows changes to be made to the entry, including giving it a new IP address if needed.

**Figure 29.5**
You can Add, Delete, and Edit your hostnames from the Manage Hosts screen.

To add a new host, click the Add button. Figure 29.6 shows the intermediate screen that will appear before you can enter any details. Do not change any options on this screen. Several of the functions are not yet available, and a Static Host is most likely what you want anyway. Click the Next button to continue.

**Figure 29.6**
Do not change any options on this screen; click Next to continue.

The next screen, shown in Figure 29.7, is where the configuration of your host is carried out. There are five fields, only two of which are critical to setting your hostname.

The available options are as follows:

■ **Domain**—This is the domain in which you are registering. The only domain offered by dhs.org at the time of this writing is dhs.org. You may want to check here, however, to see if new domains have been added.

**Figure 29.7**
All of your hostname options are configured here.

- **Hostname**—The hostname that you want to use with your computer. In Figure 29.7, the hostname is set to `poisontooth`. This means that the registered machine name will be `poisontooth.dhs.org`.

- **IP**—The IP address of the computer being registered. You'll need to check with your network administrator or check your TCP/IP settings to find out what this value is. This value can be changed at any time, but is only updated once a day with the DNS service running from `dhs.org`.

- **Mail Exchanger**—If you would like another machine (aside from the hostname you're registering) to receive email that is sent to the machine, enter the hostname of the mail server here. For example, in Figure 29.7, a mail exchanger of `poisontooth.com` is specified. This means that email sent to `blah@poisontooth.dhs.org` will actually be sent to `blah@poisontooth.com`.

- **Wildcards**—If the wildcards option is activated, then you can use multiple names that will resolve to the same hostname. If the hostname is `poisontooth.dhs.org` and wildcards are active, you can use names like `www.poisontooth.dhs.org` or `robyn.poisontooth.dhs.org` and they will resolve to the same machine. While this may not seem useful at first, it can, in fact, be used to serve multiple Web sites based on the same hostname from your computer. This is called *virtual hosting*.

After you have set all of your options appropriately, click the Addbutton. If the hostname isn't already taken, you will be sent a confirmation that your host is correctly added into the database, as well as a message telling you when the DNS servers will be updated to contain your new addition. This can take up to a day, so be patient.

To test your new hostname, you can use the nslookup utility from the command line. Used interactively, `nslookup` prompts you for hostnames or IP addresses to resolve until you type the word exit. You can also use the program directly with a hostname or IP address as an argument.

Be sure to learn the options of nslookup. The nslookup command will be your best friend while setting up a nameserver. The command can be used to perform any type of query on any nameserver, including domain transfers, which will dump all available information from a domain. There are far more options than covered in this chapter. The nslookup manpage provides an excellent reference.

For example, to look up linux.dhs.org, use the command nslookup linux.dhs.org as shown here:

```
[jray@pointy jray]$ nslookup linux.dhs.org
Server: iwaynet.iwaynet.net
Address: 198.30.29.7

Name:  linux.dhs.org
Address: 203.35.180.120
```

From this, you can tell if your IP address has been correctly mapped to your hostname. In this example, linux.dhs.org has been assigned to the IP address 203.35.180.120.

You can also verify that features such as a mail exchanger have been set. To do this, run nslookup interactively and use the set query=MX option to look up mail exchange records. Using linux.dhs.org as an example again, here are the results of a search for its MX records:

```
[jray@pointy jray]$ nslookup
Default Server: iwaynet.iwaynet.net
Address: 198.30.29.7

> set query=MX
> linux.dhs.org
Server: iwaynet.iwaynet.net
Address: 198.30.29.7

linux.dhs.org  preference = 5, mail exchanger = mail.borgs.net
dhs.org nameserver = ns1.dhs.org
dhs.org nameserver = ns2.dhs.org
ns1.dhs.org   internet address = 209.249.50.99
ns2.dhs.org   internet address = 207.71.8.95
```

Here you can see that the mail exchanger for linux.dhs.org is mail.borgs.net. Mail that is sent to linux.dhs.org will actually be delivered to a corresponding account on the machine called mail.borgs.net. Of course, mail.borgs.net must be configured to receive this email!

Let's take a look at how the wildcard feature works. Theoretically, you should be able to look up names such as fluffy.linux.dhs.org and snuffy.linux.dhs.org and have them resolve to the same address as the linux.dhs.org (203.35.180.120) as shown here:

```
[jray@pointy jray]$ nslookup
Default Server: iwaynet.iwaynet.net
```

```
Address: 198.30.29.7

> snuffy.linux.dhs.org
Server: iwaynet.iwaynet.net
Address: 198.30.29.7

Name:  snuffy.linux.dhs.org
Address: 203.35.180.120

> fluffy.linux.dhs.org
Server: iwaynet.iwaynet.net
Address: 198.30.29.7

Name:  fluffy.linux.dhs.org
Address: 203.35.180.120
```

Sure enough, the wildcard feature works exactly as expected.

Once your `dhs.org` account is configured and working, you can use your new hostname to access your machine on the Internet. Although this doesn't quite give you a full domain name of your own, it is more than enough for many purposes. If you prefer `dyndns.org` to be your domain name as opposed to `dhs.org`, head over to `http://www.dyndns.org` and sign up for that service—the two are quite similar in features and setup.

> **Tip**
>
> Don't use a dynamic DNS hosting service for commercial sites! The dynamic hosting sites are offered for free, and are not a guaranteed service. Basing a "for-profit" site off of one of these domain-names is not a wise move. If the site goes down, you'll have to re-establish your site's identity. These services are excellent for small low-traffic sites, but don't base a business on them!

## USING NETWORK SOLUTIONS TO REGISTER A DOMAIN NAME

The procedure you just went through with `dhs.org` is trivial compared to registering for a domain name with Network Solutions. The benefit, however, is that with Network Solutions, you have full control over your registration, and can choose any domain name you like. Many ISPs offer registration services for you; this is, quite honestly, the easiest way to become registered. Most ISPs that perform this feature will also supply DNS servers for your use as well, eliminating the need for your own dedicated servers. You are required to run at least two nameservers for a domain. There are ways around this, but DNS service needs to be reliable, and redundant servers provide that reliability. The previously mentioned service, `dhs.org`, runs its own DNS servers for you, so there is no need to run your own. If you are going to run your own DNS servers, skip to the configuration screen now. If not, you should have the IP addresses of your servers and contact information for the server operators available before registering for a domain name.

### FINDING AN AVAILABLE DOMAIN NAME

This, surprisingly, can be a bit more difficult than it sounds! Domain names can be up to 26 characters long, including the .com or .net ending. There are fewer and fewer names available each day, and names that you can't imagine being registered are already gone. You can use the whois command to check to see if a domain is registered and who it is registered to.

For example, try running the command whoispoisontooth.com@networksolutions.com. This will search Network Solutions and report domain name registration information for the domain poisontooth.com:

```
[jray@pointy jray]$ whois poisontooth.com@networksolutions.com
[networksolutions.com]
...
Registrant:
John Ray (POISONTOOTH-DOM)
  XXXX Rhapsody Drive
  Dublin, OH 43016

  Domain Name: POISONTOOTH.COM

  Administrative Contact:
   Ray, John (JR10134) jay@DIFFERENT.AG.OHIO-STATE.EDU
   614-718-XXXX
  Technical Contact, Zone Contact:
   Singh, David K (DKS) dsigh@IWAYNET.NET
   (614)294-XXXX (FAX) (614)291-XXXX
  Billing Contact:
   Ray, John (XX10134) jay@DIFFERENT.AG.OHIO-STATE.EDU
   614-718-XXXX

  Record last updated on 03-Sep-1998.
  Record created on 16-Jun-1998.
  Database last updated on 10-Jan-2000 13:07:57 EST.

  Domain servers in listed order:

  NS1.IWAYNET.NET       198.30.29.7
  NS2.IWAYNET.NET       198.30.29.8
```

This displays all of the available information for the poisontooth.com domain, including the administrative contact (usually the person registering the name), the technical contact (the person running the nameservers serving the domain), and a billing contact (you can figure that one out!). Also listed are the nameservers that service the domain. This is precisely the information that you will be requested to give when you complete a registration form, so, if any of this looks confusing, I highly suggest you consult with the ISP providing your connectivity. Chances are, your ISP can provide answers to any questions that you may have.

### COMPLETING THE REGISTRATION

Let's say you've found a domain name that is free, rancidtomato.com, and are ready to register it. Head over to the Network Solutions Web site at http://www.networksolutions.com. Enter your domain name into the Register a Web Address box at the top of the page, as shown in Figure 29.8, and then click the Go! button to continue.

**Figure 29.8**
Choose your domain name, and then click Go!

You will now need to make your way through several intermediate screens. On the next screen, shown in Figure 29.9, you are given the option of choosing several variations of the domain name you just entered. Don't assume that clicking the addresses will get you the domains for free—they won't. Each domain will cost you $70 for two years of use. Click Continue to go on.

**Figure 29.9**
If you want to also register a variation of your domain name, here's where you do it.

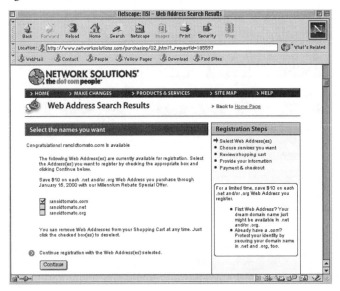

You should now be at a product selection screen (see Figure 29.10). Here you can choose among the three separate services offered by Network Solutions. The option you want (assuming you've made arrangements for DNS service or are running your own servers) is the ISP-hosted Web Address.Click the Continue button located beside this product to move on.

On the next screen, you'll be asked you have the information necessary to register your domain name (the names and IP addresses of your two DNS servers). Click the Continue button under the I Have the Information section to finish up the registration procedure.

**Figure 29.10**
The best value (and what you want) is the ISP-hosted Web Address.

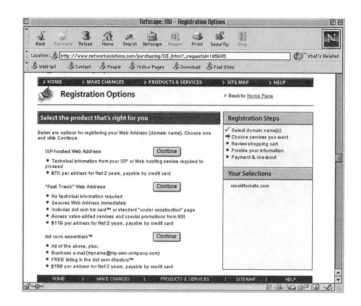

Now you'll need to enter your account information. This is simply your name and address, as shown in Figure 29.11. After entering your contact data, click Continue.

**Figure 29.11**
Fill in your name and address accordingly.

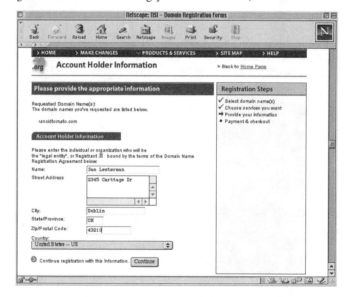

Here is where things start to get tricky. Once you've registered with Network Solutions, you are assigned a "handle" that is used to identify you on the system. If you already have a handle, you can fill in the Returning Customers portion of the form; otherwise, you'll want to fill out the New Customers section at the bottom, as shown in Figure 29.12. If you are using your ISP's DNS servers, you should get the technical contact information for the server operator from them and supply that information in the Returning Customers section as well.

Don't worry if you forget to enter your technical contact's handle. As a last step you can go back and edit your registration information and supply the handle then. If *you* are the technical contact, then don't worry about a thing! Click the Continue button to fill out the last form of the registration process.

**Figure 29.12**
Enter in the contact information or handles for the contacts.

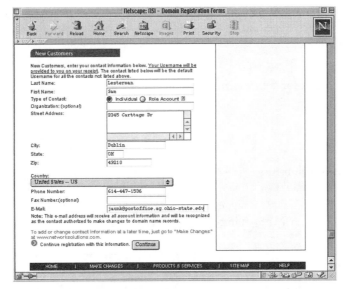

You should now be on the last page of the registration process: specifying your nameservers. If you've already set up your nameservers or have DNS service through your ISP, this should be simple. The only required fields on this form are the nameservers and an email address that will receive information about the status of the registration request (see Figure 29.13). Click Continue to finish up.

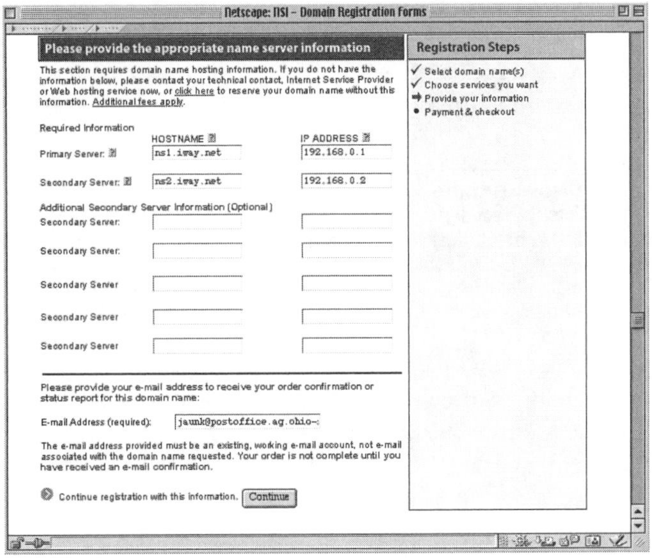

**Figure 29.13**
Enter your DNS information here.

After clicking Continue, you will be given a chance to review your data and make any changes. Once you're satisfied with the settings you can proceed to the checkout phase and pay for the registration with a credit card. The turnaround time for registration is typically shaky, so give them a few days to get your domain name up and running. Don't register and expect it to be up the next day. Sometimes it is, but more often it isn't. You will receive email from Network Solutions as the registration is processed. Pay attention to it because there may be important information or steps you need to take before the registration can be completed.

The most telling sign that your signup process has been completed is to check whois as you did earlier (to check for domain name registrations) and, if your information shows up, you're in luck!

# SETTING UP YOUR OWN DNS USING BIND

Setting up your own nameserver can be quite a hassle—in fact, unless you are planning to maintain a large number of A records or CNAME records, it is probably wise to leave DNS services up to your ISP. The biggest reason for maintaining your own is that relying on someone else to keep a large number of entries up to date can be a bit of a pain.

---

**A Good Reason for Running Your Own DNS**
One of the best reasons for "hiding" numeric addresses behind symbolic addresses is so that, as the administrator, you can move services between different machines without needing to give your customers new addresses for connecting. Relying on a remote DNS means that your ability to reconfigure your servers depends entirely on the support staff of your ISP. DNS is a "mission-critical" service; some people don't like placing that responsibility in someone else's hands.

---

If you do choose to run your own DNS service, you should research the topic before setting up a production server. Many references, both printed and online, discuss DNS configuration issues. This chapter will show you how to create a simple configuration, but should not be considered a definite reference on the subject. While it is easy to get something up and running, it isn't necessarily easy to get it up and running *right*.

---

**A Good Reason for Not Running Your Own DNS**
If this is your first foray into the wonderful world of serving the Internet from Linux, running your own DNS can be quite a hassle. If problems occur, they can be extremely difficult to diagnose. Commercial software packages have been written to diagnose faulty DNS configurations. Trying to find misconfigurations in a large DNS setup by hand can be a nightmare. Red Hat Linux includes a LinuxConf module for configuring your DNS server, but you may run into circumstances where you need to configure things by hand.

---

An alternative to running your own DNS but still having full access to your DNS records may also be possible. Ask your ISP if they offer dynamic DNS updating. By using a properly configured DNS server and an API like the DynDNS Perl module, you can easily update

DNS records on a remote server at any time. You will still need to understand the basic format of records in a DNS server, but you won't have to deal with managing your own server.

Tip

Another possible option is to have your ISP listed as running your nameservers with your domain name registration. Set up your own primary DNS, then have the ISP's DNS act as a secondary, retrieving updates from your server. This, of course, is dependent on your ISP's willingness to do this.

Some decent DNS resources that you may want to browse before continuing this chapter are listed here:

- `http://www.isc.org/products/BIND/`—The Internet Software Consortium's Web page dedicated to the nameserver that comes with Linux.

- `http://www.acmebw.com/askmr.htm`—Ask Mr. DNS—A database of users' questions about DNS, configuration, and so forth.

- `http://www.dns.net/dnsrd`—The DNS Resources directory. Everything you never wanted to know about DNS.

## WHAT IS BIND?

Before we get into the meat of configuration, it's probably a good idea to get a handle of what is being configured. In the case of your Red Hat Linux system, the software we'll be working with is the *BIND* package (*Berkeley Internet Name Domain*). The BIND software is over 15 years old and was developed at the Berkeley University on a DARPA-funded grant. Since its creation, BIND has provided most of the DNS service that is in use on the Internet. Luckily for you, a copy is included with Red Hat Linux, along with a handy configuration module for LinuxConf that will make setting up your server much easier.

If you chose to install Linux as a workstation, you may not have the BIND RPM on your system. You can quickly check this using the RPM query command `rpm -q bind`, shown here:

```
[jray@pointy jray]$ rpm -q bind
bind-8.2.2_P5-1
```

The actual program that you will be running is called `named` (the name daemon). Once you have BIND installed, make sure that `named` will start at bootup by using `chkconfig` to add it to your runlevel: `chkconfig --add named`.

You can now reboot your machine, or start the process manually by typing `/etc/rc.d/init.d/named start`.

## SETTING UP A CACHING-ONLY NAMESERVER

The very simplest nameserver that you can run is a caching nameserver. As discussed earlier, DNS servers can cache hostnames and IP addresses that they have looked up from other servers. A caching-only server only serves information from its cache; you cannot make additions or changes to the information that it is serving.

"Why then," you ask, "would I want to run such a beast?" The answer is simple: speed. Performing DNS lookups takes time. The farther away a nameserver is, the longer it takes to receive a response. If you are running log analysis software that looks up all the hostnames of people who have visited your Web site, the log processing can take quite a toll on a nameserver. By installing a caching server, local machines can request name lookups from it. Once it has cached a name, the server won't need to consult with your ISP's server in order to respond to a request. The result is a faster response time on your network and less load/bandwidth-utilization on your ISP's DNS server.

By default, Red Hat Linux comes with a caching-only setup. This means that, out of the box, you can use your Red Hat system to serve other computers on your network. If you're mainly concerned about providing fast DNS resolution for local clients, this is all you really need to do! Since this is about as simple a setup as possible, we'll look at the individual files that make up the configuration. This will introduce you to the format of the files so you aren't surprised if you ever have to configure things manually.

To check to see if the server is working, use `server <your server's name or ip>` in the interactive mode of nslookup:

```
[jray@pointy jray]$ nslookup
Default Server: iwaynet.iwaynet.net
Address: 198.30.29.7

> server poisontooth.com
Default Server: poisontooth.com
Address: 24.93.97.21

> www.cnn.com
Server: poisontooth.com
Address: 24.93.97.21

Non-authoritative answer:
Name:  cnn.com
Addresses: 207.25.71.27, 207.25.71.28, 207.25.71.29, 207.25.71.30
     207.25.71.82, 207.25.71.199, 207.25.71.245, 207.25.71.246, 207.25.71.5
     207.25.71.6, 207.25.71.7, 207.25.71.8, 207.25.71.9, 207.25.71.12
     207.25.71.20, 207.25.71.22, 207.25.71.23, 207.25.71.24, 207.25.71.25
     207.25.71.26
Aliases: www.cnn.com
```

In this example, `nslookup` is invoked, and then switched to use a vanilla Red Hat Linux 6.2 installation as its DNS server. Once switched to the Linux server, it is queried with `www.cnn.com`and responds appropriately.

You can also see that the query response is designated as a "Non-authoritative answer," which is exactly as it should be. Since `poisontooth.com` does not run the official CNN nameserver, the best it can do is respond in a non-authoritative way.

**I Performed a Similar Lookup on My Machine and It Doesn't Say It Is Non-Authoritative. Why Is That?**

The first time your computer looks up a name, it isn't in the named cache. The response it gets *is* authoritative because it was just looked up. Subsequent lookups of the same name will show up as non-authoritative since the original server is no longer queried.

If you'd like to check to see what's in your cache in a mostly human readable format, you can use kill to send the SIGINT signal to named and dump the cache to the file /var/named/named_dump.db. Here is an example of a few entries in the contents of named_dump.db:

```
[root@pointy /etc]# ps axg ¦ grep named
 522 ?    S    0:13 named
15411 pts/1  S   0:00 grep named
[root@pointy /etc]# kill -SIGINT 522
[root@pointy /etc]# more /var/named/named_dump.db
...
$ORIGIN ADKNOWLEDGE.com.
NS1   165672 IN   A    205.180.221.67 ;NT=85 Cr=addtnl
$ORIGIN NS0.com.
NS0   90255 IN    A    209.197.64.1  ;NT=130 Cr=addtnl
$ORIGIN MACOSRUMORS.com.
www   13546 IN    A    206.170.14.55  ;Cr=auth
$ORIGIN engagetech.com.
cyberweb   10255 IN   A    205.139.29.102 ;Cr=auth
$ORIGIN RR.com.
columbus   259    IN   NS   vector.columbus.rr.com. ;Cr=addtnl
     259   IN   NS  pantera.columbus.rr.com.    ;Cr=addtnl
$ORIGIN columbus.RR.com.
vector 259   IN   A    204.210.252.252 ;Cr=addtnl
viper  259   IN   A    204.210.252.254 ;Cr=answer
pantera 259   IN   A    204.210.252.250 ;Cr=addtnl
cmhnews 259   IN   CNAME viper.columbus.rr.com. ;Cr=answer
news-server   259   IN   CNAME cmhnews.columbus.rr.com.   ;Cr=auth
$ORIGIN EZGREEN.com.
NS1   12121 IN    A    209.75.20.21  ;NT=83 Cr=addtnl
...
```

You should easily be able to make out several of the nameserver record types that were mentioned earlier—namely A, NS, and CNAME records.

There are two files that should be configured for caching operation—the named.conf file and a named.local file that defines your local domain. Let's take a look at /etc/named.conf as it appears on default Red Hat Linux 6.2 systems:

**Why Do I Have a File Called** named.boot **in My** /etc **Directory?**

This file is left over from BIND v4. It can be converted to the named.conf file used in BIND v8 with the bind-bootconf command. This is useful if you happen to be migrating from an old server configuration.

```
options {
#
# a caching only nameserver config
#
```

```
      directory "/var/named";
};

zone "." {
   type hint;
   file "named.ca";
};

zone "0.0.127.in-addr.arpa" {
   type master;
   file "named.local";
};
```

The configuration is divided into three sections:

- **options**—The options section lets you configure things that globally affect your DNS server's operation. In this example, the directory keyword is used to set the data directory of named to /var/named.

- **zone "."**—The zones define a series of hosts that the server will operate for. The first zone, indicated by a dot within quotation marks, is a wildcard denoting the current zone of the type hint—this zone defines the cache. The file named.ca contains a list of root nameservers that are used to provide lookup information for the cache. This file is provided with your BIND distribution.

- **zone "0.0.127.in-addr.arpa"**—This zone provides reverse address-to-name mappings for IP addresses in the 127.0.0 domain—your loopback address. Because this address is internal to your computer, it makes sense that named can be the master server for this zone. This zone is defined by the file named.local.

You could remove the "0.0.127.in-addr.arpa" zone from the named.conf file and you'd still have a working system. Since, however, this zone is included, you'll need to create the /var/named/named.local file. Once again, if you're running Red Hat Linux 6.2, this file should already be created. Take a look at it now (line numbers are added for clarity):

```
1:@      IN   SOA   localhost.   root.localhost. (
2:            1997022700 ; serial
3:            28800 ; refresh
4:            14400 ; retry
5:            3600000 ; expire
6:            86400 ; default_ttl
7:            )
8:@      IN   NS    localhost.
9:1      IN   PTR   localhost.
```

This may look a bit scary, but let's take a look at it, line by line:

- **Line 1:** The start of the Start Of Authority record. This denotes the start of the localhost domain.

- **Line 2:** A serial number for the data file. This number should be updated each time the data is changed in the file.

- **Line 3:** A refresh period (in seconds) after which a secondary server will check the primary server to see if an update is needed.
- **Line 4:** A retry period (in seconds) for a secondary server to wait if a failure occurs during update.
- **Line 5:** The amount of time (in seconds) for a secondary server to wait before expiring data from the primary server.
- **Line 6:** The default Time To Live in seconds. This value is used for individual records in this domain if they neglect to specify their own TTL value.
- **Line 7:** Ends the SOA record.
- **Line 8:** Defines a nameserver record for the localhost domain. Obviously localhost is the nameserver for localhost.
- **Line 9:** Another record of the type PTR—or *domain name pointer*. Used to point special names to other places; in this case it doesn't really do anything interesting.

If this were the primary domain for a specialized domain name, you'd see address records, CNAME records, and other goodies, but the basic format of the file is much the same. To test that the caching server is working, use nslookup and the server localhostoption to see if your computer is responding to name queries as shown here:

```
[root@pointy vnc]# nslookup
Default Server: iwaynet.iwaynet.net
Address: 198.30.29.7

> server localhost
Default Server: localhost.poisontooth.com
Address: 127.0.0.1

> www.cnn.com
Server: localhost.poisontooth.com
Address: 127.0.0.1

Name:  cnn.com
Addresses: 207.25.71.20, 207.25.71.22, 207.25.71.23, 207.25.71.24
    207.25.71.25, 207.25.71.26, 207.25.71.27, 207.25.71.28, 207.25.71.29
    207.25.71.30, 207.25.71.82, 207.25.71.199, 207.25.71.245, 207.25.71.246
    207.25.71.5, 207.25.71.6, 207.25.71.7, 207.25.71.8, 207.25.71.9
    207.25.71.12
Aliases: www.cnn.com
```

Looks like it works! Now that you've seen the scary side of BIND, let's see how LinuxConf will make setting up a primary master server.

---

**Tip**

Even if you don't plan to run a DNS that serves "the world," you might still want to run a DNS for your internal network. This is enables you to keep track of your internal clients by name, rather than IP address. If you have a few internal addresses, it's probably not necessary—a few hundred, and it's a necessity.

# CASE STUDY: USING LINUXCONF TO SET UP A PRIMARY MASTER SERVER

LinuxConf is an all-around wonder, and its beauty shines through again in the configuration of DNS server information on Linux. The steps of setting of a primary domain usually involve creating files similar to those we just looked at, but by hand.

For the sake of clarity, the domain you'll be seeing in the setup has these properties:

- The domain name `testdomain.com`
- A mail forwarder (MX record) that forwards mail for the domain to `poisontooth.com`
- A network subnet of `192.168.0`
- An administrator email account of `jray@poisontooth.com`
- A primary nameserver of `contempt.ag.ohio-state.edu`
- A host `www.testdomain.com` with the IP address `192.168.0.10`
- A host `ftp.testdomain.com` with the IP address `192.168.0.50`
- A CNAME that points `samba.testdomain.com` to `ftp.testdomain.com`

To start, make sure that you are running as root. Next start X Window on the server or if you can view X Window remotely, start the LinuxConf application, and follow these steps:

1. Traverse the LinuxConf hierarchy as such Config, Networking, Server tasks, Domain Name Server (DNS), Config, Domains. Figure 29.14 shows the primary domain addition screen.

**Figure 29.14**
From the Primaries DNS configuration screen you can add new primary domains.

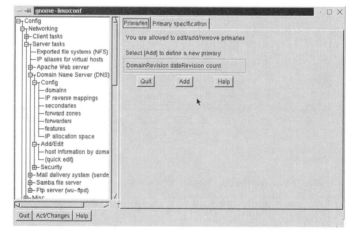

2. Click the Add button and fill in the Primary Specification tab (see Figure 29.15). The Domain is the name of the domain you're adding. The Main Server sets the main DNS for the domain. Administrator Email is a working email address for the person running the domain (that is, you).

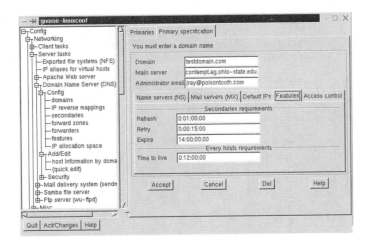

**Figure 29.15**
Every aspect of the SOA record can be set in LinuxConf.

3. You can click through the available tabs for the primary specification and add any records for the domain you'd like. Under Mail Servers (MS) you can add the name of the server that you'd like to receive email for testdomain.com. If you plan to have a secondary server, the Access Control tab lets you set hosts that can download domain data from your machine. Default IPsare IP addresses that should resolve to the name testdomain.com. Lastly, Features sets the Refresh, Retry, Expire, and TTL values for the domain.

4. Next, click the Primary Specification tab. Here you must set the network number of the domain you're adding. The sample network shown in Figure 29.16 is set to 192.168.0.

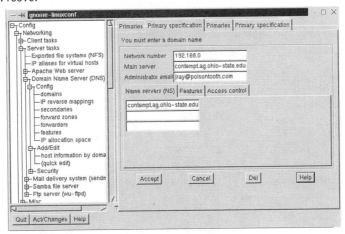

**Figure 29.16**
You must set the network identity of your domain.

5. Click Accept when you're satisfied with your settings.

6. Now you're ready to set a few hostnames in the new domain. Traverse a bit further down the LinuxConf hierarchy and choose Add/Edit, Host Information by Domain. The screen shown in Figure 29.17 should be displayed.

**Figure 29.17**
The
`testdomain.com`
domain is ready
for new hosts!

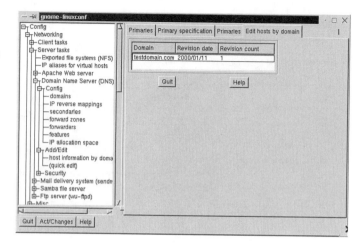

7. Double-click the domain in which you want to add/edit hosts. A new screen with a list of the currently defined hosts should appear. Double-click a host to edit it, click Add to add a new host. Click Addnow.

8. Enter the fully qualified domain name of the host you are adding, and then click the Accept button.

9. Here you can enter all of the necessary information for a record. The simplest entry is an IP Address. If you would like to add a nameserver or mail server records for the domain name, you can click the Name Servers (NS) and Mail Servers (MX) tabs to enter the IP address. If you are adding an alias (CNAME), you only need to fill out the nickname for (CNAME) field. Figure 29.18 shows the definition of `www.testdomain.com` with the IP address `192.168.0.10`.

**Figure 29.18**
Enter your indivi-
dual host infor-
mation for each
host in your do-
main.

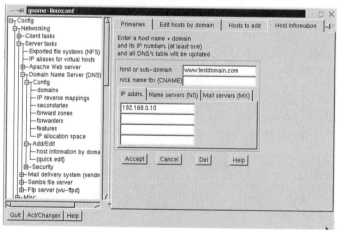

10. If you'd like your test domain to match the example, add a second host called `ftp.testdomain.com` with the IP address `192.168.0.50` and a CNAME record called `samba.testdomain.com` that points to `ftp.testdomain.com` by repeating steps 7-9.

11. When you're finished, your host listing display should look very similar to Figure 29.19. CNAME records are represented with an arrow pointing to a "real" record.

**Figure 29.19**
The defined records for the domain are clearly displayed.

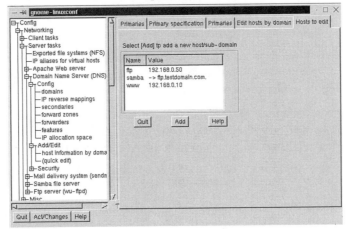

12. Click the Act/Changes or Quit button to exit and save your changes. My system did not restart `named` on exiting LinuxConf, so you may want to do it manually:

`/etc/rc.d/init.d/named restart`

That's it! You've just set up your own primary nameserver. Secondary servers can also be defined from within LinuxConf —you simply give them the IP address of the primary and give them access to the primary server from within its configuration. You might be interested in taking a look at the files that were created in the process of running LinuxConf.

First, the `/etc/named.conf` file has changed; these new zones were added to the original caching-only configuration:

```
zone "testdomain.com"{
    type master;
    file "testdomain.com";
    notify no;
};
zone "0.168.192.IN-ADDR.ARPA"{
    type master;
    file "192.168.0";
    notify no;
};
```

These two zone definitions are necessary for a single domain! The `"testdomain.com"` definition contains the information needed to map hostnames to IP addresses. Here it is:

```
[root@contempt .vnc]# more /var/named/testdomain.com
@       IN   SOA   contempt.ag.ohio-state.edu.   jray@poisontooth
.com (
          2000011102 ; serial
          3600 ; refresh
          900 ; retry
          1209600 ; expire
          43200 ; default_ttl
```

```
            )
@       IN  MX    5     poisontooth.com.
@       IN  NS    contempt.ag.ohio-state.edu.
www     IN  A     192.168.0.10
ftp     IN  A     192.168.0.50
samba   IN  CNAME ftp.testdomain.com.
```

Although this is not as clear as the LinuxConf interface, you can still probably make out what is going on in this file. You're probably also wondering how anyone would ever keep their sanity defining these files by hand!

The second zone definition "0.168.192.IN-ADDR.ARPA" is used to map IP addresses to hostnames. This is called a *reverse lookup*. You might figure that a single file would be enough for both hostname, IP and IP, hostname lookups. Alas, it isn't. This file should look like this:

```
[root@contempt .vnc]# more /var/named/192.168.0
@       IN  SOA   contempt.ag.ohio-state.edu.   jray@poisontooth
.com (
             2000011102 ; serial
             3600 ; refresh
             900 ; retry
             1209600 ; expire
             43200 ; default_ttl
             )
@       IN  NS    contempt.ag.ohio-state.edu.
10      IN  PTR   www.testdomain.com.
50      IN  PTR   ftp.testdomain.com.
```

Once again, it's pretty easy to see where the data you enter has gone. Just imagine going through this process manually. For each entry you make, you'd need to edit multiple files. Thank goodness for LinuxConf!

You can verify that the server is operating correctly using nslookup. First, the MX record for testdomain.com:

```
> set query=MX
> testdomain.com
Server: contempt.ag.ohio-state.edu
Address: 140.254.85.226

testdomain.com preference = 5, mail exchanger = poisontooth.com
testdomain.com nameserver = contempt.ag.ohio-state.edu
contempt.ag.ohio-state.edu   internet address = 140.254.85.226
```

You can see that the MX record is set to forward mail to poisontooth.com. Next, verify that www.testdomain.com resolves to the IP address 192.168.0.10:

```
> www.testdomain.com
Server: contempt.ag.ohio-state.edu
Address: 140.254.85.226

Name:  www.testdomain.com
Address: 192.168.0.10
```

Now, let's see where 192.168.0.50 is pointing (this will verify that reverse lookup is working and should return ftp.testdomain.com):

```
> 192.168.0.50
Server: contempt.ag.ohio-state.edu
Address: 140.254.85.226

Name:  ftp.testdomain.com
Address: 192.168.0.50
```

Yep, all is well! Lastly, check to see if the CNAME `samba.testdomain.com` is working as an alias to `ftp.testdomain.com`:

```
> samba.testdomain.com
Server: contempt.ag.ohio-state.edu
Address: 140.254.85.226

Name:  ftp.testdomain.com
Address: 192.168.0.50
Aliases: samba.testdomain.com
```

All is well with `testdomain.com`!

**Tip**

If you are configuring internal DNS services, be sure that you've used LinuxConf to disable serving the internal subnet to the outside world. By querying responding nameservers, potential crackers can gain information about your internal network. For example, my ISP is serving information about it's internal subnet from it's primary nameservers. I can look up traditional private IP addresses like 192.168.0.2 and the server will return `customerdb.theisp.com` (changed to protect the innocent). Obviously, this gives crackers a view of what is available on the inside, without even needing to compromise any machines.

Hopefully, this has given you a start on configuring your own nameserver. There are many options available in the BIND package that you cannot configure from within LinuxConf. Although configuration may seem easy, there may be settings that apply to your network that you should know. Please take the time to research BIND before creating a production server.

# CHAPTER 30

# USING APACHE TO SERVE THE WEB

**In this chapter**

# WHY USE LINUX AND APACHE TO SERVE THE WEB?

One of the benefits of Red Hat Linux is its reliability. Linux Administrators take pride in the number of days, weeks, months (and even years!) that their servers have been running. And in no area of serving the Internet is reliability more important than the $24 \times 7$ environment of the Web. If your Web server is not available 99.9% of the time (or more), chances are someone will notice.

This chapter introduces you to a few of the popular Linux Web servers, discusses why Apache is perhaps the best choice, then instructs you on installing, configuring and running the most popular Web server on the Internet: the Apache HTTP Server. You will then see how simple it is to post and serve Web pages from your new server. Later you will have a chance to get under the hood and see how the Web works. This chapter ends with two projects. The first is a chance for you to configure and compile Apache directly from the source code. The second project allows you to learn all you ever wanted to know about Apache, and Web servers in general.

## THE POPULAR LINUX WEB SERVERS

There are many Web server products out there from which to choose. This section briefly describes a few of the most popular Linux compatible Web servers:

- **AOLserver**—A small, free server with support for Web application development. Cost: Free (open source). (http://www.aolserver.com/server/)
- **Apache**—The Internet's most popular Web server. Feature rich, modular, and includes the source code. Cost: Free (open source). (http://www.apache.org)
- **Boa**—A small, very fast, single-tasking Web server. Cost: Free (GPL). (http://www.boa.org/)
- **Roxen**—A powerful, secure Web server. Cost: Free (GPL). (http://www.roxen.com/)
- **Stronghold**—A commercial, secure version of Apache. Cost: Around $995. (http://www.c2.net/products/stronghold/)
- **Zeus**—A full-featured Web server with support for secure virtual servers. Cost: Around $1,600. (http://www.zeus.co.uk/products/zeus3/)

---

**Open Source Software**

As a Linux user, you are no doubt familiar with the open source movement. One of the main ideas behind open source is that thousands of programmers can collectively foster the growth and improvement process of a software program better than one small group of corporate programmers. Apache and Linux both benefit greatly from being the cornerstone products of the open source movement.

According to www.opensource.org, "Open source promotes software reliability and quality by supporting independent peer review and rapid evolution of source code."

It is important to remember, however, that freeware and open source software have very little in common beyond their price tag.

---

For more information on these specific Web servers and many more, please refer to the URLs included in the previous list or check out the following sites:

- Web Server Compare, the definitive guide to HTTP server specs: `http://webcompare.internet.com/`

- Server Watch, the quintessential resource for Internet servers: `http://serverwatch.internet.com/`

PART

V

CH

30

> **Tip**
>
> Check out the Linux Software Map (LSM) at `http://www.linux.org/apps/lsm.html`. It's a database of information about software programs, device drivers, and other packages that have been developed for use under Linux. The LSM is a great place to fill all your Linux software needs.

## WEB SERVERS COMPARED

There are several very important criteria to consider when choosing a Web server. They include the following:

- Reliability
- Speed
- Features
- Cost
- Platform availability
- Technical support

A very large majority of the Linux development community, as well as a large share of Internet Web server administrators have chosen the open source Apache HTTP Server due to its outstanding performance, features, availability, and cost.

An Internet consulting firm, Netcraft Ltd, regularly surveys the Web to see the types of Web server software that Web sites are running. Table 30.1 shows the results of the most recent Netcraft survey (`http://www.netcraft.com/`).

**TABLE 30.1    WEB SERVER MARKET SHARE FOR FEBRUARY 2000 (11,161,854 SITES SURVEYED)**

| Server | Market Share |
|---|---|
| Apache | 58.1% |
| Microsoft IIS | 21.9% |
| Netscape Enterprise | 7.8% |

Due to popular consensus (and the fact that Apache comes with Red Hat), it is Apache that we will be considering in depth in the remainder of this chapter.

**Web Server Nomenclature**

These are some of the Web server-related terms that you will see either later in this chapter, or in other Web server documentation:

**Browser**–The client program of the Web. Common browsers include: Lynx, Netscape Communicator, Opera, and Microsoft Internet Explorer.

**CGI**–Common Gateway Interface. A method used to get information from a Web page to the Web server or some other resource. See Chapter 35, "CGI and Perl Programming," for more information.

**Document root**–The top location on the Web server from where Web pages are served. This is the directory explored given a URL of the form: `http://www.yourserver.com/`.

**Homepage**–The starting point of a Website. For example, the homepage of the Apache Group is `http://www.apache.org/index.html`. From there you can click into other areas and subcategories.

**HTML**–Hypertext Markup Language. The primary presentation language used on the Web.

**HTTP**–Hypertext Transfer Protocol. The TCP/IP protocol that specifies how the Web works. The official language spoken among Web servers and browsers.

**Multipurpose Internet Mail Extensions (MIME)**–MIME allows Web servers and browsers to exchange files that are not in HTML or ASCII format such as Microsoft Word documents and images.

**Port**–TCP/IP services use "ports" to make connections and pass information. By default HTTP uses port 80, although it can be configured to use any port number between 0 and 65535.

**Secure Sockets Layer (SSL)**–A protocol developed by Netscape to allow data to be sent over the Web securely. SSL uses public-key technology to encrypt the data passed over the connection.

**Server root**–The location on the computer where the Web server resides. Traditionally, all log and configuration files, as well as the daemon and other supporting documents were placed below the root. Example: `/usr/local/apache` or `/etc/httpd`.

**URL**–A universal address used to reference Web pages. Example: `http://www.apache.org/`.

**Virtual host (or virtual server)**–Most Web servers have the ability to represent more than one domain. This is done using the concept of virtual hosts, in which one Web server can serve multiple sites. Virtual hosts are commonly used by Internet service providers (ISPs) as a low cost alternative to having a separate Web server for every customer.

**Web server**–A computer that serves documents (Web pages) over the Internet using the HTTP protocol. The term *Web server* can be used to refer to the computer (a combination of hardware and Web server software) or to the software package itself (such as the Apache Web server).

See the later section "A Quick Look at How Web Servers Work" for more detailed information about the protocol that Web servers use to communicate with us.

# INSTALLING THE APACHE HTTP WEB SERVER

If you are running the Red Hat Linux operating system, there is a very good chance that your installation included the Apache Web server. If it did, great. Let's get started.

**Tip**

It may be to your benefit to uninstall Apache and start over for two reasons: 1) The version that came with your installation may be outdated or improperly configured; and 2) downloading and installing Apache yourself will give you some insight into how it works.

The next section provides details about downloading and installing a new Apache RPM file. You can also see the section "Installing Apache the Old-Fashioned Way" later in this chapter for information on compiling your own Apache.

You can verify that Apache is installed by running the command:

```
rpm -q apache
```

You should see output similar to the following:

```
apache-1.3.12.2
```

That means Apache is there and you can skip ahead to the section on "Configuring Apache." However, if you do not have Apache installed, or your installation is outdated or otherwise in need of replacement, the next section will show you how to download and install a new Apache package.

## Downloading and Installing the Apache RPM File (If Necessary)

The Linux Red Hat Package Manager (RPM) makes it very simple to add and remove software from a Linux system. It is no surprise, due to the popularity of the Apache Web server, that it does come in the form of an RPM file. You can obtain the latest Apache RPM file from the official RPM repository: `http://rpmfind.net/linux/RPM/`.

> **Tip**
>
> If you don't have Apache installed, you can install it fairly quickly if you still have your distribution CD. Just boot from your CD, specify that you want to "upgrade," and then tell the installer to add Apache (you will find it under "System Environment/Daemons"). This could save you the time it would take to locate, download, and install the Apache RPM.

You will first want to remove the original package (if one exists). The command for doing this is the following:

```
rpm -e apache
```

To install the new Apache package, run this command:

```
rpm -i <package_name>
```

*<package_name>* is the name of the Apache package—for example:

```
rpm -i apache-1.3.12.2.i386.rpm
```

For specific directions on working with RPM files, please refer to Chapter 13, "Managing Packages with RPM."

Table 30.2 lists the directories that the Apache RPM will create.

**TABLE 30.2  DIRECTORIES CREATED BY THE APACHE RPM**

| Directory | Contents |
| --- | --- |
| /etc/httpd/conf | Configuration files |
| /etc/httpd/logs | Log files (linked to /var/log/httpd) |

**TABLE 30.2    CONTINUED**

| Directory | Contents |
|---|---|
| /etc/httpd/modules | Module include files (linked to /usr/lib/apache) |
| /var/log/httpd | Log files (see /etc/httpd/logs) |
| /home/httpd/html | Web (HTML) pages |
| /home/httpd/cgi-bin | CGI programs |
| /home/httpd/icons | Miscellaneous icons |

A sample home page named index.html will be installed in /home/httpd/html, and several sample CGI programs will be installed in /home/httpd/cgi-bin. You can run the following command to see a complete list of the files installed:

```
rpm -ql apache
```

# CONFIGURING APACHE

Apache traditionally relies on three configuration files:

- **access.conf**—Controls access to your Web server's resources.
- **httpd.conf**—The primary configuration file. Tells Apache how to run.
- **srm.conf**—Specifies which resources you want to offer on your site.

With Red Hat 6.2, all configuration is moved to a single file, httpd.conf. All of the configuration that was spread across three files is now consolidated into one.

To get your server up and running initially, this file needs very little editing if any at all. Some of the configuration items, or server directives, that may need editing are detailed in the following sections. The configuration file is very well documented, and you should be able to identify the directives that need to be changed by reading through the file. Refer to http://www.apache.org/docs/ for more information on configuring Apache.

**Tip**

Assuming your Web server is up and running already, you will find some helpful Apache documentation at the URL http://localhost/manual/.

**Tip**

Traditionally, all of the Apache files were stored under one primary root: /usr/local/apache/. The Red Hat Linux distribution has its own standard for laying out the filesystem (such as library files in /usr/lib, administration binaries in /usr/sbin, logs in /var/log, and so on). Do not be surprised to find references to a

**Note**

different way of doing things in Apache documentation. A perfect example is the `httpd` man page, which incorrectly roots all of the related files under `/usr/local/apache/`.

You will need to keep this in mind when you compile your own Apache in the section "Installing Apache the Old-Fashioned Way."

## THE httpd.conf FILE

The `httpd.conf` file contains the directives that tell Apache how to run. The following are some of the directives that may need your attention:

- **ServerName**—The name of your Web server:

  ServerName www.mydomain.com

- **ServerType**—Options are `standalone` or `inetd`. A standalone server will run all the time. A `ServerType` of `inetd` will cause the server to run only when it is requested. `standalone` is recommended for best performance:

  ServerType standalone

- **Port**—By default HTTP servers run on port 80. Valid port numbers are 0-65535, although typically the first 1024 are reserved:

  Port 80

**Tip**

You can sort of "hide" your Web server by running it on a port other than 80 (the default). For example, if you were to run it on port 8080, you would access the server using a URL of the following form:

http://www.mydomain.com:8080/

Note that this is not a secure way of hiding the server. Simple port scanning programs will find it, regardless of the port it is running on.

- **User**—This specifies the user that the Apache server will run as. There are security implications to this directive, as Apache will take on the privileges of its controlling user. Many UNIX systems have a user called "nobody" just for this purpose. If your system does not have an unprivileged user, you should create one:

  User nobody

- **ServerAdmin**—This should be set to the administrative user. Apache will send mail to this user in the event of any problems:

```
ServerAdmin root
```

- **ServerRoot**—The root directory of the Apache installation. All of your configuration files and log files will be stored under this root unless you instruct Apache otherwise:

```
ServerRoot /etc/httpd
```

- **ErrorLog**—The location and name of the error logfile:

```
ErrorLog logs/error.log
```

- **TransferLog**—The location and name of the transfer (or access) logfile:

```
TransferLog logs/access.log
```

- **Timeout**—The length of time (in seconds) that the Web server will wait for a browser to respond before assuming the connection is dead. The default value is 300 seconds:

```
Timeout 300
```

The following directives are used to control Apache's resources, and are traditionally stored in the `srm.conf` file. Some of the more interesting directives are as follows:

- **DocumentRoot**—The root directory of your Web server's document tree:

```
DocumentRoot /usr/local/apache/htdocs/
```

- **DirectoryIndex**—If a user requests a URL from your server that ends in a path, the Web server will attempt to serve a document that matches DirectoryIndex. For example, loading `http://www.apache.org/` results in the file `index.html` being served to your browser. If you want the file `home.html` to be served by default, enter it here:

```
DirectoryIndex index.html, index.cgi, home.html, home.htm, index.htm
```

- **IndexIgnore**—By default, if a user requests a URL from your server that ends in a path and there is no `index.html` file available, the Web server will present the user with a listing of files in the directory. There may be files there that you don't want displayed (such as `.htaccess` or `README` files). The server will not display files set in the `IndexIgnore` directive:

```
IndexIgnore .??* *~ *# HEADER* README* RCS CVS *,v *,t
```

The `access.conf` file is historically where you would set up access rules to control access to your entire Web server, or parts thereof.

Consider the following block:

```
<Directory />
  Options FollowSymLinks
  AllowOverride None
</Directory>
```

Controls access attributes for a directory. The `<Directory />` opens the container. Every directive in the file before a `</Directory>` will apply to the directory `/`. In this example Apache is instructed to follow symbolic links for this directory and to prohibit other control files from overriding settings.

Consult the Apache documentation that came with your Web server for more information on how to control access to your site.

## CONFIGURING APACHE WITH LINUXCONF

While it is perfectly normal to edit the Apache configuration files "by hand"—that is, using your favorite text editor—you may prefer to use LinuxConf instead.

You will find the Apache configuration information under the "Config/Networking/Server tasks/Apache Web server" heading. Under "Defaults," you will find the configuration parameters mentioned in the previous section.

PART

**V**

CH

**30**

> **Tip**
>
> There are tools available that will allow you to take a more graphical approach to managing Apache. The two most notable are *Comanche* and *Vision for Apache*. For more information on these tools, or on the Apache GUI project in general, refer to the following sites:
>
> http://comanche.com.dtu.dk/comanche/
>
> http://www.focus-array.com/products/VisionForApache/
>
> http://gui.apache.org/

# STARTING AND STOPPING APACHE

Once Apache is installed and configured, you are ready to go. You can start Apache by running the following command:

```
#/etc/rc.d/init.d/httpd start
```

A quick check of the system processes should verify that it was started. The number of the process that starts is specified as the StartServers parameter in the httpd.conf file. The default is 10, which is fine for now:

```
# ps -ax ¦ grep http
444 ? S  0:00 httpd
447 ? S  0:00 httpd
448 ? S  0:00 httpd
449 ? S  0:00 httpd
450 ? S  0:00 httpd
...
```

The httpd daemon takes several optional parameters. A couple of the more interesting ones include:

- **-f config**—Specify the location of the configuration file. This is handy if you want to start your Web server using an alternate configuration.
- **-t**—Test the syntax of the configuration files only. This is useful if you have made changes to your configuration files and you want to be sure all is well.

See the httpd man page for a complete list of options.

Using your Web browser, point to your newly installed Web server by loading the ServerName URL (http://www.yourdomain.com/ or http://localhost/). If Apache is properly configured and running you will see the test page, as shown in Figure 30.1.

**Figure 30.1**
The Apache test page.

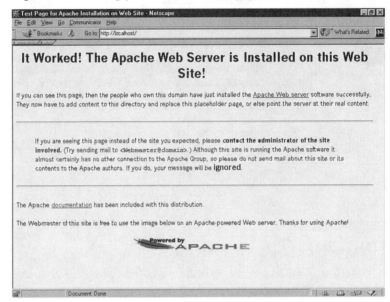

You can stop Apache by running the command:

```
#/etc/rc.d/init.d/httpd stop
```

The file /var/run/httpd.pid contains the process ID of the httpd daemon. The location and name of this file is configured using the PidFile parameter in the httpd.conf file.

## /etc/rc.d

You can use the rc.d system to automatically start Apache for you. You should have a file named /etc/rc.d/init.d/httpd already installed.

**Tip**

> You can use the `/etc/rc.d/init.d/httpd` to manually stop, start, and restart the Apache server at any time. Just run the command
>
> `# /etc/rc.d/init.d/httpd <command>`
>
> `<command>` is one of `start`, `stop`, `reload`, `restart`, or `status`.

To make sure that the Apache webserver is configured to start up when your computer boots, simply issue this command at any prompt:

```
chkconfig --add httpd
```

That's all there is to it!

## WHAT IF APACHE WON'T START?

Most of the problems you will have when starting Apache have one thing in common: a missing resource. One example happens when the daemon is unable to find a file it is looking for. This could be either a configuration file, or a DocumentRoot directory. A second example is when Apache is unable to bind to its defined port.

### MISSING FILES OR USERS

Suppose if, upon starting Apache, you see an error message similar to the following:

```
DocumentRoot must be a directory
```

Check your `httpd.conf` file for the declaration of the `DocumentRoot`. Make sure it is a valid directory.

Similarly, you may receive this error:

```
fopen: no such file or directory
httpd: could not open document config file
```

This could indicate that your configuration files are not where they should be. Locate your configuration files and put them in the default directory.

You may get this error:

```
httpd: bad user name <username>
```

In this example, `<username>` is the name of the user you specified that Apache should assume when running. Make sure this is a valid user.

### PORT PROBLEMS

The most common port problem you will experience is when Apache finds its port (by default, port 80) in use by another service. You may see an error message similar to the following:

```
httpd: could not bind to port
```

This could indicate that another service is running on the specified port (maybe even another instance of Apache!). Check to see if Apache is running already. If so, stop it and try again.

This type of message could also indicate that you are trying to run the Web server on a port that you do not have permission to use. Only root can start services that bind to the ports below 1024. Therefore, if you use the default port 80, you must start the Apache daemon as root.

# SERVING CONTENT

Now that Apache is installed, properly configured, and running, it's time to post some real content to your server. As we mentioned before, the default DocumentRoot is /home/httpd/html/. This is the directory that you will want to put your HTML Web pages.

## POSTING YOUR FIRST FILE

If you don't know HTML, check the "HTML Resources" section later for a few references that may help. Here's some basic HTML to help you get your first page started:

```
<HTML>
  <HEAD>
    <TITLE>My First Web Page</TITLE>
  </HEAD>
  <BODY>
    <H1>This is my first Web page...</H1>
  </BODY>
</HTML>
```

You can use your favorite HTML or plain text editor to create your first page. Table 30.3 lists several HTML editors that run under Linux.

### TABLE 30.3   HTML EDITORS AVAILABLE FOR LINUX

| HTML Editor | URL for More Information |
| --- | --- |
| Netscape Composer | http://home.netscape.com/communicator/composer/ |
| asWedit | http://www.advasoft.com/ |
| EZ-Edit | http://relative-web.com/dynamic/ |

Of course, a simple text editor like vi will work fine for now.

Once you have created your first page, copy it into your DocumentRoot. You can either call it index.html and overwrite the index.html that was distributed with Apache, or give it a different name. Once it's there, open a Web browser and give it a try.

Now experiment a little. Try adding some more text, or maybe a graphic or two (look in the DocumentRoot or the /icons directory for the graphics that came with Apache).

## PUTTING YOUR WEB SERVER TO WORK

This section will discuss a few of the ways that you can use your new Web server.

## CONTENT-ONLY SITES

You can use the Web to tell your friends and customers anything you want them to know about you. Information you may want to include on a content-only site includes the following:

- Pictures of your family or dog
- Contact information
- Mission statements
- Description of products and services

The content-only site provides you with a great chance to test the waters, so to speak. There are very few security concerns, maintenance is easy, and not much technical expertise is required.

## GATHERING INFORMATION FROM YOUR VIEWERS

The Web can also be used to gather information from your audience. Types of information you can gather include the following:

- Customer comments and/or complaints
- Requests for information
- Surveys
- Requests for future products and services

The technology that makes this possible is discussed in Chapter 35, "CGI and Perl Programming"

## INTRANETS

An intranet is a finite, closed network of computers that use Internet (Web) technologies to share data. An intranet may be a subset of the Internet with access controls in place to keep out the uninvited. For that matter, an intranet doesn't have to be connected to the Internet at all.

The ways in which your intranet can help make the members of your organization more efficient and productive are just about endless. Here are some typical uses of intranet technology:

- Human resources
- Forms collection
- Project management
- Inventory tracking
- Office file management

---

**Extranets: The Next Step**

Whereas intranets are intended to allow members of a company or organization to share information among themselves, the extranet goes one step further. Extranets are actually intranets that securely open their doors to an invited group of outsiders. One practical use of the extranet is to allow companies to share information with strategic partners, such as customers, shippers, or suppliers.

---

## WEB APPLICATIONS

As you get a little more advanced in your Web development, you will be able to create and use Web applications to create dynamic pages full of on-demand information for your users. Example Web applications include the following and more:

- Searchable telephone directories
- Inventory systems
- Online surveys and registration systems

### E-COMMERCE

Another increasingly common use of the Web is the selling of goods and services. Sites like *Amazon.com* have made the Web-based shopping cart a household item. You too can put this technology to use, selling your wares worldwide. Web-based e-commerce tools can allow you to do the following:

- Employ Web-based shopping carts
- Accept online credit card transactions
- Debit and credit bank accounts
- Schedule and coordinate shipping

# A QUICK LOOK AT HOW WEB SERVERS WORK

The World Wide Web works largely due to a TCP/IP protocol called the *Hypertext Transmission Protocol* (HTTP). HTTP is a request/response service that allows clients (browsers) and Web servers to exchange information. A Web server is a software program that listens for requests from a browser, and in the most basic case provides data in HTML format via HTTP. A typical HTTP session operates as follows:

- The browser connects to the server.
- The browser requests a file or some other information.
- The server responds and drops the connection.

HTTP makes request/response communication possible between the server and the client.

## THE REQUEST

A client request contains the following information:

- Request method
- Request header
- Request data

The request method is the program to be applied to the specified Web page. The methods available are shown in Table 30.4.

### TABLE 30.4 HTTP REQUEST METHODS

| Method | Description |
| --- | --- |
| GET | Requests the specified document |
| HEAD | Requests only the document header |
| POST | Requests that the server accept the specified document as an executable and pass it some information |
| PUT | Replaces the contents of the specified document with data from the client |
| DELETE | Requests that the server delete the specified page |
| OPTIONS | Allows the client to see the capabilities or requirements of the server |
| TRACE | Used for testing—allows the client to see how the message was retrieved |

The header information is optional, and is used to provide the server with additional information about the client. Request headers are shown in Table 30.5.

### TABLE 30.5  HTTP REQUEST HEADERS

| Header | Description |
| --- | --- |
| Accept | The type of data the client will accept |
| Authorization | Includes authentication information like username and password |
| User-Agent | The type of client software being used |
| Referer | The Web page from which the user is coming (yes, it is misspelled) |

If the method requires data from the client (as does POST) the client follows the header with data. Otherwise, the client waits for a response from the server.

## THE RESPONSE

Server responses also contain several essential items:

- Status code
- Response header
- Response data

HTTP defines several groups of status codes to communicate back to the browser. Table 30.6 lists the more common of these codes.

### TABLE 30.6   HTTP STATUS CODES

| | |
|---|---|
| *Informational (1xx)* | |
| 100 | Continue |
| *Successful (2xx)* | |
| 200 | OK |
| *Redirection (3xx)* | |
| 301 | Moved Permanently |
| 302 | Moved Temporarily |
| *Client Error (4xx)* | |
| 400 | Bad Request |
| 401 | Unauthorized |
| 403 | Forbidden |
| 404 | Not Found |
| *Server Error (5xx)* | |
| 500 | Internal Server Error |

Response headers provide the client with information about the server and/or the requested document and are shown in Table 30.7. All headers are terminated with a blank line.

### TABLE 30.7   HTTP RESPONSE HEADERS

| Method | Description |
|---|---|
| Server | Information about the Web server |
| Date | The current date/time |
| Last Modified | The date/time that the requested document was last modified |
| Expires | The date/time that the requested document expires |

**TABLE 30.7  CONTINUED**

| Method | Description |
|---|---|
| Content-type | The MIME type of the data |
| Content-length | The size (in bytes) of the data |
| WWW-authenticate | Used to tell the client the information that is required for authentication (such as username and password) |

If the client has requested data, it will follow. Otherwise, the server closes the connection.

Consider the following example:

```
GET /index.html HTTP/1.1
Accept: text/plain
Accept: text/html
User-Agent: Mozilla/4.5 (WinNT)
    (blank line)
```

The browser sends a GET request for the file index.html. The header includes the types of data that the browser will accept, as well as some information about the browser. The server answers with an HTTP response that includes the requested file:

```
HTTP/1.1 200 OK
Date Friday, 14-Jan-2000 12:16:03 GMT
Server: Apache/1.3.6
MIME-version: 1.0
Content-type: text/html
Last-modified: Thursday, 13-Jan-2000 10:43:56 GMT
Content-length: 1423
    (blank line)
<HTML>
<HEAD>
<title>Example Server-Browser Communication</title>
</HEAD>
<BODY>
...
```

Once the file is transmitted the connection is closed. HTTP is a stateless protocol, meaning no information about the browser or the session is maintained (beyond what the server writes to its log file).

By default, HTTP runs on TCP well-known port 80.

## UNIFORM RESOURCE LOCATORS

The key to finding information on the Web is knowing how to retrieve it. The Web uses an address scheme known as the Uniform Resource Locator (URL) to identify Web pages and other resources.

Here is an example URL:

```
http://www.w3c.org/Protocols/index.html
```

This URL, which would take you to the Web site of the World Wide Web Consortium, is broken down into the following segments:

*Protocol://  servername.domain/  directory/  file*

In the example the segments are as follows:

- Protocol: `http`
- Full domain name: `www.w3c.org`
- Directory: `Protocols`
- File: `index.html`

> **Note**
>
> Most Web servers are configured to provide default pages. In most cases the default page is called `index.html`. However, other defaults include `home.html`, `default.html`, `home.htm`, and `index.htm`. With this option turned on and configured, a URL for `http://www.w3c.org/Protocols/` would return the `index.html` file found in the Protocols directory. In Apache, this is set using the `DirectoryIndex` directive, as discussed in the earlier "Configuring Apache" section.

The following are some other common URLs:

```
ftp://servername/directory/file
ftp://username@servername/directory/file
telnet://servername
news://newsservername/newsgroup
```

These examples represent URLs that request a document via anonymous FTP, request a document via FTP using "username," request telnet access to a server, and request access to the Usenet newsgroup, respectively.

It is also possible to pass data within a URL to be used by the server. A typical use of this would be the passing of parameters to a server-side program. For example:

```
http://servername/directory/file.html?username=Jamison&uid=300
```

This URL would send to the page `file.html` two key-value pairs: a username of Jamison and a UID of 300.

Sometimes it is necessary to include special characters such as spaces or slashes (/) in the URL. In this case these special characters must be "encoded" to prevent problems on the server end. The process of encoding (sometimes referred to as hexadecimal encoding) involves replacing these special characters with their hexadecimal equivalents. For example, suppose we want to pass a user's full name on the URL:

```
http://servername/directory/file.html?name=Neal%20Jamison
```

In the preceding example, the space between Neal and Jamison has been replaced with its hexadecimal equivalent 20. This practice of passing information on the URL is frequently used with Common Gateway Interface (CGI) programs. For more about CGI refer to Chapter 35, "CGI and Perl Programming."

# INSTALLING APACHE THE OLD-FASHIONED WAY

There's no better way to learn about Apache than to do it the "old-fashioned" way. By that, I mean downloading the source, configuring, and compiling your own Apache.

PART
**V**

CH
**30**

**Note**  This is an advanced topic, and requires some knowledge of programming tools like C compilers, `make`, and so on. This project may not be for everyone.

Take note of a few requirements:

- **Disk Space**—You will need at least 12MB of temporary disk space. After installation, Apache will require approximately 3MB of space, plus whatever space is required to store your Web pages.
- **ANSI C Compiler**—You will need to have an ANSI C compiler installed and properly configured. The GNU C compiler is recommended. See `http://www.gnu.org/` to obtain GCC. You should have everything you need if you've installed Linux with C Development support.

## DOWNLOAD THE APACHE SOURCE

You will first need to download the Apache source.

**Tip**  If you are working from somewhere other than the United States, it may be faster to download from a mirror site that is geographically closer to you. See `http://www.apache.org/mirrors/` for a list of mirror sites.

Go to `http://www.apache.org/dist/`. There you will see a list of available files. Select the version you want to download, and click it to begin the download. You will want to save the file to a temporary working directory:

```
apache_1.3.11.tar.Z      21-Jan-2000 17:12   2.6M   1.3.11 compressed source
apache_1.3.11.tar.Z.asc  21-Jan-2000 17:12    1k    PGP signature
apache_1.3.12.tar.gz     21-Jan-2000 17:12   1.6M   1.3.11 gzipped source
apache_1.3.12.tar.gz.asc 21-Jan-2000 17:12    1k    PGP signature
apache_1.3.9.tar.Z       19-Aug-1999 12:17   2.3M   1.3.9 compressed source
apache_1.3.9.tar.Z.asc   19-Aug-1999 12:17    1k    PGP signature
apache_1.3.9.tar.Z.md5   19-Aug-1999 12:17    1k    1.3.9 compressed source
apache_1.3.9.tar.gz      19-Aug-1999 12:17   1.4M   1.3.9 gzipped source
apache_1.3.9.tar.gz.asc  19-Aug-1999 12:17    1k    PGP signature
apache_1.3.9.tar.gz.md5  19-Aug-1999 12:17    1k    1.3.9 gzipped source
...
```

**Tip**

> You can use the MD5 checksum to ensure that you are getting the actual package as intended by the authors. This is especially important if you are downloading a precompiled binary. Doing this will depend upon your operating environment. In Linux, you can run the following command:
>
> # md5sum apache_1.3.12.gz
>
> b4114ed78f296bfe424c4ba05dccc643 apache_1.3.12.tar.gz
>
> Compare the output with the contents of the MD5 file on the Apache site (in this case apache_1.3.12.gz.md5). If they are the same, everything is fine. If they differ you should attempt the download again.

For this example I have chosen to download the Apache_1.3.12 release, in "gzipped" format. Once you have the Apache package downloaded into a temporary directory you will need to expand the archive using gzip or uncompress (which ever corresponds to the format you downloaded), and tar.

**Note**

> gzip (GNU zip, also known as gunzip) is a "free" compression tool provided under GNU's General Public License. Due to its superior compression abilities, it is very popular in the UNIX and Internet communities.
>
> To obtain gzip or to learn more about this popular utility refer to http://www.gzip.org/.

## COMPILING APACHE

The easiest way to compile and install Apache is by using the APACI (Apache Autoconf-style Interface) available with Apache versions 1.3 and higher. The APACI provides an "out-of-the-box" type installation process.

**Note**

> You can still compile and install Apache using the older method. Instructions for doing this are in the INSTALL file in the src directory.

To install Apache using the APACI, change directory to the new temporary directory that contains the Apache files. In most cases you will not need to edit the Configuration file unless you want to install any special modules beyond those that are installed by default. However, if you receive installation errors, read through the documentation in the Configuration file. Common options that may need attention include EXTRA_CFLAGS, LIBS, LDFLAGS, INCLUDES, and CC. Review the INSTALL file in this directory for more information.

To begin the installation process, run the following command:

```
# ./configure -prefix=PREFIX
```

PREFIX is the target root directory for your Web server (for example, `/etc/http/`).

Then build the Apache package using `make`:

```
# make
```

> **Tip**
>
> If you get a `command not found` response that probably indicates that `make` is not in your path. (It is most likely in `/usr/bin/` or `/usr/ccs/bin`). The procedure for modifying your path will vary based on the shell you are running. For bash, run the following commands:
> ```
> # PATH=$PATH:/usr/ccs/bin/
> # export PATH
> ```

`make` will take several minutes to do its thing, depending on the speed of your system. Once it is complete you are ready to install Apache. Run the `make` command again passing it the `install` directive:

```
# make install
```

This will install the Apache Web server and its related files under the PREFIX directory specified in the first step. Once this step is complete you are ready to configure Apache for your specific environment. Refer to the section "Configuring Apache" for details.

# PROJECT: FINDING MORE INFORMATION

You may want to explore the vast subject of Internet Web servers further. If so, the following Web sites, books, and documents will provide you with a wealth of information on Apache, Linux, and Web servers in general.

## LINUX, APACHE, AND OTHER WEB SERVER-RELATED INFORMATION ONLINE

Home of the Linux Documentation Project: `http://www.linuxdoc.org/docs.html`

WWW-related HOWTOs:

`http://linuxdoc.org/HOWTO/WWW-HOWTO.html`

`http://linuxdoc.org/HOWTO/mini/Apache+SSL+PHP+fp.html`

The Apache Group: `http://www.apache.org/`

ApacheWeek, the essential resource for anyone running an Apache server: `http://www.apacheweek.com/`

Apache Server FAQ: http://www.apache.org/docs/misc/FAQ.html

Apache 1.3 User's Guide: http://www.apache.org/docs/

Apache Security Tips: http://www.apache.org/docs/misc/security_tips.html

Red Hat's On-Line Technical Support: http://www.redhat.com/support/docs/howto/

RFC 2616: Hypertext Transfer Protocol—HTTP/1.1: ftp://ftp.isi.edu/in-notes/rfc2616.txt

## LINUX/APACHE-RELATED BOOKS

*Linux: A Network Solution for Your Office* (Sams, Toth, Viktor T. ISBN: 0672316285)

*Professional Apache* (Wainwright, Peter. ISBN: 1861003021)

*Apache Server: Administrator's Handbook* (Kabir, Mohammed J. ISBN: 0764533061)

## OPEN SOURCE INFORMATION

*Open Sources: Voices from the Open Source Revolution* (Dibona, Chris, et al. ISBN: 1565925823) Available online at http://www.oreilly.com/catalog/opensources/book/toc.html

The Official Open Source Website: http://opensource.org/

## HTML RESOURCES

Webmonkey, The Web Developer's Resource: http://webmonkey.com/authoring/html_basics/

*Sams Teach Yourself HTML 4 in 24 Hours* (Oliver, Dick. ISBN: 0672317249)

*HTML 4 Unleashed* (Sams, Darnell, Rick. ISBN: 0672313472)

# CHAPTER 31

# SETTING UP EMAIL SERVICES

## In this chapter

# INTRODUCTION TO EMAIL SERVERS

Running a mail server is a big responsibility. Instead of serving data off of your computer, you're allowing data to come in and leave your system. Unless you're careful, this can lead to problems both on the computer acting as a server and on the clients.

## SECURITY

The biggest catch in serving email is serving it securely. This means more than just being secure from crackers—it means security of service and security of data as well.

The most common mistake when running a mail server is to leave it as an open server that can be used by anyone as a relay. An open relay is often used by spammers to send out thousands of messages to email addresses gathered from newsgroups or mailing lists around the Net. If you have a high bandwidth connection, the spammers will love you!

---

**A True Story: The X-Rated Officemate**

One day I was contacted by university security and informed that a user on my network was sending advertisements for adult Web sites at a rate that was saturating the building bandwidth during the evenings. They gave me the name of the machine that was sending the messages and left me to track down the individual causing the problem. Luckily, I didn't have to look very far. The offending machine was the OS/2 workstation used by the guy in the office next to mine. He had recently reinstalled OS/2 and had turned on its mail software without any protection. In a period of fewer than five days his machine was discovered as an open relay and put to "good" use! University security services, however, were not amused.

---

Depending on your circumstances, allowing a mail server to be used as an open relay could have serious consequences. In many companies this would be considered negligence and may cost you more than a few apologies.

Besides the threat of this kind of attack on your server, you also have to concern yourself with the security of data. If you are allowing login accounts on your machine, it is important that users cannot simply browse other users' email messages. You'll probably also want to make sure that you have a well-defined and documented backup procedure. Telling your users that you do nightly backups will make them feel good—but as soon as someone actually needs to retrieve data, you'd better be sure that you've actually been following your nightly backup procedure. Apologizing to a user who just lost a very important document in email is not going to be a pleasant experience. As with every type of Internet service, don't make promises that your server can't keep!

Another form of security that you should be aware of is security of service. Imagine that you are running a corporate email server with several thousand email accounts on it. It's noon on a Monday and the server starts sizzling in your machine room. What should you do? If you're lucky, you shouldn't have to do much at all because your secondary mail server will pick up the slack. If you don't have a secondary server, you'll probably want to lock yourself in your office for a while.

---

**A True Story: Email to Go**
Recently I was working on a consulting job for a local company that wanted to streamline its Internet services. It was operating Web and mail servers on a variety of equipment that was obviously hastily thrown together. During my stay there, the disk on the email server began to fail. Approximately every hour the server would die. You could then shut it down for 45 minutes, restart it, and get another hour's worth of service. The company was in a panic. There was zero redundancy of servers. I ended up copying 1,500 email accounts to my laptop (a Toshiba Pentium 166) and used Red Hat on the laptop to serve email until a new machine arrived. People would wander into the room look at the dead server and ask, "Where is the email being served from?" I'd point to the machine on my lap and smile. They were frightened.

---

## RESOURCES AND SCALABILITY

Other issues need to be considered besides security—namely making sure that you have the resources available to scale your server as growth occurs. While offering free email accounts to the public may seem like a neat gimmick to attract new users to your Web site or to advertise your services, be aware that there are *lots* of people (a few million at last count) who are equipped to take advantage of your offer. The department that I work for at OSU has gone from serving fewer than 200 email accounts three years ago to several thousand accounts today. Another consideration is that email messages aren't what they used to be. Roughly one year ago I gave up my text-only email world. Email is now, undeniably, a multimedia experience. Graphics, sounds, and even video are sent through email. Attachments are commonplace. Previously, a 1MB or 2MB mail quota would allow a user to have several hundred text messages. Today, 1 MB-2MB is barely enough for a single message. The advent of higher-speed connections has led to much larger messages being sent and received. Just during the writing of this paragraph, for example, I received an email attachment with the latest Windows "attachment of the day" sized at about 1.5MB.

The increased size of email also leads to a decrease in available bandwidth. The average number of messages that are sent or relayed by our server daily is approximately 20,000. If each transaction (messages and protocol communications) averages 10KB in size, roughly 200MB of data is sent out of the mail server each day. This doesn't take into account incoming messages that are roughly double the number of outgoing messages. In total, between 3-4 gigabytes of mail traffic are passed over our network each week. Add in the traffic from the Web, applications, and database servers and you've got a pretty busy network! Be sure that you have both the network and disk capacity to grow your userbase.

## OTHER RISKS

Since mail servers allow arbitrary data to be sent to your internal computers, there is a risk that harmful information could be transmitted to or through your mail server. The Melissa virus is probably the best example of what can happen with the help of a mail server. The Melissa macro virus worked by running macros in an attached document that caused copies of itself to be sent to other users, and so on. There is little that the server operator can do to guard against these attacks. There are some commercial software packages available that scan incoming messages to check for viruses—but these are only as good as the current virus definitions.

Sometimes things happen that aren't meant to be malicious, but end up bringing your server to its knees. Mail loops, for example, happen when two email accounts (usually on different servers) end up forwarding messages to each other. One of the most common occurrences of this is when a user who is subscribed to a mailing list leaves on a vacation and sets an auto-respond message on his or her account. You can easily see the problem set into motion:

1. Mail comes from the mailing list for the vacationing user.

2. The user's auto-responder emails the mailing list back with the I'm on vacation message.

3. The mailing list receives the new messages and forwards it to everyone on the list, including the missing user.

4. Go back to step 1.

This is a sure-fire way to watch your disk space quickly diminish.

In order to be prepared for these sorts of happenings, you need to be fully familiar with your email server software. You should know how to hold items in your server's queue before they are delivered and remove offending items. Much of this comes with practice—but don't assume that since your server is working fine today that something bizarre won't happen tomorrow.

> **Tip**
>
> As with the DNS server, you should seriously consider whether running your own mail server is worth it. If you have an office of ten or so people, your ISP will probably be able to host your email and eliminate the hassle for you. There is no shame in not serving something yourself. The only inconvenience in outsourcing services is when there are frequent changes to the information being served.

# TYPES OF SERVERS

The funny thing about email is that it generally takes more than one type of server to effectively serve email. How do you get your email? On the Web? From an email client? How does the email get to the server that serves your client? This section of the text will focus on the different types of servers and what you need to set up in order to deliver email the way you want. At the minimum, you'll probably want to run at least two different sorts of server processes—and maybe up to four! Let's take a look at these server types now.

## SMTP—SIMPLE MAIL TRANSFER PROTOCOL

For all intents and purposes, SMTP is *the* email protocol. SMTP is responsible for making sure that hundreds of thousands of email messages that are sent daily make their way around the world and end up in your mailbox. The UNIX-based sendmail is the father of all email servers and is included with every copy of Red Hat Linux. The process of getting email where it needs to be can be very complex—mail can bounce around the Internet from server to server before it is finally delivered. If you're running a simple mail server, there is little you'll need to do, however, other than register your mail server with a DNS. SMTP handles receiving an incoming message and passing it on to its final destination.

SMTP runs on port 25 of your server and can easily be demonstrated simply by telneting to your mail server and trying a few commands in the SMTP vocabulary. Understanding how these protocols work is important in debugging potential problems with your configuration. If you learn the basic commands of email of the mail protocols, you'll quickly be able to test your services at a slightly lower level than firing up Netscape Communicator and verifying that it isn't working.

The basic SMTP command set is simple and you'll quickly be able to guess what most of the commands do without ever using them. It's surprising to think of the strangely English-like conversations that happen every day as mail moves over the network:

- **HELO**—Before you can do anything with an SMTP server, you must say "HELO" to identify yourself.

- **MAIL FROM**—Identifies the person that a piece of mail is from.

- **RCPT TO**—The email address of the person who an email is addressed to. You can specify multiple recipients for a single piece of email.

- **DATA**—The body of the email message. You can enter as much data as you'd like, after which you need to enter a "." on a blank line to denote the end.

- **QUIT**—Ends the connection.

The following are optional commands not necessarily supported by all servers:

- **RSET**—Resets all of the information that has been entered into the server previously.

- **HELP**—Requests help for a command.

- **VRFY**—Checks an email address to see if it is a valid recipient. This is often shut off because it poses a security risk—it enables hackers to find usernames for later hacking.

- **EXPN**—Expands an alias on the server. Aliases are lists of addresses that a single address references. For example, `webmaster@testdomain.com` might expand to multiple different addresses for a group of people who maintain the `testdomain.com` Web server.

To test out a server, you can `telnet` into port 25 and try sending yourself a piece of mail. For example, the following is a session with an SMTP server that sends a piece of email from `jray@poisontooth.com` to `jray@ag.ohio-state.edu`.

First, connect to the server:

```
telnet contempt.ag.ohio-state.edu 25
```

The server identifies itself and waits for a command:

```
Trying 140.254.85.226...
Connected to contempt.ag.ohio-state.edu.
Escape character is '^]'.
```

```
220 localhost.localdomain ESMTP sendmail 8.9.3/8.8.7;
Wed, 12 Jan 2000 19:41:42 -0500
```

The first command to send is HELO, followed by your machine name:

```
HELO poisontooth.com
```

The SMTP responds quite pleasantly! It's ready to receive a piece of email for delivery:

```
250 localhost.localdomain Hello poisontooth.com [24.93.97.21],
➥pleased to meet you
```

Specify the recipient using the MAIL FROM command:

```
MAIL FROM: jray@poisontooth.com
```

The server indicates that the sender is okay with a 250 response message:

```
250 jray@poisontooth.com... Sender ok
```

If an error occurs, the server would respond with a 550 numbered message. Since the system now has a sender, it needs a recipient. Add one with the RCPT TO function:

```
RCPT TO: jray@ag.ohio-state.edu
```

The system indicates that the recipient is also acceptable:

```
250 jray@ag.ohio-state.edu... Recipient ok
```

You're now ready to use the DATA keyword to prepare the system for the text of your message:

```
DATA
```

The systems responds as follows:

```
354 Enter mail, end with "." on a line by itself
```

Type your message now, using the period on a blank line to end the email:

```
This is a test of the email server.
--- John

.
```

That's all there is to it:

```
250 TAA19451 Message accepted for delivery
```

To finish up the session, you can just type QUIT to close the connection:

```
QUIT
```

The system answers back with the following message:

```
221 localhost.localdomain closing connection
Connection closed by foreign host.
```

If a problem occurs during the process of sending mail, you now know how to telnet into your SMTP server and check to see where the problem appears.

SMTP is the one email server process that you'll definitely want installed on your computer. It is also the server with the most extensive setup procedure. The software you will be configuring is called sendmail. You'll learn how to use LinuxConf to create a basic configuration later in the chapter. If you install only SMTP service, you'll need to allow users to log in to your system and use Linux-hosted email software such as mail, elm, or pine to check your messages.

## POP—POST OFFICE PROTOCOL

The POP3 protocol is used to move email from the server that holds a user's mailbox onto their computer. If you've used Eudora, Netscape, or any other popular email clients, you've probably connected to a POP server. One of the advantages of running a POP server is that email is moved to the client's computer each time they connect. This lessens the need for the host computer to store thousands of messages. Of course, if the users don't check their mail, it will remain on the server.

One of POP's strongest points is also one of its weakest. By not leaving mail on the server, a user's email is tied to the computer that he or she used to read it. If you check your email on a computer at work, then drive home and check it again on your home computer, you won't see the messages that were received at work. Most POP clients offer a Leave on Server check box, but this is a less-than-perfect solution and requires you to actually remember to use the Leave on Server setting wherever you happen to be. Another protocol called IMAP solves this problem—you'll learn about it shortly.

Like SMTP, the POP3 protocol is simple to use and, in a snap, can be diagnosed using a Telnet session. Running on port 110, POP3 uses these commands to transfer email from the client to the server:

- **USER**—Used during the authentication portion of a POP session, the USER command tells the server what user is connecting to collect their email.
- **PASS**—Also used during the authentication phase, PASS sends the password for the account.
- **STAT**—This command returns information (number of messages and size of messages) about the mailbox on the server.
- **LIST**—LIST is used to show a list of all of the messages and their sizes in a mailbox. Used with a specific message number, it shows the size of that message.
- **RETR**—Retrieves a message from the server. This does not remove the message after deletion.
- **DELE**—Marks a message number for deletion. Any messages that are marked cannot be listed or retrieved.
- **RSET**—Resets messages that are marked for deletion.

- **NOOP**—Performs no operation. Used by client software to generate an OK response from the server.
- **QUIT**—Finishes the POP session and closes the connection.

The optional commands are as follows:

- **TOP**—Rather than retrieving an entire message, the TOP command can return a portion of a message.
- **UIDL**—The UIDL command generates a list of message numbers followed by a unique identifier for each message. This unique identifier is used when the client requests that messages are left on the server. The client software stores the unique IDs of messages it has seen and doesn't download them from the server. Since some POP3 servers don't support this command, you may find your email client downloading multiple copies of mail.

To test a POP3 server, telnet to port 110 of the machine running the service. The following is an example session that shows a message being retrieved from my email account:

```
telnet poisontooth.com 110
```

The server has identified itself and is now waiting for the client to authenticate:

```
Trying 24.93.97.21...
Connected to poisontooth.com.
Escape character is '^]'.
+OK CommuniGate Pro POP3 Server 3.2 ready <4.947728634@ag.ohio-state.edu>
```

Use the USER command to send your username:

```
USER jray
```

The system responds with the following message:

```
+OK please send the PASS
```

The PASS function is needed to transmit the account's password:

```
PASS guessagain
```

The server has authenticated the command, displayed the number of available messages, and is waiting for a command:

```
+OK 438 messages in queue
```

If an error occurs, the server will respond with a negative -ERR prefixed message. To list the available messages and their sizes, use the LIST command now:

```
LIST
```

The system lets you know here that there are 438 messages in the mailbox, so this list is obviously abbreviated:

```
+OK 438 messages
1 2454
```

```
2 7743
3 1404
4 786
5 1228
...
434 903
435 6156
436 2673
437 20971
438 452782
.
```

As you can see, the list consists simply of a message number and a size. The only way to retrieve information about a message is to use the TOP command or RETR to download the message. Let's try using RETR now:

```
RETR 4
```

The systems responds with the following message:

```
+OK message follows
Return-Path: <wray@test.ag.ohio-state.edu>
Received: from [140.254.85.74] (HELO different.ag.ohio-state.edu)
  by ag.ohio-state.edu (CommuniGate Pro SMTP 3.1b4)
  with SMTP id 60011 for jray@poisontooth.com; Wed, 14 Jul 1999 22:10:42 -0400
Received: from [207.54.134.168] ([207.54.134.168] verified) by
  different.ag.ohio-state.edu (Stalker SMTP Server 1.7b2) with SMTP
  id S.0000065705; Wed, 14 Jul 1999 21:07:09 -0500
Subject: Yaa
Date: Wed, 14 Jul 99 22:11:48 -0400
x-mailer: Claris Emailer 1.1
From: Wm Ray <wray@bigmac.ag.ohio-state.edu>
To: "Will Ray" <ray@soyokaze.biosci.ohio-state.edu>,
  "john" <jray@poisontooth.com>
Mime-Version: 1.0
Content-Type: text/plain; charset="US-ASCII"
Message-ID: <auto-000000060011@ag.ohio-state.edu>

Moms home.......

Love Dad
```

Now that the message has been downloaded, you can use the DELE command to erase it:

```
DELE 4
```

The system answers back:

```
+OK marked deleted
```

Finally, use QUIT to complete the session and exit from the server:

```
QUIT
```

The system accepts the command and responds with the following:

```
+OK CommuniGate Pro POP3 Server connection closed
Connection closed by foreign host.
```

PART

V

CH

31

POP is, by far, the most common means for delivering email to client computers. If you are offering email accounts to large numbers of people, it's probably a necessity. Red Hat Linux includes a very capable POP server that works with your existing sendmail configuration. However, if disk space is not an issue and you have the capability to train your users, IMAP may be the protocol for you.

## IMAP—Internet Message Access Protocol

IMAP is quickly becoming a necessity in the workplace. IMAP addresses the "Where's my mail?" issues of the POP protocol. IMAP returns to the idea of keeping mail on the server, not on the client machine. Only the header information for a message is downloaded to the client—the rest of the message is left on the server until the user explicitly tries to read that message. After a message is read, it is tagged as read on the server. When a message is deleted from the client, it is deleted from the server.

The server can maintain multiple folders of email. You're probably quite familiar with the idea of using folders within your email client to keep your email sorted. With IMAP, the folders are maintained on the server, rather than on the client. What's more, the folders can be shared between multiple users. This means that you can create a single mailbox called, for example, "Customer Feedback" that contains all of your user feedback. This mailbox can be shared between all of your customer support personnel. As new messages come in, they are immediately accessible to everyone. If a message is deleted, it disappears from the common folder on each machine.

Since mail is stored on the server, any machine that you configure as an IMAP recipient displays exactly the same message, folders, and so forth, no matter where you are. There is no need to worry about leaving mail at work—when you get home, it will be there. I use IMAP exclusively for my personal email—I can't imagine going back to the POP way of doing things.

The IMAP protocol vocabulary is far more complex than either SMTP or POP, and will not be discussed here for space reasons. Unlike POP, IMAP includes commands to move messages between mailboxes and to perform very complex searches on the server. If you'd like to learn more about the protocol, check out RFC 2060 at http://freesoft.org/CIE/RFC/Orig/rfc2060.txt.

As with the other protocols, Linux includes an IMAP server that can easily be turned on or off with little configuration needed to get up and running. The included IMAP server has gone through many revisions due to security issues, but for the most part, it is now a stable and reliable implementation.

## Web-Based Delivery

The final type of mail service that you may want to offer your users is a Web-based service. You're probably familiar with services such as Hotmail or Yahoo-Mail that offer free email accounts with Web-based access. Offering a Web interface to your mail server enables your users to walk up to a terminal anywhere in the world and check their messages without reconfiguring an email client. For business connectivity, this is a must.

Most Web-based software is proprietary and is not based on any particular protocol. If you're into CGI programming, writing your own Web email client is an interesting exercise. Later in the chapter you'll be introduced to a simple Web client called Majora, written by yours truly, and available as a free download off the Net.

# SETTING UP SENDMAIL

Now that you understand the different services that you can offer, it's time to actually configure your machine to run SMTP, POP, and IMAP. Red Hat Linux comes with everything you need to get up and running within seconds of installation. In fact, if you've installed Red Hat in a server configuration, you already *are* running all the services that you need. If not, you may need to install a few RPMs from your Red Hat installation CD-ROM.

To configure your computer as an SMTP server and give it the capability to send and receive mail, you need the sendmail RPM installed. Use `rpm -q sendmail` to verify that your system has this package:

```
[root@contempt jray]# rpm -q sendmail
sendmail-8.9.3-20
```

If the RPM is not installed, load it from your Red Hat Linux system CD-ROM now, along with the RPMs for `sendmail-cf`, `sendmail-doc`, and `procmail`. When you're sure that sendmail is installed, you need to add it to your runlevel so that it will be started at bootup. To do this, use `chkconfig –add sendmail`. Last, start the service by typing `/etc/rc.d/init.d/sendmail start`.

> **Tip**
>
> If you are running a mail server on the host `mail.testdomain.com` and you want messages that are sent directly to the domain (`blah@testdomain.com`) to go to your mail server, make sure that you have an MX record set in your DNS. Chapter 29, "Setting Up Domain Name Servers," explains DNS and MX records. The mail server needs this to be set on the DNS before it will work correctly. If you're only interested in receiving email on the hostname you've set up, you won't need any MX records.

Most likely your mail server is now up and running! The Red Hat Linux sendmail configuration comes ready to go, but with very little security enabled. Luckily, you can set everything you need for a simple mail server from within LinuxConf. Depending on the complexity of your mail system, you may want to look at additional sendmail documentation. Like the DNS server BIND, sendmail is quite a beast and offers enough features that many books have been written devoted to its configuration. Extensive sendmail information can be found at the official sendmail Web site: `http://www.sendmail.org`.

Before getting into the actual settings, it's best to define a few things that you'll be seeing in the setup:

- **Aliases**—Email usernames that do not point to an actual mailbox. An alias can deliver mail to an external program for processing. It can also expand an email address to multiple recipients—a mini-mailing list.

- **Domain Aliases**—Other names by which your mail server can be called. You might think that if you have 10 different CNAMES aliasing your mail server, you can send email to any of those names; that is not the case. You need to explicitly tell the server which domain names it should accept email for.

- **Mail Server**—The mail server for your network. Since you're configuring the server, this is simply the name of the machine that you are working on. If you want to allow users on other Linux machines to send email, you'll need to configure those computers to have the name of your central mail server.

- **Mail Gateway**—A machine that serves to link email from an internal network to the Internet. If your email server does not have direct access to the Internet, it may need to use a mail gateway.

- **Message Limit**—A limit to the size of messages that are being processed by the SMTP server. If you're worried about gigantic attachments filling your mailboxes, you should probably set a message limit.

- **Queue**—The messages that are waiting for delivery. On most servers, the queue should remain relatively empty. If the queue starts to fill, it's a good sign that somewhere a receiving mail server has failed.

- **Recipient Limit**—A limit to the number of recipients that a message can have. In the example sending mail with the SMTP, multiple recipients could be added using RCPT TO multiple times. Rather than sending thousands of messages separately, most spammers send a single message to thousands of people simultaneously. You should always put a reasonable limit on the number of recipients—even if it is just a count of all the users on your email system.

- **Relaying**—*Relaying* is the process of accepting an incoming message and moving it toward its destination. You need your server to act as a relay for the clients on your network, but not for outside users.

- **Routing**—*Routing* is the process of changing the destination of email (either the destination user, machine, or both). Misconfigured routing rules can disrupt your email system and be difficult to diagnose. Routing is best covered by a sendmail-dedicated textbook.

- **Virtual Domains**—Virtual domains are not covered in this chapter but at some point you may be interested in running virtual domains. *Virtual domains* are domain names that differ from your primary domain, but are hosted on your email server. For example, if your main domain is testdomain.com, you could configure your machine to receive and process email for `anotherdomain.com`. As with routing, if this topic interests you, I urge you to buy a book dedicated to the topic of sendmail configuration.

Now, let's see about configuring some of these things inside LinuxConf. Go ahead and start LinuxConf now, navigating through the hierarchy to the Config, Networking, Server Tasks, Mail Delivery System (sendmail), Basic, Basic Information settings. This configuration screen is shown in Figure 31.1.

**Figure 31.1**
Most of your basic sendmail configuration is done on this screen.

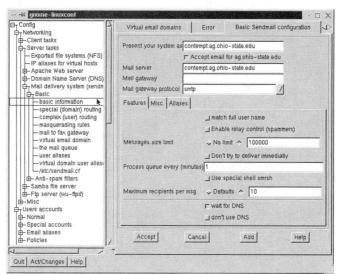

In this example, the name of the mail server is `contempt.ag.ohio-state.edu`. It is configured to limit email messages to 100,000 bytes (a little less than 100KB) and the number of recipients per message to 10 people. You'll want to raise these limits to whatever you feel is appropriate for your situation. Pay close attention to the `Accept Email for ag.ohio-state.edu` setting—this tells sendmail that it will be accepting email for the entire domain. If you've configured an MX record for your domain that points to your email server, make sure that this is clicked in your configuration as well. And last, you will almost certainly want to click Enable Relay Control (spammers). We'll take a look at the relay configuration options in a moment. Now, click the Aliases tab contained on the basic configuration pane. Your screen should now look similar to Figure 31.2.

If there are any aliases that you want to be able to send email to, enter them in this dialog box. Clicking the Add button will create more alias fields if you need them. I've found that it is incredibly easy to add aliases to a machine and forget to add them to the server's alias listing. If you try sending email to your machine and it doesn't work, make sure that the alias you're using to reference it is included here. You do not need to change any other settings in this dialog. Next, click the User Aliases item from the LinuxConf menu (see Figure 31.3).

User aliases enable a piece of email to reach multiple recipients from a single address (a mailing list) or be processed by a program. To edit one of the listed aliases, double-click it.

Click the Add button to create a new alias. Figure 31.4 shows a new `testlist` that is being added to the system.

**Figure 31.2**

If you have any aliases for your main server, you should add them here.

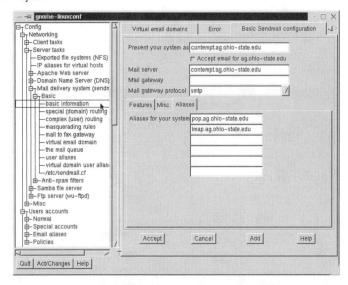

**Figure 31.3**

There are many user aliases already defined.

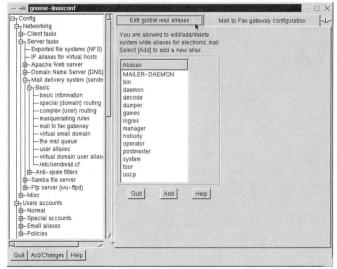

Alias configuration is very easy. First, configure an alias name—this will be the name that you send email to in order for the message to be distributed to multiple recipients. Next, add the names of the users that you want the address to send to into the available fields. If you run out of fields, clicking Add will give you more entry points. A second option for listing names is to enter the name of a text file into the List File field. This file should be a plain text file that contains a list of email addresses. It's an easy way to allow a user on your system to administrate a simple mailing list.

**Figure 31.4**
Aliases can be used as simple mailing lists.

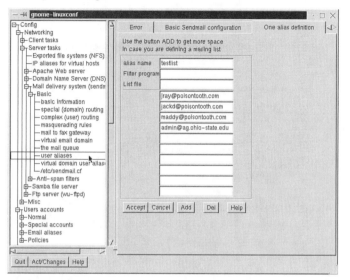

If, instead of being forwarded to several accounts, you'd prefer that a program process the mail, put the complete path of your program in the Filter Program field. The program will receive the incoming messages on standard input.

When you're done configuring your aliases, finish up the configuration process by expanding the Anti-Spam Filters in the LinuxConf section and clicking one of the available filter options. These sections are virtually identical in operation, but perform slightly different functions:

- **Rejected Senders**—If you have a known hostname or IP address that is sending spam to your clients, you can enter the offending address here. This can be either a fully qualified hostname, an IP address, a domain, or a portion of an IP address. Incoming mail will be rejected with an error message that you define.

- **Relay for by IP**—You can enter IP addresses (or portions of IP addresses) for the hosts that you plan to provide relay service for. If you have customers that need to check their email through dial-up connections, you'll need to make sure that their ISP's networks are included here.

- **Relay for by Name**—Identical to the previous setting, except you can set information by hostname or domain name.

- **Relay to Hosts**—If you want to choose where messages can be relayed to, this section is for you. A good way to keep your server unattractive to spammers—but useful for business communications—is to limit the relay service to addresses on your local subnet. This will allow communications *to* local addresses, but will not let messages be relayed to outside servers. This is a bit restrictive, however, unless your email is solely for internal support.

PART

**V**

CH

**31**

Each of these configuration screens works by adding entries to a list of restrictions. Choose the spam filter option you want and click Add, enter the appropriate host or IP information, and then click Accept. Figure 31.5 shows the process of adding a rejected sender at baddomain.com to the system.

**Figure 31.5**
LinuxConf allows you to configure several anti-spam options in send-mail.

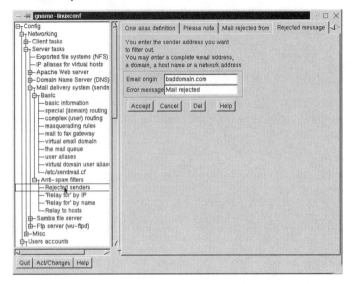

With your sendmail options set, you can quit from LinuxConf and test your mail server. You should be able to send email to your computer and read it with a local client. Now let's configure your system so it can be retrieved with a POP or IMAP client.

**Tip**

To learn more about spam prevention techniques, check out http://www.abuse.net/, the Network Abuse Clearinghouse. You can also look into the real-time blacklisting services offered by the Mail Abuse Prevention System at http://maps.vix.com/. This free service maintains an updated list of known spammers that can be queried automatically by sendmail.

# SETTING UP POP AND IMAP SERVERS

Reading email using mail is probably not the best user experience in the world, so you'll want to get a POP or IMAP server up and running as quickly as possible. Once again, Red Hat Linux comes through. You've already got the software to be up and running in a matter of seconds—the ipopd and imapd servers. In order to use POP or IMAP, you need to have the IMAP RPM installed. You can query your system for the package with rpm -q imap:

```
[jray@contempt jray]$ rpm -q imap
imap-4.5-4
```

If you don't have the RPM, you'll need to install it now. After the servers are installed, you'll need to make sure that the appropriate entries have been added to the `/etc/inetd.conf`-configuration file.

---

**What Is** `inetd.conf`**?**
This is probably the first time you've heard of the `inetd.conf` file, but it is very important for server operations. Some servers, such as your DNS, Apache, and sendmail processes are started when you first boot your computer and run constantly. There are other processes such as POP, IMAP, Telnet, and FTP that only run when necessary. The `inetd` or *Internet daemon* process monitors your machine for incoming connections and starts the appropriate server software. This process is configured through the `/etc/inetd.conf` file.

---

Open the `/etc/inetd.conf`file in your favorite text editor. Look for a section in the file that looks like this (if you can't find it, you'd better add it!):

```
#
# Pop and imap mail services et al
#
#pop-2   stream  tcp     nowait  root    /usr/sbin/tcpd ipop2d
pop-3    stream  tcp     nowait  root    /usr/sbin/tcpd ipop3d
imap     stream  tcp     nowait  root    /usr/sbin/tcpd imapd
```

PART

**V**

CH

**31**

These lines control the activation of the POP2, POP3, and IMAP servers. If you don't want to run a particular service, you can comment it out from this file by putting # in front of the appropriate line. The sample configuration here has POP2 commented out. POP2 is the first implementation of the Post Office Protocol and is no longer in use. If your clients are using software written in the past four years, they're using POP3 clients.

With `inetd.conf` set up, you need to tell the inetd process to reread its configuration file. The easiest way to do this is to send an interrupt signal (`-1`) to the process—`killall -1 inetd`.

That's all there is to it! If you have a POP or IMAP client, you should be able to access your email immediately. There's still one more thing you need to worry about, though—security!

## Securing Your POP or IMAP Server

Looking back at the entries you just edited in `/etc/inetd.conf`, you may notice that at the end of each line a program called `/usr/sbin/tcpd` is referenced before the actual IMAP or POP server program. This is a special piece of software called a TCP wrapper that sits in between the incoming connection and the server process. The TCP wrappers determine whether a connection should be considered valid based on IP address or hostname, and even performs checks to see if the incoming connection is being spoofed. If the software rules that the connection is bad, then it is dropped immediately. If not, it is forwarded to the server program for processing.

---

**What Is a Spoofed Connection?**
A *spoofed* connection is a connection that appears to be from a specific host, but is actually coming from somewhere else. Hacking software often includes the capability to spoof the source of an attack.

---

The files that control the operation of the TCP wrappers are /etc/hosts.allow and /etc/hosts.deny. As you may have guessed, hosts.allow is a list of hosts that should be allowed to access your server, and /etc/hosts.deny is a list of those that shouldn't. Typically, you'd want to deny everything and only allow connections that you know.

Here is an example of my /etc/hosts.deny file:

```
#
# hosts.deny    This file describes the names of the hosts which are
#               *not* allowed to use the local INET services, as decided
#               by the '/usr/sbin/tcpd' server.
#
# The portmap line is redundant, but it is left to remind you that
# the new secure portmap uses hosts.deny and hosts.allow.  In particular
# you should know that NFS uses portmap!
ALL:ALL
```

All connections for all processes are denied. Creating your deny file like this will serve you well, at least until your server is up and running. Red Hat Linux installs many processes that can be accessed through inetd—unless you protect your machine soon after installation, you're almost certainly going to get hacked.

Once you've locked your system down, you need to open service up to domains that should be about to access inetd processes. You can enter complete hostnames, IP addresses, or partial domains and IP addresses in the control list of either file.

The following is an example /etc/hosts.allow file:

```
#
# hosts.allow   This file describes the names of the hosts which are
#               allowed to use the local INET services, as decided
#               by the '/usr/sbin/tcpd' server.
#
ALL: LOCAL, 164.107.34.2, postoffice.ag.ohio-state.edu, 192.168.0., 140.254.85.,
 199.18.97.68, .erienet.net, 24.93.121.242
```

Here, inetd services are opened up to several different hosts and domains. The LOCAL keyword allows connections to be made by machine on the local subnet. Remember to take into account customers who will be dialing in on outside ISPs who will need to access the system. If it becomes too difficult to define who should access the services, you may have to use hosts.deny to deny access to specific hosts. You can learn more about the format of these files by reading the hosts_access man page: man 5 hosts_access.

# CASE STUDY: WEB ACCESS TO EMAIL

You've got your email server up and running, and now you want to enable users to read their email from elsewhere. Unfortunately, there isn't much built-in support for this functionality in Red Hat 6.2. There are commercial packages, including the incredible CommuniGate Pro (http://www.stalker.com), that offer excellent Web interfaces to email servers. Commercial solutions, however, are often priced out of reach of a startup company and contain functionality that isn't needed.

As a potential solution, I'm offering my Web-based POP client for free downloading from my Web site at `http://jray.ag.ohio-state.edu/`. The software is written in Perl, works with existing POP servers, and provides a very simple Web-based front end to an email system. I'm quite positive that it also has its share of bugs, but it's open for you to explore and modify as you see fit.

The software's name is Majora, and it allows remote users equipped with a Web browser to check their POP email (it does not delete messages from the server unless explicitly told to) and compose and send replies (see Figure 31.6).

There are several other packages you might want to look into for creating a Web-based email services, such as IMP and TWIG. Check out LinuxApps at `http://www.linuxapps.com/` for an extensive list of mail-related software.

**Figure 31.6**
Majora offers a simple Web interface to POP email servers.

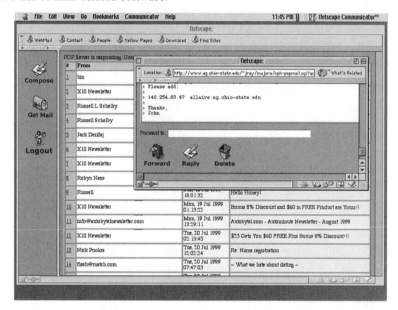

To get Majora up and running on your system, first download and decompress the Majora archive file: `tar -zxfmajora.tar.gz`.

You should now have a single directory called `majora` that contains all of the support files necessary to run the software. This directory needs to be placed within a Web-accessible area that has CGI-Execute permissions turned on. Check out Chapter 30, "Using Apache to Serve the Web," for more information on how to set up a Web server.

Before you can use the software, you'll need to configure a few variables in the `nph-popmail.cgi` file to match your system. Open the `nph-popmail.cgi` file in your text editor and look at it now:

```
#!/usr/bin/perl

#### Color information for the display
```

```
$NormalColor="BGCOLOR=\"#FFFFE9\"'";
$SelectedColor="BGCOLOR=\"#A0A0DD\"'";
$HeadingColor="BGCOLOR=\"#D3D3FA\"'";
$NumberColor="BGCOLOR=\"#CDCDDD\"'";
$SubjectColor="BGCOLOR=\"#FFEDED\"'";
$DateColor="BGCOLOR=\"#EDFFED\"'";

#### Largest message (in bytes) to allow the user to view online
$bigmessage=10000;

#### URL to this CGI
$popmailcgi="http://www.ag.ohio-state.edu/~jray/majora/nph-popmail.cgi";

#### SMTP server used to send mail... go ahead use leviathan, see if I care :)
$smtpserver="leviathan.ag.ohio-state.edu";

#### This server's hostname (in case `hostname` doesn't work)
$thishost="leviathan.ag.ohio-state.edu";

#### Directory with support files - now all in the same dir w/ everything else
$support=".";  # Now the same dir as the script
```

Most of the information in the configuration can be left as is except for the variables $thishost, $smtpserver, and $popmailcgi. Set these to the hostname running the CGI, the SMTP server you want to use to send mail, and the URL that is used to access the CGI on your machine. You can also limit the size of messages that can be viewed online (no sense in letting someone download a 50MB file to their Web browser) and the colors for the generated pages.

Once configured, simply point your Web browser toward the Majora directory and away you go!

Please note, however, that this is not a perfect solution to the email access issue, nor is it offered with any guarantee. If you choose to use the software, you do so at your own risk. Feel free to make any changes you see fit. Majora was originally created to allow people visiting a local convention to check their email. It served its purpose and has since been released into the public domain.

> **Tip**
>
> When trying to determine what mail services to run, try to balance your resources with your users' needs. If you support users who must access email from multiple places (mobile users), IMAP will probably work best for you. If disk space is an issue, POP3 helps keep your disk and network usage to a minimum. Web-based email offers some of the benefits of each—access from anywhere without the constant network connection of IMAP.

After you've mastered a basic configuration as discussed here, be sure to take the time to read the man pages for sendmail and its configuration files. Email serving is yet another case of "a minute to learn" and two or three lifetimes to master.

# SETTING UP TELNET AND FTP SERVICES

**In this chapter**

# INTRODUCTION TO TELNET, RLOGIN, SSH, AND FTP

As the administrator of a network server, you almost certainly need to provide a means by which your users (and yourself) can access the server. You need to have the ability to control your server remotely and to transfer files to and from it.

While these may seem like obvious functions, they're not necessarily up and running on your computer. This chapter will cover the basics of making sure your machine has remote access turned on. In Chapter 28, "Building an Internet Server," you learned about VNC as a means of controlling your computer—this is a perfectly acceptable alternative to using command-line remote access.

**Tip**

> VNC stands for "Virtual Network Computing." The VNC server package is offered free for many computing platforms including Linux. It enables you to remotely view your desktop with remarkable speed. This is often a friendlier alternative to command-line based access methods. Chapter 28 deals with the installation and configuration of VNC.

## THE REMOTE TERMINALS: TELNET, RLOGIN, SSH

By now, you're quite familiar with accessing the command line of your Red Hat Linux computer to run and configure applications. The trio of remote terminal access programs—Telnet, rlogin, and ssh—gives you this same ability from remote locations. Telnet and rlogin are very easy to use and require little configuration. The problem with these protocols is that they are clear-text protocols. All the information that you use to access your computer is visible to a cracker that happens to be sniffing your network connection.

---

**What Is a Sniffer?**

A *sniffer*, or *packet sniffer*, is usually a computer whose network interface card is running in "promiscuous" mode. This is a special mode of operation that enables the computer to collect all information on the network. If you share a single network backbone with other Linux computers and one happens to be compromised, it could easily be used to collect passwords from your network. I've recently experienced "sniffs" around campus that have collected hundreds of passwords. Besides passwords, a sniffer can monitor a particular computer to determine what software is installed, what it is used for, and whether the machine is a good target for hacking.

---

Depending on your network security, this might not bother you—I have several machines behind a firewall between which I feel very comfortable telneting. If, on the other hand, you share your network with other users or have a direct connection to the Internet, it would be very wise to avoid these plain-text protocols entirely.

So, what does that leave in order to connect to your machine? Wouldn't it be nice if there were a terminal utility that encrypted data *before* it was sent over the network? Luckily, there is! The secure shell program or ssh solves the problem of allowing dangerous network traffic to be encrypted before it "hits the wire."

**Tip**

You'll immediately eliminate a ton of security risks if you eliminate the need for your users to connect to the server at a command-line level. Most users will probably be maintaining their email on their client computers. The only real reason that most people need to remotely access their computers is to transfer files for Web sites and such. If this is the case for your setup, consider not allowing remote terminal access at all. Apache, for example, can be configured to allow Netscape users to save and edit Web pages directly from their browser. If it turns out that users do need to access command-line utilities, consider replacing the standard shells with something that limits their ability to run software to a known set of applications.

## FTP: THE REMOTE FILE TRANSFER PROTOCOL SOFTWARE

Telnet, rlogin, and ssh handle your command-line connections, but they aren't very good for transferring files (actually, that isn't entirely correct, but we'll get back to that in a moment). FTP, or *File Transfer Protocol*, is the foundation of file transfer on the Internet. If a client has an Internet-connected computer, it will have an FTP utility. Typically, FTP programs for desktop computer platforms are extremely easy to use. A list of files is shown on the remote system and on the local computer—and you can move files between these lists. FTP has very little overhead and is extremely fast. If you're used to copying files using Windows SMB-based networking, you're going to be impressed with the speed gains that FTP has to offer.

**Know Your Clients.**
You're not going to like this. FTP is a great protocol, and is precisely what is used to maintain many Web servers. Your average Linux user will pull up a command prompt and move files around with FTP with no problem. Unfortunately, we do not yet live in a Linux world. If you're supporting Windows clients, it's likely that you're going to have to support SMB (Samba) services as well. While this may sound like a bit of a gripe (and it is), I've come to recognize it as a sad fact. Proprietary protocols drive Windows; in order to attract people to using Linux servers and desktops, you must support these protocols as well. Chapter 24, "Sharing Linux/Windows Resources with Samba," is a good read if you're going to support Windows clients.

Unfortunately, even though FTP is a simple, fast protocol, it is, like Telnet, an unsecure protocol. If each user on the system has FTP access, their passwords are just as likely to be sniffed. Even so, if you are in control of what is plugged into the network that gives your computer connectivity, this isn't an issue. Arbitrary computers on the Internet can't just sniff packets from your computer. The network traffic must exist on the same network with the sniffing computer in order to be compromised.

If secure network transfers are indeed necessary, you can use the scp application that comes with ssh to quickly copy files between different machines that are also running ssh.

# SETTING UP TELNET AND RLOGIN

If you've installed Linux, you've got Telnet and rlogin installed. (That was pretty simple, wasn't it?) There is very little configuration that you need to perform with these utilities other than turning them on and off and limiting their access. Nonetheless, let's take a look at them now.

## TELNET

Telnet is activated through the Internet daemon, `inetd`, upon an incoming connection on port 23. To enable Telnet service on your machine, edit your `/etc/inetd.conf` file:

```
#
# These are standard services.
#
telnet   stream  tcp    nowait  root    /usr/sbin/tcpd    in.telnetd
```

Make sure that the telnet line in the configuration file is not commented out (with a #); if it is you'll need to restart `inetd` upon making the changes to the configuration file - `killall -1 inetd`.

To test the Telnet service on your local machine, go ahead and attempt an initial connection to `localhost`:

```
[jray@kottmandhcp jray]$ telnet localhost
Trying 127.0.0.1...
Connected to localhost.
Escape character is '^]'.

Red Hat Linux release 6.2 (Zoot)
Kernel 2.2.14-5.0 on an i586
login:
```

If Telnet service has been disabled on a computer, the connection will be refused. If you're moving from a Telnet-accessible system to a more secure system like ssh, you may want to add a warning message that is displayed before the connection is dropped. To do this, create a small program that displays your warning message and exits by following these steps:

1. For starters, enter this program into a text editor and save it as `noconnect.c`.

   ```c
   #include <stdio.h>

   void main() {
     printf("This server does not allow telnet connections.\n");
     printf("Please contact jray@poisontooth.com for access information.\n\n");
     printf("1999/2000 - PoisonTooth.com\n");
   }
   ```

2. Compile the software with `cc -o noconnect noconnect.c`.

3. Move the resulting noconnect binary to a common path, like `/usr/local/bin`.

4. Edit your `/etc/inetd.conf` file to look like this:

   ```
   #
   # These are standard services.
   ```

```
#
telnet  stream  tcp    nowait  root    /usr/sbin/tcpd /usr/local/bin/noconnect
```

5. Restart `inetd` with this command: `killall -1 inetd`.

6. Now, upon telneting into your computer, you should be greeted with the following:

```
[root@contempt /root]# telnet poisontooth.com
Trying 24.93.97.21...
Connected to poisontooth.com.
Escape character is '^]'.
This server does not allow telnet connections.
Please contact jray@poisontooth.com for access information.

1999/2000 - PoisonTooth.com
Connection closed by foreign host.
```

That's it for Telnet! Now let's take a look at another method of connecting your remote systems—rlogin.

## RLOGIN

rlogin stands for `remote login`. Like Telnet, it is also included on every Red Hat Linux system. For the end user, the biggest difference between Telnet and rlogin is that Telnet is a universally accessible protocol. rlogin is typically used to communicate between Linux and UNIX computers. Client platforms other than UNIX and its derivatives may have difficulty communicating with your system.

As with Telnet, you first need to edit your `/etc/inetd.conf` file to enable the remote shell if it is disabled:

```
#
# Shell, login, exec, comsat and talk are BSD protocols.
#
login   stream  tcp    nowait  root    /usr/sbin/tcpd in.rlogind
```

Remove any comment that is in front of the login line, and then restart the `inetd` process with `killall -1 inetd`.

Now, try `rlogin localhost` to connect to your rlogin-enabled server. You'll notice that you are not prompted for a username—rlogin assumes that you want to log into the remote host (or, in this case, the same host) with the same username under which you have connected.

```
[jray@contempt jray]$ rlogin localhost
Password:
Last login: Sat Jan 15 21:53:34 from dhcp9397021.columbus.happy.com
```

If you're on a Linux-only network, using rlogin may be a better solution than Telnet. It is a less frequently used protocol than Telnet, which makes it at least slightly less vulnerable to hacking—security through obscurity. Remember that you can also secure processes that are started through `inetd` by limiting access to them with TCP wrappers. Chapter 31, "Setting Up Email Services," discusses securing IMAP and POP3 servers using this technique.

PART

V

CH

32

## SETTING UP SSH

The secure shell is the best way to provide remote access to your computer. Data is encrypted during transfer, and there is no need to be concerned about network packet sniffing. ssh can be used to encrypt any network traffic—not just a terminal session. This section of the chapter, however, focuses on using ssh to securely connect to a remote computer and to securely copy files between them.

Unlike Telnet and rlogin, ssh does not come on your system—you need to install it before you can use it. ssh can be downloaded from `http://www.cs.hut.fi/ssh`.

The current major version number of ssh is version 2. I prefer to stick with version 1 of the software due to compatibility issues with some client software. Make sure that no matter which version you choose to install, you keep it consistent on all of your platforms. From my experience, version 1 is still, by far, the most common installation of the software.

The version of software referenced in this text is 1.2.27. Installation of future versions should be very similar. Follow these steps in your installation:

1. Decompress and unarchive the software with this command:

   `tar -zxf ssh-1.2.27.tar.gz.`

2. Change your working directory so that you are in the root level of the source code distribution:

   `cd ssh-1.2.27`

3. Run the configure program, which will configure the source distribution so that it is ready to be compiled: `./configure`. This process may take several minutes depending on the speed of your machine.

   ```
   [root@contempt ssh-1.2.27]# ./configure
   creating cache ./config.cache
   checking host system type... i686-unknown-linux
   checking cached information... ok
   checking for gcc... gcc
   checking whether the C compiler (gcc  ) works... yes
   checking whether the C compiler (gcc  ) is a cross-compiler... no
   checking whether we are using GNU C... yes
   checking whether gcc accepts -g... yes
   ...
   creating ./config.status
   creating Makefile
   creating demos/Makefile
   creating mpbsd/Makefile
   creating mpf/Makefile
   creating mpf/tests/Makefile
   creating mpn/Makefile
   creating mpn/tests/Makefile
   creating mpq/Makefile
   creating mpq/tests/Makefile
   creating mpz/Makefile
   creating mpz/tests/Makefile
   ```

4. Use the `make` command to compile the software. Once again, this may take a while; feel free to take a coffee break now.

```
root@contempt ssh-1.2.27]# make
gcc -pipe -c -I.  -I./gmp-2.0.2-ssh-2 -I./zlib-1.0.4 -DHAVE_CONFIG_H
-DHOST_KEY_FILE=\"/etc/ssh_host_key\" -DHOST_CONFIG_FILE=\"/etc/ssh_
➥config\"
-DSERVER_CONFIG_FILE=\"/etc/sshd_config\" -DSSH_PROGRAM=\"/usr/local/bin/
➥ssh1\"
-DETCDIR=\"/etc\" -DPIDDIR=\"/var/run\" -DSSH_BINDIR=\"/usr/local/bin\"
-DTIS_MAP_FILE=\"/etc/sshd_tis.map\" -D_GNU_SOURCE -g -O2 -I/usr/X11R6/
➥include ssh.c
gcc -pipe -c -I.  -I./gmp-2.0.2-ssh-2 -I./zlib-1.0.4 -DHAVE_CONFIG_H
-DHOST_KEY_FILE=\"/etc/ssh_host_key\" -DHOST_CONFIG_FILE=\"/etc/
➥ssh_
➥config\"
-DSERVER_CONFIG_FILE=\"/etc/sshd_config\" -DSSH_PROGRAM=\"/usr/local/bin/
Vssh1\''
-DETCDIR=\"/etc\" -DPIDDIR=\"/var/run\V -DSSH_BINDIR=\"/usr/local/bin\"
-DTIS_MAP_FILE=\"/etc/sshd_tis.map\V -D_GNU_SOURCE -g -O2
-I/usr/X11R6/include sshconnect.c
...
gcc -pipe -c -I.  -I./gmp-2.0.2-ssh-2 -I./zlib-1.0.4 -DHAVE_CONFIG_H
-DHOST_KEY_FILE=\"/etc/ssh_host_key\" -DHOST_CONFIG_FILE=\"/etc/
➥ssh_config\"
-DSERVER_CONFIG_FILE=\"/etc/sshd_config\V -DSSH_PROGRAM=\"/usr/local/bin/
➥ssh1\"
-DETCDIR=\"/etc\V -DPIDDIR=\"/var/run\V -DSSH_BINDIR=\"/usr/local/bin\"
-DTIS_MAP_FILE=\"/etc/sshd_tis.map\'' -D_GNU_SOURCE -g -O2 -I/usr/X11R6/
➥include ssh
-askpass.c
rm -f ssh-askpass
gcc -pipe  -o ssh-askpass ssh-askpass.o xmalloc.o -L/usr/X11R6/lib -lSM
➥-lICE -lX11
-lnsl -lbsd -lcrypt -L/usr/local/lib  -lutil
```

5. When the process is finished, you'll need to install the newly created binaries. This is as simple as typing `make install` in the source code directory. Make sure that you are logged in to the system as root; otherwise the installation will fail. During the installation process, the software will generate random keys to be used in the encryption process.

```
[root@contempt ssh-1.2.27]# make install
umask 022; if test '!' -d /usr/local; then \
  mkdir /usr/local; fi; \
if test '!' -d /usr/local; then \
  mkdir /usr/local; fi; \
if test '!' -d /etc; then \
  mkdir /etc; fi; \
if test '!' -d /usr/local/bin; then \
  mkdir /usr/local/bin; fi; \
...
Generating 1024 bit host key.
Initializing random number generator...
Generating p:  ..++ (distance 30)
Generating q:  ..........++ (distance 106)
Computing the keys...
Testing the keys...
```

```
Key generation complete.
Your identification has been saved in /etc/ssh_host_key.
Your public key is:
1024 33 1196233549929895873726625347634779763525307589323493013721558 7067
➥191374220044065672351861
1763051793621726739436183210621528013587073895558471320715653963559350340
➥4482220004230058
448000195654582808288324407156412085080932773033515903076336256406174201
➥06926073991917975
966570275442301395179661279834712188738849 root@contempt.ag.ohio-state.edu
Your public key has been saved in /etc/ssh_host_key.pub
```

6. The last step is to configure the software to start when your machine boots. Unlike Telnet and rlogin, ssh requires a process to be running at all times. You will need to add an entry to /etc/rc.d/rc.local that starts the /usr/local/sbin/sshd process. The following listing is a file that can be added to your /etc/rc.d/init.d directory to enable you to easily start and stop the software. Name the file sshd.

```sh
#!/bin/sh
#
# sshd          This shell script takes care of starting and stopping
#               ssh.
#
# chkconfig: 345 60 60
# description: sshd is the secure shell daemon.  It is needed by slogin and
#              scp.
# Source function library.
. /etc/rc.d/init.d/functions
# Source networking configuration.
. /etc/sysconfig/network
# Check that networking is up.
[ ${NETWORKING} = "no" ] && exit 0
[ -f /usr/local/sbin/sshd ] || exit 0
# See how we were called.
case "$1" in
  start)
        # Start daemons.
        echo -n "Starting sshd: "
        /usr/local/sbin/sshd
        RETVAL=$?
        echo
        [ $RETVAL -eq 0 ] && touch /var/lock/subsys/sshd
        ;;
  stop)
        # Stop daemons.
        echo -n "Shutting down sshd: "
        killall -9 sshd
        RETVAL=$?
        echo
        [ $RETVAL -eq 0 ] && rm -f /var/lock/subsys/sshd
        ;;
  restart|reload)
        $0 stop
        $0 start
        RETVAL=$?
        ;;
  *)
```

```
            echo "Usage: sshd {start¦stop¦restart}"
            exit 1
    esac
    exit $RETVAL
```

7. Add sshd to your runlevel by typing chkconfig --add sshd.

8. Start your new service by typing /etc/rc.d/init.d/sshd start.

You should now be able to connect to your computer using ssh. The program you'll use to do this is slogin. Type slogin localhost to test your installation now.

```
[root@contempt ssh-1.2.27]# slogin localhost
root@127.0.0.1's password:
Last login: Sat Jan 15 20:41:14 2000 from dhcp9397021.columbus.happy.com
You have new mail.
```

As you can see, the process is very similar to Telnet and rlogin—the difference is that the connection and anything that I type is encrypted. Since the password is securely transmitted, logging in directly as root is possible without representing the security risk that was present in Telnet.

> **Tip**
>
> The sshd process offers a variety of advanced options that you may want to learn about. For example, if you want to turn off the capability for root to log in, you must edit the /etc/sshd_config file and alter the PermitRootLogin yes line to read PermitRootLogin no. Many other parameters that affect the operation are also included in the file. Please read the sshd man page for more information.

PART
V

CH
32

In order to connect to your other machines, you'll need to complete this process on each one.

### scp

Without knowing it, you may have also just eliminated the need to use FTP on your system. ssh has installed another utility on your system called scp, or *secure copy*. Secure copy is exactly what it sounds like—it copies data between computers using an entirely encrypted connection. Using FTP to transfer a document that contains text will make that text visible to anyone on the network who happens to have sniffers running.

To use scp, you use the following format for the command:

scp *filename1 username@remotehostname:remotefilename*.

For example, to copy a file named README from contempt.ag.ohio-state.edu to the account of user jray on poisontooth.com, you would issue the following command:

```
[root@contempt test]# scp README jray@poisontooth.com:newREADME
Host key not found from the list of known hosts.
Are you sure you want to continue connecting (yes/no)? yes
Host 'poisontooth.com' added to the list of known hosts.
jray@poisontooth.com's password:
README                        ¦      5 KB ¦  5.3 kB/s ¦ ETA: 00:00:00 ¦ 100%
```

To make things even better, scp can copy files between two remote machines, not just your local connection and a remote machine. To do this, use the entire username@hostname:filename pattern in place of the initial filename.

The first time that you connect to an unknown host using scp or slogin, it will ask you if it should add the host's public key to the list of known keys on your system. This is harmless and will only occur the first time you connect.

### WHAT ARE THESE KEYS ANYWAY?

The key system is a very common and important method of encrypting and transmitting data. There are two keys that are used when encrypting and decrypting data: the public key and the private key. These keys are related, but cannot be derived from one another. They are generated by software and, chances are, you've already seen people passing public PGP keys around in email. The public key is distributed to anyone who needs to decrypt your data. The private key is just that—private. The process of encrypting and decrypting data goes something like this:

1. You transmit your public key to the computer or party that needs to be able to encrypt data. The data is then encrypted with your public key. Interestingly enough, the persons or things encrypting the data cannot decrypt what they just encoded! They can only encrypt it.

2. You receive the data and can decrypt it using your private key.

3. If you want to send data, you reverse the process, sending the data encrypted with the remote site's public key.

If the private key is ever compromised, data is no longer safe—third parties could then decrypt the data.

This process is handled internally by your ssh software, although it is possible to manually set your public keys.

> **Tip**
>
> SSH has a great deal more functionality than was was discussed here. You can use ssh to secure any network traffic, including traffic generated by applications such as VNC. You can also install your keys on other machines to allow password-less access. SSH is a very complete package for encrypting your network communications. Be sure to read the included documentation for more information.

# SETTING UP FTP

If you've decided that you do indeed need to run an FTP server, you're in luck because Red Hat has included one of the most popular FTP servers in the world, wu-ftpd, with your copy of Linux. If you didn't install Red Hat Linux as a server machine, you may need to add a few

RPMs before you are ready to start the server. You need to define what kind of FTP service you want to offer in order to choose the right RPM combinations.

- **Authenticated service**—If you intend to offer FTP service only to users who have accounts on your system you will need only the `wu-ftpd` RPM.

- **Anonymous service**—Anonymous FTP service means that anyone can connect to your computer. You've probably logged into anonymous sites before using "anonymous" as the username and your email address as the password. You'll need both the `wu-ftpd` and the `anonftp` RPMs.

---

**Be Wary of Running an Anonymous Server!**
Anonymous FTP servers allow *anyone* in the world (unless you explicitly lock out individual IP addresses or domains) to connect to your system. If you enable write access for anonymous users, you're opening up your system to becoming a pirate storage site. Monitor your system carefully if you must run an anonymous server.

---

Check to see if these RPMs are installed on your machine using `rpm -q anonftp` and `rpm -q wu-ftpd`:

```
[root@pointy jray]# rpm -q anonftp
anonftp-3.0-3
[root@pointy jray]# rpm -q wu-ftpd
wu-ftpd-2.6.0-3
```

Make sure you've installed these files before continuing. When you've got the FTP server installed on your system, you need to make sure that the FTP server is enabled in the `/etc/inetd.conf` file. Open the file in your favorite editor and look for the section related to FTP:

```
#
# These are standard services.
#
ftp     stream tcp    nowait root    /usr/sbin/tcpd  in.ftpd -l -a
```

Be sure that the line is not commented out with the # symbol. As a last step, restart the `inetd` process: `killall -1 inetd`.

The FTP server should now be up and running. No matter what your choice as an install method, you should be able to `ftp` into your own account on the machine `localhost`:

```
[root@pointy jray]# ftp localhost
Connected to localhost.
220 pointy FTP server (Version wu-2.6.0(1) Mon Feb 28 10:30:36 EST 2000) ready.
Name (localhost:jray): jray
331 Password required for jray.
Password:
230 User jray logged in.
Remote system type is UNIX.
Using binary mode to transfer files.
ftp>
```

If you did install anonymous FTP support, you should be able to `ftp` in anonymously. Try doing this now:

```
[root@pointy jray]# ftp localhost
Connected to localhost.
220 pointy FTP server (Version wu-2.6.0(1) Mon Feb 28 10:30:36 EST 2000) ready.
Name (localhost:jray): anonymous
331 Guest login ok, send your complete e-mail address as password.
Password:
230 Guest login ok, access restrictions apply.
Remote system type is UNIX.
Using binary mode to transfer files.
```

Looks like everything is working! Now there are a few things you might want to enable on your computer so that you can better manage your server.

## ANONYMOUS WRITES

First, if you have anonymous FTP service running, it may be nice to enable remote users to write to a directory. As it is, the anonymous FTP server installation does not add write permission to the pub directory in the ~ftp/ directory structure. If you want to allow anonymous writes on your machine, create a directory that belongs to the group ftp and enable write access for the group: chmod g+w <directory-name>.

## LIMITED USER ACCESS

If you'd like to lock out certain user accounts from incoming FTP access, you can edit the /etc/ftpusers file and include the usernames that should not be able to connect. As you expand your server, you're likely to add new user accounts that run certain processes such as database or other servers. These accounts are not real people and should never have access to the system. By default, /etc/ftpusers already includes several usernames—including root. If you'd like to enable root access through ftp (this isn't recommended!), remove root's name from the file.

```
 [root@pointy jray]# more /etc/ftpusers
root
bin
daemon
adm
lp
sync
shutdown
halt
mail
news
uucp
operator
games
nobody
```

## CUSTOMIZE YOUR SERVER SETTINGS

The file /etc/ftpaccess contains most of the options that configure how your FTP server works. A sample configuration file is included here:

```
[root@pointy jray]# more /etc/ftpaccess
```

```
class    badnet    anonymous     140.254.85.*
class    local    real        *
class    remote anonymnous    *

limit badnet 0 Any
limit remote 2 Any
limit local 10 Any
deny !nameserved

email    jray@poisontooth.com
loginfails 3
message /welcome.msg       login
message .message       cwd=*

chmod      no    anonymous
delete      no    anonymous
overwrite     no    anonymous
rename      no    anonymous

log transfers anonymous,real inbound,outbound
passwd-check rfc822 warn
```

Let's take a look at what this means, each section at a time. First, three classes of connections are defined using the class keyword: badnet, local, and remote. Each class definition includes a type of user, real or anonymous, and a list of network addresses that are included in that class. For example, the class badnet is comprised of anonymous users who are connecting from the 140.254.85 subnet. Defining classes enables you to better track connections with the ftpwho command:

```
[root@pointy jray]#ftpwho
Service class badnet:
   -   0 users (  0 maximum)
Service class local:
 5636  ?  S    0:00 ftpd: snafu.poisontooth.com: jray: IDLE
   -   1 users ( 10 maximum)
Service class remote:
 4799  ?  S    0:00 ftpd: cruddy.poisontooth.com: anonymous/jray@: IDLE
   -   1 users (  2 maximum)
```

If you're expecting a large number of connections, categorizing them into classes makes it easier to monitor your server's usage.

Moving on in the configuration file, you may have already guessed what the limit option sets. Limit is used to set a maximum number of a certain class of connection that can occur. The badnet, remote, and local classes are set to a maximum of 0, 2, and 10 users respectively. The Any option sets the time of day that the classes are limited to. These three classes are able to connect at any time. You can set these to ranges of hours—be sure to read the ftpd man page for more information on configuration options.

Next, deny !nameserved denies connections that do not have a hostname associated with their IP address. Tracing connections by an IP address can be a bit of a hassle. If you deny connection attempts from IP addresses that do not have an associated hostname, you provide a basic level of security in the form of a trackable hostname. Unfortunately, this may cause problems for some users whose ISPs have not set up reverse DNS correctly.

An administrator email address is set with the email jray@poisontooth.com. The FTP server will present this information publicly, so if you have a rather busy server, you'll probably want your server feedback messages to go to an email account other than your primary personal account.

To limit the number of attempts a username can make at logging into the system, you can set loginfails to the value you feel is appropriate. Setting this value to something high will give crackers an easy entry point for checking usernames and passwords—keep it reasonable.

Sending greetings to users as they connect is as simple as setting message /welcome.msg login. You will need to create the welcome message file, of course. You can also send a different message each time the users enter a new directory. This is a good way to notify the users of the types of files contained in a specific directory. The message .message cwd=* setting will display a .message file, if available, in any directory a user enters.

We're closing in on the end of this simple configuration now. The chmod, delete, overwrite, and rename options are straightforward. These settings let you limit these low-level functions depending on the type of connection. In the case of the example configuration file, these four functions are disabled entirely for the anonymous users.

Next, you'll certainly want to log the transfers that are made to and from your server. The line log transfers anonymous,real inbound,outbound configures the server to log everything that goes on—whether from anonymous or real users that are sending or receiving files.

To round things out, the passwd-check rfc822 warn option provides an interesting function. When anonymous users are prompted for their email address, they're usually tempted to just press Enter and skip the prompt. To try to convince them otherwise, the passwd-check option can be added to warn the users if their password doesn't match the RFC822 specification for a valid email address. This, however, doesn't guarantee that users will enter their *real* address.

There are many more options that can be set for the wu-ftpd process. The difficulty in providing a few chapters on system administration is that there is so much that cannot be covered in the space allotted. As I've urged all along, be sure to read the man pages and HOWTO documentation for the various system services.

## PROJECT: USING LINUXCONF WITH wu-ftpd

Before closing out this chapter, I will briefly look at the LinuxConf FTP configuration module. This utility is far from complete and doesn't give you access to many of the options of the server. Help files have yet to be written for the configuration utility, so this is a "use at your own risk" utility. I recommend sticking to the command line for FTP server configuration for now.

Opening the Config, Networking, Server Tasks, Ftp Server (`wu-ftpd`), Base Configuration hierarchy in LinuxConf will display the configuration screen for a few of the simple `ftpd` options. Figure 32.1 shows a basic server setup with administrator email, welcome message, and shutdown message files listed.

**Figure 32.1**
The LinuxConf `ftpd` configuration options are rather sparse.

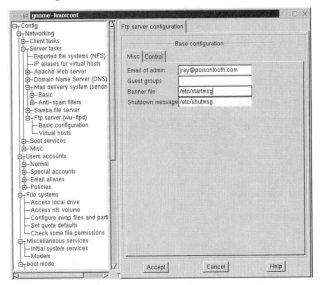

Clicking the Control tab in this window will take you to a more useful screen—the access control configuration (see Figure 32.2). These options enable you to shut off access options for different types of connections. This is identical to options like `chmod`, `delete`, and `rename` that we looked at earlier.

**Figure 32.2**
The LinuxConf `ftpd` module allows you to set access controls for types of users.

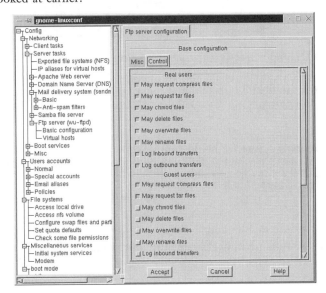

PART

**V**

CH

**32**

The last (and most useful) option that you can configure graphically is a virtual FTP host. This was not covered in the manual configuration section (although it *can* be configured manually)—but is very simple to do here. A virtual FTP host behaves as if it is its own dedicated server, depending on the name under which the server was accessed. For example, on my machine poisontooth.com, I can host an FTP site that appears entirely independent using another domain assigned to my server: brevardmpo.com. This is similar to a single machine that can host multiple different Web sites.

To configure virtual FTP servers, click the VirtualHosts option in the LinuxConf configuration. You can now click existing listed servers to edit or delete them. To add a new virtual host, click the Add button. Figure 32.3 shows the virtual host addition window.

**Figure 32.3**
Virtual hosts are just like real hosts, only not so real.

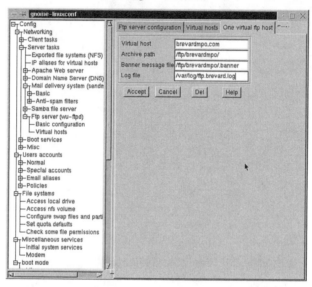

This example in this figure shows a virtual host being configured for the domain name brevardmpo.com. A path to the root of the FTP archive is defined, as well as a welcome banner for the site. Accesses to the FTP server are stored in a separate log file, which is also specified here. Once configured, click the Accept button to add the new virtual host to your system.

---

**Can I Use Any Domain Name for My Virtual Hosts?**
No. You must only use names that have already been assigned to your computer. The names themselves are real—the "virtual" part of a virtual host is nothing more than the server's ability to pretend to be a unique machine for each domain assigned to it.

---

Be sure to pay close attention to your FTP server during its operation. I've had to deal with users on my own network who got the bright idea of running FTP "warez" (pirate software) sites from their own accounts. These sites will typically make themselves known in two very obvious ways—fast growth of logfiles and a fast decrease in the available bandwidth on your network.

If you can convince your users, I still recommend using `slogin` and `scp` to control your computers and transfer files. The servers discussed in this chapter (aside from ssh) are critical in hackers gaining access to your system. Eliminating them from the picture entirely is the best thing you can do for security on your network.

CHAPTER **33**

# SETTING UP ADDITIONAL SERVERS

## In this chapter

# ADDING VALUE TO YOUR SERVER

You now know how to set up the most common servers that you might need when starting your own Internet presence. This chapter rounds things out by taking a brief look at a few servers that can add even more value to your Internet setup.

This section of the book has shown you quite a few server applications, and you're about to add some more. It may be tempting to add as many different servers as you can, but restraint is the key to running a successful and secure site. When the latest and greatest protocol-of-the-day comes along, it's fun to install and try it out. As I've said all along, however, the less you have running, the more secure your server will be. Often, however, your customers will dictate what you run—and you may need to expand your services beyond the traditional email and Web services.

# USING THE INN USENET SERVER

People run news servers for one of two reasons: to provide a full or partial Usenet newsfeed to their customers or to provide a customized news service.

If you've ever used a newsreader (and, if you've been following this book closely, you most certainly have!), you've seen what the Usenet looks like—thousands of newsgroups on thousands of topics. Typically these newsfeeds are provided by an ISP and are for end users. If you are planning to run your own ISP, this is what you probably want to run. The problem with this type of setup is that you will need a large amount of disk space, and you must pay a monthly access fee in order to receive a newsfeed for your server. You should contact your ISP to find out how to receive a full "pushed" newsfeed for your server.

---

**What Are the Resource Requirements of a Full Newsfeed?**
Although I cannot provide this information first hand, a close friend works at the Ohio's second largest ISP. This ISP carries a full newsfeed that includes well over 30,000 different newsgroups. The ISP maintains 30GB of hard drive space and must expire old messages on a daily basis to keep up with the influx of new information.

---

This chapter looks at the more practical news server—a customized server that provides newsgroups for a specific purpose. This is an excellent way to broadcast messages to your clients without filling up an email server with multiple copies of email.

## INSTALLING INN

As with most everything else, if you installed Red Hat Linux as a server, you've already got INN, the InterNetNews daemon, on your system. Check to see if the RPM is installed on your machine by typing `rpm -q inn`.

If you don't have the software on your machine, you'll need to find the INN RPM and install it now. Once you're sure INN is available, add it your runlevel with `chkconfig -add innd`. Then start it: `/etc/rc.d/init.d/innd start`.

## SETTING ACCESS CONTROL

The first thing you're going to want to do is change the access restrictions on your server. By default, the server ships with read and post access available from localhost and all access denied from everywhere else. You can limit the newsgroups that a user has access to as well as the hosts that can access a newsgroup. For even greater control, you can force users to log into the news server with a username and password. The nnrp.access man page has full details on all of the access options available. The default access control file is /etc/news/ nnrp.access. Go ahead and open this file up in a text editor now. You'll see this:

```
# Default to no access
*:: -no- : -no- :!*
# Allow access from localhost
localhost:Read Post:::*
```

The fields in this configuration file are separated by the : character and are as follows:

- **Hostname**—The hostname or domain to which the access control applies.
- **Permissions**—The level of ability that the user/domain should have. Read access allows the users to read postings. Post access, obviously, lets the user contribute to a newsgroup.
- **Username**—A username to use for authentication.
- **Password**—The corresponding password for authentication.
- **Newsgroup access**—The list of newsgroups that can be accessed, separated by commas. This can include wildcards, such as alt.*. You can also deny access to groups by putting an exclamation mark in front of the group name.

To add full news access to the subnet 192.168.0.*, you'd add a line like this to the file:

```
192.168.0.*:Read Post:::*
```

Once your access is configured, you can go about adding a few newsgroups to your server. The command to add groups to your server is ctlinnd.

## ADDING NEWSGROUPS TO YOUR SERVER

Adding new groups to your server is pretty simple. For example, suppose you want to add the group fun.stuff to your news server and you want to allow posting from anyone. The creator email address for the newsgroup is root@mydomain.com. The command to do this is ctlinnd newgroup fun.stuff y root@mydomain.com.

```
[root@contempt /root]# ctlinnd newgroup fun.stuff y root@mydomain.com
Ok
```

The only portion of this command that may require an explanation is the y. This can actually be one of several different options:

- **Y**—Local posting allowed. Any machine may post to the newsgroup.
- **N**—Local postings are disabled, only remote postings are enabled.
- **M**—The group is moderated and only approved postings can be put on the server.

If you want to add other groups, now is the time to do it. Once you've added the groups you want, you can attempt to post to one of them.

If there are groups that you'd like to remove, use `ctlinnd` in the rmgroup mode. For example, to remove the `fun.stuff` group that was just created, use `ctlinnd remove fun.stuff`.

## POSTING A SAMPLE MESSAGE

To post a sample message to a newsgroup, you can use the `rnews` command. First, you'll need to create a sample post. Create a text file called `testpost` that contains the following:

```
Path: localhost
From: root@localhost
Message-ID: <200001010450.ABC2000@localhost>
Subject: test
Date: Mon, 17 Jan 2000 09:30:00 -0500 (GMT)
Newsgroups: fun.stuff
NNTP-Posting-Host: localhost

This is a test
```

To post the message to the server, you use the `rnews` command as shown here:

```
rnews -r localhost < testpost
```

So far, so good! Now you should be able to use your newsreader to check the newsgroup to see if the article has indeed been posted. You should also be able to connect to the news server using any client you'd like. Any newsgroups that you've added to the system should also be available to the software.

If you want to remove the message that you just posted, you can use the `ctlinnd` command again, this time using it with the `cancel` command. For example, to remove the message that was just posted (it has the message ID `200001010450.ABC2000`), you'd use the following:

```
ctlinnd cancel 200001010450.ABC2000
```

`ctlinnd` responds with the following:

```
[root@contempt /root]# ctlinnd cancel 200001010450.ABC2000
Ok
```

Checking the newsgroup with your newsreader will reveal that the message is no longer on the server.

If you want to run a news server that provides only local newsgroups, this is all you need to know. If you'd like to add incoming newsfeeds, you should read the man pages for `innd` and its associated files.

If you're looking into INN just to set up a newgroup or two for an organization, you might be passing up a few easier, more manageable solutions. Mailing lists allow you to distribute messages to multiple people and do not require the user to use a special program to access them. You can easily set up simple mailing lists using sendmail's aliases. Another possible solution is to use shared IMAP mailboxes. IMAP enables you to share a mailbox amongst many users, allowing them all to see the messages contained within.

INN is a very powerful set of programs that can perform any news functions that you might need. There is quite a bit of documentation available for the software—a good place to start learning more about the system is available from the INN Web page at `http://www.isc.org/products/INN/`.

# RUNNING THE LEAFNODE NNTP SERVER

Okay, INN is a heavy-duty server that can do just about anything—but it can be a pain to configure. Getting a full newsfeed for your server can be costly and will take up large amounts of disk space on your server. Would you like to be able to offer a full newsfeed and *not* have to deal with extensive configuration options? If so, perhaps a server like Leafnode is what you need.

*Leafnode* is a news server that receives its incoming messages from an NNTP server, just like a news client. Messages are posted through the NNTP server as well. Furthermore, in order to conserve space, Leafnode downloads messages only as they are needed. This means that your news server can carry as many newsgroups as it wants and disk space will only be taken up if the groups are in use.

The Leafnode software can be downloaded from `http://wpxx02.toxi.uni-wuerzburg.de/~krasel/leafnode.html`.

## INSTALLING LEAFNODE

Once you've downloaded the Leafnode archive, you'll need to compile and install the software. Follow these steps to be up and running in a matter of minutes:

1. Unarchive and uncompress the Leafnode software with this:
   ```
   tar -zxf leafnode-1.9.9.tar.gz
   ```
2. Change your working directory into the root level of the Leafnode distribution:
   ```
   cd leafnode-1.9.9
   ```
3. Run the configure script to prepare the software for compilation:
   ```
   ./configure
   ```

The configuration process may take a few minutes and will look a bit like this:

```
[root@contempt leafnode-1.9.9]# ./configure
creating cache ./config.cache
checking for mawk... mawk
checking for gcc... gcc
checking whether the C compiler (gcc ) works... yes
checking whether the C compiler (gcc ) is a cross-compiler... no
```

```
checking whether we are using GNU C... yes
checking whether gcc accepts -g... yes
...
updating cache ./config.cache
creating ./config.status
creating Makefile
creating pcre/Makefile
creating config.h
```

4. Run make to compile Leafnode. Leafnode is a relatively small program and should only take a minute or two to compile. It will look like the following:

```
[root@contempt leafnode-1.9.9]# make
gcc -I. -DHAVE_CONFIG_H -Wall -Wstrict-prototypes -Wmissing-prototypes
-g  -c nntputil.c -o nntputil.o
gcc -I. -DHAVE_CONFIG_H -Wall -Wstrict-prototypes -Wmissing-prototypes
-g  -c configutil.c -o configutil.o
...
gcc -c -I. -DHAVE_CONFIG_H -Wall -Wstrict-prototypes -Wmissing-prototypes
-g ./newsq.c
gcc -I. -DHAVE_CONFIG_H -Wall -Wstrict-prototypes -Wmissing-prototypes
-g -o newsq newsq.o config.o -L. -llnutil
gcc -c -I. -DHAVE_CONFIG_H -Wall -Wstrict-prototypes -Wmissing-prototypes
-g ./lsort.c
gcc -I. -DHAVE_CONFIG_H -Wall -Wstrict-prototypes -Wmissing-prototypes

-g -o lsort lsort.o config.o -L. -llnutil
```

5. Run make install to install the software on your computer as shown here:

```
[root@contempt leafnode-1.9.9]# make install
/usr/bin/install -c -d -o root -g 0 -m 755 /usr/local/man/man1
/usr/bin/install -c -d -o root -g 0 -m 755 /usr/local/man/man7
/usr/bin/install -c -d -o root -g 0 -m 755 /usr/local/man/man8
/usr/bin/install -c -d -o root -g bin -m 755 /usr/local/sbin
...
cp ./config.example /etc/leafnode
chown root:news /etc/leafnode/config.example
chmod 640 /etc/leafnode/config.example
chmod 2755 /var/spool/news
Edit /etc/inetd.conf to start /usr/local/sbin/leafnode and restart inetd
If you update from a leafnode version < 1.9.3, do a "make update"
```

Leafnode is now installed and ready to be configured—so let's get to it!

## STARTING LEAFNODE

Leafnode requires that several pieces of software be in place before it is ready to use. First, you'll need to edit the /etc/leafnode/config file to include information about the server that you want to receive news from. Copy the file /etc/leafnode/config.example to /etc/leafnode/config. Then open the file in your favorite text editor. You will, at the least, need to change the name of the news server that is being referenced. For example, here is a working configuration for my system:

```
## This is the NNTP server leafnode fetches its news from.
## You need read and post access to it. Mandatory.
server = news-server.columbus.rr.com
```

```
## Unread discussion threads will be deleted after this many days if
## you don't define special expire times. Mandatory.
expire = 10

## This is another news server which stores some groups that are not
## available on the first one. You can define username, password and port
## for each server separately.
supplement = nntp.service.ohio-state.edu
username = nota
password = chance
```

This creates a server that reads its primary news files from `news-server.columbus.rr.com` and expires message threads in about 10 days. It also uses the server `nntp.service.ohio-state.edu` to supplement the primary newsfeed. This server requires a username and password.

Next, you need to configure the server so that articles will expire appropriately and not be left on the server indefinitely, and to pick up new messages from a remote server. To do this, edit a new crontab file called `leafnode.crontab` and include this line:

```
0 0 * * * /usr/local/sbin/texpire
*/10 * * * /usr/local/sbin/fetchnews
```

Now, submit this crontab to the system with `crontab -u news leafnode.crontab`. This will run the expiration software every night at midnight from the user account `news` and will fetch new news articles every 10 minutes.

Last, but not least, Leafnode must be set up so that it can accept incoming connections on your machine. Unlike INN, it is started using `inetd` rather than run as a background daemon. Add the following line to your `/etc/inetd.conf` file:

```
nntp  stream tcp   nowait news  /usr/sbin/tcpd /usr/local/sbin/leafnode
```

Restart `inetd` using `killall -1 inetd`.

Now all you have to do is sit back and wait. The first time that the `fetchnews` process runs from the `crontab` file, it will download all of the newsgroups on the servers that were configured. You can then point your newsreader toward your server and subscribe to any of the groups.

The first time you attempt to read messages in a group, there will be nothing present. This is quite all right. The server only retrieves messages after they have been requested. Once the newsgroup is visited, the next time `fetchnews` runs, it will retrieve messages from the group and they will be available for reading.

This is a much simpler and faster method of getting a full news service up and running on your Linux server. Unless you are an ISP, this should be an excellent alternative to the rather complex INN. To make configuration even simpler, a graphical front end to Leafnode has been created for the KDE desktop environment called Keafnode. The Keafnode homepage is located at `http://www.sbox.tu-graz.ac.at/home/v/vogel/lin-apps/keafnode/keaf1.html`.

PART

**V**

CH

**33**

## INSTALLING AND USING KEAFNODE

Keafnode does not have a Red Hat Linux RPM available, but the installation process is relatively simple with just the source code. Download the latest version from `http://www.sbox.tu-graz.ac.at/home/v/vogel/lin-apps/keafnode/src/`, and then follow these directions to install the package:

1. Decompress and unarchive the source code package:

   ```
   tar -zxf keafnode-0.4.tar.gz
   ```

2. Change to the root level of the source code distribution:

   ```
   cd keafnode-0.4
   ```

3. Run the auto configuration utility to prepare the package for installation:

   ```
   ./configure
   ```

   The configuration process may take a few minutes and will look a bit like this:

   ```
   [root@contempt keafnode-0.4]# ./configure
   creating cache ./config.cache
   checking for gcc... gcc
   checking whether the C compiler (gcc ) works... yes
   checking whether the C compiler (gcc ) is a cross-compiler... no
   checking whether we are using GNU C... yes
   ...
   creating Makefile
   creating keafnode/Makefile
   creating keafnode/docs/Makefile
   creating keafnode/docs/en/Makefile
   creating po/Makefile
   creating config.h
   ```

4. Run make to compile Keafnode:

   ```
   [root@contempt keafnode-0.4]# make
   make all-recursive
   make[1]: Entering directory `/root/keafnode-0.4`
   Making all in keafnode
   make[2]: Entering directory `;/root/keafnode-0.4/keafnode`
   ...
   ```

5. Run make install to finish the installation:

   ```
   [root@contempt keafnode-0.4]# make install
   mkdir /en
   mkdir /en/kcontrol
   mkdir /en/kcontrol/keafnode
   /usr/bin/install -c -m 644 index-1.html /en/kcontrol/keafnode/index-1.html
   /bin/sh ../../../mkinstalldirs /en/kcontrol/keafnode/
   /usr/bin/install -c -m 644 index-2.html /en/kcontrol/keafnode/index-2.html
   /bin/sh ../../../mkinstalldirs /en/kcontrol/keafnode/
   ...
   ```

After installing Keafnode, you can access it from the main KDE menu under the Settings, Network menu selection. Figure 33.1 shows the Keafnode main configuration window.

**Figure 33.1**
Keafnode lets you configure all of Leafnode's options.

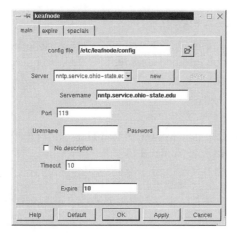

You can add new servers and edit existing news servers from the main panel. The Expiretab is used to expire messages in specific newsgroups, whereas the Specials tab allows you to set the number of articles that are fetched at a time, maximum number of bytes to download, and so forth. There is also extensive online help if you run into trouble.

> **Tip**
>
> Keafnode lets you easily set up configurations that otherwise might be a bit "hairy" by hand. The software lets you control every configurable aspect of Leafnode, so I highly recommend you install it. Memorizing the options of all the configuration files you use in Linux can be a chore—you might as well use the good GUI solutions when they are available.

The use of Keafnode makes Leafnode all the more easy to configure for your network. Hopefully, the information provided here is enough to get you started with your own Usenet news server.

PART

V

CH

33

# USING THE POSTGRESQL SERVER

If you're running a Web server, it will only be a matter of time before you need to provide database connectivity to the server. There are many ways to connect a database—including using PHP (http://www.php.org/) or directly from Perl. The backbone of a Web database server, however, is the database itself. Red Hat Linux ships with a very powerful and popular database server: PostgreSQL. PostgreSQL (or *Postgres* for short) is an SQL, or *Structured Query Language*, server. It has features that rival high-end databases like Oracle or Microsoft SQL Server, but it is entirely free for your use. You can visit the server's Web site at http://www.postgresql.org.

One of the biggest benefits of using the PostgreSQL server is that ODBC drivers are readily available for the system. You can easily connect a server on your database to a client computer that is running Microsoft Access. This sort of connectivity is a must in the corporate environment. Let's take a look at the installation and configuration of PostgreSQL right now.

## INSTALLING AND CONFIGURING POSTGRESQL

Getting PostgreSQL up and running on your system will only a take a few minutes. The Postgres package may or may not be installed already. Use RPM to query for the package with `rpm -q postgresql` as shown here:

```
[jray@pointy /var]$ rpm -q postgresql
postgresql-6.5.3-6
```

If the package is not installed, install it now from your Red Hat Linux CD. You'll also want to call `chkconfig` to include the file in your runlevel like this:

```
chkconfig --add postgresql
```

Next, start the PostgreSQL server by typing `/etc/rc.d/init.d/postgres start`.

### ADDING USERS

Once the server is started, you'll need to add a user or two to the system. These are people who can create and destroy databases, or add and delete other users. The command that you'll use to make users is `createuser`. Alternatively, you can remove users with the somewhat harsh command `destroyuser`.

There are five options to the `createuser` function that you will want to know and use each time a user is created:

- **-u**—Allows the user to create other users. This is usually reserved for administrative accounts.
- **-U**—Explicitly forbids the users from creating other accounts. Most users will fall under this category.
- **-d**—Allows the user to create databases. Usually reserved for administrative accounts.
- **-D**—Disables database creation for a user.
- **-i** *<userid>*—Sets a user ID for the user being added. If this option is not used, you will be prompted for the user ID that you want to use.

A typical user is created with the `-U` and `-D` options. Administrators are created using `-u` and `-d`. The user creation tool also includes an interactive mode, but you'll grow tired of using this mode if you're creating several users. The first thing you'll want to do is create an administrative account for yourself. The initial setup includes only the `postgres` user, so you'll need to add `su postgres` in order to run `createuser` for the first time as shown here:

```
[root@contempt jray]# su postgres
[postgres@contempt jray]$ createuser hardy
Enter user's postgres ID or RETURN to use unix user ID: 505 ->
Is user "hardy" allowed to create databases (y/n) y
Is user "hardy" a superuser? (y/n) y
createuser: hardy was successfully added
```

Here a user named `"hardy"` is created that has all of the access rights possible for a PostgreSQL user. A simplified way of adding the same user account is to use `createuser -u -d -i 505 hardy`.

## CREATING AND POPULATING A DATABASE

Once you've created a username for yourself in Postgres, you can get to the process of creating a database or two. Be sure that you are logged into the system under the user account that you just set up. Any user can have superuser PostgreSQL privileges—they don't have to have any special privileges on their Linux account.

To create a database, use the `createdb` command. Likewise, deleting a database is performed with `destroydb`. Go ahead and create a database named `testdatabase` right now. The command to do this is `createdb testdatabase`.

With the database created, you can now create tables within the database to hold your data. A table defines the different types of data that make up a "piece" of data. Multiple tables can be defined within a single database. Although this is not a book about SQL, you can probably pick up what is going on very quickly. If you'd like to learn more about SQL, an excellent reference is *Sams Teach Yourself SQL in 10 Minutes*.

Let's assume that you want to create a database with two tables. One table will hold a customer number, his name, address, and phone number. A second table will have a customer number and an item description of something he has ordered. First, define these tables in a text file called `testtables.txt` as shown here:

```
create table customers (
          FirstName    varchar(20),
          LastName     varchar(20),
          Street1      varchar(50),
          Street2      varchar(50),
          City         varchar(20),
          State        varchar(2),
          Zip          varchar(10),
          CustomerID   int,
          primary key  (CustomerID)
);

create table purchases (
    CustomerID   int,
    Product      varchar(120),
    primary key  (CustomerID,Product)
);
```

You can now create these tables by piping the `testtables.txt` file into the command-line PostgreSQL monitor `psql`. The psql software lets you interact with a specific database. Rather than using a pipe like `cat testtables.txt ¦ psql testdatabase` to create the tables, you can simply invoke `psql testdatabase` and type the tables in manually. I've found, however, that keeping a copy of the creation statements around is handy in case the database ever needs to be re-created. Here is the result of piping `testtables.txt` to `psql`:

PART

**V**

CH

**33**

```
[hardy@contempt hardy]$ cat testtables.txt ¦ psql testdatabase
create table customers (
        FirstName       varchar(20),
        LastName        varchar(20),
        Street1         varchar(50),
        Street2         varchar(50),
        City            varchar(20),
        State           varchar(2),
        Zip             varchar(10),
        CustomerID      int,
        primary key     (CustomerID)
);
NOTICE: CREATE TABLE/PRIMARY KEY will create implicit index 'customers_pkey'
 for table 'customers'
CREATE

create table purchases (
        CustomerID      int,
        Product         varchar(120),
        primary key     (CustomerID,Product)
);
NOTICE: CREATE TABLE/PRIMARY KEY will create implicit index
'purchases_pkey' for table 'purchases'
CREATE

EOF
```

You can verify that these tables are indeed in your database by opening it with psql
testdatabase, and then using the \dt option to show the tables in the database. Consider the
following, for example:

```
[hardy@contempt hardy]$ psql testdatabase
Welcome to the POSTGRESQL interactive sql monitor:
  Please read the file COPYRIGHT for copyright terms of POSTGRESQL
[PostgreSQL 6.5.2 on i686-pc-linux-gnu, compiled by gcc egcs-2.91.66]

   type \? for help on slash commands
   type \q to quit
   type \g or terminate with semicolon to execute query
 You are currently connected to the database: testdatabase

testdatabase=> \dt
Database  = testdatabase
 +.................+...........................................+..........+
 ¦ Owner           ¦                  Relation                 ¦ Type     ¦
 +.................+...........................................+..........+
 ¦ hardy           ¦ customers                                 ¦ table    ¦
 ¦ hardy           ¦ purchases                                 ¦ table    ¦
 +.................+...........................................+..........+
```

Use the \q command from within psql to quit out of the interactive monitor.

You can issue any SQL command you'd like from within psql. This is typically where you
would manually insert data into the database using an SQL INSERT command. For example,
let's take a look at inserting a record into the two tables that have just been created.

First, look at the customer table. An insert command is structured as follows: INSERT INTO <TABLENAME> VALUES ('field1','field2','fieldn');. Carrying this logic through, the command to insert a record for myself into the customer table would look like this: INSERT INTO customers VALUES ('John','Ray','Vivian Hall','Fyffe Road', 'Columbus','OH','43210',1);. The value for the customer ID (1) is not in quotes because it is a numeric value rather than a string. Try inserting a record now as shown here:

```
testdatabase=> INSERT INTO CUSTOMERs VALUES ('John','Ray','Vivian Hall','Fyffe
 Road','Columbus','OH','43210',1);
INSERT 51680 1
```

If PostgreSQL follows up the command with an INSERT response, the record has been added successfully. You can view all of the records in your database by using a SELECT statement to retrieve data. To display all of the information within the table customers, SELECT it like this:

```
SELECT * FROM customers;
```

If all goes well, Postgres should respond as follows:

```
testdatabase=> select * from customers;
firstname |lastname |street1     |street2     |city     |state | zip |customerid
----------+---------+------------+------------+---------+------+-----+-----------
John      |Ray      |Vivian Hall|Fyffe Road|Columbus|OH   |43210|    1
(1 row)
```

The record that was just added is indeed stored in the database's table. Now let's add a record to the second table: purchases. Once again, use an INSERT statement to add some arbitrary data. Be sure that the customer ID from the customers record matches the record you add here. You'll find out why it's important in a moment:

```
testdatabase=> insert into purchases values (1,'3 Pomeranian Puppies');
INSERT 51681 1
```

---

**Does Capitalization Matter?**
PostgreSQL is *not* case sensitive with regard to commands or fieldnames. I've made an attempt to capitalize the text to differentiate between keywords and user-supplied information.

---

Verify that the data was successfully stored using another SELECT statement like this:

```
testdatabase=> select * from purchases;
customerid |product
-----------+----------------------
          1|3 Pomeranian Puppies
(1 row)
```

Now that both tables are populated with data, you can start to explore the power of SQL relations. Although this is a simple example, it should demonstrate the power that can be found in SQL. There are two tables in the database—both tables have a customer ID field. Since this piece of information relates to the two tables, we can query the database so that the two tables are "joined" and a combination of data is returned. For example, let's assume you want to generate a list of customer names and what they've purchased. This calls for a SELECT statement, which looks something like this:

```
SELECT customers.FirstName,customers.LastName,purchases.Product FROM
 customers,purchases where customers.customerid=purchases.customerid;
```

Feeding that statement into Postgres results in the following:

```
testdatabase=> SELECT customers.FirstName,customers.LastName,purchases.Product
 FROM customers,purchases where customers.customerid=purchases.customerid;
firstname¦lastname¦product
..........+.........+.......................
John   ¦Ray   ¦3 Pomeranian Puppies
(1 row)
```

Pretty nifty, huh? In PostgresSQL you can carry this logic one step further by creating a "virtual" table called a view. A *view* is nothing more than a SELECT statement that acts as if it is its own table—returning updated data each time it is accessed. To create a view, you use the CREATE VIEW SQL statement and a SELECT statement to provide the relationship that will populate the table. For example, to create a view called customerpurchases using the SELECT statement that relates customers and purchases, you'd use the following:

```
CREATE VIEW customerpurchases AS SELECT customers.FirstName,customers.LastName,
 purchases.Product FROM customers,purchases where
 customers.customerid=purchases.customerid;
```

Postgres should respond with the following:

```
testdatabase=> CREATE VIEW customerpurchases AS SELECT
 customers.FirstName,customers.LastName,purchases.Product FROM
 customers,purchases where customers.customerid=purchases.customerid;
CREATE
```

Verify that the view has been created by using the \dt command in PostgreSQL to display the available tables like this:

```
testdatabase=> \dt
Database  = testdatabase
  +----------------+-----------------------------------+----------+
  ¦ Owner          ¦          Relation                 ¦  Type  ¦
  +----------------+-----------------------------------+----------+
  ¦ hardy          ¦ customerpurchases                 ¦ view?  ¦
  ¦ hardy          ¦ customers                         ¦ table  ¦
  ¦ hardy          ¦ purchases                         ¦ table  ¦
  +----------------+-----------------------------------+----------+
```

Now that the view is active, you can query the view in the same way that you would query any table. The only real limitation is that you cannot insert data into the view as you would with a table. This feature is slated for an upcoming version of PostgreSQL.

If you like what you see, be sure to learn more about SQL. The language is an extremely effective means for creating highly relational databases, and PostgreSQL offers excellent performance for a large number of users. But, you might be asking, how do I *serve* the data once it is in the database. Don't worry, we're getting to it!

**Tip**

Don't underestimate the power of PostgreSQL. PostgreSQL is a free database solution, but don't let that fool you. The simple examples shown here are just that—"simple" examples. The database itself is capable of maintaining millions of pieces of data in very complex database schemas. You shouldn't be afraid of trusting PostgreSQL to high-end tasks because of its price. In 1999, PostgreSQL beat out Oracle 8i to win the LinuxWorld Editor's Choice award.

## CONNECTING TO A POSTGRESQL SERVER

Most of your customers will probably want to access their data through traditional database-like access or through a Web site. Before you can do this, however, you'll need to enable access to the system for PostgreSQL users. You do this by editing the file /var/lib/pgsql/ pg_hba.conf. The pg_hba.conf file enables access from remote machines to the PostgreSQL server. To enable access from any remote server using a valid account, you would add this line to the file:

```
host    all    0.0.0.0    0.0.0.0    ident    sameuser
```

This should enable the "hardy" user to connect using his or her UNIX account password. Once you've added the line to the file, you need to restart PostgreSQL. Do this by typing /etc/rc.d/init.d/postgresql restart at the command line.

### WEB-ENABLING YOUR DATABASE

One way that you might want to access your database is through a Web site. This is actually much easier than you might imagine. You must have some knowledge of Perl, however, before attempting this. You must make sure that the Perl DBI module is correctly installed on your system and that the PostgreSQL DBD driver is installed. For more information about Perl and installing Perl modules, head over to the Comprehensive Perl Archive Network (CPAN) at http://www.cpan.org/.

The DBI Perl module provides a very programmer-friendly interface to supported databases. You can issue SQL commands directly to the databases on your system and retrieve the results into arrays within Perl. You can also turn to tools like PHP to Web-enable your database, but Perl is a more popular language and is simple enough to set up that most beginners can be accessing their databases within a few hours. A simple program to display all of the tables and all of the data stored in those tables is listed here:

```perl
#!/usr/bin/perl

use DBI;
use DBI qw(:sql_types);

print "Content-type: text/html\n\n";

#
# Connect
#
```

**PART**

**V**

**CH**

**33**

```
my $dbh = DBI->connect("DBI:Pg:dbname=testdatabase","hardy","party",
        {
          RaiseError => 1,
          AutoCommit => 0
        }
      ) || die "Database connection failed: $DBI::errstr";

my @names = $dbh->tables;
for ($x=0;$x<@names;$x++) {
  if (!($names[$x]=~/^MSys/)) {
  my $sth=$dbh->prepare("select * from $names[$x]"');
  $sth->execute;
  $results=$sth->fetchall_arrayref;
  my @fields=@{$sth->{NAME}};

  print "<P>Table: $names[$x]<P>";
  print "<TABLE BORDER=1><TR>";
  for ($y=0;$y<@fields;$y++) {
    print "<TH>$fields[$y]</TH>\n";
  }
  print "</TR>";
  my @resultset=@{ $results };
  for ($y=0;$y<@resultset;$y++) {
    my @row=@{$resultset[$y]};
    print "<TR>\n";
    for ($z=0;$z<@fields;$z++) {
      print "<TD>$row[$z]</TD>\n";
    }
    print "</TR>\n";
  }
  print "</TABLE>";
  $sth->finish;
}
}
$dbh->disconnect();
```

For this program to work on your system, you'll need to change the name of the database being connected to (unless you want to connect to testdatabase) and provide an appropriate username and password. In the example code, hardy/smart is the username/password pair. The program should run as a CGI on your Web server and will format the output data in HTML table form.

## PROJECT: CONNECTING USING ODBC ON WINDOWS

If the Web isn't where you want to serve your database and you'd like to make things available to a traditional desktop database application like MS Access or any other ODBC compliant program, you can do that as well. (Actually, you can do both if you'd like!) The first thing you'll need to do is install the PostgreSQL ODBC drivers on your Windows computer. The latest version of the PostgreSQL driver is located at ftp://ftp.postgresql.org/pub/odbc/latest/postdrv.exe.

To install the driver, double-click the postdrv.exe application after it has been downloaded. The software will take you through a typical Windows wizard-style installation. Once the software is installed, you'll need to add an ODBC data source for the database that you'd like to connect to. To do this, open the Windows control panels and double-click the 32-bit ODBC icon. Once the ODBC window opens, click the System tab. Figure 33.2 shows a window similar to what you should see.

**Figure 33.2**
You'll need to add a data source to the ODBC setup.

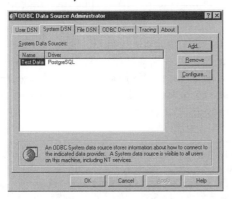

Click the Add button to add a new data source to the system. This will describe the remote database that the ODBC driver will connect to. Highlight the PostgreSQL driver from the list of available ODBC drivers and click Finish. A screen much like the one in Figure 33.3 will be shown. You'll need to fill in information that will tell the system how to contact PostgreSQL. The available fields are as follows:

- **Data Source**—This is an arbitrary name by which the system will reference your database.
- **Database**—The name of the database to which you will be connecting. In the examples the database name is `testdatabase`.
- **Description**—A description (for your benefit) of the database that you are defining. This field is not necessary.
- **Server**—The hostname or IP address of your PostgreSQL server.
- **Port**—The port that your PostgreSQL server is running on. You do not need to change this from its default value.
- **User Name**—The name of the user that you've set up to access the database.
- **Password**—The corresponding password for the user account.

**Figure 33.3**
Fill in the information needed to describe the remote database.

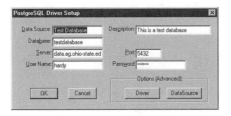

The rest of the fields can be left alone. You may want to click on the Driver button before continuing. The Driver screen lists a few driver-level functions that you may want to change.

PART
**V**

CH
**33**

Most notably, you can disable Read-Only access—allowing remote machines (that have access, of course) to write data to your database.

Once you've entered the information for your database, click the OK button to continue. Click OK again to exit from the ODBC driver setup.

That's all you need to do. You can now access your remote database from any program that supports ODBC data access. Under MS Access, you can choose Get External Data and Link Tables to connect to your defined data source. You can even use this technique to use PostgreSQL to be the back-end server for things like Active Server Pages on Windows NT. (Why you'd want to use NT, however, is an entirely different story.)

**Tip**

If you have trouble, don't fret. Be sure to check out the pg_hba.conf file on your Linux machine to be sure that you've correctly enabled access to the remote Windows machine. If you are connecting to the database as someone other than the owner, you might also need to use the SQL command "grant" to give access to the other user.

The servers in this chapter are not usually necessary to have an Internet presence. They provide extra value to the customers you serve and hopefully extra functionality that you may not have considered when you decided to set up your own Internet server.

# PROGRAMMING LINUX

# CHAPTER 34

# SHELL PROGRAMMING AND SCRIPTING

## In this chapter

# WHAT IS SHELL SCRIPTING?

You've just reached the programming section of *Special Edition Using Red Hat Linux*, and you're not a programmer. Should you continue reading? Absolutely. This part of the book will focus on programming from several different aspects. In the upcoming chapters you're going to learn about how to use various programming languages under Linux. Although it is impractical to try to teach C, C++, and Java in a single chapter, it is very nice to know how to use these languages to compile and run existing code on your system. Each chapter in Part VI of the book will focus on giving you the most knowledge in the available space. Obviously, if you want to learn a programming language, you're going to need other resources. If, however, you want to learn how to *use* programming languages on your system, you should find everything you need to know (and more) in this section.

In this chapter, you're going to be learn how to control your computer through the use of *shell scripts*. The text will assume that you are a non-programmer and will introduce you to many of the terms that you're going to be seeing in other chapters and even other books. You're probably not going to be able to rewrite StarOffice when you're done, but you'll be able to better control your computer and put its processor to good use.

So, let's start with the obvious question: *What is shell scripting?* To answer this, let's break the question up into two parts—*What is a shell?* and *What is scripting?*

## WHAT IS A SHELL?

You may not be aware of it, but each time you open a terminal session and start typing commands into your computer, you're using a "shell." The shell accepts commands from the user and processes them, returning the results. There are many different shells that come with Linux; the most popular shell is *bash*, or the *Bourne Again Shell*. Some people prefer to run older shells like *sh* or *csh* for compatibility between Linux and other UNIX systems.

There is nothing really special about a shell—it is just another program that runs on your operating system. What differentiates the shells is the syntax in which you issue commands to them. Thus far in the book, you've just been typing a command and waiting for a response. This hasn't really given you much insight into what the command line (shell) can do for you other than run a program. In fact, most shells can do much more than that—they can be programmed or *scripted* to carry out a wide variety of functions on your computer.

## WHAT IS A SCRIPT?

A script is the program that you give to a shell, or another interpreted language, which is processed on-the-fly, without the need for compiling. Scripting languages allow you to create programs just by editing text files and including commands. A script that is written for bash on Linux will also run on bash for Solaris or bash for Macintosh OS X. This is entirely unlike a compiled piece of software that would require a different version for each platform that it runs on. The drawback to using scripting languages is that they are typically slower and cannot be secured in the way that other languages can. Nonetheless, some of the most popular languages that exist right now are scripting languages: Perl, PHP, Tcl, and so forth.

---

**Compiled Versus Interpreted Languages**

A *compiled* language is one in which the source code is processed by the computer to create a binary executable file in the native language of the computer. The executable can be distributed between like computers and will run without any additional support software.

*Interpreted* scripts are left "as is" and are read and run by an interpreter each time they are used. In order to distribute interpreted programs, you must make sure that all of the computers that need to run it have the necessary interpreter installed.

There are some interpreters (Perl, for example) that compile the code internally as it is being run in order to provide speed increases. The script file being run, however, remains in its original format throughout the process.

---

## WHAT CAN I DO WITH A SHELL SCRIPT?

You can't write a word processor (at least not a very good one) with a shell script and you're not going to be able to write the next great Quake clone, but you can do things that these programs can't do. Shell scripts are typically used as "glue" to bind several existing applications together and use them in an entirely new way. For example, if you wanted to create a program that searches through your hard drive, finds files that are greater than a certain size, and then emails complaints to the people who own those files, you most certainly can. Or, if you want to create a folder that will zip up files that are placed in it, you can do that as well.

Shell scripts tend to be small in size and are often accessible to even nonprogrammers. The size of the shell's programming language is usually kept to a minimum since more traditional programming languages are used for more complex tasks. Because of this, you'll find that after looking at a few scripts and following a few examples, you can understand most things that come your way.

Shell scripts are programs that you "plan" on writing. Usually necessity drives their creation. In fact, once you finish this chapter, you might find yourself wondering what in the world you can write. The best way to answer this question is by keeping track of how you use your Linux computer. When you find yourself performing a series of actions over and over, you can probably automate the process using a shell script. If you often take the output of one program and feed it into another, a shell script may be able to do it for you.

The people who are most likely to benefit from the creation of shell scripts are system administrators. Keeping users and servers under control is much of the challenge of being a system administrator. Scripts can be used to verify that programs are running correctly or fix problems if they occur. You can even use simple scripts to provide status reports for your computer. For example, you're probably familiar with the uptime command—it tells you how long your computer has been online and what the current load average is. If you wanted, you could create a simple shell script that displayed the output of uptime through a Web browser.

PART

**VI**

CH

**34**

The resulting script is nothing more than creating a file called `uptime.cgi` that consists of the following:

```
#!/bin/bash

echo "Content-type: text/html"
echo
uptime
```

If that seems pretty simple, that's because it is! By the end of this chapter, you'll be comfortable creating similar scripts that are far more complex.

> **Tip**
>
> Although the shell scripting you learn in this chapter can be used to make CGIs, you'd probably be better off looking at Chapter 35, "CGI and Perl Programming." Learning the basics of Perl is, in many ways, easier than shell scripting (which is more verbose). But Perl requires significantly more time to master. Perl also requires a much larger memory footprint and can use valuable resources on a not-so-well-equipped machine.

# INTRODUCTION TO PROGRAMMING BASICS

Before jumping into the process of creating shell scripts, it's best to understand a bit of the concept behind programming. The next few pages introduce you to the basic pieces of a programming language and what they will do for you. This section is not specific to shell scripts and even includes information that does not necessarily pertain to creating shell scripts. It does, however, prepare you for the rest of the programming chapters and will help you understand some of the buzzwords that float around every day.

## WHAT IS A PROGRAMMING LANGUAGE?

A programming language is a structured series of commands that let you control your computer. Although the commands vary from incredibly English-like to the very arcane, depending on the language, they all perform the same purpose —they tell your machine what to do. Once you know how to program in one language, moving to another language is rarely difficult. There are two popular styles of programming that you've probably heard of: traditional and object-oriented.

### TRADITIONAL PROGRAMMING

*Traditional*, or *linear*, programming is exactly what it sounds like. The program logic flows from top to bottom. This is the type of programming that you will use when you learn how to program bash later in this chapter. The problem with traditional programming is that it does not adequately allow for easy maintenance of the code or reuse of existing code. The most wonderful routine for sorting data might be buried deep in your program, but it's going to need to be rewritten in order to use it in your next big project. It isn't uncommon for linear programming methods to produce source code that is extremely large and exists totally in one file. For some jobs, this is fine, but often it can lead to a debugging nightmare.

After you've been programming for a while, you'll find that writing a quick program using the traditional style most easily solves simple tasks. Once you start working on an ongoing and ever-expanding project (especially a collaborative effort), however, you'll realize the shortcomings of this style. The solution to the problems of linear programming is *OOP*, or *Object-Oriented Programming*.

## OBJECT-ORIENTED PROGRAMMING

Object-oriented programming is not more difficult than traditional programming, but the concepts can seem a bit strange at first. OOP attempts to provide a more real-world model for programming. In the real world, machines are made up of small parts—all of these parts have characteristics that are unique and, although related to other parts in the machine, can be described outside of the context of the whole. For example, a car is composed of several things: an engine, a frame, controls—you get the picture. In fact, there are several car manufacturers that use the same engine and frame with different body designs. These cars are sold as different models, yet they are virtually identical. Since the manufacturers know how the different parts interface, they can change the parts out to change the specifications of the resulting car. The very same concept applies to OOP.

In OOP, instead of defining the program as a whole, it is defined by the parts that comprise it. Each of the parts can be built independently of the other parts as long as a common interface is defined ahead of time. Later, the parts can be updated or upgraded without even touching the rest of the program. This is an extremely useful feature when working with other people on a project. Rather than designing a program that is "glued" together at the end, pieces of a program can be built, tested, and then assembled when they are ready.

Another benefit of OOP is that data can be hidden from other parts of a program. Sometimes programmers get lazy and, rather than access data in a way that is intended, they take shortcuts and use their intimate knowledge of the program to change data directly. As a result, if the program is ever modified, their shortcuts might stop working, requiring someone to track down the problem and rewrite the necessary code. In object-oriented programming, other parts of the program cannot necessarily "see" how the individual components work internally—they can only see the portions that are exposed to the other programmers.

Here is some of the terminology that you may encounter when reading about object-oriented programming:

- **Class**—An encapsulation of the functionality of a program unit; also called an *object*. For example, a button object might know how to highlight itself if clicked, play a sound, and so forth. All of the functionality of the unit is programmed within the unit itself, not in the main program.

- **Data hiding**—Keeping the representation of an object internal to itself and not allowing outside programmers access to internal data.

- **Data abstraction**—Although not only applicable to object-oriented programming languages, data abstraction is most easily demonstrable in OOP. This is the process of breaking a program down into its functional units (the objects).

- **Event**—Most traditional programs actively check for user events—did the user click the mouse? Did she push a key? Event-driven programs are much more intuitive. An object like a button might have an on-click method that is executed when the mouse clicks; the program is triggered by events, rather than polling to see if an event has occurred.

- **Inheritance**—Since you can't access the contents of some classes (data hiding), there needs to be a means by which functionality can be added to an object. You can do this by "subclassing" a class. A subclass of a class inherits all of the functionality of the original object and allows you to build on your own methods. For example, if you want to create a button that turns purple after it is clicked, you could subclass an existing button object, add on your customized code and be done. Traditionally, you would have to rewrite the button code from scratch.

- **Instance**—A class that is currently being used.

- **Method**—A procedure that is attached to an object. The button object might have a method called `highlight` that would place the button into its clicked state.

You're most likely to see object-oriented programming terms when you use languages like C++ or Java, which are discussed in Chapter 36, "Programming with C, C++, and Java." You won't be using these things just yet—but now you know what they are.

## COMMON PROGRAMMING CONSTRUCTS

We've covered what a programming language is and what it does, but how does it work? Luckily, there are only a few basic concepts that you need to learn before you can pick up any programming book and quickly construct simple programs. These concepts apply to any programming language, although they may be referred to by different names depending on the language. Let's take a look at these concepts now.

### VARIABLES

Programs are only useful because they can store and manipulate data faster than a human can by hand. *Variables* store data so that it can be reused and operated on by a program. Variables also tap into the limited resources of your computer.

Programming languages such as C, C++, and Java require that you *declare a variable* before it can be used. Declaring a variable sets aside space in your computer's memory (real or virtual) and prepares it for storage of whatever data you want to use. At the time of declaration, you are also required to tell the computer what type of data will be stored in a variable. These constraints force the programmer into structuring his programs to be as memory efficient as possible.

Scripting languages such as Perl deal with variables in an entirely different manner. These languages let you "play" with data. If you want to store data in a variable, you just "do it." You don't need to declare your variables or set aside memory space. Because of this freedom, you can run into trouble by assuming that whatever data you want to store in a variable will always fit. The Perl programming language will let you store entire files in a variable. The problem is that memory is a finite resource and is exhausted faster than you'd imagine. If you write a program that reads all the files in a directory into variables, it may work for a while. As the number of files grow, however, the program will get slower and slower, and eventually you may reduce your computer to a standstill by thrashing the hard drive.

---

**What Is Thrashing?**
Sounds kinda cool, huh? Unfortunately, thrashing isn't a good thing. When your computer runs out of real memory and becomes completely bogged down by the process of moving data between real and virtual memory, it is *thrashing*.

---

Variables are best used responsibly. In order to be able to move between different programming languages easily, practice keeping variable use clearly defined and conservative.

### EXPRESSIONS

Computers are binary creatures—they understand the concept of "on" and "off" or "true" and "false." Much of programming is spent evaluating expressions and acting on the result. Most common expressions are in the form of traditional algebraic comparisons. For example, "one equals zero" is an expression that evaluates to "false." Depending on the programming language, expressions usually have to be between variables that contain the same type of data. You can't (usually) compare things like "one" and "1" and show them to be equal. You could, however, write your own function to do just that.

Functions within the program can return true or false depending on the their outcome and can also be used in the place of traditional expressions. This enables the programmers to extend the functionality of the expression beyond the usual "something equals something else."

So what does a computer do with an expression once it is evaluated? In most cases it uses a conditional statement to determine what should happen next.

### CONDITIONAL STATEMENTS

*Conditional statements* take the result of an expression and act on it. If an expression evaluates to true, the program takes one direction; if it is false, then it takes another. Some conditional statements (rather than *executing* different pieces of code depending on how an expression evaluates) evaluate the same piece of code until the expression evaluates differently—this is called a *loop*. The common conditional and looping types are listed here. Be warned: The names of these statements are not necessarily identical in all programming languages—but the concepts are the same:

- **IF <expression is true> THEN <do this> ELSE <do that>**—The simplest type of conditional statement. IF an expression evaluates to true, THEN one block of code is run. ELSE, another piece of the program is executed.

- **WHILE <expression is true> DO <this>**—Rather than executing a single block of code once depending on the evaluation of an expression, a WHILE loop will execute code over and over while an expression is true. Presumably, something in the loop will change the result of the expression. When the expression evaluates as false, the looping will stop.

- **DO <this> UNTIL <expression>**—The DO UNTIL looping construct is the inverse of the WHILE loop. Rather than executing a statement while an expression evaluates as true, the DO UNTIL statement loops until the expression evaluates as false.

- **FOR <incrementing expression> NEXT**—The FOR NEXT loop is the most common loop in programming. Instead of relying on something inside the loop to change in order for the loop to exit, the loop itself changes a value until it evaluates as false. For example, a FOR loop might increment a value in the range of 1 to 10, until it exceeded the range.

## SUBROUTINES, PROCEDURES, AND FUNCTIONS

The terms *subroutine*, *procedure*, and *function* are often used interchangeably in languages like Perl. Traditionally, however, subroutines and procedures are synonymous, while functions are slightly different.

Rather than build all of the program logic into a program each time you need it, you can clean things up a bit and provide basic code reuse if you use these constructs. For example, if you must print the same information at the top of each page that your program generates, it makes sense to be able to use the same code to print the header rather than repeating it multiple times. To do this, you could put the code in a procedure, perhaps called printHeader, that will display your header information when the procedure is referenced in your code. You can also pass data to a procedure—perhaps a page number for printHeader—that alters the way that the procedure operates.

The difference between a procedure (or subroutine) and a function is that a function returns data. For example, if you write code that returns the number of days between two dates, you could turn it into a function and call it from anywhere in your program. You can use functions in expressions if they return true or false data.

Functions and procedures can often be stored in files outside of your main source code. This is a very basic form of the data abstraction that is used in object-oriented programming. The ability to keep libraries of your own functions enables you to debug peripheral code, put it aside, and concentrate on your main projects.

## I/O

You can manipulate data as much as you want and calculate pi to three trillion places, but it isn't going to do you much good if you can't do anything with the result. All programming languages need to provide the means to input data from the user and to export data from the program.

In Linux, data input is usually from a specific file or from standard input. *Standard Input* (STDIN) is the standard input stream. Usually, this is the keyboard when you are logged into a terminal. You can, however, redirect the contents of a file to provide STDIN to a program. This means that you can write a program to be operated under human control and later use a shell script or other program to automate the operation of the software. This is an extremely powerful feature of UNIX and Linux that enables software to be used in ways that the original authors maybe never intended.

*Standard Output* (STDOUT), operates in a very similar way. Usually, STDOUT is sent to the controlling terminal of a program (your screen). It can, however, be redirected so that it goes to lpr, is saved to a file, is sent in an email, or one of hundreds of other possibilities. Rather than building your program to save to a specific format, you can write the output to STDOUT and be sure that the user will be able to adapt it to whatever his or her needs might be.

Of course, most languages also support the traditional concept of files. You can open a file and read or output data to the file using its *filehandle*. Storing data to a file is usually very similar to printing data to the screen, except instead of letting the program assume you want to print to STDOUT, you explicitly tell it which filehandle should be used.

### BASIC OPERATORS

Lastly, all programming languages need to provide some basic functionality before you can do anything useful with them. For example, you need to have the ability to operate on the various built-in data types. You must be able to change information in strings and perform math operations on numeric data. Often programming languages include additional libraries that provide functions that are missing in the basic programming language.

With this background under your belt, you're ready to start looking at what makes up the bash programming language. Once you're familiar with bash, other languages such as Perl and C are only a few steps away.

# BASH SCRIPTING SYNTAX

In learning the bash programming syntax, we'll loosely follow the topics that we just covered and see how they apply to the bash scripting language. To start with, you're going to need to know how to store data in bash, so let's see how bash defines a variable.

## USING VARIABLES

Bash uses variables a little bit differently than programming languages that you may have used before. All variables are identical and do not need to be declared or initialized before they can be used. You can use any alphanumeric string to make up your variable name. Depending on how you are using your variable, there are two ways to reference it:

- **Assignment**—If you are assigning data to a variable, you reference the variable directly by its name. For example, if I wanted to assign my name "John" to the variable, `name`, I would do so with the command:

  `name="John"`

- **Value**—When you're ready to output the contents of a variable, you must prefix the name of the variable with a $ in order to tell the shell that you want the value of the variable to be returned. To reference the *contents* of the variable `name`, I would refer to it as $name.

### export

Most variables that you use only need to be used in the instance of the shell that you declare them—these variables are called *local* variables and are the default variable type in bash. Sometimes, however, you may need to start scripts from within scripts and have data accessible between the several different running shell scripts. You can do this by creating an *environment* variable in your script. An environment variable is valid for any shells that are started under the shell in which it was defined. To create an environment variable from an existing variable, you use the command `export`. To turn the `name` variable into an environment variable, you would type:

`export name`

Once the shell or script that defined an environment variable exists, the contents of the variable are lost.

## USING I/O

After you know how to store data, it is useful to understand how to move it into and out of a program. Providing feedback to the user is of utmost importance when writing scripts. Users are much more likely to accept and use shell scripts if they behave like traditional programs and provide status, usage, and error messages. Allowing input enables the program to adapt itself to different situations rather than being "hard coded" for a specific task.

### echo

To "print" data from a shell script, you use the `echo` command. `echo` takes the string that follows it (including variables) and sends the result to standard output (usually the screen). To make your life easier, `echo` also prints a line feed following its output. Sometimes, however, it is less than desirable to move down a line—especially when you are prompting the user for input. To prevent `echo` from moving down a line, invoke it with the `-n` option.

For example, to print the contents of the variable without a line feed at the `name`, you would use something like:

```
echo -n "Your name is $name" .
```

### cat AND INPUT REDIRECTION

If you happen to have a great deal of text that you want to print out (instructions for using the shell script, for example), it might be a bit tedious to use `echo` repeatedly to get the job done. Instead, you can use the `cat` command to redirect text between two points to standard output as shown here in this example:

```
cat << STOPPINGPOINT
This is a line of text.
This is another line.
STOPPINGPOINT
```

This code fragment would print the lines of text between the line containing `cat` and the arbitrarily defined tag called `STOPPINGPOINT`. Any variables contained in the lines would also be evaluated. This is a useful shortcut if you have to include large amounts of textual output in your program.

### read

The `read` command lets you read information from standard input and store it in a variable in your script. This enables you to prompt the user for information and act on the information. For example, to read data into the variable `name`, you would use the following:

```
read name
```

If you'd like to break the input up into multiple parts by word, that's just as simple as reading into multiple variables. For instance, if I wanted the user to enter her city, state, and zip all on one line, I could `read` this information separately with a command like this:

```
read city state zip
```

This would divide the input up by words and store the first word in `city`, the second in `state`, and the third in `zip`. If there were additional words on the input line, they would be stored in the last referenced variable—in this case, `zip`.

### ARGUMENTS TO A COMMAND

Sometimes requiring the user to input data while a program is running is not desirable. For example, if you have a program that asks for a variety of file attributes, searches for files matching these attributes, and then finally prompts you for an email to send the results of its search to, you're going to spend a lot of time waiting around to input data into prompts. (Of course, you could ask for the email address up front, but that's beside the point.) It's also more difficult to use scripts like this inside of other scripts. To get around the problem of constantly prompting for data, you can specify that your shell script accept input as command-line arguments.

Most Linux/UNIX utilities, even those that have an interactive prompting mode, offer support for feeding the program the important parameters via the command line. For example, you can pass data to the program doit by adding the parameters that you want to pass to it at the end of the command line. Typically, these parameters are separated by spaces. If you'd like to use a space in one of the parameters, enclose that parameter in quotes. For example, this is how I'd pass several pieces of data to the doit program:

```
doit "John Ray" 43210
```

Two parameters are passed to blah—the first parameter is "John Ray", while the second is a number, 43210. Since the first has a space in it, the quotes are necessary. In order to access these parameters from within a bash script, you use the special positional variables: $1, $2, and so forth. The first parameter is in $1, the second in $2, and so on. The name of the command that was invoked is $0. You can also reference *all* of the parameters through the special $*.

---

**Why Would I Need to Know the Name by Which a Program Was Called ($0) ?**
Sometimes programs are written to serve multiple purposes (usually because of a significant amount of code overlap that would exist between two separate programs). The program executable is then aliased to several different names. Depending on the name by which the program is called, it can execute slightly differently.

---

### READING THE RESULTS OF ANOTHER COMMAND

There is another interesting way that you can get data into a script that you're writing. If, for example, you have a command that prints out the results of the date command, you can store this output in a variable by using the *backtick quotes* ( ` ` ). Let's say that you want to store the output of date in the variable timeandday, you could do this:

```
timeandday=`date`
```

## USING EXPRESSIONS

Writing expressions in bash is pretty straightforward. There are two different ways to evaluate conditions in the bash shell. The first method, using test, enables you to check variables to see what they contain, and so forth. The second technique is to rely on the exit status code generated by other programs to determine what course of action to take.

### test

The test command will evaluate expressions and return a true or false value depending on the parameters that are supplied to test and the mode that it is operating in. For example, to check a variable for equality, you could do this:

```
test "$name" = "John"
```

The text contained in the variable name must exactly evaluate to "John" (capitalization matters!) in order to be considered true. Typically, to test to see if an expression *isn't* true, you use the ! character to negate a test. To check to see if `"$name"`*isn't* equal to `"John"`, the following code would do the trick:

```
test "$name" != "John"
```

There are many other ways that `test` can operate—several of which are listed here. For full information about `test`, read its man page. Test options include the following:

- **test $variable**—Checks to see if the variable is storing any data. If it is, the test evaluates to true.

- **test -z $variable**—Tests a variable for zero length (no data). Returns true if the variable is empty.

- **test $variable1 -eq $variable2**—Tests for equality between integers. Returns true if `$variable1` and `$variable2` are equal.

- **test $variable1 -ge $variable2**—Tests to see if `$variable1` is greater than or equal to `$variable2`.

- **test $variable1 -gt $variable2**—Returns true if `$variable1` is greater than `$variable2`.

- **test $variable1 -le $variable2**—Returns true if `$variable1` is less than or equal to `$variable2`.

- **test $variable1 -ne $variable2**—Returns true if the variables are not equal.

- **test $file1 -nt $file2**—Checks modification dates of two files. Returns true if `$file1` is newer than `file2`.

- **test -e $file**—Checks to see if the file named in `$file` exists.

- **test -d $file**—Checks to see if the named file is a directory and exists.

### EVALUATING THE RESULTS OF A COMMAND

Commands exit with a status code that is equivalent to "true" if the command completed successfully, or "false" if not. You can use these exit codes as an expression. For example, you simply input a username into the variable `username` to see if the user is included in the system's password file. If you're familiar with the `grep` command, this simple line would take care of your problem:

```
grep "$username" /etc/passwd > /dev/null
```

The `> /dev/null` portion of the line ensures that any output from the `grep` command isn't displayed.

The capability to use existing programs to make decisions within your program is a very valuable part of the process of shell scripting.

## USING CONDITIONAL AND LOOPING STATEMENTS

Once you can evaluate expressions, you need to be able to act on them. There are several different conditional and looping statements that can alter the way your program flows.

```
if...then...else...fi
```

The `if...then...else` construct is the easiest conditional that you can use. This is where, however, the code samples are going to start to grow a little bit. For example, let's say you've got a variable called `name` and you want to see if it holds the value `John`. If it does, you'll print `"Hi John"`—if not, `"Get Lost!"` You may need to refer back to the "Using I/O" and "Expressions" portions of this discussion if you have any questions about this:

```
if test "$name" = "John"
then
  echo "Hi John"
else
  echo "Get Lost!"
fi
```

You can use multiple `if...then...else` statements inside one another. A shortcut for writing `else if` is `elsif`—the rest of the syntax remains exactly the same.

```
&&
```

A shortcut conditional statement is `&&`—this can very quickly shorten your code if you only want to write a quick and dirty `if...then` statement. If you'd like to test to see whether `name` is `John` and then print `Howdy!` if it is, you can shorten the whole shebang to the following:

```
test "$name" = "John" && echo "Howdy!"
```

If the first expression evaluates to true, then the code immediately following the `&&` is executed. Pretty nifty, isn't it?

```
||
```

Similar to the previous statement, the `||` will execute the second statement if the first statement fails. For example, let's modify the code we just looked at so that it will print `You aren't John!` if the variable `name` isn't `John`:

```
test "$name" = "John" || echo "You aren't John!"
```

```
case...in...esac
```

If you've got a bunch of possible conditions, one way to get around tons of `if...then...else` statements is to use a `case` statement. The `case` statement lets you compare a variable to a variety of possible matches and then execute specific commands if a match are made. A default case is also available that will match anything, if none of the specific matches are made. For example, if you want to personalize messages for the three users who might use your program, you could use something like this:

```
case $name in
John) echo "Hi John, how's everything?"
;;
Robyn) echo "Hey Rowbin!"
;;
Jack) echo "Wake up Jack!"
;;
```

```
*) echo "I have no idea who you are!"
esac
```

If you've got a ton of conditional statements in your code, see if a `case` statement can clean things up a bit.

### while...do...done

The `while` statement lets a portion of your program execute repeatedly while a certain condition is true. Let's say—for the sake of providing an utterly ridiculous example—that you want to keep prompting a user for his name as long as he keeps typing in the name `Barney`. (This might be useful if you refuse to let any user use the name Barney, which is entirely reasonable.) It will look like the following:

```
name="Barney"
while test "$name" = "Barney"
do
echo -n "Enter your name, Barney is unacceptable: "
read name
done
```

This example will keep asking the user to enter his name for as long as he enters the name "Barney." You might notice that the program starts by assigning the value `Barney` to `name`. This is necessary so that the first time the `while` statement executes, the expression is true.

### until...do...done

The `until` statement is very similar to `while` except that it executes *until* an expression becomes true—not *while* an expression is true. A useful example for an `until` statement would be a loop when you want to accept user input until they type a certain word. Let's look at the last example again, except this time we'll only accept input until the word "Barney" is typed, shown here:

```
until test "$name" = "Barney"
do
echo -n "Enter your name, Barney is unacceptable: "
read name
done
```

You can use the `while` loop to do the same thing as the `until` loop by inverting the tested condition, but using `until` and `while` separately leads to much more readable code.

### for...in...do...done AND "*"

The shell scripting implementation of the `for` loop is a bit different from what you might be expecting if you've used `for...next` loops before. The `for` command cycles through a list of "words" (filenames, usernames, and the like—not necessarily actual words) and allows you to operate on each word in the list.

Before looking at how this is used, it's a good idea to understand what the `*` character does. This character tells the shell to expand the `*` into a list of matching filenames. For example, typing `*` is shorthand for "a list of files in the current directory." Typing `*html` would expand to all of the files ending in "html" in the current directory. This is a very easy and useful way to generate a list.

For an example of these two constructs, how about a loop that cycles through all the html files in the current directory, storing each one (temporarily) in the variable `filename` while using the wc command to print out the number of lines in the file:

```
for filename in *html
do
  echo -n "Filename: $filename contains "
  wc -l $filename
done
```

You can also use the special `$*` variable to cycle through all of the parameters that the user specified on the command line.

There's a bit more that you can do with bash, but this should be more than enough to get started. The functions that you've learned can be used to immediately create shell scripts that make your life easier and make the command line experience a bit more fun.

# CASE STUDY: A SAMPLE SCRIPT

Let's quickly take a look at a sample script that demonstrates many of the features of shell scripting and might come in handy on your system. Remember that a script is executable just like any program on your system; if you create something that is useful, you can copy it to your /usr/local/bin directory and allow all the users on your system to share in the wonder of your creation. Ready? Let's go ahead and start.

If you run a multiuser system and allow individuals to run software on your Linux computer, you may want to keep track of how often a piece of software is being run. Or, perhaps you'd like to know when it is run. The following script can help (line numbers are included to aid in the description; you shouldn't type them). Save this program on your system as watcher. Here it is:

```
1: #!/bin/bash

2: echo -n "Enter a process name to watch for: "
3: read processname

4: until ps axg ¦ grep "$processname'' ¦ grep -v "grep" > /dev/null
5: do
6: sleep 5
7: done
8: echo "$processname is now running!"
```

Let's take a look at this, line by line:

1. Every script should start with the line #!/bin/bash (assuming you're using the bash shell). This tells the computer what interpreter it should be using to execute your script. We've been using bash so we need to tell the computer where to find it.

2. Print a prompt for the user to enter the name of a process he wants to wait for.

3.  This line is a little bit tricky. We need to search the process listing for anything that matches the given process name, but, at the same time, we know that the very grep command that we're using to search for the pattern is going to match itself (for example, if we search for the process happy, we're going to see the process grep "happy" in the process listing, which, unfortunately, is a match).

4.  Because of this, we need to take the output of the first grep command and look at its output for any process that doesn't include grep in the name—thus the two grep statements. Until the process appears, a loop will be executed.

5.  Begin the until loop.

6.  Pause for five seconds before checking for the process again.

7.  Finish the until loop.

8.  Print a message that the process is now running.

If you've followed that, you're ready to make a slightly more potent version of the script. This time, rather than notifying you that a user has run a certain program, let's log the "run" to a logfile, kill the offending process, and email a listing of the offending process to someone. The program will run constantly on your computer. You can start it and walk away; it will continue to work until you manually stop it. It will look something like this:

```
1: #!/bin/bash

2: echo -n "Enter a process name to watch for: "
3: read processname
4: echo -n "Enter an email address to warn when the process runs: "}
5: read email

6: while true
7: do

8: until ps axg ¦ grep "$processname" ¦ grep -s -v "grep" ¦
   grep -s -v "watcher" > /dev/null
9: do
10: sleep 5
11: done

12: dayandtime=`date`
13: echo "$processname was running on $dayandtime" >> /var/log/watchprocess

14: ps axgu ¦ grep "$processname" ¦ grep -v "grep" ¦ /bin/mail -s "Uh Oh!" "$email"
15: killall -9 $processname

16: done
```

Much of this code is the same as the last version, but nonetheless, let's see what's going on, line by line:

1.  Tell the computer which interpreter to use to evaluate the program.

2.  Prompt the user for a process name to watch for.

3.  Read in the variable processname.

PART

VI

CH

34

4. Prompt the user for an email address to send mail to.

5. Read in the variable `email`.

6. Create a `while` loop that will execute indefinitely. This will keep the program running until you manually stop it. The `true` expression always evaluates to true and can be used to create loops like this.

7. Start the `while` loop.

8. Search for the process name to appear in the process listing. Execute an `until` loop until it does. Besides just avoiding finding the process we're looking for in the `grep` command, we now need to filter out the `watcher` command as well (the name of the script) because it is invoked with the process name that we're looking for and will generate a match in the `until` loop.

9. Start the `until` loop.

10. Pause for five seconds.

11. End the `until` loop.

12. Store the output of the `date` command in the variable `dayandtime`.

13. Print a message that the process was running and when it was running; redirect this message to a file `/var/log/watchprocess`.

14. Find the line in process listing that shows who is running the evil process, pipe that line to the mail program and send it to the email address specified in `email`.

15. Use `killall` to kill the process by process name.

16. End the `while` loop.

As you can see, this is starting to be a pretty powerful script. But wait! Let's make one more change that will make this even easier to use for a system administrator. This time, instead of rewriting everything, we'll just rewrite the beginning of the program—lines 2–5, and change the `until` loop a bit, as shown here:

```
1: #!/bin/bash

2: if test -z $2
3: then
4: echo -n "Enter a process name to watch for:"
5: read processname
6: echo -n "Enter an email address to warn when the process runs: "
7: read email
8: else
9: processname=$1
10: email=$2
11: fi

12: while true
13: do

14: until ps axg ¦ grep "$processname" ¦ grep -s -v "grep" ¦
    grep -s -v "watcher" > /dev/null
15: do
16: sleep 5
```

```
17: done

18: dayandtime=`date`
19: echo "$processname was running on $dayandtime" >> /var/log/watchprocess

20: ps axgu ¦ grep ''$processname" ¦ grep -v "grep" ¦ /bin/mail -s "Uh Oh!"
"$email"
21: killall -9 $processname

22: done
```

Instead of going through the entire script one more time, let's just look at the lines that have changed:

- **2**—Test to see if there are two arguments that have been specified on the command line by checking the variable that would hold the second parameter to see if it is empty.

- **3-7**—If there aren't command-line arguments given, then just use ask the user for the data the same way that we have been doing.

- **8-11**—If there *are* two arguments on the command line, set the variable "processname" to the first parameter and "email" to the second. This will let you run the process from the command line without being prompted for any parameters.

- **14**—Line 14 is almost the same as in the last example. This time, however, there is an important change that must be made. If you run the process with command-line arguments, it will show up in the process listing with the string that you are searching for. When you get to the loop that checks for the process, you'll accidentally match this script instead of the process you're looking for. Because of this, we must filter out the name of the script ("watcher") in the exact same way we filtered out the command grep from the process listing. To do this, add another grep statement to the string of pipes that will output anything that doesn't match the name of the script.

That's it; those are the only changes required to convert this to a program that doesn't require any direct user interaction.

This script, as you can see, is incredibly simple, but it performs a variety of tasks. It accepts user input, searches the process table for a command—if it isn't running, it waits for it to start. To round things out, it also saves data to a file and emails a user-specified email address with the information about the running process. Then it kills the process. All of this in only 22 lines.

Hopefully, you now feel comfortable enough with the process of shell scripting to create your own scripts. Most of a script's power comes from existing Linux command-line utilities such as grep. The more familiar you become with the capabilities of Linux, the more powerful the scripts you will be able to write.

PART

**VI**

CH

**34**

# CHAPTER 35

# CGI AND PERL PROGRAMMING

## In this chapter

# CGIs AND PERL

If you've never programmed CGI (Common Gateway Interface) applications and never used Perl, you may wonder why these two topics are included in the same chapter. To understand this, you need to know what a CGI is, and what Perl can do to make CGI programming easier.

## WHAT IS A CGI?

A CGI is an application that operates between the Web server on your computer (Apache) and a user's browser. Rather than delivering a static page from a server, a CGI executes and produces results that are sent back to the client's browser. CGIs can accept data from forms and process user input. If you've ever submitted an order online, you've used a CGI of some type. CGIs do not, however, provide a way to instantly interact with a user. There is always a "submit" stage that must occur before data is acted on. If you're interested in immediate feedback, the programming languages that you should be checking out are JavaScript and Java.

---

**If CGIs Can't Provide Immediate Gratification, Why Bother?!**
It's true that CGIs are not an instant feedback method of processing data, but they are a guaranteed way to interact with the user. If you've ever configured a browser (and I assume you have), you know that you can turn off the capability to run Java and JavaScript applications. Users often turn off these features to increase the security and speed of their browser. If you create an application that relies on Java or JavaScript, you've immediately shut yourself off from many potential users.

---

For all intents and purposes, a CGI is just like any other application on your computer. It can be written using any language that you'd like—in fact, in Chapter 34, "Shell Programming and Scripting," there is a simple CGI that is written as a shell script. Let's take a look at that script again:

```
1: #!/bin/bash

2: echo "Content-type: text/html"
3: echo

4: uptime
```

---

**Why Do I Hear CGI Applications Called CGI Scripts?**
You may have heard people refer to CGI programs as *CGI scripts* and are wondering what the difference is between a normal CGI and a CGI script. A CGI script is a CGI that was programmed using a scripting language. Unfortunately, however, many people just assume that *any* CGI is written in a scripting language. CGIs can be written in any language you'd like—C, Pascal, Bash, Perl, Tcl, and so on. If a program is written to work as a CGI, just call it a CGI, no matter what the language.

---

From Chapter 34, you should be able to figure out exactly what this script does. Here is a quick breakdown:

1.  Tell the computer which interpreter to use to run the script.

2.  Print the text `"Content-type: text/html"` followed by a carriage return.

3.  Print another carriage return.

4.  Execute the command `uptime` to show current server statistics.

So, what makes this simple shell script a CGI? You may have noticed that I spelled out the carriage returns that are "printed" in lines 2 and 3. That's because lines 2 and 3 make all the difference.

### SENDING DATA FROM A CGI

CGIs are just like any other program, except they must input and output data slightly differently. To send data back to a browser, you must first "tell" the browser program what type of data you are sending. These data types are a subset of the MIME (Multipurpose Internet Mail Extensions) types. There is a MIME type for just about anything you could ever want to send to a user:

- `audio/mpeg`—MPEG audio streams, MP2, MP3, and so on.
- `application/zip`—Zip files
- `image/jpeg`—JPEG images
- `image/png`—Portable Network Graphic image files
- `text/plain`—Plain text
- `text/html`—HTML files
- `text/rtf`—Rich Text Format files

There are many more types than have been defined. You can take a look at a more complete list by looking at `/etc/mime.types`.

To tell the browser what type of data you're about to send, you must first send a header that contains the appropriate MIME type for your information. Most often, this is the `text/html` type.

The `text/html` MIME type is for sending HTML to the browser. Assuming you want to display an on-the-fly created Web page, this is the type you'd use. To send this information, you use the Content-type header: `Content-type: text/html`. This must be the very first thing that you print from within your program; otherwise, you will probably not see any results from within the Web browser when your CGI is run. Another interesting twist is that the Content-type header must be followed by two carriage returns.

After the initial header is sent, you can send data to the browser as you would normally. For programs that are only used to output information, the only difference between them and their locally run counterparts is the initial header. Inputting data into the CGI is a very different story.

PART

**VI**

CH

**35**

## RECEIVING DATA FROM WITHIN A CGI

The biggest difference between a normal program and a CGI is the way that you input data into a CGI. There are no built-in input routines for a CGI. You can't simply prompt the user for input and then read it into your program. Instead, users must input data into a form and submit it to the Web server. The server, in turn, takes the data and sends it to the CGI. The data arrives at the CGI in one of two forms: as an environment variable that is available to the CGI or as standard input to the CGI. The data is encoded so that special characters can be transmitted correctly.

Luckily, all of the hard work of decoding the data being sent to a CGI has already been done. The routines for making form data easily accessible in a CGI are widely available for any programming language you'd like, and are not that difficult to write from scratch if necessary.

The server also creates several environment variables that enable you, the CGI programmer, to access information about the client that is connecting to your computer. Some of the most common environment variables are listed here:

- **HTTP_USER_AGENT**—The type of browser being used to access the CGI. This usually contains the operating system as well. For example, for a Macintosh using Netscape 4.7, the environment variable is set to `"Mozilla/4.7 (Macintosh; U; PPC)"`.

- **REMOTE_HOST**—The hostname of the computer that is connected to the CGI/Web server.

- **REMOTE_ADDR**—The IP address of the computer that is connected to the CGI/Web server.

- **HTTP_REFERER**—The URL that was used to reach the current location. This is the URL of the last page visited before your page.

## THE PROBLEM WITH CGIs

To successfully understand the process of writing a CGI, you've got to put yourself in a different frame of mind. It's easy to design a program in your mind: First display an input screen for a username and password; if the password checks out, display a second form, and then process the user's data, and so on. This is the typical train of thought for a programmer that is used to programming command-line or graphical applications. Unfortunately, CGIs can't work the same way.

CGIs must obey the rules of the HTTP protocol, which was never really intended to run remote applications. The problem is this: HTTP is made for retrieving one page at a time. The process of connecting to a Web server goes something like this:

1. The client browser opens a connection to a Web server and sends a page request.
2. The server responds with the requested data.
3. If the server supports v1.1 of the HTTP protocol, it can leave the connection open for any other data the client might request (graphics for the page, and so on).

4.  Once all the data for the page is collected, the connection between the client and the server is terminated.

So, what's the problem, you ask? Simple. If you are designing a program where a user logs in, inputs some information, and then disconnects, you must realize that the chain of events is not a continuous execution of a program. Instead it needs to be broken up into several different connections and executions, like this:

1.  The user connects to a login page. This is connection number 1 and is probably just a static page on the server.

2.  The user inputs the data into the login page and clicks Submit. Connection 2 is made to the server and data is transmitted to the CGI.

3.  The CGI responds by sending information back to the client—probably the "You've successfully logged in, now enter some data" page. This is still connection 2.

4.  The now-logged-in user fills in the new form and clicks another button to submit it. The browser connects to the server again to send the data. This is connection 3.

5.  The CGI is started and the data is processed and results are sent back to the client. This is still connection 3.

To perform the task that would be incredibly simple in a traditional programming language, three different connections have to be made to the server and a minimum of two different executions of the CGI must be performed. If this sounds strange, don't worry—it's going to sound even more bizarre in a moment.

To make matters worse for the programmer, each connection to the server is an entirely unique event. From the server's perspective, each connection is brand new and has absolutely nothing to do with the previous connection. If you've ever seen the SNL skit *Mr. Short-Term Memory*, you should get the idea: "Hello, I'm the Web server, who are you? Nice to meet you, Mr. Client! Hello, I'm the Web server! Who are you? Nice to meet you...."

Taking this even further, you can see the worst problem of all—the CGI itself has no memory of who is using it in between each execution! This means variables are reset, files are closed, and so on. Each time the CGI is called—even if it is by the same client and the connections are immediately one after the other, the CGI starts from scratch. When you log in to a Web site, you aren't actually "logged in" to anything. There is no connection between your computer and the remote computer—in fact, you can probably unplug the network wire, walk away for five minutes, plug it back in, and still be "logged in."

Obviously, however, a mechanism does exist to adequately simulate the process of logging into a site. Unfortunately, this mechanism usually must be implemented entirely by hand.

In order for a CGI to maintain information between the different connections and executions by a client, it must store the data it needs to continue executing before it disconnects from the client. It must also have the capability to recognize an incoming connection and re-read the stored information that matches that connection. Furthermore, it must keep track of what it needs to be doing each time the client connects. The first time it must be verifying login information, the second time it needs to process data from an input form, and so on. So, how can this be done? There are three primary ways of doing this; let's take a look at the advantages and disadvantages of each one.

## COOKIES

A *cookie* is a piece of information that can be stored on a user's computer when he visits a Web page. The cookie can contain information that tells the CGI who is connecting, and so forth. This all happens completely transparently to the user. Of all the solutions, this one is the most clean for the end user. Unfortunately, many people do not like the fact that remote sites can store information on their computers and they disable cookies altogether. Even if cookies are enabled, you run into trouble if multiple people try to access the CGI from the same machine (unless they are using different logins)—the cookies can't tell that a different person is using the computer and might recognize the user as someone he isn't.

## IP ADDRESSES

Each computer that accesses a Web site has a different IP address. If your CGI keeps track of the address that a connection is coming from, it can store information on the server that relates a specific IP address to a specific execution state. This is also completely transparent to the user. Unfortunately, IP addresses are not always associated with the right machine. For example, if a machine must use an IP-masquerading server or a proxy server to access the outside world, its IP address probably will appear to the Web server as the same IP address as the proxy or masquerading server. All the other machines behind the same server/proxy will also appear to have that IP address. Attempted connections from any of these machines will result in the CGI thinking that the same single computer has connected. You run into the same problem with multiple users using the same computer. This time, however, even multiuser systems will have problems because the system will have the same IP address no matter who is using the computer.

## SESSION IDs

The term *session ID* refers to an identification number that is assigned to a user the first time she connects to a CGI. In each subsequent connection, the browser tells the CGI: "Hey, remember me, I'm session ID 123." The CGI looks up its stored data for that session ID and continues execution. Although this may sound like a good solution (and it is), it does require a bit of work on the programmer's part. The challenge is to pass the session ID each time the user accesses the CGI. To do this, every time the user's browser contacts the CGI, it must send the ID as part of the form that the user is submitting. This means that the form itself must be modified to include the ID on-the-fly as it is sent to the user. It's not quite as bad as it sounds, but it can be a difficult concept to grasp if you've never programmed CGIs before. The disadvantage to using session IDs is that, if improperly programmed, it becomes easy for users to hack session IDs and break into other users' login sessions. The use of session IDs usually also leads to ugly-looking URLs in the URL field of the user's Web browser. For example, the URL for an active session on a CGI that uses session IDs might look something like this:

```
http://data.ag.ohio-state.edu/urs/webdb.cgi?SID=982344358&PREV=NMgQ
```

From the standpoint of the user, this might be a bit confusing, but it doesn't impede functionality in the slightest. From the perspective of a hacker, it immediately raises two questions: *What are the variables "SID" and "PREV"?* and *What happens if I change them?* Passing session IDs inevitably will expose some of the internal information of your CGI to the user. The key to making sure that nothing can be done with this information is adequately protecting your CGI so that faking a session ID, at worst, would do nothing—or better, it would log the anomaly as an intrusion attempt.

> **Tip**
>
> If you happen to have the luxury of configuring your customer's browsers, or you know that all of your clients are going to be connecting from a particular network and don't share their computers, then, by all means, use a simpler technique than session IDs for your CGIs. If you can ensure that everyone has cookies enabled, then use them! There's no need to make life difficult if you don't have to. If you're designing a Web site for the general public, however, you're going to want to write something that you know will work on any computer—in that case, session IDs are the way to go.

## PERL AND CGI PROGRAMMING

So, you've got a pretty good idea of what CGIs are for, but why do you have to use Perl to get the job done? There are lots of programming languages—what makes Perl any better than a nice BASIC interpreter?

### ERROR CORRECTION

Much of CGI programming is the processing of data between the user and the server. The user is expected to be able to input data in a format that is recognizable to the server. There is no method (other than JavaScript) for checking the validity of data from within a browser. If data is inaccurate, how is it caught? The CGI must catch the faulty data and ask the user to re-enter whatever is wrong. If the user makes a mistake again, the process needs to be repeated.

If the problem with a piece of data is something along the lines of forgetting to put parentheses around the area code in a phone number, wouldn't it just be easier to recognize the missing parenthesis and correct the problem on-the-fly?

Perl enables you to do just that—extract "good" data from information that didn't arrive in the format you might have intended. Perl stands for *Practical Extraction and Report Language*—the "extraction" part is what makes it incredibly valuable to the CGI programmer.

PART

**VI**

CH

**35**

Regular expressions are the key to Perl's capabilities. Perl has an excellent regular expression engine that lets you compare data that is input to the server and extract the information that is important to you—as long as it exists somewhere in the data. For example, suppose you have a field on a form for entering a phone number. Rather than forcing the user to enter it in a certain format, you could just use a single freeform field (this is assuming U.S.-style phone numbers). You could then use a regular expression like this to extract the data from the input of a form. For example, let's take a look at this simple Perl script called `phone.pl` that you execute from the command line:

```perl
#!/usr/bin/perl

print "Input a phone number:";
$a=<STDIN>;
chomp($a);

if ($a=~/.*?1{0,1}([0-9]{3,3}).*?([0-9]{3,3}).*?([0-9]{4,4})/) {
  print "($1) ($2)-($3)\n";
} else {
  print "No valid number found!\n";
}
```

This seemingly simple script can turn a piece of garbage into perfectly usable data. Try entering this program and feeding it a few phone numbers. The regular expression will strip leading 1s, find the area code, local prefix, and remaining digits, and then print the result in a nice and neat format. Try throwing in hyphens between the numbers. Add some parentheses. You'll find that it is quite difficult to trick it into not finding a valid phone number. As long as it finds two strings of three numbers followed by a string of four numbers, it will return a valid phone number. As you can see, when you're dealing with input that you can't immediately check, Perl is a wonderful tool for "correcting" simple typing mistakes.

## SPEED OF DEVELOPMENT

Since Perl is an interpreted language, it doesn't require compiling each time you make a change to the code. When you're developing an online application, you'll spend a lot of time filling in forms in a Web browser, clicking Submit, waiting, and then making some changes to your code. Then you'll repeat the process. The amount of time between changing the code and seeing the results is much higher than in traditional programming. If you use Perl, you eliminate the recompile time and can get applications up and running faster. Because of this, Perl is often used to prototype applications that are destined to be written in C.

I've found that many applications that I originally thought would have to be translated to a compiled language run perfectly well in Perl. Often times your Perl prototype will evolve into your final product.

## AVAILABILITY OF RESOURCES

Perl is a hot language. There are thousands of Perl developers around the world who, each day, make new Perl libraries and modules available for other programmers. Perl libraries/modules enable you to extend the programming language to perform a wide variety of tasks.

Modules exist that link Perl to the KDE window system, enabling you to write KDE applications entirely in Perl. There are also modules that let you access ODBC databases on your Linux server, or even on a Windows machine.

The availability of thousands of prewritten scripts and utilities is one of the best reasons to use Perl for scripting. There's no sense in writing something yourself if it has already been done and is readily available for your use. Once you've written a few programs yourself, you can share your work with the world.

### Cross-Platform Capabilities

Suppose you're sitting at work waiting for your new Linux computer to arrive and you're faced with the unthinkable—a Windows desktop. Luckily, you can still install Perl on your computer and start developing software that will work without changes when your Linux computer arrives. Perl is available for most popular platforms—Windows, Macintosh OS, and just about any UNIX platform you might want to use. I have a Macintosh OS X laptop that I use for much of my personal use, including writing this chapter. I can write a Perl application under Macintosh OS X, test and debug it. Then, finally, I can deploy it on our primary Linux server.

Other languages, such as the Microsoft Visual series must be deployed on the Microsoft platform. Perl enables you to work on the system you'd want to and deploy anywhere you'd like.

# A Quick and Dirty Perl Reference

This chapter is not meant to teach you how to program Perl—it's quite a large programming language. However, this section will provide a quick and dirty reference to the language so that you can more easily determine what is going on in the sample CGI. I strongly urge you to pick up a Perl book if you'd like to learn the language. It is, in a word, astounding.

## Variables

There are several types of variables that can be used in Perl. Here we'll focus on the most common. In Perl, variable names are case sensitive and do not need to be declared before they can be used. This often leads to trouble because you can store values in a variables with similar names (like $Mytest and $MyTest) and later confuse them in your program. Perl is also unique in that variables don't need to be "typed." You can operate on a variable as a number in one line, and then, in the next, use it as a string. The variables you're most likely to see look a bit like this:

- **$variable**—A simple variable that can hold anything is prefixed with a $. You can use these variables as strings or numbers. These are the most common variables.
- **FILEHANDLE**—Filehandles hold a reference to a file that you are writing or reading. Typically these are expressed in uppercase and do not have the $ prefix.

■ **@array**—The @ references an array of variables. The array does not need to be pre-dimensioned and can grow to whatever size memory allows. You reference individual elements of an array as $array[0], $array[1], $array[2], and so on, whereas the array as a whole is referenced as @array.

■ **%array**—This is another type of an array—an associative array. *Associative arrays* are another one of Perl's "power features." Rather than using numbers to reference the values stored in this array, you use any string you'd like. For example, if you have 3 apples, 2 oranges, and 17 grapefruit, you could store these values in the associative array as $array{apple}=3, $array{orange}=2, $array{grapefruit}=17. The only difference between the use of a normal array and an associate array (besides the method of referencing a value) is the type of brackets used. Associate arrays use curly {} brackets to access individual elements whereas standard arrays use square [] brackets.

## I/O

Getting data into and out of Perl is very simple. Whether you're dealing with reading or writing to a file, the ways to do it are similar. Let's look at these functions now.

### READING FROM AN INPUT STREAM

To input data into a variable from a file, you use $variable=<FILEHANDLE>. This inputs data a line at a time into the named variable. For reading input directly from a command prompt, you just use the special filehandle STDIN. STDIN always points to the standard input stream. After reading in data, the variable is often processed with the chomp command to remove a trailing return character if there is one as shown in this example:

```
$name=<STDIN>;
chomp($name);
```

To read data in from another filehandle, the first thing you need to do is open the file with open FILEHANDLE, "filename". For example, use the following to read the first line of a file named test.txt:

```
open FILEHANDLE, "test.txt";
$line1=<FILENAME>;
close FILEHANDLE;
```

When you've finished reading from a file, you should use close followed by the filehandle that you want to close.

### OUTPUTTING DATA

To output data, you can use print to display a string or the contents of memory. The print command will display its arguments on standard out. You can embed special characters in a print statement that are otherwise unprintable, like this:

```
print "My name is $name\n";
```

Here, the \n represents a newline character—this moves the cursor down a line so that subsequent output occurs on a new line, rather than the same line as the current print statement. Other special characters include the following:

- \r—The return character
- \t—A tab
- \"—A double quote
- \\—The backslash character itself

Since some characters such as double quotes (") have a special meaning in Perl, if you want to refer to them literally you must prefix them with a backslash (\). If you aren't sure whether you can use a character directly, you can prefix it with the backslash, as in \", and you should be safe.

If you'd rather output data to a file, you're going to need to open the file first. This is done identically to the open used to read data, except for one difference. When writing to a file, you must prefix the name of the file with one of two different character strings:

- >—Output to a file, overwriting its contents
- >>—Output to a file, adding to its end if it already exists

Once the file is open for writing, you must "print" data to it by using the print command, the filehandle, and finally the output data. For example, the following saves the word *Hello* to a file named Greeting.txt:

```
open MYFILE, "> Greeting.txt";
print MYFILE "Hello\n";
close MYFILE;
```

As with reading data, you should use close to tell the system when you are done working with the file.

### Results of External Programs

You can use the results of any external program as the value of a variable. This enables you to use programs to provide you with data that otherwise may have no output mechanism. For example, to quickly and easily assign the time and date to a variable, you can just use the UNIX date command like this:

```
$dayandtime=`date`;
```

The backtick ( ` ) character should be placed around the command to capture. The Perl program will wait until the external program has finished running.

This is both a dangerous and powerful tool. You can easily read an entire file into a variable by using $file=`cat filename`. Unfortunately, it's easy to forget that this does use a significant amount of memory. Be aware of the resources you are working with before dumping entire files into your variables.

## EXPRESSIONS

Perl's expressions are very much like most languages. They evaluate to true or false and can be used in conditional statements (which we'll see in a minute). Although the variables can hold numbers or strings, you still need to perform the appropriate type of comparison on the values (shown here) in order to write a properly behaved program:

- **$var1==$var2**—Compares two numbers for equality.
- **$var1!=$var2**—Compares two numbers for inequality.
- **$var1<$var2**—Checks $var1 to see if it is less than $var2.
- **$var1>$var2**—Tests $var1 to see if it is a larger number than $vars.
- **$var1>=$var2**—Tests $var1 to see if it is greater than or equal to $var2.
- **$var1<=$var2**—Compares $var1 to see if it is less than or equal to $var2.
- **$var1 eq $var2**—Checks two strings for equality.
- **$var1 ne $var2**—Checks two strings for inequality.
- **$var1 lt $var2**—Checks to see if the string in $var1 is less than (by ASCII value) $var2.
- **$var1 gt $var2**—Tests the string in $var1 to see if it is greater than $var2.
- **()**—Parentheses can be used to group the elements of an expression together to force an evaluation order or provide clarity to the code.
- **&&/and**—Used to connect two expressions so that both must evaluate to true in order for the complete expression to be true.
- **¦¦/or**—Used to connect two expressions so that if either evaluates to true, the entire expression will evaluate to true.
- **!**—Used to negate an expression. If the expression previously evaluated to true, you can place an exclamation mark (!) in front of the expression to force it to be false—or vice versa.

As I mentioned earlier, this chapter is not to be taken as a complete guide to Perl. The language is quite verbose and enables many different coding styles, including different ways to write expressions.

## REGULAR EXPRESSIONS

Unlike the expressions you just read about, regular expressions look significantly different and, although they do evaluate to a true or false state, they are usually used to extract and manipulate string data.

Let's assume that the variable $testme contains the information My name is John.

If you simply wanted to provide an expression that returned true or false depending on whether $testme contained John, you could write this:

```
$testme=~/John/i
```

Although this line might look like an assignment statement, it is in fact looking inside of the variable $testme for the pattern John. The pattern that a regular expression matches is—unless changed by the programmer—contained within the forwardslash (/) characters. The i after the expression tells Perl that it should ignore the case of the letters when making the comparison. This means that if $testme contained JoHN, johN, or any other combination of capitalization, it would still evaluate to true. No changes to the $testme variable are made during this evaluation.

## PATTERNS

Regular expressions are far more powerful than just enabling you to check to see if a specific sequence of characters is in a string. The pattern that is matched can also be defined symbolically using these special characters and character strings:

- **$**—Matches the end of a string
- **^**—Matches the beginning of a string
- **.**—Matches any character in the string
- **[]**—Matches any of the characters within the square brackets
- **\s**—Matches any type of whitespace
- **\n**—Matches the newline character
- **\r**—Matches the return character
- **\t**—Matches the tab character
- **\w**—Matches a word character
- **\d**—Matches a digit

The bracket characters allow you to clearly define the characters that you want to match, if a specific sequence doesn't already exist. For example, if you'd like to match any of the capital alphabetic characters or any of the digits, you could write:

```
[A-Z\d]
```

Rather than having to type in all of the capital alphabetic characters, you can represent a contiguous sequence of letters or numbers as a range—specifying the start and end characters of the range, separated by a hyphen (-).

The original pattern, $testme= /John/i, can easily be rewritten to return true if any four-letter word ends the string, rather than just John, like this:

```
$testme=~/\s\w\w\w\w$/i;
```

This will match a space (\s) followed by four word characters (\w) that occur at the end of the string ($). This expression will evaluate to true with any sentence ending in a four-letter word.

PART

**VI**

CH

**35**

## PATTERN REPETITION

With the capability to write patterns, you can match arbitrary strings within a character sequence. Unfortunately, so far you can only match patterns of a specific length. Luckily, instead of having to explicitly match each individual character in a sequence, you can match a range of characters by following what you're matching with repetition operators, shown here:

- ■ *—Match any number (including 0) of copies of a character
- ■ +—Match at least 1 copy of a character
- ■ {x,y}—Match at least "x" characters and as many as "y"

  If one of these repetition sequences is followed by a ?, the sequence will match as few characters as possible to be considered true. The previous regular expression, written to match only a four-letter word at the end of a sentence can now be written to match any sentence that ends in, say, a word between four and eight characters:

```
$testme=~/\s\w{4,8}$/i;
```

The capability to match an arbitrary number of characters enables the programmer to deal with information that he may not be expecting.

## EXTRACTING INFORMATION FROM A PATTERN

Thus far, you've seen how to match patterns, but not how to get information from them. To extract pieces of information from a match, you surround the pattern that you want to extract with parentheses (). To see this in action, let's go back to the original telephone number program that introduced Perl in this chapter. In that program, there is a single regular expression that does all of the work of extracting a phone number from data. It looks like this:

```
$a=~/.*?1{0,1}([0-9]{3,3}).*?([0-9]{3,3}).*?([0-9]{4,4})/
```

Let's analyze this pattern bit by bit. You should be able to recognize all of the characters used in this regular expression:

- ■ .*?—Match any characters (as few as possible, however) at the start of the pattern.
- ■ 1{0,1}—Match zero or one occurrences of the numeral 1. This lets the pattern match a "1" in front of the phone number, if it exists.
- ■ ([0-9]{3,3})—Match exactly three digits (the area code). Notice that this is the first piece of data we want to extract, so it is enclosed in parentheses.
- ■ .*?—Match any characters (but as few as possible in order to make the match true). If there are characters separating the area code from the rest of the number, this will match them.
- ■ ([0-9]{3,3})—Match another three numbers. This portion of the pattern is also included in parentheses since we want to extract it.

- .*?—Match any characters (but as few as possible in order to make the match true). If there are characters separating the local prefix code from the rest of the number, this will match them.

- ([0-9]{4,4})—Match the last four digits of the phone number. This is the last part of the pattern that is important to us, so it is included in parentheses.

There are three portions of the pattern that are enclosed within parentheses. This equates to the three parts of the number that we want to extract. If the contents of the variable $a do match the specified regular expression, the phone number is immediately accessible to the programmer through the special variables $1, $2, and $3. These variables contain the matching portions of the pattern that were found in the parentheses.

For each set of parentheses used in the pattern, a $# variable is created that corresponds to the order in which the parentheses are found. Since the area code is the first set of parentheses in the example, it is $1, the local prefix is $2, and so on.

### SEARCHING AND REPLACING

Since you can easily find a pattern in a string, wouldn't it be nice if you could replace it with something else? Perl lets you do just that by writing your regular expression line a little bit differently:

```
$a=~s/searchpattern/replacepattern/
```

This simple change lets you modify data in a variable so that it is exactly what you're expecting—removing extraneous data. For example, if you'd like to match a phone number in the variable "$a", and then change it to a standard format, you could do this:

```
$a=~s/.*?1{0,1}([0-9]{3,3}).*?([0-9]{3,3}).*?([0-9]{4,4})/($1) ($2)-($3)/
```

Whatever phone number is found in the original string is replaced with a number in the format of xxx xxx-xxxx. This functionality enables you to take "bad" data and turn it into something useful.

This is but a small subset of the regular expression capabilities of Perl. If it seems strange now, don't worry—many people are befuddled by regular expressions at first. After a bit of use, however, you'll be amazed at what they can do for you.

## CONDITIONALS AND LOOPING

Like other languages, Perl has all of the same constructs that make it easy to act on the results of an expression. You can use these constructs with traditional expressions or to evaluate whether or not a regular expression match was made.

### if...then...else

Perl lets you evaluate expressions using the same "if/then" logic as other programming languages. You can embed multiple if...then statements within each other. For example, to

PART

**VI**

CH

**35**

test to see if the variable $a contains the string John anywhere in it and print Hello John if it does, you could write something like:

```
if ($a=~/John/i) {
  print "Hello John\n";
} else {
  print "I don't know you!\n";
}
```

You've probably noticed that the then in the if...then statement is implied. You can also see that the portions of the code that should be executing following the condition are enclosed in curly brackets ({}). The curly brackets denote the portion of code that a conditional, looping, or subroutine construct applies to.

### unless...then...else

The unless statement is identical to the if...then statement, except that it operates on the inverse of the expression. To change the previous example so that it uses unless, you would write the following:

```
unless ($a=~/John/i) {
  print "I don't know you!\n";
} else {
  print "Hello John\n";
}
```

This is primarily used to maintain clarity of your coding. If you think of a condition as happening *unless* something is true, you can express it in the code accordingly.

### while

The while loop enables you to execute *while* a condition remains true. For example, to continue running a section of your code while the day of the week is Tuesday, you could do this:

```
$a=`date`;
while ($a=~/tue/i) {
  print "Today is still Tuesday\n";
  sleep 60;
  $a=`date`;
}
```

This code fragment will store the output of the date command in the variable $a, and then will execute the while loop as long as tue (Tuesday) is in the output of date, sleeping 60 seconds in between each check.

### for

Perl also offers the traditional for loop construct. This lets you cycle through values until a particular condition is met. If you wanted to print out the values between 1 and 10, this for loop would suit you well:

```perl
for ($x=1;$x<11;$x++) {
  print "$x\n";
}
```

The start of each `for` loop is separated into three segments, separated by semicolons. These three portions determine how the loop operates.

The first segment, in this case `$x=1`, initializes the loop. For this example, it sets the variable `$x` so that it equals 1.

The next part, `$x<11`, is the stopping condition. As long as this condition evaluates to `true`, the loop will continue to execute.

The last segment, `$x++`, provides an update to a variable, presumably the same variable that is compared in the stopping condition.

## SUBROUTINES

Subroutines enable you to divide your code into functional units that you can then call repeatedly to perform calculations. You can directly call a subroutine from within a conditional statement if it returns a true or false value.

A subroutine is started with the `sub` keyword and the name by which the subroutine should be called. The body of the subroutine is enclosed in curly brackets {}. For example, here is a simple subroutine that prints "Hi".

```perl
sub printhi {
  print "Hi!\n";
}
```

You can include subroutines anywhere in your source code and call them at any time by prefixing their names with an ampersand (as in, `&printhi`). You can also pass values to a subroutine and receive results back from its execution. This subroutine calculates the sum of two values and returns the following results:

```perl
sub addition {
  my ($x,$y)=@_;
  return ($x+$y);
}
```

To determine the sum of 5 and 6, the function call would be

```perl
$result=&addition(5,6);
```

To get data into the subroutine, the line `my($x,$y)=@_` assigns the two incoming pieces of data (5 and 6, abstractly represented by `@_` to the local variables `$x` and `$y`, respectively. The result of adding these two numbers is returned to the variable `$result`.

I hope that this section has given you enough information to better understand Perl programs that you might run into.

PART

**VI**

CH

**35**

## USEFUL PERL CGI CODE

Before actually looking at a simple Perl CGI, there is one tiny little thing that needs to be addressed. As you've already seen, there is no input mechanism that works for CGIs in the same way that standard input works on the command line. There are, however, simple prewritten routines that make getting input into a program much easier.

These are not pieces of code that I've written—they've been around for years on the Internet and will make your life much easier. You can include the following code in a file cgi.pl on your computer and then use require "cgi.pl" from within your CGI programs to automatically include these routines in your own code:

```perl
#!/usr/bin/perl


sub MethGet {
 return ($ENV{'REQUEST_METHOD'} eq "GET");
}

sub MethPost {
 return ($ENV{'REQUEST_METHOD'} eq "POST");
}

sub ReadParse {
 local (*variable) = @_ if @_;
 local ($i, $key, $val);

 # Read in text
 if (&MethGet) {
  $variable = $ENV{'QUERY_STRING'};
 } elsif (&MethPost) {
  read(STDIN,$variable,$ENV{'CONTENT_LENGTH'});
 }

 @variable = split(/[&;]/,$variable);

 foreach $i (0 .. $#variable) {
  # Handle \+ to space conversion
  $variable[$i] =~ s/\+/ /g;

  ($key, $val) = split(/=/,$variable[$i],2); # split on the ='s

  # Convert back from hex.
  $key =~ s/%(..)/pack("c",hex($1))/ge;
  $val =~ s/%(..)/pack("c",hex($1))/ge;
  # Associate key and value
  $variable{$key} .= "\0" if (defined($variable{$key})); #
  $variable{$key} .= $val;
 }
 return scalar(@in);
}

1;
```

This code will automatically process incoming data in your CGI simply by including the line &ReadParse at the start of your program. You'll see exactly how to use it next.

---

### Hey, I Write Perl CGIs; What About the CGI Module?

Perl does indeed include a CGI module that can also perform the same function as this code. The CGI module, however, is not intuitive to users who are beginning Perl programming. The information contained in this chapter is designed to help the user better understand what is actually happening in the transactions between Perl and the client browser.

---

Once you have entered the code into a file on your machine, you're ready to look at a simple CGI. Let's go ahead and try to make one now.

## CASE STUDY: A SAMPLE CGI

Earlier in the chapter, there was a discussion on the creation of a Web site that would allow a user to "log in," fill out a form, and then process the data in the form. Let's see how to make a very simple CGI to do just that.

First, start with the code to output the login form and check its input. This CGI will encapsulate all of the HTML that is needed, so there will be no other files needed outside of the source code for the CGI. Be sure to name this file test.cgi and place it in a directory that includes ExecCGI permissions. The lines in the following example are numbered for clarity—you should not number your version:

```
1: #!/usr/bin/perl

2: require "cgi.pl";

3: print "Content-type: text/html\n\n"';
4: &ReadParse;

5: if ($variable{login} eq "") {
6:     print "<BODY BGCOLOR=\"#FFFFFF\">\n";
7:     print "<FORM ACTION=\"test.cgi\" METHOD=POST>\n"';
8:     print "<CENTER>\n";
9:     print "login name: <INPUT TYPE=text name=\"name\"><BR>\n";
10:    print "password: <INPUT TYPE=password name=\"pass\"><BR>\n";
11:    print "<INPUT TYPE=submit name=\"login\" value=\"login\">\n";
12:    print "</CENTER>\n";
13:    print "</FORM>\n";
14:    print "</BODY>\n";
15:    exit 1;
16:} else {
17:    if (($variable{name} eq "jray") && ($variable{pass} eq "test")) {
18:        $loggedin=1;
19:    }
20:}

21:if ($loggedin==1) {
22:    print "Successfull login!";
23:} else {
```

```
24:    print "Access denied!";
25:}
```

This code is rather straightforward, but is designed so that it operates differently depending on how it is run. Let's take a look at the important lines now:

- **1**—Tell the computer that Perl should be used to interpret the program.
- **2**—Include the special code to process incoming data.
- **13**—Send the type of data that will be sent back to the browser. This program will always use the text/html type.
- **4**—&ReadParse calls a procedure in cgi.pl. This code figures out if there is any incoming data, and then reads it into the associative array %variable. The name of the form variable is used to index into the array and find its value.
- **5-15**—Check to see if there is any incoming data in $variable{login}. If there isn't any data, it's the first time the CGI has run, so output the HTML form. Once the form is displayed, the program exits.
- **16**—If there is data, then the system has already displayed the login screen and accepted input. It should now check to see if the name and password are valid.
- **17-20**—Check to see if $variable{name} is "jray" and $variable{pass} is "test". If so, set the $loggedin variable to 1.
- **21-25**—If $logged in is equal to 1, print out a successful login statement; otherwise print out an access denied message.

As you can see, by checking to see what data has been returned, the CGI can figure out what "state" it is in (pre-login, login, and so on). We can take this one step further by expanding the program as follows:

```
1: #!/usr/bin/perl

2: require "cgi.pl";


3: print "Content-type: text/html\n\n";
4: &ReadParse;

5: if ($variable{submit} ne "") {
6:      print "<BODY BGCOLOR=\"#FFFFFF\">\n";
7:      print "Hello again $variable{name}<BR>\n";
8:      print "Thank you for your comments:<BR><PRE>$variable{comments}</PRE>\n";
9:      print "Have a nice day!\n";
10:     print "</BODY>\n"';
11:     exit 1;
12:}

13:if ($variable{login} eq "") {
14:     print "<BODY BGCOLOR=\"#FFFFFF\">\n";
15:     print "<FORM ACTION=\"test.cgi\" METHOD=POST>\n";
16:     print "<CENTER>\n";
17:     print "login name: <INPUT TYPE=text name=\"name\"><BR>\n";
18:     print "password: <INPUT TYPE=password name=\"pass\"><BR>\n";
```

```
19:    print "<INPUT TYPE=submit name=\"login\" value=\"login\">\n";
20:    print "</CENTER>\n";
21:    print "</FORM>\n";
22:    print "</BODY>\n";
23:    exit 1;
24:} else {
25:    if (($variable{name} eq "jray") && ($variable{pass} eq "test")) {
26:        $loggedin=1;
27:    }
28:}

29:if ($loggedin==1) {
30:    print "<BODY BGCOLOR=\"#FFFFFF\">\n";
31:    print "<FORM ACTION=\"test.cgi\'' METHOD=POST>\";
32:    print "<CENTER>\n";
33:    print "Hello $variable{name}!<BR>\n";
34:    print "Please enter your comments:\n";
35:    print "<TEXTAREA name=\"comments\" rows=10 cols=60></TEXTAREA>\n";
36:    print "<INPUT TYPE=submit name=\"submit\" value=\"submit\">\n";
37:    print "<INPUT TYPE=hidden name=\"name\" value=\"$variable{name}\">\n";
38:    print "</CENTER>\n";
39:    print "</FORM>\n";
40:    print "</BODY>\n";
41:} else {
42:        print "Access denied!";
43:}
```

Most of this version of the CGI is identical to the previous version, with some notable exceptions. Picking up where the last one left off, rather than printing a you've logged in message, this version of the code prints out a new form for the newly logged-in user (lines 30-40). This form enables the user to enter comments that could later be stored. The most notable thing about this form is that line 37 includes a hidden field—this field is the user's name. Since the CGI can't remember this between executions, it must be passed along somehow. Here I chose to pass it as a hidden field.

The other change to the program is the addition of the lines 5-12. These lines check to see if $variable{submit} has a value. If it does, the CGI knows that it is being executed after information has been filled out on the comments form. If $variable{submit} is defined, the program prints out the comment that was submitted and the name of the user that sent the comment (remember, the username was input on the first page—two executions ago!). Figures 35.1, 35.2, and 35.3 show the series of screens that are all handled by this single CGI. Take a close look at the URL in all three figures; notice that just a single URL is taking care of everything.

Obviously, this isn't a very useful CGI as it exists now, but it does give a bit of insight into the programming style that you will need to adopt in order to create an interactive user experience. In this example, I passed the variable name as a hidden field in one of the forms—this is exactly what you might do with a session ID in a CGI. The session ID could be the name of a file that contains even more data that would be read in when the CGI executes. It's up to you to find what you consider to be the best solution for maintaining state between difference executions of the CGI code.

PART

VI

CH

35

**Figure 35.1**
Log into the CGI.

**Figure 35.2**
The CGI recognizes a correct login and allows data entry.

**Figure 35.3**
Finally, the user is logged out of the CGI.

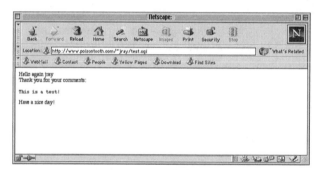

I sincerely hope that this chapter has interested you in CGI programming and the Perl language. Together they make a very powerful online application development environment.

# CHAPTER 36

# PROGRAMMING WITH C, C++, AND JAVA

## In this chapter

# USES FOR C, C++, AND JAVA

So far, we've looked at bash and Perl and their strong points. Bash is great for developing small scripts to tie together pieces of existing software. Perl, on the other hand, is a wonderful tool for deploying Web applications or quickly prototyping future software development.

So, with tools like these, who needs C, C++, and Java? I'm guessing that you do! Even if you aren't a C or C++ programmer, you'll still find it necessary to know how to use these compilers on your system. Read on to find out why.

## C AND C++

Red Hat Linux 6.2 includes the Experimental GNU Compiler System (EGCS), version 1.1.2. This is a new version of the compiler system that has shipped with earlier versions of Linux. EGCS is a completely standards-based compiler system—if you're looking to compile applications in a visual environment, this is not for you. EGCS, however, is very powerful, and an excellent place to start if you're interested in learning cross-platform C or C++.

If you've never programmed in C before, this chapter is going to be of little use to you. The C and C++ languages are very extensive and cannot be covered to the extent that Perl and bash were covered in previous chapters. This chapter will look at how C and C++ can be used to compile software and produce executables for your system. This is actually very useful information even if you don't know C or C++. Most of the software that is distributed for UNIX systems is distributed in the form of source code. The source code can then be recompiled on your computer.

C and C++ differ from Perl in that they are *compiled* languages. Instead of declaring variables on-the-fly, they must be predeclared at the start of every program. These languages give you the ability to shoot yourself in the foot. The benefits, however, are significant.

Once compiled, a C/C++program runs much faster than a Perl application and requires far less memory. Perl requires that the interpreter be loaded each time the script is run—this amounts to roughly a 5MB memory hit on top of whatever your program requires. An equivalent C program doesn't require this extra memory, and, on a machine that is RAM hungry, will perform far better.

### WHAT IS THE DIFFERENCE BETWEEN C AND C++?

There is very little difference in the two languages in regard to basic language syntax. C++, however, supports object-oriented programming. Object-oriented programming, which was defined in Chapter 34, "Shell Programming and Scripting," promotes the reuse of code and a responsible programming style.

Rather than writing code in the traditional "top-down" model, object-oriented programs build their functionality into units called *objects*. An object encapsulates functionality that is specific to that type of object. Keeping program logic from intermingling throughout the source code enables programmers to share source code and more easily divide the work on a particular project.

From the perspective of learning to program, it's often said that it's easier to learn C++ if you don't already know C. Although this is probably true for some people, I don't necessarily agree. Object-oriented programming is a state of mind. In order to get there, it's helpful to understand programming logic. If you've never programmed, picking up the logic might be the tough part for you—throwing in the object-oriented nature of C++ may just confuse things.

## JAVA

Java is a very different language from C or C++, but is also a very important language to understand. Java is a "new" language that was developed by Sun Microsystems in the 1990s. Java is far different from traditional compiled languages. Most languages (C and C++ included) are compiled for a particular type of computer. If you're running Linux on a i386 class machine (which you probably are), the code is compiled specifically for that processor. If you're using LinuxPPC, the source code is compiled into an application that will only work on other PPC-based computers.

Furthermore, besides being hardware-dependent, the application is also operating system-dependent. You can't compile an application under Linux, and then boot into Windows and use it. Each operating system has different ways to load executables as well as different APIs (Application Programmer Interfaces) that must be adhered to.

Because of these problems, Sun created Java in an entirely different way. Java introduces the concept of a universal *virtual machine* (the JVM). The JVM is exactly what it sounds like—a virtual machine within your existing machine. This virtual machine behaves just like a regular computer—executing Java applications like you would execute regular Linux applications on your Linux computer. The JVM, however, can be implemented on any computer and any operating system. This enables the programmer to target any computer that has a Java implementation. A single Java binary will run on Linux, Mac OS, Windows—any place that Java can be found.

Java provides a very extensive API that can be used to develop full GUI applications, access the network, and just about everything else that you could want to do. Rather than writing a program that can only run under Linux, by using Java you can deploy on other traditional operating systems as well. Java is the programmer's dream language.

Java is fully object-oriented and is quite easy to pick up for someone who has experience in C++. Java is actually easier than C/C++ in some aspects. It doesn't allow the direct access to memory that C/C++ does, and as such, eliminates much of the shooting-yourself-in-the-foot that can happen otherwise. If you're a new programmer, Java is an excellent language to know. It is not, however, without its problems. Java is slower than traditional compiled languages. Most Java implementations now include JIT (Just In Time) compilers that convert Java to native code as it is being executed. This helps, but doesn't solve the problem. Java also has some problems being truly cross-platform because of some inconsistencies that appear across platforms. The most obvious problems occur when developing user interfaces. The good news is that the problems are getting smaller and smaller as time goes by. The Java language and virtual machine implementations continue to evolve and become more refined with each new version.

# USING THE C/C++ COMPILER

Using the EGCS C/C++ compiler is very simple. The compiler system recognizes the type of file you're working with based on the file extension. There are two programs that you'll use to compile programs on your machines:

- **gcc**—This is the primary C/C++ compiler. It is capable of compiling both C and C++ applications, but it assumes, by default, that the program being compiled is a C application.

- **g++**—The g++ program is actually a script that calls the gcc compiler so that it knows it will be compiling C++.

The file extensions that these programs support are listed here:

- **.c**—C source
- **.C**—C++ source
- **.cc**—C++ source
- **.cxx**—C++ source
- **.m**—Objective-C source
- **.i**—Preprocessed C
- **.ii**—Preprocessed C++
- **.s**—Assembler source
- **.S**—Assembler source
- **.h**—Preprocessor file
- **.o**—Object file
- **.a**—Archive file

Let's look at a very simple C program to see how the compiler actually works in practice. Enter the following code into a file named helloworld.c on your computer:

```
#include <stdio.h>

int main() {
  printf ("Hello world.  This is my first C program.\"");
  printf ("Hopefully it won't be my last.\n");
}
```

To compile this simple program, just invoke gcc like this:

```
gcc -o helloworld helloworld.c
```

The compiler should very quickly compile the program and create the file helloworld in the same directory with your source code. You can then run helloworld and it should do exactly what you would guess (print a hello world message). In this compilation, the -o option was used to tell gcc what to name the final compiled program. If the output name is not specified, the default name is a.out.

There are several options that you can use with the gcc compiler to enable features that might be useful to your programming. Here are a few of the features that are supported:

- **-o**—Sets the output filename for whatever results gcc is creating. This includes binary executables, object files, and so forth.

- **-ansi**—Forces the compiler to act as an ANSI compiler. ANSI C is supported on many platforms but does not support all of the features that are offered in the standard compilation mode—including inline assembly language. If you are concerned with making sure that your code will run on the widest variety of platforms, compile it with this option on in order to show where your code is noncompliant.

- **-w**—Inhibits warning messages. There are many times that you may find yourself compiling C code and getting tons of warning messages even with perfectly legal code—such as type casting. To turn off all warning messages, you can use this option.

- **-O<0-3>**—Enables or disables code optimization. The gcc compiler can often produce machine code that is more optimized than a straight compilation would produce. To enable the compiler optimization, use -O followed by the level of optimization that you would like to use. 0 disables optimization whereas 3 enables full optimization.

- **-g**—Generates debugging code. By default, the binary that results from a compilation is "clean" and contains none of the information that was used to generate it. Debugging code adds some bulk to the binary that lets you use a debugger along with your executable to trace problems while executing the program.

- **-c**—Do not try to link the program after it has compiled. Generate an object (.o) file instead.

If you've never worked much with C/C++, the last option may leave you scratching your head. Why would you want to compile a file and not produce an executable? Let's take a look at a modified version of the helloworld.c program to figure out why. First, create a new file on your computer called hellomoon.c and put the following code into it:

```
#include <stdio.h>

void showend(void) {
  printf ("The program is now finished executing!\n");
}
```

You'll notice that this program defines a procedure called showend but does not include the required main that is necessary in an executable. Instead, this source code file compiles to an object file:

```
gcc -c hellomoon.c
```

The resulting file from this compilation will be named `hellomoon.o`. This file now contains a compiled version of the procedure defined in `hellomoon.c`. You can use this object file to distribute a compiled version of routines that you might not want to make available to the public. To use this object file in a program, you simply use the procedure in the code and include the object file in the compilation line. For example, change `helloworld.c` so that it looks like this:

```
#include <stdio.h>

int main() {
  printf ("Hello world.  This is my first C program.\n");
  printf ("Hopefully it won't be my last.\n");
  showend();
}
```

The `showend()` call is added to the end of the code, but is not defined anywhere in the source code for `helloworld.c`. If you attempt to compile `helloworld.c` as you did previously, you'll end up getting an error message like this:

```
[jray@pointy c]$ gcc -o helloworld helloworld.c
/tmp/ccgIV9fd.o: In function 'main':
/tmp/ccgIV9fd.o(.text+0x1e): undefined reference to 'showend'
collect2: ld returned 1 exit status
```

During linking, an undefined reference to `showend` was found, so the compilation process failed. In order to make things work, the compiler needs to be told where it should look for the compiled version of the `showend` procedure like this:

```
gcc -o helloworld helloworld.c hellomoon.o
```

Including the object files at the end of the compilation line will enable the linker to search these files for the appropriate functions to link into the final code.

Considering that compilers for other platforms cost in the hundreds of dollars, you'll be pleased by the speed and reliability of the EGCS software. Although gcc/g++ does not offer a visual environment for development, it does allow you to write high-powered software for free.

## USING C++

Using the C++ compiler is just as easy as using gcc—in fact, it *is* gcc. You can invoke g++ to compile your C++ source code files. You can also use the same options with g++ that you used with gcc. Let's try compiling a simple C++ file. Here's another basic hello world program written in C++ that you can use to test the g++ compiler. Enter this program into a file called `helloworld2.cpp` like this:

```
#include <iostream.h>

int main()
{
  cout << "Hello world!\n";
  cout << "This is a C++ program\";
}
```

Now, compile the program using the same options that you used for the original helloworld.c program except replace the gcc with g++:

```
g++ -o helloworld2 helloworld2.cpp
```

You should end up with an executable helloworld2 application, just as you would expect. Remember that you can also turn on optimization, compile to an object file, and so forth—exactly the same as you can when using the compiler with standard C files.

# USING MAKEFILES

If you have a large amount of source code that you must manage, you can easily automate the process of compiling the final executable by maintaining a *makefile* for your particular project. Not only does this make updating and compiling software easier for you, it makes it much easier for anyone that you might distribute the source code to.

The makefile defines the relationship between the different pieces of source code that make up your software distribution. If an object file needs to be created before another file can be compiled, the makefile contains the information needed to compile things in the right order.

Makefiles are simple text files and are quite easy to create. You can name the makefile one of three different names: makefile, Makefile, or GNUmakefile. The preferred name is usually Makefile because it will be listed near the start of your source code directory, rather than mingled with the files.

Let's go ahead and create a Makefile for the helloworld.c and hellomoon.c files that will enable you to compile the helloworld application with a single command. Enter the following into your favorite text editor and save it as Makefile inside the same directory as the helloworld source code. When entering the file, make sure that the indented lines are indented with a single tab character and no spaces! If you use spaces, the makefile will not work! The line numbers should not be entered. Create the Makefile for the helloworld.c and hellomoon.c files like this:

```
1: all: helloworld
2:      @echo "Successfully compiled!"

3: helloworld: hellomoon.o
4:      gcc -o helloworld helloworld.c hellomoon.o

5: hellomoon.o: hellomoon.c
6:      gcc -c hellomoon.c

7: clean:
8:      rm helloworld hello*.o *~
```

The format for the makefile is very simple. The first line of each section defines an object and the files that are needed in order for that object to be built. The subsequent indented line contains the commands needed to build the named object. For example, let's look at this makefile, line by line:

- **1**—Defines an entity called `all`. This is an arbitrary word chosen to represent "all" of the project. In order for `all` to be built, it needs the `helloworld` executable.

- **2**—If the files needed for `all` exist, then the last thing to do is display a message saying that we're finished.

- **3**—The `helloworld` application requires that the `hellomoon.o` object exists.

- **4**—To build `helloworld`, executes the command `gcc -o helloworld helloworld.c hellomoon.o`.

- **5**—In order to build `hellomoon.o`, the `hellomoon.c` file must exist.

- **6**—Builds `hellomoon.o` by executing `gcc -c hellomoon.c`.

- **7**—Defines `clean` (an object)—it doesn't rely on anything existing.

- **8**—When the `clean` object is "made," it will remove the `helloworld` application, all of the object files, and any edited ~ files. This "cleans" the source code distribution.

Once the `Makefile` is entered, you can type `make all` on the command line to create the `helloworld` application like this:

```
gcc -c hellomoon.c
gcc -o helloworld helloworld.c hellomoon.o
Successfully compiled!
```

To make any part of the program, just type `make` followed by the object name that you want to create. To clean up the files in your directory, type `make clean`.

Makefiles are very nice in that if you make a change to one part of your code that doesn't require all the code to be recompiled, it will automatically detect the change and determine other files that rely on that file. Only the necessary compilations will be done. Maintaining a makefile for your projects will ensure that they are properly compiled and will end up saving you a ton of time.

# USING THE GDB DEBUGGER

If you've compiled your code using the `-g` option to generate debugging code, you can use the GDB application to help debug any problems that may be occurring in your code.

The GDB debugger offers a great deal of flexibility and extensive online help. To get an idea of how it can simplify your life, take a look at the following example, `crash.c`:

```
#include <stdio.h>

int main() {
  int a,b,c;
  a=0;b=0;c=0;
  printf("This program should crash.\n");
  b=3;
  a=5/0;
  c=10;
  printf("An answer that doesn't exist %d\",a);
}
```

Obviously this program is not going to work. The line a=5/0 should generate a floating point exception. Unfortunately, in thousands of lines of code this condition might be difficult to detect—especially if variables are used instead of numbers. Running this program from the command line generates this:

```
[jray@pointy c]$ ./crash
This program should crash.
Floating point exception (core dumped)
```

Indeed, the program does do an admirable job of crashing—but the output gives you no idea where. Now, let's try running crash from within the debugger. Invoke gdb with the name of the program that you are going to debug, like this:

```
[jray@pointy c]$ gdb crash
GNU gdb 4.18
Copyright 1998 Free Software Foundation, Inc.
GDB is free software, covered by the GNU General Public License, and you are
welcome to change it and/or distribute copies of it under certain conditions.
Type "show copying" to see the conditions.
There is absolutely no warranty for GDB.  Type "show warranty" for details.
This GDB was configured as "i386-redhat-linux"...
(gdb)
```

Next, type the run command to execute crash from within the debugger as shown here:

```
(gdb) run
Starting program: /home/jray/c/crash
This program should crash.

Program received signal SIGFPE, Arithmetic exception.
0x80483ff in main () at crash.c:8
8          a=5/0;
(gdb)
```

At this point you can also take a look at the values of the variables that were defined before the program crashed. Use the inspect command to show the value of a variable like this:

```
(gdb) inspect a
$2 = 0
(gdb) inspect b
$3 = 3
(gdb) inspect c
$4 = 0
```

Here the contents of the variables a, b, and c are shown to be 0, 3, and 0, respectively. With the capability to display the internals of the program, it should quickly become obvious what a powerful tool gbd can be. Here are a few of the other commands that you can use while running the debugger:

- **break #**—Sets a breakpoint at a particular line number. This will stop a program before it executes the given line number.
- **clear #**—Clears a breakpoint.
- **next**—Steps through one instruction.

- **jump #**—Jumps ahead to a specific line number in the program. You can use this in conjunction with a breakpoint to actually skip past an offending part of the program.

- **set var**—Sets the value of a variable in the program. For example, in the sample crash program, the line a=5/0 causes the crash. I can set a breakpoint at the offending line, use a set var a=# and jump to line 9—allowing the program to continue executing with a valid value.

You're going to want to play with GDB to get the hang of it. It offers far more control than covered here, but this should be a good start and enable you to perform simple debugging on your code without reading through the extensive GDB documentation.

# PROJECT: USING THE JAVA COMPILER AND INTERPRETER

So, you're ready to try using the Java capabilities of your system? Great! The Java virtual machine that is included on your Red Hat Linux 6.2 system is the Kaffe Java virtual machine. *Kaffe* is a free and open implementation of Java that offers compatibility with Java 1.1 (Java 2 or version 1.2 support is in the works.) The Linux distribution of Kaffe includes the full AWT (Abstract Window Toolkit) as well as a Just In Time compiler to speed up the execution of Java applications.

> **Tip**
>
> To see if Kaffe is already installed, enter the command `rpm -q kaffe`. If you don't see `kaffe-1.0.b4-2` or something similar, you can use rpm or GnoRPM to install Kaffe from the Red Hat Linux CD-ROM #1. Mount the CD-ROM and enter the command `rpm -Uvh /mnt/cdrom/RedHat/RPMS/kaffe*.rpm`.

There are two pieces of software that you will use to compile and run Java applications on your computer: java and javac. The java program will execute a compiled Java classfile, whereas the javac program is the Java class compiler.

---

**I Thought Java Didn't Run Natively—So Why Does It Need a Compiler?**
The Java compiler does not compile to native code for your processor, but it does compile to a type of "native" code. The Java compiler produces output called *bytecode*. The Java bytecode is "native" to the virtual machine. It can be run on any compliant JVM.

---

Let's try creating and compiling a simple Java application. For example, let's use the standard helloworld example one more time. Here's a nice and simple Java helloworld application. Enter this into your Linux computer as helloworld.java:

```
public class helloworld {

    public static void main (String args[]) {
```

```
        System.out.println("Hello World!\n");
    }
}
```

Next, compile the program using the javac compiler. This is as simple as typing javac helloworld.java. If you'd like to get a bit of feedback during the compilation stage, you can use the -verbose keyword to show the Java classes as they are loaded during the compilation as shown here:

```
[jray@pointy java]$ javac -verbose helloworld.java
[parsing helloworld.java 104ms]
[loading /usr/share/kaffe/Klasses.jar(java/lang/Object.class)]
[loading /usr/share/kaffe/Klasses.jar(java/lang/String.class)]
[loading /usr/share/kaffe/Klasses.jar(java/lang/System.class)]
[loading /usr/share/kaffe/Klasses.jar(java/io/PrintStream.class)]
[loading /usr/share/kaffe/Klasses.jar(java/io/FilterOutputStream.class)]
[loading /usr/share/kaffe/Klasses.jar(java/io/OutputStream.class)]
[wrote helloworld.class]
[total 720ms]
```

Finally, you should end up with the helloworld.class file in your directory along with the source code. This is the file that the virtual machine will execute. To run the program, just use java helloworld to start the program:

```
[jray@pointy java]$ java helloworld
Hello World!
```

**Caution**

When executing a classfile, do not use the .class extension! The java program assumes that the filename you give it has a .class extension. If you attempt to run a filename.class, it will try to load filename.class.class and will throw an error.

No problem! Everything worked exactly as it should. Now let's move along to something that requires a bit more muscle. I've mentioned several times that one of the amazing things about Java is that it can create applications that run on multiple processors and multiple operating systems. Being able to do this within a full windowing environment is what makes the language very appealing to developers. So, just to be sure that the Kaffe implementation of Java can do this, let's try compiling and running a simple graphical version of the helloworld application.

Here's a simple graphical application; it opens a window and scrolls a childish message down the window, and then exits. It should be named helloframe.java on your system and will look like the following:

```
import java.awt.*;

class helloframe extends Frame {
    Font thefont=new Font("TimesRoman", Font.BOLD, 24);
    static int x=0;
```

```
    public void paint (Graphics g) {
        g.setFont(thefont);
        g.drawString("Java RULZ!",30,x);
    }

    static public void main (String s[]) throws Exception {
        helloframe testframe = new helloframe();
        testframe.setSize(200,200);
        testframe.setVisible(true);
        for (x=0;x<200;x++) {
            testframe.repaint();
            Thread.sleep(50);
        }
        System.exit(0);
    }
}
```

Once again, compile the program using javac:

```
[jray@pointy java]$ javac -verbose helloframe.java
[parsing helloframe.java 127ms]
[loading /usr/share/kaffe/Klasses.jar(java/awt/Frame.class)]
[loading /usr/share/kaffe/Klasses.jar(java/awt/Window.class)]
[loading /usr/share/kaffe/Klasses.jar(java/awt/Container.class)]
[loading /usr/share/kaffe/Klasses.jar(java/awt/Component.class)]
[loading /usr/share/kaffe/Klasses.jar(java/awt/
➥Component$DefaultSerialization.class)]
[loading /usr/share/kaffe/Klasses.jar(java/awt/Component$TreeLock.class)]
[loading /usr/share/kaffe/Klasses.jar(java/lang/Object.class)]
[loading /usr/share/kaffe/Klasses.jar(java/awt/image/ImageObserver.class)]
[loading /usr/share/kaffe/Klasses.jar(java/awt/MenuContainer.class)]
[loading /usr/share/kaffe/Klasses.jar(java/io/Serializable.class)]
[loading /usr/share/kaffe/Klasses.jar(java/awt/Font.class)]
[loading /usr/share/kaffe/Klasses.jar(java/awt/Graphics.class)]
[loading /usr/share/kaffe/Klasses.jar(java/lang/String.class)]
[loading /usr/share/kaffe/Klasses.jar(java/lang/Exception.class)]
[loading /usr/share/kaffe/Klasses.jar(java/lang/Thread.class)]
[loading /usr/share/kaffe/Klasses.jar(java/lang/Runnable.class)]
[loading /usr/share/kaffe/Klasses.jar(java/lang/InterruptedException.class)]
[loading /usr/share/kaffe/Klasses.jar(java/lang/Throwable.class)]
[loading /usr/share/kaffe/Klasses.jar(java/lang/System.class)]
[wrote helloframe.class]
[total 951ms]
```

This time you can see that the Java compiler is importing functions from the AWT—that's good, because we want the application to draw something, and the AWT manages Java's graphic system.

To run the program, you'll need to be in X Windows, and start the application from the command line with the usual java helloframe. Assuming that everything went as planned, you should see something very similar to Figure 36.1 on your screen.

**Figure 36.1**
You can create graphical applications using the Linux Java implementation.

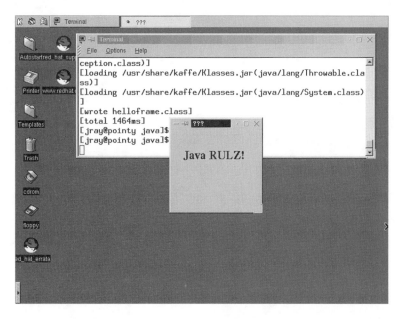

Pretty nifty, isn't it? The Red Hat Linux distribution gives you access to tons of programming languages: Perl, C, C++, the shells, Fortran 77 (f77), Tcl, Python, and more!

If you had experience in C or Java before reading this chapter, you should now have the knowledge necessary to use the compiler tools on the system for programming. If you're a beginner, you should have enough information to follow along with any beginner book and use your Linux computer as the tool to learn a new language.

# CHAPTER 37

# CONFIGURING THE KERNEL

**I**n this chapter

# WHAT IS THE KERNEL?

The *kernel* of the Linux operating system makes everything that you do with your computer possible. It provides an interface between the hardware that makes up your machine and the hundreds of programs that make up what you know as "Linux." Instead of programs directly accessing pieces of hardware on your computer, they access routines in the kernel or in kernel modules which, in turn, exchange information with the pieces of hardware. There are significant benefits to operating systems that are kernel-based—most notable are stability and portability.

## STABILITY

Most operating system crashes are caused by programs that access hardware or memory that they shouldn't. For example, you don't want to run a multiuser Linux system, and then allow any user on the system to, at will, access the hard drive controller and rewrite sectors of the drive, bit by bit. By "hiding" the hardware behind a kernel API, the most the end user can do is request that actions be carried out on the computer. If the user doesn't have the appropriate permission, the computer can deny them access.

Most modern operating systems have a kernel base—Windows 95/98 (unfortunately, these lack true protected memory), Windows NT/2000, and Macintosh OS X. Linux sports a modular kernel that allows drivers for new hardware to be loaded and unloaded on-the-fly—no rebooting necessary. (Try that on NT.)

---

**Bad Kernel Choices?**
In Windows NT 4.0, Microsoft moved the GUI code from a subsystem that ran on top of the kernel directly into the kernel. As a result, if the Windows GUI crashes, the only means for recovery is a reboot. Previously, if the GUI crashed, the kernel was not affected.

---

## PORTABILITY

The second big plus for kernel-based systems is that they are extremely portable. You've probably noticed that the Linux operating system has been ported to just about every hardware platform in the world—including the PalmPilot. This wouldn't be possible if each application that ran on Linux were dependent on the hardware it was running on. Since the applications access the kernel, they are completely insulated from the hardware. If the Linux kernel can be ported to a new CPU, all that remains is a simple recompile of the Linux support applications. Portability is precisely why applications are often distributed as source code rather than just in binary format.

You might be wondering—if other operating systems are kernel-based, why don't they run on multiple hardware platforms? Actually, until the release of Windows 2000, the Windows NT operating system was available for MIPS, PPC, Alpha, and Intel processor platforms. Unfortunately, the proprietary nature of most Windows applications doesn't make portability possible for many applications. Much of Linux software is portable because it is open source and can be recompiled on other Linux implementations. Windows and other "closed" operating systems rely on the sales of software for income, so releasing software as source code is not possible. The time needed to maintain multiple binary versions of a piece of software is also problematic. As a result, the only truly viable NT platform is an Intel-based installation.

## WHY DO I WANT TO CONFIGURE THE KERNEL?

Your system is up and running, you're happy with how it's working, the world is a wonderful place. Why, oh why, would you even want to consider changing the kernel? You wouldn't! If you're happy with your machine the way it is, there's no reason to change anything. Reconfiguring and compiling your kernel can lead to disastrous consequences if not done properly. Even if you've compiled and installed the kernel one hundred times successfully, all it takes is one misconfigured option out of hundreds to make your machine unbootable.

So, what in the world makes all this work worthwhile? Truthfully, if you have a working system, very little. There are times, however, that your system might include features that are only supported under Linux with a kernel patch. Or, perhaps you'd like to build a kernel that includes support for all of your hardware devices, rather than relying on kernel modules to support them. Compiling modules into the kernel gives you a single file that contains all of the information necessary to run your system.

Another reason you might want to recompile the kernel is if critical problems are found in the existing code. For example, if a network exploit is found, the problem is most likely to be fixed by a patch posted to a newsgroup before Red Hat addresses it with an official update. If there is ever a serious problem with your system—patching and recompiling might be your only option.

---

**Before Going Any Further...**
If you've decided to give the recompiling process a try, make sure you've got a boot disk ready in case of failure. We'll look at precautionary measures that will enable you to recover from a misconfigured kernel compile—but it's always wise to create a boot disk in case all else fails. You can use the `mkbootdisk` command to do this.

---

Although this chapter falls in the part of the book on "Programming Linux," you don't need to know anything about programming in order to use it. Linux is unique because it allows you to change the source code as you see fit. If you are a programmer, this can be great fun! If not, there are still the advantages we already discussed that might make configuring and compiling the kernel worthwhile to anyone.

**Tip**

As you may have guessed, reconfiguring and recompiling the kernel requires superuser status. You need to be logged in as root to mess with the kernel.

# CONFIGURING COMPILE-TIME OPTIONS

When you're ready to compile your kernel, the first thing that you should do is make a list of the hardware that is installed on your computer. You need to make sure that the appropriate modules are compiled to recognize your devices. Critical components of your system might fail if the corresponding module is not compiled.

---

**What Is a Module?**
Think of a kernel module as the "driver" for the components on your system. Unlike most operating systems, Linux is capable of probing for hardware and loading/unloading drivers on-the-fly.

---

If you're sure you've got a handle on what's installed, you can move to the configuration process. To configure your kernel, you need to have the source code installed. Check to see if the kernel source is available by typing `rpm -q kernel-source` like this:

```
[jray@pointy jray]$ rpm -q kernel-source
kernel-source-2.2.14-5.0
```

If the kernel source isn't on your machine, install it from your CD-ROM now. You're almost ready. Before proceeding, make sure that you have a reasonably large amount of disk space available. The kernel compilation process will produce lots of temporary object files. If your `/usr/src` directory has less than 50MB, free some space.

Let's start configuring the kernel. There are actually several interfaces to the configuration process, including a graphical X Windows-based system. This section will document the basic configuration since it can be done remotely and is much easier to document than the other methods.

Your Linux source code is located in the `/usr/src/linux` directory. The configuration procedure consists of answering hundreds of questions that will determine how your computer operates. These questions are divided into sections, and usually include very extensive help for each configuration option. The biggest problem in documenting the kernel configuration is that the options are constantly changing. It's likely that there will be updates to the kernel by the time you read this, and, as a result, the options shown here will have changed. Therefore, I'll talk generally about the main purpose of each configuration section and show many of the prompts (in their default state). Configuring certain "primary" options often enables several suboptions. Only the primary options are listed here.

Start the configuration script on your computer by typing `make config` in the main Linux source directory. Pressing the Enter key at a prompt chooses the capitalized (default) option. You can also press Y to compile an option into the kernel, N to not use the option, or M to compile the option as a module. Certain options do not include all choices. If you get confused by any of the prompts, just press ? to get help.

## CODE MATURITY LEVEL OPTIONS

There is only one code maturity option—and that is whether or not you want to be prompted for developmental configuration options. Many of these options are stable, so you'd probably want to choose Y here:

```
Prompt for development and/or incomplete code/drivers (CONFIG_EXPERIMENTAL) [Y/n/?]
```

## PROCESSOR TYPE AND FEATURES

Set various options about the processor and memory configuration on your computer. SMP and processor type are set here. It's quite acceptable to go with the default options. The processor and memory prompt will look like this:

```
Processor family (386, 486/Cx486, 586/K5/5x86/6x86, Pentium/K6/TSC,
➥PPro/6x86MX) [386]
 defined CONFIG_M386
Maximum Physical Memory (1GB, 2GB) [1GB]
 defined CONFIG_1GB
Math emulation (CONFIG_MATH_EMULATION) [Y/n/?]
MTRR (Memory Type Range Register) support (CONFIG_MTRR) [Y/n/?]
Symmetric multi-processing support (CONFIG_SMP) [N/y/?]
```

## LOADABLE MODULE SUPPORT

These options enable your kernel to dynamically load driver modules. You'll want to leave these enabled. The prompt will look like this:

```
Enable loadable module support (CONFIG_MODULES) [Y/n/?]
Set version information on all symbols for modules (CONFIG_MODVERSIONS) [Y/n/?]
Kernel module loader (CONFIG_KMOD) [Y/n/?]
```

## GENERAL SETUP

The general setup prompts for information about your computer hardware. If you do not need network support or are not running on PCI hardware, you can disable it here. Various BIOS options, including support for power management are included here. Linux is also capable of recognizing several file types as executable applications, such as the standard ELF binary format, and even Java programs. You'll probably want to enable kernel support for these features. As always, the default options can be considered safe. The general setup prompt looks like:

```
Networking support (CONFIG_NET) [Y/n/?] y
PCI support (CONFIG_PCI) [Y/n/?] y
PCI access mode (BIOS, Direct, Any) [Any] y
PCI access mode (BIOS, Direct, Any) [Any]
MCA support (CONFIG_MCA) [N/y/?]
SGI Visual Workstation support (CONFIG_VISWS) [N/y/?]
System V IPC (CONFIG_SYSVIPC) [Y/n/?]
BSD Process Accounting (CONFIG_BSD_PROCESS_ACCT) [Y/n/?]
Sysctl support (CONFIG_SYSCTL) [Y/n/?]
Kernel support for a.out binaries (CONFIG_BINFMT_AOUT) [M/n/y/?]
Kernel support for ELF binaries (CONFIG_BINFMT_ELF) [Y/m/n/?]
Kernel support for MISC binaries (CONFIG_BINFMT_MISC) [M/n/y/?]
```

```
Kernel support for JAVA binaries (obsolete) (CONFIG_BINFMT_JAVA) [M/n/y/?]
Parallel port support (CONFIG_PARPORT) [M/n/y/?]
Advanced Power Management BIOS support (CONFIG_APM) [Y/n/?]
```

## PLUG AND PLAY SUPPORT

If your system includes Plug and Play components, you'll want to make sure that support is enabled here:

```
Plug and Play support (CONFIG_PNP) [Y/n/?]
 Auto-probe for parallel devices (CONFIG_PNP_PARPORT) [M/n/?]
```

## BLOCK DEVICES

What kind of storage devices are you planning to use in your Linux computer? Floppy disk support? IDE support? You'll tell the configuration utility which sorts of traditional storage hardware you'll want supported at this prompt:

```
Normal PC floppy disk support (CONFIG_BLK_DEV_FD) [Y/m/n/?]
Enhanced IDE/MFM/RLL disk/cdrom/tape/floppy support (CONFIG_BLK_DEV_IDE) [Y/m/n/?]
```

## ADDITIONAL BLOCK DEVICES

More of the same. The additional block devices include network devices, RAID configurations, RAM disks, and Parallel port IDE devices, as shown here:

```
Loopback device support (CONFIG_BLK_DEV_LOOP) [M/n/y/?]
Network block device support (CONFIG_BLK_DEV_NBD) [M/n/y/?]
Multiple devices driver support (CONFIG_BLK_DEV_MD) [Y/n/?]
Autodetect RAID partitions (CONFIG_AUTODETECT_RAID) [Y/n/?]
RAM disk support (CONFIG_BLK_DEV_RAM) [Y/m/n/?]
XT hard disk support (CONFIG_BLK_DEV_XD) [M/n/y/?]
Mylex DAC960/DAC1100 PCI RAID Controller support (CONFIG_BLK_DEV_DAC960) [M/n/y/?]
Parallel port IDE device support (CONFIG_PARIDE) [M/n/?]
```

## NETWORKING OPTIONS

Are you intending to use your Linux computer as a firewall? Would you like to perform socket filtering or use IP masquerading to serve your internal network? If so, be sure that you've enabled it here:

```
Packet socket (CONFIG_PACKET) [Y/m/n/?]
Kernel/User netlink socket (CONFIG_NETLINK) [Y/n/?] Routing messages
➥(CONFIG_RTNETLINK) [Y/n/?]
Netlink device emulation (CONFIG_NETLINK_DEV) [Y/m/n/?]
Network firewalls (CONFIG_FIREWALL) [Y/n/?]
Socket Filtering (CONFIG_FILTER) [Y/n/?]
Unix domain sockets (CONFIG_UNIX) [Y/m/n/?]
TCP/IP networking (CONFIG_INET) [Y/n/?]
The IPv6 protocol (EXPERIMENTAL) (CONFIG_IPV6) [N/y/m/?]
Appletalk DDP (CONFIG_ATALK) [M/n/y/?]
CCITT X.25 Packet Layer (EXPERIMENTAL) (CONFIG_X25) [N/y/m/?]
LAPB Data Link Driver (EXPERIMENTAL) (CONFIG_LAPB) [N/y/m/?]
Bridging (EXPERIMENTAL) (CONFIG_BRIDGE) [N/y/?]
802.2 LLC (EXPERIMENTAL) (CONFIG_LLC) [N/y/?]
```

```
Acorn Econet/AUN protocols (EXPERIMENTAL) (CONFIG_ECONET) [N/y/m/?]
WAN router (CONFIG_WAN_ROUTER) [M/n/y/?]
Fast switching (read help!) (CONFIG_NET_FASTROUTE) [N/y/?]
Forwarding between high speed interfaces (CONFIG_NET_HW_FLOWCONTROL) [N/y/?]
CPU is too slow to handle full bandwidth (CONFIG_CPU_IS_SLOW) [N/y/?]
QoS and/or fair queueing (CONFIG_NET_SCHED) [N/y/?]
```

In the middle of these options, you'll be prompted for the information specific to the IP and IPX protocols. Unless you completely understand the implementation of these protocols, it's best to go with the defaults.

## SCSI SUPPORT TYPE

Many server systems use SCSI drives because of the speed, fault tolerance, and command queuing that makes them more appealing than IDE drives. If you plan to support SCSI on your system, you can include the drivers for your system here. I usually compile the SCSI driver into the kernel rather than as a loadable module. Linux supports a large number of SCSI drivers, so I've left the individual drivers out of the following listing:

```
SCSI disk support (CONFIG_BLK_DEV_SD) [Y/m/n/?]
SCSI tape support (CONFIG_CHR_DEV_ST) [M/n/y/?]
SCSI CD-ROM support (CONFIG_BLK_DEV_SR) [Y/m/n/?]
SCSI generic support (CONFIG_CHR_DEV_SG) [M/n/y/?]
Probe all LUNs on each SCSI device (CONFIG_SCSI_MULTI_LUN) [N/y/?]
Verbose SCSI error reporting (kernel size +=12K) (CONFIG_SCSI_CONSTANTS) [Y/n/?]
```

## NETWORK DEVICE SUPPORT

This is the general type of network hardware that you'll be using with your computer. After answering these questions, you'll be prompted for the specific type of hardware that you have installed. If you'd like support for AppleTalk and token-ring networks, Packet Radio, ISDN, and IrDA—these options are included here:

```
Network device support (CONFIG_NETDEVICES) [Y/n/?]
ARCnet support (CONFIG_ARCNET) [N/y/m/?]
Dummy net driver support (CONFIG_DUMMY) [M/n/y/?]
EQL (serial line load balancing) support (CONFIG_EQUALIZER) [M/n/y/?]
Ethertap network tap (CONFIG_ETHERTAP) [M/n/y/?]
General Instruments Surfboard 1000 (CONFIG_NET_SB1000) [M/n/y/?] *
Ethernet (10 or 100Mbit) (CONFIG_NET_ETHERNET) [Y/n/?]
Apple/Farallon LocalTalk PC support (CONFIG_LTPC) [M/n/?]
Appletalk-IP driver support (CONFIG_IPDDP) [M/n/?]
IP to Appletalk-IP Encapsulation support (CONFIG_IPDDP_ENCAP) [Y/n/?]
Appletalk-IP to IP Decapsulation support (CONFIG_IPDDP_DECAP) [Y/n/?]
PLIP (parallel port) support (CONFIG_PLIP) [M/n/?]
PPP (point-to-point) support (CONFIG_PPP) [M/n/y/?]
SLIP (serial line) support (CONFIG_SLIP) [M/n/y/?]
CSLIP compressed headers (CONFIG_SLIP_COMPRESSED) [Y/n/?]
Wireless LAN (non-hamradio) (CONFIG_NET_RADIO) [Y/n/?]
Token Ring driver support (CONFIG_TR) [Y/n/?]
Amateur Radio support (CONFIG_HAMRADIO) [N/y/?]
IrDA subsystem support (CONFIG_IRDA) [M/n/y/?]
ISDN support (CONFIG_ISDN) [M/n/y/?]
```

## Old CD-ROM Drivers

Remember the old days when you got your first CD-ROM? It probably plugged into a funny port on your sound card or someplace else equally bizarre. If you'd like to use this old device with your system, Linux is going to let you do it! Just choose the device from this list:

```
Support non-SCSI/IDE/ATAPI CDROM drives (CONFIG_CD_NO_IDESCSI) [Y/n/?]
Aztech/Orchid/Okano/Wearnes/TXC/CyDROM CDROM support
➥(CONFIG_AZTCD) [M/n/y/?]
Goldstar R420 CDROM support (CONFIG_GSCD) [M/n/y/?]
Matsushita/Panasonic/Creative, Longshine, TEAC CDROM support (CONFIG_SBPCD) [M/n/
y/?]
Mitsumi (standard) [no XA/Multisession] CDROM support (CONFIG_MCD) [M/n/y/?]
Mitsumi [XA/MultiSession] CDROM support (CONFIG_MCDX) [M/n/y/?]
Optics Storage DOLPHIN 8000AT CDROM support (CONFIG_OPTCD) [M/n/y/?]
Philips/LMS CM206 CDROM support (CONFIG_CM206) [M/n/y/?]
Sanyo CDR-H94A CDROM support (CONFIG_SJCD) [M/n/y/?]
ISP16/MAD16/Mozart soft configurable cdrom interface support
➥(CONFIG_ISP16_CDI) [M/n/y/?]
Sony CDU31A/CDU33A CDROM support (CONFIG_CDU31A) [M/n/y/?]
Sony CDU535 CDROM support (CONFIG_CDU535) [M/n/y/?]
```

## Character Devices

Do you need support for a lot of serial ports, or do you need specialized port support? Linux can use serial extension boards and other hardware to increase your connectivity. Unless you're going to be running a terminal server or another very specialized serial application, it's unlikely most of these will be needed. There are a few, however, that you'll probably be interested in—mouse support and parallel ports shown here:

```
Virtual terminal (CONFIG_VT) [Y/n/?]
Support for console on virtual terminal (CONFIG_VT_CONSOLE) [Y/n/?]
Standard/generic (dumb) serial support (CONFIG_SERIAL) [Y/m/n/?]
  Support for console on serial port (CONFIG_SERIAL_CONSOLE) [Y/n/?]
Extended dumb serial driver options (CONFIG_SERIAL_EXTENDED) [Y/n/?]
  Support more than 4 serial ports (CONFIG_SERIAL_MANY_PORTS) [Y/n/?]
Non-standard serial port support (CONFIG_SERIAL_NONSTANDARD) [Y/n/?]
Unix98 PTY support (CONFIG_UNIX98_PTYS) [Y/n/?]
Maximum number of Unix98 PTYs in use (0-2048) (CONFIG_UNIX98_PTY_COUNT) [256]
Parallel printer support (CONFIG_PRINTER) [M/n/?]
Mouse Support (not serial mice) (CONFIG_MOUSE) [Y/n/?]
```

## Mouse Support

Unless you're running a headless server, you've probably got a mouse hooked up to your computer. Choose the type of mouse support you'd like from this list:

```
ATIXL busmouse support (CONFIG_ATIXL_BUSMOUSE) [M/n/y/?]
Logitech busmouse support (CONFIG_BUSMOUSE) [M/n/y/?]
Microsoft busmouse support (CONFIG_MS_BUSMOUSE) [M/n/y/?]
PS/2 mouse (aka "auxiliary device") support (CONFIG_PSMOUSE) [Y/n/?]
C&T 82C710 mouse port support (as on TI Travelmate)
➥(CONFIG_82C710_MOUSE) [M/n/y/?]
PC110 digitizer pad support (CONFIG_PC110_PAD) [M/n/y/?]
```

## VIDEO FOR LINUX

Macintosh OS has QuickTime, Windows has Video For Windows (or QuickTime if you're serious), and, at long last, Linux has Video For Linux. Linux video support has a long way to go, but already supports several video input devices. If you've got one, here is where you tell the config utility:

```
Video For Linux (CONFIG_VIDEO_DEV) [M/n/y/?]
AIMSlab RadioTrack (aka RadioReveal) support (CONFIG_RADIO_RTRACK) [M/n/?]
AIMSlab RadioTrack II support (CONFIG_RADIO_RTRACK2) [M/n/?]
Aztech/Packard Bell Radio (CONFIG_RADIO_AZTECH) [M/n/?]
ADS Cadet AM/FM Tuner (CONFIG_RADIO_CADET) [M/n/?]
Miro PCM20 Radio (CONFIG_RADIO_MIROPCM20) [M/n/?]
GemTek Radio Card support (CONFIG_RADIO_GEMTEK) [M/n/?]
Trust FM Radio (CONFIG_RADIO_TRUST) [M/n/?]
BT848 Video For Linux (CONFIG_VIDEO_BT848) [M/n/?]
Quickcam BW Video For Linux (CONFIG_VIDEO_BWQCAM) [M/n/?]
Colour QuickCam Video For Linux (EXPERIMENTAL) (CONFIG_VIDEO_CQCAM) [M/n/?]
Mediavision Pro Movie Studio Video For Linux (CONFIG_VIDEO_PMS) [M/n/?]
SAA5249 Teletext processor (CONFIG_VIDEO_SAA5249) [M/n/?]
SF16FMI Radio (CONFIG_RADIO_SF16FMI) [M/n/?]
Typhoon Radio (a.k.a. EcoRadio) (CONFIG_RADIO_TYPHOON) [M/n/?]
Zoltrix Radio (CONFIG_RADIO_ZOLTRIX) [M/n/?]
Zoran ZR36057/36060 support (CONFIG_VIDEO_ZORAN) [M/n/?]
```

## JOYSTICK SUPPORT

Another wonderful addition to Linux is the support for a variety of different joysticks. It's a wonderful feeling to go into an Electronics Boutique and see Quake III for Linux in a box and on the shelf. Now you can play *and* control games under Linux. Here's where you configure your joystick support:

```
Joystick support (CONFIG_JOYSTICK) [M/n/y/?]
  Classic PC analog joysticks and gamepads (CONFIG_JOY_ANALOG) [M/n/?]
  FPGaming and MadCatz A3D controllers (CONFIG_JOY_ASSASIN) [M/n/?]
  Gravis GrIP joysticks and gamepads (CONFIG_JOY_GRAVIS) [M/n/?]
  Logitech Digital joysticks and gamepads (CONFIG_JOY_LOGITECH) [M/n/?]
  Microsoft SideWinder, Genius Digital joysticks and gamepads
  ➡(CONFIG_JOY_SIDEWINDER) [M/n/?]
  ThrustMaster DirectConnect joysticks and gamepads
  ➡(CONFIG_JOY_THRUSTMASTER) [M/n/?]
  PDPI Lightning 4 gamecards (CONFIG_JOY_LIGHTNING) [M/n/?]
  NES, SNES, PSX, Multisystem joysticks and gamepads (CONFIG_JOY_CONSOLE) [M/n/?]
  Sega, Multisystem joysticks and gamepads (CONFIG_JOY_DB9) [M/n/?]
  TurboGraFX Multisystem joystick interface (CONFIG_JOY_TURBOGRAFX) [M/n/?]
Double Talk PC internal speech card support (CONFIG_DTLK) [M/n/y/?]
```

## FTAPE, THE FLOPPY TAPE DEVICE DRIVER

There is a very popular (at one time) type of tape backup system that uses the floppy control to drive the tape unit. Most current backup units use the parallel port, SCSI, or IDE controllers. If you have a floppy controlled mechanism, support is found here:

```
Ftape (QIC-80/Travan) support (CONFIG_FTAPE) [M/n/y/?]
Zftape, the VFS interface (CONFIG_ZFTAPE) [M/n/?]
```

```
Default block size (CONFIG_ZFT_DFLT_BLK_SZ) [10240]
Number of ftape buffers (EXPERIMENTAL) (CONFIG_FT_NR_BUFFERS) [3]
Enable procfs status report (+2kb) (CONFIG_FT_PROC_FS) [N/y/?]
Debugging output (Normal, Excessive, Reduced, None) [Normal]
Floppy tape controllers (Standard, MACH-2, FC-10/FC-20, Alt/82078) [Standard]
Default FIFO threshold (EXPERIMENTAL) (CONFIG_FT_FDC_THR) [8]
Maximal data rate to use (EXPERIMENTAL) (CONFIG_FT_FDC_MAX_RATE) [2000]
```

## FILESYSTEMS

Linux offers support for a wide range of filesystems—from the Macintosh HFS filesystem to the various Windows FAT systems, NTFS, and the like. If you'd like to be able to use disks or drives containing these filesystems on your computer, configure the appropriate options here. Support for filesystem quotas is also turned on here:

```
Quota support (CONFIG_QUOTA) [Y/n/?]
Kernel automounter support (CONFIG_AUTOFS_FS) [M/n/y/?]
ADFS filesystem support (read only) (EXPERIMENTAL) (CONFIG_ADFS_FS) [N/y/m/?]
Amiga FFS filesystem support (CONFIG_AFFS_FS) [N/y/m/?]
Apple Macintosh filesystem support (experimental) (CONFIG_HFS_FS) [M/n/y/?]
DOS FAT fs support (CONFIG_FAT_FS) [M/n/y/?]
 MSDOS fs support (CONFIG_MSDOS_FS) [M/n/?]
 UMSDOS: Unix-like filesystem on top of standard MSDOS filesystem
   (CONFIG_UMSDOS_FS) [M/n/?]
VFAT (Windows-95) fs support (CONFIG_VFAT_FS) [M/n/?] ISO 9660 CDROM filesystem
   support (CONFIG_ISO9660_FS) [Y/m/n/?]
Microsoft Joliet CDROM extensions (CONFIG_JOLIET) [Y/n/?]
Minix fs support (CONFIG_MINIX_FS) [M/n/y/?]
NTFS filesystem support (read only) (CONFIG_NTFS_FS) [N/y/m/?] OS/2 HPFS
   filesystem support (read only) (CONFIG_HPFS_FS) [M/n/y/?]
/proc filesystem support (CONFIG_PROC_FS) [Y/n/?]
/dev/pts filesystem for Unix98 PTYs (CONFIG_DEVPTS_FS) [Y/n/?]
QNX filesystem support (EXPERIMENTAL) (CONFIG_QNX4FS_FS) [N/y/m/?]
ROM filesystem support (CONFIG_ROMFS_FS) [M/n/y/?]
Second extended fs support (CONFIG_EXT2_FS) [Y/m/n/?]
System V and Coherent filesystem support (CONFIG_SYSV_FS) [M/n/y/?]
UFS filesystem support (CONFIG_UFS_FS) [M/n/y/?]
SGI EFS filesystem support (read only) (experimental) (CONFIG_EFS_FS) [N/y/m/?]
```

## NETWORK FILE SYSTEMS

Besides traditional file systems, Linux supports the capability to mount and serve network filesystems, including the Windows SMB filesystem, natively on your computer. Choose filesystem support here:

```
Coda filesystem support (advanced network fs) (CONFIG_CODA_FS) [M/n/y/?]
NFS filesystem support (CONFIG_NFS_FS) [M/n/y/?]
NFS server support (CONFIG_NFSD) [M/n/y/?]
SMB filesystem support (to mount WfW shares etc.) (CONFIG_SMB_FS) [M/n/y/?]
NCP filesystem support (to mount NetWare volumes) (CONFIG_NCP_FS) [M/n/y/?]
```

## PARTITION TYPES

Besides being able to read and write a filesystem, you'll probably need support for being able to read partition tables off of foreign drives. If you don't need support for foreign file systems, you really won't need this stuff. Here's what the partition table support prompts look like:

```
BSD disklabel (BSD partition tables) support (CONFIG_BSD_DISKLABEL) [N/y/?]
Macintosh partition map support (CONFIG_MAC_PARTITION) [N/y/?]
SMD disklabel (Sun partition tables) support (CONFIG_SMD_DISKLABEL) [N/y/?]
Solaris (x86) partition table support (CONFIG_SOLARIS_X86_PARTITION) [N/y/?]
Unixware slices support (EXPERIMENTAL) (CONFIG_UNIXWARE_DISKLABEL) [N/y/?]
```

## NATIVE LANGUAGE SUPPORT

Need native support for foreign language character sets? Choose what you want from the following:

```
Codepage 437 (United States, Canada) (CONFIG_NLS_CODEPAGE_437) [M/n/y/?]
Codepage 737 (Greek) (CONFIG_NLS_CODEPAGE_737) [M/n/y/?] ?
Codepage 737 (Greek) (CONFIG_NLS_CODEPAGE_737) [M/n/y/?]
Codepage 775 (Baltic Rim) (CONFIG_NLS_CODEPAGE_775) [M/n/y/?]
Codepage 850 (Europe) (CONFIG_NLS_CODEPAGE_850) [M/n/y/?]
Codepage 852 (Central/Eastern Europe) (CONFIG_NLS_CODEPAGE_852) [M/n/y/?]
Codepage 855 (Cyrillic) (CONFIG_NLS_CODEPAGE_855) [M/n/y/?]
Codepage 857 (Turkish) (CONFIG_NLS_CODEPAGE_857) [M/n/y/?]
Codepage 860 (Portuguese) (CONFIG_NLS_CODEPAGE_860) [M/n/y/?]
Codepage 861 (Icelandic) (CONFIG_NLS_CODEPAGE_861) [M/n/y/?]
Codepage 862 (Hebrew) (CONFIG_NLS_CODEPAGE_862) [M/n/y/?]
Codepage 863 (Canadian French) (CONFIG_NLS_CODEPAGE_863) [M/n/y/?]
Codepage 864 (Arabic) (CONFIG_NLS_CODEPAGE_864) [M/n/y/?]
Codepage 865 (Norwegian, Danish) (CONFIG_NLS_CODEPAGE_865) [M/n/y/?]
Codepage 866 (Cyrillic/Russian) (CONFIG_NLS_CODEPAGE_866) [M/n/y/?]
Codepage 869 (Greek) (CONFIG_NLS_CODEPAGE_869) [M/n/y/?]
Codepage 874 (Thai) (CONFIG_NLS_CODEPAGE_874) [M/n/y/?]
NLS ISO 8859-1 (Latin 1; Western European Languages) (CONFIG_NLS_ISO8859_1)
    [M/n/y/?]
NLS ISO 8859-2 (Latin 2; Slavic/Central European Languages) (CONFIG_NLS_
    ISO8859_2) [M/n/y/?]
NLS ISO 8859-3 (Latin 3; Esperanto, Galician, Maltese, Turkish) (CONFIG_NLS_
    ISO8859_3) [M/n/y/?]
NLS ISO 8859-4 (Latin 4; Estonian, Latvian, Lithuanian) (CONFIG_NLS_ISO8859_4)
    [M/n/y/?]
NLS ISO 8859-5 (Cyrillic) (CONFIG_NLS_ISO8859_5) [M/n/y/?]
NLS ISO 8859-6 (Arabic) (CONFIG_NLS_ISO8859_6) [M/n/y/?]
NLS ISO 8859-7 (Modern Greek) (CONFIG_NLS_ISO8859_7) [M/n/y/?]
NLS ISO 8859-8 (Hebrew) (CONFIG_NLS_ISO8859_8) [M/n/y/?]
NLS ISO 8859-9 (Latin 5; Turkish) (CONFIG_NLS_ISO8859_9) [M/n/y/?]
NLS ISO 8859-14 (Latin 8; Celtic) (CONFIG_NLS_ISO8859_14) [M/n/y/?]
NLS ISO 8859-15 (Latin 9; Western European Languages with Euro) (CONFIG_NLS_
    ISO8859_15) [M/n/y/?]
NLS KOI8-R (Russian) (CONFIG_NLS_KOI8_R) [M/n/y/?]
```

## CONSOLE DRIVERS

In order to present you with a login console, Linux must be able to drive your video card. There is very little chance that it won't be able to do this, out of the box. There are, however, special options that can be configured here if you have the appropriate sort of video card:

```
VGA text console (CONFIG_VGA_CONSOLE) [Y/n/?]
Video mode selection support (CONFIG_VIDEO_SELECT) [Y/n/?]
MDA text console (dual-headed) (EXPERIMENTAL) (CONFIG_MDA_CONSOLE) [M/n/y/?]
Support for frame buffer devices (EXPERIMENTAL) (CONFIG_FB) [Y/n/?]
Permedia2 support (experimental) (CONFIG_FB_PM2) [N/y/?]
VESA VGA graphics console (CONFIG_FB_VESA) [Y/n/?]
VGA 16-color graphics console (CONFIG_FB_VGA16) [N/y/?]
Matrox acceleration (CONFIG_FB_MATROX) [M/n/y/?]
ATI Mach64 display support (CONFIG_FB_ATY) [N/y/?]
Virtual Frame Buffer support (ONLY FOR TESTING!) (CONFIG_FB_VIRTUAL) [N/y/m/?]
Advanced low level driver options (CONFIG_FBCON_ADVANCED) [N/y/?]
Support only 8 pixels wide fonts (CONFIG_FBCON_FONTWIDTH8_ONLY) [N/y/?]
Select compiled-in fonts (CONFIG_FBCON_FONTS) [N/y/?]
```

## SOUND

What is a computer without sound? Linux offers support for many different types of sound hardware. From the original Sound Blaster to the current PCI offerings—you'll find the drivers here:

```
Sound card support (CONFIG_SOUND) [M/n/y/?]
Support for C-Media PCI audio chips (Experimental) (CONFIG_SOUND_CMPCI) [M/n/?]
Enable legacy FM (CONFIG_SOUND_CMPCI_FM) [N/y/?]
Enable legacy MPU-401 (CONFIG_SOUND_CMPCI_MIDI) [Y/n/?]
Ensoniq AudioPCI (ES1370) (CONFIG_SOUND_ES1370) [M/n/?]
Creative Ensoniq AudioPCI 97 (ES1371) (CONFIG_SOUND_ES1371) [M/n/?]
ESS Solo1 (Experimental) (CONFIG_SOUND_ESSSOLO1) [M/n/?]
Support for Turtle Beach MultiSound Pinnacle, Fiji (CONFIG_SOUND_MSNDPIN) [M/n/?]
OSS sound modules (CONFIG_SOUND_OSS) [M/n/?]
ProAudioSpectrum 16 support (CONFIG_SOUND_PAS) [M/n/?]
100% Sound Blaster compatibles (SB16/32/64, ESS, Jazz16) support (CONFIG_SOUND_SB)
  [M/n/?]
Generic OPL2/OPL3 FM synthesizer support (CONFIG_SOUND_ADLIB) [M/n/?]
...there's a lot!...
Ensoniq SoundScape support (CONFIG_SOUND_SSCAPE) [M/n/?]
MediaTrix AudioTrix Pro support (CONFIG_SOUND_TRIX) [M/n/?]
VIA 82C686 Audio Codec (CONFIG_SOUND_VIA82CXXX) [M/n/?]
Support for OPTi MAD16 and/or Mozart based cards (CONFIG_SOUND_MAD16) [M/n/?]
Support MIDI in older MAD16 based cards (requires SB)
➥(CONFIG_MAD16_OLDCARD) [Y/n/?]
Support for Aztech Sound Galaxy (non-PnP) cards (CONFIG_SOUND_SGALAXY) [M/n/?]
Support for AD1816 based cards (EXPERIMENTAL) (CONFIG_SOUND_AD1816) [M/n/?]
Yamaha OPL3-SA1 audio controller (CONFIG_SOUND_OPL3SA1) [M/n/?]
SoftOSS software wave table engine (CONFIG_SOUND_SOFTOSS) [M/n/?]
FM synthesizer (YM3812/OPL-3) support (CONFIG_SOUND_YM3812) [M/n/?]
Loopback MIDI device support (CONFIG_SOUND_VMIDI) [M/n/?]
6850 UART support (CONFIG_SOUND_UART6850) [M/n/?]
NM256AV/NM256ZX audio support (CONFIG_SOUND_NM256) [M/n/?]
```

When you've finally reached the end of the options (it's gonna take a while!), you're ready to start the compilation process. There are a few steps to this, but they're relatively simple.

## OTHER CONFIGURATION METHODS

Before moving on, I'd like to point out that there are two other means by which you can configure the kernel that might be a bit more appealing to some people. The first method is a text, cursor-controlled setup screen. If you've used LinuxConf, you'll be at home with the hierarchical configuration stuff. A sample configuration screen for this method is shown in Figure 37.1. To start using the menu-based configuration, just type make menuconfig instead of the make config option that you used previously. You must be in the /usr/src/linux directory to do this.

**Figure 37.1**
Running make menuconf allows you to configure the system much like LinuxConf.

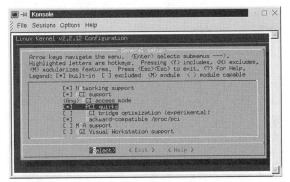

If you'd like to configure the kernel compilation in an entirely graphical environment, you've got that option as well. From within your preferred X Window environment, type make xconfig at the command line—be sure that you're in the /usr/linux/src directory first. Each kernel configuration section is represented by a button. Clicking the button of the portion you'd like to configure will bring up a secondary window with the appropriate options. Figure 37.2 shows the GUI version of the kernel configuration.

After you've finished your configuration with either the text-based menu system or X Windows interface, you can save the configuration options, and then proceed with the compilation from the command line.

# COMPILING AND INSTALLING A NEW KERNEL

The kernel compilation actually consists of several different steps. You can safely combine these into two steps—compiling and installing. These two steps can take a considerable amount of time, so you can take a breather while the system does its thing.

To compile the kernel, type make dep clean bzImage modules from within the /usr/src/linux directory:

```
make[1]: Entering directory '/usr/src/linux-2.2.14/arch/i386/boot'
make[1]: Nothing to be done for 'dep'.
make[1]: Leaving directory '/usr/src/linux-2.2.14/arch/i386/boot'
```

```
scripts/mkdep init/*.c > .depend
scripts/mkdep 'find /usr/src/linux-2.2.14/include/asm /usr/src/linux-2.2.14/
    include/linux /usr/src/linux-2.2.14/include/scsi /usr/src/linux-2.2.14/include/
    net -follow -name \*.h ! -name modversions.h -print· > .hdepend
make _sfdep_kernel _sfdep_drivers _sfdep_mm _sfdep_fs _sfdep_net _sfdep_ipc _
    sfdep_lib _sfdep_arch/i386/kernel _sfdep_arch/i386/mm _sfdep_arch/i386/lib _
    sfdep_arch/i386/math-emu _FASTDEP_ALL_SUB_DIRS="kernel drivers mm fs net ipc
    lib arch/i386/kernel arch/i386/mm arch/i386/lib arch/i386/math-emu"
make[1]: Entering directory '/usr/src/linux-2.2.14'
make -C kernel fastdep
make[2]: Entering directory '/usr/src/linux-2.2.14/kernel'
...
```

**Figure 37.2**
Use `make`
`xconfig` to con-
figure the kernel
using an X Win-
dows interface.

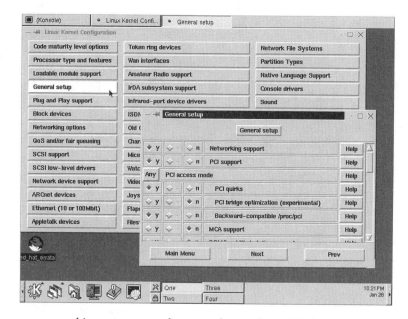

On a slow computer, this process can take more than an hour. Today's Pentium systems should have the procedure completed within 10 minutes or so.

When the compilation is completed, it's time to finish things up. Before going any further, however, make sure that you've created backups of your old kernel file. The default kernel filename under Red Hat 6.2 is `vmlinuz-2.x.x`. Make a copy of this—just in case!

Finally, type `make modules_install install`. This will copy both the modules and the kernel to their appropriate spots on your drive.

## SETTING UP `/etc/lilo.conf`

In order to finish up the installation of the kernel, you'll need to edit the `/etc/lilo.conf` file so that your boot loader knows where to find the appropriate kernel. For example, your initial configuration might look at bit like this (line numbers are added for clarity):

```
1: boot=/dev/hda
2: map=/boot/map
3: install=/boot/boot.b
```

```
4: prompt
5: timeout=50
6: default=linux

7: image=/boot/vmlinuz-2.2.14-5.0
8:     label=linux
9:     read-only
10:    root=/dev/sda1
```

The important part of this file is at the end—lines 7-10. These lines define the kernel file that will be used at bootup. If you've compiled a new kernel named, for example, vmlinuz-2.5.0, you could change the lilo.conf file to include it as an option at bootup:

```
1: boot=/dev/hda
2: map=/boot/map
3: install=/boot/boot.b
4: prompt
5: timeout=50
6: default=linux

7: image=/boot/vmlinuz-2.2.14-5.0
8:     label=linux
9:     read-only
10:    root=/dev/sda1

11:image=/boot/vmlinuz-2.5.0
12:     label=newlinux
13:     read-only
14:     root=/dev/sda1
```

The additional lines are the same, but reference the new kernel. Notice also that line 12 names the new configuration option newlinux. When you first boot your computer, you'll be able to type newlinux at the LILO: prompt to boot using the new kernel. If you find that the new kernel works the way you want, just change line 6 to set the new default kernel to newlinux.

After /etc/lilo.conf is configured, you need to have LILO read the new configuration file. To do this, run /sbin/lilo:

```
[root@contempt /root]# /sbin/lilo
Added linux *
Added newlinux
```

That's it! Reboot and enjoy.

Tip

> If you have a SCSI-based system, there are some situations where you might need to create a RAM disk file that is loaded with modules before your system boots. This is usually necessary if you have SCSI drivers that are being loaded as modules. If you do have a SCSI system, check the man pages for mkinitrd for more information.

# APPENDIXES

# Dual Booting Windows and Linux

## In this appendix

# WHY DUAL BOOT?

Many of you may be accomplished Windows users who would like to explore and learn about Linux, but at the same time still have access to Windows and all your favorite programs so that you can be productive when you're not exploring and learning Linux. In that case, you want to be able to *dual boot*. What that means is, whenever you first start your computer, you'll be given the option to use either Windows or Linux as your OS.

Dual booting is recommended only if you're planning to set up Linux as a workstation. A server-class installation will automatically wipe out everything on your hard disk, so there's no point in trying to dual boot if you're planning to set up a server. Besides, the whole idea behind most servers is to provide access to resources seven days a week, 24 hours a day. If allowed to dual boot, the server would be "down" whenever you were running it with any operating system other than Linux.

If you're new to Linux, you'd do well to start off with a workstation installation anyway. With a workstation installation you get access to the graphical GNOME interface, used throughout Part I of this book. And it's there you'll learn all the basics. If you decide to set up a Linux server after you've learned the basics, no problem. Simply reinstall Linux as a server at that time. Just remember that once you do set up Linux as a server, you won't be able to dual boot with Windows, or any other operating system, after that point.

# BACKING UP YOUR HARD DISK

If you want to be able to dual boot, each OS on your hard drive must exist in its own *partition*. A partition is an area of the disk that's reserved for a specific operating system and its files. If your Windows PC is like most, it has one hard disk that's formatted as a single partition, which Windows refers to as drive C:. In order to dual boot, you should really have a hard disk with at least 4GB of storage. Windows can occupy about 2GB of that drive, and the rest can be dedicated to Linux.

When you repartition a disk, you lose everything on that disk! So making a backup of everything you'd like to have access to in the future is vitally important. There are Windows products, such as Partition Magic, that will allow you to repartition a disk without losing all the data on it. However, you may still want to make a backup of your disk prior to repartitioning even with a product like that, just in case something goes wrong.

If your hard disk is an overcrowded, disorganized mess, you may not really want to back it up and restore it after partitioning. You might, instead, want to do a little housekeeping. Just back up the things you really need, and dump any junk you don't need anymore. As you think about what you do—and don't—want to back up and restore, keep the following points in mind:

- Any documents you've created yourself—including word processing documents, spreadsheets, databases, and so forth—absolutely must be backed up if you want to get them back after partitioning.

■ Commercial programs (including Windows) can be reinstalled from their original CD-ROMs or floppy disks, so it's not absolutely necessary to back up each and every program on your hard disk. However, some program installations require a CD Key or serial number. You'll be able to reinstall such programs after repartitioning only if you have the program's CD Key or serial number!

■ If you don't back up program files, but instead reinstall them from scratch after partitioning, don't forget that all "personal" settings you've made in those programs will be returned to their default values.

■ Programs that maintain a database, such as Microsoft Outlook, Microsoft Money, and so forth, usually offer some kind of backup for the data. If you plan to reinstall such programs from scratch, be sure to back up the data in those programs first.

■ Some programs maintain lists for you. For example, Web browsers and email programs maintain Favorites, Bookmarks, and Addresses. If you don't back up those programs, you stand to lose those lists.

PART

VII

APP

A

**Caution**  Make sure you have your original Windows CD-ROM so that you can reinstall Windows after repartitioning. You cannot reinstall Windows without that CD! You will probably need the original CD jacket as well, which contains the Product Key code that you need to enter to install Windows.

Once you've decided what you do—and don't—want to bring back to your hard disk after repartitioning, you need to make your backup files. Exactly how you do that depends on what kind of back up hardware you have. You may be able to backup your entire hard disk to a tape. If you have a CD-writer, you can place files on a CD-R. In a LAN, you can simply copy whatever you need to another PC's hard drive. The procedure you use to make your backups is entirely up to you. Just remember that you stand to lose everything that you don't back up prior to repartitioning your drive.

If you have multiple Windows hard disks, such as C: and D:, I would recommend you back up everything on the additional drives as well. There's a chance you could lose everything on the extra Windows drives during the repartitioning procedure. And you wouldn't want that to happen without a backup to restore from.

## DECIDING ON PARTITION SIZES

After you've made backups of important Windows files, you're ready to repartition your drive. Your first decision will be how large you want each partition to be. There are some limitations to consider right off the bat:

- The maximum size of the Windows boot partition will be about 2000MB (about 2GB) because the computer cannot dual boot if the first partition is greater than that size. The technical reason for this is that the typical PC BIOS (Basic Input/Output System) requires that the boot partition not extend beyond cylinder 1023, which corresponds to about two gigabytes in size.

**Tip**

> The Windows boot partition is essentially your Windows drive C: Even though the boot partition is limited to 2GB, you can create additional Windows partitions of virtually any size. For example, you can create a Windows drive D: of virtually any size, and perhaps use it to store all your documents. It's sort of an entire drive for your My Documents folder.

- The minimum size for the Windows boot partition is about 1GB, depending on which version of Windows you're using and what additional programs you plan to add to the Windows partition. I wouldn't recommend going below 1GB, though.

- The minimum size for all Linux partitions will be 600MB, although I wouldn't recommend going below 1GB (1024MB). In fact, if at all possible, you should go for a minimum of 2GB.

- There is no maximum size limit for the Linux partitions.

If your hard disk is GB or greater in size, the decision is pretty simple. Give Windows its 2000MB maximum size and devote the rest to Linux. If your hard drive is less than 4GB in size, perhaps divide the drive up 50/50—half for Windows, half for Linux. If you have a lot of disk space, you can devote about 2000MB to Windows and the rest to Linux. Or, as discussed in this appendix, you can create a 2GB Primary DOS Partition (drive C:) for Windows, and also an Extended DOS Partition (drive D:) for additional Windows files. That drive D; can be any size you want, provided you leave at least a gigabyte or two for Linux.

If your drive is really small—say, less than 2GB—dual booting may not be an option. Fortunately, hard drives are pretty cheap these days. So you could probably upgrade to a 4GB or greater drive for about $150 or so. Any computer dealer or repair shop can give you a more accurate estimate. If you're not too savvy on building PCs or upgrading hardware components, I'm sure the dealer will be happy to do the labor as well...for a fee, of course.

If you don't want to have to mess with additional partitions for Linux, with Red Hat 6.2, one of the installation options is to actually install on an existing Windows/DOS partition. This is a good way to "play" with the system without a big investment in configuration time. The drawback is that you don't get the advantages of running on the efficient ext2 filesystem that Linux provides, and you can only allocate a maximum of around 4GB of storage space. The Linux system files are stored in a single file on the Windows partition, making it very simple to "uninstall" if you so desire.

# CREATING A WINDOWS STARTUP DISK

Before you repartition your hard disk, you'll want to be able to boot from a Windows startup disk. Grab a blank floppy disk (or a floppy disk that contains stuff you don't want anymore), and label it "Windows Startup Disk." With so many versions of Windows floating around these days, it's hard to give specific instructions on creating that disk. But if you're using Windows 98 or Windows 95, you'll find the option to create a startup disk in the Add/ Remove Programs dialog box in Control Panel. To get there, click the Windows Start button, choose Settings, Control Panel, and open the Add/Remove Programs icon. Click the Startup Disk tab, click the Create Disk button, and follow the instructions that appear on the screen. After you've created the startup disk, remove it from the floppy drive. You can close any open windows or dialog boxes on the Windows desktop.

PART

**VII**

APP

**A**

### Deleting Linux Partitions

The FDISK program that comes with Windows can't delete Linux partitions. If you've already created some Linux partitions and want to get rid of them, you'll need to use Linux to do that. You'll also be able to remove Windows partitions with Linux. But don't forget that when you remove a partition, you remove all data with it. Don't delete any partitions that contain data you need.

You can use the Linux Setup procedure to remove existing partitions. Shut down your computer, put your Red Hat Linux boot disk in drive A: and your Red Hat Linux CD in your CD-ROM drive. Start the computer, and go through the steps as though you were going to install Linux from scratch (just keep pressing Enter to choose the default selection). When you get to the option to perform a Workstation, Server, or Custom Install, choose Custom. Then choose Disk Druid when asked which partitioning tool to use.

In Disk Druid, you can delete any partition by moving the highlight bar to it, and then pressing F4 (or tab to the Delete button and press Enter). After you've deleted all partitions, press F12 to choose OK. You'll see a message saying that you need to assign a root (/) partition if you want to install Linux. However, you want to install Windows first, so the message isn't really relevant. Press Enter to choose OK, and then select the Back button. Answer Yes when asked about saving changes to the partition table.

When you get back to the Disk Setup options, pull the Red Hat disks from the CD-ROM and floppy drives, and put your Windows Emergency Boot Disk in floppy drive A. Then bail out of Linux setup by pressing Ctrl+Alt+Del. Your computer will boot to an A:\> prompt. You're then ready to run the Windows FDISK to create Windows partitions.

# REPARTITIONING YOUR HARD DRIVE

Now comes the part where you repartition your disk using FDISK. If you prefer to use a third-party program like Partition Magic, *do not proceed* with these instructions. Instead, follow whatever instructions are provided by your third-party program. Make sure you make the primary DOS partition (a.k.a., Windows drive C:) no larger than 2000 megabytes. When you've finished, you can go straight to Appendix B, "Installing Red Hat Linux" to install Linux.

If you do plan to use FDISK to repartition your hard disk, continue reading. You're approaching the point of no return here: Once you start partitioning your hard disk, you'll lose anything and everything that's on that disk. So don't proceed unless you're sure you've backed up everything you want to be able to bring back into Windows and that you know how to get files from whatever backup medium you used. The steps you need to follow to repartition your hard disk, using Windows' FDISK program, are as follows:

1. Put the Windows startup disk into floppy drive A:.

2. If Windows is currently running, click the Start button and choose Shut Down, Restart, and then click the OK button. If the computer is already shut down, simply start up your computer in the usual manner, but with the Windows startup disk still in drive A:.

3. Your computer will go through its normal Power On Self-Test and you'll be given options to start the computer with or without CD-ROM support. Press Enter to choose the first option—Start Computer with CD-ROM Support. Or, just wait a few seconds to have that first option selected automatically.

4. Some more information will go by on the screen as Windows tries to figure out which driver is needed to activate your CD-ROM drive. In a minute or so you should end up with some messages and a DOS A:\> prompt looking something like the following:

```
The diagnostic tools were successfully loaded to drive D:.

...

Drive E: Driver MSCD001 unit 0

To get help, type HELP and press Enter.

A:\>
```

When you boot from a floppy disk, the procedure creates a *RAM disk* (a chunk of memory made to look like a disk to the system) with the name *D:*. If you already have a drive named D (such as your CD-ROM drive), it will be temporarily renamed to *E:*. Any drives beyond that will also move up a letter (for example, your old drive E: will become drive F: temporarily). Don't worry about that, though. When all the repartitioning is done and Windows is reinstalled, all your drives above drive C: will go back to their original names.

> **Note**
> If drive C: has no partitions defined, you'll see a message to that effect, followed by a lot of possible causes when you boot from the floppy. Your RAM disk will probably be set to drive D:. Don't worry about any of that though. You can still run FDISK and create partitions.

## STARTING WINDOWS FDISK

To start FDISK, type the following at the A:\> prompt:

```
FDISK
```

Now press Enter. You'll see a long message about large disk support and several caveats to be aware of, including the fact that you may not be able to dual boot if you enable large disk support. The long message is followed by the prompt:

```
Do you wish to enable large disk support (Y/N)...?[Y]
```

You can choose either Yes or No. Just keep in mind that if you allow large disk support, you'll still need to make your Primary DOS partition 2GB or less, even though FDISK will allow you to go to the full capacity of the drive. After you make your selection, you'll then be taken to a menu containing the following options:

- Create DOS Partition or Logical DOS Drive
- Set Active Partition
- Delete Partition or Logical DOS Drive
- Display Partition Information

If you want to see how your hard disk is currently partitioned, choose option 4 (type 4 and press Enter). The hard disk's partition table appears (see Figure A.1). The partition table is a list of all the partitions that currently exist on the hard disk. If your Windows PC is configured so that the entire hard disk is defined as drive C, your screen will look something like Figure A.1. Only one partition exists, and its type is PRI DOS (Primary DOS partition).

PART

**VII**

APP

**A**

**Figure A.1**
All of this hard drive is currently partitioned as the Primary DOS partition, better known as drive C: in Windows.

If you had two or more hard drives dedicated to Windows, (for example, a second hard disk named D:), those drives will be listed as the type EXT DOS (Extended DOS partitions). After viewing the partition information, press Escape to return to the FDISK Options menu.

## DELETING PARTITIONS

Next, you'll need to delete the existing partition(s) to make room for new ones. Once you delete a partition, there's no hope of recovering whatever was on the disk before, so make sure you understand you are about to delete, forever, everything on your C drive. To delete your primary DOS partition, choose option 3, Delete Partition or Logical DOS Drive. Then choose option 1, Delete Primary DOS Partition. A warning message appears to let you know that you have really reached the point of no return. Press Enter to proceed, thereby opting to delete partition 1 (which is your C: drive). To play it safe, FDISK makes you type in the drive's volume label. The volume label appears near the top of the partition table, just to the right of PRI DOS on the primary DOS partition. You must type the partition name exactly as shown. If the partition has no volume label, just leave the Volume Label prompt on the screen blank. Press Enter.

One more time, FDISK asks if you're sure. (It's dutifully paranoid!) Type Y and press Enter to proceed. You'll see a message indicating that the primary DOS partition has been deleted. Press Escape to return to the FDISK Options menu.

To make sure that you deleted all DOS partitions, choose option 4 from FDISK's menu to see which partitions are currently defined. If you see No partitions defined near the bottom of the screen, you have finished deleting partitions. Your hard disk is as naked as a newborn baby. Press Escape to return to the FDISK Options menu, and you can now go to the next section in this appendix, "Creating a New Primary DOS Partition."

> **Note** Microsoft's FDISK program will not allow you to delete Linux partitions. Refer to the sidebar titled "Deleting Linux Partitions" in this appendix if you need to get rid of any existing Linux partitions.

If your hard disk was divided into two or more drive letters (for example, C:, D:, and so on), each of those drive letters will be represented as a partition. If you backed them up as well and really want to start from a clean slate, you should delete all the remaining partitions. Be aware, however, that when you delete the partition, you permanently delete everything on the corresponding drive. To delete any remaining partitions, use option 3 again. The extra partitions will most likely be defined as extended DOS partitions and/or logical DOS drives. You need to delete any logical DOS drives within a partition before you can delete the partition itself.

Just keep deleting logical DOS drives and partitions until choosing option 3 leads to the message No Partitions to Delete. At that point, your hard disk is completely "clean," and you can press Escape to return to the FDISK options.

## CREATING A NEW PRIMARY DOS PARTITION

Now you're ready to create a new Primary DOS Partition for Windows. This partition will be your Windows drive C:. Assuming you're at FDISK's main menu right now, here's how to proceed:

1. Choose option 1, Create DOS Partition or Logical DOS Drive, by typing 1 and pressing Enter. A new menu appears.

2. From the next menu that appears, choose option 1, Create Primary DOS Partition. There will be a brief disk verification test. Then you'll see an option asking if you want to use the maximum available size for the Primary DOS Partition. Type N for No and press Enter.

3. The next prompt asks you to enter a partition size in megabytes or as a percentage of disk space. If you want to set aside the maximum 2000MB for Windows, type `2000`. If need be, you can make the partition smaller by typing in a smaller number, although I wouldn't recommend going any lower than 1GB (1000MB). Press Enter after typing the number.

4. The partition table appears on the screen as well as the message `Primary DOS Partition Created`. Press Esc to return to the FDISK Options menu.

5. Next, select option 2, Set Active Partition, by typing `2` and pressing Enter.

6. Type `1` to indicate that you want to make partition 1 the active partition. (This tells the computer to boot from that partition.) Press Enter. The message `Partition 1 made active` appears near the bottom of the screen.

7. Press Escape to return to the FDISK Options menu.

For the time being, keep your new partition as the only Windows partition on your hard drive. If you like, you'll be able to create a drive D: for additional Windows files later during the Linux installation. Appendix B will explain how when the opportunity arises. For now, press Escape to exit FDISK. You'll see a message indicating that you must restart your computer for the changes to take effect. Go ahead and press Escape to exit FDISK.

## RESTARTING YOUR COMPUTER

Next, you need to restart the computer to make the new partitions permanent. Leave the Windows startup disk in floppy drive A:, turn off the computer, wait a few seconds, and then turn the computer back on. The computer will once again go through its Power-On Self Test and ask if you want to start with, or without, CD-ROM support. Again, you can choose the first option—With CD-ROM Support. Eventually, you'll be taken back to the DOS A:\> prompt, where you'll be able to format your new partition (or partitions), as discussed in the next section.

## FORMATTING THE C DRIVE

Your new Primary DOS partition needs to be formatted before you can put Windows on it. To format that partition, type the following command:

```
format c:
```

Next press Enter. You'll see a warning that you'll lose all data on the drive. That message is actually a moot point by now because you already wiped the disk clean when you deleted its original partitions. So you can just type the letter Y and press Enter to proceed with the format. This part may take a few minutes. The screen will keep you informed of the format's progress. When the disk is completely formatted you'll see the message:

```
Volume label (11 characters, ENTER for none)?
```

The volume label is entirely optional and can be any text you like (but no blank spaces) up to 11 characters in length. I usually label my C: drive as the computer's name followed by an underscore and the letter C (`_C`). For example, on the computer named BiGBoy, I'd enter

BiGBoy_C as the volume label. This makes it easy to identify the drive later on down the road, when you're browsing around through computers in your network. Press Enter after typing the volume label. You're returned to the DOS A:\> prompt.

**Tip**
> There's nothing permanent about the volume label you enter here. After you reinstall Windows, you can change the volume label if you want. In Windows 95/98, open My Computer, right-click the drive's icon, choose Properties, and change the Label entry on the General tab.

# REINSTALLING WINDOWS

Now you can reinstall Windows. Gather up your original Windows CD-ROM or floppy disks. If you are installing from a CD-ROM, put the Windows CD-ROM in your CD-ROM drive. If you're installing from floppies, put the Windows #1 disk in drive A:. Then follow these steps:

- If you're installing from a CD-ROM, type E:\setup where *E* is the drive letter for your CD-ROM drive, and then press Enter. Don't forget, though, that your CD-ROM drive will be one letter higher than normal because booting from the Windows startup disk creates a RAM drive. So to reinstall Windows from your Windows CD-ROM, you'll most likely need to type E:\setup and press Enter to start setup.exe.

- If you're installing from a floppy disk, just type setup and press Enter.

Follow the instructions on the screen to install Windows. If you're installing from a CD-ROM, you can remove the floppy disk from drive A: as soon as you see the main setup screen for the Windows installation. There's nothing special to be done here; simply install Windows as you would on any PC that has only Windows as its operating system. When asked about where to put Windows, you can choose the suggested default C:\Windows. Just follow the instructions on the screen until you see the message indicating that Windows has been successfully installed.

# TESTING YOUR WINDOWS INSTALLATION

When the installation is finished, you're taken to the Windows desktop, and perhaps the Welcome to Windows dialog box. No more installation activity will occur. To verify that all went well, shut down and restart your computer from drive C: like this:

1. Remove any floppy disks and CD-ROMs from their drives.
2. Click the Windows Start button and choose Shut Down, Restart, and then click the OK button.

3. When the computer restarts and you're returned to the Windows desktop, open your My Computer icon.

4. You should see a drive icon for drive C:. Your CD-ROM drive should be back to being drive D:, as in Figure A.2.

Now you can start restoring files you backed up before repartitioning your drive. Or you can install Linux by flipping to Appendix B now. The choice is yours; it doesn't matter which you do first.

There is one last little caveat to be aware of, though. If you used a CD-R to make your backup files, you can use the typical drag-and-drop method in File Manager or Windows Explorer to recopy those files to drive C:. However, be aware that anything copied from a CD-ROM disk is automatically flagged as Read-Only on your hard disk. This means you won't be able to change the copies that are on your hard disk. You'll have to get rid of the Read-Only flags on all the files you copied back to your hard disk in order for those files to function normally again. Fortunately, that's easy to do. Just use My Computer or Windows Explorer to open any folder that contains files that you copied from the CD-ROM. Select all the files in that folder (press Ctrl+A). Then right-click any one of the selected files and choose Properties. On the General tab of the dialog box that appears, clear the Read-Only check box, and then click the OK button. Remember to do this for all the files you copied from a CD-ROM back to your hard disk. You won't need to do anything to the files in your C:\Windows directory though. The setup program that installed Windows has already taken care of the Read-Only flags in that directory.

PART

**VII**

APP

**A**

**Figure A.2**

Windows drive C: and CD-ROM drive D: in My Computer.

# INSTALLING RED HAT LINUX

## In this appendix

# GATHERING INFORMATION ABOUT YOUR COMPUTER

Some people say installing Linux is no more difficult than installing any other operating system. Others say it's like trying to pull teeth from an angry alligator with your bare hands. I'm sort of in the middle on that. Usually, the installation goes smoothly and doesn't cause any headaches. However, occasionally—especially if your computer contains any Linux-incompatible hardware—installation can be difficult. My goal in this appendix is to help make your own installation of Linux as smooth and painless as possible. To start, two important points:

- If you want to use both Windows and Linux on the same computer, you must repartition your hard disk and install Windows first, as discussed in Appendix A.

- Obviously, if you bought a computer that already has Linux installed on it, you can skip this entire Appendix and go straight to Chapter 1.

Installing Linux properly may require quite a bit of knowledge about the hardware in your computer. I say "may require" because the installation program is pretty good at figuring out, on its own, what kind of hardware is installed in your PC. (And I do mean pretty good, not outstanding.) To play it safe you should try to gather as much information as you can before you begin the installation, so that you're not looking around for it during the installation procedure.

## SOURCES OF HARDWARE INFORMATION

The following sources of information will help you discover everything you need to know about your basic hardware configuration:

- The written documentation that came with your computer
- Any stickers on the hardware itself, particularly the monitor and mouse
- Your computer manufacturer's tech support or customer service line or Web site
- The Windows System Information program, if Windows is installed on the computer
- The DOS MSD program (if you have DOS or an older version of Windows installed already)

As you gather information about your hardware, fill in the second column of Table B.1 with the make and model of your specific hardware components. If you simply can't find a specific piece of information, or don't even understand what you're supposed to be looking for, leave it blank. There's a good chance that you'll be able to complete the setup without the information.

TABLE B.1    HARDWARE INFORMATION

| Component | Your Hardware |
|---|---|
| Amount of memory (RAM) | |
| Is hard disk IDE or SCSI? | |
| Is CD-ROM SCSI or other? | |
| SCSI Adapter (if any) make and model | |
| Graphics card make and model | |
| Memory on graphics card | |
| Graphics card chipset | |
| Monitor make and model | |
| Mouse make and model | |
| Mouse connection (serial or PS/2) | |
| Sound, video, and game controllers | |
| Network adapter make and model (if any) | |
| Is there a DHCP server available in your LAN? | |
| IP address (if no DHCP) | |
| Subnet Mask (if no DHCP) | |
| Gateway IP address | |
| DNS (name) server address(es) | |
| Domain name | |
| Hostname (computer name) | |

## USING WINDOWS TO GATHER INFORMATION

If Windows is currently installed on the computer, the System Information program will come in very handy. To open the System Information dialog box, just right-click the My Computer icon on the Windows desktop. Then choose Properties from the shortcut menu that appears. The System Properties dialog box opens (see Figure B.1). Initially, the General tab is opened. Under Computer on that tab, you can see how much memory (RAM) your system has.

If you click the Device Manager tab of the System Information dialog box, you can get more detailed information about installed hardware. If you select View Devices by Type from the dialog box, you'll see the different types of components installed in your computer. Most have a plus sign (+) to the left. Clicking that plus sign expands the category type to show specific make and model information for most components. For example, in Figure B.2 I've expanded the CDROM, Disk Drives, Display Adapters, and Network Adapters categories.

The Device Manager tab also offers a Print button. In addition to filling in Table B.1 as we go along here, you may also want to print both a System Summary and a more detailed system report. Click the Print button, choose one report type or the other, and then click the OK button.

**Figure B.1**

The General tab of the Windows System Properties dialog box.

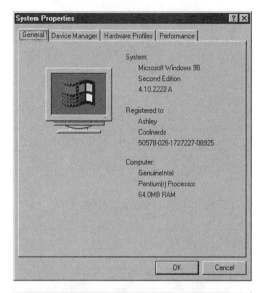

**Figure B.2**

The Device Manager tab of the Windows System Information dialog box.

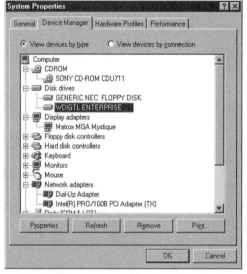

To determine whether your hard disk is IDE or SCSI, expand the Disk Drives category in System Information. Ignore the Floppy Disk entry, and focus on the other. If the name of the hard drive includes the letters IDE, then you have an IDE hard drive. If you don't see the letters IDE in the drive name, the hard disk is probably SCSI. If your hard disk is indeed SCSI, there should also be a SCSI controller card listed in System Information.

To see whether or not your computer has a SCSI adapter in it, scroll down to and expand (if it's available) the SCSI category. If you do have a SCSI controller, be sure to jot down in

Table B.1 the make and model of the adapter exactly as it appears in System Information after you've expanded the SCSI Controllers category.

Graphics card information can be a little harder to come by. Typically, when you expand the Display Adapters category in System Information, all you get is the basic make and model. For example, referring to Figure B.2, the computer there contains a Matrox MGA Mystique display card. If you have printed documentation for the graphics card, you can probably also find out its chip set and the amount of memory the card has. If you can't find that information, try visiting the manufacturer's Web site to see if you can dig up additional information. If you cannot find the chipset and memory information, don't worry about it. There's a good chance the installation program will be able to figure that information out on its own.

The System Information dialog box can tell you some basic information about your mouse and monitor. But to get more detail, look around at the back of the monitor for specific make and model information. Likewise, flip your mouse over to see if there's a sticker on the bottom indicating the make and model of the mouse. If you're not sure whether your mouse is serial or PS/2 compatible, follow the mouse cable to the back of the PC. If the plug on that end of the mouse is round, you have a PS/3 connection. If that plug is rectangular, you have a serial connection. If your computer has sound, expand the Sound, Video, and Game Controllers type to discover the make and model of your sound card.

## LAN INFORMATION

If your computer is connected to a LAN, your company's network administrator probably knows the most about the hardware and software used in the LAN. If you *are* the network administrator (or there isn't one around), you can gather some information from the Network Properties dialog box in Windows. Right-click the Network Neighborhood icon on the Windows desktop, and choose Properties. You'll probably see a *binding* that links the TCP/IP protocol to your Ethernet adapter. It will look something like this:

```
TCP/IP -> 3Com EtherLink III
```

3Com EtherLink III will normally be replaced by the make of your own computer's network interface adapter. (Don't use the binding that points to Dial-Up Adapter.) Click the binding and then choose Properties. You'll come to the TCP/IP Properties dialog box, shown in Figure B.3.

On the IP Address tab, if the Obtain an IP Address Automatically option is selected, then there must be a DHCP server somewhere on the LAN that's giving each computer an IP address automatically. In that case, you can mark the *Is there a DHCP server available in your LAN?* box in Table B.1 with a Yes. If the Specify an IP Address option in that dialog box is selected, the computer's IP address and subnet mask will be shown below that option. Mark the DHCP row in Table B.1 "No," and use the information in the dialog box to fill in the IP Address and Subnet Mask rows of Table B.1.

On the Gateway tab, you can gather information about your gateway IP addresses (if any). If several gateways are listed, the first one will be the default gateway, which you'll want to jot down in Table B.1. If several gateways are listed, jot down the default gateway in the table, and perhaps make a list of the others on a separate sheet of paper.

On the DNS Configuration tab, you'll find information about Domain Name Servers. If Disable DNS is selected, then don't worry about it. If Enable DNS is selected, jot down the information from the Host, Domain, and DNS server IP addresses in Table B.1.

**Figure B.3**
The IP Address tab of the TCP/IP Properties dialog box shows your computer's IP Address and Subnet Mask.

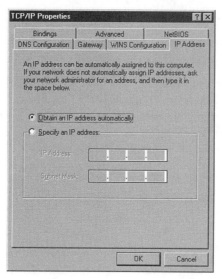

**Note**

If a DHCP server has already given your computer an IP address, you can find out that address by going clicking the Start button, choosing Run, and entering the command `winipcfg` (or `ipconfig` on some versions of Windows NT). Be sure to choose your Ethernet adapter, not your PPP Adapter from the drop-down list that appears. Jot down the IP address, subnet mask, and default gateway (if any) in Table B.1.

# CHECKING THE HARDWARE COMPATIBILITY LIST

After you've gathered as much information as you can, check the Red Hat Linux Hardware Compatibility list to see if all of your hardware is compatible. If you discover an incompatible component, there's a chance you may have to swap the component out for a compatible component. However, before you go to the time and expense, you might try doing the installation anyway. Linux has built-in support for a lot of hardware, so there's a good chance you'll get lucky and the installation will go smoothly the first time. If you do want to check out the Hardware Compatibility List anyway, visit www.redhat.com/support/hardware.

# INSTALLING LINUX FROM A CD-ROM

Some of you may already have the Red Hat Linux 6.2 boxed set. Some of you may have bought this book instead. If you *don't* have the boxed set, you can easily install Red Hat Linux from the CD-ROM at the back of this book. If your computer is capable of booting from the CD-ROM drive, you can follow these steps to get started:

1. Remove any floppy disk from the floppy drive.

2. Insert the CD-ROM from the back of this book into your CD-ROM drive.

3. Reboot (or shut down, then start) your computer.

---

**Book CD, Package CD—What's the Difference?**

Buying the Red Hat Linux boxed set is truly optional. You can get the same Red Hat Linux Version 6.2 for free by downloading it off the Internet, or from the CD at the back of this book. The incentives to buy the Red Hat Linux 6.2 Standard Edition boxed set are as follows:

- 90 days of Web-based installation support. (Support dealing with anything other than installation is not free.)

- 30 days of free priority access to `priority.redhat.com`, which is less crowded than the `public.redhat.com` site.

- Almost 1,000 pages of written documentation that comes in the package.

- A boot diskette that's ready to use.

- A second CD with source code for programmers who want to modify C++ code (those are also available online for free though.)

- Email telling you when new packages are available for download, and the Official Red Hat e-newsletter "Under the Brim."

The Deluxe and Professional editions provide even more incentives. However, they're also considerably more expensive than the Standard edition. Whether or not the incentives justify the added cost of purchasing the boxed set is a decision you need to make for yourself.

---

PART

**VII**

APP

**B**

Even if your computer has the ability to boot from the CD-ROM drive, its BIOS settings might not be set to allow that. To check your options and settings, you need to run your BIOS Setup program. Unfortunately, I can't tell you exactly how to do that, because there are lots of different BIOS and Setup programs out there. But as a rule, you want to watch the screen closely right after you start the computer. Then look for a message that says something like "Press <F1> to run Setup," "Press F2 to run Setup," or "Press Del to run setup." You'll only have a few seconds to press the appropriate key. If you get it in time, you'll be taken to your BIOS setup program before the computer completes the booting-up process. Once you're in your BIOS settings, you'll need to navigate around using your keyboard (the Tab, arrow, and Enter keys) to look for your boot-up options. When you find them, you want to make sure the computer attempts to boot from the CD-ROM drive before booting from the hard disk. Then save your current selections and exit your BIOS setup programs by following any instructions on your screen.

If you're able to boot from the CD-ROM drive, you'll eventually come to a screen titled "Welcome to Red Hat Linux 6.2!" Go straight to the section titled "Using the Graphical Installer" later in this appendix. You don't need to create or use a boot disk.

## CAN'T BOOT FROM CD-ROM DRIVE?

If you can't boot from your CD-ROM drive, you'll need to make a startup floppy disk to boot from. First, you'll need to grab a blank, formatted floppy disk (or a disk that contains files that you definitely don't need any more), and label it *Red Hat Linux 6.2 Boot Diskette*. Exactly how you proceed from there depends on whether Windows, or Linux, is currently installed on your computer. Read whichever of the following sections is appropriate to the operating system that's currently installed on your computer.

> **Note**
>
> The program that you'll use to create your boot disk permanently deletes all files currently on the floppy disk. So don't use a floppy that contains files that you might need at some time in future!

## CREATING A BOOT DISK FROM WINDOWS

If Windows is currently installed on your computer, you can work right from the Windows desktop. If you're not already at the Windows desktop, want to boot up normally, with your floppy and CD-ROM drives empty. Grab the Red Hat Linux CD-ROM from the back of this book. Then follow the steps below to create a Red Hat Linux 6.2 boot disk:

1. Insert the CD-ROM from the back of this book into your CD-ROM drive.

2. Place the floppy disk you labeled *Red Hat Linux 6.2 Boot Diskette* into your floppy disk drive.

3. Click the Windows Start button and choose Programs, MS-DOS Prompt.

4. Type the command *d*:\dosutils\rawrite but replace the leading *d*: with the appropriate drive letter for your CD-ROM drive. For example, if your CD-ROM drive is E: then you'd want to type e:\dosutils\rawrite.

5. Click the OK button in the Run dialog box. An MS-DOS window will open and start displaying prompts.

6. In response to the prompt that reads *"Enter disk image source file name:"* type d:\images\boot.img again replacing the leading *d*: with the appropriate letter for your CD-ROM drive. Then press Enter.

7. In response to the prompt "Enter target diskette drive" type a: and press Enter. (If you're not using drive A:, substitute the appropriate drive letter.)

8. The last prompt will ask you to insert a formatted disk and press Enter. Assuming you've already inserted the disk (back in step 2), you can just press Enter.

It might take a couple of minutes for rawrite to create the floppy disk. When the floppy disk's drive light stops showing activity, and you get back to the DOS prompt on your screen, you're done. In the MS-DOS window you can type the command exit and then press Enter to close that window. Now you can skip to the section "Booting from the Floppy Disk" in this appendix to start your installation.

## CREATING A BOOT DISK FROM LINUX

If you currently have some version of Linux (or UNIX) installed on your computer, you can create a startup using the dd program available in virtually all Linux and UNIX distributions. The exact steps are as follows:

1. Insert the CD-ROM from the back of this book into your CD-ROM drive.

2. Mount that CD according to your current Linux or UNIX version. For example, if you have an older version of Red Hat Linux installed, you'd enter the command `mount /dev/cdrom /mnt/cdrom`.

3. Place the floppy disk you labeled *Red Hat Linux 6.2 Boot Diskette* into your floppy disk drive.

4. Get to the Linux command prompt. If you're in an X GUI like GNOME, KDE, or some window manager, you can just open a terminal window.

5. Type the following command, but replace the italicized text with information that's appropriate to your system, as described in the following list:

   `dd if=/mnt/cdrom/images/boot.img of=/dev/fd0 bs=1440k`

   - */mnt/cdrom*: Replace this with the actual mount point for your CD-ROM drive, if it's not /mnt/cdrom.

   - *fd0:* If you're not using the first (or only) floppy disk drive, change the *0* to the appropriate drive. For example, if your system has two floppy drives and you're using the second drive to create the floppy, change *fd0* to *fd1*.

   - *1440*k: If you're not using the standard 1.44MB 3.5-inch floppy disk, replace the 1440 with the appropriate capacity of your floppy disk.

6. Press Enter after typing your command.

7. Wait for the command prompt to reappear, and all floppy disk drive activity to stop, before removing the floppy disk from the floppy drive.

Now you can skip to the section titled "Booting from the Floppy Disk" to get started with your installation.

## IF YOU HAVE THE RED HAT LINUX 6.2 BOXED SET

If you have the Red Hat Linux boxed set, it should already contain a floppy disk labeled *Red Hat Linux Boot Diskette*. You don't need to create anything else—just use that floppy disk to start your computer. When you start the installation procedure, make you use the CD-ROM labeled as number 1.

## BOOTING FROM THE FLOPPY DISK

Assuming you need to boot from the Red Hat Linux 6.2 Boot Diskette (either one you created yourself, or the one from the Red Hat package), booting up will be simple. Put the disk labeled Red Hat Linux 6.2 Boot Diskette into your floppy disk drive. Then restart (or reboot) your computer. For example, if your computer currently has Windows installed, you can click the Start button and choose Shutdown, Restart, and then click the OK button. If your computer is currently running Linux or UNIX, get to a command prompt and enter the command shutdown -r now. Once the computer boots up you'll be taken to a screen titled "Welcome to Red Hat Linux 6.2!". Now you're ready to start installing.

## USING THE GRAPHICAL INSTALLER

By this point, you should be at the screen titled "Welcome to Red Hat Linux 6.2" that has the boot: prompt at the bottom of the screen. If you just press Enter, or do nothing for several seconds, you'll be taken to the first page of the installation program, which asks that you choose a language. Click on the language of your choice, then click on the Next button. Or, if your mouse isn't working yet, use the ~UA and ~DA keys to move the highlighter to the language of your choice (such as English), and then press Enter.

> **Tip**
> If you're an experienced user, and would prefer to use some other method of installing Linux, you'll need to type the appropriate keyword at the boot: prompt (such as text). Then press Enter to start that installation procedure.

A second screen will ask what type of keyboard you're using. The default, US, is typical of keyboards made for use with the English language. Again, if your mouse is working you can click the keyboard of your choice, then click the Next button. Or, use the ~UA and ~DA keys to highlight the language your keyboard is defined for, and then press Enter.

The next screen will ask whether you're installing from a local CD-ROM or hard disk. Assuming you're installing from the either the CD-ROM from the back of this book, or the Red Hat Linux CD-ROM, put the CD into your CD-ROM drive, close the drive door, wait a few seconds for the CD-ROM drive light to stop blinking. Then press Enter to accept the default setting, Local CD-ROM. Some more gobbledygook, which you can ignore, will whiz by on the screen. Next, go straight to the following section "Mouse Configuration."

If you chose the Hard Disk option instead, you'll need to specify the drive and directory to which you've already copied all the Red Hat Linux files from the Red Hat CD-ROM. See "Alternative Installations" later in this appendix for more information on installing from a hard disk.

## MOUSE CONFIGURATION

One of the first things the installer will want to know is what kind of mouse is connected to your computer (see Figure B.4). You should choose the appropriate mouse manufacturer and model from the options provided. Use the Online Help in the left column if you need more information.

> **Tip**
>
> To expand or collapse an option that has a plus (+) or minus (-) sign to the left, click the plus or minus sign.

## Mouse Doesn't Work

Sometimes the installation program won't read your mouse or video card correctly at startup. The screen might be a little fuzzy. Your mouse pointer might be completely invisible or look like a bar code label. If, for whatever reason, you can't use your mouse in the installation program, you can use the following keys instead:

- **Tab:** Moves to the next option, button, or group of options.
- **Shift+Tab:** Moves back to the previous option, button, or group of options.
- **~UA, ~DA, ~LA, ~RA:** Moves from option to option within a group of options.
- **Spacebar:** Selects or de-selects the current option if it's a toggle, which means it's an option that can be turned on/off, a button that can be selected (pushed in) or de-selected (popped out).
- **Enter:** Selects the currently highlighted option. For example, to use the Next button (if your mouse doesn't work), press Tab until that button is highlighted. Then press Enter to "push" the button.
- **+ (plus sign):** If the plus sign at the top of a collapsed list is currently highlighted, pressing the + key expands the list.
- **- (hyphen or minus sign):** If the minus sign at the top of a list is highlighted, pressing the - key collapses the list.

**Figure B.4**

The Mouse Configuration screen and Online Help in the left column allow you to tell Linux what kind of mouse you're using.

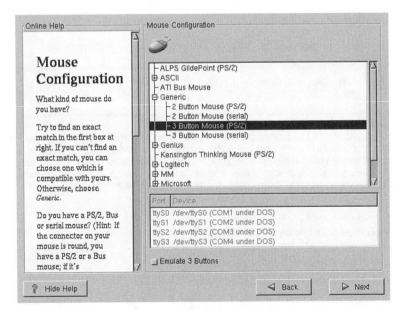

If you're using a two-button mouse, and the Emulate 3 Buttons option near the bottom of the screen is available, select that option so its button looks pushed in. Not all mouse devices will allow that option, though. So if you can't select it, don't worry about it. Click the Next button to move on to the next installation screen. You'll come to a System Installer screen with some more information to read in the left column. Click the Next button to move on after reading that column.

## INSTALLATION TYPE

The Install Type screen, shown in Figure B.5, appears next. You want to make your selection carefully based on the information presented in the left pane and summarized here:

- **GNOME Workstation:** Sets up Linux as a workstation (regular PC), with the GNOME graphical user interface installed. This is an excellent choice for beginners.

- **KDE Workstation:** Sets up Linux as a workstation with the KDE graphical user interfaces installed.

- **Server:** A terrible choice for beginners, this option performs a bare-minimum installation with no graphical user interface at all. This option also takes over the entire hard disk and will destroy your Windows installation if you were planning to dual-boot. Recommended only for hard-core Linux experts.

- **Custom:** Another tough installation recommended for hardcore Linux experts only.

- **Upgrade:** Select this option only if you're upgrading from an earlier version of Red Hat Linux, and want to keep as many options and settings as possible from that previous installation.

If you selected GNOME Workstation, KDE Workstation, or Server, go straight to the section "Automatic Partitioning." If you opted for a Custom installation, you'll be taken to the Disk Druid screen, described under "Using Disk Druid" later in this appendix.

---

**Virtual Consoles During Installation**

If you're familiar with the concept of virtual consoles from earlier Linux experience, you may find it interesting to know that you can view various behind-the-scenes messages during the installation process just by visiting other consoles. If you're really experienced with Linux, you might even find information within those consoles that will help you fix any problems encountered during the installation. The virtual consoles available to you, and the keys used to get to those consoles, are summarized here:

- Console 1, installation dialog (Ctrl+Alt+F1)
- Console 2, shell prompt (Ctrl+Alt+F2)
- Console 3, installation log (Ctrl+Alt+F3)
- Console 4, system log (Ctrl+Alt+F4)
- Console 5, other messages (Ctrl+Alt+F5)
- Console 7, X graphical installation display (Ctrl+Alt+F7)

If you have no idea what I'm talking about here, don't worry about it. Viewing virtual consoles is strictly optional and probably of interest only to very experienced Linux gurus.

---

**Figure B.5**
The Install Type screens lets you decide how you want to set up Linux on your computer.

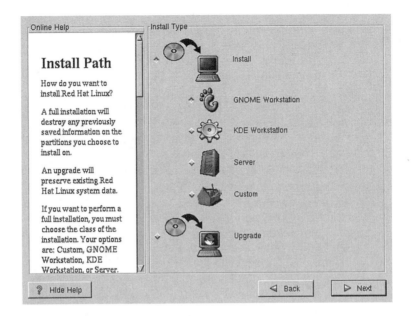

## AUTOMATIC PARTITIONING

The next screen, shown in Figure B.6, asks how you want to handle disk partitioning. You'll want to choose Remove Data if any of the following is true:

- You're installing Linux for the first time.
- You've installed Linux before, but haven't created and saved anything of great importance in Linux (or you've backed up those files already).
- You don't know a disk partition from a bologna sandwich.

> **Note**
>
> If you selected Server in the previous screen, choosing Remove Data here will destroy *all* Windows partitions and remove Windows from your computer. However, if you chose GNOME Workstation or KDE Workstation from the previous screen, your Windows partitions will be just fine, even if you select Remove Data.

Since Remove Data is the default selection, you can simply press the Next button to move onto the next screen. Then go straight to the section titled "Network Configuration" later in this appendix.

You might want to choose Manually Partition if any of the following is true:

- You're a Linux/disk partitioning guru, and you want to set up your own custom partitions.

**Figure B.6**
The Automatic Partitioning screen lets you decide whether or not to let the installer set up Linux partitions for you automatically.

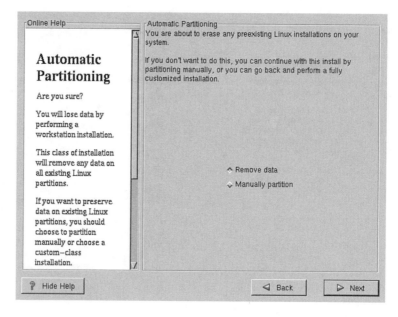

- You're a Linux/disk partitioning guru, and you want to preserve data on some of your existing Linux partitions.

- You're masochistic, and want to try to learn the esoteric subject of disk partitioning right now, despite the fact that getting Linux installed would be a much better use of your time at this point.

If you want help setting up your manual disk partitions, see the section "Using Disk Druid" in this appendix now.

Starting with Red Hat 6.2, there is a new option for those of you who already have Windows installed and aren't ready to commit to using Linux. You can now choose your existing Windows partition (if you have one) from the partition list in Disk Druid. This will create a single file in the Windows partition that holds all of the Linux system files. Unfortunately, you will lose the benefits of running on the native Linux filesystem, so the performance you see will not be indicative of a native partition installation.

## NETWORK CONFIGURATION

If the installer detects a network card in your computer, you'll see the screen shown in Figure B.7. Fill in whatever blanks you can. If you don't know a piece of information, leave it blank. You'll learn how to configure your network card in Chapter 22. Or, if you're adding this computer to an existing network that someone else maintains, ask that person (typically, job titled network administrator) for the appropriate numbers for filling in the blanks. Click the Next button after filling in the blanks (or leaving them blank).

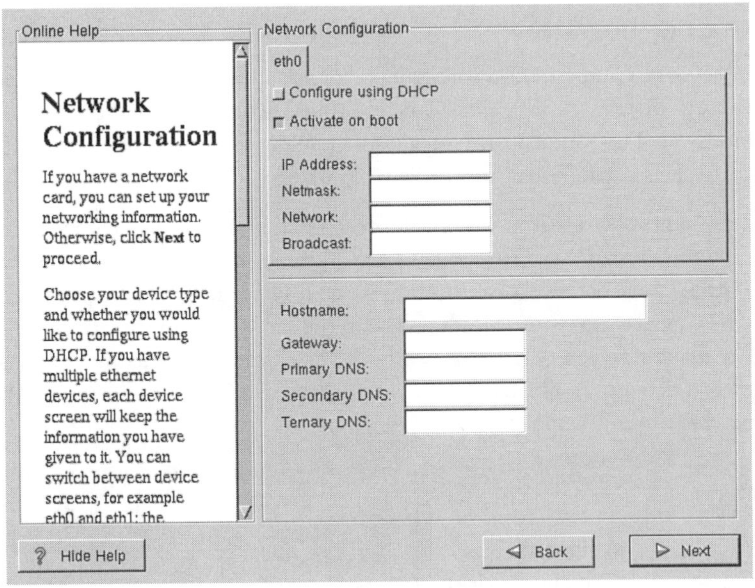

**Figure B.7**
The Network Configuration options appear only if your computer has a network interface card installed in it.

**TIME ZONE SELECTION**

The Time Zone Selection screen, shown in Figure B.8, is pretty much a no-brainer. Just choose your time zone from the scrolling list beneath the world map. If your system clock uses Universal Coordinated Time (UTC), choose the System Clock Uses UTC option. Then click the UTC Offset tab and select your UTC offset. Click the Next button, where you'll define the root password and any additional user accounts for this computer.

**Figure B.8**
The Time Zone configuration screen.

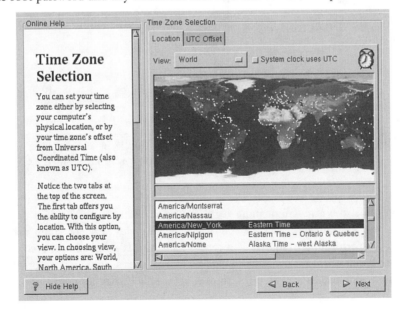

## ACCOUNT CONFIGURATION

The Account Configuration screen lets you set up a password for the superuser (a.k.a. "the root user" or just "root"), as well as additional accounts for other "regular" users (see Figure B.9). The root user is typically the person who installed Red Hat Linux and has free reign over its capabilities—most likely, yourself.

Type in a password that you won't forget. Make it at least six characters long, and don't use any blank spaces. Passwords are case-sensitive, so make sure you also remember where you used uppercase and lowercase letters. You won't be able to see the password as you type (only asterisks appear), so type carefully. Type in the same password a second time next to Confirm, just to make sure you typed it correctly the first time. Then do yourself a favor and write the password down on a piece of paper. Keep that piece of paper in your wallet or file it somewhere that it won't get lost.

**Figure B.9**
The Account Con-
figuration screen
lets you define the
password for the
root user (a.k.a.
the superuser), as
well as an addi-
tional user ac-
count you might
want to enter.

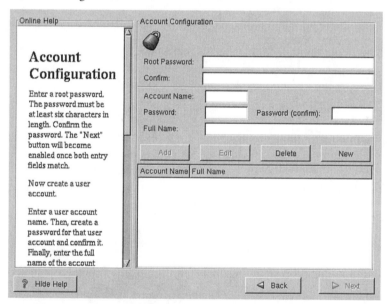

If, after typing your password twice, the Next button is still dimmed and unavailable, your passwords probably don't match. Retype the password twice again.

You can also create one or more regular user accounts. A user account doesn't have all the freedom and privileges that the root user has. The idea here is to limit the less experienced users to performing tasks that won't mess up Linux. It's a good idea even to create a regular user account for yourself. You can log in with that user account whenever you won't be doing system administration type tasks, to prevent yourself from accidentally messing things up.

**Tip** Any time you type a password, you won't see the actual password on the screen. This is to prevent "shoulder surfing," where someone can learn your password simply by looking over your shoulder as you type.

To create a user account, type in a username next to Account Name. It's customary to use the person's first initial and last name (all lowercase, no blank spaces) for usernames. For example, asimpson or kjones. Give the user a password. Again, make it at least six characters in length, no spaces, and type it in twice for confirmation—once in the Password field, and then again in the Password (Confirm) field. Then, type the user's full name in the Full Name field. Then click the Add button to add the user to the list of users below the button. If the Add button is dimmed and unavailable, the Password and Password (Confirm) entries for this user don't match. Retype those passwords and try again.

You can add as many user accounts as you want in this manner. Just remember to jot down every username and password you create. Otherwise you're likely to forget later. Click the Next button when you're finished with the Account Configuration screen.

If you're performing a Custom installation, you'll be taken to the Authentication Configuration screen. If you need help with that, see the section "Authentication Configuration" later in this appendix. If you're performing a GNOME, KDE, or Server installation, just continue reading.

## X CONFIGURATION

The X Configuration screen lets you configure your X options. X is short for the *X Window System*, which is a suite of programs that allows your Linux machine to have a graphical user interface (GUI), like Windows and the Macintosh. Without X, you'd be back to 1960s-style computing where you have to enter one cryptic little command at a time to get anything done. Not good, particularly if you're new to Linux.

**Tip** The version of the X Window systems that comes with Red Hat Linux 6.2 is known as Xfree86. The 86 refers to the fact that the system was designed for Intel *x*86-type processors, like the 386, 486, all the different types of Pentium chips, AMD's K6 and Athlon chips, and the Cyrix chips. It has since been ported to run on many systems, including the PowerPC, Alpha, Sparc, and MIPS processors.

In the X Configuration screen, shown in Figure B.10, pay attention to the Video Card, Video RAM (if shown), and X Server information displayed at the top of the dialog box. If you weren't able to gain that information while filling out Table B.1 near the beginning of this appendix, you can fill in the graphics card make and model and perhaps memory on graphics card options, just for future reference. Click the Next button.

**Figure B.10**
The X Configuration screen lets you tweak your X server settings for graphics. Your best bet, at this point, would probably be to ignore all options and just click the Next button.

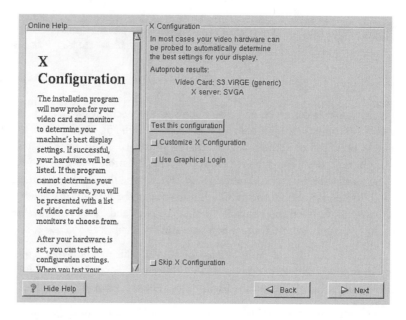

As to the Test This Configuration button, Customize X Configuration, Use Graphical Login, and Skip X Configuration options, I suggest you leave all those options in their default unselected state, and then click the Next button.

## ABOUT TO INSTALL

The About to Install window appears next, telling you that a log of your installation will be placed in the file /tmp/install.log. All you need to do is click the Next button. Then, wait as Linux installs all the files necessary to set up Linux the way you want it.

## CONGRATULATIONS

When the file installation is complete, you'll be taken to a Congratulations screen. Remove the floppy disk from your disk drive (if any). Then press Enter. Remove the CD while the computer is rebooting. The Eject button may not work at first. Press the Eject button every few seconds until the door opens, and then remove the CD. Before you do anything else, I suggest you check and fix up your X configuration, as discussed next.

# GETTING YOUR GUI WORKING

After you've completed the installation, your computer will boot up in Linux. Wait for the prompt that looks something like this:

```
Red Hat Linux release 6.2 (Zoot)
Kernel 2.2.14-5.0 on an ix86

localhost login:
```

Type in the word root as your username, and then press Enter. You'll see the following prompt:

Password:

Type in the root password that you provided back in Figure B.9 (the one I asked you to jot down on a piece of paper), and then press Enter. You'll come to a prompt that looks something like this:

[root@localhost /root]#

That's it—Linux is booted up and ready for action. In fact, the screen won't do another thing until you tell it what to do next. Pretty exciting, huh? (Yeah, right.) I suggest that you start out by running the Xconfigurator program, to get ready for GNOME or KDE, the graphical user interface which will be quite a bit more inviting than that [root@localhost /root]# prompt. To run Xconfigurator, type the following command and press Enter:

Xconfigurator

If you get an error message like command not found, you've just learned a profound and often irritating thing about Linux. Everything is case-sensitive. This means when I show you a command to type, you must type it exactly as shown. For example, the Xconfigurator program will only run if you type the command with an uppercase *X* and all the rest of the letters lowercase. If you didn't get it right the first time, just try again.

A Welcome screen will appear on your screen, describing (in technical terms) what the Xconfigurator program will do for you. Press Enter to move onto the next screen, which will probe your system for the video card you have installed. If successful, you'll see a message describing that card and an OK button. Just press Enter to choose OK. You'll then be taken to the Monitor Setup screen (see Figure B.11). You can press the first letter of your monitor manufacturer's name to jump to that section of the list. Then use the ~UA and ~DA keys to highlight the exact make and model of your monitor.

PART

**VII**

APP

**B**

**Figure B.11**
The Monitor Setup screen of Xconfigurator lets you choose the make and model of your computer's monitor.

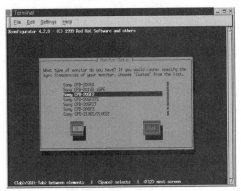

If you can't find your exact model of monitor, you might want to check the documentation that came with the monitor to see if there are any compatible monitors that you can choose. If you can't even find your monitor's manufacturer, your best bet would be to highlight the Generic Multisync. Then press Enter.

The next screen to appear will give you the option to probe, or not to probe. Your best bet would be to press Tab and then Enter to select the Probe option. You'll see a message telling you that the screen is going to blink a bunch of times. When the screen is finished blinking, you'll see a message telling you that Xconfigurator has chosen a default video mode for you, perhaps something like this:

```
Color depth: 16 bits per pixel
Resolution: 1600x1200
```

Unfortunately, Xconfigurator knows nothing about the size or your monitor and how good your eyesight is, so you might want to give yourself some flexibility here. If you're using a 17-inch or smaller monitor, a high resolution will make everything on the screen appear to be very small, perhaps too small for comfort. If you'd like to be able to switch among different resolutions, to find whatever's most comfortable for you, press Tab and then press Enter to select Let Me Choose, and you'll come to a screen that looks something like Figure B.12. Your screen may have more or fewer options, depending on your video card.

**Figure B.12**
This screen lets you choose any combination of color depths and screen resolutions that your video hardware can support.

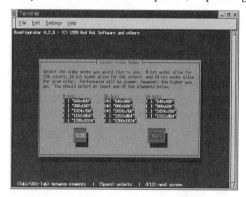

If possible, I suggest you choose settings of 640 × 480, 800 × 600, and 1024 × 768, at one or more color depths. The 1024 × 768 resolution is good because it will give you the best view of the entire desktop. But if your screen is small, everything will be pretty tiny. Adding the 640 × 480 and 800 × 600 resolutions will allow you to zoom in on portions of the desktop to magnify whatever you're working on. As to choosing a color depth, the 16-bit and 24-bit depths are best if you'll be viewing lots of photographs and such. The 8-bit resolution provides for only 256 unique colors. But it's fast, and sufficient for most applications that don't involve real-life photography or video. To choose depths, use the arrow and Tab keys to move from option to option. Press the spacebar to select or de-select the currently highlighted option. When you're finished choosing options, press the Tab key until the OK button is highlighted, and then press OK.

The next screen will give you the option to test your settings, get your hand ready to use the mouse, and press Enter to start the test. You should see a message that says Can You See This Message?. If you don't see it, or only see part of it, move the mouse pointer around the screen, and off the edges, until the message appears. Then click the Yes button or just press the Enter key to choose Yes.

The next screen will ask if you want to start X automatically when you boot up. I suggest you choose No (you can always change your mind later, when you have a better understanding of what that means). A final message describing the roles of certain keys will appear. But you needn't be too concerned with those right now. Just press the Enter key. The Xconfigurator program terminates, and you're ready to move onto Chapter 1 right now, and you can ignore the sections that follow in this appendix.

## USING DISK DRUID

If you're reading this, I assume you've opted to create your own Linux disk partitions. Initially you'll be faced with the Disk Druid options screen, which look something like Figure B.13. What you'll need to do here is set up at least three mount points for Linux.

But first, if you plan to dual-boot with Windows, you'll notice at least one partition of the type Win 95 FAT or FAT 32. You do *not* want to delete any of those partitions. Instead, just change their Mount Point names. For example, if you have a single Windows partition, you can click its name, click the Edit button, type in something like /winc (short for Windows C: drive) as its mount point, and then click the OK button. If you have several Windows partitions, select the one that appears to represent your Windows drive C:, based on its size. For example, if you created a Windows Primary DOS partition that's 2Gb in size, the Windows partition that's somewhere in the range of 1900-2000M in size would be your Windows C: drive. Also, your Windows C: drive is likely to have a smaller device number (such as hda1 or sda1).

Since you're the proud owner of Red Hat 6.2, you can also install directly onto the Windows FAT partition without creating additional partitions. All you need to do is select the FAT partition in Disk Druid and set it as the root mount point. Disk Druid will prompt you for the size of the Linux file system you want to create and the size of the swapfile. Installing Linux with this method will not erase or harm your Windows installation in any way. If you're planning on running a server, you SHOULDN'T use this option—it is mainly for first-time users who plan on spending more time in Windows than in Linux.

PART
**VII**

APP
**B**

> **Caution**
>
> Make sure you always type a forward slash (/) and never a backslash (\) when you're entering Disk Druid options. Both UNIX and Linux use forward slashes, whereas DOS and Windows typically use backslashes. Remember, too, the upper/lowercase is important in Linux. So always type things *exactly* as shown in this book.

If you do have a second Windows partition, you should highlight it, click the Edit button, and give that partition a mount point name as well. For example, /wind (short for Windows D: drive) would be good. Then choose OK. Then don't mess with the Windows partitions any more.

**Figure B.13**
The Disk Druid screen lets you set up partitions for your Linux installation.

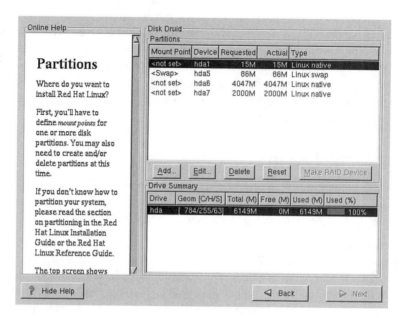

For Linux, you'll need to create at least three mount points, with one called /swap, of the type Linux swap. The size of that one should be roughly equal to the amount of RAM you have in your computer because Linux uses that mount point to swap information into and out of RAM for faster handling of jobs that require lots of RAM.

Another mount point, named /boot, is needed to hold files used to boot the Linux operating system. That one should be at least 15M in size, of the type Linux native.

**Caution**

If your hard drive is larger than 8GB, be aware that the /boot partition *must* be placed somewhere within the first 8GB of the disk.

A third partition, named simply / of the type Linux native, can take up the remaining space. If you're already a Linux guru and have a reason to create additional partitions, you're certainly welcome to do so. But if you want to keep things simple, I suggest that you simply highlight the mount point named <not set> that's roughly 15-64M in size, click the Edit button, and change its name to /boot. Then press the OK button. If you have more than one partition named <not set> left, I suggest you delete all but one of those by highlighting their names and clicking the Delete button. When you get down to just one remaining Linux Native partition named <not set>, click its name and then click the Edit button. Give this partition the mount point name of simply / (a forward slash, *not* a backslash).

If the Grow to Fill Disk button is not dimmed, select it by clicking that button, and then click OK. Thus, in addition to any Windows partitions that you may have seen initially in Disk Druid, you should end up with the partitions that look something like the ones in Table B.2.

Although the sizes of your partitions will vary depending on how much disk space and RAM your computer has.

**TABLE B.2  LINUX NEEDS MOUNT POINTS NAMED / AND /boot, AS WELL AS A <swap> PARTITION OF THE TYPE LINUX SWAP**

| Mount Point | Actual (Size) | Type |
| --- | --- | --- |
| /boot | 23M | Linux native |
| / | 4290M | Linux native |
| <swap> | 62M | Linux native |

When you're finished filling in the Disk Druid options, click the Next button. You'll see a screen asking which partitions you want to format. All but the /swap partition will be selected for formatting, and you should leave it that way unless you already have some important data on one of those partitions. In this case, you'll want to de-select that partition so that it doesn't get reformatted (and thereby erased). Click the Next button. Where you go next depends on the type of installation you're performing:

- If you're performing a GNOME or KDE Workstation, or Server Installation, go to the section titled "Network Configuration" earlier in this appendix.

- If you're performing a Custom installation, continue on to the next section, "LILO Configuration."

## LILO CONFIGURATION

LILO, short for *Linux Loader*, is a program that lets you choose how you want to start Linux. If you have multiple operating systems installed, LILO is also the program that lets you choose which operating system you want to run as the computer is booting up. My suggestion is that you leave all these options in their default settings and just click the Next button.

If you have a network interface card installed in your computer, you'll be taken to the Network Configuration dialog box discussed under Network Configuration earlier in this appendix. If you need help with network configuration, you'll want to skip to that section now. Otherwise, continue reading below.

## AUTHENTICATION CONFIGURATION

The Authentication Configuration screen, shown in Figure B.14, appears next. As described in the left column of this screen, these options let you set up network passwords. If your network isn't set up to use Network Information Services (NIS), then you should select the first two options only: Enable MD5 Passwords and Enable Shadow Passwords. Both options allow for better network security.

If the computer you're configuring right now is connected to a network that has NIS services running, then you should choose Enable NIS instead. Then choose options and fill in the

PART

**VII**

APP

**B**

**Figure B.14**
The Authentication Configuration screen lets you decide how you want to handle network passwords.

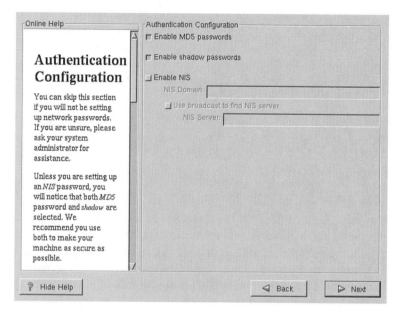

blanks beneath that option. If you don't know, for sure, what these are all about, you'll need to ask your company's network administrator for some help. Only they (or the person who built the network) will know whether or not NIS is installed, and what the NIS Domain and NIS Server names would be. Click the Next button when you're done.

## Package Group Selection

The Custom installation assumes that you know exactly which packages you do and don't want to install. And therefore it presents a long list of choices, part of which appears in Figure B.15. You can select entire package groups by scrolling through the list and selecting the package groups you want to install. If you're an old pro at this and know exactly which specific programs you want to install, choose the Select Individual Packages button at the bottom of the screen and click the Next button. You'll be taken to screens that allow you to select individual packages to install.

If you're not quite experienced enough to select individual packages, then just click the Next button. If you opted to install the X Window system, you'll be taken to the X Configuration screen. For help with that screen, see the section "X Configuration" earlier in this appendix.

# Alternatives to CD-ROM Installation

If your computer is connected to a network, you can install Red Hat Linux via the network. But you'll need to use a boot disk other than the one that came in your Red Hat Linux box. Likewise, if you're using a laptop or other computer that connects to a CD-ROM drive or network via a PC Card, the boot disk that came with your Linux package won't work. You'll need one or the other of the following disks to perform your installation:

**Figure B.15**
The Package Group Selection screen lets you choose which major package groups you want to install when you're performing a Custom installation.

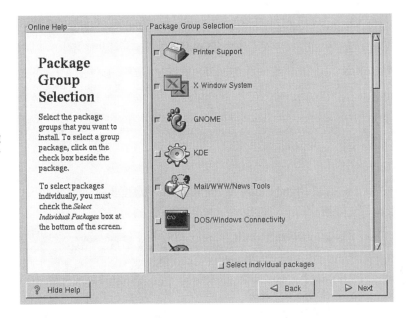

- **Network boot disk**—Required if you plan to install Linux from a network using the NFS, FTP, or HTTP installation method.
- **PCMCIA boot disk**—If your computer connects to a CD-ROM drive or a network through a PC card, you'll need the PCMCIA boot disk. (Note that this disk allows you to install from the connected CD-ROM drive or hard disk, as well as an NFS, FTP, or HTTP server on the network.)

You'll need to create these disks from disk images provided on the Red Hat Linux CD-ROM. You may want to check the Red Hat site for newer versions of these images.

> **Tip**
>
> If they update the disk images again, the version number in the file name will change. Use that newer file name throughout all the instructions that follow.

Once you've either downloaded the .img file of your choosing or have the Red Hat Linux CD-ROM in your hand, you can create the new boot disk using either a Windows or Linux computer. (Although it will have to be a fully functioning computer—not one that has no operating system yet!) Both alternatives are described in the sections that follow.

## CREATING AN ALTERNATIVE BOOT DISK FROM WINDOWS

To make a Network or PCMCIA boot disk on a Windows (or DOS) computer, first insert the Red Hat Linux 6.2 CD-ROM disk into the CD-ROM drive of your Windows computer. Next, grab a blank, formatted 3.5-inch floppy disk, and label it something like "Red Hat

Linux 6.2 Network Boot Disk" or "Red Hat Linux 6.2 PCMCIA Boot Disk," whichever is most appropriate to the disk you are creating. Place that disk into your floppy drive A:.

Get to the MS-DOS command prompt on your Windows computer, and switch to your CD-ROM drive. For example, if your CD-ROM drive is drive D:, type the command:

```
d:
```

And then press Enter. Switch to the dosutils directory on the CD-ROM drive by entering the following command:

```
cd \dosutils
```

Start the rawrite program by entering the following command:

```
rawrite
```

You'll see a prompt asking for the name of the disk image source file. You must type the complete path to the disk image file. For example:

- To create a Network boot disk from the CD-ROM currently in drive D:, enter D:\images\bootnet.img.

- To create a PCMCIA boot disk from the CD-ROM currently in drive D:, enter D:\images\pcmcia.img.

Press Enter after typing the location, and you'll see a prompt stating the following:

```
Enter target diskette drive:
```

Type the drive letter for the blank floppy disk (such as A) and press Enter. Finally, you'll see these instructions:

```
Please insert a formatted diskette into drive A: and press --ENTER--
```

Go ahead and press the Enter key, and follow any additional instructions that appear on the screen. Then, to boot from that disk, put it into the floppy drive of the computer that you plan to install Linux on, and turn on (or reboot) that computer.

## CREATING AN ALTERNATIVE BOOT DISK FROM LINUX

If you have a working Linux (or Linux-like) computer to work with, you can use that to create the new boot disk. You should log in as root on the Linux computer, or at least make sure you have permission to write to the floppy drive. Grab a blank, formatted 3.5-inch floppy disk and label it either "Red Hat Linux 6.2 Network Boot Disk" or "Red Hat Linux 6.2 PCMCIA Boot Disk," depending on which type of disk you plan to create. Place that disk into a floppy disk drive, such as /dev/fd0 (the equivalent to drive A: on a Windows computer). It's not necessary to mount the floppy disk.

Put the Red Hat Linux 6.1 CD-ROM into your CD-ROM drive and mount it (enter the command `mount /mnt/cdrom`). Then enter the `dd` command with the following syntax:

`dd if=diskimage of=/dev/fd0 bs=1440k`

However, substitute the path to the disk image file for `diskimage`. For example:

- To create a Network boot disk from the CD-ROM, enter `dd if=/mnt/cdrom/images/bootnet.img of=/dev/fd0 bs=1440k`.

- To create a PCMCIA boot disk from the CD-ROM, enter `dd if=/mnt/cdrom/images/pcmcia.img of=/dev/fd0 bs=1440k`.

- To create a Network boot disk from an image file you downloaded to your Linux hard drive, enter `dd if=/path/netbootdiskname.img of=/dev/fd0 bs=1440k` but substitute the path to the downloaded image file where `path` is shown.

- To create a PCMCIA boot disk from an image file you downloaded to your Linux hard drive enter `dd if=/path/pcmciadistance.img of=/dev/fd0 bs=1440k` but substitute the path to the downloaded image file where `path` is shown.

After the boot disk is created, you can put the floppy disk into the disk drive on which you want to install Linux. Then start (or reboot) the computer to begin the installation process. When the computer boots up, you'll be given different options depending on how you want to perform the installation. If you're performing an installation over a network, you'll be prompted to enter basic network information about the computer you're installing Linux on at the moment. Eventually, you'll get to a screen that asks for the specific location of the files needed for installation. In particular, if you're installing over a network, you'll need to choose a method (CD-ROM, Hard Disk, NFS, FTP, or HTTP). If you choose anything other than CD-ROM, you'll then need to provide more information:

- **Hard Drive:** If you've opted to install from a hard drive, you must specify the drive and directory to which you've already copied all the files from the Red Hat Linux CD-ROM.

- **NFS Image:** If you've opted to install from an NFS share, you must specify the NFS server name and the directory containing the Red Hat Linux installation files.

- **FTP Server:** If you are installing from an FTP server, you'll need to supply the FTP site name and the directory containing the Red Hat Linux 6.1 installation files.

- **HTTP Server:** If you are installing directly from an HTTP Web server, you'll need to specify the IP address, or hostname of your Web server, as well as the directory that contains the Red Hat Linux installation files.

When the installer locates the files, you'll be taken to the Welcome screen. You can then complete the installation by following the directions starting at the section titled "Using the Graphical Installer" near the beginning of this appendix.

PART

**VII**

APP

**B**

# STILL MORE ON INSTALLATION

My goal in this appendix has been to make the installation of Linux as painless and productive as possible for the majority of users out there. But, as you may have deduced, there are lots of ways to install Linux, partition your drive, and so forth. If you need more information on partitioning your hard disk, installing Linux, and other related issues, feel free to check out the following resources:

- Installing and Upgrading Red Hat Linux 6.2 FAQs, Gotchas, and more at `http://www.redhat.com/support/docs/howto`.

- Red Hat Errata at `http://www.redhat.com/support/errata/index.html`.

- *The Linux Installation HOWTO* by Eric S. Raymond at `http://www.redhat.com/mirrors/LDP/HOWTO/Installation-HOWTO.html` and on the Red Hat CD-ROM as `/doc/HOWTO/Installation-HOWTO`.

- LinuxCare's *Installation and Configuration Issues* at `http://lc.experts-exchange.com/Computers/Operating_Systems/Linux/Setup`.

- *Red Hat 6.2 Installation Guide* that comes with the Red Hat boxed set (if you have it). Also available online at `http://www.redhat.com/support/manuals/RHL-6.2-Manual/install-guide`.

- Part II Installation-Related Reference in the *Official Red Hat Linux 6.2 Reference Guide* that comes with the Red Hat boxed set (if you have it). Also available online at `http://www.redhat.com/support/manuals/RHL-6.2-Manual/ref-guide/`.

# X-Compatible Video Cards

X-Compatible Video Cards

This appendix lists X-compatible video cards, and the Xserver software each requires. Typically, Red Hat Linux will automatically detect these cards and install the appropriate server during installation. But in the event that the installation procedure doesn't detect your card, you can use the information presented here to choose the best Xserver for your card.

Cards *not* listed are either incompatible or not supported. You can try using the generic XF86_SVGA Xserver with those cards, but there's no guarantee that it will work. For a more recent list of X-compatible video cards and other types of compatible hardware, see the Red Hat 6.2 Hardware Compatibility List at `http://www.redhat.com/support/hardware`.

| Card | XServer |
| --- | --- |
| 2 the Max MAXColor S3 Trio64V+ | XF86_S3 |
| 3DLabs Oxygen GMX | XF86_3DLabs |
| 928Movie | XF86_S3 |
| AccelStar Permedia II AGP | XF86_3DLabs |
| Actix GE32+ 2MB | XF86_S3 |
| Actix GE32i | XF86_S3 |
| Actix GE64 | XF86_S3 |
| Actix ProStar | XF86_SVGA |
| Actix ProStar 64 | XF86_SVGA |
| Actix Ultra | XF86_S3 |
| Acumos AVGA3 | XF86_SVGA |
| AGX (generic) | XF86_AGX |
| ALG-5434 | XF86_SVGA |
| Alliance ProMotion 6422 | XF86_SVGA |
| Ark Logic ARK1000PV (generic) | XF86_SVGA |
| Ark Logic ARK1000VL (generic) | XF86_SVGA |
| Ark Logic ARK2000MT (generic) | XF86_SVGA |
| Ark Logic ARK2000PV (generic) | XF86_SVGA |
| ASUS 3Dexplorer | XF86_SVGA |
| ASUS PCI-AV264CT | XF86_Mach64 |
| ASUS PCI-V264CT | XF86_Mach64 |
| ASUS Video Magic PCI V864 | XF86_S3 |
| ASUS Video Magic PCI VT64 | XF86_S3 |
| AT25 | XF86_SVGA |
| AT3D | XF86_SVGA |
| ATI 3D Pro Turbo | XF86_Mach64 |
| ATI 3D Pro Turbo PC2TV | XF86_Mach64 |
| ATI 3D Xpression | XF86_Mach64 |
| ATI 3D Xpression+ | XF86_Mach64 |
| ATI 3D Xpression+ PC2TV | XF86_Mach64 |
| ATI 8514 Ultra (no VGA) | XF86_Mach8 |
| ATI All-in-Wonder | XF86_Mach64 |
| ATI All-in-Wonder Pro | XF86_Mach64 |

| | |
|---|---|
| ATI Graphics Pro Turbo | XF86_Mach64 |
| ATI Graphics Pro Turbo 1600 | XF86_Mach64 |
| ATI Graphics Pro Turbo w/ AT&T 20C408 | XF86_Mach64 |
| RAMDAC ATI Graphics Pro Turbo w/ ATI68860 | XF86_Mach64 |
| RAMDAC ATI Graphics Pro Turbo w/ ATI68860B | XF86_Mach64 |
| RAMDAC ATI Graphics Pro Turbo w/ ATI68860C | XF86_Mach64 |
| RAMDAC ATI Graphics Pro Turbo w/ ATI68875 | XF86_Mach64 |
| RAMDAC ATI Graphics Pro Turbo w/ CH8398 RAMDAC | XF86_Mach64 |
| ATI Graphics Pro Turbo w/ STG1702 RAMDAC | XF86_Mach64 |
| ATI Graphics Pro Turbo w/ STG1703 RAMDAC | XF86_Mach64 |
| ATI Graphics Pro Turbo w/ TLC34075 RAMDAC | XF86_Mach64 |
| ATI Graphics Ultra | XF86_Mach8 |
| ATI Graphics Ultra Pro | XF86_Mach32 |
| ATI Graphics Xpression | XF86_Mach64 |
| ATI Graphics Xpression w/ AT&T 20C408 | XF86_Mach64 |
| RAMDAC ATI Graphics Xpression w/ ATI68860 RAMDAC | XF86_Mach64 |
| ATI Graphics Xpression w/ ATI68860B RAMDAC | XF86_Mach64 |
| ATI Graphics Xpression w/ ATI68860C RAMDAC | XF86_Mach64 |
| ATI Graphics Xpression w/ ATI68875 RAMDAC | XF86_Mach64 |
| ATI Graphics Xpression w/ CH8398 RAMDAC | XF86_Mach64 |
| ATI Graphics Xpression w/ Mach64 CT (264CT) | XF86_Mach64 |
| ATI Graphics Xpression w/ STG1702 RAMDAC | XF86_Mach64 |
| ATI Graphics Xpression w/ STG1703 RAMDAC | XF86_Mach64 |
| ATI Graphics Xpression w/ TLC34075 RAMDAC | XF86_Mach64 |
| ATI integrated on Intel Maui MU440EX motherboard | XF86_Mach64 |
| ATI Mach32 | XF86_Mach32 |
| ATI Mach64 (and Mach64 GB) | XF86_Mach64 |
| ATI Mach64 215GB | XF86_Mach64 |
| ATI Mach64 3D Rage II | XF86_Mach64 |
| ATI Mach64 3D Rage II+DVD | XF86_Mach64 |
| ATI Mach64 3D Rage IIC | XF86_Mach64 |
| ATI Mach64 3D Rage Pro (NOT the Rage LT Pro) | XF86_Mach64 |
| ATI Mach64 CT (264CT), Internal RAMDAC | XF86_Mach64 |
| ATI Mach64 GT (264GT), a.k.a. 3D RAGE, Int | XF86_Mach64 |
| RAMDAC ATI Mach64 VT (264VT), Internal RAMDAC | XF86_Mach64 |
| ATI Mach64 w/ AT&T 20C408 RAMDAC | XF86_Mach64 |
| ATI Mach64 w/ ATI68860 RAMDAC | XF86_Mach64 |
| ATI Mach64 w/ ATI68860B RAMDAC | XF86_Mach64 |
| ATI Mach64 w/ ATI68860C RAMDAC | XF86_Mach64 |
| ATI Mach64 w/ ATI68875 RAMDAC | XF86_Mach64 |

PART

VII

APP

C

| | |
|---|---|
| ATI Mach64 w/ CH8398 RAMDAC | XF86_Mach64 |
| ATI Mach64 w/ IBM RGB514 RAMDAC | XF86_Mach64 |
| ATI Mach64 w/ Internal RAMDAC | XF86_Mach64 |
| 2ATI Mach64 w/ STG1702 RAMDAC | XF86_Mach64 |
| ATI Mach64 w/ STG1703 RAMDAC | XF86_Mach64 |
| ATI Mach64 w/ TLC34075 RAMDAC | XF86_Mach64 |
| ATI Pro Turbo+PC2TV, 3D Rage II+DVD | XF86_Mach64 |
| ATI Rage 128 | XF86_Mach64 |
| ATI Rage Mobility | XF86_Mach64 |
| ATI Ultra Plus | XF86_Mach32 |
| ATI Video Xpression | XF86_Mach64 |
| ATI Video Xpression+ | XF86_Mach64 |
| ATI Win Boost w/ AT&T 20C408 RAMDAC | XF86_Mach64 |
| ATI Win Turbo | XF86_Mach64 |
| ATI WinBoost | XF86_Mach64 |
| ATI WinBoost w/ ATI68860 RAMDAC | XF86_Mach64 |
| ATI WinBoost w/ ATI68860B RAMDAC | XF86_Mach64 |
| ATI WinBoost w/ ATI68860C RAMDAC | XF86_Mach64 |
| ATI WinBoost w/ ATI68875 RAMDAC | XF86_Mach64 |
| ATI WinBoost w/ CH8398 RAMDAC | XF86_Mach64 |
| ATI WinBoost w/ Mach64 CT (264CT) | XF86_Mach64 |
| ATI WinBoost w/ STG1702 RAMDAC | XF86_Mach64 |
| ATI WinBoost w/ STG1703 RAMDAC | XF86_Mach64 |
| ATI WinBoost w/ TLC34075 RAMDAC | XF86_Mach64 |
| ATI WinCharger | XF86_Mach64 |
| ATI WinCharger w/ AT&T 20C408 RAMDAC | XF86_Mach64 |
| ATI WinCharger w/ ATI68860 RAMDAC | XF86_Mach64 |
| ATI WinCharger w/ ATI68860B RAMDAC | XF86_Mach64 |
| ATI WinCharger w/ ATI68860C RAMDAC | XF86_Mach64 |
| ATI WinCharger w/ ATI68875 RAMDAC | XF86_Mach64 |
| ATI WinCharger w/ CH8398 RAMDAC | XF86_Mach64 |
| ATI WinCharger w/ Mach64 CT (264CT) | XF86_Mach64 |
| ATI WinCharger w/ STG1702 RAMDAC | XF86_Mach64 |
| ATI WinCharger w/ STG1703 RAMDAC | XF86_Mach64 |
| ATI WinCharger w/ TLC34075 RAMDAC | XF86_Mach64 |
| ATI WinTurbo w/ AT&T 20C408 RAMDAC | XF86_Mach64 |
| ATI WinTurbo w/ ATI68860 RAMDAC | XF86_Mach64 |
| ATI WinTurbo w/ ATI68860B RAMDAC | XF86_Mach64 |
| ATI WinTurbo w/ ATI68860C RAMDAC | XF86_Mach64 |
| ATI WinTurbo w/ ATI68875 RAMDAC | XF86_Mach64 |
| ATI WinTurbo w/ CH8398 RAMDAC | XF86_Mach64 |
| ATI WinTurbo w/ Mach64 CT (264CT) | XF86_Mach64 |
| ATI WinTurbo w/ STG1702 RAMDAC | XF86_Mach64 |

| | |
|---|---|
| ATI WinTurbo w/ STG1703 RAMDAC | XF86_Mach64 |
| ATI WinTurbo w/ TLC34075 RAMDAC | XF86_Mach64 |
| ATI Wonder SVGA | XF86_SVGA |
| ATI Xpert 98 | XF86_Mach64 |
| ATI Xpert XL | XF86_Mach64 |
| ATI Xpert@Play 98 | XF86_Mach64 |
| ATI Xpert@Play PCI and AGP, 3D Rage Pro | XF86_Mach64 |
| ATI Xpert@Work, 3D Rage Pro | XF86_Mach64 |
| ATrend ATC-2165A | XF86_SVGA |
| Avance Logic 2101 | XF86_SVGA |
| Avance Logic 2228 | XF86_SVGA |
| Avance Logic 2301 | XF86_SVGA |
| Avance Logic 2302 | XF86_SVGA |
| Avance Logic 2308 | XF86_SVGA |
| Avance Logic 2401 | XF86_SVGA |
| Binar Graphics AnyView | XF86_SVGA |
| Boca Vortex (Sierra RAMDAC) | XF86_AGX |
| California Graphics SunTracer 6000 | XF86_SVGA |
| Canopus Co Power Window 3DV | XF86_SVGA |
| Canopus Total-3D | XF86_SVGA |
| Cardex Challenger (Pro) | XF86_SVGA |
| Cardex Cobra | XF86_SVGA |
| Cardex Trio64 | XF86_S3 |
| Cardex Trio64Pro | XF86_S3 |
| Chips & Technologies CT64200 | XF86_SVGA |
| Chips & Technologies CT64300 | XF86_SVGA |
| Chips & Technologies CT65520 | XF86_SVGA |
| Chips & Technologies CT65525 | XF86_SVGA |
| Chips & Technologies CT65530 | XF86_SVGA |
| Chips & Technologies CT65535 | XF86_SVGA |
| Chips & Technologies CT65540 | XF86_SVGA |
| Chips & Technologies CT65545 | XF86_SVGA |
| Chips & Technologies CT65546 | XF86_SVGA |
| Chips & Technologies CT65548 | XF86_SVGA |
| Chips & Technologies CT65550 | XF86_SVGA |
| Chips & Technologies CT65554 | XF86_SVGA |
| Chips & Technologies CT65555 | XF86_SVGA |
| Chips & Technologies CT68554 | XF86_SVGA |
| Chips & Technologies CT69000 | XF86_SVGA |
| Cirrus Logic GD542x | XF86_SVGA |
| Cirrus Logic GD543x | XF86_SVGA |
| Cirrus Logic GD5446 (no-name card) 1MB upg to 2MB | XF86_SVGA |
| Cirrus Logic GD544x | XF86_SVGA |

PART
VII

APP
C

| | |
|---|---|
| Cirrus Logic GD5462 | XF86_SVGA |
| Cirrus Logic GD5464 | XF86_SVGA |
| Cirrus Logic GD5465 | XF86_SVGA |
| Cirrus Logic GD5480 | XF86_SVGA |
| Cirrus Logic GD62xx (laptop) | XF86_SVGA |
| Cirrus Logic GD64xx (laptop) | XF86_SVGA |
| Cirrus Logic GD754x (laptop) | XF86_SVGA |
| Colorgraphic Dual Lightning | XF86_SVGA |
| COMPAQ Armada 7380DMT | XF86_S3 |
| COMPAQ Armada 7730MT | XF86_S3 |
| Creative Labs 3D Blaster Exxtreme | XF86_3DLabs |
| Creative Labs 3D Blaster PCI (Verite 1000) | XF86_SVGA |
| Creative Labs Graphics Blaster 3D | XF86_SVGA |
| Creative Labs Graphics Blaster Eclipse (OEM Model CT6510) | XF86_SVGA |
| Creative Labs Graphics Blaster MA201 | XF86_SVGA |
| Creative Labs Graphics Blaster MA202 | XF86_SVGA |
| Creative Labs Graphics Blaster MA302 | XF86_SVGA |
| Creative Labs Graphics Blaster MA334 | XF86_SVGA |
| DataExpert DSV3325 | XF86_SVGA |
| DataExpert DSV3365 | XF86_S3 |
| Dell onboard ET4000 | XF86_SVGA |
| Dell S3 805 | XF86_S3 |
| DFI-WG1000 | XF86_SVGA |
| DFI-WG5000 | XF86_SVGA |
| DFI-WG6000 | XF86_SVGA |
| Diamond Edge 3D | XF86_SVGA |
| Diamond Fire GL 1000 | XF86_3DLabs |
| Diamond Fire GL 1000 PRO | XF86_3DLabs |
| Diamond Fire GL 3000 | XF86_3DLabs |
| Diamond Multimedia Stealth 3D 2000 | XF86_SVGA |
| Diamond Multimedia Stealth 3D 2000 PRO | XF86_SVGA |
| Diamond SpeedStar (Plus) | XF86_SVGA |
| Diamond SpeedStar 24 | XF86_SVGA |
| Diamond SpeedStar 24X * | XF86_SVGA |
| Diamond SpeedStar 64 | XF86_SVGA |
| Diamond SpeedStar A50 | XF86_SVGA |
| Diamond SpeedStar HiColor | XF86_SVGA |
| Diamond SpeedStar Pro (not SE) | XF86_SVGA |
| Diamond SpeedStar Pro 1100 | XF86_SVGA |
| Diamond SpeedStar Pro SE (CL-GD5430/5434) | XF86_SVGA |
| Diamond SpeedStar64 Graphics 2000/2200 | XF86_SVGA |
| Diamond Stealth 24 | XF86_S3 |

| | |
|---|---|
| Diamond Stealth 32 | XF86_SVGA |
| Diamond Stealth 3D 2000 | XF86_SVGA |
| Diamond Stealth 3D 2000 PRO | XF86_SVGA |
| Diamond Stealth 3D 3000 | XF86_SVGA |
| Diamond Stealth 3D 4000 | XF86_SVGA |
| Diamond Stealth 64 DRAM SE | XF86_S3 |
| Diamond Stealth 64 DRAM w/ S3 SDAC | XF86_S3 |
| Diamond Stealth 64 DRAM w/ S3 Trio64 | XF86_S3 |
| Diamond Stealth 64 Video VRAM (TI RAMDAC) | XF86_S3 |
| Diamond Stealth 64 VRAM | XF86_S3 |
| Diamond Stealth II S220 | XF86_SVGA |
| Diamond Stealth Pro | XF86_S3 |
| Diamond Stealth Video 2500 | XF86_SVGA |
| Diamond Stealth Video DRAM | XF86_S3 |
| Diamond Stealth VRAM | XF86_S3 |
| Diamond Stealth64 Graphics 2001 series | XF86_SVGA |
| Diamond Stealth64 Graphics 2xx0 series (864 + SDAC) | XF86_S3 |
| Diamond Stealth64 Graphics 2xx0 series (Trio64) | XF86_S3 |
| Diamond Stealth64 Video 2001 series (2121/2201) | XF86_S3 |
| Diamond Stealth64 Video 2120/2200 | XF86_S3 |
| Diamond Stealth64 Video 3200 | XF86_S3 |
| Diamond Stealth64 Video 3240/3400 (IBM RAMDAC) | XF86_S3 |
| Diamond Stealth64 Video 3240/3400 (TI RAMDAC) | XF86_S3 |
| Diamond Viper 330 | XF86_SVGA |
| Diamond Viper 550 | XF86_SVGA |
| Diamond Viper PCI 2MB | XF86_P9000 |
| Diamond Viper Pro Video | XF86_SVGA |
| Diamond Viper VLB 2MB | XF86_P9000 |
| Digital 24-plane TGA (ZLXp-E2) | XF86_TGA |
| Digital 24-plane+3D TGA (ZLXp-E3) | XF86_TGA |
| Digital 8-plane TGA (UDB/Multia) | XF86_TGA |
| Digital 8-plane TGA (ZLXp-E1) | XF86_TGA |
| DSV3325 | XF86_SVGA |
| DSV3326 | XF86_S3 |
| EIZO (VRAM) | XF86_AGX |
| ELSA ERAZOR II | XF86_SVGA |
| ELSA Gloria Synergy | XF86_3DLabs |
| ELSA Gloria-4 | XF86_S3 |

| | |
|---|---|
| ELSA Gloria-8 | XF86_S3 |
| ELSA Gloria-L | XF86_3DLabs |
| ELSA Gloria-L/MX | XF86_3DLabs |
| ELSA Gloria-S | XF86_3DLabs |
| ELSA Gloria-XL | XF86_3DLabs |
| ELSA Victory 3D | XF86_SVGA |
| ELSA Victory 3DX | XF86_SVGA |
| ELSA Victory ERAZOR | XF86_SVGA |
| ELSA Winner 1000 R3D | XF86_SVGA |
| ELSA Winner 1000/T2D | XF86_S3 |
| ELSA Winner 1000AVI (AT&T 20C409 version) | XF86_S3 |
| ELSA Winner 1000AVI (SDAC version) | XF86_S3 |
| ELSA Winner 1000ISA | XF86_S3 |
| ELSA Winner 1000PRO w/ S3 SDAC | XF86_S3 |
| ELSA Winner 1000PRO w/ STG1700 or | XF86_S3 |
| AT&T RAMDAC ELSA Winner 1000PRO/X | XF86_S3 |
| ELSA Winner 1000TRIO | XF86_S3 |
| ELSA Winner 1000TRIO/V | XF86_S3 |
| ELSA Winner 1000TwinBus | XF86_S3 |
| ELSA Winner 1000VL | XF86_S3 |
| ELSA Winner 2000 | XF86_S3 |
| ELSA Winner 2000/Office | XF86_3DLabs |
| ELSA Winner 2000AVI | XF86_S3 |
| ELSA Winner 2000AVI/3D | XF86_SVGA |
| ELSA Winner 2000PRO/X-2 | XF86_S3 |
| ELSA Winner 2000PRO/X-4 | XF86_S3 |
| ELSA Winner 2000PRO/X-8 | XF86_S3 |
| ELSA Winner 2000PRO-2 | XF86_S3 |
| ELSA Winner 2000PRO-4 | XF86_S3 |
| ELSA Winner 3000 | XF86_SVGA |
| ELSA Winner 3000-L-42 | XF86_SVGA |
| ELSA Winner 3000-M-22 | XF86_SVGA |
| ELSA Winner 3000-S | XF86_SVGA |
| EPSON CardPC (onboard) | XF86_SVGA |
| ET3000 (generic) | XF86_SVGA |
| ET4000 (generic) | XF86_SVGA |
| ET4000 W32i, W32p (generic) | XF86_SVGA |
| ET4000/W32 (generic) | XF86_SVGA |
| ET6000 (generic) | XF86_SVGA |
| ET6100 (generic) | XF86_SVGA |
| ExpertColor DSV3325 | XF86_SVGA |
| ExpertColor DSV3365 | XF86_S3 |
| Generic VGA compatible | XF86_VGA16 |

| | |
|---|---|
| Genoa 5400 | XF86_SVGA |
| Genoa 8500VL(-28) | XF86_SVGA |
| Genoa 8900 Phantom 32i | XF86_SVGA |
| Genoa Phantom 64i w/ S3 SDAC | XF86_S3 |
| Genoa VideoBlitz III AV | XF86_S3 |
| Hercules Dynamite | XF86_SVGA |
| Hercules Dynamite 128/Video | XF86_SVGA |
| Hercules Dynamite Power | XF86_SVGA |
| Hercules Dynamite Pro | XF86_SVGA |
| Hercules Graphite HG210 | XF86_AGX |
| Hercules Graphite Power | XF86_AGX |
| Hercules Graphite Pro | XF86_AGX |
| Hercules Graphite Terminator 64 | XF86_S3 |
| Hercules Graphite Terminator 64/DRAM | XF86_S3 |
| Hercules Graphite Terminator Pro 64 | XF86_S3 |
| Hercules Stingray | XF86_SVGA |
| Hercules Stingray 128 3D | XF86_SVGA |
| Hercules Stingray 64/V w/ ICS5342 | XF86_SVGA |
| Hercules Stingray 64/V w/ ZoomDAC | XF86_SVGA |
| Hercules Stingray Pro | XF86_SVGA |
| Hercules Stingray Pro/V | XF86_SVGA |
| Hercules Terminator 3D/DX | XF86_SVGA |
| Hercules Terminator 64/3D | XF86_SVGA |
| Hercules Terminator 64/Video | XF86_S3 |
| Hercules Thriller3D | XF86_SVGA |
| Integral FlashPoint | XF86_SVGA |
| Intel 5430 | XF86_SVGA |
| Interay PMC Viper | XF86_SVGA |
| Jaton Video-58P | XF86_SVGA |
| Jaton Video-70P | XF86_SVGA |
| JAX 8241 | XF86_S3 |
| Jazz Multimedia G-Force 128 | XF86_SVGA |
| LeadTek WinFast 2300 | XF86_3DLabs |
| LeadTek WinFast 3D S600 | XF86_SVGA |
| LeadTek WinFast 3D S680 | XF86_SVGA |
| LeadTek WinFast S200 | XF86_SVGA |
| LeadTek WinFast S430 | XF86_S3 |
| LeadTek WinFast S510 | XF86_S3 |
| Matrox Comet | XF86_SVGA |
| Matrox G400 (Only first head and no TV out support) | XF86_SVGA |
| Matrox Marvel II | XF86_SVGA |
| Matrox Millennium (MGA) | XF86_SVGA |

| | |
|---|---|
| Matrox Millennium 2/4/8MB | XF86_SVGA |
| Matrox Millennium G200 4/8/16MB | XF86_SVGA |
| Matrox Millennium G200 SD 4/8/16MB | XF86_SVGA |
| Matrox Millennium II 4/8/16MB | XF86_SVGA |
| Matrox Millennium II AGP | XF86_SVGA |
| Matrox Mystique | XF86_SVGA |
| Matrox Mystique G200 4/8/16MB | XF86_SVGA |
| Matrox Productiva G100 4/8MB | XF86_SVGA |
| MediaGX | XF86_SVGA |
| MediaVision Proaxcel 128 | XF86_SVGA |
| MELCO WGP-VG4S | XF86_SVGA |
| MELCO WGP-VX8 | XF86_SVGA |
| Mirage Z-128 | XF86_SVGA |
| Miro Crystal 10SD w/ GenDAC | XF86_S3 |
| Miro Crystal 12SD | XF86_S3 |
| Miro Crystal 16S | XF86_S3 |
| Miro Crystal 20SD PCI w/ S3 SDAC | XF86_S3 |
| Miro Crystal 20SD VLB w/ S3 SDAC (BIOS 3 xx) | XF86_S3 |
| Miro Crystal 20SD w/ ICD2061A (BIOS 2 xx) | XF86_S3 |
| Miro Crystal 20SD w/ ICS2494 (BIOS 1 xx) | XF86_S3 |
| Miro Crystal 20SV | XF86_S3 |
| Miro Crystal 22SD | XF86_S3 |
| Miro Crystal 40SV | XF86_S3 |
| Miro Crystal 80SV | XF86_S3 |
| Miro Crystal 8S | XF86_S3 |
| Miro Crystal DVD | XF86_SVGA |
| Miro miroCRYSTAL VRX | XF86_SVGA |
| Miro miroMedia 3D | XF86_SVGA |
| Miro MiroVideo 20TD | XF86_SVGA |
| Miro Video 20SV | XF86_S3 |
| MSI MS-4417 | XF86_SVGA |
| NeoMagic 2070 (MagicGraph128) | XF86_SVGA |
| NeoMagic 2090 (MagicGraph128V) | XF86_SVGA |
| NeoMagic 2093 (MagicGraph128ZV) | XF86_SVGA |
| NeoMagic 2097 (MagicGraph128ZV+) | XF86_SVGA |
| NeoMagic 2160 (MagicGraph128XD) | XF86_SVGA |
| NeoMagic 2200 (MagicMedia256AV) | XF86_SVGA |
| Number Nine FX Motion 331 | XF86_S3 |
| Number Nine FX Motion 332 | XF86_SVGA |
| Number Nine FX Motion 531 | XF86_S3 |
| Number Nine FX Motion 771 | XF86_S3 |
| Number Nine FX Vision 330 | XF86_S3 |

| | |
|---|---|
| Number Nine GXE Level 10/11/12 | XF86_S3 |
| Number Nine GXE Level 14/16 | XF86_S3 |
| Number Nine GXE64 | XF86_S3 |
| Number Nine GXE64 Pro | XF86_S3 |
| Number Nine GXE64 w/ S3 Trio64 | XF86_S3 |
| Number Nine Imagine I-128 (2-8MB) | XF86_I128 |
| Number Nine Imagine I-128 Series 2 (2-4MB) | XF86_I128 |
| Number Nine Imagine I-128-T2R | XF86_I128 |
| Number Nine Revolution 3D AGP (4-8MB SGRAM) | XF86_I128 |
| Number Nine Visual 9FX Reality 332 | XF86_SVGA |
| nVidia GeForce 256 | XF86_SVGA |
| nVidia 128 | XF86_SVGA |
| nVidia NV1 | XF86_SVGA |
| nVidia RIVA INTEGRATED | XF86_SVGA |
| nVidia RIVA TNT | XF86_SVGA |
| nVidia RIVA TNT2 | XF86_SVGA |
| nVidia RIVA ULTRA TNT2 | XF86_SVGA |
| nVidia RIVA ULTRA VANTA | XF86_SVGA |
| nVidia RIVA VANTA | XF86_SVGA |
| nVidia STG2000 | XF86_SVGA |
| Oak 87 ISA (generic) | XF86_SVGA |
| Oak 87 VLB (generic) | XF86_SVGA |
| Oak ISA Card (generic) | XF86_SVGA |
| Ocean (octek) VL-VGA-1000 | XF86_SVGA |
| Octek AVGA-20 | XF86_SVGA |
| Octek Combo-26 | XF86_SVGA |
| Octek Combo-28 | XF86_SVGA |
| Octek VL-VGA-26 | XF86_SVGA |
| Octek VL-VGA-28 | XF86_SVGA |
| Orchid Celsius (AT&T RAMDAC) | XF86_AGX |
| Orchid Celsius (Sierra RAMDAC) | XF86_AGX |
| Orchid Fahrenheit 1280 | XF86_S3 |
| Orchid Fahrenheit VA | XF86_S3 |
| Orchid Fahrenheit-1280+ | XF86_S3 |
| Orchid Kelvin 64 | XF86_SVGA |
| Orchid Kelvin 64 VLB Rev A | XF86_SVGA |
| Orchid Kelvin 64 VLB Rev B | XF86_SVGA |
| Orchid P9000 VLB | XF86_P9000 |
| Orchid Technology Fahrenheit Video 3D | XF86_SVGA |
| Paradise Accelerator Value | XF86_SVGA |
| Paradise/WD 90CXX | XF86_SVGA |
| PC-Chips M567 Mainboard | XF86_SVGA |
| PixelView Combo TV 3D AGP (Prolink) | XF86_SVGA |

PART

VII

APP

C

| | |
|---|---|
| PixelView Combo TV Pro (Prolink) | XF86_SVGA |
| Rendition Verite 1000 | XF86_SVGA |
| Rendition Verite 2x00 | XF86_SVGA |
| Revolution 3D (T2R) | XF86_I128 |
| S3 801/805 (generic) | XF86_S3 |
| S3 801/805 w/ ATT20c490 RAMDAC | XF86_S3 |
| S3 801/805 w/ ATT20c490 RAMDAC and | XF86_S3 |
| ICD2061A S3 801/805 w/ Chrontel 8391 | XF86_S3 |
| S3 801/805 w/ S3 GenDAC | XF86_S3 |
| S3 801/805 w/ SC1148{2,3,4} RAMDAC | XF86_S3 |
| S3 801/805 w/ SC1148{5,7,9} RAMDAC | XF86_S3 |
| S3 864 (generic) | XF86_S3 |
| S3 864 w/ ATT 20C498 or 21C498 | XF86_S3 |
| S3 864 w/ SDAC (86C716) | XF86_S3 |
| S3 864 w/ STG1703 | XF86_S3 |
| S3 868 (generic) | XF86_S3 |
| S3 868 w/ ATT 20C409 | XF86_S3 |
| S3 868 w/ ATT 20C498 or 21C498 | XF86_S3 |
| S3 868 w/ SDAC (86C716) | XF86_S3 |
| S3 86C260 (generic) | XF86_SVGA |
| S3 86C280 (generic) | XF86_SVGA |
| S3 86C325 (generic) | XF86_SVGA |
| S3 86C357 (generic) | XF86_SVGA |
| S3 86C365 (Trio3D) | XF86_VGA16 |
| S3 86C375 (generic) | XF86_SVGA |
| S3 86C385 (generic) | XF86_SVGA |
| S3 86C391 (Savage3D) | XF86_VGA16 |
| S3 86C764 (generic) | XF86_S3 |
| S3 86C765 (generic) | XF86_S3 |
| S3 86C775 (generic) | XF86_S3 |
| S3 86C785 (generic) | XF86_S3 |
| S3 86C801 (generic) | XF86_S3 |
| S3 86C805 (generic) | XF86_S3 |
| S3 86C864 (generic) | XF86_S3 |
| S3 86C868 (generic) | XF86_S3 |
| S3 86C911 (generic) | XF86_S3 |
| S3 86C924 (generic) | XF86_S3 |
| S3 86C928 (generic) | XF86_S3 |
| S3 86C964 (generic) | XF86_S3 |
| S3 86C968 (generic) | XF86_S3 |
| S3 86C988 (generic) | XF86_SVGA |
| S3 86CM65 | XF86_S3 |
| S3 911/924 (generic) | XF86_S3 |

| | |
|---|---|
| S3 924 w/ SC1148 DAC | XF86_S3 |
| S3 928 (generic) | XF86_S3 |
| S3 964 (generic) | XF86_S3 |
| S3 968 (generic) | XF86_S3 |
| S3 Aurora64V+ (generic) | XF86_S3 |
| S3 Savage3D, Savage4 * | XF86_SVGA |
| S3 Savage2000, Savage4 * | XF86_SVGA |
| Trio32 (generic) | XF86_S3 |
| S3 Trio3D, Trio3D/2X * | XF86_SVGA |
| S3 Trio64 (generic) | XF86_S3 |
| S3 Trio64V+ (generic) | XF86_S3 |
| S3 Trio64V2 (generic) | XF86_S3 |
| S3 Trio64V2/DX (generic) | XF86_S3 |
| S3 Trio64V2/GX (generic) | XF86_S3 |
| S3 ViRGE (generic) | XF86_SVGA |
| S3 ViRGE (old S3V server) | XF86_SVGA |
| S3 ViRGE/DX (generic) | XF86_SVGA |
| S3 ViRGE/GX2 (generic) | XF86_SVGA |
| S3 ViRGE/MX (generic) | XF86_SVGA |
| S3 ViRGE/MX+ (generic) | XF86_SVGA |
| S3 ViRGE/VX (generic) | XF86_SVGA |
| S3 Vision864 (generic) | XF86_S3 |
| S3 Vision868 (generic) | XF86_S3 |
| S3 Vision964 (generic) | XF86_S3 |
| S3 Vision968 (generic) | XF86_S3 |
| SHARP 9080 | XF86_S3 |
| SHARP 9090 | XF86_S3 |
| Sierra Screaming 3D | XF86_SVGA |
| Sigma Concorde | XF86_SVGA |
| Sigma Legend | XF86_SVGA |
| Silicon Motion Lynx chipsets | XF86_SVGA |
| SiS 3D PRO AGP | XF86_SVGA |
| SiS 540/630 | XF86_SVGA |
| SiS 300 | XF86_SVGA |
| SiS 5597 | XF86_SVGA |
| SiS 5598 | XF86_SVGA |
| SiS 6326 * | XF86_SVGA |
| SiS SG86C201 | XF86_SVGA |
| SiS SG86C205 | XF86_SVGA |
| SiS SG86C215 * | XF86_SVGA |
| SiS SG86C225 * | XF86_SVGA |
| SNI PC5H W32 | XF86_SVGA |
| SNI Scenic W32 | XF86_SVGA |

PART

**VII**

APP

**C**

| | |
|---|---|
| Some S3 ViRGE/GX (generic) | XF86_SVGA |
| Some S3 ViRGE/GX (generic) Cards * | XF86_S3V |
| SPEA Mercury 64 | XF86_S3 |
| SPEA Mirage | XF86_S3 |
| SPEA/V7 Mercury | XF86_S3 |
| SPEA/V7 Mirage P64 | XF86_S3 |
| SPEA/V7 Mirage P64 w/ S3 Trio64 | XF86_S3 |
| SPEA/V7 Mirage VEGA Plus | XF86_SVGA |
| SPEA/V7 ShowTime Plus | XF86_SVGA |
| Spider Black Widow | XF86_AGX |
| Spider Black Widow Plus | XF86_AGX |
| Spider Tarantula 64 | XF86_S3 |
| Spider VLB Plus | XF86_SVGA |
| STB Horizon | XF86_SVGA |
| STB Horizon Video | XF86_SVGA |
| STB LightSpeed | XF86_SVGA |
| STB LightSpeed 128 | XF86_SVGA |
| STB MVP-2 | XF86_SVGA |
| STB MVP-2 PCI | XF86_SVGA |
| STB MVP-2X | XF86_SVGA |
| STB MVP-4 PCI | XF86_SVGA |
| STB MVP-4X | XF86_SVGA |
| STB Nitro (64) | XF86_SVGA |
| STB Nitro 3D | XF86_SVGA |
| STB Nitro 64 Video | XF86_SVGA |
| STB nvidia 128 | XF86_SVGA |
| STB Pegasus | XF86_S3 |
| STB Powergraph 64 | XF86_S3 |
| STB Powergraph 64 Video | XF86_S3 |
| STB Powergraph X-24 | XF86_S3 |
| STB Systems Powergraph 3D | XF86_SVGA |
| STB Systems Velocity 3D | XF86_SVGA |
| STB Velocity 128 | XF86_SVGA |
| STB Velocity 64 Video | XF86_S3 |
| TechWorks Thunderbolt | XF86_SVGA |
| TechWorks Ultimate 3D | XF86_SVGA |
| Toshiba Tecra 540CDT | XF86_SVGA |
| Toshiba Tecra 550CDT | XF86_SVGA |
| Toshiba Tecra 750CDT | XF86_SVGA |
| Toshiba Tecra 750DVD | XF86_SVGA |
| Trident 3DImage975 (generic) | XF86_SVGA |
| Trident 3DImage975 AGP (generic) | XF86_SVGA |
| Trident 3DImage985 (generic) | XF86_SVGA |

| | |
|---|---|
| Trident 8900/9000 (generic) | XF86_SVGA |
| Trident 8900D (generic) | XF86_SVGA |
| Trident Cyber 9382 (generic) | XF86_SVGA |
| Trident Cyber 9385 (generic) | XF86_SVGA |
| Trident Cyber 9388 (generic) | XF86_SVGA |
| Trident Cyber 9397 (generic) | XF86_SVGA |
| Trident TGUI9400CXi (generic) | XF86_SVGA |
| Trident TGUI9420DGi (generic) | XF86_SVGA |
| Trident TGUI9430DGi (generic) | XF86_SVGA |
| Trident TGUI9440 (generic) | XF86_SVGA |
| Trident TGUI9660 (generic) | XF86_SVGA |
| Trident TGUI9680 (generic) | XF86_SVGA |
| Trident TGUI9682 (generic) | XF86_SVGA |
| Trident TGUI9685 (generic) | XF86_SVGA |
| Trident TVGA 8800BR | XF86_VGA16 |
| Trident TVGA 8800CS | XF86_VGA16 |
| Trident TVGA9200CXr (generic) | XF86_SVGA |
| Unsupported VGA-compatible | XF86_VGA16 |
| VI720 | XF86_SVGA |
| VideoLogic GrafixStar 300 | XF86_S3 |
| VideoLogic GrafixStar 400 | XF86_S3 |
| VideoLogic GrafixStar 500 | XF86_S3 |
| VideoLogic GrafixStar 550 | XF86_SVGA |
| VideoLogic GrafixStar 560 (PCI/AGP) | XF86_SVGA |
| VideoLogic GrafixStar 600 | XF86_SVGA |
| VideoLogic GrafixStar 700 | XF86_S3 |
| VidTech FastMax P20 | XF86_S3 |
| ViewTop PCI | XF86_SVGA |
| VL-41 | XF86_S3 |
| WD 90C24 (laptop) | XF86_SVGA |
| WD 90C24A or 90C24A2 (laptop) | XF86_SVGA |
| Weitek P9100 (generic) | XF86_SVGA |
| WinFast 3D S600 | XF86_SVGA |
| WinFast 3D S600 | XF86_SVGA |
| WinFast S200 | XF86_SVGA |
| WinFast S430 | XF86_S3 |
| WinFast S510 | XF86_S3 |
| XGA-1 (ISA bus) | XF86_AGX |
| XGA-2 (ISA bus) | XF86_AGX |

*Cards marked with an asterisk are compatible, supported by Red Hat Support.*

PART

VII

APP

C

# LINUX-COMPATIBLE ETHERNET CARDS

LINUX-COMPATIBLE ETHERNET CARDS

This appendix lists Linux-compatible Ethernet cards and the module (driver) that each requires. In most cases, Linux will detect your Ethernet card and load the appropriate module automatically. So you may not have to concern yourself with choosing the right driver. For any Ethernet card not listed here, or discrepancies, see the Red Hat 6.2 Hardware Compatibility list at www.redhat.com/support/hardware. Also, check the card manufacturer's Web site for new or updated Linux drivers.

The Tier column indicates the level of compatibility each card provides, as summarized here:

- **Tier 1:** Hardware that Linux can detect and use. It is known to be reliable at Red Hat as well as in the field. If you've purchased the official Red Hat Linux 6.2/Intel boxed set, you can expect a reasonable level of support when installing the software for these cards.

- **Tier 2:** Hardware that should be detected and usable with Linux kernel, but some users have reported problems with either the hardware or the hardware's interaction with other hardware. Official Red Hat Linux 6.2/Intel boxed set owners can expect limited installation support for this hardware, including how to determine if Linux is recognizing the device and how to enter configuration data into the installation program or the /etc/conf.modules configuration file.

- **Tier 3:** Hardware that is compatible, but not supported by Red Hat Linux Support. Owners of the official Red Hat Linux 6.2/Intel boxed set can expect support on determining whether Linux recognizes the hardware and which included drivers to use. Drivers are not always available from Red Hat, and Red Hat offers no support for third-party drivers.

| Device | Module | Tier |
|---|---|---|
| 100VG-AnyLan Network | hp100.o | 2 |
| 3Com 3c501 | 3c501.o | 3 |
| 3Com 3c503 | 3c503.o | 2 |
| 3Com 3c503/16 | 3c503.o | 2 |
| 3Com 3c579 | 3c59x.o | 1 |
| 3Com 3c59x | 3c59x.o | 1 |
| 3Com 3c900 | 3c59x.o | 1 |
| 3Com 3c905 | 3c59x.o | 1 |
| 3Com EtherLink 16 | 3c507.o | 2 |
| 3Com EtherLink III | 3c509.o | 1 |
| 3Com EtherLink PCI III/XL "Corkscrew" | 3c59x.o | 1 |
| 3Com EtherLink Plus (3c505) | 3c505.o | 2 |
| 3Com ISA EtherLink XL | 3c501.o | 3 |
| Aironet Arlan 655 | arlan.o | 2 |
| Allied Telesis LA100PCI-T | tulip.o | 1 |
| Allied Telesis AT1500 | lance.o | 2 |
| Allied Telesis AT1700 | at1700.o | 2 |
| Alteon AceNIC Gigabit | acenic.o | 2 |

| | | |
|---|---|---|
| AMD Lance/PCnet | lance.o | 2 |
| AMD PCnet32 | pcnet32.o | 2 |
| AMD PCnetPCI | pcnet32.o | 2 |
| Ansel Communications AC3200 EISA | Ac3200.o | 2 |
| Apricot Xen-II | 82596.o | 2 |
| AT&T GIS WaveLAN ISA | wavelan.o | 2 |
| Boomerage 3c595 | 3c59x.o | 1 |
| Boomerage 3c900 | 3c59x.o | 1 |
| Boomerage 3c905 | 3c59x.o | 1 |
| Cabletron E2100 series | e2100.o | 2 |
| Cogent EM110 | tulip.o | 1 |
| Compaq Integrated NetFlex 3/P | tlan.o | 2 |
| Compaq Netelligent 10 T PCI UTP | tlan.o | 2 |
| Compaq Netelligent 10 T/2 PCI UTP/Coax | tlan.o | 2 |
| Compaq Netelligent 10/100 TX Embedded 3UTP | tlan.o | 2 |
| Compaq Netelligent 10/100 TX PCI UTP | tlan.o | 2 |
| Compaq Netelligent 10/100 TX UTP | tlan.o | 2 |
| Compaq Netelligent Dual 10/100 TX PCI UTP | tlan.o | 2 |
| Compaq Netelligent Integrated 10/100 TX UTP | tlan.o | 2 |
| Compaq NetFlex 3/P | tlan.o | 2 |
| Compex ReadyLink | hp100.o | 2 |
| Compex RL2000 | ne2k-pci.o | 2 |
| Comtrol Hostess SV11 | hostess_sv11.o | 2 |
| COPS LT-95 | cops.o | 2 |
| Crystal LAN CS8900 | cs89x0.o | 2 |
| Crystal LAN CS8920 | cs89x0.o | 2 |
| Danpex EN-9400 | tulip.o | 1 |
| Dayna DL2000 | cops.o | 2 |
| DaynaTalk PC (HL) | cops.o | 2 |
| Daystar Digital LT-200 | cops.o | 2 |
| DE434 TP PCI | De4x5.o | 1 |
| DE435/450 | De4x5.o | 1 |
| DE500 10/100 PCI | De4x5.o | 1 |
| DEC EtherWorks 10 PCI(DE450) | tulip.o | 1 |
| DEC EtherWorks 100/10 PCI(DE500-XA) | tulip.o | 1 |
| DEC QSILVER's | tulip.o | 1 |
| Digi Intl. RightSwitch SE-X EISA | dgrs.o | 2 |
| Digi Intl. RightSwitch SE-X PCI | dgrs.o | 2 |
| Digital 2104x Tulip chip | tulip.o | 1 |
| Digital 2114x Tulip chip | tulip.o | 1 |
| Digital 21x4x Tulip PCI Ethernet cards | tulip.o | 1 |
| Digital DC21041 [A] chipset | De4x5.o | 1 |
| Digital DC21140 [A] chipset | De4x5.o | 1 |

| | | |
|---|---|---|
| Digital DC21142 chipset | De4x5.o | 1 |
| Digital DC21143 chipset | De4x5.o | 1 |
| Digital DE100 | depca.o | 2 |
| Digital DE101 | depca.o | 2 |
| Digital DE200 Turbo | depca.o | 2 |
| Digital DE201 Turbo | depca.o | 2 |
| Digital DE202 Turbo | depca.o | 2 |
| Digital DE202 Turbo TP/BNC | depca.o | 2 |
| Digital DE210 | depca.o | 2 |
| Digital DE422 | depca.o | 2 |
| Digital DE422 EISA | depca.o | 2 |
| Digital DE425 | De4x5.o | 1 |
| Digital DE434 | De4x5.o | 1 |
| Digital DE435 | De4x5.o | 1 |
| Digital DE450 | De4x5.o | 1 |
| Digital DE500 | De4x5.o | 1 |
| DIGITAL DEPCA & EtherWORKS | depca.o | 2 |
| D-Link DE-600 Pocket | de600.o | 2 |
| D-Link DE-620 Pocket | de600.o | 2 |
| D-Link DFE-930-TX PCI 10/100 | via-rhine.o | 2 |
| ENET100-VG4 | hp100.o | 2 |
| EtherWORKS 3 DE203 | ewrk3.o | 2 |
| EtherWORKS 3 DE204 | ewrk3.o | 2 |
| EtherWORKS 3 DE205 | ewrk3.o | 2 |
| EtherWORKS DE425 TP/COAX EISA | De4x5.o | 1 |
| Farallon PhoneNET PC II & III | cops.o | 2 |
| FreedomLine 100/VG | hp100.o | 2 |
| Fujitsu FMV-181 | fmv18x.o | 2 |
| Fujitsu FMV-182 | fmv18x.o | 2 |
| Fujitsu FMV-183 | fmv18x.o | 2 |
| Fujitsu FMV-184 | fmv18x.o | 2 |
| General Instruments SB1000 | sb1000.o | 3 |
| G-NIC PCI Gigabit Ethernet | z85230.o | 2 |
| adapter Z8530-based HDLC cards for AX.25 | | |
| HP AnyLAN, 10/100VG | hp.o | 2 |
| HP J2405A | lance.o | 2 |
| HP J2573 | hp100.o | 2 |
| HP J2585A | hp100.o | 2 |
| HP J2585B | hp100.o | 2 |
| HP J2970 | hp100.o | 2 |
| HP J2973 | hp100.o | 2 |
| HP NE2100 | lance.o | 2 |
| HP NE2500 | lance.o | 2 |

| | | |
|---|---|---|
| HP PC-LAN 27245B | hp.o | 2 |
| HP PCLAN 27248B | hp.o | 2 |
| HP PC-LAN 27*xxx* series | hp.o | 2 |
| HP PCLAN J2573 | hp.o | 2 |
| HP PCLAN J2577 | hp.o | 2 |
| HP PCLAN/plus | hp-plus.o | 2 |
| ICL EtherTeam 16i/32 | eth16i.o | 2 |
| Intel EEPro100 (PCI) | eepro100.o | 1 |
| Intel EtherExpress 16 (i82586) | eexpress.o | 2 |
| Intel EtherExpress i82558 PCI Pro/10+ | eepro100.o | 1 |
| Intel EtherExpress i82595 Pro10/10+ (ISA only) | eepro.o | 2 |
| IntelEtherExpress i82557 PCI Pro/10+ | eepro100.o | 1 |
| Kingston SMC8432 | De4x5.o | 1 |
| Kingston SMC9332 | De4x5.o | 1 |
| KTI ET32P2 | ne2k-pci.o | 2 |
| MiCom-Interlan NI5010 | ni5010.o | 2 |
| Mylex LNE390 EISA | lne390.o | 2 |
| Mylex LNE390A | lne390.o | 2 |
| Mylex LNE390B | lne390.o | 2 |
| NE1000 | ne.o | 2 |
| NE2000 (non-PCI) | ne.o | 2 |
| NE2000 (PCI) | ne2k-pci.o | 2 |
| NetVin NV5000SC | ne2k-pci.o | 2 |
| NI5210 (i82586 Ethernet chip) | ni52.o | 2 |
| NI6510 EtherBlaster | ni65.0 | 2 |
| Novell NL-10000 | cops.o | 2 |
| Novell NE3210 EISA Network Adapter | ne3210.o | 2 |
| Olicom OC-2183 | tlan.o | 2 |
| Olicom OC-2325 | tlan.o | 2 |
| Olicom OC-2326 | tlan.o | 2 |
| PureData PDUC8028 | wd.o | 2 |
| Racal-Interlan ES3210 EISA | es3210.o | 2 |
| RealTek cards using RTL8129 or | rtl8139.o | 2 |
| RTL8139 Fast Ethernet chipsets RealTek RTL-8029 | ne2k-pci.o | 2 |
| RedCreek Communications PCI | rcpci.o | 2 |
| Sangoma ES502A | sdladrv.o | 2 |
| Sangoma S502/S508 multi-protocol FR | sdla.o | 2 |
| Sangoma S502A | sdladrv.o | 2 |
| Sangoma S502E | sdladrv.o | 2 |
| Sangoma S503 | sdladrv.o | 2 |
| Sangoma S507 | sdladrv.o | 2 |
| Sangoma S508 | sdladrv.o | 2 |
| Sangomw S509 | sdladrv.o | 2 |

| | | |
|---|---|---|
| SeaLevel Systems 4012 | `sealevel.o` | 3 |
| SeaLevel Systems 4021 | `sealevel.o` | 3 |
| SiS 900 PCI | `sis900.o` | 3 |
| SMC 9000 series | `smc9194.o` | 2 |
| SMC DEC21041 | `tulip.o` | 1 |
| SMC EtherEZ ISA (8K, 83c790) | `smc-ultra.o` | 2 |
| SMC EtherPower 10 PCI(8432T/8432BT) | `tulip.o` | 1 |
| SMC EtherPower 10/100 PCI(9332DST) | `tulip.o` | 1 |
| SMC EtherPower II 9432 PCI(83c170/175 EPIC series) | `epic100.o` | 2 |
| SMC PCI EtherPower | `tulip.o` | 1 |
| SMC Ultra | `smc-ultra.o` | 2 |
| SMC Ultra32 EISA (32K) | `smc-ultra32.o` | 2 |
| SureCom NE3 | `ne2k-pci.o` | 2 |
| Tangent ATB-II | `cops.o` | 2 |
| VIA 82C926 | `ne2k-pci.o` | 2 |
| VIA Rhine PCI Fast Ethernet with 3043 Rhine-I | `via-rhine.o` | 2 |
| VIA Rhine PCI Fast Ethernet with VIA VT86c100A Rhine-II PC | `via-rhine.o` | 2 |
| Vortex 3c590 | `3c59x.o` | 1 |
| Vortex 3c592 | `3c59x.o` | 1 |
| Vortex 3c595 | `3c59x.o` | 1 |
| Vortex 3c597 | `3c59x.o` | 1 |
| Western Digital WD8003 | `wd.o` | 2 |
| Western Digital WD8013 | `wd.o` | 2 |
| Winbond 89C940 | `ne2k-pci.o` | 2 |
| Yellowfin Packet Engines | `yellowfin.o` | 2 |
| Znyx 312 etherarray | `tulip.o` | 1 |
| Znyx31 [45] | `De4x5.o` | 1 |
| Znyx346 10/100 cards w/ DC21040 (no SROM) | `De4x5.o` | 1 |

# INDEX

# Installing the CD-ROM

## CD-ROM Boot

1. Insert CD-ROM in the CD drive.

2. Restart your computer.

3. You may need to change your BIOS settings to boot from the CD-ROM. Typically, you enter your BIOS setup program with the F2 or Delete keys.

4. Make your changes (if any) and exit the BIOS setup utility.

5. If your CD drive is capable of booting from CD-ROMs, you will boot into Red Hat's setup program.

6. Follow the onscreen prompts to complete the installation.

## Installing from Boot Floppies

The first step in getting Red Hat's distribution of Linux onto a system is finding a way of starting the installation program. The usual method of doing so is to create an installation disk, although if you are installing from CD-ROM, and your system's BIOS supports it, you should be able to boot directly into the installation program from the CD.

Otherwise, to create an installation disk, you'll need to copy boot.img (which is simply an image of an ext2-formatted Linux boot disk with an additional installation program) onto a floppy disk. The boot.img file can be obtained from the /images directory of the Red Hat CD-ROM disk.

You can create the boot disk either from a DOS or Windows system, or from an existing Linux or UNIX system. For your destination disk, you can use either an unformatted or a pre-formatted disk—it makes no difference.

Under DOS, assuming your CD-ROM is accessible as drive E:, you can type the following:

```
e: cd\images\dosutils\rawrite
```

For the source file, enter boot.img. For the destination file, enter a: (assuming the disk you are created is inserted into the A: drive). The rawrite program will then copy the boot.img file onto the disk.

After rawrite has finished, reboot the computer with the floppy disk inserted. If your computer is set up properly, you will boot into the Red Hat setup program. Follow the onscreen prompts to complete the installation.